THE BELL CURVE

THE BELL CURVE

*Intelligence and Class Structure
in American Life*

RICHARD J. HERRNSTEIN
CHARLES MURRAY

THE FREE PRESS
New York London Toronto Sydney Tokyo Singapore

The Free Press
A Division of Simon & Schuster Inc.
866 Third Avenue, New York, N.Y. 10022

Printed in the United States of America

printing number
1 2 3 4 5 6 7 8 9 10

Library of Congress Cataloging-in-Publication Data
Herrnstein, Richard J.
    The bell curve : intelligence and class structure in American life
/ Richard J. Herrnstein, Charles Murray.
        p.   cm.
    ISBN 0–02–914673–9
    1. Intellect.   2. Nature and nurture,   3. Intelligence levels—
Social aspects.   4. Educational psychology.   I. Murray, Charles A.
II. Title.
BF431.H398   1994
305.9'082—dc20
                                                        94–29694
                                                          CIP

For
JULIA,
MAX,
JAMES,
NARISARA,
SARAWAN,
ANNA,
AND BENNETT
We wrote with your world in our thoughts

There is a most absurd and audacious Method of reasoning avowed by some Bigots and Enthusiasts, and through Fear assented to by some wiser and better Men; it is this. They argue against a fair Discussion of popular Prejudices, because, say they, tho' they would be found without any reasonable Support, yet the Discovery might be productive of the most dangerous Consequences. Absurd and blasphemous Notion! As if all Happiness was not connected with the Practice of Virtue, which necessarily depends upon the Knowledge of Truth.

EDMUND BURKE
A Vindication of Natural Society

Contents

List of Illustrations

List of Tables

A Note to the Reader

We have designed *The Bell Curve* to be read at several levels.

At the simplest level, it is only about thirty pages long. Each chapter except the Introduction and the final two chapters opens with a precis of the main findings and conclusions minus any evidence for them, written in an informal style free of technical terms. You can get a good idea of what we have to say by reading just those introductory essays.

The next level is the main text. It is accessible to anyone who enjoys reading, for example, the science section of the news magazines. No special knowledge is assumed; everything you need to know to follow all of the discussion is contained within the book. The main text does include considerable technical material, however. The documentation becomes especially extensive when we come to a topic so controversial that many readers will have a "This can't possibly be true" reaction.

Sprinkled throughout the book are boxes that add more detail, discuss alternative ways of thinking about the data, or relate tidbits that don't quite fit in the text. You may skip any of these without interrupting the flow of the narrative, but we think they add something (or they wouldn't be there), and we encourage you to dip into them.

The endnotes provide the usual scholarly references. Some of them, indicated in text by endnote numbers enclosed in brackets, add short discussions that will be of interest mostly to specialists.

Finally, the appendixes elaborate on key issues. For example, readers who come to the book unfamiliar with statistics will find that Appendix 1 supplies the basics; if you want to know more about the debate over cultural bias in intelligence tests, Appendix 5 guides you through the literature on that issue; and so on. Other appendixes lay out the statistical detail that could not be fit into the main text and was too bulky for a note.

Regarding those pesky impersonal third-person singular pronouns and other occasions when the authors must assign a gender to a fictitious person used to illustrate a point, it seems to us there is a simple, fair solution, which we hereby endorse: Unless there are obvious reasons not to, use the gender of the first author. We use *he* throughout.

Preface

This book is about differences in intellectual capacity among people and groups and what those differences mean for America's future. The relationships we will be discussing are among the most sensitive in contemporary America—so sensitive that hardly anyone writes or talks about them in public. It is not for lack of information, as you will see. On the contrary, knowledge about the connections between intelligence and American life has been accumulating for years, available in the journals held by any good university library and on the computer tapes and disks of public use databases.

People have shied from the topic for many reasons. Some think that the concept of intelligence has been proved a fraud. Others recall totalitarian eugenic schemes based on IQ scores or worry about such schemes arising once the subject breaks into the open. Many fear that discussing intelligence will promote racism.

The friends and colleagues whose concerns we take most seriously say something like this: "Yes, we acknowledge that intelligence is important and that people differ. But the United States is founded on the principle that people should be equal under the law. So what possible relevance can individual differences in intelligence have to public policy? What good can come of writing this book?" In answer, we ask these friends and you, the reader, to share for a moment our view of the situation, perhaps suppressing some doubts and assuming as true things that we will subsequently try to prove are true. Here is our story:

A great nation, founded on principles of individual liberty and self-government that constitute the crowning achievement of statecraft, approaches the end of the twentieth century. Equality of rights—another central principle—has been implanted more deeply and more successfully than in any other society in history. Yet even as the principle of equal rights triumphs, strange things begin to happen to two small segments of the population.

In one segment, life gets better in many ways. The people in this group are welcomed at the best colleges, then at the best graduate and professional schools, regardless of their parents' wealth. After they complete their education, they enter fulfilling and prestigious careers. Their incomes continue to rise even when income growth stagnates for everyone else. By their maturity, these fortunate ones commonly have six-figure incomes. Technology works in their behalf, expanding their options and their freedom, putting unprecedented resources at their command, enhancing their ability to do what they enjoy doing. And as these good things happen to them, they gravitate to one another, increasingly enabled by their affluence and by technology to work together and live in one another's company—and in isolation from everybody else.

In the other group, life gets worse, and its members collect at the bottom of society. Poverty is severe, drugs and crime are rampant, and the traditional family all but disappears. Economic growth passes them by. Technology is not a partner in their lives but an electronic opiate. They live together in urban centers or scattered in rural backwaters, but their presence hovers over the other parts of town and countryside as well, creating fear and resentment in the rest of society that is seldom openly expressed but festers nonetheless.

Pressures from these contrasting movements at the opposite ends of society put terrific stress on the entire structure. The mass of the nation belongs to neither group, but their lives are increasingly shaped by the power of the fortunate few and the plight of the despairing few. The culture's sense of what is right and wrong, virtuous and mean, attainable and unattainable—most important, its sense of how people are to live together—is altered in myriad ways. The fragile web of civility, mutual regard, and mutual obligations at the heart of any happy society begins to tear.

In trying to think through what is happening and why and in trying to understand thereby what ought to be done, the nation's social scientists and journalists and politicians seek explanations. They examine changes in the economy, changes in demographics, changes in the culture. They propose solutions founded on better education, on more and better jobs, on specific social interventions. But they ignore an underlying element that has shaped the changes: human intelligence—the way it varies within the American population and its crucially changing role in our destinies during the last half of the twentieth century. To try to come to grips with the nation's problems without understanding the role of intelligence is to see through a glass darkly indeed, to grope with symptoms instead of causes, to stumble into supposed remedies that have no chance of working.

We are not indifferent to the ways in which this book, wrongly construed, might do harm. We have worried about them from the day we set to work. But there can be no real progress in solving America's social problems when they are as misperceived as they are today. What good can come of understanding the relationship of intelligence to social structure and public policy? Little good can come without it.

Acknowledgments

The first thing that made this book possible was our good fortune in being where we are—Harvard University and the American Enterprise Institute. Different as they are in many ways, these two splendid institutions gave us a gift that is too often taken for granted: freedom and support to pursue our inquiries wherever they took us.

For learned and often creative advice for dealing with methodological issues, our thanks go to James Heckman, Derek Neal, Robert Rosenthal, Donald Rubin, Christopher Winship, and the Harvard Psychology Department's Seminar on the Analysis of Psychological Data. The staff of the Center for Human Resource Research—Paula Baker must be singled out—were unfailingly ready to answer our questions about the intricacies of the National Longitudinal Survey of Youth. In the world of psychometrics and testing, we benefited especially from the advice of Robert Forsyth, Arthur Jensen, Richard Lynn, Len Ramist, Malcolm Ree, and Frank Schmidt. Others who have read chapters or listened to us try to explain what we're up to and then have offered advice, or at least raised their eyebrows usefully, are Douglas Besharov, Eileen Blumenthal, John Bunzel, John DiIulio, Christopher DeMuth, David Ellwood, Richard Epstein, Ronald Haskins, James Herrnstein, Karl Hess, Michael Horowitz, Fred Jewett, Michael Joyce, Cheryl Keller, Robert Klitgaard, Irving Kristol, Richard Larry, Marlyn Lewis, Glenn Loury, Harvey Mansfield, Frank Miele, Michael Novak, Warren Reed, Daniel Seligman, Irwin Stelzer, Joan Kennedy Taylor, Abigail Thernstrom, Daniel Vining, Dean Whitla, James Wilson, and Douwe Yntema. Along with some of those already mentioned, John Bishop, Philip Cook, George Borjas, Robert Frank, Sandra Scarr, and Richard Weinberg provided us with drafts of their ongoing work that filled in missing pieces of the puzzle.

We took unblushing advantage of the energy and good nature of research assistants, with Kris Kirby and Ira Carnahan taking on some huge tasks early in the work, followed by the invaluable help of Kristin

Caplice, Joseph Fazioli, and one other who asked to remain anonymous out of his wish to preserve, as he put it, a viable political future.

All of these people, and others whom we have surely forgotten over the years, deserve our thanks for their help, but not the risk of being held accountable for what we've done with it.

We were lucky to have Erwin Glikes as our editor and Amanda Urban as our agent—the best in the business, and utterly undaunted by the hazards of this enterprise. *The Bell Curve* is Erwin's title, and its manuscript was the last he completed editing before his death.

In a list of acknowledgments, we would be remiss not to mention each other. We decided to write this book in November of 1989, and since the spring of 1990 have been working at it nearly full time, for long stretches much more than full time, in continual collaboration. Our partnership has led to a more compelling intellectual adventure and a deeper friendship than we could have imagined. Authorship is alphabetical; the work was symbiotic.

At last, how shall we express our thanks to Susan Herrnstein and Catherine Cox? They could not be, and were not, overjoyed to see their husbands embark on a project as controversial as this one. But they have endured our preoccupation with the book and its intrusion into our families' lives with love and humor. Beyond that, each of them read the entire manuscript, persuasively but affectionately pressing on us the benefit of their fine judgment, their good sense, and their honesty. In more ways than one, this book could not have been written without their help.

Richard J. Herrnstein
Charles Murray
3 June 1994

Introduction

That the word *intelligence* describes something real and that it varies from person to person is as universal and ancient as any understanding about the state of being human. Literate cultures everywhere and throughout history have had words for saying that some people are smarter than others. Given the survival value of intelligence, the concept must be still older than that. Gossip about who in the tribe is cleverest has probably been a topic of conversation around the fire since fires, and conversation, were invented.

Yet for the last thirty years, the concept of intelligence has been a pariah in the world of ideas. The attempt to measure it with tests has been variously dismissed as an artifact of racism, political reaction, statistical bungling, and scholarly fraud. Many of you have reached this page assuming that these accusations are proved. In such a context comes this book, blithely proceeding on the assumption that intelligence is a reasonably well-understood construct, measured with accuracy and fairness by any number of standardized mental tests. The rest of this book can be better followed if you first understand why we can hold such apparently heterodox views, and for this it is necessary to know something about the story of measured intelligence.

INTELLIGENCE ASCENDANT

Variation in intelligence became the subject of productive scientific study in the last half of the nineteenth century, stimulated, like so many other intellectual developments of that era, by Charles Darwin's theory of evolution. Darwin had asserted that the transmission of inherited intelligence was a key step in human evolution, driving our simian ancestors apart from the other apes. Sir Francis Galton, Darwin's young cousin and already a celebrated geographer in his own right, seized on this idea and set out to demonstrate its continuing relevance by using the great families of Britain as a primary source of data. He presented evidence that intellectual capacity of various sorts ran in families in

1

Hereditary Genius, published just a decade after the appearance of *Origin of Species* in 1859. So began a long and deeply controversial association between intelligence and heredity that remains with us today.[1]

Galton realized that he needed a precise, quantitative measure of the mental qualities he was trying to analyze, and thus he was led to put in formal terms what most people had always taken for granted: People vary in their intellectual abilities and the differences matter, to them personally and to society.[2] Not only are some people smarter than others, said Galton, but each person's pattern of intellectual abilities is unique. People differ in their talents, their intellectual strengths and weaknesses, their preferred forms of imagery, their mental vigor.

Working from these observations, Galton tried to devise an intelligence test as we understand the term today: a set of items probing intellectual capacities that could be graded objectively. Galton had the idea that intelligence would surface in the form of sensitivity of perceptions, so he constructed tests that relied on measures of acuity of sight and hearing, sensitivity to slight pressures on the skin, and speed of reaction to simple stimuli. His tests failed, but others followed where Galton had led. His most influential immediate successor, a French psychologist, Alfred Binet, soon developed questions that attempted to measure intelligence by measuring a person's ability to reason, draw analogies, and identify patterns.[3] These tests, crude as they were by modern standards, met the key criterion that Galton's tests could not: Their results generally accorded with common understandings of high and low intelligence.

By the end of the nineteenth century, mental tests in a form that we would recognize today were already in use throughout the British Commonwealth, the United States, much of continental Europe, and Japan.[4] Then, in 1904, a former British Army officer named Charles Spearman made a conceptual and statistical breakthrough that has shaped both the development and much of the methodological controversy about mental tests ever since.[5]

By that time, considerable progress had been made in statistics. Unlike Galton in his early years, investigators in the early twentieth century had available to them an invaluable number, the *correlation coefficient* first devised by Galton himself in 1888 and elaborated by his disciple, Karl Pearson.[6] Before the correlation coefficient was available, scientists could observe that two variables, such as height and weight, seemed to vary together (the taller the heavier, by and large), but they had no way of saying exactly how much they were related. With Pearson's r, as the coefficient was labeled, they now could specify "how much" of a relationship existed, on a scale ranging from a minimum of −1 (for perfectly inverse relationships) to +1 (for perfectly direct relationships).

Spearman noted that as the data from many different mental tests were accumulating, a curious result kept turning up: If the same group of people took two different mental tests, anyone who did well (or poorly) on one test tended to do similarly well (or poorly) on the other. In statistical terms, the scores on the two tests were positively correlated. This outcome did not seem to depend on the specific content of the tests. As long as the tests involved cognitive skills of one sort or another, the positive correlations appeared. Furthermore, individual items within tests showed positive correlations as well. If there was any correlation at all between a pair of items, a person who got one of them right tended to get the other one right, and vice versa for those who got it wrong. In fact, the pattern was stronger than that. It turned out to be nearly impossible to devise items that plausibly measured some cognitive skill and were *not* positively correlated with other items that plausibly measured some cognitive skill, however disparate the pair of skills might appear to be.

The size of the positive correlations among the pairs of items in a test did vary a lot, however, and it was this combination—positive correlations throughout the correlation matrix, but of varying magnitudes—that inspired Spearman's insight.[7] Why are almost all the correlations positive? Spearman asked. Because, he answered, they are tapping into the same general trait. Why are the magnitudes different? Because some items are more closely related to this general trait than others.[8]

Spearman's statistical method, an early example of what has since become known as factor analysis, is complex, and we will explore some of those complexities. But, for now, the basis for factor analysis can be readily understood. Insofar as two items tap into the same trait, they share something in common. Spearman developed a method for estimating how much sharing was going on in a given set of data. From almost any such collection of mental or academic test scores, Spearman's method of analysis uncovered evidence for a unitary mental factor, which he named *g*, for "general intelligence." The evidence for a general factor in intelligence was pervasive but circumstantial, based on statistical analysis rather than direct observation. Its reality therefore was, and remains, arguable.

Spearman then made another major contribution to the study of intelligence by defining what this mysterious *g* represented. He hypothesized that *g* is a general capacity for inferring and applying relationships drawn from experience. Being able to grasp, for example, the relationship between a pair of words like *harvest* and *yield*, or to recite a list of digits in reverse order, or to see what a geometrical pattern would look like upside down, are examples of tasks (and of test items) that draw on *g* as Spearman conceived of it. This definition of intelligence differed subtly from the more prevalent idea that intelligence is the ability to learn and to generalize what is learned. The course of learning is affected by intelligence, in Spearman's view, but it was not the thing in itself. Spearmanian intelligence was a measure of a person's capacity for complex mental work.

Meanwhile, other testers in Europe and America continued to refine mental measurement. By 1908, the concept of *mental level* (later called *mental age*) had been developed, followed in a few years by a slightly more sophisticated concept, the intelligence quotient. IQ at first was just a way of expressing a person's (usually a child's) mental level relative to his or her contemporaries. Later, as the uses of testing spread, IQ became a more general way to express a person's intellectual performance relative to a given population. Already by 1917, soon after the concept of IQ was first defined, the U.S. Army was administering intelligence tests to classify and assign recruits for World War I. Within a few years, the letters "IQ" had entered the American vernacular, where they remain today as a universally understood synonym for intelligence.

To this point, the study of cognitive abilities was a success story, representing one of the rare instances in which the new soft sciences were able to do their work with a rigor not too far short of the standards of the traditional sciences. A new specialty within psychology was created, psychometrics. Although the debates among the psychometricians were often fierce and protracted, they produced an expanded understanding of what was involved in mental capacity. The concept of *g* survived, embedded in an increasingly complex theory of the structure of cognitive abilities.

Because intelligence tests purported to test rigorously an important and valued trait about people (including ourselves and our loved ones), IQ also became one of the most visible and controversial products of social science. The first wave of public controversy occurred during the first decades of the century, when a few testing enthusiasts proposed using the results of mental tests to support outrageous racial policies. Sterilization laws were passed in sixteen American states between 1907 and 1917, with the elimination of mental retardation being one of the prime targets of the public policy. "Three generations of imbeciles are enough," Justice Oliver Wendell Holmes declared in an opinion upholding the constitutionality of such a law.[9] It was a statement made possible, perhaps encouraged, by the new enthusiasm for mental testing.

In the early 1920s, the chairman of the House Committee on Immigration and Naturalization appointed an "Expert Eugenical Agent" for his committee's work, a biologist who was especially concerned about keeping up the American level of intelligence by suitable immigration policies.[10] An assistant professor of psychology at Princeton, Carl C. Brigham, wrote a book entitled *A Study of American Intelligence* using the results of the U.S. Army's World War I mental testing program to conclude that an influx of immigrants from southern and eastern Europe would lower native American intelligence, and that immigration therefore should be restricted to Nordic stock (see the box about tests and immigration).[11]

Fact and Fiction About Immigration and Intelligence Testing

Two stories about early IQ testing have entered the folklore so thoroughly that people who know almost nothing else about that history bring them up at the beginning of almost any discussion of IQ. The first story is that Jews and other immigrant groups were thought to be below average in intelligence, even feebleminded, which goes to show how untrustworthy such tests (and the testers) are. The other story is that IQ tests were used as the basis for the racist immigration policies of the 1920s, which shows how dangerous such tests (and the testers) are.[12]

The first is based on the work done at Ellis Island by H. H. Goddard, who explicitly preselected his sample for evidence of low intelligence (his purpose was to test his test's usefulness in screening for feeblemindedness), and did not try to draw any conclusions about the general distribution of intelligence in immigrant groups.[13] The second has a stronger circumstantial case: Brigham published his book just a year before Congress passed the Immigration Restriction Act of 1924, which did indeed tip the flow of immigrants toward the western and northern Europeans. The difficulty with making the causal case is that a close reading of the hearings for the bill shows no evidence that Brigham's book in particular or IQ tests in general played any role.[14]

Critics responded vocally. Young Walter Lippmann, already an influential columnist, was one of the most prominent, fearing power-hungry intelligence testers who yearned to "occupy a position of power which no intellectual has held since the collapse of theocracy."[15] In a lengthy exchange in the *New Republic* in 1922 and 1923 with Lewis Terman, premier American tester of the time and the developer of the Stanford-Binet IQ test, Lippmann wrote, "I hate the impudence of a claim that in fifty minutes you can judge and classify a human being's predestined fitness in life. I hate the pretentiousness of that claim. I hate the abuse of scientific method which it involves. I hate the sense of superiority which it creates, and the sense of inferiority which it imposes."[16]

Lippmann's characterization of the tests and the testers was sometimes unfair and often factually wrong, as Terman energetically pointed out.[17] But while Terman may have won the technical arguments, Lippmann was right to worry that many people were eager to find connections between the results of testing and the more chilling implications of social Darwinism. Even if the psychometricians generally made modest claims for how much the tests predicted, it remained true that "IQ" —that single number with the memorable label—was seductive. As Lippmann feared, people did tend to give more credence to an individual's specific IQ score and make broader generalizations from it than was appropriate. And not least, there was plenty to criticize in the psychometricians' results. The methods for collecting and analyzing quantitative psychological data were still new, and some basic inferential mistakes were made.

If the tests had been fatally flawed or merely uninformative, they would have vanished. Why this did not happen is one of the stories we will be telling, but we may anticipate by observing that the use of tests endured and grew because society's largest institutions—schools, military forces, industries, governments—depend significantly on measurable individual differences. Much as some observers wished it were not true, there is often a need to assess differences between people as objectively, fairly, and efficiently as possible, and even the early mental tests often did a better job of it than any of the alternatives.

During the 1930s, mental tests evolved and improved as their use continued to spread throughout the world. David Wechsler worked on the initial version of the tests that would eventually become the Wechsler Adult Intelligence Scale and the Wechsler Intelligence Scale for Children, the famous WAIS and WISC. Terman and his associates published an improved version of the Stanford-Binet. But these tests were individually administered and had to be scored by trained personnel, and they were therefore too expensive to administer to large groups of people. Psychometricians and test publishers raced to develop group-administered tests that could be graded by machine. In the search for practical, economical measurements of intelligence, testing grew from a cottage industry to big business.

World War II stimulated another major advance in the state of the art, as psychologists developed paper-and-pencil tests that could accurately identify specific military aptitudes, even ones that included a significant element of physical aptitude (such as an aptitude for flying airplanes). Shortly after the war, psychologists at the University of Minnesota developed the Minnesota Multiphasic Personality Inventory, the first machine-gradable standardized test with demonstrated validity as a predictor of various personality disorders. Later came the California Psychological Inventory, which measured personality characteristics within the normal range—"social presence" and "self-control," for example. The testing industry was flourishing, and the annual *Mental Measurements Yearbook* that cataloged the tests grew to hundreds of pages. Hundreds of millions of people throughout the world were being psychologically tested every year.

Attacks on testing faded into the background during this period. Though some psychometricians must have known that the tests were capturing human differences that had unsettling political and social implications, no one of any stature was trying to use the results to promote discriminatory, let alone eugenic, laws. And though many intellectuals outside the testing profession knew of these results, the political agendas of the 1940s and 1950s, whether of New Deal Democrats or Eisenhower Republicans, were more pragmatic than ideological. Yes, intelligence varied, but this was a fact of life that seemed to have little bearing on the way public policy was conducted.

INTELLIGENCE BESIEGED

Then came the 1960s, and a new controversy about intelligence tests that continues to this day. It arose not from new findings but from a new outlook on public policy. Beginning with the rise of powerful social democratic and socialist movements after World War I and accelerating across the decades until the 1960s, a fundamental shift was taking place in the received wisdom regarding equality. This was most evident in the political arena, where the civil rights movement and then the War on Poverty raised Americans' consciousness about the nature of the inequalities in American society. But the changes in outlook ran deeper and broader than politics. Assumptions about the very origins of social problems changed profoundly. Nowhere was the shift more pervasive than in the field of psychology.

Psychometricians of the 1930s had debated whether intelligence is almost entirely produced by genes or whether the environment also plays a role. By the 1960s and 1970s the point of contention had shifted dramatically. It had somehow become controversial to claim, especially in public, that genes had any effect at all on intelligence. Ironically, the evidence for genetic factors in intelligence had greatly strengthened during the very period when the terms of the debate were moving in the other direction.

In the psychological laboratory, there was a similar shift. Psychological experimenters early in the century were, if anything, more likely to concentrate on the inborn patterns of human and animal behavior than on how the learning process could change behavior.[18] But from the 1930s to the 1960s, the leading behaviorists, as they were called, and their students and disciples were almost all specialists in learning theory. They filled the technical journals with the results of learning experiments on rats and pigeons, the tacit implication being that genetic endowment mattered so little that we could ignore the differences among species, let alone among human individuals, and still discover enough about the learning process to make it useful and relevant to human concerns.[19] There are, indeed, aspects of the learning process that cross the lines between species, but there are also enormous differences, and these differences were sometimes ignored or minimized when psychologists explained their findings to the lay public. B. F. Skinner, at Harvard University, more than any other of the leading behaviorists, broke out of the academic world into public attention with books that applied the findings of laboratory research on animals to human society at large.[20]

To those who held the behaviorist view, human potential was almost perfectly malleable, shaped by the environment. The causes of human deficiencies in intelligence—or parenting, or social behavior, or work behavior—lay outside the individual. They were caused by flaws in society. Sometimes capitalism was blamed, sometimes an uncaring or incompetent government. Further, the causes of these deficiencies could be fixed by the right public policies—redistribution of wealth, better education, better housing and medical care. Once these environmental causes were removed, the deficiencies should vanish as well, it was argued.

The contrary notion—that individual differences could not easily be diminished by government intervention—collided head-on with the enthusiasm for egalitarianism, which itself collided head-on with a half-century of IQ data indicating that differences in intelligence are intractable and significantly heritable and that the average IQ of various socioeconomic and ethnic groups differs.

In 1969, Arthur Jensen, an educational psychologist and expert on testing from the University of California at Berkeley, put a match to this volatile mix of science and ideology with an article in the *Harvard Educational Review*.[21] Asked by the *Review's* editors to consider why compensatory and remedial education programs begun with such high hopes during the War on Poverty had yielded such disappointing results, Jensen concluded that the programs were bound to have little success because they were aimed at populations of youngsters with relatively low IQs, and success in school depended to a considerable degree on IQ. IQ had a large heritable component, Jensen also noted. The article further disclosed that the youngsters in the targeted populations were disproportionately black and that historically blacks as a population had exhibited average IQs substantially below those of whites.

The reaction to Jensen's article was immediate and violent. From 1969 through the mid-1970s, dozens of books and hundreds of articles appeared denouncing the use of IQ tests and arguing that mental abilities are determined by environment, with the genes playing a minor role and race none at all. Jensen's name became synonymous with a constellation of hateful ways of thinking. "It perhaps is impossible to exaggerate the importance of the Jensen disgrace," wrote Jerry Hirsch, a psychologist specializing in the genetics of animal behavior who was among Jensen's more vehement critics. "It has permeated both science and the universities and hoodwinked large segments of government and society. Like Vietnam and Watergate, it is a contemporary symptom of serious affliction."[22] The title of Hirsch's article was "The Bankruptcy of 'Science' Without Scholarship." During the first few years after the *Harvard Educational Review* article was published, Jensen could appear in no public forum in the United States without triggering something perilously close to a riot.

The uproar was exacerbated by William Shockley, who had won the Nobel Prize in physics for his contributions to the invention of the transistor but had turned his attention to human variation toward the end of his career. As eccentric as he was brilliant, he often recalled the eugenicists of the early decades of the century. He proposed, as a "thought exercise," a scheme for paying people with low IQs to be sterilized.[23] He supported (and contributed to) a sperm bank for geniuses. He seemed to relish expressing sensitive scientific findings in a way that would outrage or disturb as many people as possible. Jensen and Shockley, utterly unlike as they were in most respects, soon came to be classed together as a pair of racist intellectual cranks.

Then one of us, Richard Herrnstein, an experimental psychologist at Harvard, strayed into forbidden territory with an article in the September 1971 *Atlantic Monthly*.[24] Herrnstein barely mentioned race, but he did talk about heritability of IQ. His proposition, put in the form of a syllogism, was that because IQ is substantially heritable, because economic success in life depends in part on the talents measured by IQ tests, and because social standing depends in part on economic success, it follows that social standing is bound to be based to some extent on inherited differences. By 1971, this had become a controversial thing to say. In media accounts of intelligence, the names Jensen, Shockley, and Herrnstein became roughly interchangeable.

That same year, 1971, the U.S. Supreme Court outlawed the use of standardized ability tests by employers unless they had a "manifest relationship" to the specific job in question because, the Supreme Court held, standardized tests acted as "built-in headwinds" for minority groups, even in the absence of discriminatory intent.[25] A year later, the National Education Association called upon the nation's schools to impose a moratorium on all standardized intelligence testing, hypothesizing that "a third or more of American citizens are intellectually folded, mutilated or spindled before they have a chance to get through elementary school because of linguistically or culturally biased standardized tests."[26] A movement that had begun in the 1960s gained momentum in the early 1970s, as major school systems throughout the country, including those of Chicago, New York, and Los Angeles, limited or banned the use of group-administered standardized tests in public schools. A number of colleges announced that they would no longer require the Scholastic Aptitude Test as part of the admissions process. The legal movement against tests reached its apogee in 1978 in the case of *Larry P.* Judge Robert Peckham of the U.S. District Court in San Francisco ruled that it was unconstitutional to use IQ tests for placement of children in classes for the educably mentally retarded if the use of those tests resulted in placement of "grossly disproportionate" numbers of black children.[27]

Meanwhile, the intellectual debate had taken a new and personalized turn. Those who claimed that intelligence was substantially inherited were not just wrong, the critics now discovered, they were charlatans as well. Leon Kamin, a psychologist then at Princeton, opened this phase of the debate with a 1974 book, *The Science and Politics of IQ.* "Patriotism, we have been told, is the last refuge of scoundrels," Kamin wrote in the opening pages. "Psychologists and biologists might consider the possibility that heritability is the first."[28] Kamin went on to charge that mental testing and belief in the heritability of IQ in particular had been fostered by people with right-wing political views and racist social views. They had engaged in pseudoscience, he wrote, suppressing the data they did not like and exaggerating the data that agreed with their preconceptions. Examined carefully, the case for the heritability of IQ was nil, concluded Kamin.

In 1976, a British journalist, Oliver Gillie, published an article in the *London Sunday Times* that seemed to confirm Kamin's thesis with a sensational revelation: The recently deceased Cyril Burt, Britain's most eminent psychometrician, author of the largest and most famous study of the intelligence of identical twins who grew up apart, was charged with fraud.[29] He had made up data, fudged his results, and invented coauthors, the *Sunday Times* declared. The subsequent scandal was as big as the Piltdown Man hoax. Cyril Burt had not been just another researcher but one of the giants of twentieth-century psychology. Nor could his colleagues find a ready defense (the defense came later, as described in the box). They protested that the revelations did not compromise the great bulk of the work that bore on the issue of heritability, but their defenses sounded feeble in the light of the suspicions that had preceded Burt's exposure.

For the public observing the uproar in the academy from the sidelines, the capstone of the assault on the integrity of the discipline occurred in 1981 when Harvard paleobiologist Stephen Jay Gould, author of several popular books on biology, published *The Mismeasure of Man.*[32] Gould examined the history of intelligence testing, found that it was

---

The Burt Affair

It would be more than a decade before the Burt affair was subjected to detailed reexamination. In 1989 and 1991, two accounts of the Burt allegations, by psychologist Robert Joynson and sociologist Ronald Fletcher, written independently, concluded that the attacks against Burt had been motivated by a mixture of professional and ideological antagonism and that no credible case of data falsification or fictitious research or researchers had ever been presented.[30] Both authors also concluded that some of Burt's leading critics were aware that their accusations were inaccurate even at the time they made them. An ironic afterword centers on Burt's claim that the correlation between the IQs of identical twins reared apart is +.77. A correlation this large almost irrefutably supports a large genetic influence on IQ. Since the attacks on Burt began, it had been savagely derided as fraudulent, the product of Burt's fiddling with the data to make his case. In 1990, the Minnesota twin study, accepted by most scholars as a model of its kind, produced its most detailed estimates of the correlation of IQ between identical twins reared apart. The procedure that most closely paralleled Burt's yielded a correlation of +.78.[31]

---

peopled by charlatans, racists, and self-deluded fools, and concluded that "determinist arguments for ranking people according to a single scale of intelligence, no matter how numerically sophisticated, have recorded little more than social prejudice."[33] *The Mismeasure of Man* became a best-seller and won the National Book Critics Circle Award.

Gould and his allies had won the visible battle. By the early 1980s, a new received wisdom about intelligence had been formed that went roughly as follows:

> *Intelligence is a bankrupt concept. Whatever it might mean—and nobody really knows even how to define it—intelligence is so ephemeral that no one can measure it accurately. IQ tests are, of course, culturally biased, and so are all the other "aptitude" tests, such as the SAT. To the extent that tests such as IQ and SAT measure anything, it certainly is not an innate "intelligence." IQ scores are not constant; they often change significantly over an individual's life span. The scores of entire populations can be expected to change over time—look at the Jews, who early in the twentieth century scored below average on IQ scores and now score well above the*

average. Furthermore, the tests are nearly useless as tools, as confirmed by the well-documented fact that such tests do not predict anything except success in school. Earnings, occupation, productivity—all the important measures of success—are unrelated to the test scores. All that tests really accomplish is to label youngsters, stigmatizing the ones who do not do well and creating a self-fulfilling prophecy that injures the socioeconomically disadvantaged in general and blacks in particular.

INTELLIGENCE REDUX

As far as public discussion is concerned, this collection of beliefs, with some variations, remains the state of wisdom about cognitive abilities and IQ tests. It bears almost no relation to the current state of knowledge among scholars in the field, however, and therein lies a tale. The dialogue about testing has been conducted at two levels during the last two decades—the visible one played out in the press and the subterranean one played out in the technical journals and books.

The case of Arthur Jensen is illustrative. To the public, he surfaced briefly, published an article that was discredited, and fell back into obscurity. Within the world of psychometrics, however, he continued to be one of the profession's most prolific scholars, respected for his meticulous research by colleagues of every theoretical stripe. Jensen had not recanted. He continued to build on the same empirical findings that had gotten him into such trouble in the 1960s, but primarily in technical publications, where no one outside the profession had to notice. The same thing was happening throughout psychometrics. In the 1970s, scholars observed that colleagues who tried to say publicly that IQ tests had merit, or that intelligence was substantially inherited, or even that intelligence existed as a definable and measurable human quality, paid too high a price. Their careers, family lives, relationships with colleagues, and even physical safety could be jeopardized by speaking out. Why speak out when there was no compelling reason to do so? Research on cognitive abilities continued to flourish, but only in the sanctuary of the ivory tower.

In this cloistered environment, the continuing debate about intelligence was conducted much as debates are conducted within any other academic discipline. The public controversy had surfaced some genuine issues, and the competing parties set about trying to resolve them. Controversial hypotheses were put to the test. Sometimes they were confirmed, sometimes rejected. Often they led to new questions, which were then explored. Substantial progress was made. Many of the issues that created such a public furor in the 1970s were resolved, and the study of cognitive abilities went on to explore new areas.

This is not to say that controversy has ended, only that the controversy within the professional intelligence testing community is much different from that outside it. The issues that seem most salient in articles in the popular press (Isn't intelligence determined mostly by environment? Aren't the tests useless because they're biased?) are not major topics of debate within the profession. On many of the publicly discussed questions, a scholarly consensus has been reached.[34] Rather, the contending parties within the professional community divide along other lines. By the early 1990s, they could be roughly divided into three factions for our purposes: the classicists, the revisionists, and the radicals.

The Classicists: Intelligence as a Structure

The classicists work within the tradition begun by Spearman, seeking to identify the components of intelligence much as physicists seek to identify the structure of the atom. As of the 1990s, the classicists are for practical purposes unanimous in accepting that *g* sits at the center of the structure in a dominating position—not just as an artifact of statistical manipulation but as an expression of a core human mental ability much like the ability Spearman identified at the turn of the century. In their view, *g* is one of the most thoroughly demonstrated entities in the behavioral sciences and one of the most powerful for understanding socially significant human variation.

The classicists took a long time to reach this level of consensus. The ink on Spearman's first article on the topic in 1904 was barely dry before others were arguing that intellectual ability could not be adequately captured by *g* or by any other unitary quantity—and understandably so, for common sense rebels against the idea that something so important about people as their intellects can be captured even roughly by variations in a single quantity. Many of the famous names in the history of psychometrics challenged the reality of *g*, starting with Galton's most eminent early disciple, Karl Pearson, and continuing with many other creative and influential psychometricians.

In diverse ways, they sought the grail of a set of primary and mutually independent mental abilities. For Spearman, there was just one such primary ability, *g*. For Raymond Cattell, there are two kinds of *g*, *crystallized* and *fluid*, with crystallized *g* being general intelligence transformed into the skills of one's own culture, and fluid *g* being the all-purpose intellectual capacity from which the crystallized skills are formed. In Louis Thurstone's theory of intelligence, there are a half-dozen or so *primary mental abilities*, such as verbal, quantitative, spatial, and the like. In Philip Vernon's theory, intellectual capacities are arranged in a hierarchy with *g* at its apex; in Joy Guilford's, the structure of intellect is refined into 120 or more intellectual components. The theoretical alternatives to unitary, general intelligence have come in many sizes, shapes, and degrees of plausibility.

Many of these efforts proved to have lasting value. For example, Cattell's distinction between fluid and crystallized intelligence remains a useful conceptual contrast, just as other work has done much to clarify what lies in the domain of specific abilities that *g* cannot account for. But no one has been able to devise a set of tests that do not reveal a large general factor of intellectual ability—in other words, something very like Spearman's *g*. Furthermore, the classicists point out, the best standardized tests, such as a modern IQ test, do a reasonably good job of measuring *g*. When properly administered, the tests are not measurably biased against socioeconomic, ethnic, or racial subgroups. They predict a wide variety of socially important outcomes.

This is not the same as saying that the classicists are satisfied with their understanding of intelligence. *g* is a statistical entity, and current research is probing the underlying neurologic basis for it. Arthur Jensen, the archetypal classicist, has been active in this effort for the last decade, returning to Galton's intuition that performance on elementary cognitive tasks, such as reaction time in recognizing simple patterns of lights and shapes, provides an entry point into understanding the physiology of *g*.

The Revisionists: Intelligence as Information Processing

A theory of intelligence need not be structural. The emphasis may be on process rather than on structure. In other words, it may try to figure out what a person is *doing* when exercising his or her intelligence, rather than what elements of intelligence are put together. The great Swiss psychologist, Jean Piaget, started his career in Alfred Binet's laboratory trying to adapt Cyril Burt's intelligence tests for Parisian children. Piaget discovered quickly that he was less interested in how well the children did than in what errors they made.[35] Errors revealed what the underlying processes of thought must have been, Piaget believed. It was the processes of intelligence that fascinated him during his long and illustrious career, which led in time to his theory of the stages of cognitive development.

Starting in the 1960s, research on human cognition became the preoccupation of experimental psychologists, displacing the animal learning experiments of the earlier period. It was inevitable that the new experimentalists would turn to the study of human intelligence in natural settings. John B. Carroll and Earl B. Hunt led the way from the cognition laboratory to the study of human intelligence in everyday life. Today Yale psychologist Robert Sternberg is among the leaders of this development.

The revisionists share much with the classicists. They accept that a general mental ability much like Spearman's *g* has to be incorporated into any theory of the structure of intelligence, although they would not agree that it accounts for as much of the intellectual variation among people as many classicists claim. They use many of the same statistical tools as the classicists and are prepared to subject their work to the same standards of rigor. Where they differ with the classicists, however, is their attitude toward intellectual structure and the tests used to measure it.

Yes, the revisionists argue, human intelligence has a structure, but is it worth investing all that effort in discovering what it is? The preoccupation with structure has engendered preoccupation with summary scores, the revisionists say. That, after all, is what an IQ score represents: a composite of scores that individually measure quite distinct intellectual processes. "Of course," Sternberg writes, "a tester can always average over multiple scores. But are such averages revealing, or do they camouflage more than they reveal? If a person is a wonderful visualizer but can barely compose a sentence, and another person can write glowing prose but cannot begin to visualize the simplest spatial images, what do you really learn about these two people if they are reported to have the same IQ?"[36]

By focusing on processes, the revisionists argue, they are working richer veins than are those who search for static structure. What really counts about intelligence are the ways in which people process the information they receive. What problem-solving mechanisms do they employ? How do they trade off speed and accuracy? How do they combine different problem-solving resources into a strategy? Sternberg has fashioned his own thinking on this topic into what he calls a "triarchy of intelligence," or "three aspects of human information processing."[37]

The first part of Sternberg's triarchy attempts to describe the internal architecture of intellectual functioning, the means by which humans translate sensory inputs into mental representations, allocate mental resources, infer conclusions from raw material, and acquire skills. This architectural component of Sternberg's theory bears a family resemblance to the classicists' view of the dimensions of intelligence, but it emphasizes process over structure.

The second part of the triarchic theory addresses the role of intelligence in routinizing performance, starting with completely novel tasks that test a person's insightfulness, flexibility, and creativity, and eventually converting them to routine tasks that can be done without conscious thought. Understand this process, Sternberg argues, and we have leverage not just for measuring intelligence but for improving it.

The third part of Sternberg's triarchy attacks the question that has been central to the controversy over intelligence tests: the relationship of intelligence to the real world in which people function. In Sternberg's view, people function by means of three mechanisms: *adaptation* (roughly, trying to make the best of the situation), *shaping* the external environment so that it conforms more closely to the desired state of affairs, or *selecting* a new environment altogether. Sternberg laments the inadequacies of traditional intelligence tests in capturing this real-world aspect of intelligence and seeks to develop tests that will do so—and, in addition, lead to techniques for teaching people to raise their intelligence.

The Radicals: The Theory of Multiple Intelligences

Walter Lippmann's hostility toward intelligence testing was grounded in his belief that this most important of all human qualities was too diverse, too complex, too changeable, too dependent on cultural context, and, above all, too subjective to be measured by answers to a mere list of test questions. Intelligence seemed to him, as it does to many other thoughtful people who are not themselves expert in testing, more like beauty or justice than height or weight. Before something can be measured, it must be defined, this argument goes.[38] And the problems of definition for beauty, justice, or intelligence are insuperable. To people who hold these views, the claims of the intelligence testers seem naive at best and vicious at worst. These views, which are generally advanced primarily by nonspecialists, have found an influential spokesman from the academy, which is mainly why we include them here. We refer here to the theory of multiple intelligences formulated by Howard Gardner, a Harvard psychologist.

Gardner's general definition of intelligent behavior does not seem radical at all. For Gardner, as for many other thinkers on intelligence, the notion of problem solving is central. "A human intellectual competence must entail a set of skills of problem solving," he writes, "enabling the individual to *resolve genuine problems or difficulties* that he or she encounters and, when appropriate, to create an effective product— and also must entail the potential for *finding or creating problems*— thereby laying the groundwork for the acquisition of new knowledge."[39]

Gardner's view is radical (a word he uses himself to describe his theory) in that he rejects, virtually without qualification, the notion of a general intelligence factor, which is to say that he denies g. Instead, he argues the case for seven distinct intelligences: linguistic, musical, logical-mathematical, spatial, bodily-kinesthetic, and two forms of "personal intelligence," the intrapersonal and the interpersonal, each based on its own unique computational capacity.[40] Gardner rejects the criticism that he has merely redefined the word *intelligence* by broadening it to include what may more properly be called talents: "I place no particular premium on the word *intelligence*, but I do place great importance on the equivalence of various human faculties," he writes. "If critics [of his theory] were willing to label language and logical thinking as talents as well, and to remove these from the pedestal they currently occupy, then I would be happy to speak of multiple talents."[41]

Gardner's approach is also radical in that he does not defend his theory with quantitative data. He draws on findings from anthropology to zoology in his narrative, but, in a field that has been intensely quantitative since its inception, Gardner's work is uniquely devoid of psychometric or other quantitative evidence. He dismisses factor analysis: "[G]iven the same set of data, it is possible, using one set of factor-analytic procedures, to come up with a picture that supports the idea of a 'g' factor; using another equally valid method of statistical analysis, it is possible to support the notion of a family of relatively discrete mental abilities."[42] He is untroubled by the fact that tests of the varying intelligences in his theory seem to be intercorrelated: "I fear . . . that I cannot accept these correlations at face value. Nearly all current tests are so devised that they call principally upon linguistic and logical facility. . . . Accordingly, individuals with these skills are likely to do well even in tests of musical or spatial abilities, while those who are not especially facile linguistically and logically are likely to be impaled on such standardized tests."[43] And in general, he invites his readers to disregard the thorny complexities of the classical and revisionist approaches: "When it comes to the interpretation of intelligence testing, we are faced with an issue of taste or preference rather than one on which scientific closure is likely to be reached."[44]

THE PERSPECTIVE OF THIS BOOK

Given these different ways of understanding intelligence, you will naturally ask where our sympathies lie and how they shape this book.

We will be drawing most heavily from the classical tradition. That body of scholarship represents an immense and rigorously analyzed body of knowledge. By accepted standards of what constitutes scientific evidence and scientific proof, the classical tradition has in our view given the world a treasure of information that has been largely ignored in trying to understand contemporary policy issues. Moreover, because our topic is the relationship of human abilities to public policy, we will be dealing in relationships that are based on aggregated data, which is where the classical tradition has the most to offer. Perhaps an example will illustrate what we mean.

Suppose that the question at issue regards individuals: "Given two 11 year olds, one with an IQ of 110 and one with an IQ of 90, what can you tell us about the differences between those two children?" The answer must be phrased very tentatively. On many important topics, the answer must be, "We can tell you nothing with any confidence." It is well worth a guidance counselor's time to know what these individual scores are, but only in combination with a variety of other information about the child's personality, talents, and background. The individual's IQ score all by itself is a useful tool but a limited one.

Suppose instead that the question at issue is: "Given two sixth-grade classes, one for which the average IQ is 110 and the other for which it is 90, what can you tell us about the difference between those two classes and their average prospects for the future?" Now there is a great deal to be said, and it can be said with considerable confidence—not about any one person in either class but about average outcomes that are important to the school, educational policy in general, and society writ large. The data accumulated under the classical tradition are extremely rich in this regard, as will become evident in subsequent chapters.

If instead we were more concerned with the development of cognitive processes than with aggregate social and economic outcomes, we would correspondingly spend more time discussing the work of the revisionists. That we do not reflects our focus, not a dismissal of their work.

With regard to the radicals and the theory of multiple intelligences, we share some common ground. Socially significant individual differences include a wide range of human talents that do not fit within the classical conception of intelligence. For certain spheres of life, they matter profoundly. And even beyond intelligence and talents, people vary temperamentally, in personality, style, and character. But we confess to reservations about using the word *intelligence* to describe such factors as musical abilities, kinesthetic abilities, or personal skills. It is easy to understand how intelligence (ordinarily understood) is part of some aspects of each of those human qualities—obviously, Bach was engaging in intelligent activity, and so was Ted Williams, and so is a good used-car salesman—but the part intelligence plays in these activities is captured fairly well by intelligence as the classicists and revisionists conceive of it. In the case of music and kinesthetics, *talent* is a word with a domain and weight of its own, and we are unclear why we gain anything by discarding it in favor of another word, *intelligence*, that has had another domain and weight. In the case of intrapersonal and interpersonal skills, conventional intelligence may play some role, and, to the extent that other human qualities matter, words like *sensitivity, charm, persuasiveness, insight*—the list could go on and on—have accumulated over the centuries to describe them. We lose precision by using the word *intelligence* to cover them all. Similarly, the effect that an artist or an athlete or a salesman creates is complex, with some aspects that may be dominated by specific endowments or capacities, others that may be the product of learned technique, others that may be linked to desires and drives, and still others that are characteristic of the kind of cognitive ability denoted by intelligence. Why try to make *intelligence* do triple or quadruple duty?

We agree emphatically with Howard Gardner, however, that the concept of intelligence has taken on a much higher place in the pantheon of human virtues than it deserves. One of the most insidious but also widespread errors regarding IQ, especially among people who have high IQs, is the assumption that another person's intelligence can be inferred from casual interactions. Many people conclude that if they see someone who is sensitive, humorous, and talks fluently, the person must surely have an above-average IQ.

This identification of IQ with attractive human qualities in general is unfortunate and wrong. Statistically, there is often a modest correlation with such qualities. But modest correlations are of little use in sizing up other individuals one by one. For example, a person can have a terrific sense of humor without giving you a clue about where he is within thirty points on the IQ scale. Or a plumber with a measured IQ of 100—only an average IQ—can know a great deal about the functioning of plumbing systems. He may be able to diagnose problems, discuss them articulately, make shrewd decisions about how to fix them, and, while he is working, make some pithy remarks about the president's recent speech.

At the same time, high intelligence has earmarks that correspond to a first approximation to the commonly understood meaning of *smart*. In our experience, people do not use *smart* to mean (necessarily) that a person is prudent or knowledgeable but rather to refer to qualities of mental quickness and complexity that do in fact show up in high test scores. To return to our examples: Many witty people do not have unusually high test scores, but someone who regularly tosses off impromptu complex puns probably does (which does not necessarily mean that such puns are very funny, we hasten to add). If the plumber runs into a problem he has never seen before and diagnoses its source through inferences from what he does know, he probably has an IQ of more than 100 after all. In this, language tends to reflect real differences: In everyday language, people who are called very smart tend to have high IQs.

All of this is another way of making a point so important that we will italicize it now and repeat elsewhere: *Measures of intelligence have reliable statistical relationships with important social phenomena, but they are a limited tool for deciding what to make of any given individual.* Repeat it we must, for one of the problems of writing about intelligence is how to remind readers often enough how little an IQ score tells about whether the human being next to you is someone whom you will admire or cherish. This thing we know as IQ is important but not a synonym for human excellence.

Idiot Savants and Other Anomalies

To add one final complication, it is also known that some people with low measured IQ occasionally engage in highly developed, complex cognitive tasks. So-called idiot savants can (for example) tell you on what day Easter occurred in any of the past or future two thousand years.[45] There are also many less exotic examples. For example, a study of successful track bettors revealed that some of them who used extremely complicated betting systems had below-average IQs and that IQ was not correlated with success.[46] The trick in interpreting such results is to keep separate two questions: (1) If one selects people who have already demonstrated an obsession and success with racetrack betting systems, will one find a relationship with IQ (the topic of the study in question)? versus (2) if one selects a thousand people at random and asks them to develop racetrack betting systems, will there be a relationship with IQ (in broad terms, the topic of this book)?

Howard Gardner has also convinced us that the word *intelligence* carries with it undue affect and political baggage. It is still a useful word, but we shall subsequently employ the more neutral term *cognitive ability* as often as possible to refer to the concept that we have hitherto called *intelligence*, just as we will use *IQ* as a generic synonym for *intelligence test score*. Since *cognitive ability* is an uneuphonious phrase, we lapse often so as to make the text readable. But at least we hope that it will help you think of *intelligence* as just a noun, not an accolade.

We have said that we will be drawing most heavily on data from the classical tradition. That implies that we also accept certain conclusions undergirding that tradition. To draw the strands of our perspective together and to set the stage for the rest of the book, let us set them down explicitly. Here are six conclusions regarding tests of cognitive ability, drawn from the classical tradition, that are by now beyond significant technical dispute:

1. There is such a thing as a general factor of cognitive ability on which human beings differ.
2. All standardized tests of academic aptitude or achievement measure this general factor to some degree, but IQ tests expressly designed for that purpose measure it most accurately.
3. IQ scores match, to a first degree, whatever it is that people mean when they use the word *intelligent* or *smart* in ordinary language.

4. IQ scores are stable, although not perfectly so, over much of a person's life.
5. Properly administered IQ tests are not demonstrably biased against social, economic, ethnic, or racial groups.
6. Cognitive ability is substantially heritable, apparently no less than 40 percent and no more than 80 percent.

All six points have an inverse worth noting. For example, some people's scores change a lot; cognitive ability is not synonymous with test scores or with a single general mental factor, and so on. When we say that all are "beyond significant technical dispute," we mean, in effect, that if you gathered the top experts on testing and cognitive ability, drawn from all points of view, to argue over these points, away from television cameras and reporters, it would quickly become apparent that a consensus already exists on all of the points, in some cases amounting to near unanimity. And although dispute would ensue about some of the points, one side—the side represented by the way the points are stated—would have a clear preponderance of evidence favoring it, and those of another viewpoint would be forced to lean heavily on isolated studies showing anomalous results.

This does not mean that the experts should leave the room with their differences resolved. All six points can be accurate as general rules and still leave room for differences in the theoretical and practical conclusions that people of different values and perspectives draw from them (and from the mass of material about cognitive ability and testing not incorporated in the six points). Radicals in the Gardner mold might still balk at all the attention being paid to intelligence as the tests measure it. But these points, in themselves, are squarely in the middle of the scientific road.

Having said this, however, we are left with a dilemma. The received wisdom in the media is roughly 180 degrees opposite from each of the six points. To prove our case, taking each point and amassing a full account of the evidence for and against, would lead us to write a book just about them. Such books have already been written. There is no point in our trying to duplicate them.[47]

We have taken two steps to help you form your own judgments within the limits of this book. First, we deal with specific issues involving the six points as they arise in the natural course of the discussion—cultural bias when discussing differences in scores across ethnic groups, for example. Second, we try to provide a level of detail that will satisfy different levels of technical curiosity through the use of boxed material (you have already come across some examples), notes, and appendixes. Because we expect (and fear) that many readers will go directly to chapters that especially interest them rather than read the book from cover to cover, we also insert periodic reminders about where discussion of certain key topics may be found.

PART I

The Emergence of a Cognitive Elite

The twentieth century dawned on a world segregated into social classes defined in terms of money, power, and status. The ancient lines of separation based on hereditary rank were being erased, replaced by a more complicated set of overlapping lines. Social standing still played a major role, if less often accompanied by a sword or tiara, but so did out-and-out wealth, educational credentials, and, increasingly, talent.

Our thesis is that the twentieth century has continued the transformation, so that the twenty-first will open on a world in which cognitive ability is the decisive dividing force. The shift is more subtle than the previous one but more momentous. Social class remains the vehicle of social life, but intelligence now pulls the train.

Cognitive stratification takes different forms at the top and the bottom of the scale of intelligence. Part II will look at the bottom. In Part I, we look at the top. Its story line is that modern societies identify the brightest youths with ever increasing efficiency and then guide them into fairly narrow educational and occupational channels. These channels are increasingly lucrative and influential, leading to the development of a distinct stratum in the social hierarchy, which we hereby dub the Cognitive Elite. The isolation of the brightest from the rest of society is already extreme; the forces driving it are growing stronger rather than weaker. Governments can influence these forces but cannot neutralize them.

This does not mean that a member of the cognitive elite never crosses paths with a person with a low IQ, but the encounters that matter tend to be limited. The more intimate or more enduring the human relationship is, the more likely it is to be among people similar in intellectual level. That the brightest are identified has its benefits. That they become so isolated and inbred has its costs. Some of these costs are already visible in American society, while others lie over the horizon.

25

Human society has always had some measure of cognitive stratification. The best hunters among the Bushmen of the Kalahari tend to score above the average of their tribe on modern intelligence tests and so, doubtless, would have the chief ministers in Cheop's Egypt.[1] The Mandarins who ran China for centuries were chosen by examinations that tested for understanding of the Confucian classics and, in so doing, screened for intelligence. The priests and monks of medieval Europe, recruited and self-selected for reasons correlated with cognitive ability, must have been brighter than average.

This differentiation by cognitive ability did not coalesce into cognitive classes in premodern societies for various reasons. Clerical celibacy was one. Another was that the people who rose to the top on their brains were co-opted by aristocratic systems that depleted their descendants' talent, mainly through the mechanism known as primogeniture. Because parents could not pick the brightest of their progeny to inherit the title and land, aristocracies fell victim to regression to the mean: children of parents with above-average IQs tend to have lower IQs than their parents, and their children's IQs are lower still. Over the course of a few generations, the average intelligence in an aristocratic family fell toward the population average, hastened by marriages that matched bride and groom by lineage, not ability.

On the other hand, aristocratic societies were not as impermeable to social mobility as they tried to be. They allowed at least some avenues for ability to rise toward the top, whereupon the brains of the newcomer were swapped in marriage for family connections and titles. England was notably sagacious in this regard, steadily infusing new talent into the aristocracy by creating peerages for its most successful commoners. The traditional occupations for the younger sons of British peers—army, navy, church, and the administration of the empire—gave the ablest younger sons in the aristocracy a good chance to rise to the top and help sustain the system. Indeed, the success of some English families in sustaining their distinction over several generations was one of the factors that prompted Francis Galton to hypothesize that intelligence was inherited. But only a minority of aristocratic families managed this trick. It remained true even in England that, after a few generations, the holder of any given aristocratic title was unlikely to be smarter than anyone else. When one observer wrote of the aristocracy in Queen Victoria's day that "all the social talk is stupid and insipid," he was being more accurate than perhaps he realized.[2]

Even in less rigidly stratified societies, stratification by cognitive ability has been weak and inconsistent until this century because the number of very bright people was so much greater than the specialized jobs for which high intelligence is indispensable. A true cognitive elite requires a technological society. This raises a distinction that is so important, and forgetting it can so easily lead to needless misunderstanding, that it is worth emphasizing: *To say that most of the people in the cognitively demanding positions of a society have a high IQ is not the same as saying that most of the people with high IQs are in such positions.* It is possible to have cognitive screening without having cognitive classes. Mathematical necessity tells us that a large majority of the smart people in Cheop's Egypt, dynastic China, Elizabethan England, and Teddy Roosevelt's America were engaged in ordinary pursuits, mingling, working, and living with everyone else. Many were housewives. Most of the rest were farmers, smiths, millers, bakers, carpenters, and shopkeepers. Social and economic stratification was extreme, but cognitive stratification was minor.

So it has been from the beginning of history into this century. Then, comparatively rapidly, a new class structure emerged in which it became much more consistently and universally advantageous to be smart. In the next four chapters, we examine that process and its meaning.

Chapter 1

Cognitive Class and Education, 1900–1990

In the course of the twentieth century, America opened the doors of its colleges wider than any previous generation of Americans, or other society in history, could have imagined possible. This democratization of higher education has raised new barriers between people that may prove to be more divisive and intractable than the old ones.

The growth in the proportion of people getting college degrees is the most obvious result, with a fifteen-fold increase from 1900 to 1990. Even more important, the students going to college were being selected ever more efficiently for their high IQ. The crucial decade was the 1950s, when the percentage of top students who went to college rose by more than it had in the preceding three decades. By the beginning of the 1990s, about 80 percent of all students in the top quartile of ability continued to college after high school. Among the high school graduates in the top few percentiles of cognitive ability, the chances of going to college already exceeded 90 percent.

Perhaps the most important of all the changes was the transformation of America's elite colleges. As more bright youngsters went off to college, the colleges themselves began to sort themselves out. Starting in the 1950s, a handful of institutions became magnets for the very brightest of each year's new class. In these schools, the cognitive level of the students rose far above the rest of the college population.

Taken together, these trends have stratified America according to cognitive ability.

A perusal of Harvard's Freshman Register for 1952 shows a class looking very much as Harvard freshman classes had always looked. Under the photographs of the well-scrubbed, mostly East Coast, overwhelmingly white and Christian young men were home addresses from places like Philadelphia's Main Line, the Upper East Side of New York, and Boston's Beacon Hill. A large proportion of the class came from a handful of America's most exclusive boarding schools; Phillips Exeter and Phillips Andover alone contributed almost 10 percent of the freshmen that year.

And yet for all its apparent exclusivity, Harvard was not so hard to get into in the fall of 1952. An applicant's chances of being admitted were about two out of three, and close to 90 percent if his father had gone to Harvard.[1] With this modest level of competition, it is not surprising to learn that the Harvard student body was not uniformly brilliant. In fact, the mean SAT-Verbal score of the incoming freshmen class was only 583, well above the national mean but nothing to brag about.[2] Harvard men came from a range of ability that could be duplicated in the top half of many state universities.

Let us advance the scene to 1960. Wilbur J. Bender, Harvard's dean of admissions, was about to leave his post and trying to sum up for the board of overseers what had happened in the eight years of his tenure. "The figures," he wrote, "report the greatest change in Harvard admissions, and thus in the Harvard student body, in a short time—two college generations—in our recorded history."[3] Unquestionably, suddenly, but for no obvious reason, Harvard had become a different kind of place. The proportion of the incoming students from New England had dropped by a third. Public school graduates now outnumbered private school graduates. Instead of rejecting a third of its applicants, Harvard was rejecting more than two-thirds—and the quality of those applicants had increased as well, so that many students who would have been admitted in 1952 were not even bothering to apply in 1960.

The SAT scores at Harvard had skyrocketed. In the fall of 1960, the average verbal score was 678 and the average math score was 695, an increase of almost a hundred points for each test. The average Harvard freshman in 1952 would have placed in the bottom 10 percent of the incoming class by 1960. In eight years, Harvard had been transformed from a school primarily for the northeastern socioeconomic elite into a school populated by the brightest of the bright, drawn from all over the country.

The story of higher education in the United States during the twentieth century is generally taken to be one of the great American success stories, and with good reason. The record was not without blemishes, but the United States led the rest of the world in opening college to a mass population of young people of ability, regardless of race, color, creed, gender, and financial resources.

But this success story also has a paradoxically shadowy side, for education is a powerful divider and classifier. Education affects income, and income divides. Education affects occupation, and occupations divide. Education affects tastes and interests, grammar and accent, all of which divide. When access to higher education is restricted by class, race, or religion, these divisions cut across cognitive levels. But school is in itself, more immediately and directly than any other institution, the place where people of high cognitive ability excel and people of low cognitive ability fail. As America opened access to higher education, it opened up as well a revolution in the way that the American population sorted itself and divided itself. Three successively more efficient sorting processes were at work: the college population grew, it was recruited by cognitive ability more efficiently, and then it was further sorted among the colleges.

THE COLLEGE POPULATION GROWS

A social and economic gap separated high school graduates from college graduates in 1900 as in 1990; that much is not new. But the social and economic gap was not accompanied by much of a cognitive gap, because the vast majority of the brightest people in the United States had not gone to college. We may make that statement despite the lack of IQ scores from 1900 for the same reason that we can make such statements about Elizabethan England: It is true by mathematical necessity. In 1900, only about 2 percent of 23-year-olds got college degrees. Even if all of the 2 percent who went to college had IQs of 115 and above (and they did not), seven out of eight of the brightest 23-year-olds in the America of 1900 would have been without college degrees. This situation barely changed for the first two decades of the new century. Then, at the close of World War I, the role of college for American youths began an expansion that would last until 1974, interrupted only by the Great Depression and World War II.

The three lines in the figure show trends established in 1920–1929, 1935–1940, and 1954–1973, then extrapolated. They are there to high-

In the twentieth century, the prevalence of the college degree goes from one in fifty to a third of the population

New bachelor's degrees as a percentage of 23-year-olds

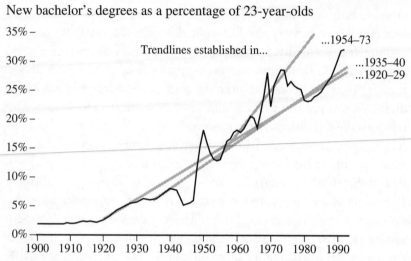

Sources: 1900–1959: U.S. Bureau of the Census 1975, H751–765. 1960–1992: DES, 1992, Table 229.

light the three features of the figure worth noting. First, the long perspective serves as a counterweight to the common belief that the college population exploded suddenly after World War II. It certainly exploded in the sense that the number of college students went from a wartime trough to record highs, but this is because two generations of college students were crowded onto campuses at one time. In terms of trendlines, World War II and its aftermath was a blip, albeit a large blip. When this anomalous turmoil ended in the mid-1950s, the proportion of people getting college degrees was no higher than would have been predicted from the trends established in the 1920s or the last half of the 1930s (which are actually a single trend interrupted by the worst years of the depression).

The second notable feature of the figure is the large upward tilt in the trendline from the mid-1950s until 1974. That it began when it did—the Eisenhower years—comes as a surprise. The GI bill's impact had faded and the postwar baby boom had not yet reached college age. Presumably postwar prosperity had something to do with it, but the explanation cannot be simple. The slope remained steep in periods as different as Eisenhower's late 1950s, LBJ's mid-1960s, and Nixon's early 1970s.

After 1974 came a peculiar plunge in college degrees that lasted until 1981—peculiar because it occurred when the generosity of scholarships and loans, from colleges, foundations, and government alike, was at its peak. This period of declining graduates was then followed by a steep increase from 1981 to 1990—also peculiar, in that college was becoming harder to afford for middle-class Americans during those years. As of 1990, the proportion of students getting college degrees had more than made up for the losses during the 1970s and had established a new record, with B.A.s and B.S.s being awarded in such profusion that they amounted to 30 percent of the 23-year-old population.

MAKING GOOD ON THE IDEAL OF OPPORTUNITY

At first glance, we are telling a story of increasing democracy and intermingling, not of stratification. Once upon a time, the college degree was the preserve of a tiny minority; now almost a third of each new cohort of youths earns it. Surely, it would seem, this must mean that a broader range of people is going to college—including people with a broader, not narrower, range of cognitive ability. Not so. At the same time that many more young people were going to college, they were also being selected ever more efficiently by cognitive ability.

A compilation of the studies conducted over the course of the century suggests that the crucial decade was the 1950s. The next figure shows the data for the students in the top quartile (the top 25 percent) in ability and is based on the proportion of students entering college (though not necessarily finishing) in the year following graduation from high school.

Again, the lines highlight trends set in particular periods, here 1925–1950 and 1950–1960. From one period to the next, the proportion of bright students getting to college leaped to new heights. There are two qualifications regarding this figure. First, it is based on high school *graduates*—the only data available over this time period—and therefore drastically understates the magnitude of the real change from the 1920s to the 1960s and thereafter, because so many of the top quartile in ability never made it through high school early in the century (see Chapter 6). It is impossible to be more precise with the available data, but a reasonable estimate is that as of the mid-1920s, only about 15 percent of all of the nation's youth in the top IQ quartile were going on to college.[4] It is further the case that almost all of those moving on

At mid-century America abruptly becomes more efficient in getting the top students to college

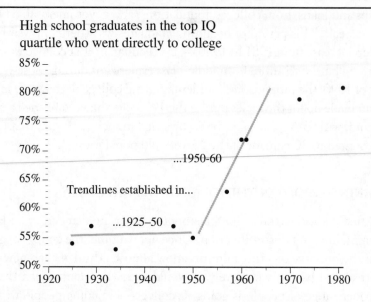

High school graduates in the top IQ
quartile who went directly to college

Sources: Eagle 1988b; Taubman and Wales 1972; authors' analysis of the National Longitudinal Survey of Youth (NLSY). See below and the introduction to Part II.

to college in the 1920s were going to four-year colleges, and this leads to the second qualification to keep in mind: By the 1970s and 1980s, substantial numbers of those shown as continuing to college were going to a junior college, which are on average less demanding than four-year colleges. Interpreting all the available data, it appears that the proportion of all American youth in the top IQ quartile who went directly to four-year colleges rose from roughly one youth in seven in 1925 to about two out of seven in 1950 to more than four out of seven in the early 1960s, where it has remained, with perhaps a shallow upward trend, ever since.[5]

But it is not just that the top quartile of talent has been more efficiently tapped for college. At every level of cognitive ability, the links between IQ and the probability of going to college became tighter and more regular. The next figure summarizes three studies that permit us to calculate the probability of going to college throughout the ability range over the last seventy years. Once again we are restricted to high school

Between the 1920s and the 1960s, college attendance becomes much more closely pegged to IQ

High school graduates going directly to college

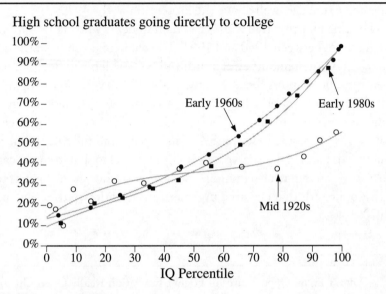

Source: Taubman and Wales 1972, Figures 3, 4; and authors' analysis of NLSY students who graduated from high school in 1980–1982.

graduates for the 1925 data, which overstates the probability of going to college during this period. Even for the fortunate few who got a high school degree in 1925, high cognitive ability improved their chances of getting to college—but not by much.[6] The brightest high school graduates had almost a 60 percent chance of going to college, which means that they had more than a 40 percent chance of not going, despite having graduated from high school and being very bright. The chances of college for someone merely in the 80th percentile in ability were no greater than classmates who were at the 50th percentile, and only slightly greater than classmates in the bottom third of the class.

Between the 1920s and the 1960s, the largest change in the probability of going to college was at the top of the cognitive ability distribution. By 1960, a student who was really smart—at or near the 100th percentile in IQ—had a chance of going to college of nearly 100 percent.[7] Furthermore, as the figure shows, going to college had gotten more dependent on intelligence at the bottom of the distribution, too.[8] A student at the 30th percentile had only about a 25 percent chance of going to college—*lower* than it had been for high school graduates in the 1920s. But a student in the 80th percentile had a 70 percent chance of going to college, well above the proportion in the 1920s.

The line for the early 1980s is based on students who graduated from high school between 1980 and 1982. The data are taken from the National Longitudinal Survey of Youth (NLSY), which will figure prominently in the chapters ahead. Briefly, the NLSY is a very large (originally 12,686 persons), nationally representative sample of American youths who were aged 14 to 22 in 1979, when the study began, and have been followed ever since. (The NLSY is discussed more fully in the introduction to Part II.) The curve is virtually identical to that from the early 1960s, which is in itself a finding of some significance in the light of the many upheavals that occurred in American education in the 1960s and 1970s.

Didn't Equal Opportunity in Higher Education Really Open Up During the 1960s?

The conventional wisdom holds that the revolution in higher education occurred in the last half of the 1960s, as part of the changes of the Great Society, especially its affirmative action policies. We note here that the proportion of youths going to college rose about as steeply in the 1950s as in the 1960s, as shown in the opening figure in this chapter and the accompanying discussion. Chapter 19 considers the role played by affirmative action in the changing college population of recent decades.

Meanwhile, the sorting process continued in college. College weeds out many students, disproportionately the least able. The figure below shows the situation as of the 1980s.[9] The line for students entering college reproduces the one shown in the preceding figure. The line for students completing the B.A. shows an even more efficient sorting process. A high proportion of people with poor test scores—more than 20 percent of those in the second decile (between the 10th and 20th centile), for example—entered a two- or four-year college. But fewer than 2 percent of them actually completed a bachelor's degree. Meanwhile, about 70 percent of the students in the top decile of ability were completing a B.A.

**Cognitive sorting continues from the time that students
enter college to the time they get a degree**

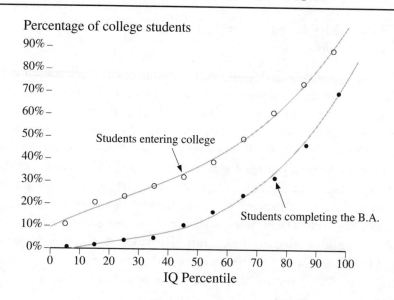

So a variety of forces have combined to ensure that a high proportion of the nation's most able youths got into the category of college
graduates. But the process of defining a cognitive elite through education is not complete. The socially most significant part of the partitioning remains to be described. In the 1950s, American higher
education underwent a revolution in the way that sorted the college
population itself.

THE CREATION OF A COGNITIVE ELITE WITHIN THE COLLEGE SYSTEM

The experience of Harvard with which we began this discussion is a
parable for the experience of the nation's university system. Insofar as
many more people now go to college, the college degree has become
more democratic during the twentieth century. But as it became democratic, a new elite was developing even more rapidly within the system.
From the early 1950s into the mid-1960s, the nation's university system
not only became more efficient in bringing the bright youngsters to col-

lege, it became radically more efficient at sorting the brightest of the bright into a handful of elite colleges.

The Case of Ivy League and the State of Pennsylvania: The 1920s Versus the 1960s

Prior to World War II, America had a stratum of elite colleges just as it has now, with the Ivy League being the best known. Then as now, these schools attracted the most celebrated faculty, had the best libraries, and sent their graduates on to the best graduate schools and to prestigious jobs. Of these elite schools, Harvard was among the most famous and the most selective. But what was true of Harvard then was true of the other elite schools. They all had a thin layer of the very brightest among their students but also many students who were merely bright and a fair number of students who were mediocre. They tapped only a fragment of the cognitive talent in the country. The valedictorian in Kalamazoo and the Kansas farm girl with an IQ of 140 might not even be going to college at all. If they did, they probably went to the nearest state university or to a private college affiliated with their church.

One of the rare windows on this period is provided by two little-known sources of test score data. The first involves the earliest SATs, which were first administered in 1926. As part of that effort, a standardized intelligence test was also completed by 1,080 of the SAT subjects. In its first annual report, a Commission appointed by the College Entrance Examination Board provided a table for converting the SAT of that era to IQ scores.[10] Combining that information with reports of the mean SAT scores for entrants to schools using the SAT, we are able to approximate the mean IQs of the entering students to the Ivy League and the Seven Sisters, the most prestigious schools in the country at that time.[11]

Judging from this information, the entering classes of these schools in 1926 had a mean IQ of about 117, which places the average student at the most selective schools in the country at about the 88th percentile of all the nation's youths and barely above the 115 level that has often been considered the basic demarcation point for prime college material.

In the same year as these SAT data were collected, the Carnegie Foundation began an ambitious statewide study of high school seniors and their college experience in the entire state of Pennsylvania.[12] By happy coincidence, the investigators used the same form of the Otis Intelligence Test used by the SAT Commission. Among other tests, they reported means for the sophomore classes at all the colleges and universities in Pennsylvania in 1928. Pennsylvania was (then as now) a large state with a wide variety of public and private schools, small and large, prestigious and pedestrian. The IQ equivalent of the average of all Pennsylvania colleges was 107, which put the average Pennsylvania student at the 68th percentile, considerably below the average of the elite schools. But ten Pennsylvania colleges had freshman classes with mean IQs that put them at the 75th to 90 percentiles.[13] In other words, students going to any of several Pennsylvania colleges were, on average, virtually indistinguishable in cognitive ability from the students in the Ivy League and the Seven Sisters.

Now let us jump to 1964, the first year for which SAT data for a large number of Pennsylvania colleges are available. We repeat the exercise, this time using the SAT-Verbal test as the basis for analysis.[14] Two important changes had occurred since 1928. The average freshman in a Pennsylvania college in 1964 was much smarter than the average Pennsylvania freshman in 1928—at about the 89th percentile. At the same time, however, the elite colleges, using the same fourteen schools represented in the 1928 data, had moved much further out toward the edge, now boasting an average freshman who was at the 99th percentile of the nation's youth.

Cognitive Stratification Throughout the College System by the 1960s

The same process occurred around the country, as the figure below shows. We picked out colleges with freshman SAT-Verbal means that were separated by roughly fifty-point intervals as of 1961.[15] The specific schools named are representative of those clustering near each break point. At the bottom is a state college in the second echelon of a state system (represented by Georgia Southern); then comes a large state university (North Carolina State), then five successively more selective private schools: Villanova, Tulane, Colby, Amherst, and Harvard. We have placed the SAT scores against the backdrop of the overall distribution of SAT scores for the entire population of high school seniors (not just those who ordinarily take the SAT), using a special study that the College Board conducted in the fall of 1960. The figure points to the general phenomenon already noted for Harvard: By 1961, a large

Cognitive stratification in colleges by 1961

The SAT Distribution for All High School Seniors

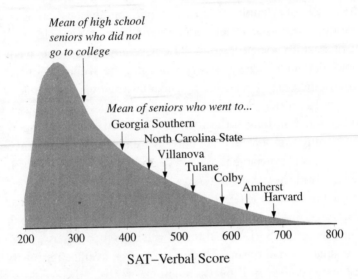

Mean of high school seniors who did not go to college

Mean of seniors who went to...
Georgia Southern
North Carolina State
Villanova
Tulane
Colby
Amherst
Harvard

200   300   400   500   600   700   800

SAT–Verbal Score

Source: Seibel 1962; College Entrance Examination Board 1961.

gap separated the student bodies of the elite schools from those of the public universities. Within the elite schools, another and significant level of stratification had also developed.

As the story about Harvard indicated, the period of this stratification seems to have been quite concentrated, beginning in the early 1950s.[16] It remains to explain why. What led the nation's most able college age youth (and their parents) to begin deciding so abruptly that State U. was no longer good enough and that they should strike out for New Haven or Palo Alto instead?

If the word *democracy* springs to your tongue, note that democracy—at least in the economic sense—had little to do with it. The Harvard freshman class of 1960 comprised fewer children from low-income families, not more, than the freshman class in 1952.[17] And no wonder. Harvard in 1950 had been cheap by today's standards. In 1950, total costs for a year at Harvard were only $8,800—in 1990 dollars, parents of to-day's college students will be saddened to learn. By 1960, total costs there had risen to $12,200 in 1990 dollars, a hefty 40 percent increase. According to the guidelines of the times, the average family could, if it stretched, afford to spend 20 percent of its income to send a child to Harvard.[18] Seen in that light, the proportion of families who could afford Harvard *decreased* slightly during the 1950s.[19] Scholarship help increased but not fast enough to keep pace.

Nor had Harvard suddenly decided to maximize the test scores of its entering class. In a small irony of history, the Harvard faculty had decided in 1960 *not* to admit students purely on the basis of academic potential as measured by tests but to consider a broader range of human qualities.[20] Dean Bender explained why, voicing his fears that Harvard would "become such an intellectual hot-house that the unfortunate aspects of a self-conscious 'intellectualism' would become dominant and the precious, the brittle and the neurotic take over." He asked a very good question indeed: "In other words, would being part of a super-elite in a high prestige institution be good for the healthy development of the ablest 18- to 22-year-olds, or would it tend to be a warping and narrowing experience?"[21] In any case, Harvard in 1960 continued, as it had in the past and would in the future, to give weight to such factors as the applicant's legacy (was the father a Harvard alum?), his potential as a quarterback or stroke for the eight-man shell, and other nonacademic qualities.[22]

The baby boom had nothing to do with the change. The leading edge of the baby boomer tidal wave was just beginning to reach the campus by 1960.[23]

So what had happened? With the advantage of thirty additional years of hindsight, two trends stand out more clearly than they did in 1960.

First, the 1950s were the years in which television came of age and long-distance travel became commonplace. Their effects on the attitudes toward college choices can only be estimated, but they were surely significant. For students coming East from the Midwest and West, the growth of air travel and the interstate highway system made travel to school faster for affluent families and cheaper for less affluent ones. Other effects may have reflected the decreased psychic distance of Boston from parents and prospective students living in Chicago or Salt Lake City, because of the ways in which the world had become electronically smaller.

Second, the 1950s saw the early stages of an increased demand that results not from proportional changes in wealth but from an expanding number of affluent customers competing for scarce goods. Price increases for a wide variety of elite goods have outstripped changes in the consumer price index or changes in mean income in recent decades, sometimes by orders of magnitude. The cost of Fifth Avenue apartments, seashore property, Van Gogh paintings, and rare stamps are all examples. Prices have risen because demand has increased and supply cannot. In the case of education, new universities are built, but not new Princetons, Harvards, Yales, or Stanfords. And though the proportion of families with incomes sufficient to pay for a Harvard education did not increase significantly during the 1950s, the raw number did. Using the 20-percent-of-family-income rule, the number of families that could afford Harvard increased by 184,000 from 1950 to 1960. Using a 10 percent rule, the number increased by 55,000. Only a small portion of these new families had children applying to college, but the number of slots in the freshmen classes of the elite schools was also small. College enrollment increased from 2.1 million students in 1952 to 2.6 million by 1960, meaning a half-million more competitors for available places. It would not take much of an increase in the propensity to seek elite educations to produce a substantial increase in the annual applications to Harvard, Yale, and the others.[24]

We suspect also that the social and cultural forces unleashed by World War II played a central role, but probing them would take us far afield. Whatever the combination of reasons, the basics of the situation were straightforward: By the early 1960s, the entire top echelon of American universities had been transformed. The screens filtering their students from the masses had not been lowered but changed. Instead of the old screen—woven of class, religion, region, and old school ties—the new screen was cognitive ability, and its mesh was already exceeding fine.

Changes Since the 1960s

There have been no equivalent sea changes since the early 1960s, but the concentration of top students at elite schools has intensified. As of the early 1990s, Harvard did not get four applicants for each opening, but closer to seven, highly self-selected and better prepared than ever. Competition for entry into the other elite schools has stiffened comparably.

Philip Cook and Robert Frank have drawn together a wide variety of data documenting the increasing concentration.[25] There are, for example, the Westinghouse Science Talent Search finalists. In the 1960s, 47 percent went to the top seven colleges (as ranked in the *Barron's* list that Cook and Frank used). In the 1980s, that proportion had risen to 59 percent, with 39 percent going to just three colleges (Harvard, MIT, and Princeton).[26] Cook and Frank also found that from 1979 to 1989, the percentage of students scoring over 700 on the SAT-Verbal who chose one of the "most competitive colleges" increased from 32 to 43 percent.[27]

The degree of partitioning off of the top students as of the early 1990s has reached startling proportions. Consider the list of schools that were named as the nation's top twenty-five large universities and the top twenty-five small colleges in a well-known 1990 ranking.[28] Together, these fifty schools accounted for just 59,000 out of approximately 1.2 million students who entered four-year institutions in the fall of 1990—fewer than one out of twenty of the nation's freshmen in four-year colleges. But they took in twelve out of twenty of the students who scored in the 700s on their SAT-Verbal test. They took in seven out of twenty of students who scored in the 600s.[29]

The concentration is even more extreme than that. Suppose we take just the top ten schools, as ranked by the number of their freshmen who scored in the 700s on the SAT-Verbal. Now we are talking about schools that enrolled a total of only 18,000 freshmen, one out of every sixty-seven nationwide. Just these ten schools—Harvard, Yale, Stanford, University of Pennsylvania, Princeton, Brown, University of California at Berkeley, Cornell, Dartmouth, and Columbia—soaked up 31 percent of the nation's students who scored in the 700s on the SAT-Verbal. Harvard and Yale alone, enrolling just 2,900 freshmen—roughly 1 out of every 400 freshmen—accounted for 10 percent. In other words, scoring above 700 is forty times more concentrated in the freshman classes at Yale and Harvard than in the national SAT population at large—and the national SAT population is already a slice off the top of the distribution.[30]

HOW HIGH ARE THE PARTITIONS?

We have spoken of "cognitive partitioning" through education, which implies separate bins into which the population has been distributed. But there has always been substantial intellectual overlap across educational levels, and that remains true today. We are trying to convey a situation that is as much an ongoing process as an outcome. But before doing so, the time has come for the first of a few essential bits of statistics: the concepts of distribution and standard deviation. If you are new to statistics, we recommend that you read the more detailed explanation in Appendix 1; you will enjoy the rest of the book more if you do.

A Digression: Standard Deviations and Why They Are Important

Very briefly, a distribution is the pattern formed by many individual scores. The famous "normal distribution" is a bell-shaped curve, with most people getting scores in the middle range and a few at each end, or "tail," of the distribution. Most mental tests are designed to produce normal distributions.

A standard deviation is a common language for expressing scores. Why not just use the raw scores (SAT points, IQ points, etc.)? There are many reasons, but one of the simplest is that we need to compare results on many different tests. Suppose you are told that a horse is sixteen hands tall and a snake is quarter of a rod long. Not many people can tell you from that information how the height of the horse compares to the length of the snake. If instead people use inches for both, there is no problem. The same is true for statistics. The standard deviation is akin to the inch, an all-purpose measure that can be used for any distribution. Suppose we tell you that Joe has an ACT score of 24 and Tom has an SAT-Verbal of 720. As in the case of the snake and the horse, you need a lot of information about those two tests before you can tell much from those two numbers. But if we tell you instead that Joe has an ACT score that is .7 standard deviation above the mean and Tom has an SAT-Verbal that is 2.7 standard deviations above the mean, you know a lot.

How big is a standard deviation? For a test distributed normally, a person whose score is one standard deviation *below* the mean is at the 16th percentile. A person whose score is a standard deviation *above* the mean is at the 84th percentile. Two standard deviations from the mean mark the 2d and 98th percentiles. Three standard deviations from the mean marks the bottom and top thousandth of a distribution. Or, in short, as a measure of distance from the mean, one standard deviation means "big," two standard deviations means "very big," and three standard deviations means "huge." Standard deviation is often abbreviated "SD," a convention we will often use in the rest of the book.

Understanding How the Partitions Have Risen

The figure below summarizes the situation as of 1930, after three decades of expansion in college enrollment but before the surging changes of the decades to come. The area under each distribution is composed of peo-

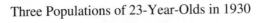

Americans with and without a college degree as of 1930

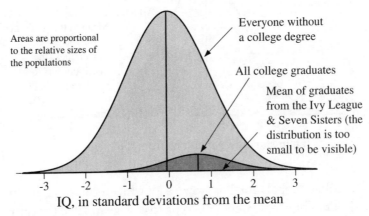

Three Populations of 23-Year-Olds in 1930

Areas are proportional to the relative sizes of the populations

Everyone without a college degree

All college graduates

Mean of graduates from the Ivy League & Seven Sisters (the distribution is too small to be visible)

IQ, in standard deviations from the mean

Sources: Brigham, 1932; Learned and Wood, 1938.

ple age 23 and is proportional to its representation in the national population of such people. The vertical lines denote the mean score for each distribution. Around them are drawn normal distributions—bell curves—expressed in terms of standard deviations from the mean.[31]

It is easy to see from the figure above why cognitive stratification was only a minor part of the social landscape in 1930. At any given level of cognitive ability, the number of people without college degrees dwarfed the number who had them. College graduates and the noncollege population did not differ much in IQ. And even the graduates of the top universities (an estimate based on the Ivy League data for 1928) had IQs well within the ordinary range of ability.

The comparable picture sixty years later, based on our analysis of the NLSY, is shown in the next figure, again depicted as normal distributions.[32] Note that the actual distributions may deviate from perfect normality, especially out in the tails.

Americans with and without a college degree as of 1990

Three Populations of 23-Year-Olds in 1990

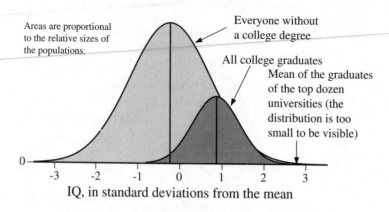

Areas are proportional to the relative sizes of the populations.

Everyone without a college degree

All college graduates

Mean of the graduates of the top dozen universities (the distribution is too small to be visible)

0—

-3   -2   -1   0   1   2   3

IQ, in standard deviations from the mean

The college population has grown a lot while its mean IQ has risen a bit. Most bright people were not going to college in 1930 (or earlier)—waiting on the bench, so to speak, until the game opened up to them. By 1990, the noncollege population, drained of many bright youngsters, had shifted downward in IQ. While the college population grew, the gap between college and noncollege populations therefore also grew. The largest change, however, has been the huge increase in the intelligence of the average student in the top dozen universities, up a standard deviation and a half from where the Ivies and the Seven Sisters were in 1930. One may see other features in the figure evidently less supportive of cognitive partitioning. Our picture suggests that for every person within the ranks of college graduates, there is another among those without a college degree who has just as high an IQ—or at least almost. And as for the graduates of the dozen top schools,[33] while it is true that their mean IQ is extremely high (designated by the +2.7 SDs to which the line points), they are such a small proportion of the nation's population that they do not even register visually on this graph, and they too are apparently outnumbered by people with similar IQs who do not graduate from those colleges, or do not graduate from college at all. Is there anything to be concerned about? How much partitioning has really occurred?

Perhaps a few examples will illustrate. Think of your twelve closest friends or colleagues. For most readers of this book, a large majority will be college graduates. Does it surprise you to learn that the odds of having even *half* of them be college graduates are only six in a thousand, if people were randomly paired off?[34] Many of you will not think it odd that half or more of the dozen have advanced degrees. But the odds against finding such a result among a randomly chosen group of twelve Americans are actually more than a million to one. Are any of the dozen a graduate of Harvard, Stanford, Yale, Princeton, Cal Tech, MIT, Duke, Dartmouth, Cornell, Columbia, University of Chicago, or Brown? The chance that even one is a graduate of those twelve schools is one in a thousand. The chance of finding two among that group is one in fifty thousand. The chance of finding four or more is less than one in a billion.

Most readers of this book—this may be said because we know a great deal about the statistical tendencies of people who read a book like this—are in preposterously unlikely groups, and this reflects the degree of partitioning that has already occurred.

In some respects, the results of the exercise today are not so different from the results that would have been obtained in former years. Sixty years ago as now, the people who were most likely to read a book of this nature would be skewed toward those who had friends with college or Ivy League college educations and advanced degrees. The differences between 1930 and 1990 are these:

First, only a small portion of the 1930 population was in a position to have the kind of circle of friends and colleagues that characterizes the readers of this book. We will not try to estimate the proportion, which would involve too many assumptions, but you may get an idea by examining the small area under the curve for college graduates in the 1930 figure, and visualize some fraction of that area as representing people in 1930 who could conceivably have had the educational circle of friends and colleagues you have. They constituted the thinnest cream floating on the surface of American society in 1930. In 1990, they constituted a class.

Second, the people who obtained such educations changed. Suppose that it is 1930 and you are one of the small number of people whose circle of twelve friends and colleagues included a sizable fraction of college graduates. Suppose you are one of the even tinier number whose circle came primarily from the top universities. Your circle, selective and uncommon as it is, nonetheless will have been scattered across a wide range of intelligence, with IQs from 100 on up. Given the same educational profile in one's circle today, it would consist of a set of people with IQs where the bottom tenth is likely to be in the vicinity of 120, and the mean is likely to be in excess of 130—people whose cognitive ability puts them out at the edge of the population at large. What might have been a circle with education or social class as its most salient feature in 1930 has become a circle circumscribing a narrow range of high IQ scores today.

The sword cuts both ways. Although they are not likely to be among our readers, the circles at the bottom of the educational scale comprise lower and narrower ranges of IQ today than they did in 1930. When many youngsters in the top 25 percent of the intelligence distribution who formerly would have stopped school in or immediately after high school go to college instead, the proportion of high-school-only persons whose intelligence is in the top 25 percent of the distribution has to fall correspondingly. The occupational effect of this change is that bright youngsters who formerly would have become carpenters or truck drivers or postal clerks go to college instead, thence to occupations higher on the socioeconomic ladder. Those left on the lower rungs are therefore likely to be lower and more homogeneous intellectually. Likewise their neighborhoods, which get drained of the bright and no longer poor, have become more homogeneously populated by a less bright, and even poorer, residuum. In other chapters we focus on what is happening at the bottom of the distribution of intelligence.

The point of the exercise in thinking about your dozen closest friends and colleagues is to encourage you to detach yourself momentarily from the way the world looks to you from day to day and contemplate how extraordinarily different your circle of friends and acquaintances is from what would be the norm in a perfectly fluid society. This profound isolation from other parts of the IQ distribution probably dulls our awareness of how unrepresentative our circle actually is.

With these thoughts in mind, let us proceed to the technical answer to the question, How much partitioning is there in America? It is done by expressing the overlap of two distributions after they are equated for size. There are various ways to measure overlap. In the following table we use a measure called *median overlap*, which says what proportion of IQ scores in the lower-scoring group matched or exceeded the median score in the higher-scoring group. For the nationally representative

Overlap Across the Educational Partitions	
Groups Being Compared	**Median Overlap**
High school graduates with college graduates	7%
High school graduates with Ph.D.s, M.D.s, or LL.B.s	1%
College graduates with Ph.D.s, M.D.s, and LL.Bs	21%

NLSY sample, most of whom attended college in the late 1970s and through the 1980s, the median overlap is as follows: By this measure, there is only about 7 percent overlap between people with only a high school diploma and people with a B.A. or M.A. And even this small degree of overlap refers to all colleges. If you went to any of the top hundred colleges and universities in the country, the measure of overlap would be a few percentage points. If you went to an elite school, the overlap would approach zero.

Even among college graduates, the partitions are high. Only 21 percent of those with just a B.A. or a B.S. had scores as high as the median for those with advanced graduate degrees. Once again, these degrees of overlap are for graduates of all colleges. The overlap between the B.A. from a state teachers' college and an MIT Ph.D. can be no more than a few percentage points.

What difference does it make? The answer to that question will unfold over the course of the book. Many of the answers involve the ways that the social fabric in the middle class and working class is altered when the most talented children of those families are so efficiently extracted to live in other worlds. But for the time being, we can begin by thinking about that thin layer of students of the highest cognitive ability who are being funneled through rarefied college environments, whence they go forth to acquire eventually not just the good life but often an influence on the life of the nation. They are coming of age in environments that are utterly atypical of the nation as a whole. The national percentage of 18-year-olds with the ability to get a score of 700 or above on the SAT-Verbal test is in the vicinity of one in three hundred. Think about the consequences when about half of these students are going to universities in which 17 percent of their classmates also had

SAT-Vs in the 700s and another 48 percent had scores in the 600s.[35] It is difficult to exaggerate how different the elite college population is from the population at large—first in its level of intellectual talent, and correlatively in its outlook on society, politics, ethics, religion, and all the other domains in which intellectuals, especially intellectuals concentrated into communities, tend to develop their own conventional wisdoms.

The news about education is heartening and frightening, more or less in equal measure. Heartening, because the nation is providing a college education for a high proportion of those who could profit from it. Among those who graduate from high school, just about all the bright youngsters now get a crack at a college education. Heartening also because our most elite colleges have opened their doors wide for youngsters of outstanding promise. But frightening too. When people live in encapsulated worlds, it becomes difficult for them, even with the best of intentions, to grasp the realities of worlds with which they have little experience but over which they also have great influence, both public and private. Many of those promising undergraduates are never going to live in a community where they will be disabused of their misperceptions, for after education comes another sorting mechanism, occupations, and many of the holes that are still left in the cognitive partitions begin to get sealed. We now turn to that story.

Chapter 2

Cognitive Partitioning by Occupation

People in different jobs have different average IQs. Lawyers, for example, have higher IQs on the average than bus drivers. Whether they must have higher IQs than bus drivers is a topic we take up in detail in the next chapter. Here we start by noting simply that people from different ranges on the IQ scale end up in different jobs.

Whatever the reason for the link between IQ and occupation, it goes deep. If you want to guess an adult male's job status, the results of his childhood IQ test help you as much as knowing how many years he went to school.

IQ becomes more important as the job gets intellectually tougher. To be able to dig a ditch, you need a strong back but not necessarily a high IQ score. To be a master carpenter, you need some higher degree of intelligence along with skill with your hands. To be a first-rate lawyer, you had better come from the upper end of the cognitive ability distribution. The same may be said of a handful of other occupations, such as accountants, engineers and architects, college teachers, dentists and physicians, mathematicians, and scientists. The mean IQ of people entering those fields is in the neighborhood of 120. In 1900, only one out of twenty people in the top 10 percent in intelligence were in any of these occupations, a figure that did not change much through 1940. But after 1940, more and more people with high IQs flowed into those jobs, and by 1990 the same handful of occupations employed about 25 percent of all the people in the top tenth of intelligence.

During the same period, IQ became more important for business executives. In 1900, the CEO of a large company was likely to be a WASP born into affluence. He may have been bright, but that was not mainly how he was chosen. Much was still the same as late as 1950. The next three decades saw a great social leveling, as the executive suites filled with bright people who could maximize corporate profits, and never mind if they came from the wrong side of the tracks or worshipped at a temple instead of a church. Meanwhile, the college degree became a requirement for many business positions, and graduate education went from a rarity to a commonplace among senior executives.

When one combines the people known to be in high-IQ professions with estimates of the numbers of business executives who are drawn from the top tenth in cognitive ability, the results do not leave much room for maneuver. The specific proportions are open to argument, but the main point seems beyond dispute: Even as recently as midcentury, America was still a society in which most bright people were scattered throughout the wide range of jobs. As the century draws to a close, a very high proportion of that same group is now concentrated within a few occupations that are highly screened for IQ.

Jobs sort people by their IQs, just as college does. But there is a difference between educational and occupational sorting. People spend only one to two decades in school. School may seem like forever when we are there, but we spend most of our lives with the sorting that centers on work and carries over into circles of friends and colleagues, and into communities—if not physically the same workplaces, communities, and friends throughout the life span, then generically similar ones. In this chapter, we continue our discussion of the contours of the intellectual landscape. An examination of occupational sorting will carry us through to the end of Part I.

JOBS AND INTELLIGENCE

No one decreed that occupations should sort us out by our cognitive abilities, and no one enforces the process. It goes on beneath the surface, guided by its own invisible hand. Testers observe that job status and intelligence test scores have gone together since there were intelligence tests to give.[1] As tests evolved and as the measurement of status was formalized, studying the relation between the jobs and intelligence became a cottage industry for social scientists. By now, the relation has been confirmed many times, in many countries, and in many approaches to the data.[2]

This is not to say that the experts find nothing to quarrel about. The technical literature is replete with disagreement. Aside from the purely technical bones of contention, the experts argue about whether the IQ-job status connection is a by-product of a more fundamental link between educational level and job status. For example, it takes a law degree to be a lawyer, and it takes intelligence to get into and through law school, but aside from that, is there any good reason why lawyers need to have higher IQs on average than, say, bus drivers? At the height of egalitarianism in the 1970s, the received wisdom in many academic circles was "no," with Christopher Jencks's *Inequality* the accepted text.[3] A related argument, stated forcefully by James Fallows, arises over whether an IQ score is a credential for certain jobs, like a union card for a musician, or whether there is a necessary link between job status and intelligence, like a good ear.[4] By the time we get to the end of Part I, our answers to such questions should be clear. Here we review a few of the more illuminating findings, to push the discussion beyond the fact that occupational status is correlated with IQ.

One notable finding is that the correlation between IQ and job status is just about as high if the IQ test is given in childhood, decades before people enter the job market, as it is among young adults who are taking an intelligence test after years of education. For example, in a small but elegant longitudinal study of childhood intelligence and adult outcomes, the boys and girls in the sample were given IQ tests in childhood and then their job statuses and levels of schooling were measured on standard scales after they were at least 26 years old.[5] The IQ scores they got when they were 7 or 8 years old were about as correlated with the status level of their adult jobs as their adult IQs would have been.[6] Inasmuch as childhood IQ is more correlated with status than completed education, as it is in some studies, the thesis that IQ scores really just measure educational level is weakened.

Family members typically resemble each other in their occupational status.[7] We are talking here not about a son or a niece or a brother-in-law going into the family business but about job status, however measured. On rating scales that categorize jobs from those with the highest status to those with the lowest, family members tend to land at similar levels. There are many exceptions; we all hear occasionally about families with several members who are doctors and lawyers plus another who is a blue-collar worker, or vice versa. But such stories call attention to themselves because they describe rarities. Mostly, relatives occupy neighboring, if not the same, rungs on the job status ladder, and the closer the relationship is, the nearer they are. Such commonplace findings have many possible explanations, but an obvious one that is not mentioned or tested often by social scientists is that since intelligence runs in families and intelligence predicts status, status *must* run in families. In fact, this explanation somehow manages to be both obvious and controversial.[8]

One useful study of family resemblance in status comes from Denmark and is based on several hundred men and women adopted in or around Copenhagen between 1924 and 1947.[9] Four out of five of these adopted people had been placed with their adopting families in their first year of life; the average age of placement overall was 3 months. To all intents and purposes, then, the adoptees shared little common environment with their biological siblings, but they shared a home environment with their adoptive siblings. In adulthood, they were compared with both their biological siblings and their adoptive siblings, the idea being to see whether common genes or common home life determined where they landed on the occupational ladder. The biologically related siblings resembled each other in job status, even though they grew up in different homes. And among them, the full siblings had more similar job status than the half siblings. Meanwhile, adoptive siblings were *not* significantly correlated with each other in job status.[10]

THE GROWTH OF HIGH-IQ PROFESSIONS

The above comments apply to all sorts of occupations, from low status to high. But the relationship of IQ to occupations changes as the job becomes more cognitively demanding. Almost anyone can become a ditch digger (if he has a strong enough back); many can become cabinetmakers (if they have good enough small-motor skills), but only people from a fairly narrow range of cognitive ability can become lawyers. If lawyering pays more than cabinetmaking, what happens as the number of lawyering jobs increases, as it has in America? More people with high IQs are diverted to lawyering, which means that they are not going to become cabinetmakers or ditch diggers.

Now imagine that process writ large, and consider what has happened within the handful of occupations that are most highly screened for IQ. We will concentrate here on a dozen such occupations, which we will refer to as "high-IQ professions." Some of them have existed as long as IQ tests and are included in the list of occupations for the 1900 census: accountants, architects, chemists, college teachers, dentists, engineers, lawyers, and physicians. Others have emerged more recently or are relabeled in more recent occupational breakdowns: computer scientists, mathematicians, natural scientists, and social scientists.

The mean IQ of people entering those fields is about 120, give or take a few points.[11] The state of knowledge is not perfect, and the sorting process is not precise. Different studies find slightly different means for these occupations, with some suggesting that physicians have a mean closer to 125, for example.[12] Theoretical physicists probably average higher than natural scientists in general. Within each profession, the range of scores may be large. Even an occupation with a high mean may include individuals with modest scores; it will certainly include a sizable proportion below its mean—50 percent of them, if the distribution is symmetrical above and below its mean.[13]

Nonetheless, 120 is a good ballpark figure for estimating the mean person in these high-IQ professions, and it also has the advantage of marking the cutoff point for approximately the top tenth of the entire population in IQ.[14] Armed with this information plus a few conjectures, we may explore how cognitive stratification at the top of the American labor market has changed over the years. The figure below shows the answer for the twentieth century to date.

Once again, the portrait of American society depends on vantage point. Let us begin with the bottom line, showing the percentage of the entire labor force that is engaged in high-IQ professions. There has been a proportional increase during the twentieth century, but these people still constituted only about one out of fifteen Americans in the labor force as of 1990.

Now consider Americans in the top 10 percent (the top decile, in other words) in cognitive ability—everyone over the age of 25, including housewives, the retired, and others who are not counted as being part of the labor force. These people are represented by the middle line in the graph. In 1900, the number of jobs in the high-IQ professions soaked up only about one out of twenty of these talented people. By 1990, they soaked up almost five times as many, or one out of four.

Finally, consider the top line in the graph, which is limited to Americans who are in both the top decile of IQ and the labor force. In 1900, about one out of eleven was in one of the high-IQ professions; by 1990, more than one out of three. This still leaves almost two out of three of them unaccounted for, but we will get to them in the next section of the chapter.

The top IQ decile becomes rapidly more concentrated in high-IQ professions from 1940 onward

People in the high-IQ occupations, expressed as a percentage of...

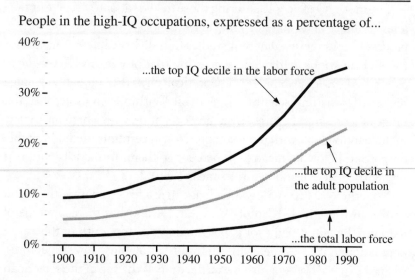

Source: U.S. Bureau of the Census 1975, Table D233–682; SAVS 1981, Table 675; U.S. Department of Labor, 1991, Table 22.

Note: Included are accountants, architects, chemists, college teachers, computer scientists, dentists, engineers, lawyers, mathematicians, natural scientists, physicians, and social scientists. Assumes 50 percent of persons in these professions have IQs of 120 or higher.

The specific proportions should be taken with a grain of salt, based, as they are, on estimates of IQs within the occupations. But we have a way of checking the 1990 estimate against actual experience, using the National Longitudinal Survey of Youth (described fully in the introduction to Part II), and our estimate fits quite closely.[15] In any case, the basic trends are unmistakable. Unlike the steep slopes we saw for educational changes in the first half of the century, the high-IQ professions gained proportionally little of the working force through 1940. But after 1940, the trickle swelled to a flood, shown by the nonlinear upward sweep of the proportion in the top IQ decile who have more recently gone to work in this limited number of jobs.

The High-IQ Professions and the Cognitive Elite

We have been discussing the top decile: everyone with an IQ of 120 or higher. What about people in the even more rarefied cognitive elite, the top fraction of a centile who are so concentrated in a handful of universities during their college years? We have little to tell us exactly what is happening now, but we know what the situation was fifty years ago, through Lewis Terman's famous study of 1,500 highly gifted children who were born in the early 1900s and followed throughout their lives. Their average IQs were over three standard deviations above the mean, meaning that the Terman sample represented about 1/300th of the population. As of 1940, the members of the Terman sample who had finished their schooling were engaged in high-IQ professions at three times the rate of people in the top 10 percent—24 percent for the Terman sample against 8 percent for the top decile in 1940, as the preceding figure shows.[16] If that was the case in 1940, when fewer than one in twelve people in the top decile were working in high-IQ professions, what might be the proportion for a comparable sample today? Presumably much higher, though how much higher is impossible to estimate with the available data.[17]

COGNITIVE SCREENS IN THE EXECUTIVE SUITE

The changes in our twelve high-IQ professions understate how much occupational cognitive segregation there has been in this century. We lack data about other professions and occupations in which mean IQ may be comparably high (e.g., military officers, writers, journalists). But the biggest omission involves business executives. For while the mean IQ of all people who go into business cannot be near 120,[18] both common sense and circumstantial evidence suggest that people who rise to the upper echelons of large businesses tend to have high IQs and that this tendency has increased during the course of the century.

One source of circumstantial evidence that ties success in major business to intelligence is the past and present level of education of business executives.[19] In 1900, more than two-thirds of the presidents and chairmen of America's largest corporations did not have even a college degree—not because many of them were poor (few had risen from outright poverty) but because a college degree was not considered important for running a business.[20] A Wall Street tycoon (himself a Harvard alumnus) writing in 1908 advised parents that "practical business is the best school and college" for their sons who sought a business career and that, indeed, a college education "is in many instances not only a hindrance, but absolutely fatal to success."[21]

The lack of a college education does not mean that senior executives of 1900 were necessarily less bright than their counterparts in 1990. But other evidence points to a revolution in the recruitment of senior executives that was not much different from the revolution in educational stratification that began in the 1950s. In 1900, the CEO of a large company was likely to be the archetype of the privileged capitalist elite that C. Wright Mills described in *The Power Elite*: born into affluence, the son of a business executive or a professional person, not only a WASP but an Episcopalian WASP.[22] In 1950, it was much the same. The fathers' occupations were about the same as they had been in 1900, with over 70 percent having been business executives or professionals, and, while Protestantism was less overwhelmingly dominant than it had been in 1900, it remained the right religion, with Episcopalianism still being the rightest of all. Fewer CEOs in 1950 had been born into wealthy families (down from almost half in 1900 to about a third), but they were continuing to be drawn primarily from the economically comfortable part of the population. The proportion coming from poor families had not changed. Many CEOs in the first half of the century had their jobs because their family's name was on the sign above the factory door; many had reached their eminent positions only because they did not have to compete against more able people who were excluded from the competition for lack of the right religion, skin color, national origin, or family connections.

In the next twenty-five years, the picture changed. The proportion of CEOs who came from wealthy families had dropped from almost half in 1900 and a third in 1950 to 5.5 percent by 1976.[23] The CEO of 1976 was still disproportionately likely to be Episcopalian but much less so than in 1900—and by 1976 he was also disproportionately likely to be Jewish, unheard of in 1920 or earlier. In short, social and economic background was no longer nearly as important in 1976 as in the first half of the century. Educational level was becoming the high road to the executive suite at the same time that education was becoming more de-

**In fifty years, the education of the typical CEO
increases from high school to graduate school**

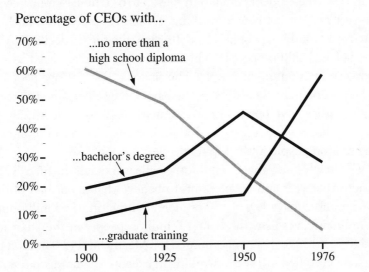

Percentage of CEOs with...

...no more than a high school diploma

...bachelor's degree

...graduate training

1900   1925   1950   1976

Source: Burck 1976, p. 172; Newcomer 1955, Table 24.

pendent on cognitive ability, as Chapter 1 showed. The figure above traces the change in highest educational attainment from 1900 to 1976 for CEOs of the largest U.S. companies.

The timing of the changes is instructive. The decline of the high school-educated chief executive was fairly steady throughout the period. College-educated CEOs surged into the executive suite in the 1925–1950 period. But as in the case of educational stratification, the most dramatic shift occurred after 1950, represented by the skyrocketing proportion of chief executives who had attended graduate school.[24] By 1976, 40 percent of the Fortune 500 companies were headed by individuals whose background was in finance or law, fields of study that are highly screened for intelligence. So we are left with this conservative interpretation: Nobody knows what the IQ mean or distribution was for executives at the turn of the century, but it is clear that, as of the 1990s, the cognitive screens were up. How far up? The broad envelope of possibilities suggests that senior business executives soak up a large proportion of the top IQ decile who are not engaged in the dozen high-IQ professions. The constraints leave no other possibility. Here are the constraints and the arithmetic:

In 1990, the resident population ages 25 to 64 (the age group in which the vast majority of people working in high-IQ professions fall) consisted of 127 million people.[25] By definition, the top IQ decile thus consisted of 12.7 million people. The labor force of persons aged 25 to 64 consisted of 100 million people. The smartest working-age people are disproportionately likely to be in the labor force (especially since career opportunities have opened up for women). As a working assumption, suppose that the labor force of 100 million included 11 million of the 12.7 million people in the top IQ decile.

We already know that 7.3 million people worked in the high-IQ professions that year and have reason to believe that about half of those (3.65 million) have IQs of 120 or more. Subtracting 3.65 million from 11 million leaves us with about 7.4 million people in the labor force with IQs of 120 or more unaccounted for. Meanwhile, 12.9 million people were classified in 1980 as working in executive, administrative, and managerial positions.[26] A high proportion of people in those positions graduated from college, one screen. They have risen in the corporate hierarchy over the course of their careers, which is probably another screen for IQ. What is their mean IQ? There is no precise answer. Studies suggest that the mean for the job category including all white-collar and professionals is around 107, but that category is far broader than the one we have in mind. Moreover, the mean IQ of four-year college graduates in general was estimated at about 115 in 1972, and senior executives probably have a mean above that average.[27]

At this point, we are left with startlingly little room for maneuver. How many of those 12.9 million people in executive, administrative, and managerial positions have IQs above 120? Any plausible assumption digs deep into the 7.4 million people with IQs of 120 or more who are not already engaged in one of the other high-IQ professions and leaves us with an extremely high proportion of people of the labor force with IQs above 120 who are already working in a high-IQ profession or in an executive or managerial position. One could easily make a case that the figure is in the neighborhood of 70 to 80 percent.

Cognitive sorting has become highly efficient in the last half century, but has it really become *that* efficient? We cannot answer definitely yes, but it is difficult to work back through the logic and come up with good reasons for thinking that the estimates are far off the mark.

It is not profitable to push much further along this line because the uncertainties become too great, but the main point is solidly established in any case: In midcentury, America was still a society in which a large proportion of the top tenth of IQ, probably a majority, were scattered throughout the population, *not* working in a high-IQ profession and *not* in a managerial position. As the century draws to a close, some very high proportion of that same group is concentrated within those highly screened jobs.

Chapter 3

The Economic Pressure
to Partition

What accounts for the way that people with different levels of IQ end up in different occupations? The fashionable explanation has been education. People with high SAT scores get into the best colleges; people with the high GRE, MCAT, or LSAT test scores get into professional and graduate schools; and the education defines the occupation. The SAT score becomes unimportant once the youngster has gotten into the right college or graduate school.

Without doubt, education is part of the explanation; physicians need a high IQ to get into medical school, but they also need to learn the material that medical school teaches before they can be physicians. Plenty of hollow credentialing goes on as well, if not in medicine then in other occupations, as the educational degree becomes a ticket for jobs that could be done just as well by people without the degree.

But the relationship of cognitive ability to job performance goes beyond that. A smarter employee is, on the average, a more proficient employee. This holds true within professions: Lawyers with higher IQs are, on the average, more productive than lawyers with lower IQs. It holds true for skilled blue-collar jobs: Carpenters with high IQs are also (on average) more productive than carpenters with lower IQs. The relationship holds, although weakly, even among people in unskilled manual jobs.

The magnitude of the relationship between cognitive ability and job performance is greater than once thought. A flood of new analyses during the 1980s established several points with large economic and policy implications:

Test scores predict job performance because they measure g, Spearman's general intelligence factor, not because they identify "aptitude" for a specific job. Any broad test of general intelligence predicts proficiency in most common occupations, and does so more accurately than tests that are narrowly constructed around the job's specific tasks.

The advantage conferred by IQ is long-lasting. Much remains to be learned, but usually the smarter employee tends to remain more productive than the less smart employee even after years on the job.

An IQ score is a better predictor of job productivity than a job interview, reference checks, or college transcript.

Most sweepingly important, an employer that is free to pick among applicants can realize large economic gains from hiring those with the highest IQs. An economy that lets employers pick applicants with the highest IQs is a significantly more efficient economy. Herein lies the policy problem: Since 1971, Congress and the Supreme Court have effectively forbidden American employers from hiring based on intelligence tests. How much does this policy cost the economy? Calculating the answer is complex, so estimates vary widely, from what one authority thinks was a lower-bound estimate of $80 billion in 1980 to what another authority called an upper-bound estimate of $13 billion for that year.

Our main point has nothing to do with deciding how large the loss is or how large the gain would be if intelligence tests could be freely used for hiring. Rather, it is simply that intelligence itself is importantly related to job performance. Laws can make the economy less efficient by forbidding employers to use intelligence tests, but laws cannot make intelligence unimportant.

To this point in the discussion, the forces that sort people into jobs according to their cognitive ability remain ambiguous. There are three main possibilities, hinted at in the previous chapter but not assessed.

The first is the standard one: IQ really reflects education. Education imparts skills and knowledge—reading, writing, doing arithmetic, knowing some facts. The skills and knowledge are valuable in the workplace, so employers prefer to hire educated people. Perhaps IQ, in and of itself, has something to do with people's performance at work, but probably not much. Education itself is the key. More is better, for just about everybody, to just about any level.

The second possibility is that IQ is correlated with job status because we live in a world of artificial credentials. The artisan guilds of old were replaced somewhere along the way by college or graduate degrees. Most parents want to see their children get at least as much education as they got, in part because they want their children to profit from the valuable credentials. As the society becomes richer, more children get more education. As it happens, education screens for IQ, but that is largely incidental to job performance. The job market, in turn, screens for educational credentials. So cognitive stratification occurs in the workplace, but it reflects the premium put on education, not on anything inherent in either education or cognitive ability itself.

The third possibility is that cognitive ability itself—sheer intellectual horsepower, independent of education—has market value. Seen from this perspective, the college degree is not a credential but an indirect measure of intelligence. People with college degrees tend to be smarter than people without them and, by extension, more valuable in the marketplace. Employers recruit at Stanford or Yale not because graduates of those schools know more than graduates of less prestigious schools but for the same generic reason that Willie Sutton gave for robbing banks. Places like Stanford and Yale are where you find the coin of cognitive talent.

The first two explanations have some validity for some occupations. Even the brightest child needs formal education, and some jobs require many years of advanced training. The problem of credentialing is widespread and real: the B.A. is a bogus requirement for many management jobs, the requirement for teaching certificates often impedes hiring good teachers in elementary and secondary schools, and the Ph.D. is irrelevant to the work that many Ph.D.s really do.

But whatever the mix of truth and fiction in the first two explanations, the third explanation is almost always relevant and almost always ignored. The process described in the previous chapter is driven by a characteristic of cognitive ability that is at once little recognized and essential for understanding how society is evolving: intelligence is fundamentally related to productivity. This relationship holds not only for highly skilled professions but for jobs across the spectrum. The power of the relationship is sufficient to give every business some incentive to use IQ as an important selection criterion.

That in brief is the thesis of the chapter. We begin by reviewing the received wisdom about the links between IQ and success in life, then the evidence specifically linking cognitive ability to job productivity.

THE RECEIVED WISDOM

"Test scores have a modest correlation with first-year grades and no correlation at all with what you do in the rest of your life," wrote Derek Bok, then president of Harvard University, in 1985, referring to the SATs that all Harvard applicants take.[1] Bok was poetically correct in ways that a college president understandably wants to emphasize. A 17-year-old who has gotten back a disappointing SAT score should not think that the future is bleak. Perhaps a freshman with an SAT math score of 500 had better not have his heart set on being a mathematician, but if instead he wants to run his own business, become a U.S. senator, or make a million dollars, he should not put aside those dreams because some of his friends have higher scores. The link between test scores and those achievements is dwarfed by the totality of other characteristics that he brings to his life, and that's the fact that individuals should remember when they look at their test scores. Bok was correct in that, for practical purposes, the futures of most of the 18-year-olds that he was addressing are open to most of the possibilities that attract them.

President Bok was also technically correct about the students at his own university. If one were to assemble the SATs of the incoming freshmen at Harvard and twenty years later match those scores against some quantitative measure of professional success, the impact could be modest, for reasons we shall discuss. Indeed, if the measure of success was the most obvious one, cash income, then the relationship between IQ and success among Harvard graduates could be less than modest; it could be nil or even negative.[2]

Finally, President Bok could assert that test scores were meaningless as predictors of what you do in the rest of your life without fear of contradiction, because he was expressing what "everyone knows" about test scores and success. The received wisdom, promulgated not only in feature stories in the press but codified in landmark Supreme Court decisions, has held that, first of all, the relation between IQ scores and job performance is weak, and, second, whatever weak relationship there is depends not on general intellectual capacity but on the particular mental capacities or skills required by a particular job.[3]

There have been several reasons for the broad acceptance of the conclusions President Bok drew. Briefly:

A Primer on the Correlation Coefficient

We have periodically mentioned the "correlation coefficient" without saying much except that it varies from −1 to +1. It is time for a bit more detail, with even more to be found in Appendix 1. As in the case of standard deviations, we urge readers who shy from statistics to take the few minutes required to understand the concept. The nature of "correlation" will be increasingly important as we go along.

A correlation coefficient represents the degree to which one phenomenon is linked to another. Height and weight, for example, have a positive correlation (the taller, the heavier, usually). A positive correlation is one that falls between zero and +1, with +1 being an absolutely reliable, linear relationship. A negative correlation falls between 0 and −1, with −1 also representing an absolutely reliable, linear relationship, but in the inverse direction. A correlation of 0 means no linear relationship whatsoever.[4]

A crucial point to keep in mind about correlation coefficients, now and throughout the rest of the book, is that correlations in the social sciences are seldom much higher than .5 (or lower than −.5) and often much weaker—because social events are imprecisely measured and are usually affected by variables besides the ones that happened to be included in any particular body of data. A correlation of .2 can nevertheless be "big" for many social science topics. In terms of social phenomena, modest correlations can produce large aggregate effects. Witness the prosperity of casinos despite the statistically modest edge they hold over their customers.

Moderate correlations mean many exceptions. We all know people who do not seem all that smart but who handle their jobs much more effectively than colleagues who probably have more raw intelligence. The correlations between IQ and various job-related measures are generally in the .2 to .6 range. Throughout the rest of the book, keep the following figure in mind, for it is what a highly significant correlation in the social sciences looks like. The figure uses actual data from a randomly selected 1 percent of a nationally representative sample, using two variables that are universally acknowledged to have a large and socially important relationship, income and education, with the line showing the expected change in income for each increment in years of education.[5] For this sample, the correlation was a statistically significant .33, and the expected value of an additional year of education was an additional $2,800 in family income—a major substantive increase. Yet look at how

The variation among individuals that lies behind a significant correlation coefficient

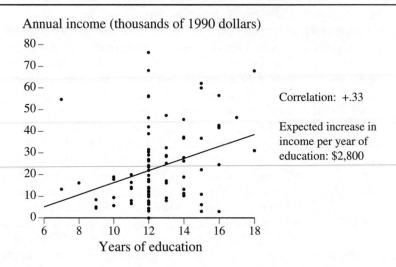

Annual income (thousands of 1990 dollars)

Correlation: +.33

Expected increase in income per year of education: $2,800

Years of education

numerous are the exceptions; note especially how people with twelfth-grade educations are spread out all along the income continuum. *For virtually every topic we will be discussing throughout the rest of the book, a plot of the raw data would reveal as many or more exceptions to the general statistical relationship, and this must always be remembered in trying to translate the general rule to individuals.*

The exceptions associated with modest correlations mean that a wide range of IQ scores can be observed in almost any job, including complex jobs such as engineer or physician, a fact that provides President Bok and other critics of the importance of IQ with an abundant supply of exceptions to any general relationship. The exceptions do not invalidate the importance of a statistically significant correlation.

Restriction of range. In any particular job setting, there is a restricted range of cognitive ability, and the relationship between IQ scores and job performance is probably very weak *in that setting*. Forget about IQ for a moment and think about weight as a qualification for being an offensive tackle in the National Football League. The All-Pro probably is not the heaviest player. On the other hand, the lightest tackle in the league weighs about 250 pounds. That is what we mean by restriction of range. In terms of correlation coefficients, if we were to rate the performance of every NFL offensive tackle and then correlate those ratings with their weights, the result would probably be a correlation near zero. Should we then approach the head coaches of the NFL and recommend that they try out a superbly talented 150-pound athlete at offensive tackle? The answer is no. We would be right in concluding that performance does not correlate much with weight among NFL tackles, whose weights range upward from around 250, but not about the correlation in the general population. Imagine a sample of ordinary people drawn from the general population and inserted into an offensive line. The correlation between the performance of these people as tackles in football games and their weights would be large indeed. The difference between these two correlations—one for the actual tackles in the NFL and the other a hypothetical one for people at large—illustrates the impact of restriction of range on correlation coefficients.[6]

Confusion between a credential and a correlation. Would it be silly to require someone to have a minimum score on an IQ test to get a license as a barber? Yes. Is it nonetheless possible that IQ scores are correlated with barbering skills? Yes. Later in the chapter, we discuss the economic pros and cons of using a weakly correlated score as a credential for hiring, but here we note simply that some people confuse a well-founded opposition to credentialing with a less well-founded denial that IQ correlates with job performance.[7]

The weaknesses of individual studies. Until the last decade, even the experts had reason to think that the relationship must be negligible. Scattered across journals, books, technical reports, conference proceedings, and the records of numberless personnel departments were thousands of samples of workers for whom there were two measurements: a cognitive ability test score of some sort and an estimate of proficiency or productivity of some sort. Hundreds of such findings were published, but every aspect of this literature confounded any attempt to draw general conclusions. The samples were usually small, the measures of performance and of worker characteristics varied and were more or less unreliable and invalid, and the ranges were restricted for both the test score and the performance measure. This fragmented literature seemed to support the received wisdom: Tests were often barely predictive of worker performance and different jobs seemed to call for different predictors. And yet millions of people are hired for jobs every year in competition with other applicants. Employers make those millions of choices by trying to guess which will be the best worker. What then is a fair way for the employer to make those hiring decisions?

Since 1971, the answer to that question has been governed by a landmark Supreme Court decision, *Griggs* v. *Duke Power Co.*[8] The Court held that any job requirement, including a minimum cutoff score on a mental test, must have a "manifest relationship to the employment in question" and that it was up to the employer to prove that it did.[9] In practice, this evolved into a doctrine: Employment tests must focus on the skills that are specifically needed to perform the job in question.[10] An applicant for a job as a mechanic should be judged on how well he does on a mechanical aptitude test, while an applicant for a job as a clerk should be judged on tests measuring clerical skills, and so forth. So decreed the Supreme Court, and why not? In addition to the expert testimony before the Court favoring it, it seemed to make good common sense.

THE RECEIVED WISDOM OVERTURNED

The problem is that common sense turned out to be wrong. In the last decade, the received wisdom has been repudiated by research and by common agreement of the leading contemporary scholars.[11] The most comprehensive modern surveys of the use of tests for hiring, promotion, and licensing, in civilian, military, private, and government occupations, repeatedly point to three conclusions about worker performance, as follows.

1. Job training and job performance in many common occupations are well predicted by any broadly based test of intelligence, as compared to narrower tests more specifically targeted to the routines of the job. As a corollary: Narrower tests that predict well do so largely because they happen themselves to be correlated with tests of general cognitive ability .
2. Mental tests predict job performance largely via their loading on g.
3. The correlations between tested intelligence and job performance or training are higher than had been estimated prior to the 1980s. They are high enough to have economic consequences.

We state these conclusions qualitatively rather than quantitatively so as to span the range of expert opinion. Whereas experts in employee selection accept the existence of the relationship between cognitive ability and job performance, they often disagree with each other's numerical conclusions. Our qualitative characterizations should be acceptable to those who tend to minimize the economic importance of general cognitive ability and to those at the other end of the range.[12]

Why has expert opinion shifted? The answer lies in a powerful method of statistical analysis that was developing during the 1970s and came of age in the 1980s. Known as meta-analysis, it combines the results from many separate studies and extracts broad and stable conclusions.[13] In the case of job performance, it was able to combine the results from hundreds of studies. Experts had long known that the small samples and the varying validities, reliabilities, and restrictions of range in such studies were responsible to some extent for the low, negligible, or unstable correlations. What few realized was how different the picture would look when these sources of error and underestimation were taken into account through meta-analysis.[14] Taken individually, the studies said little that could be trusted or generalized; properly pooled, they were full of gold. The leaders in this effort—psychologists John Hunter and Frank Schmidt have been the most prominent—launched a new epoch in understanding the link between individual traits and economic productivity.

THE LINK BETWEEN COGNITIVE ABILITY AND JOB PERFORMANCE

We begin with a review of the evidence that an important statistical link between IQ and job performance does in fact exist. In reading the discussion that follows, remember that job performance does vary in the real world, and the variations are not small. Think of your own workplace and of the people who hold similar jobs. How large is the difference between the best manager and the worst? The best and worst secretary? If your workplace is anything like ours have been, the answer is that the differences are large indeed. Outside the workplace, what is it worth to you to have the name of a first-rate plumber instead of a poor one? A first-rate auto mechanic instead of a poor one? Once again, the common experience is that job performance varies widely, with important, tangible consequences for our everyday lives.

Nor is variation in job performance limited to skilled jobs. Readers who have ever held menial jobs know this firsthand. In restaurants, there are better and worse dishwashers, better and worse busboys. There are better and worse ditch diggers and garbage collectors. People who work in industry know that no matter how apparently mindless a job is, the job can still be done better or worse, with significant economic consequences. If the consequences are significant, it is worth knowing what accounts for the difference.

Job performance may be measured in many different ways.[15] Sometimes it is expressed as a natural quantitative measure (how many units a person produces per hour, for example), sometimes as structured ratings by supervisors or peers, sometimes as analyses of a work sample. When these measures of job productivity are correlated with measures of intelligence, the overall correlation, averaged over many tests and many jobs, is about .4. In the study of job performance and tests, the correlation between a test and job performance is usually referred to as the *validity* of the test, and we shall so refer to it for the rest of the discussion.[16] Mathematically, validity and the correlation coefficient are identical. Later in the chapter we will show that a validity of .4 has large economic implications, and even validities half as large may warrant worrying about.

This figure of .4 is no more than a point of reference. As one might expect, the validities are higher for complex jobs than for simple ones. In Edwin Ghiselli's mammoth compilation of job performance studies, mostly from the first half of the century, a reanalysis by John Hunter found a mean validity of .53 for the job family labeled "manager" and .46 for a "trades and crafts worker." Even an "elementary industrial worker" had a mean validity of .37.[17]

The Ghiselli data were extremely heterogeneous, with different studies using many different measures of cognitive ability, and include data that are decades old. A more recent set of data is available from a meta-analysis of 425 studies of job proficiency as predicted by the General Aptitude Test Battery (GATB), the U.S. Labor Department's cognitive ability test for the screening of workers. The table below summarizes the results of John and Ronda Hunter's reanalysis of these databases.[18]

The average validity in the meta-analysis of the GATB studies was .45.[19] The only job category with a validity lower than .40 was the in-

The Validity of the GATB for Different Types of Jobs			
	GATB Validity for:		% of U.S.
	Proficiency	Training	Workers in These
Job Complexity	Ratings	Success	Occupations
General job families			
High			
(synthesizing/coordinating)	.58	.50	14.7
Medium			
(compiling/computing)	.51	.57	62.7
Low (comparing/copying)	.40	.54	17.7
Industrial job families			
High (setup work)	.56	.65	2.5
Low (feeding/offbearing)	.23	NA	2.4

Source: Hunter and Hunter 1984, Table 2.

dustrial category of "feeding/offbearing"—putting something into a machine or taking it out—which occupies fewer than 3 percent of U.S. workers in any case. Even at that bottom-most level of unskilled labor, measured intelligence did not entirely lose its predictiveness, with a mean validity of .23.

The third major database bearing on this issue comes from the military, and it is in many ways the most satisfactory. The AFQT (Armed Forces Qualification Test) is extracted from the scores on several tests that everyone in the armed forces takes. It is an intelligence test, highly loaded on *g*. Everyone in the military goes to training schools, and everyone is measured for training success at the end of their schooling, with "training success" based on measures that directly assess job performance skills and knowledge. The job specialties in the armed forces include most of those found in the civilian world, as well a number that are not (e.g., combat). The military keeps all of these scores in personnel files and puts them on computers. The resulting database has no equal in the study of job productivity.

We will be returning to the military data for a closer look when we turn to subjects for which they are uniquely suited. For now, we will simply point out that the results from the military conform to the results in the civilian job market. The results for training success in the four ma-

The Validity of the AFQT for Military Training	
Military Job Family	Mean Validity of AFQT Score and Training Success
Mechanical	.62
Clerical	.58
Electronic	.67
General technical	.62

Source: Hunter 1985, Table 3.

jor job families are shown in the table above. These results are based on results from 828 military schools and 472,539 military personnel. The average validity was .62. They hold true for individual schools as well. Even the lowest-validity school, combat, in which training success is heavily dependent on physical skills, the validity was still a substantial .45.[20]

The lowest modern estimate of validity for cognitive ability is the one contained in the report by a panel convened by the National Academy of Sciences, *Fairness in Employment Testing.*[21] That report concluded that the mean validity is only about .25 for the GATB, in contrast to the Hunter estimate of .45 (which we cited earlier). Part of the reason was that the Hartigan committee (we name it for its chairman, Yale statistician John Hartigan), analyzing 264 studies after 1972, concluded that validities had generally dropped in the more recent studies. But the main source of the difference in validities is that the committee declined to make any correction whatsoever for restriction of range (see above and note 6). It was, in effect, looking at just the tackles already in the NFL; Hunter was considering the population at large. The Hartigan committee's overriding concern, as the title of their report (*Fairness in Employment Testing*) indicates, was that tests not be used to exclude people, especially blacks, who might turn out to be satisfactory workers. Given that priority, the committee's decision not to correct for restriction of range makes sense. But failing to correct for restriction of range produces a misleadingly low estimate of the overall relationship of IQ to job performance and its economic consequences.[22] Had the Hartigan committee corrected for restriction of range, the estimates of the relationship would have been .35 to .40, not much less than Hunter's.

THE REASONS FOR THE LINK BETWEEN COGNITIVE ABILITY AND JOB PERFORMANCE

Why are job performance and cognitive ability correlated? Surgeons, for example, will be drawn from the upper regions of the IQ distribution. But isn't it possible that all one needs is "enough" intelligence to be a surgeon, after which "more" intelligence doesn't make much difference? Maybe small motor skills are more important. And yet "more" intelligence always seems to be "better," for large groups of surgeons and every other profession. What is going on that produces such a result?

Specific Skills or g?

As we begin to explore this issue, the story departs more drastically from the received wisdom. One obvious, commonsense explanation is that an IQ test indirectly measures how much somebody knows about the specifics of a job and that that specific knowledge is the relevant thing to measure. According to this logic, more general intellectual capacities are beside the point. But the logic, however commonsensical, is wrong. Surprising as it may seem, the predictive power of tests for job performance lies almost completely in their ability to measure the most general form of cognitive ability, g, and has little to do with their ability to measure aptitude or knowledge for a particular job.

SPECIFIC SKILLS VERSUS G IN THE MILITARY. The most complete data on this issue come from the armed services, with their unique advantages as an employer that trains hundreds of thousands of people for hundreds of job specialties. We begin with them and then turn to the corresponding data from the civilian sector.

In assigning recruits to training schools, the services use particular combinations of subtests from a test battery that all recruits take, the Armed Services Vocational Aptitude Battery (ASVAB).[23] The Pentagon's psychometricians have tried to determine whether there is any practical benefit of using different weightings of the subtests for different jobs rather than, say, just using the overall score for all jobs. The overall score is itself tantamount to an intelligence test. One of the most comprehensive studies of the predictive power of intelligence tests was by Malcolm Ree and James Earles, who had both the intelligence test scores and the final grades from military school for over 78,000 air force enlisted personnel spread over eighty-nine military specialties. The personnel were educationally homogeneous (overwhelmingly high school graduates without college degrees), conveniently "controlling" for educational background.[24]

What explains how well they performed? For every one of the eighty-nine military schools, the answer was *g*—Charles Spearman's general intelligence. The correlations between *g* alone and military school grade ranged from an almost unbelievably high .90 for the course for a technical job in avionics repair down to .41 for that for a low-skill job associated with jet engine maintenance.[25] Most of the correlations were above .7. Overall, *g* accounted for almost 60 percent of the observed variation in school grades in the average military course, once the results were corrected for range restriction (the accompanying note spells out what it means to "account for 60 percent of the observed variation").[26]

Did cognitive factors other than *g* matter at all? The answer is that the explanatory power of *g* was almost thirty times greater than of all other cognitive factors in ASVAB combined. The table below gives a sampling of the results from the eighty-nine specialties, to illustrate the

---

The Role of g in Explaining Training Success for Various Military Specialties

Enlisted Military Skill Category	Percentage of Training Success Explained by:	
	g	Everything Else
Nuclear weapons specialist	77.3	0.8
Air crew operations specialist	69.7	1.8
Weather specialist	68.7	2.6
Intelligence specialist	66.7	7.0
Fireman	59.7	0.6
Dental assistant	55.2	1.0
Security police	53.6	1.4
Vehicle maintenance	49.3	7.7
Maintenance	28.4	2.7

Source: Ree and Earles 1990a, Table 9.

two commanding findings: g alone explains an extraordinary proportion of training success; "everything else" in the test battery explained very little.

An even larger study, not quite as detailed, involving almost 350,000 men and women in 125 military specialties in all four armed services, confirmed the predominant influence of g and the relatively minor further predictive power of all the other factors extracted from ASVAB scores.[27] Still another study, of almost 25,000 air force personnel in thirty-seven different military courses, similarly found that the validity of individual ASVAB subtests in predicting the final technical school grades was highly correlated with the g loading of the subtest.[28]

EVIDENCE FROM CIVILIAN JOBS. There is no evidence to suggest that military jobs are unique in their dependence on g. However, scholars in the civilian sector are at a disadvantage to their military colleagues; nothing approaches the military's database on this topic. In one of the few major studies involving civilian jobs, performance in twenty-eight occupations correlated virtually as well with an estimate of g from GATB scores as it did with the most predictively weighted individual subtest scores in the battery.[29] The author concluded that, for samples in the range of 100 to 200, a single factor, g, predicts job performance as well as, or better than, batteries of weighted subtest scores. With larger samples, for which it is possible to pick up the effect of less potent influences, there may be some modest extra benefit of specialized weighted scores. At no level of sampling, however, does g become anything less than the best single predictor known, across the occupational spectrum. Perhaps the most surprising finding has been that tests of general intelligence often do better in predicting future job performance than do contrived tests of job performance itself. Attempts to devise measures that are specifically keyed to a job's tasks—for example, tests of filing, typing, answering the telephone, searching in records, and the like for an office worker—often yield low-validity tests, unless they happen to measure g, such as a vocabulary test. Given how pervasive g is, it is almost impossible to miss it entirely with any test, but some tests are far more efficient measures of it than others.[30]

Behind the Test Scores

Let us try to put these data in the framework of everyday experience. Why should it be that variation in general cognitive ability, g, is more important than job-specific skills and knowledge? We will use the job of busboy as a specific example, asking the question: At a run-of-the-mill family restaurant, what distinguishes a really good busboy from an average one?

Being a busboy is a straightforward job. The waiter takes the orders, deals with the kitchen, and serves the food while the busboy totes the dirty dishes out to the kitchen, keeps the water glasses filled, and helps the waiter serve or clear as required. In such a job, a high IQ is not required. One may be a good busboy simply with diligence and good spirits. But complications arise. A busboy usually works with more than one waiter. The restaurant gets crowded. A dozen things are happening at once. The busboy is suddenly faced with queuing problems, with setting priorities. A really good busboy gets the key station cleared in the nick of time, remembering that a table of new orders near that particular station is going to be coming out of the kitchen; when he goes to the kitchen, he gets a fresh water pitcher *and* a fresh condiment tray to save an extra trip. He knows which waiters appreciate extra help and when they need it. The point is one that should draw broad agreement from readers who have held menial jobs: Given the other necessary qualities of diligence and good spirits, intelligence helps. The really good busboy is engaged in using g when he is solving the problems of his job, and the more g he has, the more quickly he comes up with the solutions and can call on them when appropriate.

Now imagine devising a test that would enable an employer to choose the best busboy among applicants. One important aspect of the test would measure diligence and good spirits. Perhaps the employer should weigh the results of this part of the test more heavily than anything else, if his choice is between a diligent and cheerful applicant and a slightly smarter but sulky one. But when it comes to measuring performance in general for most applicants, it is easy to see why the results will match the findings of the literature we just discussed. Job-specific items reveal mostly whether an applicant has ever been a busboy before. But that makes very little difference to job productivity, because a bright person can pick up the basic routine in the course of a few shifts. The g-loaded items, on the other hand, will reveal whether the applicant will ever become the kind of busboy who will clear table 12 before he clears table 20 because he relates the needed task to something that happened twenty minutes earlier regarding table 15. And that is why employers who want to select productive busboys should give applicants a test of general intelligence rather than a test of busboy skills. The kind of test that would pass muster with the courts—a test of job-specific skills—is a less effective kind of test to administer. What applies to busboys applies ever more powerfully as the jobs become more complex.

DOES MORE EXPERIENCE MAKE UP FOR LESS INTELLIGENCE?

The busboy example leads to another question that bears on how we should think about cognitive ability and job productivity: How much can experience counterbalance ability? Yes, the smart busboy will be more productive than the less-smart busboy a week into the job, and, yes, perhaps there will always be a few things that the smart busboy can do that the less smart cannot. But will the initial gap in productivity narrow as the less-smart busboy gains experience? How much, and how quickly?

Separately, job performance relates to both experience and intelligence, but the relationships differ.[31] That is, people who are new to a job learn quickly at first, then more slowly. A busboy who has, say, one month on the job may for that reason outperform someone who started today, but the one-month difference in experience will have ceased to matter in six months. No comparable leveling-off effect has been observed for increasing intelligence. Wherever on the scale of intelligence pairs of applicants are, the smarter ones not only will outperform the others, on the average, but the benefit of having a score that is higher by a given amount is approximately the same throughout the range. Or, to put it more conservatively, no one has produced good evidence of diminishing returns to intelligence.[32]

But what happens when both factors are considered jointly? Do employees of differing intelligence converge after some time on the job? If the answer were yes, then it could be argued that hiring less intelligent people imposes only a limited and passing cost. But the answer seems to be closer to no than to yes, although much remains to be learned.

Some convergence has been found when SATs are used as the measure of ability and grade point average is used as the measure of achievement.[33] Students with differing SATs sometimes differ more in their freshman grades than in later years. That is why President Bok granted predictive value to the SAT only for first-year grades.[34] On the other hand, the shrinking predictive power may be because students learn which courses they are likely to do well in: They drop out of physics or third-year calculus, for example, and switch to easier courses. They find out which professors are stingy with A's and B's. At the U.S. Military Academy, where students have very little choice in courses, there is no convergence in grades.[35]

When it comes to job performance, the balance of the evidence is that convergence either does not occur or that the degree of convergence is small. This was the finding of a study of over 23,000 civilian employees at three levels of mental ability (high, medium, and low), using supervisor ratings as the measure of performance, and it extended out to job tenures of twenty years and more.[36] A study of four military specialties (armor repairman, armor crewman, supply specialist, cook) extending out to five years of experience and using three different measures of job performance (supervisor's ratings, work sample, and job knowledge) found no reliable evidence of convergence.[37] Still another military study, which examined several hundred marines working as radio repairmen, automotive mechanics, and riflemen, found no convergence among personnel of differing intelligence when job knowledge was the measure of performance but did find almost complete convergence after a year or so when a work sample was the measure.[38]

Other studies convey a similarly mixed picture.[39] Some experts are at this point concluding that convergence is uncommon in the ordinary range of jobs.[40] It may be said conservatively that for most jobs, based on most measures of productivity, the difference in productivity associated with differences in intelligence diminishes only slowly and partially. Often it does not diminish at all. The cost of hiring less intelligent workers may last as long as they stay on the job.

TEST SCORES COMPARED TO OTHER PREDICTORS OF PRODUCTIVITY

How good a predictor of job productivity is a cognitive test score compared to a job interview? Reference checks? College transcript? The answer, probably surprising to many, is that the test score is a better predictor of job performance than any other single measure. This is the conclusion to be drawn from a meta-analysis on the different predictors of job performance, as shown in the table below.

The Validity of Some Different Predictors of Job Performance	
Predictor	**Validity Predicting Job Performance Ratings**
Cognitive test score	.53
Biographical data	.37
Reference checks	.26
Education	.22
Interview	.14
College grades	.11
Interest	.10
Age	−.01

Source: Hunter and Hunter 1984.

The data used for this analysis were top heavy with higher-complexity jobs, yielding a higher-than-usual validity of .53 for test scores. However, even if we were to substitute the more conservative validity estimate of .4, the test score would remain the best predictor, though with close competition from biographical data.[41] The method that many people intuitively expect to be the most accurate, the job interview, has a poor record as a predictor of job performance, with a validity of only .14.

Readers who are absolutely sure nonetheless that they should trust their own assessment of people rather than a test score should pause to consider what this conclusion means. It is not that you would select a markedly different set of people through interviews than test scores would lead you to select. Many of the decisions would be the same. The results in the table say, in effect, that among those choices that would be different, the employees chosen on the basis of test scores will on average be more productive than the employees chosen on the basis of any other single item of information.

THE DIFFERENCE INTELLIGENCE MAKES

We arrive finally at the question of what it all means. How important is the overall correlation of .4, which we are using as our benchmark for the relation between intelligence and job performance? The temptation may be to say, not very. As we showed before, there will be many exceptions to the predicted productivity with correlations this modest. And indeed it is not very important when an employer needs just a few new employees for low-complexity jobs and is choosing among a small group of job applicants who have small differences in test scores. But the more reality departs from this scenario, the more important cognitive ability becomes.

The Dollar Value of Cognitive Ability

How much is the variation in job performance worth? To answer that question, we need a measure in dollars of how much the workers in a given occupation vary. (Some of the methods for making this measurement are recounted in the notes, to which we refer readers who would like more detail.)[42] To cut a long story short, think now of a particular worker—a secretary, let us say. You have a choice between hiring an average secretary, who by definition is at the 50th percentile, or a first-rate one—at the 84th percentile, let us say. If you were free to set their salaries at the figures you believe to reflect their true worth, how different would they be? We imagine that anyone who has worked with average secretaries and first-rate ones will answer "a lot." The consensus among experts has been that, measured in dollars, "a lot" works out, on the average, to about a 40 percent premium.

Put more technically and precisely, one standard deviation of the distribution of workers' annual productivities in a typical occupation is worth 40 percent of the average worker's annual income.[43] New work suggests the premium may actually be twice as large. Since the larger estimate has yet to be confirmed, we will base our calculations on the more conservative estimate.[44] To take a specific example, for a $20,000-a-year job, which is correctly priced for an average worker, the incremental value of hiring a new worker who is one standard deviation above the mean—at the 84th percentile—is $8,000 per year.[45] Hiring a worker for a $20,000-a-year job who is one standard deviation *below* the mean—at the 16th percentile—would cost the employer $8,000 in lost output.

The standard deviation for output is usually larger for more complex jobs.[46] This makes intuitive sense: an assembly-line worker can do his job well or poorly, but ordinarily the gap that separates the proficiency of the 16th and 84th percentiles of assembly-line workers is not as great measured in the dollar value of the output as the gap that separates the proficiency of the 16th and 84th percentiles of engineers. But when we match this fact against an additional fact—that engineers make a lot more money than assembly-line workers—we are faced with what is known in statistics as an interaction effect. Getting high quality for a complex job can be worth large multiples of what it is worth to get equally high quality for a simpler job.

We may make this concrete with some hypothetical calculations. Imagine a dental office, consisting of dentist and receptionist. Assume that the annual salary of an average dentist is $100,000 and that of the receptionist $25,000, and that these are correctly priced. For whatever reasons, society finds the dentist to be worth four times as much as the receptionist.[47] Suppose further that you are an employer—a Health Maintenance Organization (HMO), for example—who hires both dentists and receptionists. By using a certain selection procedure, you can improve the quality of your new hirees, so that instead of hiring people who are, on average, at the 50th percentile of proficiency (which is what would happen if you picked randomly from the entire pool of receptionists and dentists looking for jobs), you instead could hire people who are, on average, at the 84th percentile. What is this screening procedure worth to you?

For the value of the output produced, we use a standard deviation of .5 of the annual income for dentists and of .15 for that of receptionists, based on values actually observed.[48] The answer, given these numbers, is that it is worth $50,000 a year for the dentist and $3,750 per year for the receptionist to hire people who are one standard deviation above average in proficiency—not the ratio of four to one that separates the dentist's wages from the receptionist's but a ratio of more than thirteen to one.[49]

We are not home yet, for although we know what it is worth to hire these more proficient dentists and receptionists, we have not yet factored in the validity of the selection test. The correlation between test score and proficiency is roughly .6 for dentists and .2 for receptionists, again based on observation and approximating the top and bottom of the range illustrated in the figure below. Given that information, we may estimate the expected output difference between two dentists who score at the 50th and 84th percentiles on an intelligence test as being worth $30,000 a year.[50] The corresponding difference between two receptionists who score at the 50th and 84th percentiles in intelligence is $750 a year. And this is what we meant by an "interaction effect": the wage of the dentist is only four times that of the receptionist. But the value to the employer of hiring brighter dentists is *forty* times greater than the value of hiring comparably brighter receptionists.[51]

In a real-life situation, the value of a test (or any other selection procedure) depends on another factor: How much choice does the employer have?[52] There is no point in spending money on an intelligence test if only one applicant shows up. If ten applicants show up for the job, however, a test becomes attractive. The figure below illustrates the economic benefit of testing with different levels of competition for the job (from one to fifty applicants per job) and different tests (from a very

The advantages of hiring by test score

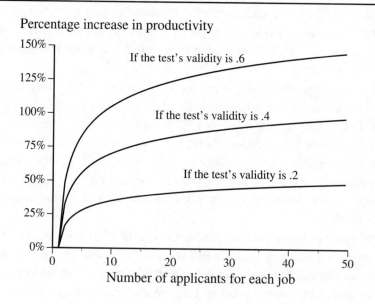

Percentage increase in productivity

If the test's validity is .6

If the test's validity is .4

If the test's validity is .2

Number of applicants for each job

poor one with a validity of .2 to a very strong one with a validity of .6).[53]
If everyone is hired, then, on average, the hired person is just at the average level of proficiency, which is a standard score of 0. But as soon as even two applicants are available per position, the value of testing rises quickly. With just two applicants per position, the employer gains 16 to 48 percent in productivity, depending on the validity of the test.[54] The curve quickly begins to flatten out; much of the potential value of testing has already been captured when there are three applicants per job. The figure above is an answer to those who claim that a correlation of, say, .4 is too small to bother with.[55] A validity of .4 (or even .6) may be unimportant if almost all applicants are hired, but even a correlation of .2 (or still smaller) may be important if only a small proportion gets hired.

The Macroeconomic Costs of Not Testing

Since the pivotal Supreme Court decision of *Griggs* v. *Duke Power Co.* in 1971, no large American employer has been able to hire from the top down based on intelligence tests. Estimates vary widely for how much the American economy loses by not doing so, from what Hunter and Hunter conclude is a minimum loss of $80 billion in 1980 (and in 1980 dollars) to what the Hartigan committee thought was a maximum loss of $13 billion for that year.[56] The wide range reflects the many imponderables in making these calculations. For one thing, many attributes of an applicant other than a test score are correlated with intelligence—educational level, for example. Schooling captures some, but not all, of the predictive value of intelligence. Or consider an employer using family connections to hire instead of tests. A bright worker is likely to have a bright sister or brother. But the average IQ score difference between siblings is eleven or twelve points, so, again, test scores would predict proficiency better than judging an applicant by the work of a brother or sister.

Modeling the economic impact of testing has additional complexities. It has been noted that the applicant pool would gradually get depleted of the top scorers when every successive employer tries to hire top down.[59] As the smart people are hired and thereby removed from the applicant pool, the validity of a test for those still on the job market may change because of, for example, restriction of range. The eco-

---

When Only the Best Will Do

A selection ratio of one in fifty may seem unrealistic, and so it is for the run-of-the-mill job. But for the most competitive jobs, much higher ratios, up to one in several hundred, are common. Consider the handful of new openings in top law firms or for internships in the most desirable research hospitals or in the richest investment banking firms for which each year's new graduates are competing. Many potential applicants select themselves out of the pool for those prized jobs, realizing that the openings will be filled by people with stronger credentials, but they must nevertheless be reckoned as being part of the applicant pool in order to get a realistic estimate of the importance of cognitive ability. This is again the issue exemplified by the weight of offensive tackles, discussed earlier in the chapter.

The question arises whether the employer gains much by a rigorous selection process for choosing among the people who actually do show up at the job interview. Aren't they already so highly screened that they are, in effect, homogeneous? The answer is intimately related to the size of the stakes. When the job is in a top Wall Street firm, for example, the dollar value of output is so high that the difference between a new hiree who is two standard deviations above the mean and one who is four standard deviations above the mean on any given predictor measure can mean a huge economic difference, even though the "inferior" applicant is already far into the top few centiles in ability.

---

nomic benefit of using a test would then decline. But if testing tended to place the smartest people in the jobs where the test-job correlations are large, the spread of the productivity distributions is broad, the absolute levels of output value are high, and the proportions hired are small, the benefits could be huge, even if the economic effects of testing the last people in the pool are negligible. In short, figuring out the net effects of testing or not testing is no small matter. No one has yet done it conclusively.

WHY PARTITIONING IS INEVITABLE

To recapitulate a complex discussion: Proficiency in most common civilian and military occupations can be predicted by IQ, with an over-

---

Choosing Police Applicants by IQ

A case study of what happens when a public service is able to hire from the top down on a test of cognitive ability, drawing on a large applicant pool, comes out of New York City. In April 1939, after a decade of economic depression, New York City attracted almost 30,000 men to a written and physical examination for 300 openings in the city's police force, a selection ratio of approximately one in a hundred.[57] The written test was similar to the intelligence test then being given by the federal civil service. Positions were offered top down for a composite score on the mental and physical tests, with the mental test more heavily weighted by more than two to one. Not everyone accepted the offer, but, times being what they were, the 300 slots were filled by men who earned the top 350 scores. Inasmuch as the performance of police officers has been shown to correlate significantly with scores on intelligence tests,[58] this group of men should have made outstanding policemen. And they did, achieving extraordinarily successful careers in and out of policing. They attained far higher than average rank as police officers. Of the entire group, four have been police chiefs, four deputy commissioners, two chiefs of personnel, one a chief inspector, and one became commissioner of the New York Police Department. They suffered far fewer disciplinary penalties, and they contributed significantly to the study and teaching of policing and law enforcement. Many also had successful careers as lawyers, businessmen, and academics after leaving the police department.

---

all validity that may conservatively be placed at .4. The more demanding a job is cognitively, the more predictive power such a test has, but no common job is so undemanding that the test totally lacks predictiveness. For the job market as a whole, cognitive ability predicts proficiency better than any other known variable describing an individual, including educational level. Intelligence tests are usually more predictive of proficiency than are paper-and-pencil tests that are specifically based on a job's activities. For selecting large numbers of workers, there may be some added predictive power, usually small, when a score on a narrower test of performance is combined with an intelligence test. For low-complexity jobs, a test of motor skill often adds materially to predictiveness. The predictive power of IQ derives from its loading on g, in Spearman's sense of general intelligence.

If we were writing a monograph for personnel managers, the appropriate next step would be to present a handbook of tables for computing when it makes economic sense to test new applicants (ignoring for the moment legislative and judicial restrictions on such testing). Such a calculation would be based on four variables: the predictive power of the test for the job at hand, the variation in worker productivity for the job at hand, the proportion of job applicants that are to be selected, and the cost of testing. The conclusion would often be that testing is profitable. Even a marginally predictive test can be economically important if only a small fraction of applicants is to be selected. Even a marginally predictive test may have a telling economic impact if the variation in productivity is wide. And for most occupations, the test is more than marginally predictive. In the average case, a test with a .4 validity, the employer who uses a cognitive test captures 40 percent of the profit that would be realized from a perfectly predictive test—no small advantage. In an era when a reliable intelligence test can be administered in twelve minutes, the costs of testing can be low—lower in terms of labor than, for example, conducting an interview or checking references.

We are not writing a monograph for personnel managers, however, and the main point has nothing to do with whether one favors or opposes the use of tests as a hiring device. The main point is rather that intelligence itself is importantly related to job performance. *Getting rid of intelligence tests in hiring—as policy is trying to do—will not get rid of the importance of intelligence.* The alternatives that employers have available to them—biographical data, reference checks, educational record, and so forth—are valid predictors of job performance in part because they imperfectly reflect something about the applicant's intelligence. Employers who are forbidden to obtain test scores nonetheless strive to obtain the best possible work force, and it so happens that the way to get the best possible work force, other things equal, is to hire the smartest people they can find. It is not even necessary for employers to be aware that intelligence is the attribute they are looking for. As employers check their hiring procedures against the quality of their employees and refine their procedures accordingly, the importance of intelligence in the selection process converges on whatever real importance it has for the job in question, whether or not they use a formal test.

Because the economic value of their employees is linked to intelligence, so ultimately are their wages. Let us consider that issue in the next chapter, along with some others that have interlocking implications as we try to foresee, however dimly, what the future holds for the cognitive elite.

Chapter 4

Steeper Ladders, Narrower Gates

Cognitive partitioning through education and occupations will continue, and there is not much that the government or anyone else can do about it. Economics will be the main reason. At the same time that elite colleges and professional schools are turning out brighter and brighter graduates, the value of intelligence in the marketplace is rising. Wages earned by people in high-IQ occupations have pulled away from the wages in low-IQ occupations, and differences in education cannot explain most of this change.

Another force for cognitive partitioning is the increasing physical segregation of the cognitive elite from the rest of society. Members of the cognitive elite work in jobs that usually keep them off the shop floor, away from the construction site, and close to others who also tend to be smart. Computers and electronic communication make it increasingly likely that people who work mainly with their minds collaborate only with other such people. The isolation of the cognitive elite is compounded by its choices of where to live, shop, play, worship, and send its children to school.

Its isolation is intensified by an irony of a mobile and democratic society like America's. Cognitive ability is a function of both genes and environment, with implications for egalitarian social policies. The more we succeed in giving every youngster a chance to develop his or her latent cognitive ability, the more we equalize the environmental sources of differences in intelligence. The irony is that as America equalizes the circumstances of people's lives, the remaining differences in intelligence are increasingly determined by differences in genes. Meanwhile, high cognitive ability means, more than ever before, that the chances of success in life are good and getting better all the time. Putting it all together, success and failure in the American economy, and all that goes with it, are increasingly a matter of the genes that people inherit.

Add to this the phenomenon known as assortative mating. Likes attract when it comes to marriage, and intelligence is one of the most important of those likes. When this propensity to mate by IQ is combined with increasingly efficient educational and occupational stratification, assortative mating by IQ has more powerful effects on the next generation than it had on the previous one. This process too seems to be getting stronger, part of the brew creating an American class system.

A s Mae West said in another context, goodness has nothing to do with it. We are not talking about what should have been but what has been. The educational system *does* sort by cognitive ability at the close of the twentieth century in a way that it did not at the opening of the century. The upper strata of intelligence *are* being sucked into a comparatively few occupations in a way that they did not used to be. Cognitive ability *is* importantly related to job productivity. All of these trends will continue under any social policy. We are optimistic enough to believe that no administration, Left or Right, is going to impede the education of the brightest, or forbid the brightest from entering the most cognitively demanding occupations, or find a way to keep employers from rewarding productivity. But we are not so optimistic that we can overlook dark shadows accompanying the trends.

To this point, we have avoided saying what social consequences might be expected. This omission has been deliberate, for part of a candid answer must be, "We aren't sure." We can be sure only that the trends are important. Cognitive stratification as a central social process is something genuinely new under the sun. One of our purposes is to bring it to public attention, hopeful that wisdom will come from encouraging more people to think about it.

It is impossible to predict all the ways in which cognitive stratification will interact with the workings of an American democracy that is in flux. We do have some thoughts on the matter, however, and in this chapter use the available scientific data to peer into the future. The data center on the dynamics that will make cognitive stratification more pronounced in the years to come—the differences greater, the overlap smaller, the separation wider. We reserve our larger speculations about the social consequences for Chapters 21 and 22.

THE CHANGING MARKET FOR ABILITY

The overriding dynamic that will shape the effects of cognitive stratification is the increasing value of intelligence in the marketplace. The smart ones are not only being recruited to college more efficiently, they are not only (on average) more productive in the workplace, their dollar value to employers is increasing and there is every reason to believe that this trend will continue. As it does so, the economic gap separating the upper cognitive classes from the rest of society will increase.

The general shape of what has been happening is shown in the figure for a representative high-IQ occupation, engineering, compared to the average manufacturing employee, starting back in 1932. As always, dollar figures are expressed in 1990 dollars. The 1950s turn out to have been the decade of hidden revolution for income, just as it was for education and status. Throughout the 1930s and 1940s, the average engineer and the average manufacturing employee remained in roughly a constant economic relationship, even converging slightly. Then from

Engineers' salaries as an example of how intelligence became much more valuable in the 1950s

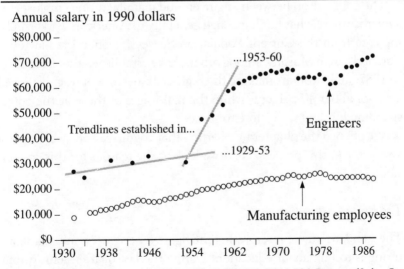

Source: U.S. Bureau of the Census 1975, Tables D802-810, D913-926; Bureau of Labor Statistics 1989, Tables 80, 106.

Were the 1980s Good or Bad for Income?

There are half a dozen different ways to view the economy during the 1980s. Because most of it fell in Ronald Reagan's presidency, an intense political struggle to characterize the decade as economically "good" or "bad" has ensued. The main source of confusion lies in the distinction between *household income*, which went up for all income groups, driven by the increase in two-income families and low unemployment, and *real wages*, which (generally) rose for white-collar workers and fell for blue-collar workers. There are also confusions that arise because the value of benefit packages rose even though cash wages did not and because of controversies over the proper calculation of changes in real purchasing power. We will not try to adjudicate these issues or the role that President Reagan's economic policies played, which have taken whole books to argue out.

1953 to 1961 the average engineer's salary nearly doubled while the manufacturing employee's salary followed the same gradually rising trend and increased by only 20 percent. By the end of the 1980s, the average manufacturing employee had to get by on about $23,000 a year while the engineer made an average of $72,000. The difference in their purchasing power had tripled since the 1940s, which is enough to put them in separate economic brackets.

The comparison between engineers and manufacturing employees is a microcosm of what has happened generally to American workers. Using data from the Current Population Surveys, economists Lawrence Katz and Kevin Murphy, among others, have established that from 1963 to 1987, male workers making the highest 10 percent of wages enjoyed a rise of about 40 percent, while the real wages of those at the corresponding low end were close to static.[1]

We opened the chapter by asserting that cognitive ability has been a key factor in this process. Next we look at the reasons for this conclusion.

The Role of Education

The standard way of interpreting the figure for engineers and manufacturing is to talk about education. During the last quarter-century, real wages rose more than twice as much for workers with college educations than for those with high school or less.[2] Trends were not uninterrupted within the interval. Following the huge expansion of the post–World War II college population, it seemed for a while that the economic benefits of education were being swamped by oversupply, as wages fell during the 1970s for college-educated people.[3] But in the 1980s, the trend reversed. Real wages for highly educated people started once again to climb and wages fell for those with twelve or fewer years of schooling.[4]

The table below gives the percentage change in real wages for full-time male workers[5] at three educational levels during the 1980s, broken out by whether they are new workers (one to five or twenty-six to thirty-five years of work experience). The dramatic changes occurred

Education, Experience, and Wages, 1979–1987	
	Percentage Change in Wages
New workers (1–5 years of experience)	
Less than 12 years of school	−15.8
High school degree	−19.8
16 or more years of school	+10.8
Old workers (26–35 years of experience)	
Less than 12 years of school	−1.9
High school degree	−2.8
16 or more years of school	+1.8

Source: Adapted from Katz and Murphy, 1990, Table 1.

among young men just coming into the labor market. High school graduates and dropouts saw their real wages plunge, while young men with college educations enjoyed a healthy increase.[6] Meanwhile, experienced older men saw little real change in income whatever their level of education. Why the difference between the age groups? Interpretively, wages for men with many years of experience reflect their work history as well as their immediate economic value. Wages for people just entering the labor force are more purely an expression of prevailing market forces. The job market reevaluated schooling during the past two decades: Educated workers, having been devalued in the 1970s, became increasingly valuable in the 1980s, in comparison with less educated workers.[7]

Why have the economic returns to education lately risen, thereby widening the income gap between the educated and the uneducated? Perhaps, say some commentators, the wage inequality problem is technological, as machines displace people from low-skill jobs. Perhaps schools are failing to teach people skills that they used to teach, or maybe the schools are doing as well as ever but the blue-collar jobs that require only low-level skills are emigrating to countries where labor is cheaper, thereby creating an oversupply of less educated workers in America. Perhaps the welfare system is eroding the need to work among the low-skill population, or the weakening labor unions are not protecting their economic interests, or a declining real minimum wage is letting the wage structure sag at the low end.

These possibilities all bear on a crucial issue: *How much good would it do to improve education for the people earning low wages?* If somehow the government can cajole or entice youths to stay in school for a few extra years, will their economic disadvantage in the new labor market go away? We doubt it. Their disadvantage might be diminished, but only modestly. There is reason to think that the job market has been rewarding not just education but intelligence.[8]

The Mysterious Residual

The indispensable database for analyzing wages over time is the Current Population Survey, the monthly national survey conducted by the Bureau of the Census and the Bureau of Labor Statistics, which asks people only about their years of education, not their IQs. But as the sophisticated statistical analyses of wage variation have accumulated, experts have come to agree that something beyond education, gender, and experience has been at work to increase income disparities in recent times.[9] The spread in real wages grew between 1963 and 1987 even after taking those other factors into account.[10] The economic term for this unexplained variation in wages is "the residual."[11]

To understand the growing wage inequality requires an account of this residual variation. Residual wage variation for both men and women started rising in about 1970 and seems still to be rising. Among economists, there is a consensus that, whatever those residual characteristics consist of, it has been mainly the *demand* for them, not their *supply*, that has been changing and causing increasing wage inequality for a generation, with no signs of abating.[12] Despite the public focus on the increasing importance of education in the workplace, most of the increasing wage inequality during the past two and a half decades is due to changes in the demand for the residual characteristics of workers rather than to changes in the demand for education or experience.[13] The job market for people lacking the residual characteristics declined, while expanding for people having them.

The Case for IQ as the Residual

What then is this residual, this X factor, that increasingly commands a wage premium over and above education? It could be a variety of factors. It could be rooted in diligence, ambition, or sociability.[14] It could be associated with different industries or different firms within industries, or different wage norms (e.g., regional variations, variations in merit pay), again insofar as they are not accounted for by the measured variables. Or it could be cognitive ability. Conclusive evidence is hard to come by, but readers will not be surprised to learn that we believe that it includes cognitive ability. There are several lines of support for this hypothesis.

As a first cut at the problem, the changing wages have something to do with the shifting occupational structure of our economy. High-status, and therefore relatively high-paying, jobs are tipped toward people with high intelligence, as Chapter 2 showed. As the high-end jobs have become more numerous, demand must rise for the intellectual abilities that they require. When demand rises for any good, including intelligence, the price (in this case, the wages) goes up. Purely on economic grounds, then, wage inequality grew as the economic demand for intelligence climbed.

We further know from the data discussed in Chapter 3 that cognitive ability affects how well workers at all levels do their jobs. If smarter workers are, on average, better workers, there is reason to believe that income within job categories may be correlated with intelligence.

Still further, we know that the correlation between intelligence and income is not much diminished by partialing out the contributions of education, work experience, marital status, and other demographic variables.[15] Such a finding strengthens the idea that the job market is increasingly rewarding not just education but intelligence.

Finally, McKinley Blackburn and David Neumark have provided

direct evidence in their analysis of white men in the National Longitudinal Survey of Youth (NLSY). Education and intelligence each contributed to a worker's income, but the smart men earned most of the extra wage benefit of education during the past decade.[16] The growing economic benefits of either schooling or intelligence are disproportionately embodied in the rising income of educated people with high test scores and in the falling wages earned by less educated people with low scores.[17]

This premium for IQ applies even within the high-IQ occupations that we discussed in Chapter 2. In the NLSY, among people holding one of these jobs, the 1989 weekly earnings (expressed in 1990 dollars) of those in the top 10 percent of IQ were $977, compared to $697 for those with IQs below the top 10 percent, for an annual income difference of over $14,000.[18] Even after extracting any effects of their specific occupations (as well as of the differing incomes of men and women), being in the top 10 percent in IQ was still worth over $11,000 in income for those in this collection of prestigious occupations.

Why Cognitive Ability Has Become More Valuable to Employers

This brings us as far as the data on income and intelligence go. Before leaving the topic, we offer several reasons why the wage premium for intelligence might have increased recently and may be expected to continue to increase.

Perhaps most obviously is that technology has increased the economic value of intelligence. As robots replace factory workers, the factory workers' jobs vanish, but new jobs pop up for people who can design, program, and repair robots. The new jobs are not necessarily going to be filled by the same people, for they require more intelligence than the old ones did. Today's technological frontier is more complex than yesterday's. Even in traditional industries like retailing, banking, mining, manufacturing, and farming, management gets ever more complex. The capacity to understand and manipulate complexity, as earlier chapters showed, is approximated by *g*, or general intelligence. We would have predicted that a market economy, faced with this turn of events, would soon put intelligence on the sales block. It has. Business consultancy is a new profession that is soaking up a growing fraction of the graduates of the elite business schools. The consultants sell mainly their trained intelligence to the businesses paying their huge fees.

A second reason involves the effects of scale, spurred by the growth in the size of corporations and markets since World War II. A person who can dream up a sales campaign worth another percentage point or two of market share will be sought after. What "sought after" means in dollars and cents depends on what a point of market share is worth. If it is worth $500,000, the market for his services will produce one range of salaries. If a point of market share is worth $5 million, he is much more valuable. If a point of market share is worth $100 million, he is worth a fortune. Now consider that since just 1960, the average annual sales, per corporation, of America's five hundred largest industrial corporations has jumped from $1.8 billion to $4.6 billion (both figures in 1990 dollars). The same gigantism has affected the value of everything from the ability to float successful bond offerings to the ability to negotiate the best prices for volume purchases by huge retail chains. The magnitude of the economic consequences of ordinary business transactions has mushroomed, and with it the value of people who can do their work at a marginally higher level of skill. All the evidence we have suggests that such people have, among their other characteristics, high intelligence. There is no reason to think that this process will stop soon.

Then there are the effects of legislation and regulation. Why are certain kinds of lawyers who never see the inside of a courtroom able to command such large fees? In many cases, because a first-rate lawyer can make a difference worth tens of millions of dollars in getting a favorable decision from a government agency or slipping through a tax loophole. Lawyers are not the only beneficiaries. As the rules of the game governing private enterprise become ever more labyrinthine, intelligence grows in value, sometimes in the most surprising places. One of our colleagues is a social psychologist who supplements his university salary by serving as an adviser on jury selection, at a consulting fee of several thousand dollars per day. Based on his track record, his advice raises the probability of a favorable verdict in a liability or patent dispute by about 5 to 10 percent. When a verdict may represent a swing of $100 million, an edge of that size makes him well worth his large fee.

We have not exhausted all the reasons that cognitive ability is becoming more valuable in the labor market, but these will serve to illustrate the theme: The more complex a society becomes, the more valuable are the people who are especially good at dealing with complexity. Barring a change in direction, the future is likely to see the rules for doing business become yet more complex, to see regulation extend still further, and to raise still higher the stakes for having a high IQ.

The End Result: Prosperity for Those Lucky Enough to Be Intelligent

After all that has gone before, it will come as no surprise to find that smart people tend to have high incomes. The advantage enjoyed by those who have high enough IQs to get into the high-IQ occupations is shown in the figure below. All of the high-IQ occupations have median wages well out on the right-hand side of the distribution.[19] Those

The high-IQ occupations also are well-paid occupations

The Recent American Wage Distribution

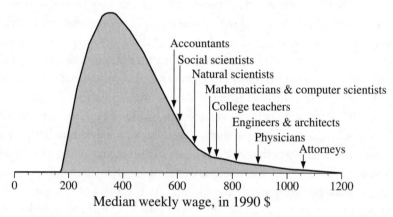

Median weekly wage, in 1990 $

Source: U.S. Department of Labor 1991.

in the top range of IQ had incomes that were conspicuously above those with lower IQs even within the high-IQ occupations. The overall median family income with a member in one of these occupations and with an IQ in the top 10 percent was $61,100, putting them at the 84th percentile of family incomes for their age group. These fortunate people were newly out of graduate school or law school or medical school, still near the bottom of their earnings trajectory as of their early thirties, whereas a large proportion of those who had gone into blue-collar jobs (disproportionately in the lower IQ deciles) have much less room to ad-

Income as a Family Trait
America has taken great pride in the mobility of generations: enterprising children of poor families are supposed to do better than their parents, and the wastrel children of the rich are supposed to fritter away the family fortune. But in modern America, this mobility has its limits. The experts now believe that the correlation between fathers' and sons' income is at least .4 and perhaps closer to .5.[21] Think of it this way: The son of a father whose earnings are in the bottom 5 percent of the distribution has something like one chance in twenty (or less) of rising to the top fifth of the income distribution and almost a fifty-fifty chance of staying in the bottom fifth. He has less than one chance in four of rising above even the median income.[22] Economists search for explanations of this phenomenon in structural features of the economy. We add the element of intellectual stratification. Most people at present are stuck near where their parents were on the income distribution in part because IQ, which has become a major predictor of income, passes on sufficiently from one generation to the next to constrain economic mobility.

vance beyond this age.[20] In other words, the occupational elite is prosperous. Within it, the cognitive elite is more prosperous still.

COGNITIVE SORTING THROUGH PHYSICAL SEPARATION

The effects of cognitive sorting in education and occupation are reified through geography. People with similar cognitive skills are put together in the workplace and in neighborhoods.

Cognitive Segregation in the Workplace

The higher the level of cognitive ability and the greater the degree of homogeneity among people involved in that line of work, the greater is the degree of separation of the cognitive elite from everyone else. First, consider a workplace with a comparatively low level of cognitive homogeneity—an industrial plant. In the physical confines of the plant, all kinds of abilities are being called upon: engineers and machinists, electricians and pipefitters and sweepers, foremen and shift supervisors, and the workers on the loading dock. The shift supervisors and engineers may have offices that give them some physical separation from the plant floor, but, as manufacturers have come to realize in recent years, they had better not spend all their time in those offices. Efficient and profitable production requires not only that very different tasks be accomplished, using people of every level of cognitive ability, but that they be accomplished cooperatively. If the manufacturing company is prospering, it is likely that a fair amount of daily intermingling of cognitive classes goes on in the plant.

Now we move across the street to the company's office building. Here the average level of intelligence is higher and the spread is narrower. Only a handful of jobs, such as janitor, can be performed by people with low cognitive ability. A number of jobs can be done by people of average ability—data entry clerks, for example. Some jobs that can be done adequately by people with average cognitive ability turn into virtually a different, and much more important, sort of job if done superbly. The job of secretary is the classic example. The traditional executive secretary, rising through the secretarial ranks until she takes charge of the boss's office, was once a familiar career path for a really capable, no doubt smart, woman. For still other jobs, cognitive ability is important but less important than other talents—among the sales representatives, for example. And finally there is a layer of jobs among the senior executives and in the R&D department for which cognitive ability is important and where the mean IQ had better be high if the company is to survive and grow in a competitive industry. In the office building, not only cognitive homogeneity has increased; so has physical separation. The executives do not spend much time with the janitors or the data entry clerks. They spend almost all their time interacting with other executives or with technical specialists, which means with people drawn from the upper portion of the ability distribution.

Although corporate offices are more stratified for intelligence than the manufacturing plant, some workplaces are even more stratified. Let's move across town to a law firm. Once again, the mean IQ rises and the standard deviation narrows. Now there are only a few job categories—for practical purposes, three: secretaries, paralegals or other forms of legal assistants, and the attorneys. The lowest categories, secretarial and paralegal work, require at least average cognitive skills for basic competence, considerably more than that if their jobs are to be done as well as they could be. The attorneys themselves are likely to be, virtually without exception, at least a standard deviation above the mean, if only because of the selection procedures in the law schools that enabled them to become lawyers in the first place. It remains true that part of the success of the law firm depends on qualities that are only slightly related to cognitive skills—the social skills involved in getting new business, for example. And attorneys in almost any law firm can be found shaking their heads over the highly paid (and smart) partner who is coasting on his subordinates' talents. But the overall degree of cognitive stratification in a good law firm is extremely high. And note an important distinction: It is not that stratification *within* the law firm is high; rather, the entire workplace represents a stratum highly atypical of cognitive ability in the population at large.

These rarefied environments are becoming more common because the jobs that most demand intelligence are increasing in number and economic importance. These are jobs that may be conducted in cloistered settings in the company of other smart workers. The brightest lawyers and bankers increasingly work away from the courtroom and the bank floor, away from all except the most handpicked of corporate clients. The brightest engineers increasingly work on problems that never require them to visit a construction site or a shop floor. They can query their computers to get the answers they need. The brightest public policy specialists shuttle among think tanks, bureaucracies, and graduate schools of public policy, never having to encounter an angry voter. The brightest youngsters launch their careers in business by getting an M.B.A. from a top business school, thence to climb the corporate ladder without ever having had to sell soap or whatever to the company's actual customers. In each example, a specialized profession within the profession is developing that looks more and more like academia in the way it recruits, insulates, and isolates members of the cognitive elite.

Residential Segregation

As soon as a town grows larger than a few dozen households in size, it starts to develop neighborhoods. As towns become cities, this tendency becomes a reliable law of human communities. People seek out comfortable neighborhoods they can afford. For some people, this will mean looking for a particular kind of setting. Parents with young children typically want parks, good schools, and neighbors with young children. Single people in their twenties and thirties making good money often gravitate toward upscale urban neighborhoods with lots of places to go and things to do.

The result is to produce neighborhoods with a high level of socioeconomic partitioning. The factory worker seldom lives next door to the executive, and this was as true in 1900 as in the last years of the century. The wealthy people have always been the most mobile. But in the late twentieth century, the most mobile people are increasingly drawn from the cognitive elite. In thinking about these changes, we will focus on their implications for the way that the children of the cognitive elite are raised, for therein lies one of the main potential sources of trouble.

First, the urbanization of the nation has meant that a much smaller proportion of the population grows up in places where socioeconomic mixing occurs naturally. Given a small enough town, there are not enough elementary schools to segregate the children efficiently. The children of the local upper crust may live on the street with the large houses, but there are not enough of them to fill up a whole school. After elementary school, every child in the town goes to the same middle school and high school. Such towns now constitute a shrinking proportion of the population, however. As of 1990, 78 percent of the overall population lived in metropolitan areas.[23]

Cognitive segregation is also being intensified by failures of government in large cities. As urban school systems deteriorate, people with money relocate to rich suburbs because that is where the good public school systems are; if they remain in the city, they send their children to private schools, which are even more homogeneous. As crime rates rise, people with money relocate to suburbs where the crime rates are low, or they concentrate ever more densely within the safer parts of the city. As urban tax rates rise, the middle class flees, leaving behind even more starkly segregated poles of rich and poor.

Bright working-class youngsters mix with children of every other level of ability in elementary school, but they are increasingly likely to be drawn away to the more intellectually homogeneous high school courses, thence to college. Much of the cognitive talent that used to be in the working-class neighborhood is being whisked up and out of the community through an educational system that is increasingly driven by academic performance. Because of residential segregation, the children of lawyers, physicians, college professors, engineers, and business executives tend to go to schools with each other's children, and seldom with the children of cab drivers or assembly-line workers, let alone with the children of welfare recipients or the chronically unemployed. They may never go to school with children representative of the whole range of cognitive ability. This tendency is exacerbated by another force working in the background, genes.

GENETIC PARTITIONING

Twenty years ago, one of us wrote a book that created a stir because it discussed the heritability of IQ and the relationship of intelligence to success in life, and foresaw a future in which socioeconomic status would increasingly be inherited. The logic of the argument was couched in a syllogism:

- If differences in mental abilities are inherited, and
- If success requires those abilities, and
- If earnings and prestige depend on success,
- Then social standing (which reflects earnings and prestige) will be based to some extent on inherited differences among people.[24]

As stated, the syllogism is not fearsome. If intelligence is only trivially a matter of genes and if success in life is only trivially a matter of intelligence, then success may be only trivially inherited.

How Much Is IQ a Matter of Genes?

In fact, IQ is substantially heritable. The state of knowledge does not permit a precise estimate, but half a century of work, now amounting to hundreds of empirical and theoretical studies, permits a broad conclusion that the genetic component of IQ is unlikely to be smaller than 40 percent or higher than 80 percent.[25] The most unambiguous direct estimates, based on identical twins raised apart, produce some of the highest estimates of heritability.[26] For purposes of this discussion, we will adopt a middling estimate of 60 percent heritability, which, by extension, means that IQ is about 40 percent a matter of environment. The balance of the evidence suggests that 60 percent may err on the low side.

Because IQ and genes has been such a sensitive topic, it is worth a short digression to give some idea of where these estimates come from and how trustworthy they are.

First, consider the question that heads this section, not its answer. What we want to know is how much of the variation in IQ in a *population*—the aggregated differences among the individuals[27]—is due to variations in genetic endowments and how much is due to variations in environment. If all the population variation in IQ is due to variations in environment, then the *heritability* is 0;[28] if half is due to environmental variations, it is .5; if none is due to environmental variations, it is 1.0. Heritability, in other words, is a ratio that ranges between 0 and 1 and measures the relative contribution of genes to the variation observed in a trait.[29]

Specialists have come up with dozens of procedures for estimating heritability. Nonspecialists need not concern themselves with nuts and bolts, but they may need to be reassured on a few basic points. First the heritability of any trait can be estimated as long as its variation in a population can be measured. IQ meets that criterion handily. There are, in fact, no other human traits—physical or psychological—that provide as many good data for the estimation of heritability as the IQ. Second, heritability describes something about a population of people, not an individual. It makes no more sense to talk about the heritability of an individual's IQ than it does to talk about his birthrate. A given individual's IQ may have been greatly affected by his special circumstances even though IQ is substantially heritable in the population as a whole. Third, the heritability of a trait may change when the conditions producing variation change. If, one hundred years ago, the variations in exposure to education were greater than they are now (as is no doubt the case), and if education is one source of variation in IQ, then, other things equal, the heritability of IQ was lower then than it is now.

This last point is especially important in the modern societies, with their intense efforts to equalize opportunity. As a general rule, *as environments become more uniform, heritability rises*. When heritability rises, children resemble their parents more, and siblings increasingly resemble each other; in general, family members become more similar to each other and more different from people in other families. It is the central irony of egalitarianism: Uniformity in society makes the members of families more similar to each other and members of different families more different.

Now for the answer to the question, How much is IQ a matter of genes? Heritability is estimated from data on people with varying amounts of genetic overlap and varying amounts of shared environment. Broadly speaking, the estimates may be characterized as direct or indirect.[30] Direct estimates are based on samples of blood relatives who were raised apart. Their genetic overlap can be estimated from basic genetic considerations. The direct methods assume that the correlations between them are due to the shared genes rather than shared environments because they do not, in fact, share environments, an assumption that is more or less plausible, given the particular conditions of the study. The purest of the direct comparisons is based on identical (monozygotic, MZ) twins reared apart, often not knowing of each other's existence. Identical twins share all their genes, and if they have been raised apart since birth, then the only environment they shared was that in the womb. Except for the effects on their IQs of the shared uterine environment, their IQ correlation directly estimates heritability. The most modern study of identical twins reared in separate homes suggests a heritability for general intelligence between .75 and .80, a value near the top of the range found in the contemporary technical literature.[31] Other direct estimates use data on ordinary siblings who were raised apart or on parents and their adopted-away children. Usually, the heritability estimates from such data are lower but rarely below .4.[32]

Indirect methods compare the IQ correlations between people with different levels of shared genes growing up in comparable environments—siblings versus half-siblings or versus cousins, for example, or MZ twins versus fraternal (dizygotic, DZ) twins, or nonadoptive siblings versus adoptive siblings. The underlying idea is that, for example, if full siblings raised in the same home and half-siblings raised in the same home differ in their IQ correlations, it is because they differ in the proportion of genes they share: full siblings share about 50 percent of genes, half siblings about 25 percent. Similarly, if siblings raised in unshared environments and cousins raised in unshared environments differ in their IQ correlations, it is because of the differing degrees of genetic overlap between cousins and siblings and not because of differing environmental influences, which are unshared by definition. And so on. Fleshed out in some sort of statistical model, this idea makes it possible to estimate the heritability, but the modeling can get complex. Some studies use mixtures of direct and indirect methods.[33]

The technical literature is filled with varying estimates of the heritability of IQ, owing to the varying models being used for estimation and to the varying sets of data. Some people seem eager to throw up their hands and declare, "No one knows (or can know) how heritable IQ is." But that reaction is as unwarranted as it is hasty, if one is content, as we are, to accept a range of uncertainty about the heritability that specialists may find nerve-racking. We are content, in other words, to say that the heritability of IQ falls somewhere within a broad range and that, for purposes of our discussion, a value of .6 ±.2 does no violence to any of the competent and responsible recent estimates. The range of .4 to .8 includes virtually all recent (since 1980) estimates—competent, responsible, or otherwise.[34]

Recent studies have uncovered other salient facts about the way IQ scores depend on genes. They have found, for example, that the more general the measure of intelligence—the closer it is to g—the higher is the heritability.[35] Also, the evidence seems to say that the heritability of IQ rises as one ages, all the way from early childhood to late adulthood.[36] This means that the variation in IQ among, say, youths ages 18 to 22 is less dependent on genes than that among people ages 40 to 44.[37] Most of the traditional estimates of heritability have been based on youngsters, which means that they are likely to underestimate the role of genes later in life.

Finally, and most surprisingly, the evidence is growing that whatever variation is left over for the environment to explain (i.e., 40 percent of the total variation, if the heritability of IQ is taken to be .6), relatively little can be traced to the shared environments created by families.[38] It is, rather, a set of environmental influences, mostly unknown at present, that are experienced by individuals as individuals. The fact that family members resemble each other in intelligence in adulthood as much as they do is very largely explained by the genes they share rather than the family environment they shared as children. These findings suggest deep roots indeed for the cognitive stratification of society.

The Syllogism in Practice

The heritability of IQ is substantial. In Chapters 2 and 3, we presented evidence that the relationship of cognitive ability to success in life is far from trivial. Inasmuch as the syllogism's premises cannot be dismissed out of hand, neither can its conclusion that success in life will be based to some extent on inherited differences among people.[39]

Furthermore, a variety of other scientific findings leads us to conclude that the heritability of success is going to increase rather than diminish. Begin with the limits that heritability puts on the ability to manipulate intelligence, by imagining a United States that has magically made good on the contemporary ideal of equality. Every child in this imaginary America experiences exactly the same environmental effects, for good or ill, on his or her intelligence. How much intellectual variation would remain? If the heritability of IQ is .6, the standard deviation of IQ in our magical world of identical environments would be 11.6 instead of 15 (see the note for how this calculation is done)—smaller, but still leaving a great deal of variation in intellectual talent that could not be reduced further by mere equalization.[40] As we noted earlier, when a society makes good on the ideal of letting every youngster have equal access to the things that allow latent cognitive ability to develop, it is in effect driving the environmental component of IQ variation closer and closer to nil.

The United States is still very far from this state of affairs at the extremes. If one thinks of babies growing up in slums with crack-addicted mothers, at one extreme, compared to children growing up in affluent, culturally rich homes with parents dedicated to squeezing every last IQ point out of them, then even a heritability of .6 leaves room for considerable change if the changes in environment are commensurably large. We take up the evidence on that issue in detail in Chapter 17, when we consider the many educational and social interventions that have attempted to raise IQ. But those are, by definition, the extremes, the two tails of the distribution of environments. Moving a child from an environment that is the very worst to the very best may make a big difference. In reality, what most interventions accomplish is to move children from awful environments to ones that are merely below average, and such changes are limited in their potential consequences when heritability so constrains the limits of environmental effects.[41]

So while we can look forward to a future in which science discovers how to foster intelligence environmentally and how to use the science humanely, inherited cognitive ability is now extremely important. In this sense, luck continues to matter in life's outcomes, but now it is more a matter of the IQ handed out in life's lottery than anything else about circumstances. High cognitive ability as of the 1990s means, more than even before, that the chances of success in life are good and getting better all the time, and these are *decreasingly* affected by the social environment, which by extension indicates that they must be *increasingly* affected by genes. Holding these thoughts in mind, now consider the phenomenon known as *assortative mating*.

Love, Marriage, and IQ

The old saw notwithstanding, opposites do not really attract when it comes to love and marriage. Likes attract. In one of the classic papers, originally published in 1943, two sociologists studied 1,000 engaged couples in Chicago, expecting to find at least some traits in which opposites did indeed attract. But out of fifty-one social characteristics studied, the sign of the correlation was positive for every single one. For all but six of the fifty-one traits, the correlations were statistically significant.[42] Modest but consistently positive correlations have been found for a wide variety of physical traits as well, ranging from stature (the correlations from many studies average about +.25) to eye color (also averaging about +.25, even within national populations).[43]

Of the many correlations involving husbands and wives, one of the highest is for IQ. In most of the major studies, the correlation of husband and wife IQ has been in the region of .4, though estimates as low as .2 and as high as .6 have been observed. Jensen's review of the literature in the late 1970s found that the average correlation of forty-three spouse correlations for various tests of cognitive ability was +.45, almost as high as the typical correlation of IQs among siblings.[44]

If the Propensity to Mate by Cognitive Ability Has Remained the Same:

When the propensity to mate by cognitive ability is combined with the educational and occupational stratification we have described, the impact on the next generation will be larger than on the previous one, *even if the underlying propensity to mate by cognitive ability remains the same*.

Consider 100 Harvard/Radcliffe marriages from the class of 1930 versus another 100 from the class of 1964. We stipulate that the propensity to marry people of similar intelligence has not changed in the intervening thirty-four years. Nonetheless, the ones who marry in 1964 will produce a set of children with considerably higher mean IQ than the ones who married in 1930, because the level of intelligence at Harvard and Radcliffe had risen so dramatically.

How much difference can it make? If the average Harvard man in the class of 1930 married the average Radcliffe woman in the same graduating class—as far as we can tell, both would have had IQs of about 117—then the expected mean IQ of their children, after taking regression to the mean into account, will be about 114, or at the 82d percentile.[45] But average Harvard and Radcliffe newlyweds in the class of 1964 were likely to have children with a mean IQ of about 124, at the 95th percentile. In terms of distributions rather than averages, about a third of the children of the Harvard newlyweds of 1930 could be expected to have IQs of less than 110—not even college material by some definitions.[46] In contrast, only 6 percent of the children of the Harvard newlyweds of 1965 could be expected to fall below this cutoff. Meanwhile, only about 22 percent of the children of the 1930 newlyweds could be expected to match or exceed the *average* of the children of the 1965 newlyweds. In such numbers lurk large social effects.

If the Propensity to Mate by Cognitive Ability Has Increased:

We have been assuming that the propensity to mate by IQ has remained the same. In reality, it has almost certainly increased and will continue to increase.

We hedge with "almost" because no quantitative studies tell whether assortative mating by intelligence has been increasing recently. But we do know from sociologist Robert Mare of the University of Wisconsin that assortative mating by educational level increased over the period from 1940 to 1987—an increase in "homogamy," in the sociologists' language. The increase in homogamy was most pronounced among college-educated persons. Specifically, the odds of a college graduate's marrying someone who was not a college graduate declined from 44 percent in 1940 to 35 percent in Mare's most recent data (for 1985 to 1987). The proportion hit a low of 33 percent in the 1980 data.[47] Because educational attainment and IQ are so closely linked and became more closely linked in the postwar period, Mare's results suggest a substantial increase in assortative mating by IQ, with the greatest change occurring at the upper levels of IQ.

Mare identifies some of the reasons for increased homogamy in the trends involving educational attainment, age at leaving school, and age at marriage. But there are a variety of other potential explanations (some of which he notes) that involve cognitive ability specifically. For example, a smart wife in the 1990s has a much greater dollar payoff for a man than she did fifty years ago.[48] The feminist movement has also increased the likelihood of marrying by cognitive ability.

First, the feminist revolution in practice (which began in the 1950s, antedating the revolution in rhetoric) drastically increased the odds that bright young women will be thrown in contact with bright young men during the years when people choose spouses. This is most obvious in college, where the proportion of women continuing to college surged from about half the proportion of men in 1950 to equality in 1975.[49] It was not just the numbers, however. All of the elite men's colleges became coeducational, as did many of elite women's colleges. Strict parietal rules gave way to coeducational dorms. Intelligence has always been an important factor for sorting among prospective mates, but comparison shopping at single-sex colleges like Vassar or Yale was a struggle; the feminist revolution in the universities led to an explosion of information, as it were, that made it easier for the brightest to pair up.

The same phenomenon extended to the workplace. Large proportions of the cognitive elite delay marriage until the later twenties or even thirties. Only a few decades ago, delay tended to dilute the chances of assortative mating by IQ. In a world where the brightest women were usually not in the work force or were in a few restricted occupations, the pool from which a man in his late twenties found a bride were moderated primarily by socioeconomic status; he found his mate among the women he encountered in his neighborhood, church, social organizations, and other settings that were matched mostly by socioeconomic status. But today background status is less important than intelligence. The young man newly graduated from his elite law school joins his elite New York firm, thereupon encountering young women, just as highly selected for cognitive ability as he was, in the adjacent offices at his own firm, at business lunches, across the table in negotiations, on a daily basis. The opportunities for propinquity to work its magic were increased in the workplace too, and will continue to increase in the years to come.

The second effect of feminism is less ponderable but may be important anyway. Not so many years ago, the cliché was true: brains were not considered sexy in a woman, and many men undervalued brains as an asset in a prospective spouse or even felt threatened by smart women. Such attitudes may linger in some men, but feminism has surely weakened them and, to some degree, freed relationships among men and women so that a woman's potential for occupational success can take as dominant a place in the man's marriage calculus as it has traditionally taken in the woman's.[50] We speculate that the effect has been most liberating among the brightest. If we are right, then the trends in educational homogamy that Mare has demonstrated are an understated reflection of what is really going on. Intermarriage among people in the top few percentiles of intelligence may be increasing far more rapidly than suspected.

THE LIMITS OF CHURNING

American society has historically been full of churning, as new groups came to this country, worked their way up, and joined the ranks of the rich and powerful. Meanwhile, some of the children of the rich and powerful, or their grandchildren, were descending the ladder. This process has made for a vibrant, self-renewing society. In depressing contrast, we have been envisioning a society that becomes increasingly quiescent at the top, as a cognitive elite moves toward the upper income brackets and runs most of the institutions of society, taking on some of the characteristics of a caste.

Is the situation really so extreme? To some extent, not yet. For example, national surveys still indicate that fewer than 60 percent in the top quartile of intelligence actually complete a bachelor's degree.[51] This would seem to leave a lot of room for churning. But when we focus instead on the students in the top few centiles of cognitive ability (from which the nation's elite colleges pick almost exclusively), an extremely high proportion are already being swept into the comfortable precincts of the cognitive elite.[52] In the NLSY, for example, 81 percent of those in the top 5 percent of IQ had obtained at least a bachelor's degree by 1990, when the youngest members of the sample were 25 years old.[53]

When we examine the remaining 19 percent who had not obtained college degrees, the efficiency of American society in pushing the most talented to the top looks even more impressive. For example, only a small portion of that 19 percent were smart students who had been raised in a low-income family and did not get to college for lack of opportunity. Only 6 percent of persons in the top five IQ centiles did not have a college degree *and* came from families in the lower half of socioeconomic status.[54]

If this 19 percent of high-IQ persons-without-B.A.s does not fit the stereotype of the deprived student, who were they? Some were becoming members of the cognitive elite even though they do not have a college degree. Bill Gates, college dropout and founder of Microsoft, is the larger-than-life prototype. Five percentage points of the 19 percent were working in one of the high-IQ occupations, indicating that they were probably of the minor-league Bill Gates variety (corroborated by their incomes, which were high). Of the remaining 14 percent who were not working in high-IQ occupations, a quarter had family incomes in excess of $50,000 while they were still only in their late twenties and early thirties, putting them in the top 20 percent of family incomes for their age group.[55] In total, roughly half of these smart non–college graduates are already taking their place among the smart college graduates, by virtue of their incomes, their occupations, or both. It seems a safe bet that the neighborhoods where they live and the way they socialize their children are going to be indistinguishable from those of most of their counterparts in the top five centiles who completed college.

There is doubtless some relatively small fraction of those in the top 5 percent intellectually who will never rise to successful positions, whether because of lack of motivation or objective barriers. But what a small percentage of the highly talented they are. And we may add a reminder that we are watching an ongoing process. Think back to Chapter 1 and imagine the trend line from 1900 to 1990 stretched out to, say, 2020. Whatever the number of the cognitive elite who slip between the cracks now, it is a much smaller figure than it was in the 1950s, radically smaller than it was in the 1900s, and presumably it will get smaller still in the future.

These observations have several implications. At a practical policy level, the most obvious is that programs to expand opportunity for the disadvantaged are not going to make much difference in getting the most talented youths to college. An extremely high proportion of those who want to go are already going. The broader implication is that the funneling system is already functioning at a high level of efficiency, thereby promoting three interlocking phenomena:

1. The cognitive elite is getting richer, in an era when everybody else is having to struggle to stay even.
2. The cognitive elite is increasingly segregated physically from everyone else, in both the workplace and the neighborhood.
3. The cognitive elite is increasingly likely to intermarry.

These phenomena are driven by forces that do not lend themselves to easy reconfiguration by politicians. As we leave Part I, here is a topic to keep in the back of your mind: What if the cognitive elite were to become not only richer than everyone else, increasingly segregated, and more genetically distinct as time goes on but were also to acquire common political interests? What might those interests be, and how congruent might they be with a free society? How decisively could the cognitive elite affect policy if it were to acquire such a common political interest?

These issues will return in the last chapters in the book. They are postponed for now, because we must first explore the social problems that might help create such a new political coalition.

PART II

Cognitive Classes and Social Behavior

Whereas Part I dealt with positive outcomes—attainment of high educational levels, prestigious occupations, high incomes—Part II presents our best estimate of how much intelligence has to do with America's most pressing social problems. The short answer is "quite a lot," and the reason is that different levels of cognitive ability are associated with different patterns of social behavior. High cognitive ability is generally associated with socially desirable behaviors, low cognitive ability with socially undesirable ones.

"Generally associated with" does not mean "coincident with." For virtually all of the topics we will be discussing, cognitive ability accounts for only small to middling proportions of the variation among people. It almost always explains less than 20 percent of the variance, to use the statistician's term, usually less than 10 percent and often less than 5 percent. What this means in English is that you cannot predict what a given person will do from his IQ score—a point that we have made in Part I and will make again, for it needs repeating. On the other hand, despite the low association at the individual level, large differences in social behavior separate groups of people when the groups differ intellectually on the average.

We will argue that intelligence itself, not just its correlation with socioeconomic status, is responsible for these group differences. Our thesis appears to be radical, judging from its neglect by other social scientists. Could low intelligence possibly be a cause of irresponsible childbearing and parenting behaviors, for example? Scholars of childbearing and parenting do not seem to think so. The 850 double-column pages of the authoritative Handbook of Marriage and the Family, for example, allude to intelligence about half a dozen times, always in passing.[1] Could low intelligence possibly be a cause of unemployment or poverty? Only a scattering of economists have broached the possibility.[2]

This neglect points to a gaping hole in the state of knowledge about social behavior. It is not that cognitive ability has been considered and found inconsequential but that it has barely been considered at all. The chapters in Part II add cognitive ability to the mix of variables that social scientists have traditionally used, clearing away some of the mystery that has surrounded the nation's most serious social problems.

We will also argue that cognitive ability is an important factor in thinking about the nature of the present problems, whether or not cognitive ability is a cause. For example, if many of the single women who have babies also have low IQ, it makes no difference (in one sense) whether the low IQ caused them to have the babies or whether the path of causation takes a more winding route. The reality that less intelligent women have most of the out-of-wedlock babies affects and constrains public policy, whatever the path of causation. The simple correlation, unadjusted for other factors—what social scientists called the zero-order correlation—between cognitive ability and social behaviors is socially important.

The chapters of Part II cover a wide range of topics, each requiring extensive documentation. Many statistics, many tables and graphs, many citations to technical journals crowd the pages. But the chapters generally follow a similar pattern, and many of the complexities will be less daunting if you understand three basics: the NLSY, our use of cognitive classes, and our standard operating procedure for statistical analysis.

THE NLSY

In Part I, we occasionally made use of the National Longitudinal Survey of Youth, the NLSY. In the chapters that follow, it will play the central role in the analysis, with other studies called in as available and appropriate.

Until a few years ago, there were no answers to many of the questions we will ask, or only very murky answers. No one knew what the relationship of cognitive ability to illegitimacy might be, or even the relationship of cognitive ability to poverty. Despite the millions of mental tests that have been given, very few of the systematic surveys, and sometimes none, gave the analyst a way to conclude with any confidence that this is how IQ interacts with behavior X for a representative sample of Americans.

Several modern sources of data have begun to answer such questions. The TALENT database, the huge national sample of high school students taken in 1961, is the most venerable of the sources, but its follow-up surveys have been limited in the range and continuity of their data. The Panel Study of Income Dynamics, begun in 1968 and the nation's longest-running longitudinal database, administered a brief vocabulary test in 1972 to part of its sample, but the scores allow only rough discriminations among people in the lower portions of the distribution of intelligence. The National Longitudinal Survey begun by the Department of Education in 1972 (not to be confused with the NLSY) provides answers to many questions associated with educational outcomes. The department's more ambitious study, High School and Beyond, conducted in the early 1980s, is also useful.

But the mother lode for scholars who wish to understand the relationship of cognitive ability to social and economic outcomes is the NLSY, whose official name is the National Longitudinal Survey of Labor Market Experience of Youth. When the study began in 1979, the participants in the study were aged 14 to 22.[3] There were originally 12,686 of them, chosen to provide adequate sample sizes for analyzing crucial groups (for example, by oversampling blacks, Latinos, and low-income whites), and also incorporating a weighting system so that analysts could determine the correct estimates for nationally representative samples of their age group. Sample attrition has been kept low and the quality of the data, gathered by the National Opinion Research Council under the supervision of the Center for Human Resources Research at Ohio State University, has been excellent.

The NLSY is unique because it combines in one database all the elements that hitherto had to be studied piecemeal. Only the NLSY combined detailed information on the childhood environment *and* parental socioeconomic status *and* subsequent educational and occupational achievement *and* work history *and* family formation *and*—crucially for our interests—detailed psychometric measures of cognitive skills.

The NLSY acquired its cognitive measures by a lucky coincidence. In 1980, a year after the first wave of data collection, the Department of Defense decided to update the national norms for its battery of enlistment tests. At the time, it was still using test scores from World War II recruits as the reference population. Because the NLSY had just gone through the technically difficult and tedious task of selecting a nationally representative sample, the Department of Defense proposed to piggyback its study on the NLSY sample.[4] And so the NLSY became the beneficiary of an expensive, well-designed set of cognitive and aptitude tests that were given under carefully controlled conditions to almost 94 percent of the 12,686 young men and women in the NLSY sample.[5]

The measure of cognitive ability extracted from this test battery was the Armed Forces Qualification Test, the AFQT. It is what the psychometricians call "highly g-loaded," meaning that it is a good measure of general cognitive ability.[6] The AFQT's most significant shortcoming is that it is truncated at the high end; about one person in a thousand gets a perfect score, which means both that the test does not discriminate among the very highest levels of intelligence and that the variance in the population is somewhat understated. Otherwise the AFQT is an excellent test, with psychometric reliability and validity that compare well with those of the other major tests of intelligence. Because the raw scores on the AFQT mean nothing to the average reader, we express them in the IQ metric (with a mean of 100 and a standard deviation of 15) or in centiles. Also, we will subsequently refer to them as "IQ scores," in keeping with our policy of using *IQ* as a generic term for intelligence test scores. When we use centiles, they are age equated. A centile score of 45, for example, means that the subject would rank in the 45th percentile of everyone born in the same year, if everyone took the AFQT.[7] A final point about the presentation of NLSY results is that *all results are based on weighted analyses*, which means that all may be interpreted in terms of a nationally representative sample of Americans in the NLSY age group. We use data collected through the 1990 interview wave.

THE DEFINITION OF COGNITIVE CLASSES

To this point, we have been referring to cognitive classes without being specific. In these chapters, we divide the world into cognitive classes— five of them, because that has been the most common number among sociologists who have broken down socioeconomic status into classes and because five allows the natural groupings of "very high," "high," "mid," "low," and "very low." We have chosen to break the intervals at the 5th, 25th, 75th, and 95th percentiles of the distribution. The figure shows how this looks for a normally distributed population.

Break points are arbitrary, but we did have some reasons for these.

Defining the cognitive classes

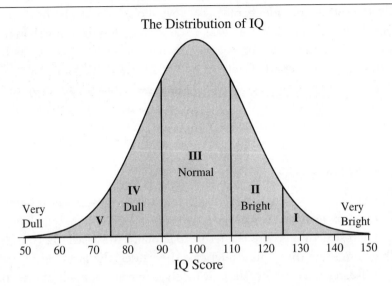

The Distribution of IQ

Mainly, we wanted to focus on the extremes; hence, we avoided a simple breakdown into quintiles (i.e., into equal cuts of 20 percent). A great deal of interest goes on within the top 20 percent and bottom 20 percent of the population. Indeed, if the sample sizes were large enough, we would have defined the top cognitive class as consisting of the top 1 or 2 percent of the population. Important gradations in social behavior occasionally separate the top 2 percent from the next 2 percent. This is in line with another of the themes that we keep reiterating because they are so easily forgotten: You—meaning the self-selected person who has read this far into this book—live in a world that probably looks nothing like the figure. In all likelihood, almost all of your friends and professional associates belong in that top Class I slice. Your friends and associates whom you consider to be unusually slow are probably somewhere in Class II. Those whom you consider to be unusually bright are probably somewhere in the upper fraction of the 99th centile, a very thin slice of the overall distribution. In defining Class I, which we will use as an operational definition of the more amorphous group called the "cognitive elite," as being the top 5 percent, we are being quite inclusive. It does, after all, embrace some 12 1/2 million people. Class III, the normals, comprises half of the population. Classes II and IV each comprises 20 percent, and Class V, like Class I, comprises 5 percent.

The labels for the classes are the best we could do. It is impossible to devise neutral terms for people in the lowest classes or the highest ones. Our choice of "very dull" for Class V sounds to us less damning than the standard "retarded" (which is generally defined as below an IQ of 70, with "borderline retarded" referring to IQs between 70 and 80). "Very bright" seems more focused than "superior," which is the standard term for people with IQs of 120 to 130 (those with IQs above 130 are called "very superior" in that nomenclature).[8]

PRESENTING STATISTICAL RESULTS

The basic tool for multivariate analysis in the social sciences is known as *regression analysis*.[9] The many forms of regression analysis have a common structure. There is a result to explain, the *dependent variable*. There are some things that might be the causes, the *independent variables*. Regression analysis tells how much each cause actually affects the result, *taking the role of all the other hypothesized causes into account*—an enormously useful thing for a statistical procedure to do, hence its widespread use.

In most of the chapters of Part II, we will be looking at a variety of social behaviors, ranging from crime to childbearing to unemployment to citizenship. In each instance, we will look first at the direct relationship of cognitive ability to that behavior. After observing a statistical connection, the next question to come to mind is, What else might be another source of the relationship?

In the case of IQ, the obvious answer is socioeconomic status. To what

---

What Is a Variable?

The word *variable* confuses some people who are new to statistics, because it sounds as if a variable is something that keeps changing. In fact, it is something that has different values among the members of a population. Consider weight as a variable. For any given observation, weight is a single number: the number of pounds that an object weighed at the time the observation was taken. But over all the members of the sample, weight has different values: It varies, hence it is a variable. A mnemonic for keeping "independent" and "dependent" straight is that the dependent variable is thought to "depend on" the values of the independent variables.

extent is this relationship really founded on the social background and economic resources that shaped the environment in which the person grew up—the parents' socioeconomic status (SES)—rather than intelligence? Our measure of SES is an index combining indicators of parental education, income, and occupational prestige (details may be found in Appendix 2). Our basic procedure has been to run regression analyses in which the independent variables include IQ and parental SES.[10] The result is a statement of the form: "Here is the relationship of IQ to social behavior X after the effects of socioeconomic background have been extracted," or vice versa. Usually this takes the analysis most of the distance it can sensibly be pushed. If the independent relationship of IQ to social behavior X is small, there is no point in looking further. If the role of IQ remains large independent of SES, then it is worth thinking about, for it may cast social behavior and public policy in a new light.

But What About Other Explanations?

We do not have the choice of leaving the issue of causation at that, however. Because intelligence has been such a taboo explanation for social behavior, we assume that our conclusions will often be resisted, if not condemned. We can already hear critics saying, "If only they had added this other variable to the analysis, they would have seen that intelligence has nothing to do with X." A major part of our analysis accordingly has been to anticipate what other variables might be invoked and seeing if they do in fact attenuate the relationship of IQ to any given social behavior. This was not a scattershot effort. For each relationship, we asked ourselves if evidence, theory, or common sense suggests another major causal story. Sometimes it did. When looking at whether a new mother went on welfare, for example, it clearly was not enough to know the general socioeconomic background of the woman's parents. It was also essential to examine her own economic situation at the time she had the baby: Whatever her IQ is, would she go on welfare if she had economic resources to draw on?

At this point, however, statistical analysis can become a bottomless pit. It is not uncommon in technical journals to read articles built around the estimated effects of a dozen or more independent variables. Sometimes the entire set of variables is loaded into a single regression equation. Sometimes sets of equations are used—modeling even more complex relationships, in which all the variables can exert mutual effects on one another.

Why should we not press forward? Why not also ask if religious background has an effect on the decision to go on welfare, for example? It is an interesting question, as are another fifty others that might come to mind. Our principle was to explore additional dynamics when there was another factor that was not only conceivably important but for clear logical reasons might be important *because of dynamics having little or nothing to do with IQ*. This last proviso is crucial, for one of the most common misuses of regression analysis is to introduce an additional variable that in reality is mostly another expression of variables that are already in the equation.

The Special Case of Education

Education posed a special and continuing problem. On the one hand, education can be important independent of cognitive ability. For example, education tends to delay marriage and childbirth because the time and commitment involved in being in school competes with the time and commitment it takes to be married or have a baby. Education shapes tastes and values in ways that are independent of the cognitive ability of the student. At the same time, however, the role of education versus IQ as calculated by a regression equation is tricky to interpret, for four reasons.

First, the number of years of education that a youth gets is *caused* to an important degree by both the parents' SES and the youth's own academic ability. In the NLSY, for example, the correlation of years of education with parental SES and youth's IQ are +.50 and +.64, respectively. This means that when years of education is used as an independent variable, it is to some extent expressing the effects of SES and IQ in another form.

Second, any role that education plays independent of intelligence is likely to be discontinuous. For example, it may make a big difference to many outcomes that a person has a college degree. But how is one to interpret the substantive difference between one year of college and two? Between one year of graduate school and two? They are unlikely to be nearly as important as the difference between "a college degree" and "no college degree."

Third, variables that are closely related can in some circumstances produce a technical problem known as *multicollinearity*, whereby the solutions produced by regression equations are unstable and often mis-leading.

Fourth and finally, to take education's regression coefficient seriously tacitly assumes that intelligence and education could vary independently and produce similar results. No one can believe this to be true in general: indisputably, giving nineteen years of education to a person with an IQ of 75 is not going to have the same impact on life as it would for a person with an IQ of 125. The effects of education, whatever they may be, depend on the coexistence of suitable cognitive ability in ways that often require complex and extensive modeling of interaction effects—once again, problems that we hope others will take up but would push us far beyond the purposes of this book.

Our solution to this situation is to report the role of cognitive ability for two subpopulations of the NLSY that each have the same level of education: a high school diploma, no more and no less in one group; a bachelor's degree, no more and no less, in the other. This is a simple, but we believe reasonable, way of bounding the degree to which cognitive ability makes a difference independent of education.

We walk through all three of these basics—the NLSY, the five cognitive classes, and the format for the statistical analysis—in a step-by-step fashion in the next chapter, where we use poverty to set the stage for the social behaviors to follow. Chapter 6 returns to education, this time not just talking about how far people got but the comparative roles of IQ and SES in determining how far someone gets in school. Then, seriatim, we take up unemployment and labor force dropout (Chapter 7), single-parent families and illegitimacy (Chapter 8), welfare dependency (Chapter 9), parenting (Chapter 10), crime (Chapter 11), and civic behavior (Chapter 12).

In these eight chapters, we limit the analysis to whites, and more specifically to non-Latino whites.[11] This is, we think, the best way to make yet another central point: Cognitive ability affects social behavior without regard to race or ethnicity. The influence of race and ethnicity is deferred to Part III.

Chapter 5

Poverty

Who becomes poor? One familiar answer is that people who are unlucky enough to be born to poor parents become poor. There is some truth to this. Whites, the focus of our analyses in the chapters of Part II, who grew up in the worst 5 percent of socioeconomic circumstances are eight times more likely to fall below the poverty line than those growing up in the top 5 percent of socioeconomic circumstances. But low intelligence is a stronger precursor of poverty than low socioeconomic background. Whites with IQs in the bottom 5 percent of the distribution of cognitive ability are fifteen times more likely to be poor than those with IQs in the top 5 percent.

How does each of these causes of poverty look when the other is held constant? Or to put it another way: If you have to choose, is it better to be born smart or rich? The answer is unequivocally "smart." A white youth reared in a home in which the parent or parents were chronically unemployed, worked at only the most menial of jobs, and had not gotten past ninth grade, but of just average intelligence—an IQ of 100—has nearly a 90 percent chance of being out of poverty by his or her early 30s. Conversely, a white youth born to a solid middle-class family but with an IQ equivalently below average faces a much higher risk of poverty, despite his more fortunate background.

When the picture is complicated by adding the effects of sex, marital status, and years of education, intelligence remains more important than any of them, with marital status running a close second. Among people who are both smart and well educated, the risk of poverty approaches zero. But it should also be noted that young white adults who marry are seldom in poverty, even if they are below average in intelligence or education. Even in these more complicated analyses, low IQ continues to be a much stronger precursor of poverty than the socioeconomic circumstances in which people grow up.

We begin with poverty because it has been so much at the center of concern about social problems. We will be asking, "What causes poverty?" focusing on the role that cognitive ability might play. Our point of departure is a quick look at the history of poverty in the next figure, which scholars from the Institute for Research on Poverty have now enabled us to take back to the 1930s.[1]

Dramatic progress against poverty from World War II through the 1960s, stagnation since then

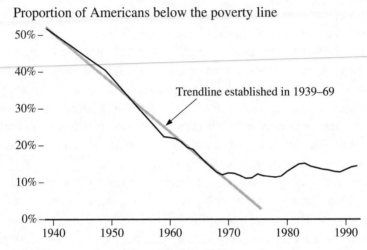

Proportion of Americans below the poverty line

Trendline established in 1939–69

Sources: SAUS, various editions; Ross and others, 1987.

In 1939, over half of the people of the United States lived in families with an income below the amount that constitutes the present poverty line—in constant dollars, of course. This figure declined steeply through World War II, and then through the Truman, Eisenhower, Kennedy, and Johnson administrations. Then came a sudden and lasting halt to progress. As of 1992, 14.5 percent of Americans were below the poverty line, within a few percentage points of the level in 1969. This history provokes three observations.

The first is that poverty *cannot* be a simple, direct cause of such problems as crime, illegitimacy, and drug abuse. Probably no single observation about poverty is at once so indisputable and so ignored. It is indisputable because poverty was endemic at a time when those problems were minor. We know that reducing poverty cannot, by itself, be expected to produce less criminality, illegitimacy, drug abuse, or the rest of the catalog of social problems, else the history of the twentieth century would have chronicled their steep decline.

The second point illustrated by the graph of poverty is that the pool of poor people must have changed over time. As late as the 1940s, so many people were poor in economic terms that to be poor did not necessarily mean to be distinguishable from the rest of the population in any other way. To rephrase the dialogue between F. Scott Fitzgerald and Ernest Hemingway, the poor were different from you and me: They had less money. But that was almost the only reliable difference. As affluence spread, people who escaped from poverty were not a random sample of the population. When a group shrinks from over 50 percent of the population to the less than 15 percent that has prevailed since the late 1960s, the people who are left behind are likely to be disproportionately those who suffer not only bad luck but also a lack of energy, thrift, farsightedness, determination—and brains.

The third point of the graph is that some perspective is in order about what happened to poverty during the 1960s and the famous War on Poverty. The trendline we show for 1936–1969 would have had about the same slope if we had chosen any of the decades in between to calculate it. The United States was not only getting richer but had been reducing the percentage of people below the modern poverty line for at least three decades before the 1960s came to a close. We will not reopen here the continuing debate about why progress came to an end when it did.

In this chapter, we explore some basic findings about the different roles that intelligence and social background play in keeping individuals out of poverty. The basics may be stated in a few paragraphs, as we did in the chapter's introduction. But we also want to speak to readers who ask, "Yes, but what about the role of. . . ," thinking of the many other potential causes of white poverty. By the end of the chapter, we will have drawn a controversial conclusion. How did we get there? What makes us think that we have got our causal ordering right? We will walk through the analyses that lie behind our conclusions, taking a more leisurely approach than in the chapters to come.

CAN AN IQ SCORE TAKEN AT AGE 15 BE A CAUSE OF POVERTY AT AGE 30?

We need to deal at once with an issue that applies to most of the topics in Part II. We want to consider poverty as an effect rather than as a cause—in social science terminology, as a dependent, not an independent, variable.[2] Intelligence will be evaluated as a factor that bears on becoming poor. But what, after all, does an intelligence test score mean for an adolescent who has grown up poor? Wouldn't his test score have been higher if his luck in home environment had been better? Can IQ be causing poverty if poverty is causing IQ?

The Stability of IQ over the Life Span

The stability of IQ over time in the general population has been studied for decades, and the main findings are not in much dispute among psychometricians. Up to about 4 or 5 years of age, measures of IQ are not of much use in predicting later IQ. Indeed, you will get a better prediction of the child's IQ at age 15 by knowing his parents' IQ than by any test of the child given before age 5.[3] Between ages 5 and 10, the tests rapidly become more predictive of adult IQ.[4] After about the age of 10, the IQ score is essentially stable within the constraints of measurement error.[5] On the comparatively rare occasions when large changes in IQ are observed, there is usually an obvious explanation. The child had been bedridden with a long illness before one of the tests, for example, or there was severe emotional disturbance at the time of one or both of the tests.

The IQ score of an individual might have been higher if he had been raised in more fortunate circumstances. Chapter 17 discusses this issue in more detail. But for purposes of Part II, the question is not what might have been but what is. In discussions of intelligence, people obsess about nature versus nurture, thinking that it matters fundamentally whether a person with a low IQ at, say, age 15 came by that IQ through a deficient environment or by bad luck in the genetic draw. But it does not matter for the kinds of issues we consider in Part II. The AFQT test scores for the NLSY sample were obtained when the subjects were 15 to 23 years of age, and their IQ scores were already as deeply rooted a fact about them as their height.[6]

SOCIOECONOMIC BACKGROUND VERSUS COGNITIVE ABILITY

For a century after poverty became a topic of systematic analysis in the mid-1800s, it was taken for granted that there were different kinds of poor people, with "deserving" and "undeserving" being one of the primary divisions.[7] Some people were poor because of circumstances beyond their control; others were poor as a result of their own behavior. Such distinctions among types of poverty were still intellectually respectable into the beginning of the Kennedy administration in 1961. By the end of the 1960s, they were not. Poverty was now seen as a product of broad systemic causes, not of individual characteristics. To say otherwise was to "blame the victim."[8] Accordingly, the technical literature about the causes of current poverty deals almost exclusively in economic and social explanations rather than with individual characteristics. Much of this literature focuses on poverty among blacks and its roots in racism and does not apply to the topic at hand: poverty among whites.

It seems easy to make the case that poverty among whites also arises from social and economic causes. Using the NLSY, we convert information about the education, occupations, and income of the parents of the NLSY youths into an index of socioeconomic status (SES) in which the highest scores indicate advanced education, affluence, and prestigious occupations. The lowest scores indicate poverty, meager education, and the most menial jobs. Suppose we then take the SES index and divide all the NLSY youngsters into five socioeconomic classes on exactly the same basis that we defined cognitive classes (split into categories of 5–20–50–20–5 percent of the population). We then ask, What percentage of people who came from those socioeconomic backgrounds were below the poverty line in their late 20s and early 30s (i.e., in 1989)? We exclude those who were still in school. The answer for non-Latino whites in the NLSY sample is shown in the following table. What could be plainer? Hardly any of the lucky 5 percent who had grown up in the most advantaged circumstances were in poverty (only

White Poverty by Parents' Socioeconomic Class	
Parents' Socioeconomic Class	Percentage in Poverty
Very high	3
High	3
Mid	7
Low	12
Very low	24
Overall average	7

3 percent). Meanwhile, the white children of parents in the lowest socioeconomic class had a poverty rate of 24 percent. Rank hath its privileges, and in the United States one of those privileges is to confer
economic benefits on your children. The way to avoid poverty in the
United States is to be born into an advantaged home.

Now we switch lenses. Instead of using socioeconomic class, we now
ask, What percentage of the people who are in the different *cognitive*
classes were below the poverty line in 1989? The answer is in the next
table. There are similarities at the top of the ladder. Those in the top

| White Poverty by Cognitive Class ||
Cognitive Class	Percentage in Poverty
I Very bright	2
II Bright	3
III Normal	6
IV Dull	16
V Very dull	30
Overall average	7

three classes—75 percent of the population—in either socioeconomic
background or intelligence had similar poverty rates. But then the story
diverges. As cognitive ability fell below average, poverty rose even more
steeply among the cognitively disadvantaged than the socioeconomically disadvantaged. For the very dull, in the bottom 5 percent in IQ,
30 percent were below the poverty line, fifteen times the rate for the
people in the top cognitive class.

Taken one variable at a time, the data fit both hypotheses: Poverty
is associated with socioeconomic disadvantage and even more strongly
with cognitive disadvantage. Which is really explaining the relationship? And so we introduce a way of assessing the comparative roles of
intelligence and socioeconomic background, which we will be using
several times in the course of the subsequent chapters.

We want to disentangle the comparative roles of cognitive ability and
socioeconomic background in explaining poverty. The dependent variable, poverty, has just two possible values: Yes, the family had an income
below the poverty line in 1989, or no, its income was above the poverty

line. The statistical method is a type of regression analysis specifically designed to estimate relationships for a yes-no kind of dependent variable.[9] In our first look at this question, we see how much poverty depends on three independent variables: IQ, age, and parental socioeconomic status (hereafter called "parental SES"). The sample consists of all whites in the NLSY who were out of school in 1989.[10] We are asking a straightforward question:

Given information about intelligence, socioeconomic status, and age, what is our best estimate of the probability that a family was below the poverty line in 1989?

for which a computer, using the suitable software, can provide an answer. Then we ask a second question:

Taking the other factors into account, how much remaining effect does any one of the independent variables have on the probability of being in poverty?

for which the computer can also provide an answer.

When we apply these questions to the NLSY data, the figure below shows what emerges. First, age in itself is not important in determining whether someone is in poverty once the other factors of intelligence and parental family background are taken into account.[11] Statistically, its impact is negligible.

This leaves us with the two competing explanations that prompted the analysis in the first place: the socioeconomic background in which the NLSY youth grew up, and his own IQ score.

The black line lets you ask, "Imagine a person in the NLSY who comes from a family of exactly average socioeconomic background and exactly average age.[12] What are this person's chances of being in poverty if he is very smart? Very dumb?" To find out his chances if he is smart, look toward the far right-hand part of the graph. A person with an IQ 2 SDs above the mean has an IQ of 130, which is higher than 98 percent of the population. Reading across to the vertical axis on the left, that person has less than a 2 percent chance of being in poverty (always assuming that his socioeconomic background was average). Now think about someone who is far below average in cognitive ability, with an IQ 2 SDs below the mean (an IQ of 70, higher than just 2 percent of the

The comparative roles of IQ and parental SES in determining whether young white adults are below the poverty line

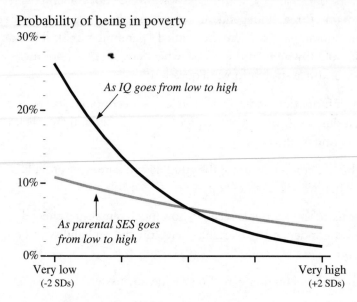

Note: For computing the plot, age and either SES (for the black curve) or IQ (for the gray curve) were set at their mean values.

population). Look at the far left-hand part of the graph. Now, our imaginary person with an average socioeconomic background has about a 26 percent chance of being in poverty. The gray line lets you ask, "Imagine a person in the NLSY who is exactly average in IQ and age. What are this person's chances of being in poverty if he came from an extremely advantaged socioeconomic background? An extremely de-

---

Refresher

1/2 standard deviation below and above the mean cuts off the 31st and 69th percentiles. A 1/2 SD difference is substantial.

1 standard deviation below and above the mean cuts off the 16th and 84th percentiles. A 1 SD difference is big.

2 standard deviations below and above the mean cuts off the 2d and 98th percentiles. A 2 SD difference is very big.

A "standard score" means one that is expressed in terms of standard deviations.

prived socioeconomic background?" As the gray line indicates, the probability of being in poverty rises if he was raised by parents who were low in socioeconomic status , but only gradually.

In general, the visual appearance of the graph lets you see quickly the result that emerges from a close analysis: Cognitive ability is more important than parental SES in determining poverty.[13]

This does not mean that socioeconomic background is irrelevant. The magnitude of the effect shown in the graph and its statistical regularity makes socioeconomic status significant in a statistical sense. To put it into policy terms, the starting line remains unequal in American society, even among whites. On the other hand, the magnitude of the disadvantage is not as large as one might expect. For example, imagine a white person born in 1961 who came from an unusually deprived socioeconomic background: parents who worked at the most menial of jobs, often unemployed, neither of whom had a high school education (a description of what it means to have a socioeconomic status index score in the 2d centile on socioeconomic class). *If that person has an IQ of 100*—nothing special, just the national average—the chance of falling below a poverty-level income in 1989 was 11 percent. It is not zero, and it is not as small as the risk of poverty for someone from a less punishing environment, but in many ways this is an astonishing statement of progress. Conversely, suppose that the person comes from the 2d centile in IQ but his parents were average in socioeconomic status—which means that his parents worked at skilled jobs, had at least finished high school, and had an average income. Despite coming from that solid background, his odds of being in poverty are 26 percent, more than twice as great as the odds facing the person from a deprived home but with average intelligence.

In sum: Low intelligence means a comparatively high risk of poverty. If a white child of the next generation could be given a choice between being disadvantaged in socioeconomic status or disadvantaged in intelligence, there is no question about the right choice.

Education

Now let us consider whether education really explains what is going on. One familiar hypothesis is that if you can only get people to stick with school long enough, they will be able to stay out of poverty even if they have modest test scores.

As in subsequent chapters, we will consider two educational groups:

In the white high school sample, high IQ makes a difference in avoiding poverty; in the college sample, hardly anyone was poor

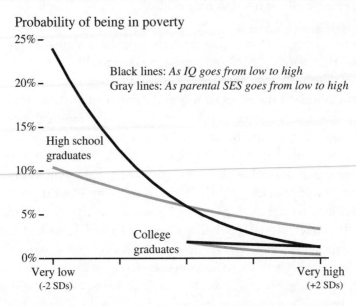

Probability of being in poverty

Black lines: *As IQ goes from low to high*
Gray lines: *As parental SES goes from low to high*

High school graduates

College graduates

Very low
(-2 SDs)

Very high
(+2 SDs)

Note: For computing the plot, age and either SES (for the black curve) or IQ (for the gray curve) were set at their mean values.

white people with a high school degree (no more, no less) and those with a bachelor's degree (no more, no less). The figure above shows the results when the poverty rates for these two groups are considered sep-arately.

First, look at the pair of lines for the college graduates. We show them only for values greater than the mean, to avoid nonsensical implications (such as showing predicted poverty rate for a college graduate with an IQ two standard deviations below the mean). The basic lesson of the graph is that people who can complete a bachelor's degree seldom end up poor, no matter what. This makes sense. Although income varies im-portantly for college graduates at different cognitive levels (as we dis-cussed in Chapters 2 through 4), the floor income is likely to be well above the poverty line. College has economic value independent of cognitive ability, whether as a credential, for the skills that are acquired, or as an indicator of personal qualities besides IQ (diligence, persis-tence) that make for economic success in life. It is impossible with these data to disentangle what contributions these different explanations make.

The two lines showing the results for high school graduates are much more informative. These people are taking a homogeneous and modest set of educational skills to the workplace. Within this group, IQ has a strong effect independent of socioeconomic background. A young adult at the bottom 2 percent of IQ had about a 24 percent change of being in poverty compared to less than a 2 percent chance for one at the top 2 percent of IQ (given average age and socioeconomic background, and just a high school diploma). The parents' background made much less difference. Cognitive ability still has a major effect on poverty even within groups with identical education.

COMPLICATING THE ISSUE: POVERTY AMONG CHILDREN

How does the information we have just presented help in trying to understand the nature of poverty in America? To illustrate, consider one of the most painful topics in recent American social policy, the growing proportion of poor who consist of children. As of the 1991 figures, 22 percent of all children under the age of 15 were below the official poverty line, twice as high as the poverty rate among those age 15 and over.[14] It is a scandalously high figure in a country as wealthy as the United States. Presumably every reader wishes for policies that would reduce poverty among children.

Why are so many children in poverty in a rich country? In political debate, the question is usually glossed over. An impression is conveyed that poverty among children is something that has grown everywhere in the United States, for all kinds of families, for reasons vaguely connected with economic troubles, ungenerous social policies during the 1980s, and discrimination against women and minority groups.

Specialists who have followed these figures know that this explanation is misleading.[15] Poverty among children has always been much higher in families headed by a single woman, whether she is divorced or never married. For families headed by a single woman, the poverty rate in 1991 was 36 percent; for all other American families, 6 percent.[16] Indeed, the national poverty rate for households headed by a single woman has been above 30 percent since official poverty figures began to be available in 1959.[17] The equation is brutally simple: The higher the proportion of children who live in households headed by single women, then, ceteris paribus, the higher the proportion of children who will live in poverty. An important part of the increasing child poverty in the United States is owed to the increasing proportion of children who live in those families.[18] The political left and right differ in their views of what policies to follow in response to this state of affairs, but recently they have broadly agreed on the joint roles of gender and changes in family structure in pushing up the figures for child poverty.

Poverty Among Children: The Role of the Mother's IQ

What does IQ add to this picture? It allows us to focus sharply on who is poor and why, and to dispense with a number of mistaken ideas. To see how, let us consider women, and specifically women with children.[19] Here is the graph that results when we ask how often mothers with differing IQs and differing family structures suffer from poverty. (In the figure, the effects of the mothers' socioeconomic background are held constant, as are the number of children, which is factored into the calculation of the poverty line.)

The first, glaring point of the figure is that marriage is a powerful poverty preventative, and this is true for women even of modest cogni-

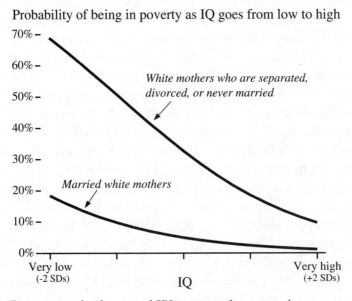

**The role of the mother's IQ in determining
which white children are poor**

Probability of being in poverty as IQ goes from low to high

*White mothers who are separated,
divorced, or never married*

Married white mothers

Very low
(-2 SDs)

IQ

Very high
(+2 SDs)

Notes: For computing the plot, age and SES were set at their mean values.

tive ability. A married white woman with children who is markedly below average in cognitive ability—at the 16th centile, say, one standard deviation below the mean—from an average socioeconomic background had only a 10 percent probability of poverty.

The second point of the graph is that to be without a husband in the house is to run a high risk of poverty, even if the woman was raised in an average socioeconomic background. Such a woman, with even an average IQ, ran a 33 percent chance of being in poverty. If she was unlucky enough to have an IQ of only 85, she had more than a 50 percent chance—five times as high as the risk faced by a married woman of identical IQ and socioeconomic background. Even a woman with a conspicuously high IQ of 130 (two standard deviations above the mean) was predicted to have a poverty rate of 10 percent if she was a single mother, which is quite high compared to white women in general. Perhaps surprisingly, it did not make much difference which of the three kinds of "nonmarriage"—separation, divorce, or no marriage at all—was involved. The results for all three groups of women were drastically different from the results for married women, and quite similar to each other (which is why they are grouped in the figure.)

The third obvious conclusion is that IQ is extremely important in determining poverty among women without a husband present. A poverty rate of 10 percent for women with IQs of 130 may be high compared to some standards, but it is tiny compared to the steeply rising probabilities of poverty that characterize women with below average cognitive ability.

Poverty Among Children: The Role of the Mother's Socioeconomic Background

Now we pursue the same issue but in terms of socioeconomic background. Remember that the steep downward curve in the figure above for unmarried mothers is the effect of IQ after holding the effects of socioeconomic status constant. What is the role of socioeconomic background after we take IQ into account? Not much, as the next figure shows.

We used the same scale on the vertical axis in both of the preceding graphs to make the comparison with IQ easier. The conclusion is that no matter how rich and well educated the parents of the mother might have been, a separated, divorced, or never-married white woman with children and an average IQ was still looking at nearly a 30 percent

The role of the mother's socioeconomic background in determining which white children are poor

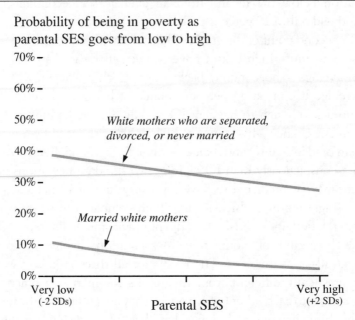

Probability of being in poverty as
parental SES goes from low to high

Note: For computing the plot, age and IQ were set at their mean values.

chance of being below the poverty line, far above the usual level for whites and far above the level facing a woman of average socioeconomic background but superior IQ. We cannot even be sure that higher socioeconomic background reduces the poverty rate at all for unmarried women after the contribution of IQ has been extracted; the downward slope of the line plotted in the graph does not approach statistical significance.[20]

There are few clearer arguments for bringing cognitive ability into the analysis of social problems. Consider the hundreds of articles written about poverty among children and about the effects of single-parent families on poverty. Of course, these are important factors: Children *are* more often poor than adults. Family breakup *is* responsible for a major portion of the increase in child poverty. But if analysts are trying to understand the high rates of poverty among children, it must be done against the background that whatever other factors increase the risk of poverty among unmarried mothers, they hit unmarried mothers at low levels of intelligence much harder than they do those at high levels of intelligence—even after socioeconomic background is held constant.

HOLDING BOTH COMPLICATIONS AND POLICY THOUGHTS AT BAY

You have been following a common process in social science. An initially simple issue becomes successively more complicated. And we have barely gotten started—an analysis in a technical journal seldom has as few independent variables as the ones we have examined. For that matter, even this simplified analysis represents only the end result of a long process. In the attached note, we describe how big the rest of the iceberg is.[21]

Complex analysis has both merits and faults. The merit is that the complications are part of reality. Einstein's injunction that solutions should be as simple as possible, but no simpler, still applies. At the same time, social science often seems more in need of the inverse injunction, to introduce as much complexity as necessary, but no more. Complications can make us forget what we were trying to understand in the first place. Here is where we believe the situation stands:

By complicating the picture, we raise additional questions: Education is important in affecting poverty; the appropriate next step is to explore how intelligence and socioeconomic status are related to years of education. Marriage is important in determining poverty; we should explore how intelligence and socioeconomic status are related to marriage. These things we shall do in subsequent chapters.

But the simple picture, with only IQ, parental SES, and age in the equation, restricted to our all-white sample, continues to tell a story of its own. A major theme in the public dialogue in the United States has been that socioeconomic disadvantage is the primary driving force behind poverty. The simple picture shows that it just isn't so for whites.[22] The high rates of poverty that afflict certain segments of the white population are determined more by intelligence than by socioeconomic background. The force and relevance of this statement does not seem to us diminished by the complications it does not embrace.

Indeed, now that we are returning to basics, let us remember something else that could be overlooked in the welter of regression analyses. The poverty rate for whites in Class V was 30 percent—a percentage usually associated with poverty in poor urban neighborhoods. Ethnically and culturally, these are supposed to be the advantaged Americans: whites of European descent. But they have one big thing working against them: they are not very smart.

Like many other disabilities, low intelligence is not the fault of the individual. Everything we know about the causes of cognitive ability, genetic and environmental, tells us that by the time people grow to an age at which they can be considered responsible moral agents, their IQ is fairly well set. Many readers will find that, before writing another word, we have already made the case for sweeping policy changes meant to rectify what can only be interpreted as a palpably unfair result.

And yet between this and the chapters that will explore those policy issues stretch a few hundred pages of intervening analysis. There is a reason for them. By adding poverty to the portrait of cognitive stratification described in Part I, we hope to have set the terms of a larger problem than income inequality. The issue is not simply how people who are poor through no fault of their own can be made not poor but how we—all of us, of all abilities and income levels—can live together in a society in which all of us can pursue happiness. Changing policy in ways that affect poverty rates may well be part of that solution. But as we observed at the outset of the chapter, poverty itself has been declining as various discontents have been rising during this century, and curing poverty is not necessarily going to do much to cure the other pains that afflict American society. This chapter's analysis should establish that the traditional socioeconomic analysis of the origins of poverty is inadequate and that intelligence plays a crucial role. We are just at the beginning of understanding how intelligence interacts with the other problems in America's crisis.

Chapter 6

Schooling

Leaving school before getting a high school diploma in the old days was usually not a sign of failure. The youngster had not dropped out but simply moved on. As late as 1940, fewer than half of 18-year-olds got a high school diploma. But in the postwar era, the high school diploma became the norm. Now, not having one is a social disability of some gravity.

The usual picture of high school dropouts focuses on their socioeconomic circumstances. It is true that most of them are from poor families, but the relationship of socioeconomics to school dropout is not simple. Among whites, almost no one with an IQ in the top quarter of the distribution fails to get a high school education, no matter how poor their families. Dropout is extremely rare throughout the upper half of the IQ distribution. Socioeconomic background has its most powerful effect at the lowest end of the social spectrum, among students who are already below average in intelligence. Being poor has a small effect on dropping out of school independent of IQ; it has a sizable independent effect on whether a person finishes school with a regular diploma or a high school equivalency certificate.

To raise the chances of getting a college degree, it helps to be in the upper half of the distribution for either IQ or socioeconomic status. But the advantage of a high IQ outweighs that of high status. Similarly, the disadvantage of a low IQ outweighs that of low status. Youngsters from poor backgrounds with high IQs are likely to get through college these days, but those with low IQs, even if they come from well-to-do backgrounds, are not.

Of all the social behaviors that might be linked to cognitive ability, school dropout prior to high school graduation is the most obvious. Low intelligence is one of the best predictors of school failure, and students who fail a grade or two are likely to have the least attachment to school. And yet this relationship, as strong as it is now, is also new.

143

The very concept of school failure is a modern invention. In the era of the one-room schoolhouse, students advanced at their own pace. There were no formal grade levels, no promotions to the next grade, hence no way to fail.[1]

"Dropping out" is an even more recent concept, created by the assumption that it is normal to remain in school through age 17. Until recently, it wasn't typical. In 1900, the high school diploma was the preserve of a tiny minority of American youth: The number of those who got one amounted to only 6 percent of the crop of potential seniors that year. This figure, known as the *graduation ratio*, is calculated as the percentage of the 17-year-old population.[2] Perhaps even more startling, it was not until the beginning of World War II that the graduation ratio first passed the 50 percent mark. The figure shows the story from 1900 to 1990.[3]

The trendlines that overlie the data indicate two broad phases in this ninety-year history. The first phase, from 1908 until the early 1920s, featured moderate expansion of high school education. It did not appear moderate at the time—the graduation rate more than doubled from 1900 to 1922—but the growth was nonetheless moderate by comparison with steep surge from 1922 until the beginning of World War II.

In the first half of the century, the high school diploma becomes the norm

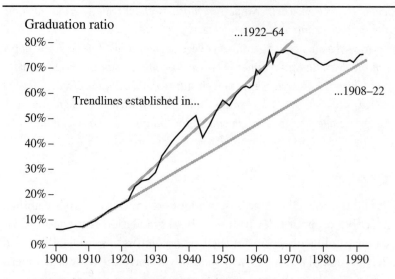

Source: DES 1992, Table 95; U.S. Bureau of the Census, 1975, Table H598-601.

This was the opening of the second growth phase, which lasted, with an interruption for World War II, until 1964. The story since 1964 has been mixed. Graduation rates stalled during the last half of the 1960s and then reversed during the 1970s. The trend since 1980 has been uncertainly and shallowly upward. As of 1992, the graduation ratio for 17-year-olds stood at 76 percent, near the 1969 high of 77 percent. The proportion of people who eventually graduate or get a high school equivalency certificate now stands at about 86 percent for the population as a whole.[4]

Americans today take it for granted that the goal is to graduate everyone and that a high school dropout rate is a social evil. But earlier thinkers, even those in our liberal tradition, were dubious about educating the entire population beyond the rudiments of literacy. Voltaire's view that "the lower classes should be guided, not educated," was typical until this century.[5] Even early in this century, many observers feared that unqualified youngsters were being educated beyond their abilities. "We must turn back the clock," one prominent educator wrote in 1936, "to take some five million boys and girls from the educational dole."[6]

And yet when the psychometricians sought to document the fear that the country was trying to educate the ineducable, they found little evidence for it. One investigator, Frank Finch, assembled all of the competent studies of the intelligence of high school students conducted from 1916 (the earliest study he could find) to 1942. The mean IQ of ninth graders in these studies was 105; the mean IQ of the twelfth graders or graduates was 107, trivially different.[7] The data suggest that the large number of youngsters who dropped out between ninth grade and high school graduation averaged less than 105 in IQ, but not by much (a calculation explained in the note).[8]

Finch found no increasing trend over time in the IQ gap between dropouts and graduates during the early part of the century. Replicating the story that we described regarding the college level in Chapter 1, the first decades of the century saw American high school education mushroom in size without having to dip much deeper into the intellectual pool. This process could not go on forever. As the high school diploma became the norm, the dropouts were likely to become more self-selected for low IQ, and so indeed it transpired.

We have not been able to determine exactly when the gap between nongraduates and graduates began to open up. Probably it was widening even by the early 1940s. By the early 1950s, a study in Iowa found a ten-point gap in IQ between dropouts and high school graduates.[9] Another study, in 1949, of 2,600 students who had been given an IQ test in the seventh grade, found a gap between the graduates and nongraduates of about thirteen IQ points, close to the IQ's standard deviation of 15.[10] The proportion of students getting a high school diploma had reached about 55 percent by then. By the spring of 1960, when 70 percent of students were graduating, the data from Project TALENT—the large, nationally representative sample of high school students mentioned in Chapter 1—indicate a gap equivalent to almost sixteen IQ points between the academic aptitude of those who graduated and those who did not, slightly more than a standard deviation.[11] This is tantamount to saying that the average dropout had an IQ that put him at the 15th centile of those who graduated.

The situation seems to have remained roughly the same since then. By the standard current definition of the population that "gets a high school education"—meaning either a diploma or by passing an equivalency examination—the NLSY data reveal that the mean score of those who get a high school education is 1.28 standard deviations higher than those who do not. Comparing those who get the ordinary high school diploma with all those who left high school before doing so (including those who later get an equivalency certificate), the gap is 1.02 standard deviations.

WHITE HIGH SCHOOL DROPOUT IN THE NLSY

Who drops out of high school these days? The following table shows the story for NLSY whites in the various cognitive classes. The results

Failure to Get a High School Education Among Whites	
Cognitive Class	Percentage Who Did Not Graduate or Pass a High School Equivalency Exam
I Very bright	0
II Bright	0[a]
III Normal	6
IV Dull	35
V Very dull	55
Overall average	9

[a] The actual figure was 0.4 percent.

could hardly be starker. Among whites in the top quartile (Classes I and II together), virtually everyone got a high school education. In the bottom quartile of the IQ distribution (Classes IV and V together), 39 percent of whites did not.[12] This huge discrepancy is also predictable, however, given the close relationship between IQ and educational attainment—so predictable that we should pause for a moment before viewing dropout rates with alarm. Is a 39 percent dropout rate for students in the lowest quartile of IQ "high"? From one perspective, it seems so, considering how essential education appears to be for making a living. From another perspective, it is remarkable that over 60 percent of white youths with IQs under 90 did get a high school education. It is particularly remarkable that nearly half of the youths in Class V, with IQs of 75 and under, completed a high school education, despite being on the borderline (or beyond) of the clinical definition of retarded.[13] Whether these figures say something about the ability of low-IQ students to learn or about the state of American secondary education is a topic we defer until Chapter 18.

What Does "A High School Education" Mean?

The standard question now arises: To what extent are we looking at an effect of cognitive ability, and to what extent are white children from poor socioeconomic backgrounds being shunted out of the school system because of their backgrounds? The answer depends on exactly how the question is asked. Specifically, it is important to be precise about what "a high school education" means. In the table above, it was defined to include anyone who graduated from high school in the normal way or who passed an equivalency examination, known generically as a GED (for General Educational Development).[14] This has become nearly standard practice when researchers and journalists alike talk about high school dropout. But recent work by economists Steven Cameron and James Heckman has demonstrated that GED youths are not equivalent to "normal" graduates in terms of their success in the job market.[15] In their unemployment rates, job tenure, and wages, the GEDs look more like dropouts than they look like high school graduates, raising the possibility that they differ from other high school graduates in a variety of ways that makes it dangerous to lump all people with "a high school education" into a single group. We know from our own analyses that the white GEDs in the NLSY had an average IQ half a standard deviation lower than the average for white high school graduates. Furthermore, apart from the specifics of the data, it is apparent that the nature of the GED student's behavior—giving up on school, then later returning to pass the examination—is different in kind from that of both the dropout who leaves school and never goes back, and from that of the youth who sticks with four consecutive years of schooling and gets a diploma.

To clinch their case for separating GED from "normal" graduates, Cameron and Heckman also point out that the size of the GED population, once negligible, has grown to become a substantial minority. In 1968, GED graduates accounted for only 5 percent of all high school certifications. By 1980, that proportion had reached more than 13 percent, where it has remained, with minor fluctuations, ever since.[16]

We are persuaded that these disparate groups need to be separated and will therefore analyze separately the relationship of IQ and socioeconomic background to each of these two types of dropouts.

The Permanent Dropouts

First, we compare students who got a high school degree through the normal process with dropouts who left school never to return, shown in the next figure.

Staying through high school to receive a diploma did not require genius or high-status parents. Dropout rates were extremely low for white students who were of at least average intelligence or socioeconomic background. But dropout rates rose rapidly when those variables fell below average, with the rise being precipitous for students with low IQ.

A closer look at these numbers dispels the stereotype of the high school dropout as the bright but unlucky youngster whose talents are wasted because of economic disadvantage or a school system that cannot hold onto him—the stereotype that people have in mind when they lament the American dropout rate because it is frittering away the nation's human capital.[17] Among whites, hardly anyone in the NLSY fit that description. Of the whites who dropped out never to return, only three-tenths of 1 percent met a realistic definition of the gifted-but-disadvantaged dropout (top quartile of IQ, bottom quartile of socioeconomic background.) Another eight-tenths of 1 percent were in the top quartile of IQ and the third quartile of the socioeconomic distribution.

**In predicting which white youths will never complete a
high school education, IQ is more important than SES**

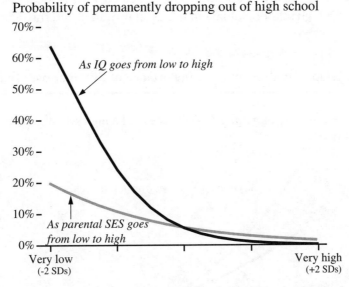

Probability of permanently dropping out of high school

70% –

60% –   *As IQ goes from low to high*

50% –

40% –

30% –

20% –

10% –   *As parental SES goes*

0% –   *from low to high*

Very low   Very high
(-2 SDs)   (+2 SDs)

Note: For computing the plot, age and either SES (for the black curve) or IQ (for the gray curve) were set at their mean values.

Even when we relax the definition to include everyone who is from the top half of the IQ distribution and the bottom half of the socioeconomic distribution—a very loose definition indeed—we are talking about a grand total of only 5.5 percent of the permanent dropouts, or half of 1 percent of American whites in the NLSY.[18]

The permanent dropout instead fits the older image, more common among the general public than intellectuals, of the youngster who is both not very smart and from the wrong side of the tracks. To put it technically, the effects of socioeconomic status and intelligence interact. A white youth who had *both* low cognitive ability and a poor socioeconomic background was at even more risk of dropout than the separate effects of each variable would lead one to expect.[19] Of white youths who were in the bottom quartile on both IQ and socioeconomic status, half permanently dropped out of school.

The Temporary Dropouts

The "temporary dropouts," who go back to get a GED, tell a different story. In the figure below, they are compared with students who received a high school diploma in the usual way. In effect, the figure says

For temporary dropouts, the importance of SES increases sharply

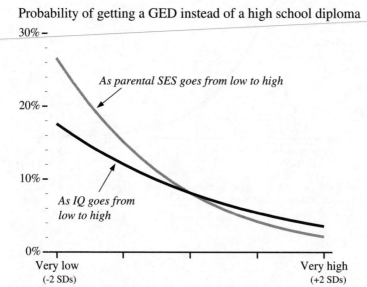

Probability of getting a GED instead of a high school diploma

As parental SES goes from low to high

As IQ goes from low to high

Note: For computing the plot, age and either SES (for the black curve) or IQ (for the gray curve) were set at their mean values.

that if you want to predict who will stay in high school through the diploma, and who will instead drop out of school and eventually get a GED, you are better off sizing up their parents than looking at their IQ scores. In speculating about what lies behind these numbers, three images come to mind. First, there are middle- and the upper-class parents who find it unthinkable that their children should drop out of high school—call the therapist, find a special school, do anything, but keep the child in school. Then one thinks of working-class parents (most of whom are somewhere around the mean on the socioeconomic index), urging their children to get an education and do better than their parents. Finally, one thinks of lower-class parents, the Pap Finns of American folklore, complaining about their children wasting all that time on book learning. The NLSY data are consistent with these popular images. For youths with a socioeconomic background anywhere near or above the mean, the high school diploma is the norm. As socioeconomic background falls below the mean, the probability that the high school certification came through a GED instead of the normal route soars.

This view also fits into the Cameron and Heckman finding that GED students are more like dropouts than high school graduates in the problems they experience in the labor market. Interpretively, the brighter dropouts may go back to get a GED, but they continue to share in common with the permanent dropouts a lower-class social background that has not inculcated a work ethic that makes for success in the labor force.[20] Thus, GEDs are more like normal graduates in their intelligence but more like other dropouts in their success in the labor force.

All of this interpretation is speculative, and we will leave it to others to determine whether these possibilities stand up to examination. Meanwhile, the results emphasize the need for more open exploration of a topic that has been almost as taboo in some circles as IQ: the possibility that "lower class" in its old-fashioned sense has an impact on how people behave.

One concrete result of this analysis bears on the presentation in this book. The differences between GED graduates and those with regular diplomas are too great to justify grouping them together. Whenever we refer to "a high school education" throughout the rest of Part II, we are referring specifically to the normal high school career, completed by a diploma. GED graduates are excluded.

THE COMPARATIVE ROLE OF IQ AND FAMILY BACKGROUND IN GETTING A COLLEGE DEGREE

As a general statement, the relationship of IQ to educational attainment seems to have been remarkably stable. Twenty years ago, one of the leading texts on the Wechsler Adult Intelligence Scale reported that the mean of high school graduates was about 105, the mean of college graduates was 115, and the mean of people getting medical degrees and Ph.D.s was about 125.[21] The book, published in 1972, was based on clinical experience in the 1950s and 1960s. This summary is virtually identical to the story told by the NLSY for whites (who correspond most closely with the college population in the 1950s and early 1960s). The mean IQ of high school graduates was 106, the mean of college graduates was 116, and the mean of people with professional degrees was 126. The relative roles of socioeconomic status and IQ in getting a bachelor's degree for youths of the late 1970s and 1980s are shown in the figure below.

**For white youths, being smart is more important
than being privileged in getting a college degree**

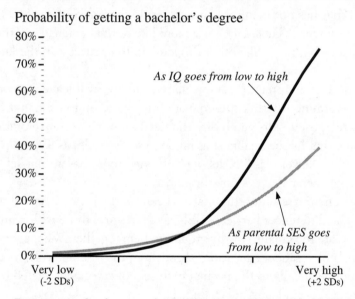

Note: For computing the plot, age and either SES (for the black curve) or IQ (for the gray curve) were set at their mean values.

Two broad implications of these results stand out. The first is suggested by the way that both curves hug the bottom throughout the left-hand side of the graph. The combination of average-or-below parental SES *or* average-or-below IQ meant that the odds of getting a college degree are minuscule. The second broad implication is that parental SES is important but not decisive. In terms of this figure, a student with very well-placed parents, in the top 2 percent of the socioeconomic scale, had only a 40 percent chance of getting a college degree if he had only average intelligence. A student with parents of only average SES—lower middle class, probably without college degrees themselves—who is himself in the top 2 percent of IQ had more than a 75 percent chance of getting a degree.

Once again, the common stereotype of the talented-but-disadvantaged-youth-denied-educational-opportunity does not seem to exist in significant numbers any longer. Only seven-tenths of 1 percent of whites in the NLSY were both "prime college material" (IQs of 115 or above) and markedly disadvantaged in their socioeconomic background (in the bottom quartile on the SES index). Among this tiny group, it is true that fewer than half (46 percent) got college degrees. Those who did not, despite having high IQs, may be seen as youths who suffered from having a disadvantaged background. But recall that this group consists of only four-tenths of 1 percent of all white youths. A category of worthy white young persons denied a college education because of circumstances surely exists to some degree, but of such small size that it does not constitute a public policy problem.

What about another stereotype, the untalented child of rich parents who gets shepherded through to a degree? Almost 5 percent of white youths had below-average IQs (under 100) and parents in the top quartile of socioeconomic status. Of those, only 12 percent had gotten college degrees, representing just six-tenths of 1 percent of white youths. Judging from these data, the common assertion that privileged white parents can make sure their children do well in school, no matter what, may be exaggerated.

SUMMING UP

The act of leaving high school before graduating is a rare event among white youths, conspicuously concentrated in the lowest quartile of cognitive ability. Among those who drop out, both socioeconomic status and cognitive ability are involved. Most dropouts with above-average intelligence go back to get a GED.[22] But socioeconomic status remains bound up with the dropout process. The children of lower-class families are more likely to end up with a GED than are the children of average or upper-class families. There is irony in this: Throughout Part II, we describe social problems that are more understandable once cognitive ability is brought into the picture and for which socioeconomic background is not as important as most people think. But the one social problem that has a widely acknowledged cause in cognitive ability—school dropout—also has a strong and complex socioeconomic link.

When it comes to explaining who gets a college education among whites, both academic merit and socioeconomic background play important roles. But while socioeconomic privilege can help if the youngster is reasonably bright, there are limits to what it can do if he is not. And if cognitive ability is high, socioeconomic disadvantage is no longer a significant barrier to getting a college degree.

Chapter 7

Unemployment, Idleness, and Injury

Economists distinguish between being unemployed and being out of the labor force. The unemployed are looking for work unsuccessfully. Those out of the labor force are not looking, at least for the time being. Among young white men in their late 20s and early 30s, both unemployment and being out of the labor force are strongly predicted by low cognitive ability, even after taking other factors into account.

Many of the white males in the NLSY who were out of the labor force had the obvious excuse: They were still in college or graduate school. Of those not in school, 15 percent spent at least a month out of the labor force in 1989. The proportion was more than twice as high in cognitive Class V as in Class I. Socioeconomic background was not the explanation. After the effects of IQ were taken into account, the probability of spending time out of the labor force went up, not down, as parental SES rose.

Why are young men out of the labor force? One obvious possibility is physical disability. Yet here too cognitive ability is a strong predictor: Of the men who described themselves as being too disabled to work, more than nine out of ten were in the bottom quarter of the IQ distribution; fewer than one in twenty were in the top quarter. A man's IQ predicted whether he described himself as disabled better than the kinds of job he had held. We do not know why intelligence and physical problems are so closely related, but one possibility is that less intelligent people are more accident prone.

The results are similar for unemployment. Among young white men who were in the labor market, the likelihood of unemployment for high school graduates and college graduates was equally dependent on cognitive ability. Socioeconomic background was irrelevant once intelligence was taken into account.

Most men, whatever their intelligence, are working steadily. However, for that minority of men who are either out of the labor force or unemployed, the primary risk factor seems to be neither socioeconomic background nor educa-tion but low cognitive ability.

Having a high IQ makes it easier to do well in a job; we followed that story in Chapter 3. But what about the relationship of cogni-tive ability to that crucially important social behavior known as "being able to get and hold a job." To what extent are dropouts from the labor force concentrated in the low-IQ classes? To what extent are the un-employed concentrated there?

In the following discussion, we limit the analysis to males. It is still accepted that women enter and leave the labor force for reasons hav-ing to do with home and family, introducing a large and complex set of issues, whereas healthy adult men are still expected to work. And yet something troubling has been happening in that area, and for a long time. The problem is shown in the figure below for a group of young men who are likely to be (on average) in the lower half of the IQ dis-tribution: men 16 to 19 years who are not enrolled in school.

**Since mid-century, teenage boys not in school are
increasingly not employed either**

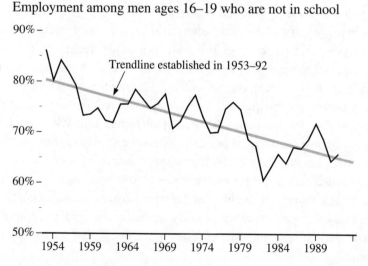

Employment among men ages 16–19 who are not in school

Sources: Bureau of Labor Statistics, 1982, Table C-42; unpublished data provided by the Bu-reau of Labor Statistics.

Although the economy has gone up and down over the last forty years and the employment of these young men with it, the long-term employment trend of their employment has been downhill. The overall drop has not been small. In 1953, the first year for which data are available, more than 86 percent of these young men had jobs. In 1992, it was just 66 percent.

Large macroeconomic and macrosocial forces, which we will not try to cover, have been associated with this trend in employment.[1] In this chapter, we are concerned with what intelligence now has to do with getting and holding a job. To explore the answer, we divide the employment problem into its two constituent parts, the unemployed and those not even looking for work. All of the analyses that follow refer exclusively to whites; in this case white males.

LABOR FORCE DROPOUT

To qualify as "participating in the labor force," it is not necessary to be employed; it is necessary only to be looking for work. Seen from this perspective, there are only a few valid reasons why a man might not be in the labor force. He might be a full-time student; disabled; institutionalized or in the armed forces; retired; independently wealthy; staying at home caring for the children while his wife makes a salary. Or, it may be argued, a man may legitimately be out of the labor force if he is convinced that he cannot find a job even if he tries. But this comes close to exhausting the list of legitimate reasons.

As of the 1990 interview wave, the members of the NLSY sample were in an ideal position for assessing labor force participation. They were 25 to 33 years old, in their prime working years, and they were indeed a hardworking group. Ninety-three percent of them had jobs. Fewer than 5 percent were out of the labor force altogether. What had caused that small minority to drop out of the labor force? And was there any relationship between being out of the labor force and intelligence?

One such relationship was entirely predictable. A few men were out of the labor force because they were still in school in their late 20s and early 30s—most of them in law school, medical school, or studying for the doctorate. They were concentrated in the top cognitive classes. But this does not tell us much about who leaves the labor force. We will exclude them from the subsequent analysis and focus on men who were out of the labor force for reasons other than school.

To structure the analysis, let us ask who spent at least a month out of the labor force during calendar year 1989. Here is the breakdown of labor force dropout by cognitive class for white males.[2] Dropout from the labor force rose as cognitive ability fell. The percentage of Class V men

Which White Young Men Spent a Month or More Out of the Labor Force in 1989?

Cognitive Class	Percentage
I Very bright	10
II Bright	14
III Normal	15
IV Dull	19
V Very dull	22
Overall average	15

who were out of the labor force was a little more than twice the percentage for men in Class I.

SOCIOECONOMIC BACKGROUND VERSUS COGNITIVE ABILITY. The next step, in line with our standard procedure, is to examine how much of the difference may be accounted for by the man's socioeconomic background. The thing to be explained (the dependent variable) is the probability of spending at least a month out of the labor force in 1989. Our basic analysis has the usual three explanatory variables: parental SES, age, and IQ. The results are shown in the figure below. In this analysis, we exclude all men who in either 1989 or 1990 reported that they were in school, the military, or were physically unable to work.

These results are the first example of a phenomenon you will see again in the chapters of Part II. If we had run this analysis with just socioeconomic background and age as the explanatory variables, we would have found a mildly interesting but unsurprising result: Holding age constant, white men from more privileged backgrounds have a modestly smaller chance of dropping out of the labor force than white men from deprived

**IQ and socioeconomic background have opposite effects
on leaving the labor force among white men**

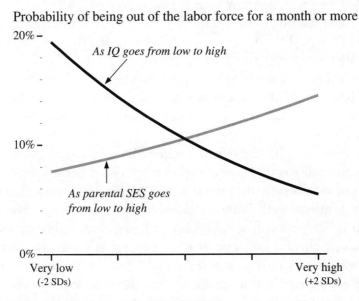

Probability of being out of the labor force for a month or more

As IQ goes from low to high

*As parental SES goes
from low to high*

Very low
(-2 SDs)

Very high
(+2 SDs)

Note: For computing the plot, age and either SES (for the black curve) or IQ (for the gray curve) were set at their mean values.

backgrounds. But when IQ is added to the equation, the role of socio-economic background either disappears entirely or moves in the opposite direction. Given equal age and IQ, a young man from a family with high socioeconomic status was *more* likely to spend time out of the labor force than the young man from a family with low socioeconomic status.[3] In contrast, IQ had a large positive impact on staying at work. A man of average age and socioeconomic background in the 2d centile of IQ had almost a 20 percent chance of spending at least a month out of the labor force, compared to only a 5 percent chance for a man at the 98th centile.

It is not hard to imagine why high intelligence helps keep a man at work. As Chapter 3 discussed, competence in the workplace is related to intelligence, and competent people more than incompetent people are likely to find the workplace a congenial and rewarding place. Hence, other things equal, they are more likely than incompetent people to be in the labor force. Intelligence is also related to time horizons. A male in his 20s has many diverting ways to spend his time, from traveling the world to seeing how many women he can romance, all of them a lot more fun than working forty hours a week at a job. A shortsighted man may be tempted to take a few months off here and there; he thinks he can always pick up again when he feels like it. A farsighted man tells himself that if he wants to lay the groundwork for a secure future, he had better establish a record as a reliable employee now, while he is young. Statistically, smart men tend to be more farsighted than dumb men.

In contrast to IQ, the role of parental SES is inherently ambiguous. One possibility is that growing up in a privileged home foretells low dropout rates, because the parents in such households socialize their sons to conventional work. But this relationship may break down among the wealthy, whose son has the option of living comfortably without a weekly paycheck. In any case, aren't working-class homes also adamant about raising sons to go out and get a job? And don't young men from lower-class homes have a strong economic incentive to stay in the labor force because they are likely to need the money? The statistical relationship with parental SES that shows up in the analysis suggests that higher status may facilitate labor force dropout, at least for short periods.

The analysis of labor force dropout is also the first example in Part II of a significant relationship that is nonetheless modest. When we know from the outset that 78 percent of white men in Class V—borderline retarded or below—did *not* drop out of the labor force for as much as a month, we can also infer that all sorts of things besides IQ are important in determining whether someone stays at work. The analysis we have presented adds to our understanding without enabling us to explain fully the phenomenon of labor force dropout.

EDUCATION. Conducting the analysis separately for our two educational samples (those with a bachelor's degree, no more and no less, and those with a high school diploma, no more and no less) does not change the picture. High intelligence played a *larger* independent role in reducing labor force dropout among the college sample than among the high school sample. And for both samples, high socioeconomic background did not decrease labor force dropout independent of IQ and age. Once again, the probability of dropout actually increased with socioeconomic background.

JOB DISABILITIES

In the preceding analysis, we excluded all the cases in which men reported that they were unable to work. But it is not that simple. Low cognitive ability increases the risk of being out of the labor force for healthy young men, but it also increases the risk of not being healthy. The breakdown by cognitive classes is shown in the following table. The rela-

Job Disability Among Young White Males		
No. per 1,000 Who Reported Being Prevented from Working by Health Problems	Cognitive Class	No. per 1,000 Who Reported Limits in Amount or Kind of Work by Health Problems
0	I Very Bright	13
5	II Bright	21
5	III Normal	37
36	IV Dull	45
78	V Very dull	62
11	Overall average	33

tionship of IQ with both variables is conspicuous but more dramatic for men reporting that their disability prevents them from working. The rate per 1,000 of men who said they were prevented from working by a physical disability jumped sevenfold from Class III to Class IV, and then more than doubled again from Class IV to Class V.

A moment's thought suggests a plausible explanation: Men with low intelligence work primarily in blue-collar, manual jobs and thus are more likely to get hurt than are men sitting around conference tables. Being injured is more likely to shrink the job market for a blue-collar worker than a for a white-collar worker. An executive with a limp can still be an executive; a manual laborer with a limp faces a more serious job impediment. This plausible hypothesis appears to be modestly confirmed in a simple cross-classification of disabilities with type of job.

More blue-collar workers reported some health limitation than did white-collar workers (38 per 1,000 versus 28 per 1,000), and more blue-collar workers reported being prevented from working than did white-collar workers (5 per 1,000 versus 2 per 1,000).

But the explanation fails to account for the relationship of disability with intelligence. For example, given average cognitive ability and age, the odds of having reported a job limitation because of health were about 3.3 percent for white men working in white-collar jobs compared to 3.8 percent for white men working in blue-collar jobs, a very minor difference. But *given that both men have blue-collar jobs*, the man with an IQ of 85 had double the probability of a work disability of a man with an IQ of 115.

Might there be something within job categories to explain away this apparent relationship of IQ to job disability? We explored the question from many angles, as described in the extended note, and the finding seems to be robust. For whatever reasons, white men with low IQs are more likely to report being unable to work because of health than their smarter counterparts, even when the occupational hazards have been similar.[4]

Why might intelligence be related to disability, independent of the line of work itself? An answer leaps to mind: The smarter you are, the less likely that you will have accidents. In Lewis Terman's sample of people with IQs above 140 (see Chapter 2), accidents were well below the level observed in the general population.[5] In other studies, the risk of motor vehicle accidents rises as the driver's IQ falls.[6] Level of education—to some degree, a proxy measure of intelligence—has been linked to accidents and injury, including fatal injury, in other activities as well.[7] Smarter workers are typically more productive workers (see Part I), and we can presume that some portion of what makes a worker productive is that he avoids needless accidents.

Whatever validity this explanation may have, however, it is unlikely to be the whole story. We will simply observe that self-reported health problems are subject to a variety of biases, especially when the question is so sensitive as one that asks, in effect, "What is your excuse for not looking for a job, young man?" The evidence in the NLSY regarding the seriousness of the ailments, whether a doctor has been consulted, and their duration raises questions about whether the self-reported disability data have the same meaning when reported by (for example) a subject who reports that he was two months out of the labor market because of a broken leg and another who reports that he has been out of the labor market for five years because of a bad back.

We leave the analysis of labor force participation with a strong case to be made for two points: Cognitive ability is a significant determinant of dropout from the labor force by healthy young men, independent of other plausibly important variables. And the group of men who are out of the labor force because of self-described physical disability tend toward low cognitive ability, independent of the physical demands of their work.

UNEMPLOYMENT

Men who are out of the labor force are in one way or another unavailable for work; unemployed men, in contrast, want work but cannot find it. The distinction is important. The nation's unemployment statistics are calculated on the basis of people who are looking for work, not on those who are out of the labor force. Being unemployed is transitory, a way station on the road to finding a job or dropping out of the work force. But it is hard to see much difference between unemployment and dropping out in the relationship with intelligence. We begin with the basic breakdown, set out in the following table. The extremes—Classes I and V—differed markedly in the frequency of unemployment lasting a month or more, with Class V experiencing six times the unemployment of Class I. Class IV also had higher unemployment than the upper three-quarters of the IQ distribution.

Which White Young Men Spent a Month or More Unemployed in 1989?

Cognitive Class	Percentage
I Very bright	2
II Bright	7
III Normal	7
IV Dull	10
V Very dull	12
Overall average	7

Socioeconomic Background Versus Cognitive Ability

The independent roles of our three basic variables are shown in the figure below. For a man of average age and socioeconomic background,
cognitive ability lowered the probability of being unemployed for a
month from 15 percent for a man at the 2d centile of IQ to 4 percent
for men at the 98th centile. Neither parental SES nor age had an appreciable (or statistically significant) independent effect.

The Role of Education

Before looking at the numbers, we would have guessed that cognitive ability would be more important for explaining unemployment
among the high school sample than among the college sample. The
logic is straightforward: A college degree supplies a credential and
sometimes specific job skills that, combined with the college gradu-

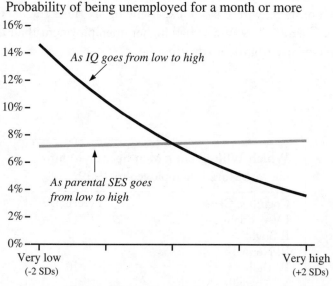

**High IQ lowers the probability of a month-long spell
of unemployment among white men, while
socioeconomic background has no effect**

Probability of being unemployed for a month or more

As IQ goes from low to high

*As parental SES goes
from low to high*

Very low   Very high
(-2 SDs)   (+2 SDs)

Note: For computing the plot, age and either SES (for the black curve) or IQ (for the gray
curve) were set at their mean values.

ate's greater average level of intelligence, should reduce the independent role of IQ in ways that would not apply as strongly to high school graduates.[8] But this logic is not borne out by the NLSY. Cognitive ability was more important in determining unemployment among college graduates than among the high school sample, although the small sample sizes in this analysis make this conclusion only tentative. Socioeconomic background and age were not independently important in explaining unemployment in the high school or college samples.

A CONCLUSION AND A REMINDER ABOUT INTERPRETING RARE EVENTS

The most basic implication of the analysis is that intelligence and its correlates—maturity, farsightedness, and personal competence—are important in keeping a person employed and in the labor force. Because such qualities are not entirely governed by economic conditions, the question of who is working and who is not cannot be answered just in terms of what jobs are available.

This does not mean we reject the relevance of structural or economic conditions. In bad economic times, we assume, finding a job is harder for the mature and farsighted as well as for the immature and the shortsighted, and it is easier to get discouraged and drop the search. Our goal is to add some leavening to the usual formulation. The state of the economy matters, but so do personal qualities, a point that most economists would probably accept if it were brought to their attention so baldly, but somehow it gets left out of virtually all discussions of unemployment and labor force participation.

As we close this discussion of cognitive ability and labor force behavior, let us be clear about what has and has not been demonstrated. In focusing on those who did drop out of the labor force and those who were unemployed, we do not want to forget that most white males at every level of cognitive ability were in the labor force and working, even at the lowest cognitive levels. Among physically able white males in Class V, the bottom 5 percent of the IQ distribution, comprising men who are intellectually borderline or clinically retarded, seven out of ten were in the labor force for all fifty-two weeks of 1989. Of those who were in the labor force throughout the year, more than eight out of ten experienced not a single week of unemployment.

Condescension toward these men is not in order, nor are glib assumptions that those who are cognitively disadvantaged cannot be productive citizens. The world is statistically tougher for them than for others who are more fortunate, but most of them are overcoming the odds.

Chapter 8

Family Matters

Rumors of the death of the traditional family have much truth in them for some parts of white American society—those with low cognitive ability and little education—and much less truth for the college educated and very bright Americans of all educational levels. In this instance, cognitive ability and education appear to play mutually reinforcing but also independent roles.

For marriage, the general rule is that the more intelligent get married at higher rates than the less intelligent. This relationship, which applies across the range of intelligence, is obscured among people with high levels of education because college and graduate school are powerful delayers of marriage.

Divorce has long been more prevalent in the lower socioeconomic and educational brackets, but this turns out to be explained better by cognitive level than by social status. Once the marriage-breaking impact of low intelligence is taken into account, people of higher socioeconomic status are more likely to get divorced than people of lower status.

Illegitimacy, one of the central social problems of the times, is strongly related to intelligence. White women in the bottom 5 percent of the cognitive ability distribution are six times as likely to have an illegitimate first child as those in the top 5 percent. One out of five of the legitimate first babies of women in the bottom 5 percent was conceived prior to marriage, compared to fewer than one out of twenty of the legitimate babies to women in the top 5 percent. Even among young women who have grown up in broken homes and among young women who are poor—both of which foster illegitimacy— low cognitive ability further raises the odds of giving birth illegitimately. Low cognitive ability is a much stronger predisposing factor for illegitimacy than low socioeconomic background.

At lower educational levels, a woman's intelligence best predicts whether she will bear an illegitimate child. Toward the higher reaches of education, almost no white women are having illegitimate children, whatever their family background or intelligence.

The conventional understanding of troubles in the American family has several story lines. The happily married couple where the husband works and the wife stays home with the children is said to be as outmoded as the bustle. Large proportions of young people are staying single. Half the marriages end in divorce. Out-of-wedlock births are soaring.

These features of modern families are usually discussed in the media (and often in academic presentations) as if they were spread more or less evenly across society.[1] In this chapter, we introduce greater discrimination into that description. Unquestionably, the late twentieth century has seen profound changes in the structure of the family. But it is easy to misperceive what is going on. The differences across socioeconomic classes are large, and they reflect important differences by cognitive class as well.

MARRIAGE

Marriage is a fundamental building block of social life and society itself and thus is a good place to start, because this is one area where much has changed and little has changed, depending on the vantage point one takes.

From a demographic perspective, the changes are huge, as shown in the next figure. The marriage rate since the 1920s has been volatile, but the valleys and peaks in the figure have explanations that do not necessarily involve the underlying propensity to marry. The Great Depression probably had a lot to do with the valley in the early 1930s, and World War II not only had a lot to do with the spike in the late 1940s but may well have had reverberations on the marriage rate that lasted into the 1950s. It could even be argued that once these disruptive events are taken into account, the underlying propensity to marry did not change from 1930 to the early 1970s. The one prolonged decline for which there is no obvious explanation *except* a change in the propensity to marry began in 1973, when marriage rates per 1,000 women began dropping and have been dropping ever since, in good years and bad. In 1987, the nation passed a landmark: Marriage rates hit an all-time low, dropping below the previous mark set in the depths of the depression. A new record was promptly set again in 1988.

This change, apparently reflecting some bedrock shifts in attitudes toward marriage in postindustrial societies, may have profound signifi-

**In the early 1970s, the marriage rate began a
prolonged decline for no immediately apparent reason**

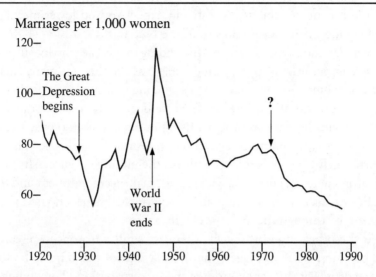

Marriages per 1,000 women

Sources: U.S. Bureau of the Census, 1975, Table B214–215; *SAUS*, 1992, Table 127, and comparable tables in various editions.

cance. And yet marriage is still alive and well in the sense that it remains a hugely popular institution. Over 90 percent of Americans of both sexes have married by the time they reach their 40s.[2]

Marriage and IQ

What does cognitive ability have to do with marriage, and is there any reason to think that it could be interacting with society's declining propensity to marry?

We know from work by Robert Retherford that in premodern societies the wealthy and successful married at younger ages than the poor and underprivileged.[3] Retherford further notes that intelligence and social status are correlated wherever they have been examined; hence, we can assume that intelligence—via social status—facilitated marriage in premodern societies.

With the advent of modernity, however, this relationship flips over. Throughout the West since the nineteenth century, people in the more privileged sector of society have married later and at lower rates than the less privileged. We examine the demographic implications of this phenomenon in Chapter 15. For now, the implication is that in late-twentieth-century America, we should expect to find lower marriage rates among the highly intelligent in the NLSY.

Everyday experience bears out this finding for people who live in academic communities or professional circles, where they see many smart men and women in their 30s and 40s who are still single and look as if they might stay that way forever. The intelligent professional woman is the most visible of this new tribe, rising in her career, too busy for, or not interested in, marriage and children. Among men, other images have recently become part of the culture: the intelligent, successful, and unmarried heterosexual male who cannot make a commitment and the intelligent, successful, and unmarried homosexual male who no longer needs to go through the motions of a marriage.

At the other end of the scale, there are similar reasons in research and common sense to suggest that marriage rates will tend to be low among people at the very bottom of the IQ distribution.[4] For a number of reasons, having to do with everything from initiative to romance to economics, people with very low IQs are likely to be at a disadvantage in competing for marriage partners.

Our first look at the NLSY data conforms to these expectations, though not dramatically. The next table shows the situation for the NLSY sample among whites who had reached the age of 30. There were surprises in these results for us, and perhaps for some of our readers. We would not have guessed that the average age of marriage for people in the top 5 percent of the intelligence distribution was only 25, for example.[5] A main point of the table is to introduce the theme threaded throughout the chapter: Our, your, and the media's impressions of the state of the American family are not necessarily accurate.

The Role of Socioeconomic Background

Note in the table below that marriage percentages are highest for people in the middle of the intelligence distribution and taper off on both ends. The same is true, though less dramatically, if the table is constructed by socioeconomic class: The percentage of whites who had married before the age of 30 declines at both extremes. Furthermore, we have good reasons for thinking that this pattern is not a sampling fluke

Which Whites Get Married When?		
Percentage who Had Ever Married Before Age 30	Cognitive Class	Average Age at First Marriage
67	I Very bright	25.4
72	II Bright	24.3
81	III Normal	22.9
81	IV Dull	21.5
72	V Very dull	21.3
78	Overall averages	22.1

but reflects underlying dynamics of marriage. This pattern makes interpreting regression results tricky, because the regression techniques we are using compute the lines in the graphs based on the assumption that the lines are not trying to make U-turns. For the record: When we run the standard initial analysis incorporating IQ, age, and socioeconomic status as predictors of marriage, IQ has no significant independent role; there is a slight, statistically insignificant downward probability of marriage as IQ goes up. Socioeconomic background has a much larger suppressive role on marriage: The richer and better educated your parents, the less likely you are to marry, according to these results, which, again, must be interpreted cautiously.

The Role of Education

The real culprit in explaining marriage rates in a young population is education. In the rest of the chapters of Part II, we point out many instances in which taking education into account does not much affect IQ's independent role. Not so with marriage. When we take education into account, the apparent relationship reverses: The probability of marrying goes up, not down, for people with high IQs—a result found in other databases as well.[6] Our standard analysis with the two educational samples, high school graduates (no more and no less) and college graduates (no more and no less) elucidates this finding.

The figure shows that neither IQ nor socioeconomic background was important in determining marriage for the college sample. In sharp con-

High IQ raises the probability of marriage for the white high school sample, while high socioeconomic background lowers it

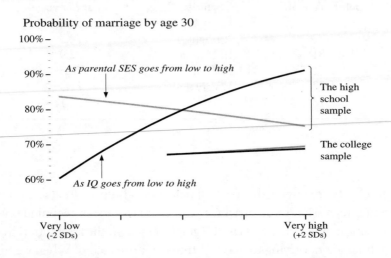

Note: For computing the plot, age, and either SES (for the black curves) or IQ (for the gray curves) were set at their mean values.

trast, IQ made a significant difference in the high school sample. A high school graduate from an average socioeconomic background who was at the bottom of the IQ distribution (2 standard deviations below the mean) had a 60 percent chance of having married. A high school graduate at the top of the IQ distribution had an 89 percent chance of having married. Meanwhile, the independent role of socioeconomic status in the high school sample was either slightly negative or nil (the downward slope is not statistically significant).

DIVORCE

People marry, but do they stay married? Here is where the change has been not only dramatic but, some would say, cataclysmic, as shown below. In 1920, only death parted husbands and wives in about 82 percent of marriages and, in any given year (the datum shown in the next figure below), only about 8 out of 1,000 married females experienced a divorce. As late as 1964, despite the sweeping changes in technology,

The divorce revolution

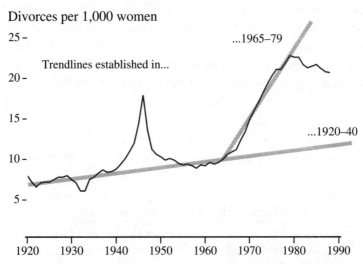

Divorces per 1,000 women

Sources: U.S. Bureau of the Census, 1975, Table B214–215; *SAUS*, 1992, Table 127, and comparable table in various editions.

wealth, and social life that had occurred in the intervening forty-four years, the number was very little changed: 10 of every 1,000. The peak divorce rates just following World War II had fully subsided, and the divorce rate still lay upon a trendline established between 1920 and 1940.

Then came the revolution. The steep upward sweep of the divorce rate from the mid-1960s through the end of the 1970s represents one of the most rapid, compressed changes in a basic social behavior that the twentieth century has witnessed. When the divorce rate hit its peak at the end of the 1970s, a marriage had more than a fifty–fifty chance of ending in divorce.[7] Despite a downward trend since 1980, divorce remains at twice the annual rate of the mid-1960s.

Divorce and IQ

We do not attempt to explain this profound change in our lives, which no doubt has roots in changing mores, changing laws, changing roles of women, changing labor markets, and who knows what else. Instead, we address the narrow question: How does divorce currently correlate with intelligence?

There are plausible reasons for expecting that cognitive ability will have an impact on divorce. For example, one may hypothesize that bright people less often marry on a whim, hence they have fewer disastrous short marriages. Bright people are perhaps less likely to act on impulse when the marriage has problems, hence are less likely to divorce precipitously during the first years of marriage. More generally, it may be argued that brighter people are better able to work out differences that might otherwise eventually destroy a marriage. We are, of course, referring to statistical tendencies for which individual exceptions abound.

Within the confines of the NLSY experience, these expectations are borne out to some degree, as shown in the table. The results are based

Which Whites Get Divorced When?	
Cognitive Class	**Percentage Divorced in First Five Years of Marriage**
I Very bright	9
II Bright	15
III Normal	23
IV Dull	22
V Very dull	21
Overall averages	20

on the first five years of marriage. Those in Class I were ten times as likely to stay married for at least five years as to get divorced; for those in Classes III, IV, and V—the bottom three-quarters of the population— the ratio of marital survival to divorce for at least five years was only 3.5 to 1.[8] Virtually all of the effect of IQ seems to have been concentrated at the top of the distribution. The divorce rates across the bottom three-quarters of the cognitive ability distribution were essentially identical.

The Role of Socioeconomic Background

Do these findings hold up when we begin to add in other considerations? The figure below shows the results for the white sample who had been married at least five years.[9] The consistent finding, represented fairly by the figure, was that higher IQ was still associated with a lower probability of divorce after extracting the effects of other variables, and parental SES had a significant *positive* relationship to divorce—that is,

IQ and socioeconomic background have opposite effects on the likelihood of an early divorce among young whites

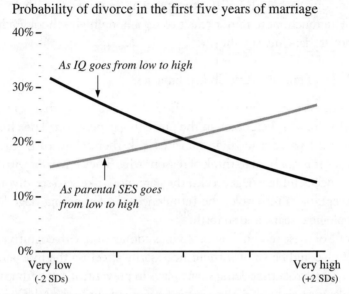

Probability of divorce in the first five years of marriage

As IQ goes from low to high

As parental SES goes from low to high

Very low (-2 SDs)

Very high (+2 SDs)

Note: In addition to IQ, age, and parental SES, the independent variables included date of first marriage. For computing the plot, age, date of first marriage, and either SES (for the black curve) or IQ (for the gray curve) were set at their mean values.

IQ being equal, children of higher-status families were more likely to get divorced than children of lower-status families.[10]

The Role of Education

It is clear to all researchers who examine the data that higher education is associated with lower levels of divorce. This was certainly true of the NLSY, where the college sample (persons with a bachelor's degree, no more and no less) had a divorce rate in the first five years of marriage that was less than half that of the high school sample: 7 percent compared to 19 percent. But this raw outcome is deceptive.[11] Holding some critical other things equal—IQ, socioeconomic status, age, and date of marriage—the divorce rate for the high school graduates in the first five years of marriage was *lower* than for college graduates.

For whom did IQ make more difference: the high school sample or the college sample? The answer is the college sample, by far. For them, the probability of divorce in the first five years plunged from 28 percent for someone with an IQ of 100 to 9 percent for someone with an IQ of 130. The much more minor effect of IQ among high school graduates was not statistically significant.[12]

Do Broken Families Beget Broken Families?

One other cause of divorce is mentioned so commonly that it requires exploration: a broken home in the preceding generation. The children of divorced parents have an elevated risk themselves of getting divorced.[13] It is not hard to think of reasons why: They have not witnessed how a successful marriage works, they are more likely to see divorce as an acceptable alternative, the turbulence of a failing marriage leaves psychological scars, and so forth.[14]

None of these reasons has an obvious connection with cognitive ability. They could be valid without necessarily affecting the independent prophylactic role that being smart plays in preventing (or perhaps simply delaying) divorce. And so indeed it worked out in the NLSY. Given a young person of average IQ and socioeconomic background, the probability of divorce within the first five years of marriage was lowest for those who at age 14 had been living with both parents (20 percent), a bit higher for those who had been living with a remarried parent (22 percent), and higher still for those living with an un-remarried or never-married mother (25 percent).[15] These are not large effects, however, and are not significant in a statistical sense. We can say only that the results supported the general proposition that, when it comes to raising children who will themselves stay married, two adults as parents are generally better than one and that two biological parents in the household are better than one or none. But it is worth noting that the introduction of these variables did nothing to change the importance of the rest of the variables. Higher cognitive ability conferred just about as much protection from, and higher status just as much risk for, divorce as in the preceding analyses.

The NLSY gives us a window on the early years of marriage, though not necessarily about marriage as a whole. Based on national divorce rates, we know that most of the divorces that the members of the NLSY will experience have yet to occur. We will have to wait and see what happens to the NLSY sample in later years.

One final point about the divorce results is worth noting, however. These findings may help explain the common observation that divorce is less likely when the husband has high education, income, or socioeconomic status or that marriages are more likely to fall apart if they start when the couple is afflicted with unemployment.[16] If we had showed a breakdown of divorce rates in the NLSY by social and economic measures alone, we too would have shown such effects. But each of those variables is correlated with cognitive ability, and the studies that examine them almost never include an independent measure of intelligence per se. Some portion of what has so often been observed about the risk factors for divorce turns out to be more narrowly the result of low cognitive ability.

ILLEGITIMACY

Childbearing touches on one of the most sensitive topics in the study of intelligence and its social consequences: fertility patterns among the smart and the dumb, and their possible long-term effects on the intellectual capital of a nation's population. We devote a full chapter to this topic (Chapter 15) in the portion of the book dealing with the national, multiracial perspective. In this chapter, the focus is on family problems, and one of the leading current problems is the failure of two-parent families to form in the first place, as denoted by births to single women—illegitimacy.

We use the older term "illegitimacy" in favor of the phrases currently in favor, "out-of-wedlock births" or "births to single women," because we think that, in the long run, the word illegitimacy will prove to be the right one. We are instructed in this by the anthropologist Bronislaw Malinowski. In his research early in the century, Malinowski observed a constant running throughout the rich diversity of human cultures and indeed throughout history. He decided that this amounted to "a universal sociological law" and called it the "principle of legitimacy." No matter what the culture might be, "there runs the rule that the father is indispensable for the full sociological status of the child as well as of the mother, that the group consisting of a woman and her offspring is sociologically incomplete and illegitimate."[17] The rule applied alike to East or West, primitive cultures or advanced ones, cultures where premarital sex was accepted or banned, where children were con-sidered an asset or a burden, where fathers could have one wife or many.

Despite our faith that Malinowski was observing something that will once again be considered true about human societies, the contemporary Western democracies, including the United States, seem intent on proving Malinowski wrong, as shown in the next figure.

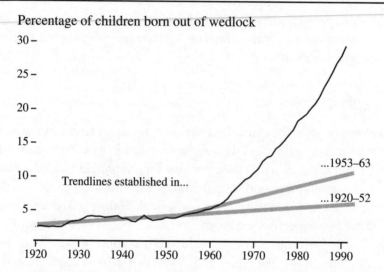

The illegitimacy revolution

Percentage of children born out of wedlock

Sources: Various editions of the Natality volume of *Vital Statistics*, compiled annually by the Public Health Service.

In the seventy-one years from 1920 to 1990, the proportion of chil-dren born to single women in the United States went from less than 3 percent, roughly where it had been throughout American history, to 30 percent.[18] It would have been about 6 percent had the trendline es-tablished from 1920 to 1952 remained unchanged. The trendline shifted upward during the 1950s, but not dramatically. If we had maintained the trendline established from 1952 to 1963, the United States would have had about 11 percent of births out of wedlock in 1991. Instead, the figure was 30 percent, the result of a steep, sustained increase that gathered steam in the mid-1960s and continued into the early 1990s. The increase for the most recent available year, 1991, was one of the largest in history. There are no signs as we write that illegitimacy is reaching an asymptote.

Anyone who is trying to understand social trends must also realize that the magic of compound interest has created an even more explosive rise in the population of unmarried mothers and children. In 1960, for example, there were just 73,000 never-married mothers between the ages of 18 and 34. In 1980, there were 1.0 million.[19] In 1990, there were approximately 2.9 million.[20] Thus the illegitimacy ratio increased by sixfold from 1960 to 1990—bad enough—but the number of never-married mothers increased fortyfold. From just 1980 to 1990, while the illegitimacy ratio was increasing by half, the number of unmarried mothers almost tripled.

Illegitimacy and IQ

If IQ is a factor in illegitimacy, as we will conclude it is, it must be in combination with other things (as common sense would suggest), because IQ itself has not changed nearly enough in recent years to account for the explosive growth in illegitimacy.[21] But we will also be exploring the possibility that some of these "other things" that have changed in the last three decades—broken homes and the welfare system being prime suspects—interact with intelligence, making it still more likely than before that a woman of low cognitive ability will have a baby out of wedlock.

Among other reasons that cognitive ability may be related to illegitimacy, we have this causal model in mind: The smarter a woman is, the more likely that she deliberately decides to have a child and calculates the best time to do it. The less intelligent the woman is, the more likely that she does not think ahead from sex to procreation, does not remember to use birth control, does not carefully consider when and under what circumstances she should have a child. How intelligent a woman is may interact with her impulsiveness, and hence her ability to exert self-discipline and restraint on her partner in order to avoid pregnancy. The result is a direct and strong relationship between high intelligence and the likelihood that a child is conceived after marriage, and between low intelligence and the likelihood that the child will be born out of wedlock.

There are, of course, objections to this explanation. Some will bristle at our identification of conception within marriage with the intelligent thing to do. But is it really controversial or even arguable? Under what circumstances can a thoughtful, coolheaded appraisal lead one to conclude that it is better to conceive a child outside marriage? If such circumstances exist, are they not exceptional? Perhaps a woman wants to conceive a child out of marriage, but how likely is it that a disinterested person would consider it to be in the best interest of all concerned, including the child's?

We begin our exploration with the overall numbers. First, how many white women are engaging in this behavior? As the next table shows, the differences among the cognitive classes are extremely large. Only 2 percent of white women in Class I had given birth to an illegitimate child as of the 1990 interview, compared to 32 percent of the women in Class V.

**The Incidence of Illegitimacy Among
Young White Women**

Cognitive Class	Percentage Who Have Given Birth to an Illegitimate Baby
I Very bright	2
II Bright	4
III Normal	8
IV Dull	17
V Very dull	32
Overall average	8

Now we switch lenses. Instead of asking how many women have ever had an illegitimate baby, we ask what proportion of first babies born to white women are illegitimate. The next table shows the results. The proportions of illegitimate first births in the top two cognitive classes are nearly the same, rounding to 7 percent—about half the proportion for Class III, a third of the proportion for Class IV, and a sixth of the proportion for Class V. Illegitimacy is again conspicuously concentrated in the lowest cognitive groups.

The Proportion of White First Births That Are Illegitimate	
Cognitive Class	Percentage of Illegitimate Births
I Very bright	7
II Bright	7
III Normal	13
IV Dull	23
V Very dull	42
Overall average	14

The relationship between intelligence and illegitimacy is strong not only in these basic respects, but also in more subtle ways, as the numbers based on the women's first births, shown in the next table, reveal.

Circumstances of the First Birth Among Whites				
Born Illegitimate			Born After Marriage	
Mother Hasn't Married[a]	Mother Eventually Married[a]	Cognitive Class	Conceived Before Marriage	Conceived After Marriage
3%	4%	I Very bright	4%	89%
3	4	II Bright	13	80
3	10	III Normal	20	67
7	16	IV Dull	22	55
17	24	V Very dull	12	47
4	10	Population averages	19	68

[a] By the time of the 1990 interview.

Not only are children of mothers in the top quartile of intelligence (Classes I and II) more likely to be born within marriage, they are more likely to have been conceived within marriage (no shotgun wedding). The differences among the cognitive classes are large, as if they lived in different worlds. For the women in Class V, only 47 percent of the first children were conceived after a marriage ceremony; for the women in Class I, 89 percent.

The table makes a strong prima facie case for a relationship between cognitive ability and illegitimacy. The question is whether it survives scrutiny when we introduce other factors into the analysis.[22]

The Role of Socioeconomic Background

The socioeconomic background of a young woman was traditionally thought to be crucial in determining whether she bore a child out of wedlock. The old-fashioned view of illegitimacy was that it occurred mostly among girls from the lower classes, with occasional and scandalous slip-ups by higher-class "good girls" who "got in trouble." But during the last few decades, as births outside marriage became more common and as examples proliferated of film stars and career women who were choosing to have babies without husbands, an alternative view spread. The sexual revolution had obviously penetrated to all levels of society, it was argued, and births out of wedlock were occurring at all levels of our sexually liberated society.

There were never any systematic data to support this view, but neither did scholars rush to check it out. A 1980 article in the *American Sociological Review* on education and fertility reported that white women with less than a high school education were twenty times more likely to have a child out of wedlock than white women with at least a college degree, but illegitimacy was only a side issue in the article and the datum never got noticed in the public dialogue.[23] The relationship of teenage illegitimacy to social and cognitive factors was first treated in detail in an analysis of the High School and Beyond survey published by the RAND Corporation in 1988.[24] The report revealed that more than three-quarters of the teenage girls in this national sample who had babies while they were still of high school age came from families in the bottom half of the socioeconomic stratum. More than half came from the bottom quartile. This finding also held true among just the white teenage girls who had babies out of wedlock, with 70 percent coming from the bottom half of the socioeconomic distribution and only 12 percent from the top quartile.[25] The RAND study was also the first to reveal that cognitive ability played an important role, independent of socioeconomic status.[26]

The data from the NLSY generally confirm those reported in the RAND analysis. On the surface, white illegitimacy is associated with socioeconomic status: About 9 percent of babies of women who come from the upper socioeconomic quartile are illegitimate, compared to about 23 percent of the children of women who come from the bottom socioeconomic quartile. But white women of varying status backgrounds differ in cognitive ability as well. Our standard analysis with IQ, age, and parental SES as independent variables helps to clarify the situation. The dependent variable is whether the first child was born out of wedlock.[27]

IQ has a large effect on white illegitimate births independent of the mother's socioeconomic background

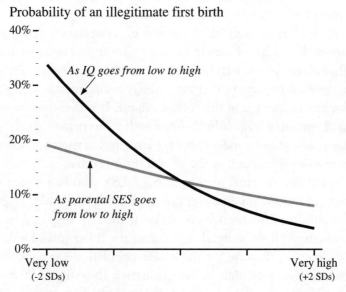

Probability of an illegitimate first birth

As IQ goes from low to high

As parental SES goes from low to high

Very low (-2 SDs)　　　　　　　　　　　Very high (+2 SDs)

Note: For computing the plot, age and either SES (for the black curve) or IQ (for the gray curve) were set at their mean values.

Higher social status reduces the chances of an illegitimate first baby from about 19 percent for a woman who came from a very low status family to about 8 percent for a woman from a very high status family, given that the woman has average intelligence. Let us compare that 11 percentage point swing with the effect of an equivalent shift in intelligence (given average socioeconomic background).[28] The odds of having an illegitimate first child drop from 34 percent for a very dull woman to about 4 percent for a very smart woman, a swing of 30 percentage points independent of any effect of socioeconomic status.

The Role of Education

Without doubt, the number of well-educated women who are deliberately deciding to have a baby out of wedlock—the name "Murphy Brown" comes to mind—has increased. The Bureau of the Census's most recent study of fertility of American women revealed that the percentage of never-married women with a bachelor's degree who had a baby had increased from 3 to 6 percent from 1982 to 1992.[29] But during the same decade, the percentage of never-married women with less than a high school education who had a baby increased from 35 to 48 percent.[30] The role of education continues to be large.

In the NLSY, the statistics contrast even more starkly. Among white women in the NLSY who had a bachelor's degree (no more, no less) and who had given birth to a child, 99 percent of the babies were born within marriage. In other words, there is virtually no independent role for IQ to play among women in the college sample. It is true that the women in that 1 percent who gave birth out of wedlock were more likely to have the lower test scores—independent of any effect of their socioeconomic backgrounds—but this is of theoretical interest only.

Meanwhile, for white women in the NLSY who had a high school diploma (no more, no less) and had given birth to a child, 13 percent of the children had been born out of wedlock (compared to 1 percent for the college sample). For them, the independent role of IQ was as large as the one for the entire population (as shown in the preceding figure). A high school graduate with an IQ of 70 had a 34 percent probability that the first baby would be born out of wedlock; a high school graduate with an IQ of 130 had less than a 3 percent chance, after extracting the effects of age and socioeconomic background. The independent effect of socioeconomic status was comparatively minor.

The Role of Broken Homes

We have already noted that family structure at the age of 14 had only modest influence on the chances of getting divorced in the NLSY sample after controlling for IQ and parental SES. Now the question is how the same characteristic affects illegitimacy. Let us consider a white woman of average intelligence and average socioeconomic background. The odds that her first child would be born out of wedlock were:

10 percent if she was living with both biological parents.

18 percent if she was living with a biological parent and a steppar-
ent.

25 percent if she was living with her mother (with or without a live-
in boyfriend).

The difference between coming from a traditional family versus anything else was large, with the stepfamily about halfway between the traditional family and the mother-only family.

As we examined the role of family structure with different breakdowns (the permutations of arrangements that can exist are numerous), a few patterns kept recurring. It seemed that girls who were still
living with their biological father at age 14 were protected from having their first baby out of wedlock. The girls who had been living with
neither biological parent (usually living with adopted parents) were
also protected. The worst outcomes seemed conspicuously associated
with situations in which the 14-year-old had been living with the
biological mother but not the biological father. Here is one such breakdown. The odds that a white woman's first baby would be born out
of wedlock (again assuming average intelligence and socioeconomic
background) were:

8 percent if the biological mother, but not the biological father, was
absent by age 14.

8 percent if both biological parents were absent at age 14 (mostly
adopted children).

10 percent if both biological parents were present at age 14.

23 percent if the biological father was absent by age 14 but not the
biological mother.

There is considerable food for thought here, but we refrain from speculation. The main point for our purposes is that family structure is clearly
important as a cause of illegitimacy in the next generation.

Did cognitive ability still continue to play an independent role? Yes,
for all the different family configurations that we examined. Indeed, the
independent effect of IQ was sometimes augmented by taking family
structure into account. Consider the case of a young woman at risk, having lived with an unmarried biological mother at age 14. Given aver-

age socioeconomic background and an average IQ, the probability that her first baby would be born out of wedlock was 25 percent. If she had an IQ at the 98th centile (an IQ of 130 or above), the probability plunged to 8 percent. If she had an IQ at the 2d centile (an IQ of 70 or below), the probability soared to 55 percent. High socioeconomic status offered weak protection against illegitimacy once IQ had been taken into account.[31]

The Role of Poverty and Welfare

In the next chapter, we discuss IQ in relation to welfare dependence. Here, we take up a common argument about welfare as a cause of illegitimacy. It is not that low IQ causes women to have illegitimate babies, this argument suggests, but that the combination of poverty and welfare causes women to have illegitimate babies. The logic is that a poor woman who is assured of clothes, shelter, food, and medical care will take fewer precautions to avoid getting pregnant, or, once pregnant, will put less pressure on the baby's father to marry her, than a woman who is not assured of support. There are two versions of the argument. One sees the welfare system as bribing women to have babies; they get pregnant so they can get a welfare check. The alternative, which we find more plausible, is that the welfare check (and the collateral goods and services that are part of the welfare system) *enables* women to do something that many young women might naturally like to do anyway: bear children.

The controversy about the welfare explanation, in either the "enabling" or "bribe" version, has been intense, with many issues still unresolved.[32] Whichever version is employed, the reason for focusing on the role of poverty is obvious: For affluent young women, the welfare system is obviously irrelevant. They are restrained from having babies out of wedlock by moral considerations or by fear of the social penalties (both of which still exist, though weakened, in middle-class circles), by a concern that the child have a father around the house, and because having a baby would interfere with their plans for the future. In the poorest communities, having a baby out of wedlock is no longer subject to social stigma, nor do moral considerations appear to carry much weight any longer; it is *not* irresponsible to have a child out of wedlock, the argument is more likely to go, because a single young woman can in fact support the child without the help of a husband.[33] And that brings the welfare system into the picture. For poor young women, the welfare system is highly relevant, easing the short-term economic penalties that might ordinarily restrain their childbearing.[34] The poorer she is, the more attractive the welfare package is and the more likely that she will think herself enabled to have a baby by receiving it.

Given this argument and given that poverty and low IQ are related, let us ask whether the apparent relationship between IQ and illegitimacy is an artifact. Poor women disproportionately have low IQs, and bear a disproportionate number of illegitimate babies. Control for the effects of poverty, says this logic, and the relationship between IQ and illegitimacy will diminish.

Let us see. First, we ask whether the initial condition is true: Is having babies out of wedlock something that is done disproportionately not only by women who come from low socioeconomic backgrounds (a fact which we already have discussed), but women who are literally poor themselves when they reach childbearing age? Even more specifically, are they disproportionately living below the poverty line *before the birth*? We use the italics to emphasize a distinction that we believe offers an important new perspective on single motherhood and poverty. It is one thing to say that single women with babies are disproportionately poor, as we discussed in Chapter 5. That makes sense, because a single woman with a child is often not a viable economic unit. It is quite another thing to say that women who are already poor become mothers. Now we are arguing that there is something about being in the state of poverty itself (after holding the socioeconomic status in which they were raised constant) that makes having a baby without a husband attractive.

To put the question in operational terms: Among NLSY white mothers who were below the poverty line in the year prior to giving birth, what proportion of the babies were born out of wedlock? The answer is 44 percent. Among NLSY white mothers who were anywhere *above* the poverty line in the year before giving birth, what proportion of the babies were born out of wedlock? The answer is only 6 percent. It is a huge difference and makes a prima facie case for those who argue that poverty itself, presumably via the welfare system, is an important cause of illegitimacy.

But now we turn to the rest of the hypothesis: that controlling for poverty will explain away at least some of the apparent relationship between IQ and illegitimacy. Here is the basic analysis—controlling for IQ, parental SES, and age—restricted to white women who were poor the year before the birth of their babies.[35]

Compare the graph below with the one before it and two points about white poor women and illegitimacy are vividly clear. First, the inde-

IQ is a more powerful predictor of illegitimacy among poor white women than among white women as a whole

Probability that the first child will be born out of wedlock for white women already below the poverty line

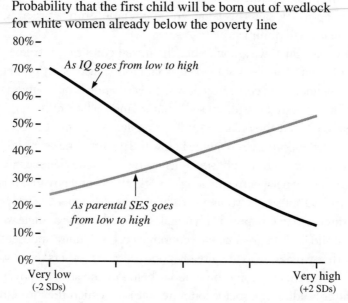

Note: For computing the plot, age and either SES (for the black curve) or IQ (for the gray curve) were set at their mean values.

pendent importance of intelligence is even greater for poor white women than for white women as a whole. A poor white woman of average socioeconomic background and average IQ has more than a 35 percent chance of an illegitimate first birth. For white women in general, average socioeconomic status and IQ resulted in less than a 15 percent chance. Second, among poor women, the role of socioeconomic background in restraining illegitimacy disappears once the role of IQ is taken into account.

The results, taken literally, suggest that illegitimacy tends to *rise* among poor women who came from higher socioeconomic background after IQ is taken into account. However, the sample of white women includes too few women who fit all of the conditions (below the poverty line, from a good socioeconomic background, with an illegitimate baby) to make much of this. The more conservative interpretation is that low socioeconomic background, independent of IQ and current poverty itself, does not increase the chances of giving birth out of wedlock among poor white women—in itself a sufficiently provocative finding for sociologists.[36]

Our main purpose has been to demonstrate that low intelligence is an important independent cause of illegitimacy, and to do so we have considered the role of poverty. In reality, however, we have also opened up many new avenues of inquiry that we cannot fully pursue without writing an entire book on this subject alone. For example, the results raise many questions to be asked about the "culture of poverty" argument. To the extent that a culture of poverty is at work, transmitting dysfunctional values from one generation to the next, it seems paradoxical that low socioeconomic background does not foster illegitimacy once poverty in the year prior to birth is brought into the picture.

But the main task posed by these results is to fill in the reason for that extremely strong relationship between low IQ and illegitimacy within the population of poor white women. The possibilities bear directly on some of the core issues in the social policy debate. For example, many people have argued that the welfare system cannot really be a cause of illegitimacy, because, in objective terms, the welfare system is a bad deal. It provides only enough to squeak by, it can easily trap young women into long-term dependence, and even poor young women would be much better off by completing their education and getting a job rather than having a baby and going on welfare. The results we have presented can be interpreted as saying that the welfare system may be a bad deal, but it takes foresight and intelligence to understand why. For women without foresight and intelligence, it may seem to be a good deal. Hence poor young women who are bright tend not to have illegitimate babies nearly as often as poor young women who are dull.

Another possibility fits in with those who argue that the best preventative for illegitimacy is better opportunities. It is not the welfare system that is at fault but the lack of other avenues. Poor young women who are bright are getting scholarships, or otherwise having positive incentives offered to them, and they accordingly defer childbearing. Poor young women who are dull do not get such opportunities; they have nothing else to do, and so have a baby. The goal should be to provide them too with other ways of seeing their futures.

Both of these explanations are stated as hypotheses that we hope others will explore. Those explorations will have to incorporate our central finding, however: Cognitive ability in itself is an important factor in illegitimacy, and the dynamics for understanding illegitimacy—and dealing with it through policy—must take that strong link into account.

THE SELECTIVE DETERIORATION OF THE TRADITIONAL FAMILY

Our goal has been to sharpen understanding of the much-lamented breakdown of the American family. The American family has been as battered in the latter decades of the twentieth century as the public rhetoric would have it, but the damage as measured in terms of divorce and illegitimacy has been far more selective than we hear. By way of summary, let us consider the children of the white NLSY mothers in the top quartile of cognitive ability (Classes I and II) versus those in the bottom quartile (Classes IV and V):

- *The percentage of households with children that consist of a married couple:* 87 percent in the top quartile of IQ, 70 percent in the bottom quartile.
- *The percentage of households with children that have experienced divorce:* 17 percent in the top quartile of IQ, 33 percent in the bottom quartile.
- *The percentage of children born out of wedlock:* 5 percent in the top quartile of IQ, 23 percent in the bottom quartile.

The American family may be generally under siege, as people often say. But it is at the bottom of the cognitive ability distribution that its defenses are most visibly crumbling.

Chapter 9

Welfare Dependency

People have had reason to assume for many years that welfare mothers are concentrated at the low end of the cognitive ability distribution, if only because they have generally done poorly in school. Beyond that, it makes sense that smarter women can more easily find jobs and resist the temptations of welfare dependency than duller ones, even if they have given birth out of wedlock.

The link is confirmed in the NLSY. Over three-quarters of the white women who were on welfare within a year of the birth of their first child came from the bottom quartile of IQ, compared to 5 percent from the top quartile. When we subdivide welfare recipients into two groups, "temporary" and "chronic," the link persists, though differently for the two groups.

Among women who received welfare temporarily, low IQ is a powerful risk factor even after the effects of marital status, poverty, age, and socioeconomic background are statistically extracted. For chronic welfare recipiency, the story is more complicated. For practical purposes, white women with above-average cognitive ability or above-average socioeconomic background do not become chronic welfare recipients. Among the restricted sample of low-IQ, low-SES, and relatively uneducated white women who are chronically on welfare, low socioeconomic background is a more powerful predictor than low IQ, even after taking account of whether they were themselves below the poverty line at the time they had their babies.

The analyses provide some support for those who argue that a culture of poverty tends to transmit chronic welfare dependency from one generation to the next. But if a culture of poverty is at work, it seems to have influence primarily among women who are of low intelligence.

A part from whether it causes increased illegitimacy, welfare has been a prickly topic in the social policy debate since shortly after the core welfare program, Aid to Families with Dependent Children (AFDC), was created in the mid-1930s. Originally AFDC was a popular idea. No one in the community was a likelier object of sympathy than the young widow with small children to raise, and AFDC seemed to be a way to help her stay home with her children until they were old enough to begin taking care of her in their turn. And if some of the women going on AFDC had not been widowed but abandoned by no-good husbands, most people thought that they should be helped too, though some people voiced concerns that helping such women undermined marriage.

But hardly anyone had imagined that never-married women would be eligible for AFDC. It came as a distressing surprise to Frances Perkins, the first woman cabinet member and a primary sponsor of the legislation, to find that they were.[1] But not only were they eligible; within a few years after AFDC began, they constituted a large and growing portion of the caseload. This created much of the general public's antagonism toward AFDC: It wasn't just the money, it was the principle of the thing. Why should hardworking citizens support immorality?

Such complaints about welfare go far back into the 1940s and even the 1930s, but, at least from our perspective in the 1990s, it was much ado about a comparatively small problem, as the next figure shows. After

The welfare revolution

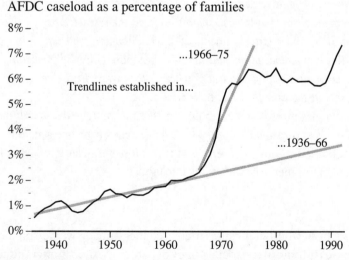

AFDC caseload as a percentage of families

Sources: U.S. Bureau of the Census, 1975, Table H 346-367; annual data published in the *Social Security Bulletin.*

a slow and meandering rise since the end of World War II, the welfare caseload was still less than 2 percent of families when John F. Kennedy took office. Then, as with so many other social phenomena, the dynamics abruptly changed in mid-1960s. In a concentrated period from 1966 to 1975, the percentage of American families on welfare nearly tripled. The growth in the caseload then stopped and even declined slightly through the 1980s. Welfare rolls have been rising steeply since 1988, apparently beginning a fourth era. As of 1992, more than 14 million Americans were on welfare.

The steep rise in the welfare population is obviously not to be explained by intelligence, which did not plummet in the 1960s and 1970s. More fundamental forces were reshaping the social landscape during that time. The surging welfare population is just one outcropping among others summarized in Part II of trouble in American society. In this chapter, the theme will be, as it is elsewhere in the book, that as society changes, some people are especially vulnerable to the changes—in this instance, to events that cause dependence on welfare. We show here that low intelligence increases a white mother's risk of going on welfare, independent of the other factors that might be expected to explain away the relationship.

IQ AND WELFARE

It has not been an openly discussed topic, but there are many good reasons for assuming that welfare mothers come mainly from the lower reaches of the distribution of cognitive ability. Women on welfare have less education than women not on welfare, and chronic welfare recipients have less education than nonchronic recipients.[2] Welfare mothers have been estimated to have reading skills that average three to five years below grade level.[3] Poor reading skills and little schooling define populations with lower-than-average IQ, so even without access to IQ tests, it can be deduced that welfare mothers have lower-than-average intelligence. But can it be shown that low IQ has an independent link with welfare itself, after taking account of the less direct links via being poor and being an unwed mother?[4]

By a direct link, we mean something like this: The smarter the woman is, the more likely she will be able to find a job, the more likely she will be able to line up other sources of support (from parents or the father of the child), and the more farsighted she is likely to be about the dangers of going on welfare. Even within the population of women who go on welfare, cognitive ability will vary, and the smarter ones will be better able to get off.

No database until the NLSY has offered the chance to test these hypotheses in detail for a representative population. We begin as usual with a look at the unadorned relationship with cognitive class.

Use of welfare is uncommon but not rare among these white mothers, as the table below shows. Overall, 12 percent of the white mothers

Which White Women Go on Welfare After the Birth of the First Child?		
Percentage of Mothers Who Went on AFDC Within a Year of First Birth	Cognitive Class	Percentage of Mothers Who Became Chronic Welfare Recipients
1	I Very bright	a
4	II Bright	2
12	III Normal	8
21	IV Dull	17
55	V Very dull	31
12	Overall average	9

[a] Sample = 17, with no one qualifying as a chronic welfare recipient. Minimum sample reported: 25.

in the NLSY received welfare within a year of the birth of their first child; 9 percent had become chronic recipients by our definition of chronic welfare recipients (meaning that they had reported at least five years of welfare income). Overall, 21 percent of white mothers had received assistance from AFDC at some point in their lives.[5] The differences among the cognitive classes are large, with a conspicuously large jump in the rates at the bottom. The proportion of women in Class IV who became chronic welfare recipients is double the rate for Class III, with another big jump for Class V, to 31 percent of all mothers.

This result should come as no surprise, given what we already know about the higher rates of illegitimate births in the lower half of the cognitive ability distribution (Chapter 8). Women without husbands are most at risk for going on welfare. We also know that poverty has a strong association with the birth status of the child. In fact, it may be asked whether we are looking at anything except a reflection of illegitimacy and poverty in these figures. The answer is yes, but a somewhat different "yes" for periodic and for chronic welfare recipiency.

GOING ON WELFARE AFTER THE BIRTH OF THE FIRST CHILD

First, we ask of the odds that a woman had received welfare by the end of the first calendar year after the birth of her first child.[6] In all cases, we limit the analysis to white women whose first child was born prior to 1989, so that all have had a sufficient "chance" to go on welfare.

If we want to understand the independent relationship between IQ and welfare, the standard analysis, using just age, IQ, and parental SES, is not going to tell us much. We have to get rid of the confounding effects of being poor and unwed. For that reason, the analysis that yielded the figure below extracted the effects of the marital status of the mother

Even after poverty and marital status are taken into account, IQ played a substantial role in determining whether white women go on welfare

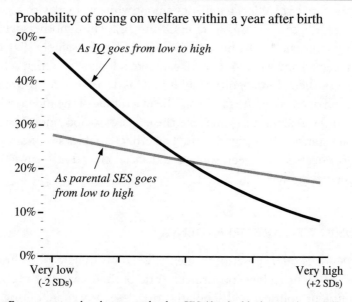

Probability of going on welfare within a year after birth

As IQ goes from low to high

As parental SES goes from low to high

Note: For computing the plot, age and either SES (for the black curves) or IQ (for the gray curves) were set at their mean values. Additional independent variables of which the effects have been extracted for the plot: marital status at the time of first birth, and poverty status in the calendar year prior to the first birth.

and whether she was below the poverty line in the year before birth, in addition to the usual three variables. The dependent variable is whether the mother received welfare benefits during the year after the birth of her first child. As the black line indicates, cognitive ability predicts going on welfare even after the effects of marital status and poverty have been extracted. This finding is worth thinking about, for it is not intuitively predictable. Presumably much of the impact of low intelligence on being on welfare—the failure to look ahead, to consider consequences, or to get an education—is already captured in the fact that the woman had a baby out of wedlock. Other elements of competence, or lack of it, are captured in the fact that the woman was poor before the baby was born. Yet holding the effects of age, poverty, marital status, and parental SES constant, a white woman with an IQ at the 2d centile had a 47 percent chance of going on welfare, compared to the 8 percent chance facing a white woman at the 98th centile.

The socioeconomic background of these mothers was not a statistically significant factor in their going on welfare.

The Role of Education

We cannot analyze welfare recipiency among white women with a bachelor's degree because it was so rare: Of the 102 white mothers with a B.A. (no more, no less) who met the criteria for the sample, 101 had never received any welfare. But we can take a look at the high school sample. For them, low cognitive ability was as decisive as for the entire population of NLSY white mothers. The magnitude of the independent effect of IQ was about the same, and the effect of socioeconomic status was again statistically insignificant. The other variables swept away all of the connections between welfare and social class that seem so evident in everyday life.

CHRONIC WELFARE DEPENDENCY

Now we focus on a subset of women who go on welfare, the chronic welfare recipients. They constitute a world of their own. In the course of the furious political and scholarly struggle over welfare during the 1980s, two stable and consistent findings emerged, each having different implications: Taking all the women who ever go on welfare, the average spell lasts only about two years.[7] But among never-married mothers (all races) who had their babies in their teens, the average time on welfare is eight or more years, depending on the sample being investigated.[8]

The white women who had met our definition of chronic welfare recipient in the NLSY by the 1990 interview fit this profile to some extent. For example, of the white women who gave birth to an illegitimate baby before they were 19 (that is, they probably got pregnant before they would normally have graduated from high school) and stayed single, 22 percent became chronic welfare recipients by our definition—a high percentage compared to women at large. On the other hand, 22 percent is a long way from 100 percent. Even if we restrict the criteria further so that we are talking about single teenage mothers who were below the poverty line, the probability of becoming a chronic welfare recipient goes up only to 28 percent.

To get an idea of how restricted the population of chronic welfare mothers is, consider the 152 white women in the NLSY who met our definition of a chronic welfare recipient and also had IQ scores. None of them was in Cognitive Class I, and only five were even in Class II. Only five had parents in the top quartile in socioeconomic class. One lone woman of the 152 was from the top quartile in ability *and* from the top quartile in socioeconomic background. White women with above-average cognitive ability or socioeconomic background rarely become chronic welfare recipients.

Keeping this tight restriction of range in mind, consider what happens when we repeat the previous analysis (including the extra variables controlling for marital status and poverty at the time of first birth) but this time comparing mothers who became chronic welfare recipients with women who never received any welfare.[9] According to the figure, when it comes to chronic white welfare mothers, the independent effect of the young woman's socioeconomic background is substantial. Whether it becomes more important than IQ as the figure suggests is doubtful (the corresponding analysis in Appendix 4 says no), but clearly the role of socioeconomic background is different for all welfare recipients and chronic ones. We spent much time exploring this shift in the role of socioeconomic background, to try to pin down what was going on. We will not describe our investigation with its many interesting byways, instead simply reporting where we came out. The answer turns out to hinge on education.

Socioeconomic background and IQ are both important in determining whether white women become chronic welfare recipients

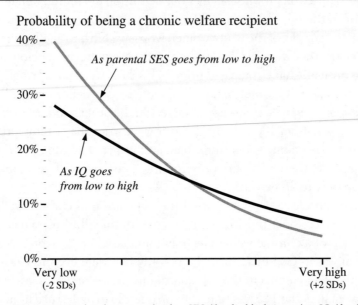

Note: For computing the plot, age and either SES (for the black curves) or IQ (for the gray curves) were set at their mean values. Additional independent variables of which the effects have been extracted for the plot: marital status at the time of first birth, and poverty status in the calendar year prior to the first birth.

The Role of Education

White chronic welfare recipients are virtually all women with modest education at best, as set out in the next table. More than half of the chronic welfare recipients had not gotten a high school diploma; only six-tenths of 1 percent had gotten a college education. As in the case of IQ and socioeconomic status, this is a radically unrepresentative sample of white women.[10] It is obviously impossible (as well as unnecessary) to analyze chronic welfare recipiency among college graduates.

The women for whom socioeconomic background was the main risk factor for being chronically on welfare are those who had not finished high school. For women with a high school diploma or more, IQ was

Educational Attainment of White Chronic Welfare Recipients	
Highest Degree	**Percentage**
Advanced degree	0
B.A. or B.S.	1
Associate degree	3
High school diploma	42
GED	16
Less than high school	38

more important than socioeconomic status (other things equal) in affecting the probability of becoming a chronic welfare recipient.[11]

Why? Apparently the women who did not finish high school and had an illegitimate child were selected for low intelligence, especially if they had the child while still in high school.[12] The average IQ of these women was about 91, and analysis tells us that further variation in cognitive ability does not have much power to predict which ones become chronic welfare cases.[13] Instead, for this narrowly screened group of women, family background matters more. Without trying to push the analysis much further, a plausible explanation is that for most white American parents, having a school-aged child go on welfare is highly stigmatizing *to them*. If the daughter of a working-class or middle-class couple has an illegitimate baby out of wedlock while still in high school, chances are that her parents will take over support for the new baby rather than let their daughter go on welfare. The parents who do not keep their school-aged daughter off welfare will tend to be those who are not deterred by the stigma or who are themselves too poor to support the new baby. Both sets of parents earn low scores on the socioeconomic status index. Hence what we are observing in the case of chronic welfare recipiency among young women who do not finish high school may reflect parental behavior as much as the young mother's behavior.[14]

Other hypotheses are possible, however. Generally these results provide evidence for those who argue that a culture of poverty transmits chronic welfare dependency from one generation to the next. Our analysis adds that women who are susceptible to this culture are likely to have low intelligence in the first place.

DRAWING TOGETHER THE FINDINGS ON ILLEGITIMACY AND WELFARE

As social scientists often do, we have spent much effort burrowing through analyses that ultimately point to simple conclusions. Here is how a great many parents around America have put it to their daughters: Having a baby without a husband is a dumb thing to do. Going on welfare is an even dumber thing to do, if you can possibly avoid it. And so it would seem to be among the white women in the NLSY. White women who remained childless or had babies within marriage had a mean IQ of 105. Those who had an illegitimate baby but never went on welfare had a mean IQ of 98. Those who went on welfare but did not become chronic recipients had a mean IQ of 94. Those who became chronic welfare recipients had a mean IQ of 92.[15] Altogether, almost a standard deviation separated the IQs of white women who became chronic welfare recipients from those who remained childless or had children within marriage.

In Chapter 8, we demonstrated that a low IQ is a factor in illegitimate births that cannot be explained away by the woman's socioeconomic background, a broken family, or poverty at the time the child was conceived. In particular, poor women of low intelligence seemed especially likely to have illegitimate babies, which is consistent with the idea that the prospect of welfare looms largest for women who are thinking least clearly about their futures. In this chapter, we have demonstrated that even among women who are poor and even among those who have a baby without a husband, the less intelligent tend to be the ones who use the welfare system.

Two qualifications to this conclusion are that (1) we have no way of knowing whether higher education or higher IQ explains why college graduates do not use welfare—all we know is that welfare is almost unknown among college-educated whites, but that for women with a high school education, intelligence plays a large independent role—and (2) for the low-IQ women without a high school education who become chronic welfare recipients, a low socioeconomic background is a more important predictor than any further influence of cognitive ability.

The remaining issue, which we defer to the discussion of welfare policy in Chapter 22, is how to reconcile two conflicting possibilities, both of which may have some truth to them: Going on welfare really is a dumb idea, and that is why women who are low in cognitive ability end up there; but also such women have little to take to the job market, and welfare is one of their few appropriate recourses when they have a baby to care for and no husband to help.

Chapter 10

Parenting

Everyone agrees, in the abstract and at the extremes, that there is good parenting and poor parenting. This chapter addresses the uncomfortable question: Is the competence of parents at all affected by how intelligent they are?

It has been known for some time that socioeconomic class and parenting are linked, both to disciplinary practices and to the many ways in which the intellectual and emotional development of the child are fostered. On both counts, parents with higher socioeconomic status look better. At the other end of the parenting continuum, neglect and abuse are heavily concentrated in the lower socioeconomic classes.

Whenever an IQ measure has been introduced into studies of parent-child relationships, it has explained away much of the differences that otherwise would have been attributed to education or social class, but the examples are sparse. The NLSY provides an opportunity to fill in a few of the gaps.

With regard to prenatal and infant care, low IQ among the white mothers in the NLSY sample was related to low birth weight, even after controlling for socioeconomic background, poverty, and age of the mother. In the NLSY's surveys of the home environment, mothers in the top cognitive classes provided, on average, better environments for children than the mothers in the bottom cognitive classes. Socioeconomic background and current poverty also played significant roles, depending on the specific type of measure and the age of the children.

In the NLSY's measures of child development, low maternal IQ was associated with problematic temperament in the baby and with low scores on an index of "friendliness," with poor motor and social development of toddlers and with behavioral problems from age 4 on up. Poverty usually had a modest independent role but did not usually diminish the contribution of IQ (which was usually also modest). Predictably, the mother's IQ was also strongly related to the IQ of the child.

Taking these data together, the NLSY results say clearly that high IQ is by no means a prerequisite for being a good mother. The disquieting finding is *that the worst environments for raising children, of the kind that not even the most resilient children can easily overcome, are concentrated in the homes in which the mothers are at the low end of the intelligence distribution.*

Parenting, in one sense the most private of behaviors, is in another the most public. Parents make a difference in the way their children turn out—whether they become law abiding or criminal, generous or stingy, productive or dependent. How well parents raise their children has much to do with how well the society functions.

But how are parents to know whether they are doing a good or a bad job as parents? The results seem to be hopelessly unpredictable. Most people know at least one couple who seem to be the ideal parents but whose teenage child ends up on drugs. Parents with more than one child are bemused by how differently their children respond to the same home and parental style. And what makes a good parent anyway? Most people also have friends who seem to be raising their children all wrong, and yet the children flourish.

The exceptions notwithstanding, the apparent unpredictability of parenting is another of those illusions fostered by the ground-level view of life as we live it from day to day. Parenting is more predictable in the aggregate than in the particular. The differences in parenting style that you observe among your friends are usually minor—the "restriction of range" problem that we discussed in Chapter 3. A middle-class mother may think that one of her friends is far too permissive or strict, but put against the full range of variation that police and social workers are forced to deal with, where "permissiveness" is converted into the number of days that small children are left on their own and "strictness" may be calibrated by the number of stitches required to close the wounds from a parental beating, the differences between her and her friend are probably small.

Despite all the differences among children and parents, there is such a thing as good parenting as opposed to bad—not precisely defined but generally understood. Our discussion proceeds from the assumption that good parenting includes (though is not restricted to) seeing to nourishment and health, keeping safe from harm, feeling and expressing love, talking with and listening to, helping to explore the world, imparting values, and providing a framework of rules enforced consistently but not inflexibly. Parents who more or less manage to do all those things, we assert, are better parents than people who do not. The touchy question of this chapter is: Does cognitive ability play any role in this? Are people with high IQs generally better parents than people with low IQs?

SOCIAL CLASS AND PARENTING STYLES

The relationship of IQ to parenting is another of those issues that social scientists have been slow to investigate. Furthermore, this is a topic for which the NLSY is limited. For unemployment, school dropout, illegitimacy, or welfare recipiency, the NLSY permits us to cut directly to the question, What does cognitive ability have to do with this behavior? But many of the NLSY indicators about parenting give only indirect evidence. To interpret that evidence, it is useful to begin with the large body of studies that have investigated whether social class affects parenting. Having described that relationship (which by now is reasonably well understood), we will be on firmer ground in drawing inferences about cognitive ability.

The first scholarly study of parenting styles among parents of different social classes dates back to 1936 and a White House conference on children.[1] Ever since, the anthropologists and sociologists have told similar stories. Working-class parents tend to be more authoritarian than middle-class parents. Working-class parents tend to use physical punishment and direct commands, whereas middle-class parents tend to use reasoning and appeals to more abstract principles of behavior. The consistency of these findings extends from the earliest studies to the most recent.[2]

In an influential article published in 1959, Melvin Kohn proposed that the underlying difference was that working-class parents were most concerned about qualities in their children that ensure respectability, whereas middle-class parents were most concerned about internalized standards of conduct.[3] Kohn argued that the real difference in the use of physical punishment was not that working-class parents punish more but that they punish differently from middle-class parents. Immediate irritants like boisterous play might evoke a whack from working-class parents, whereas middle-class parents tended to punish when the intent of the child's behavior (knowingly hurting another child, for example) was problematic.[4] Kohn concluded that "the working-class orientation . . . places few restraints on the impulse to punish the child when his behavior is out of bounds. Instead, it provides a positive rationale for punishing the child in precisely those circumstances when one might most like to do so."[5] To put it more plainly, Kohn found that working-class parents were more likely to use physical punishment impulsively, when the parents themselves needed the relief, not when it was likely to do the child the most good.

The middle-class way sounds like "better" behavior on the part of parents, not just a neutral socioeconomic difference in parenting style, and this raises a point that scholars on child development bend over backward to avoid saying explicitly: Generally, and keeping in mind the many exceptions, the conclusion to be drawn from the literature on parenting is that middle-class people are in fact better parents, on average, than working-class people. Readers who bridle at this suggestion are invited to reread the Kohn quotation above and ask themselves whether they can avoid making a value judgment about it.

Parenting differences among the social classes are not restricted to matters of discipline. Other major differences show up in the intellectual development of the child. Anthropologist Shirley Brice Heath[6] gives vivid examples in her description of parenting in "Roadville," a white lower-class community in the Carolinas, versus "Gateway," a nearby community of white middle-class parents.[7] The parents of Roadville were just as devoted to their children as the parents of Gateway. Roadville newborns came home to nurseries complete with the same mobiles, pictures, and books that the Gateway babies had. From an early age, Roadville children were held on laps and read to, talked to, and otherwise made as much the center of attention as Gateway babies. But the interactions differed, Heath found. Take bedtime stories, for example. In middle-class Gateway, the mother or father encouraged the children to ask questions and talk about what the stories meant, pointing at items on the page and asking what they were. The middle-class parents praised right answers and explained what was wrong with wrong ones.[8] It is no great stretch to argue, as Robert Sternberg and others do, that this interaction amounts to excellent training for intelligence tests. Lower-class Roadville parents did not do nearly as much of that kind of explaining and asking.[9] When the children were learning to do new tasks, the Roadville parents did not explain the "how" of things the way the Gateway parents did. Instead, the Roadville parents were more likely to issue directives ("Don't twist the cookie cutter") and hardly ever gave reasons for their instructions ("If you twist the cutter, the cookies will be rough on the edge").[10]

When they got to school, the Roadville and Gateway children continued to differ. The working-class Roadville children performed well in the early tasks of each of the first three grades. They knew the alphabet when they went to kindergarten; they knew how to sit still in class and could perform well in the reading exercises that asked them to identify specific portions of words or to link two items on the same page of the book. But if the teacher asked, "What did you like about the story?" or "What would you have done if you had been the child in that story?" the Roadville children were likely to say "I don't know" or shrug their shoulders, while the middle-class Gateway children would more often respond easily and imaginatively.[11]

Heath's conclusions drawn from her anthropological observations are buttressed by the quantitative work that has been done to date. A review of the technical literature in the mid-1980s put it bluntly: "It is an empirical fact that children from relatively higher SES families receive an intellectually more advantageous home environment. This finding holds for white, black, and Hispanic children, for children within lower- and middle-SES families, as well as for children born preterm and full-term."[12]

SOCIAL CLASS AND MALPARENTING

To this point, we have been talking about parenting within the normal range. Now we turn to child neglect and child abuse, increasingly labeled "malparenting" in the technical literature.

Abuse and neglect are distinct. The physical battering and other forms of extreme physical and emotional punishment that constitute child abuse get most of the publicity, but child neglect is far more common, by ratios ranging from three to one to ten to one, depending on the study.[13] Among the distinctions that the experts draw between child abuse and neglect are these:

- Abuse is an act of commission, while neglect is more commonly an act of omission.
- Abuse is typically episodic and of short duration; neglect is chronic and continual.
- Abuse typically arises from impulsive outbursts of aggression and anger; neglect arises from indifference, inattentiveness, or being overwhelmed by parenthood.[14]

Commonly, neglect is as simple as failure to provide a child with adequate food, clothing, shelter, or hygiene. But it can also mean leaving dangerous materials within reach, not keeping the child away from an open window, or leaving toddlers alone for hours at a time. It means not taking the child to a doctor when he is sick or not giving him the medicine the doctor prescribed. Neglect can also mean more subtle deprivations: habitually leaving babies in cribs for long periods, never talking to infants and toddlers except to scold or demand, no smiles, no bedtime stories. At its most serious, neglect becomes abandonment.

Are abusing parents also neglectful? Are neglectful parents also abusive? Different studies have produced different answers. Child abuse in some bizarre forms has nothing to do with anything except a profoundly deranged parent. Such cases crop up unpredictably, independent of demographic and socioeconomic variables.[15]

Once we move away from these exceptional cases, however, abuse and neglect seem to be more alike than different in their origins.[16] The theories explaining them are complex, involving stress, social isolation, personality characteristics, community characteristics, and transmission of malparenting from one generation to the next.[17] But one concomitant of malparenting is not in much dispute: Malparenting of either sort is heavily concentrated in the lower socioeconomic classes. Indeed, the link is such that, as Douglas Besharov has pointed out, behaviors that are sometimes classified as forms of neglect—letting a child skip school, for example—are not considered neglectful in some poor communities but part of the normal pattern of upbringing.[18] What would be considered just an overenthusiastic spanking in one neighborhood might be called abuse in another.

We realize that once again we are contradicting what everyone knows, which is that "child abuse and neglect afflict all communities, regardless of race, religion, or economic status," to pick one formulation of this common belief.[19] And in a narrow technical sense, such statements are correct, insofar as neglect and abuse are found at every social and economic level, as is every other human behavior. It is also correct that only a small minority of parents among the poor and disadvantaged neglect or abuse their children. But the way such statements are usually treated in the media, by politicians, and by child advocacy groups is to imply that child neglect and abuse are spread *evenly* across social classes, as if children have about an equal chance of being abused or neglected whether they come from a rich home or a poor one, whether the mother is a college graduate or a high school dropout. And yet from the earliest studies to the present, malparenting has been strongly associated with socioeconomic class.

The people who argue otherwise do not offer data to make their case. Instead, they argue that child neglect and abuse are reported when it happens to poor children but not rich ones. Affluent families are believed to escape the reporting net (by using private physicians, for example, who are less likely to report abuse). Social service agencies are said to be reluctant to intervene in affluent families.[20] Poor people are likely to be labeled deviant for behaviors that would go unnoted or unremarked in richer neighborhoods.[21] People are likely to think the worst of socially unattractive people and give socially attractive people the benefit of the doubt.[22]

Studies spread over the last twenty years have analyzed reporting bias in a variety of ways, including surveys to identify abuse that goes unreported through official channels. The results are consistent: The socioeconomic link with maltreatment is authentic.[23] Probably the link is stronger for neglect than for abuse.[24] But specifying exactly how strongly socioeconomic status and child maltreatment are linked is difficult because of the genuine shortcomings of official reports and because so many different kinds of abuse and neglect are involved. The following numbers give a sense of the situation:

- In an early national study (using data for 1967) 60 percent of the families involved in abuse incidents had been on welfare during or prior to the study year.[25]
- In data on 20,000 validated reports of child abuse and neglect collected by the American Humane Association for 1976, half of the reported families were below the poverty line and most of the rest were concentrated just above it.[26]
- In a 1984 study of child maltreatment in El Paso, Texas, 87 percent of the alleged perpetrators were in families with incomes under $18,000, roughly the bottom third of income. Seventy-three percent of the alleged female perpetrators were unmarried.[27]
- In the federally sponsored National Incidence Study in 1979, which obtained information on unreported as well as reported cases, the families of 43 percent of the victims of child abuse or neglect had an income under $7,000, compared to 17 percent of

---

Other Precursors of Maltreatment

Premature births, low birth weight, and illegitimacy also have links with maltreatment. Studies in America and Britain have found rates of low birth weight among abused children running at three to four times the national average.[29] Prematurity has been found to be similarly disproportionate among abused children.[30] The proportion of neglected children who are illegitimate has run far above national averages in studies from the early 1960s onward. More than a quarter of the neglected children in the mid-1960s were illegitimate, for example—almost four times the national proportion.[31] In a British sample, 36 percent of the neglected children were illegitimate compared to 6 percent in the control group.[32]

---

all American children. Only 6 percent of the abusive or neglectful families had incomes of $25,000 or more.

- The 1986 replication of the National Incidence Study found that the rate of abuse and neglect among families with incomes under $15,000 was five times that of families with incomes above $15,000. Only 6 percent of the families involved in neglect or abuse had incomes above the median for all American families.[28]

Given the one-sided nature of the evidence, why has the "myth of classlessness," in Leroy Pelton's phrase, been so tenacious? Pelton himself blamed social service professionals and politicians, arguing that both of these powerful groups have a vested interest in a medical model of child abuse, in which child abuse falls on its victims at random, like the flu.[33] Pelton does not mention another reason that seems plausible to us: Child abuse and neglect are held in intense distaste by most Americans, who feel great hostility toward parents who harm their children. People who write about malparenting do not want to encourage this hostility to spill over into hostility toward the poor and disadvantaged.

Whatever the reasons, the myth of classlessness is alive and well. It is a safe bet that at the next Senate hearing on a child neglect bill, witnesses and senators alike will agree that neglect and abuse are scattered throughout society, and the next feature story on child neglect you see on the evening news will report, as scientific fact, that child neglect is not a special problem of the poor.

PARENTAL IQ AND PARENTING

In all of these studies of socioeconomic status and parenting, the obvious but usually ignored possibility has been that the parents' cognitive ability, not their status, was an important source of the differences in parenting styles and also an important source of the relationship between malparenting and children's IQs. Indeed, even without conducting any additional studies, some sort of role for cognitive ability must be presupposed. If cognitive ability is a cause of socioeconomic status (yes) and if socioeconomic status is related to parenting style (yes), then cognitive ability must have at least some indirect role in parenting style. The same causal chain applies to child maltreatment.

Direct evidence for a link with IQ is sparse. Even the educational attainment of the abusing parents is often unreported. But a search of the literature through the early 1990s uncovered a number of fragments that point to a potentially important role for cognitive ability, if we bear in mind that cognitive ability is a stronger predictor of school dropout than is socioeconomic status (Chapter 6):

- In Gil's national study of child abuse reports, more than 65 percent of the mothers and 56 percent of the fathers had not completed high school.[34]
- A study of 480 infants of women registering for prenatal care at an urban hospital for indigent persons and their children found that the less educated mothers even within this disadvantaged population were more likely to neglect their babies.[35]
- Three studies of child maltreatment in a central Virginia city of 80,000 people found that neglecting families had an average eighth-grade education, and almost three-quarters of them had been placed in classes for the mentally retarded during their school years. In contrast with the neglecting families, the abusing families tended to be literate, high school graduates, and of normal intelligence.[36]
- A study of fifty-eight preschool children of unspecified race in the Cleveland area with histories of failure to thrive found that their mothers' IQs average was 81.[37] No comparison group was available in this study, but a mean of 81 indicates cognitive functioning at approximately the 10th centile.

- A study of twenty abusive or neglectful mothers and ten comparison mothers from inner-city Rochester, New York, found that maltreating and nonmaltreating mothers differed significantly in their judgment about child behavior and in their problem-solving abilities.[38]
- A clinical psychological study of ten parents who battered their children severely (six of the children died) classified five as having a "high-grade mental deficiency" (mentally retarded), one as dull, and another as below average. The remaining three were classified as above average.[39]
- A quantitative study of 113 two-parent families in the Netherlands found that parents with a high level of "reasoning complexity" (a measure of cognitive ability) responded to their children more flexibly and sensitively, while those with low levels of reasoning complexity were more authoritarian and rigid, independent of occupation and education.[40]

The most extensive clinical studies of neglectful mothers have been conducted by Norman Polansky, whose many years of research began with a sample drawn from rural Appalachia, subsequently replicated with an urban Philadelphia sample. He described the typical neglectful mother as follows:

> She is of limited intelligence (IQ below 70), has failed to achieve more than an eighth-grade education, and has never held . . . employment. . . . She has at best a vague, or extremely limited, idea of what her children need emotionally and physically. She seldom is able to see things from the point of view of others and cannot take their needs into consideration when responding to a conflict they experience.[41]

The specific IQ figure Polansky mentions corresponds to the upper edge of retardation, and his description of her personality invokes further links between neglect and intelligence.

Another body of literature links neglectful and abusive parents to personality characteristics that have clear links to low cognitive ability.[42] The most extensive evidence describes the impulsiveness, inconsistency, and confusion that mark the parenting style of many abusive parents.[43] The abusive parents may or may not punish their children more often or severely in the ordinary course of events than other parents (studies differ on this point),[44] but the abuse characteristically comes unpredictably, in episodic bursts. Abusive parents may punish a given behavior on one occasion, ignore it on another, and encourage it on a third. The inconsistency can reach mystifying proportions; one study of parent-child interactions found that children in abusing families had about the same chance of obtaining positive reinforcement for aggressive behaviors as for pro-social behaviors.[45]

The observed inconsistency of abusing parents was quantified in one of the early and classic studies of child abuse by Leontine Young, *Wednesday's Children*. By her calculations, inconsistency was the rule in *all* of the "severe abuse" families in her sample, in 91 percent of the "moderate abuse" families, 97 percent of the "severe neglect" families, and 88 percent of the "moderate neglect" families.[46] In one of the most extensive literature reviews of the behavioral and personality dimensions of abusive parents (as of 1985), the author concluded that the main problem was not that abusive parents were attached to punishment as such but that they were simply incompetent as parents.[47]

One might think that researchers seeing these malparenting patterns would naturally be inspired to look at the parents' intelligence as a predictor. And yet in that same literature review, examining every rigorous American study on the subject, the word *intelligence* (or any synonym for it) does not occur until the next-to-last page of the article.[48] The word finally makes its appearance as the literature review nears its end and the author turns to his recommendations for future research. He notes that in an ongoing British prospective study of parenting, "mothers in their Excellent Care group, for example, were found to be of higher intelligence . . . than parents in their Inadequate Care group," and then describes several ways in which the study found that maternal intelligence seemed to compensate for other deprivations in the child's life.[49]

With such obvious signals about such tragic problems as child neglect and abuse, perhaps an editorial comment is appropriate: The reluctance of scholars and policymakers alike to look at the role of low intelligence in malparenting may properly be called scandalous.

MATERNAL IQ AND THE WELL-BEING OF INFANTS

Combined with the literature, the NLSY lends further insight into good and bad parenting. We begin with information on the ways in which women of varying cognitive ability care for their children and then turn to the outcomes for the children themselves.

Prenatal Care

In most of the ways that are easily measurable, most white women in the different cognitive classes behaved similarly during pregnancy. Almost everyone got prenatal care, and similar proportions in all cognitive classes began getting it in the early months. If we take the NLSY mothers' self-descriptions at face value, alcohol consumption during pregnancy was about the same across the cognitive classes.[50] The risk of miscarriage or a stillbirth was also spread more or less equally across cognitive classes.

Smoking was the one big and medically important difference related to maternal intelligence: The smarter the women, the less they smoked while they were pregnant. Fifty-one percent of the women in the bottom two cognitive classes smoked, and 19 percent of them admitted to smoking more than a pack a day. In the top two cognitive classes, only 16 percent of the white women in the NLSY smoked at all, and only 4 percent admitted to smoking more than a pack a day. In Class I, no one smoked. Smarter pregnant women smoked less even after controlling for their socioeconomic backgrounds. Higher levels of education, independent of intelligence, also deterred pregnant women from smoking.[51]

Low Birth Weight

We focus here on an indicator that is known to have important implications for the subsequent health, cognitive ability, and emotional development of the child and is also affected to some degree by how well women have cared for themselves during pregnancy: low birth weight.[52] Low birth weight is often caused by behaviors during pregnancy, such as smoking, drug or alcohol abuse, or living exclusively on junk food, that are seldom caused by pure ignorance these days. The pregnant woman who never registers the simple and ubiquitous lessons about taking care of herself and her baby, fails to remember them, or fails to act on them could be willfully irresponsible or in the grip of an irresistible addiction to drugs or junk food, but slow comprehension, a short time horizon, and difficulty in connecting cause and effect are at least as plausible an explanation, and all of these betoken low IQ.

A low-birth-weight baby is defined in these analyses as an infant weighing less than 5.5 pounds at birth, excluding premature babies whose weight was appropriate for their gestational age.[53] The experience of the NLSY mothers is shown in the table below. There does not

Low Birth Weight Among White Babies	
Cognitive Class	Incidence per 1,000 Births
I Very bright	50
II Bright	16
III Normal	32
IV Dull	72
V Very dull	57
Population average	62

appear to be much of a relationship between intelligence and low birth weight; note the high rate for babies of mothers in Class I (which is discussed in the accompanying box). But the table obscures a strong overall relationship between IQ and low birth weight that emerges in the regression analysis shown in the following figure.

A white mother's IQ has a significant role in determining whether her baby is underweight while her socioeconomic background does not

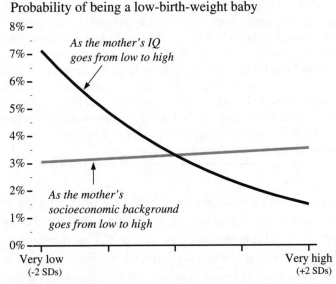

Note: For computing the plot, age and either SES (for the black curve) or IQ (for the gray curve) were set at their mean values.

A low IQ is a major risk factor, whereas the mother's socioeconomic background is irrelevant. A mother at the 2d centile of IQ had a 7 percent chance of giving birth to a low-birth-weight baby, while a mother at the 98th percentile had less than a 2 percent chance.

Adding Poverty. Poverty is an obvious potential factor when trying to explain low birth weight. Overall, poor white mothers (poor in the year before birth) had 61 low-birth-weight babies per 1,000, while other white mothers had 36. But poverty's independent role was small and statistically insignificant, once the other standard variables were taken into account. Meanwhile, the independent role of IQ remained as large, and that of socioeconomic background as small, even after the effects of poverty were extracted.

Can Mothers Be Too Smart for Their Own Good?

The case of low birth weight is the first example of others you will see in which the children of white women in Class I have anomalously bad scores. The obvious, but perhaps too obvious, culprit is sample size. The percentage of low-birth-weight babies for Class I mothers, calculated using sample weights, was produced by just two low-birth-weight babies out of seventy-four births.[54] The sample sizes for white Class I mothers in the other analyses that produce anomalous results are also small, sometimes under fifty and always under one hundred, while the sample sizes for the middle cognitive classes number several hundred or sometimes thousands.

On the other hand, perhaps the children of mothers at the very top of the cognitive distribution do in fact have different tendencies than the rest of the range. The possibility is sufficiently intriguing that we report the anomalous data despite the small sample sizes, and hope that others will explore where we cannot. In the logistic regression analyses, where each case is treated as an individual unit (not grouped into cognitive classes), these problems of sample size do not arise.

Adding mother's age at the time of birth. It is often thought that very young mothers are vulnerable to having low-birth-weight babies, no matter how good the prenatal care may be.[55] This was not true in the NLSY data for white women, however, where the mothers of low-birth weight babies and other mothers had the same mean (24.2 years).

In sum, neither the mother's age in the NLSY cohort, nor age at birth of the child, nor poverty status, nor socioeconomic background had any appreciable relationship to her chances of giving birth to a low-birth-weight baby after her cognitive ability had been taken into account.

Adding education. Among high school graduates (no more, no less) in the NLSY, a plot of the results of the standard analysis looks visually identical to the one presented for the entire sample, but the sample of low-birth-weight babies was so small that the results do not reach statistical significance. Among the college graduates, low-birth-weight babies were so rare (only six out of 277 births to the white college sample) that a multivariate analysis produced no interpretable results. We do not know whether it is the education itself, or the self-selection that goes into having more education, that is responsible for their low incidence of underweight babies.

Infant Mortality

Though we have not been able to find any studies of cognitive ability and infant mortality, it is not hard to think of a rationale linking them. Many things can go wrong with a baby, and parents have to exercise both watchfulness and judgment. It takes more than love to childproof a house effectively; it also takes knowledge and foresight. It takes intelligence to decide that an apparently ordinary bout of diarrhea has gone on long enough to make dehydration a danger; and so on. Nor is simple knowledge enough. As pediatricians can attest, it may not be enough to tell new parents that infants often spike a high fever, that such episodes do not necessarily require a trip to the hospital, but that they require careful attention lest such a routine fever become life threatening. Good parental judgment remains vital. For that matter, the problem facing pediatricians dealing with children of less competent parents is even more basic than getting them to apply good judgment: It is to get such mothers to administer the medication that the doctor has provided.

This rationale is consistent with the link that has been found between education and infant mortality. In a study of all births registered in California in 1978, for example, infant deaths per 1,000 to white women numbered 12.2 for women with less than twelve years of education, 8.3 for those with twelve years, and 6.3 for women with thirteen or more years of education, and the role of education remained significant after controlling for birth order, age of the mother, and marital status.[56]

We have been unable to identify any study that uses tested IQ as an explanatory factor, and, with such a rare event as infant mortality, even the NLSY cannot answer our questions satisfactorily. The results certainly suggest that the questions are worth taking seriously. As of the 1990 survey, the NLSY recorded forty-two deaths among children born to white women with known IQ. Some of these deaths were presumably caused by severe medical problems at birth and occurred in a hospital where the mother's behavior was irrelevant.[57] For infants who died between the second and twelfth month (the closest we can come to defining "after the baby had left the hospital"), the mothers of the surviving children tested six points higher in IQ than the mothers of the deceased babies. (The difference for mothers of children who died in the first month was not quite three points and for the mothers of children who were older than 1 year old when they died, virtually zero.) The samples here are too small to analyze in conjunction with socioeconomic status and other variables.

POVERTY THROUGHOUT EARLY CHILDHOOD

In Chapter 5, we described how the high-visibility policy issue of children in poverty can be better understood when the mother's IQ is brought into the picture. Here, we focus more specifically on the poverty in the early years of a child's life, when it appears to be an especially important factor (independent of other variables) in affecting the child's development.[58] The variable is much more stringent than simply experiencing poverty at some point in childhood. Rather, we ask about the mothers of children who lived under the poverty line throughout their first three years of life, comparing them with mothers who were not in poverty at any time during the child's first three years. The standard analysis is shown in the figure below. There are few other analyses in Part II that show such a steep effect for both intelligence and SES. If the mother has even an average intelligence and average socioeconomic background, the odds of a white child's living in poverty for his or her first three years were under 5 percent. If either of those conditions fell below average, the odds increased steeply.

**A white mother's IQ and socioeconomic background each has
a large independent effect on her child's chances of spending
the first three years of life in poverty**

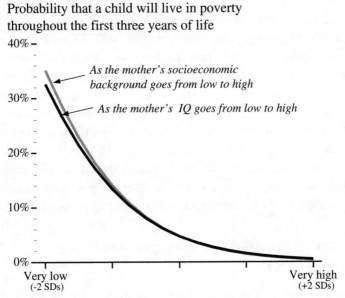

Probability that a child will live in poverty
throughout the first three years of life

As the mother's socioeconomic
background goes from low to high

As the mother's IQ goes from low to high

Very low
(-2 SDs)

Very high
(+2 SDs)

Note: For computing the plot, age and either SES (for the black curve) or IQ (for the gray
curve) were set at their mean values.

The Role of Preexisting Poverty

When we ask whether the mother was in poverty in the year prior to
birth, it turns out that a substantial amount of the effect we attribute to
socioeconomic background in the figure really reflects whether the
mother was already in poverty when the child was born. If you want to
know whether a child will spend his first three years in poverty, the single most useful piece of information is whether the mother was already
living under the poverty line when he was born. Nevertheless, adding
poverty to the equation does not diminish a large independent role for
cognitive ability. A child born to a white mother who was living under
the poverty line but was of average intelligence had almost a 49 percent
chance of living his first three years in poverty. This is an extraordinarily
high chance of living in poverty for American whites as a whole. But if
the same woman were at the 2d centile of intelligence, the odds rose to
89 percent; if she were at the 98th centile, they dropped to 10 percent.[59]

The changes in the odds were proportionately large for women who were not living in poverty when the child was born.

The Role of Education

For children of women with a high school diploma (no more, no less), the relationships of IQ and socioeconomic background to the odds that a child would live in poverty are the same as shown in the figure above—almost equally important, with socioeconomic background fractionally more so—except that the odds are a little lower than for the whole sample (the highest percentages, for mothers two standard deviations below the mean, are in the high 20s, instead of the mid-30s). As this implies, the highest incidence of childhood poverty occurs among women who dropped out of school. Among the white college sample (a bachelor's degree, no more and no less), there was nothing to analyze; only one child of such mothers had lived his first three years in poverty.

IQ AND THE HOME ENVIRONMENT FOR CHILD DEVELOPMENT

In 1986, 1988, and 1990, the NLSY conducted special supplementary surveys of the children and mothers in the sample. The children were given tests of mental, emotional, and physical development, to which we shall turn presently. The mothers were questioned about their children's development and their rearing practices. The home situation was directly observed. The survey instruments were based on the so-called HOME (Home Observation for Measurement of the Environment) index.[60]

Dozens of questions and observations go into creating the summary measures, many of them interesting in themselves. Children of the brightest mothers (who also tend to be the best educated and the most affluent) have a big advantage in many ways, especially on such behaviors as reading to the child. On other indicators that are less critical in themselves, but indirectly suggest how the child is being raised, children with smarter mothers also do better. For example, mothers in the top cognitive classes use physical punishment less often (though they agree in principle that physical punishment can be an appropriate response), and the television set is off more of the time in the homes of the top cognitive classes.

Treating the HOME index as a continuous scale running from "very bad" to "very good" home environments, the advantages of white children with smarter mothers were clear. The average child of a Class V woman lived in a home at the 32d percentile of home environment, while the home of the average child of a Class I woman was at the 76th percentile. The gradations for the three intervening classes were regular as well.[61] Overall, the correlation of the HOME index with IQ for white mothers was +.24, statistically significant but hardly overpowering.

In trying to identify children at risk, this way of looking at the relationship is not necessarily the most revealing. We are willing to assume that a child growing up in a home at the 90th centile on the HOME index has a "better" environment than one growing up at the 50th. Perhaps the difference between a terrific home environment and a merely average one helps produce children who are at the high end on various personality and achievement measures. But it does not necessarily follow that the child in the home at the 50th centile is that much more at risk for the worst outcomes of malparenting than the child at the 90th centile. Both common sense and much of the scholarly work on child development suggest that children are resilient in the face of moderate disadvantages and obstacles and, on the other hand, that parents are frustratingly unable to fine-tune good results for their children.

But resilience has its limits. Children coming from the least nurturing, most punishing environments are indeed at risk. We will therefore focus throughout this section on children who are in the bottom 10 percent on various measures of their homes.[62]

Which White Children Grow Up in the Worst Homes?	
Cognitive Class of the Mother	Percentage of Their Children Growing Up in Homes in the Bottom Decile of the HOME Index
I Very bright	0
II Bright	2
III Normal	6
IV Dull	11
V Very dull	24
All whites	6

In the case of the HOME index, the percentages of white children of mothers in the different cognitive classes who are growing up in homes that scored at the bottom are displayed in the table. It was extremely rare for children of women in the top cognitive classes to grow up in these "worst homes" and quite uncommon for children of women throughout the top three-fourths of the IQ distribution. Only in the bottom cognitive classes did the proportion of such children grow, and then the proportions rose rapidly. Nearly one out of four of the children of the dullest mothers was growing up in a home that also ranked in the bottom decile on the HOME index.[63]

The Role of Socioeconomic Background

The usual assumption about maternal behavior is that a woman's socioeconomic status is crucial—that she passes on to her children the benefits or disadvantages of her own family background. The figure below summarizes the standard analysis comparing SES and IQ.

A white mother's IQ is more important than her socioeconomic background in predicting the worst home environments

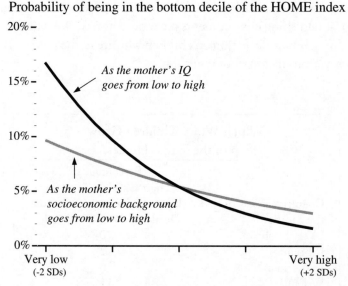

Probability of being in the bottom decile of the HOME index

Note: For computing the plot, age and either SES (for the black curve) or IQ (for the gray curve) were set at their mean values. Additional independent variables were used to control for the test year and the age of the children.

Both factors play a significant role, but once again it is worse (at least for the white NLSY population) to have a mother with a low IQ than one from a low socioeconomic background. Given just an average IQ for the mother, even a mother at the 2d centile on socioeconomic background had less than a 10 percent chance of providing one of the "worst homes" for her children. But even with average socioeconomic background, a mother at the 2d centile of intelligence had almost a 17 percent chance of providing one of these "worst homes."

The Role of Poverty and Welfare

Many of the problems experienced by poor children are usually attributed in both public dialogue and academic writings to poverty itself.[64] The reasons for this widely assumed link between poverty and developmental problems are harder to spell out than you might think. To repeat a point that must always be kept in mind when thinking about poverty: Most of the world's children throughout history have grown up poor, with "poverty" meaning material deprivation far more severe than the meaning of "below the poverty line" in today's America. Many of the disadvantages today's children experience are not the poverty itself but the contemporary correlates of poverty: being without a father, for example, or living in high-crime neighborhoods. Today, high proportions of poor children experience these correlates; fifty years ago, comparatively few poor children did.

But there are reasons to think that the HOME index might be influenced by poverty. Reading to children is a good thing to do, for example, and raises the HOME score, but children's books are expensive. It is easier to have books in the house if you can afford to buy them than if you have to trek to the library—perhaps quite far from home—to get them. Similar comments apply to many of the indicators on the HOME index that do not require wealth but could be affected by very low income. We therefore explored how the HOME index was related to the mother's poverty or welfare recipiency in the calendar year before the HOME score was obtained.[65]

Poverty proved to be important, with "being in a state of poverty" raising the odds of being in the worst decile of the HOME index from 4 percent to 11 percent, given a mother of average IQ and socioeconomic status.[66] But adding poverty to the equation did not diminish the independent role of cognitive ability. For example, if the mother had very low IQ (the 2d centile) *and* was in poverty, the odds of being in the worst decile on the HOME index jumped from 11 percent to 26 percent. Generally, adding poverty to the analysis replaced the impact of the mother's socioeconomic background, not of her intelligence.

Then we turn to welfare. The hypothesis is that going on welfare signifies personality characteristics other than IQ that are likely to make the home environment deficient—irresponsibility, immaturity, or lack of initiative, for example. Therefore, the worst homes on the HOME index will also tend to be welfare homes. This hypothesis too is borne out by the data: Welfare recipiency was a slightly more powerful predictor of being in a "worse home" than poverty—but it had as little effect on the independent role of IQ.

In trying to decide among competing explanations, the simplest thing to do is to enter both poverty and welfare in the analysis and see which wins out. We summarize the outcome by first considering a child whose mother is of average intelligence and socioeconomic background. If his mother is either poor or on welfare (but not both), the odds of having a terrible home environment (bottom decile on the HOME index) are 8 or 9 percent. If the mother has an IQ of 70, the odds shoot up to 18 to 21 percent. If the mother has very low intelligence, is poor, and is also on welfare, the odds rise further, to 34 percent. A table with some of the basic permutations is given in the note.[67]

Still, many of the causal issues remain unresolved. The task for scholars is to specify what it is about poverty that leads to the outcomes associated with it. With the data at hand, we cannot go much further in distinguishing between the effects of lack of money and the effects of other things that "being in poverty" signifies. In particular, the way that poverty and welfare interact in producing a poor home environment provides many hints that need to be followed up.

What can be said unequivocally is that low income as such does not prevent children from being raised in a stimulating, nurturing environment. Such is the story of the regression coefficients, and a conclusion that accords with child rearing throughout history. By the same token, it does not take a genius to provide a child with a stimulating, nurturing environment. The average differences in environment across the cognitive classes are large and in many ways troubling, but, in percentage terms, they explain little of the variance. Abundant examples of excellent parents may be found through all but the very lowest range of cognitive ability.

The Role of Education

We conclude, as usual, by considering the role of education through the high school graduate and college graduate subsamples. Holding maternal age and the mother's socioeconomic background constant at their means, college graduates tend to do well, no matter what their cognitive ability (within their restricted range), even though cognitive ability retains a statistically significant relationship. Within the high school sample, the effects of cognitive ability are plain; the odds of being in the bottom decile on the HOME index for the child of a mother of average socioeconomic background drop from 15 percent for a high school graduate at the 2d IQ centile to 5 percent for a comparable person at the 98th IQ centile. As in the earlier analyses, the most important impact of cognitive ability within the high school graduates seems to be at the low end. Socioeconomic background also continues to play an important independent role, but less than IQ.

DEVELOPMENTAL OUTCOMES

The NLSY also administered batteries of tests regarding the developmental outcomes for the children of NLSY mothers. We review several indicators briefly, then present a summary index showing the interrelationships the mother's cognitive ability, socioeconomic background, poverty, and welfare.

Some More Complications

The HOME inventory has two components—a Cognitive Stimulation score and an Emotional Support score—both adapted to three separate age groups (under 3, 3 to 5, and over 5 years of age). We conducted a variety of analyses to explore the subtests' roles for different age groups. Briefly, the mother's IQ had the dominant role in determining the Emotional Support score for children through the age of 5, whereas its role in determining Cognitive Stimulation was roughly coequal with education and socioeconomic background—the opposite of what one might predict. Maternal IQ was especially important for Emotional Support to the 3- to 5-year-old group. It would be worthwhile for investigators to explore with other data the NLSY's indications that parental IQ is especially important for the home environment from ages 3 to 5, and the peculiar finding that parental IQ is more important for Emotional Support than for Cognitive Stimulation.

Temperament in Very Young Children

The first of the measures applies to very young children (12 to 23 months), and consists of indexes of "difficulty" and "friendliness." Once again we focus on children who exhibit the most conspicuous signs of having problems—those in the bottom decile—as shown in the following table.[68] Generally, babies were more "difficult"—more irritable, more fearful, and less sociable—for mothers with lower cognitive ability, and they were also less friendly, as measured by this index.

Which White Toddlers Have the Worst Temperaments?		
Percentage of Children in the Most Difficult Decile on the Difficulty Index	Cognitive Class of the Mother	Percentage of Children in the Least Friendly Decile on the Friendliness Index
—	I Very bright	—
4	II Bright	3
8	III Normal	5
14	IV Dull	11
—	V Very dull	12
8	All whites	6

Motor and Social Development in Infants and Toddlers

Motor and social development is, in effect, a set of measures designed to capture whether the child is progressing in the ways described as normal in the baby manuals by Spock, Brazelton, et al. The table below shows the results for children through the age of 3. The results look like a U-shaped curve, with a big jump in Class V. Since sample sizes in both Class I and Class V are under 100 (75 and 81, respectively), this information falls in the category of interesting but uncertain.

Behavioral Problems in Older Children

For older children, the NLSY employed an instrument that measured behavioral problems, with subscales on antisocial behavior, depression,

Which White Children Are Behind in Motor and Social Development?	
Cognitive Class of the Mother	Percentage of Children in the Bottom Decile of the Motor & Social Development Index
I Very bright	10
II Bright	5
III Normal	6
IV Dull	10
V Very dull	32
All whites	7

headstrongness, hyperactivity, immature dependency, and peer conflict/social withdrawal. The table below shows the results for those who had the most severe problems—those in the worst 10 percent on these measures.

Which White Children Have the Worst Behavioral Problems?	
Cognitive Class ofthe Mother	Percentage of Children in the Worst Decile of the Behavioral Problems Index
I Very bright	11
II Bright	6
III Normal	10
IV Dull	12
V Very dull	21
All whites	10

Once again, there is the curious case of the elevated percentage for children of mothers in Class I. The most prudent assumption is that it is an artifact of small sample sizes, but the possibility remains that something else is going on worth investigating in greater detail, with larger samples.

An Index of Developmental Problems

Each of the developmental indexes we have reviewed is based on a number of individual items, which in turn lend themselves to a wide variety of analyses that would take us far beyond the scope of this discussion.

We conducted many analyses for the separate indexes, but the overall patterns were similar. For our purposes in conveying to you the general pattern of results, it is sufficient to summarize the results for a broad question: What independent role, if any, does the mother's IQ have on the probability that her child experiences a substantial developmental problem? We created a simple "developmental problem index," in which the child scores Yes if he or she were in the bottom decile of any of the four indicators in a given test year, and No if not. The results are shown in the next figure.

Both a white mother's IQ and socioeconomic background have moderate relationships with the developmental problems in the child

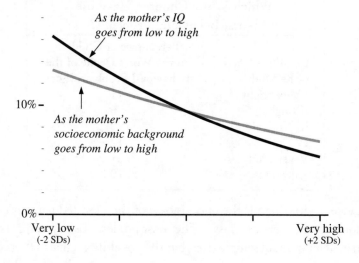

Probability of having a child in the bottom decile on one of the developmental indicators

20% –

As the mother's IQ goes from low to high

10% –

As the mother's socioeconomic background goes from low to high

0% –

Very low
(-2 SDs)

Very high
(+2 SDs)

The pattern shown in the figure generally applies to the four development indicators separately: IQ has a somewhat larger independent effect than socioeconomic background, but of modest size and marginal statistical significance.

The Role of Poverty, Welfare, and Illegitimacy

We repeated the analyses adding a poverty variable (Was the mother living in poverty in the year the developmental measures were taken?), a welfare variable (Was the mother on AFDC in the year the developmental measures were taken?), and legitimacy variable (Was the child born outside marriage?) When entered separately or in combination, each had a statistically significant independent role.[69] Consider the stark contrast between a child born to an unmarried mother, on welfare and in poverty, and a child born to a married mother, not on welfare and above the poverty line. Given a mother with average IQ and socioeconomic background, the chances that the first child had a substantial developmental problem were almost twice as high as those facing the second child—15 percent compared to 8 percent. But taking these factors into account did not wipe out the independent role of either IQ or the mother's socioeconomic background; in fact, the independent effects of IQ and socioeconomic background after extracting the independent role of poverty, illegitimacy, and welfare, is visually almost indistinguishable from the one shown above.

The Role of Education

Analyses of the college graduate sample were provocative but no more than that, because only 29 out of 470 children of white college graduates who were tested (6 percent) showed up with a substantial developmental problem. The provocative finding was that among those 29, 5 were children of women in Class I (10 percent of the 50 such children tested). Thus in the college sample, the statistical result of holding socioeconomic background constant was that higher IQ was associated with a substantially higher probability of having developmental problems. Five out of 50 is of course not enough to make much of these numbers, but we commend the finding to our colleagues who specialize in child development.

Within the high school sample, the independent roles of IQ and socioeconomic background were almost identical, and of the same order of magnitude indicated in the figure for the entire white sample.

THE COGNITIVE OUTCOME

We finally come to the intelligence of the children of white NLSY women. The measure of intelligence we shall be using is the Peabody Picture Vocabulary Test (PPVT), a widely used measure of cognitive ability in children that has the advantage of not requiring that the child be able to read. The scores for the NLSY children are expressed in terms of the national norms for the PPVT, which use a mean of 100 and a standard deviation of 15. Because IQ scores tend to be volatile for children under the age of 6, we limit the sample to children who were at least 6 when they took the test.

The unsurprising news in the next table is that the children tend to resemble their mothers in IQ.[70] But by continuing to use the "worst

---

IQ in the Mother and the Child for Whites in the NLSY

Cognitive Class of the Mothers	Mean IQ of Their Children	Percentage of Their Children in the Bottom Decile of IQ
I Very bright	—	—
II Bright	107	7
III Normal	100	6
IV Dull	95	17
V Very dull	81	39
All whites	99	10

---

decile" as a way of zeroing in on the children most at risk, the table makes another point: White parents throughout the top three-quarters of the IQ distribution have few children who fall into the bottom decile of IQ.[71] For mothers in the bottom quarter of the distribution, however, the proportion of low IQ children rises precipitously. We return to this issue in Chapter 15.

The Role of Socioeconomic Background

Consistent with the conclusions drawn in a large technical literature, the IQ of the NLSY mothers was much more important than their socioeconomic background in determining their children's IQ.[72] A white child's IQ in the NLSY sample went up by 6.3 IQ points for each increase of one standard deviation in the mother's IQ, compared to 1.7 points for each increase of one standard deviation in the mother's socioeconomic background (in an analysis that also extracted the effects of the mother's age, the test year, and the age of the child when tested). When we examine the probability that the child will fall in the bottom decile of IQ, we arrived at the results shown in the next figure.

A white mother's IQ dominates the importance of socioeconomic background in determining the child's IQ

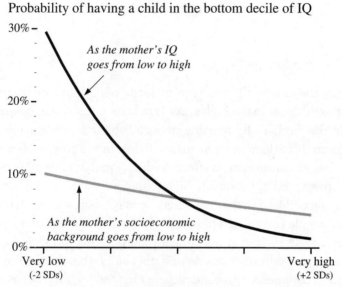

Probability of having a child in the bottom decile of IQ

As the mother's IQ goes from low to high

As the mother's socioeconomic background goes from low to high

Very low (-2 SDs) — Very high (+2 SDs)

Note: For computing the plot, age and either SES (for the black curve) or IQ (for the gray curve) were set at their mean values. Additional independent variables were used to control for the test year and the age of the children when they took the test.

A mother at the 2d IQ centile but of average socioeconomic background had a 30 percent chance that her child would be in the bottom decile of IQ, compared to only a 10 percent chance facing the woman from an equivalently terrible socioeconomic background (2d centile on the SES index) but with an average IQ.

The Role of Poverty and the Home Environment

In discussions of IQ among disadvantaged groups, it seems plausible that factors such as poverty and the aspects of the home environment would have an effect on the child's IQ. Suppose, for example, we were to ignore the mother's IQ, and look only at her socioeconomic background, her poverty status in the year before her child was tested, and her HOME index score. In that case, we could document the conventional wisdom: both socioeconomic background and the home environment have large effects on whether a child scores in the bottom IQ decile. Poverty has a smaller and statistically marginal effect. But when we add the mother's IQ, all of those other effects become both small in magnitude and statistically insignificant. After taking socioeconomic background, the HOME index, and pretest poverty into account, the independent effect of IQ remains virtually identical to the one shown on the preceding figure.

The Role of Education

None of the children in the bottom decile of IQ had a mother with a bachelor's degree. In the high school graduate sample, the independent role of the mother's IQ remains large and the independent role of socioeconomic background remains small. But in the process of exploring this issue, we came upon an effect of education that is worth exploring: Women who did not complete high school were at much higher risk of producing children in the bottom decile of IQ than women in the high school sample (meaning a high school diploma and exactly 12 years of education), even after controlling for mother's IQ and socioeconomic background. Additional analyses did not clarify what this finding might mean; we commend it to our colleagues for a full-scale analysis.

THE ASYMMETRY OF GOOD AND BAD PARENTS

Granting the many exceptions at the individual level, the relationship of cognitive ability to parenting is unmistakable. Some of these analyses have involved measures that are arguable. Can we really be sure that the indicators of what constitutes a stimulating and nurturing environment are not just reflections of the preferences of the upper middle class? We hope our readers do not take this easy way out. If the indicators that were used in the studies we have reported are indeed ones that you find valid in your own beliefs about what children need, then the conclusion follows: Over the long run and in the broad perspective, based on your best understanding of the realities of child rearing, smart parents tend to be better parents. People with low cognitive ability tend to be worse parents. This conclusion holds for a wide range of parenting behaviors, from prenatal negligence that leads to low birth weight, to postnatal treatment of the child associated with neglect and abuse, to developmental outcomes, to cognitive outcomes.

On the other hand, these data provide little or no evidence that the smartest women make the best mothers. Children can flourish in a wide variety of environments that are merely okay. But some environments are so bad that no one can seriously dispute that they are bad, and even the most resilient children have difficulty overcoming them. These truly disadvantaged homes are disproportionately associated with women at the low end of the intelligence distribution, even after other contributing factors such as poverty and socioeconomic status are taken into account.

Chapter 11

Crime

Among the most firmly established facts about criminal offenders is that their distribution of IQ scores differs from that of the population at large. Taking the scientific literature as a whole, criminal offenders have average IQs of about 92, eight points below the mean. More serious or chronic offenders generally have lower scores than more casual offenders. The relationship of IQ to criminality is especially pronounced in the small fraction of the population, primarily young men, who constitute the chronic criminals that account for a disproportionate amount of crime. Offenders who have been caught do not score much lower, if at all, than those who are getting away with their crimes. Holding socioeconomic status constant does little to explain away the relationship between crime and cognitive ability.

High intelligence also provides some protection against lapsing into criminality for people who otherwise are at risk. Those who have grown up in turbulent homes, have parents who were themselves criminal, or who have exhibited the childhood traits that presage crime are less likely to become criminals as adults if they have high IQ.

These findings from an extensive research literature are supported by the evidence from white males in the NLSY. Low IQ was a risk factor for criminal behavior, whether criminality was measured by incarceration or by self-acknowledged crimes. The socioeconomic background of the NLSY's white males was a negligible risk factor once their cognitive ability was taken into account.

Crime can tear a free society apart, because free societies depend so crucially on faith that the other person will behave decently. As crime grows, society must substitute coercion for cooperation. The first casualty is not just freedom but the bonds that make community life at-

235

tractive. Yes, it is always possible to buy better locks, stay off the streets after dark, regard every stranger suspiciously, post security guards everywhere, but these are poor substitutes for living in a peaceful and safe neighborhood.

Most Americans think that crime has gotten far too high. But in the ruminations about how the nation has reached this state and what might be done, too little attention has been given to one of the best-documented relationships in the study of crime: As a group, criminals are below average in intelligence.

As with so many of the other problems discussed in the previous six chapters, things were not always so bad. Good crime statistics do not go back very far in the United States, but we do not need statistics to remind Americans alive in the 1990s of times when they felt secure walking late at night, alone, even in poor neighborhoods and even in the nation's largest cities. In the mid-1960s, crime took a conspicuous turn for the worse. The overall picture using the official statistics is shown in the figure below, expressed as multiples of the violent crime rate in 1950.

The figure shows the kind of crime that worries most people most viscerally: violent crime, which consists of robbery, murder, aggravated assault, and rape. From 1950 through 1963, the rate for violent crime was

The boom in violent crime after the 1950s

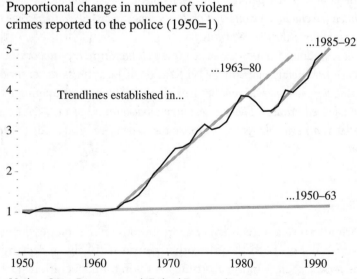

Proportional change in number of violent crimes reported to the police (1950=1)

Trendlines established in...

...1963–80

...1985–92

...1950–63

Source: Uniform Crime Reports, annual, Federal Bureau of Investigation.

almost flat, followed by an extremely rapid rise from 1964 to 1971, followed by continued increases until the 1980s. The early 1980s saw an interlude in which violent crime decreased noticeably. But the trendline for 1985–1992 is even steeper than the one for 1963–1980, making it look as if the lull was just that—a brief respite from an increase in violent crime that is now thirty years old.[1]

There is still some argument among the experts about whether the numbers in the graph, drawn from the FBI's *Uniform Crime Reports*, mean what they seem to mean. But the disagreement has limits. Drawing on sophisticated analyses of these numbers, the consensus conclusions are that victimization studies, based on interviews of crime victims and therefore including crimes not reported to the police, indicate that the increase in the total range of crimes since 1973 has not been as great as the official statistics suggest, but that the increase reflected in the official statistics is also real, capturing changes in crimes that people consider serious enough to warrant reporting to the police.[2]

DEPRAVED OR DEPRIVED?

The juvenile delinquents in Leonard Bernstein's *West Side Story* tell Officer Krupke that they are "depraved on account of we're deprived," showing an astute grasp of the poles in criminological theory: the psychological and the sociological.[3] Are criminals psychologically distinct? Or are they ordinary people responding to social and economic circumstances?

Theories of criminal behavior were mostly near the sociological pole from the 1950s through the 1970s. Its leading scholars saw criminals as much like the rest of us, except that society earmarks them for a life of criminality. Some of these scholars went further, seeing criminals as free of personal blame, evening up the score with a society that has victimized them. The most radical theorists from the sociological pole argued that the definition of crime was in itself ideological, creating "criminals" of people who were doing nothing more than behaving in ways that the power structure chose to define as deviant. In their more moderate forms, sociological explanations continue to dominate public discourse. Many people take it for granted, for example, that poverty and unemployment cause crime—classic sociological arguments that are distinguished more by their popularity than by evidence.[4]

Theories nearer the psychological pole were more common earlier in the history of criminology and have lately regained acceptance among experts. Here, the emphasis shifts to the characteristics of the offender rather than to his circumstances. The idea is that criminals are distinctive in psychological (perhaps even biological) ways. They are deficient, depending on the particular theory, in conscience or in self-restraint. They lack normal attachment to the mores of their culture, or they are peculiarly indifferent to the feelings or the good opinion of others. They are overendowed with restless energy or with a hunger for adventure or danger. In a term that was in common use throughout the nineteenth and early twentieth centuries, chronic offenders may be suffering from "moral insanity."[5] In other old-fashioned vocabularies, they have been called inhumane, atavistic, demented, monstrous, or bestial—all words that depict certain individuals as something less than human. In their most extreme form, psychological theories say that some people are born criminal, destined by their biological makeup to offend.

We are at neither of these theoretical poles. Like almost all other students of crime, we expect to find explanations from both sociology and psychology. The reason for calling attention to the contrast between the theories is that public discussion has lagged; it remains more nearly stuck at the sociological pole in public discourse than it is among experts. In this chapter, we are interested in the role that cognitive ability plays in creating criminal offenders. This by no means requires us to deny that sociology, economics, and public policy might play an important part in shaping crime rates. On the contrary, we assume that changes in those domains are likely to interact with personal characteristics.

Among the arguments often made against the claim that criminals are psychologically distinctive, two are arguments in principle rather than in fact. We will comment on these two first, because they do not require any extensive review of the factual evidence.

> Argument 1: Crime rates have changed in recent times more than people's cognitive ability or personalities could have. We must therefore find the reason for the rising crime rates in people's changing circumstances.

When crime is changing quickly, it seems hard to blame changing personal characteristics rather than changing social conditions. But bear in mind that personal characteristics need not change everywhere in society for crime's aggregate level in society to change. Consider age, for example, since crime is mainly the business of young people between 15 and 24.[6] When the age distribution of the population shifts toward more people in their peak years for crime, the average level of crime may be expected to rise. Or crime may rise disproportionately if a large bulge in the youthful sector of the population fosters a youth culture that relishes unconventionality over traditional adult values. The exploding crime rate of the 1960s is, for example, partly explained by the baby boomers' reaching adolescence.[7] Or suppose that a style of child rearing sweeps the country, and it turns out that this style of child rearing leads to less control over the behavior of rebellious adolescents. The change in style of child rearing may predictably be followed, fifteen or so years later, by a change in crime rates. If, in short, circumstances tip toward crime, the change will show up most among those with the strongest tendencies to break laws (or the weakest tendencies to obey them).[8] Understanding those tendencies is the business of theories at the psychological pole.

   Argument 2: Behavior is criminal only because society says so. There cannot be psychological tendencies to engage in behavior defined so arbitrarily.

This argument, made frequently during the 1960s and 1970s and always more popular among intellectuals than with the general public, is heard most often opposing any suggestion that criminal behavior has biological roots. How can something so arbitrary, say, as not paying one's taxes or driving above a 55 mph speed limit be inherited? the critics ask. Behavior regarding taxes and speed limits certainly cannot be coded in our DNA; perhaps even more elemental behaviors such as robbery and murder cannot either.

Our counterargument goes like this: Instead of crime, consider behavior that is less controversial and even more arbitrary, like playing the violin. A violin is a cultural artifact, no less arbitrary than any other man-made object, and so is the musical scale. Yet few people would argue that the first violinists in the nation's great orchestras are a random sample of the population. The interests, talents, self-discipline, and dedication that it takes to reach their level of accomplishment have roots in individual psychology—quite possibly even in biology. The variation across people in *any* behavior, however arbitrary, will have such roots. To that we may add that the core crimes represented in the violent crime and property crime indexes—murder, robbery, and assault—are really not so arbitrary, unless the moral codes of human cultures throughout the world may be said to be consistently arbitrary in pretty much the same way throughout recorded human history.

But even if crime is admitted to be a psychological phenomenon, why should intelligence be important? What is the logic that might lead us to expect low intelligence to be more frequently linked with criminal tendencies than high intelligence is?[9]

One chain of reasoning starts from the observation that low intelligence often translates into failure and frustration in school and in the job market. If, for example, people of low intelligence have a hard time finding a job, they might have more reason to commit crimes as a way of making a living. If people of low intelligence have a hard time acquiring status through the ordinary ways, crime might seem like a good alternative route. At the least, their failures in school and at work may foster resentment toward society and its laws.

Perhaps the link between crime and low IQ is even more direct. A lack of foresight, which is often associated with low IQ, raises the attractions of the immediate gains from crime and lowers the strength of the deterrents, which come later (if they come at all). To a person of low intelligence, the threats of apprehension and prison may fade to meaninglessness. They are too abstract, too far in the future, too uncertain.

Low IQ may be part of a broader complex of factors. An appetite for danger, a stronger-than-average hunger for the things that you can get only by stealing if you cannot buy them, an antipathy toward conventionality, an insensitivity to pain or to social ostracism, and a host of derangements of various sorts, combined with low IQ, may set the stage for a criminal career.

Finally, there are moral considerations. Perhaps the ethical principles for not committing crimes are less accessible (or less persuasive) to people of low intelligence. They find it harder to understand why robbing someone is wrong, find it harder to appreciate the values of civil and cooperative social life, and are accordingly less inhibited from acting in ways that are hurtful to other people and to the community at large.

With these preliminaries in mind, let us explore the thesis that, whatever the underlying reasons might be, the people who lapse into criminal behavior are distinguishable from the population at large in their distribution of intelligence.

THE LINK BETWEEN COGNITIVE ABILITY AND CRIMINAL BEHAVIOR: AN OVERVIEW

The statistical association between crime and cognitive ability has been known since intelligence testing began in earnest. The British physician Charles Goring mentioned a lack of intelligence as one of the distinguishing traits of the prison population that he described in a landmark contribution to modern criminology early in the century.[10] In 1914, H. H. Goddard, an early leader in both modern criminology and the use of intelligence tests, concluded that a large fraction of convicts were intellectually subnormal.[11]

The subsequent history of the study of the link between IQ and crime replays the larger story of intelligence testing, with the main difference being that the attack on the IQ/crime link began earlier than the broader attempt to discredit IQ tests. Even in the 1920s, the link was called into question, for example, by psychologist Carl Murchison, who produced data showing that the prisoners of Leavenworth had a higher mean IQ than that of enlisted men in World War I.[12] Then in 1931, Edwin Sutherland, America's most prominent criminologist, wrote "Mental Deficiency and Crime," an article that effectively put an end to the study of IQ and crime for half a century.[13] Observing (accurately) that the ostensible IQ differences between criminals and the general population were diminishing as testing procedures improved, Sutherland leaped to the conclusion that the remaining differences would disappear altogether as the state of the art improved.

The difference, in fact, did not disappear, but that did not stop criminology from denying the importance of IQ as a predictor of criminal behavior. For decades, criminologists who followed Sutherland argued that the IQ numbers said nothing about a real difference in intelligence between offenders and nonoffenders. They were skeptical about whether the convicts in prisons were truly representative of offenders in general, and they disparaged the tests' validity. Weren't tests just measuring socioeconomic status by other means, and weren't they biased against the people from the lower socioeconomic classes or the minority groups who were most likely to break the law for other reasons? they asked. By the 1960s, the association between intelligence and crime was altogether dismissed in criminology textbooks, and so it remained until recently. By the end of the 1970s, students taking introductory courses in criminology could read in one widely used textbook that the belief in a correlation between low intelligence and crime "has almost disappeared in recent years as a consequence of more cogent research findings,"[14] or learn from another standard textbook of "the practical abandonment of feeblemindedness as a cause of crime."[15]

It took two of the leading criminologists of another generation, Travis Hirschi and Michael Hindelang, to resurrect the study of IQ and criminality that Sutherland had buried. In their 1977 article, "Intelligence and Delinquency: A Revisionist View," they reviewed many studies that included IQ measures, took into account the potential artifacts, and concluded that juvenile delinquents were in fact characterized by substantially below-average levels of tested intelligence.[16] Hirschi and Hindelang's work took a while to percolate through the academy (the author of the 1982 edition of one of the textbooks quoted above continued to make no mention whatever of IQ),[17] but by the end of the 1980s, most criminologists accepted not just that an IQ gap separates offenders and nonoffenders, but that the gap is genuinely a difference in average intellectual level or, as it is sometimes euphemistically called, "academic competence." Criminology textbooks now routinely report the correlation between crime and intelligence, and although some questions of interpretation are still open, they are narrower than they used to be because the correlation itself is no longer in dispute.[18]

The Size of the IQ Gap

How big is the difference between criminals and the rest of us? Taking the literature as a whole, incarcerated offenders average an IQ of about 92, 8 points below the mean. The population of nonoffenders averages more than 100 points; an informed guess puts the gap between offenders and nonoffenders at about 10 points.[19] More serious or more chronic offenders generally have lower scores than more casual offenders.[20] The eventual relationship between IQ and repeat offending is already presaged in IQ scores taken when the children are 4 years old.[21]

Not only is there a gap in IQ between offenders and nonoffenders, but a disproportionately large fraction of all crime is committed by people toward the low end of the scale of intelligence. For example, in a twenty-year longitudinal study of over 500 hundred boys in an unidentified Swedish community, 30 percent of all arrests of the men by the age of 30 were of the 6 percent with IQs below 77 (at the age of 10) and 80 percent were of those with IQs below 100.[22] However, it stands to reason (and is supported by the data) that the population of offenders is short of very low-scoring persons—people whose scores are so low that they have trouble mustering the competence to commit most crimes.[23] A sufficiently low IQ is, in addition, usually enough to exempt a person from criminal prosecution.[24]

Do the Unintelligent Ones Commit More Crimes—or Just Get Caught More Often?

Some critics continue to argue that offenders whose IQs we know are unrepresentative of the true criminal population; the smart ones presumably slipped through the net. Surely this is correct to some degree. If intelligence has anything to do with a person's general competence, then it is not implausible that smart criminals get arrested less often because they pick safer crimes or because they execute their crimes more skillfully.[25] But how much of a bias does this introduce into the data? Is there a population of uncaught offenders with high IQs committing large numbers of crimes? The answer seems to be no. The crimes we can trace to the millions of offenders who do pass through the criminal justice system and whose IQs are known account for much of the crime around us, particularly the serious crime. There is no evidence for any other large population of offenders, and barely enough crime left unaccounted for to permit such a population's existence.

In the small amount of data available, the IQs of uncaught offenders are not measurably different from the ones who get caught.[26] Among those who have criminal records, there is still a significant negative correlation between IQ and frequency of offending.[27] Both of these kinds of evidence imply that differential arrests of people with varying IQs, assuming they exist, are a minor factor in the aggregate data.

Intelligence as a Preventative

Looking at the opposite side of the picture, those who do not commit crimes, it appears that high cognitive ability protects a person from becoming a criminal even if the other precursors are present. One study followed a sample of almost 1,500 boys born in Copenhagen, Denmark, between 1936 and 1938.[28] Sons whose fathers had a prison record were almost six times as likely to have a prison record themselves (by the age of 34–36) as the sons of men who had no police record of any sort. Among these high-risk sons, the ones who had no police record at all had IQ scores one standard deviation higher than the sons who had a police record.[29]

The protective power of elevated intelligence also shows up in a New Zealand study. Boys and girls were divided on the basis of their behavior by the age of 5 into high and low risk for delinquency. High-risk children were more than twice as likely to become delinquent by their mid-teens as low-risk children. The high-risk boys or girls who did *not* become delinquent were the ones with the higher IQs. This was also true for the low-risk boys and girls: The nondelinquents had higher IQs than the delinquents.[30]

Children growing up in troubled circumstances on Kauai in the Hawaiian chain confirm the pattern. Several hundred children were followed in a longitudinal study for several decades.[31] Some of the children were identified by their second birthday as being statistically "vulnerable" to behavioral disorders or delinquency. These were children suffering from two or more of the following circumstances: they were being raised in troubled or impoverished families; had alcoholic, psychologically disturbed, or unschooled (eight years or less of schooling) parents; or had experienced prenatal or perinatal physiological stress. Two-thirds of these children succumbed to delinquency or other psychological disturbances. But how about the other third, the ones who grew up without becoming delinquents or disturbed psychologically? Prominent among the protective factors were higher intellectual ability scores than the average for the vulnerable group.[32]

THE LINK BETWEEN COGNITIVE ABILITY AND CRIMINAL BEHAVIOR: WHITE MEN IN THE NLSY

In the United States, where crime and race have become so intertwined in the public mind, it is especially instructive to focus on just whites. To

---

The Rest of the Story

The statistically distinguishable personal characteristics of criminals go far beyond IQ. There is, for example, the enormous difference between the levels of male and female criminality, which cannot be explained by intellectual differences between the sexes. Accounts of the rapidly expanding literature on the psychological and biological correlates of criminality, which has become highly informative about everything from genes to early childhood precursors, may be tracked in numerous scientific journals and books.[33] Probably as much could be learned about individual differences beyond intelligence that characterize the chronically unemployed, unmarried mothers, neglectful parents, and others who have been the subjects of the other chapters in Part II. But that is just surmise at this point. The necessary research has either not been done at all or has been done in only the sketchiest way.[34]

---

simplify matters, we also limit the NLSY sample to males. Crime is still overwhelmingly a man's vice. Among whites in the sample, 83 percent of all persons who admitted to a criminal conviction were male.

Interpreting Self-Report Data

In the 1980 interview wave, the members of the NLSY sample were asked detailed questions about their criminal activity and their involvement with the criminal justice system. These data are known as *self-report data*, meaning that we have to go on what the respondent says. One obvious advantage of self-reports is that they presumably include information about the crimes of offenders whether or not they have been caught. Another is that they circumvent any biases in the criminal justice system, which, some people argue, contaminate official criminal statistics. But can self-report data be trusted? Criminologists have explored this question for many years, and the answer is yes, but only if the data are treated gingerly. Different racial groups have different response patterns, and these are compounded by differences between the genders.[35] [36] Other issues are discussed in the note.[36]

Our use of the NLSY self-report data sidesteps some of the problems by limiting the analysis to one ethnic group and one gender: white males. Given the remaining problems with self-report data, we will concentrate in this analysis on events that are on the public record (and the respondent knows are on the public record): being stopped by the police, formal charges, and convictions. In doing so, we are following a broad finding in crime research that official contacts with the law enforcement and criminal justice system are usefully accurate reflections of the underlying level of criminal activity.[37] At the end of the discussion, we show briefly that using self-report data on undetected crimes reinforces the conclusions drawn from the data on detected crimes.

IQ and Types of Criminal Involvement

The typical finding has been that between a third and a half of all juveniles are stopped by police at some time or another (a proportion that has grown over the last few decades) but that 5 to 7 percent of the population account for about half the total number of arrests.[38] In the case of white males in the NLSY, 34 percent admitted having been stopped at some time by the police (for anything other than a minor traffic violation), but only 3 percent of all white males accounted for half of the self-reported "stops."

Something similar applies as we move up the ladder of criminal severity. Only 18 percent of white males had ever formally been charged with an offense, and a little less than 3 percent of them accounted for half the charges. Only 13 percent of white males had ever been convicted of anything, and 2 percent accounted for half of the convictions. Based on these self-reports, a very small minority of white males had serious criminal records while they were in this 15 to 23 age range.

Like studies using all races, the NLSY results for white males show a regular relationship between IQ and criminality. The table below presents the average IQs of white males who had penetrated to varying levels of the criminal justice system as of the 1980 interview.[39] Those who

Criminality and IQ Among White Males	
Deepest Level of Contact with the Criminal Justice System	**Mean IQ**
None	106
Stopped by the police but not booked	103
Booked but not convicted	101
Convicted but not incarcerated	100
Sentenced to a correctional facility	93

reported they had never even been stopped by the police (for anything other than a minor traffic violation) were above average in intelligence, with a mean IQ of 106, and things went downhill from there. Close to a standard deviation separated those who had never been stopped by the police from those who went to prison.

A similar pattern emerges when the criminal involvements are sorted by cognitive class, as shown in the next table. Involvement with the criminal justice system rises as IQ falls from Classes I through IV. Then

The Odds of Getting Involved with the Police and Courts for Young White Males				
Percentage Who in 1980 Reported Ever Having Been:				
Cognitive Class	Stopped by the Police	Booked for an Offense	Convicted of an Offense	Sentenced to Incarceration
I Very bright	18	5	3	0
II Bright	27	12	7	1
III Normal	37	20	15	3
IV Dull	46	27	21	7
V Very dull	33	17	14	7
Overall	34	18	9	3

we reach Class V, with IQs under 75. If we take the responses at face value, the Class Vs are stopped, charged, and convicted at lower rates than the Class IVs but are sentenced to correctional facilities at rates almost exactly the same rate. We noted earlier that people at the lowest levels of intelligence are likely to be underrepresented in criminal statistics, and so it is in the NLSY. It may be that the offenses of the Class Vs are less frequent but more serious than those of the Class IVs or that they are less competent in getting favorable treatment from the criminal justice system. The data give us no way to tell.

In addition to self-reports, the NLSY provides data on criminal behavior by noting where the person was interviewed. In all the interviews from 1979 to 1990, was the young man ever interviewed in a correctional facility? The odds shown in the table below (computed from the unrounded results) that a white male had ever been interviewed in jail

The Odds of Doing Time for Young White Males	
Cognitive Class	Percentage Ever Interviewed in a Correctional Facility
I Very bright	1
II Bright	1
III Normal	3
IV Dull	7
V Very dull	12
Overall	3

were fourteen times greater for Class V than for white males anywhere in the top quartile of IQ.

Being incarcerated at the time of the interview signifies not just breaking the law and serving time but also something about the duration of the sentence, which may explain the large increase at the bottom of the ability distribution. The NLSY sample of white males echoes the scientific literature in general in showing a sizable IQ gap between offenders and nonoffenders at each level of involvement with the criminal justice system.

The Role of Socioeconomic Background

We will use both self-reports and whether the interviewee was incarcerated at the time of the interview as measures of criminal behavior. The self-reports are from the NLSY men in 1980, when they were still in their teens or just out of them. It combines reports of misdemeanors, drug offenses, property offenses, and violent offenses. Our definition of criminality here is that the man's description of his own behavior put him in the top decile of frequency of self-reported criminal activity.[40] The other measure is whether the man was ever interviewed while being confined in a correctional facility between 1979 and 1990. When we run our standard analysis for these two different measures, we get the results in the next figure.

Both measures of criminality have weaknesses but different weaknesses. One relies on self-reports but has the virtue of including uncaught criminality; the other relies on the workings of the criminal justice system but has the virtue of identifying people who almost certainly have committed serious offenses. For both measures, after con-

On two diverse measures of crime, the importance of IQ dominates socioeconomic background for white men

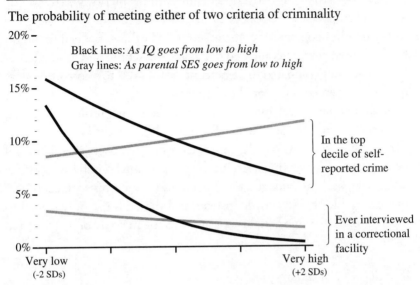

The probability of meeting either of two criteria of criminality

Black lines: *As IQ goes from low to high*
Gray lines: *As parental SES goes from low to high*

In the top decile of self-reported crime

Ever interviewed in a correctional facility

Very low (-2 SDs)

Very high (+2 SDs)

Note: For computing the plot, age and either SES (for the black curves) or IQ (for the gray curves) were set at their mean values.

trolling for IQ, the men's socioeconomic background had little or nothing to do with crime. In the case of the self-report data, higher socioeconomic status was associated with *higher* reported crime after controlling for IQ. In the case of incarceration, the role of socioeconomic background was close to nil after controlling for IQ, and statistically insignificant. By either measure of crime, a low IQ was a significant risk factor.

The Role of a Broken Home

When people think about the causes of crime, they usually think not only of the role of juvenile delinquent's age and socioeconomic background but also of what used to be called "broken homes." It is now an inadequate phrase, because many families do not even begin with a married husband and wife, and many broken homes are reconstituted (in some sense) through remarriage. But whatever the specific way in which a home is not intact, the children of such families are usually more likely to get in trouble with the law than children from intact families.[41] This was true for the NLSY white males. An intact family consisting of the biological mother and father was associated with better outcomes for their children than any of the other family arrangements. Was the young man ever stopped by the police? Thirty-two percent of white males from intact families compared to 46 percent of all others. Booked for an offense? Fifteen percent compared to 29 percent. Convicted of an offense? Eleven percent compared to 21 percent. Sentenced to a correctional facility? Two percent compared to 7 percent.

Although family setting had an impact on crime, it did not explain away the predictive power of IQ. For example, a young man from a broken family and an average IQ and socioeconomic background had a 4 percent chance of having been interviewed in jail. Switch his IQ to the 2d centile, and the odds rise to 22 percent. (Switch his socioeconomic background to the 2d centile instead, and the odds rise only from 4 to 5 percent .) The same conclusions apply to the measure of self-reported crime.

The Role of Education

Scholars have been arguing about the relationship of education to crime and delinquency for many years without settling the issue. The case of the NLSY white males is a classic example. Of those who were ever interviewed in jail, 74 percent had not gotten a high school diploma. None had a college degree. Clearly something about getting seriously involved in crime competes with staying in school. Low IQ is part of that "something" in many cases, but the relationship is so strong that other factors are probably involved—for example, the same youngster who is willing to burglarize a house probably is not the most obedient of pupils; the youngster who commits assaults on the street probably gets in fights on the school grounds; the youngster who is undeterred by the prospect of jail time probably is not much motivated by the prospect of getting a high school degree; and so forth.

Does high school dropout actually cause the subsequent crime? Many people assumed so until Delbert Elliott and Harwin Voss published a study in 1974 that concluded the opposite: Crime diminished after school dropout.[42] Since then, everyone has agreed that eventual dropouts tend to have high levels of criminal activity while they are in school, but disputes remain about whether the rates fall or rise after the dropout occurs.[43]

For our purposes, it makes little sense to examine the continuing role of IQ in our usual educational samples when the action is so conspicuously concentrated among those who fall neither in the high school nor the college graduate samples. Running our standard analysis on white males who did not get a high school diploma did not shed much more light on the matter.[44] Given the restriction of range in the sample (the mean IQ of the white male dropout sample was 91, with a standard deviation of only 12.5), not much can be concluded from the fact that the ones at the very bottom of the cognitive ability distribution were less likely to report high levels of criminal activity. For these school dropouts, the likelihood of having been interviewed in jail rose as IQ fell, but the relationship was weaker than for the unrestricted sample of white males.

CRIME, COGNITIVE ABILITY, AND CONSCIENCE

By now, you will already be anticipating the usual caution: Despite the relationship of low IQ to criminality, the great majority of people with low cognitive ability are law abiding. We will also take this opportunity to reiterate that the increase in crime over the last thirty years (like the increases in illegitimacy and welfare) cannot be attributed to changes in intelligence but rather must be blamed on other factors, which may have put people of low cognitive ability at greater risk than before.

The caveats should not obscure the importance of the relationship of cognitive ability to crime, however. Many people tend to think of criminals as coming from the wrong side of the tracks. They are correct, insofar as that is where people of low cognitive ability disproportionately live. They are also correct insofar as people who live on the right side of the tracks—whether they are rich or just steadily employed working-class people—seldom show up in the nation's prisons. But the assumption that too glibly follows from these observations is that the economic and social disadvantage is in itself the cause of criminal behavior. That is not what the data say, however. In trying to understand how to deal with the crime problem, much of the attention now given to problems of poverty and unemployment should be shifted to another question altogether: coping with cognitive disadvantage. We will return to this question in the final chapter, when we consider policy changes that might make it easier for everyone to live within the law.

Chapter 12

Civility and Citizenship

A free society demands a citizenry that willingly participates in the civic enterprise, in matters as grand as national elections and as commonplace as neighborliness. Lacking this quality—civility, in its core meaning—a society must replace freedom with coercion if it is to maintain order. This chapter examines the contribution of cognitive ability to the capacity for civility and citizenship.

Most manifestations of civility are too fleeting to be measured and studied. One realm of activity that does leave measurable traces is political involvement, which includes both participation in political activities and some knowledge and sophistication about them.

For assessing any relationship between political involvement and IQ, the best data, surprisingly, are from studies of children, and the results are consistent: Brighter children of all socioeconomic classes, including the poorest, learn more rapidly about politics and how government works, and are more likely than duller children to read about, discuss, and participate in political activities. The gap between brighter and duller children in political development widens with age, unlike the static gap across socioeconomic classes.

For adults, the standard theory of political involvement for many years has assumed that socioeconomic status is the vital link. People at higher-status levels vote more, and they know and care more about political matters than do people at lower levels of status. But the available research offers ample evidence that the key element for predicting political involvement is educational level. The people who vote least and who care the least about political issues are not so much the poor as the uneducated, whatever their income or occupation. Why does education matter so much? The fragmentary studies available indicate that education predicts political involvement in America because it is primarily a proxy for cognitive ability.

The NLSY does not have the data for pursuing this manifestation of civility, but it permits us to explore another aspect of it: To what extent is high in-

253

telligence associated with the behaviors associated with "middle-class values"?
The answer is that the brighter young people of the NLSY are also the ones
whose lives most resemble a sometimes disdained stereotype: They stick with
school, are plugging away in the workforce, and are loyal to their spouse. Insofar as intelligence helps lead people to behave in these ways, it is also a force
for maintaining a civil society.

A merica's political system relies on the civility of its citizens—"civility" not in the contemporary sense of mere politeness but according to an older meaning which a dictionary close at hand defines
as "deference or allegiance to the social order befitting a citizen."[1] The
wording of the definition is particularly apt in the American case. Civility is not obedience but rather "allegiance" and "deference"—words
with old and honorable meanings that are now largely lost. The object
of these sentiments is not the government but a social order. And these
things are required not of a subject but of a citizen. Taken together, the
elements of civility imply behavior that is both considered and consid-
erate—precisely the kind of behavior that the Founders relied upon to
sustain their creation, though they would have been more likely to use
the word *virtue* than *civility*.[2]

The point is that, given such civility, a free society as envisioned by
the Founders is possible. "Civil-ized" people do not need to be tightly
constrained by laws or closely monitored by the organs of state. Lacking such civility, they do, and society must over time become much less
free. That is why civility was relevant to the Founders' vision of a free
society and also why it remains relevant today. In Part IV, we consider
further the link between intelligence and the polity. At this point, we
ask what the differences are between people that explain whether they
are civil. Specifically, what is the role of intelligence?

Much of what could go under the heading of civility is not readily
quantified. Mowing the lawn in the summer or keeping the sidewalks
shoveled in the winter, maintaining a tolerable level of personal hygiene
and grooming, returning a lost wallet, or visiting a sick friend are not
entirely dictated by fear of lawsuits or of retaliation from outraged neighbors. They likely have an element of social engagement, of caring about
one's neighbors and community, of what we are calling civility. Most
such everyday acts of civility are too fleeting to be caught in the net of
observation that social science requires.

Fortunately, the behaviors that go into civility tend to be of a piece, and some acts leave clear traces that can be aggregated and studied. In the preceding chapter, we examined one set of such behaviors, crime. Crime is important in itself, of course, but it also captures the negative pole of disassociation from society at large and the community in particular. Everything we know about the lives of most criminals suggests that in their off-duty hours they are *not* commonly shoveling the sidewalk, visiting sick friends, or returning lost wallets—or doing the myriad other things that signify good neighbors and good citizens. In that light, the chapter on crime may be seen as a discussion of a growing incivility in American life and the contribution that low cognitive ability makes to it.

POLITICAL PARTICIPATION AS AN OUTCROPPING OF CIVILITY

Political participation is not the thing-in-itself of civility. Most of us can recall acquaintances who show up reliably at town council meetings and are hectoring, opinionated, and generally destructive of community life. But, as always, we are talking about statistical tendencies, and for that purpose political participation is not a bad indirect measure.

Consider the act of voting. We have friends, conscientious in many ways, who do not vote and who even look at us, registering and voting, often at some inconvenience, with bemused superiority. They point out with indisputable accuracy that our ballots account for less than a millionth of the overall outcome of most statewide elections, not to mention national ones, and that no major political contest in United States history has ever been decided by a single vote.[3] Are we behaving irrationally by voting?[4]

Not if we value civility. In thinking about what it means to vote, a passage in Aristotle's *Politics* comes to mind. "Man is by nature a political animal," Aristotle wrote, "and he who by nature and not by mere accident is without a state, is either a bad man or above humanity; he is like the 'tribeless, lawless, heartless one,' whom Homer denounces."[5] The polling place is a sort of civic hearth. In the aggregate (though not always in every instance) those who do not vote, or who vote less consistently, are weaker in this manifestation of civility than those who do vote consistently. Think inwardly about why you try to keep up with issues that affect your neighborhood or at least try to do some cramming as an election approaches, and why you usually manage to get to the polling place when the election arrives (or feel guilty when you do not). Are we wrong to assume that the reasons have something to do with a consciousness of the duties of being a citizen and good neighbor? Therein lies the modest claim we make here. There is nothing particularly virtuous or civil about being a political activist, but the simpler ways in which we carry on the basic political business of a democracy betoken the larger attitudes that make up civility.

DEVELOPING CIVILITY IN CHILDREN

The connection between intelligence and political involvement has been more thoroughly studied for children than for adults. In part, this is because until recently schools routinely gave IQ tests to children. With the children's intelligence test scores as a baseline, social scientists could then study whatever variables they were interested in, such as political awareness or interest. Besides being relatively easy to do, studies of childhood political development circumvented some of the questions that arise with adults; children, for example, have no vested political or economic interests (beyond the approval of parents or others) to complicate the analysis of their responses.

One major study assembled a sample of 12,000 children in grades 2 through 8, from schools in middle- or working-class neighborhoods in both large and small cities in various regions of the country in the early 1960s.[6] The children provided information about their fathers' occupations and interest in politics. School records included IQ scores for about 85 percent of the children. The heart of the study was a series of questions about the children's level and range of political development.[7] They were, for example, asked whether they knew which branch of government enacted laws, whether they understood the duties of the president and the courts, whether they ever read about politics in the newspapers or talked about it to their parents or friends, whether they felt that they were protected by the government or whether individuals could exert any political influence on their own, whether they had ever worn campaign buttons or handed out leaflets for a candidate. Their attitudes about voting, about the duties of a citizen, about political change, about legal punishment, among other things, were probed.

The results were predictable in many ways. Younger children tended to see the government in terms of individuals (government = the current president) and as a fixed and absolute entity; older children were better informed, were more likely to think in terms of institutions instead of individuals, and had a clearer sense of the duties of citizenship. The higher a child's socioeconomic background, the more rapidly his political socialization proceeded. Among the dimensions most affected by socioeconomic status—again, no surprise—was a child's sense of political efficacy.[8]

The big surprise in the study was the impact of IQ, which was larger than that of socioeconomic status. Brighter children from even the poorest households and with uneducated parents learned rapidly about politics, about how the government works, and about the possibilities for change. They were more likely to discuss, read about, and participate in political activities than intellectually slower children were. Not only was the gap in political development across cognitive classes larger than the gap across socioeconomic classes, it tended to widen with age, while the gap due to socioeconomic class did not—an important distinction in trying to understand the comparative roles of intelligence and socioeconomic status. IQ differences tend to be dynamic; socioeconomic differences, static. The more important distinction from our perspective, however, is that cognitive ability had more impact, and socioeconomic status virtually none, on a child's perception of the duties of citizenship. If this be civility, then it is most purely a result of intelligence, at least among the variables examined.

A study of older children—approximately 400 high school students—set out to determine the importance of intelligence, contrasted with socioeconomic status, as a factor in political development.[9] The survey questions tapped a wide range of political behaviors and attitudes. From the responses, scales were constructed for fourteen political dimensions. The youngsters were characterized by an overall measure of socioeconomic background, plus separate measures of parental education, family wealth, media exposure, and a measure of verbal intelligence made available from school records. To a remarkable degree and with only a few exceptions, each of the political dimensions was most strongly correlated with intelligence.[10] This was true of scales that measured political knowledge, as would be expected.[11] But the bright youngsters were also much more aware of the potentialities of government and the duties of citizenship—civility again. A multivariate analysis of the results indicated that intelligence per se, rather than socioeconomic status, was driving the relationships, and that when socioeconomic status was significantly correlated with a dimension of political involvement, it was via its effects on intelligence. It is possible that the importance of intelligence was somewhat inflated in this study because the youngsters were disproportionately from working-class backgrounds, hence underestimating the impact of socioeconomic status in more representative samples. However, the qualitative outcome leaves no doubt that intelligence, apart from the usual socioeconomic variables, has a potent effect on political behavior for teenagers, as well as for preteens.[12]

VOTING BEHAVIOR AMONG ADULTS

Social scientists do not find it easy to dragoon large samples of adult Americans and make them sit still for the kinds of assessments of political involvement that can be conducted with children. But they try nonetheless, and they have had some success, mostly centering on voting.

Depending on the election and the historical period, the turnout in elections for federal officeholders ranges from about 25 to 70 percent, with the recent level in presidential elections in the 45 to 60 percent range. It may or may not be a pity that so many of our fellow citizens fail to vote, but it is a boon to social scientists. With the deep split between voters and nonvoters, voting has been an invaluable resource for gaining a glimpse into the nature of this manifestation of civility.[13]

Voting and Socioeconomic Class

The literature on voting repeats the familiar story: Most of the analysis has focused on socioeconomic class, not cognitive ability. The standard model of political participation, including voting, is that it is highly dependent on socioeconomic status.[14] "College graduates vote more than high school graduates; white-collar workers vote more than blue-collar workers; and the rich vote more than the poor," as Wolfinger summarized it.[15] The connection between political participation and social status is so strong that almost any measure of it, no matter how casual, will pick up some part of the relationship. The impression we all have that elections are settled mostly by the votes of the middle and upper classes broadly construed is confirmed by careful scrutiny, if socioeconomic status is the only measure taken of potential voters.

When we are able to look behind the isolated vote to broader kinds of political behavior, the same relationship prevails. The landmark study on this topic was conducted by Sidney Verba and Norman Nie, who polled several thousand people representing the national population in 1967 not only about their voting but also about other political activities—campaigning, demonstrating, contacting officials, and so on.[16] Verba and Nie identified six categories of political activity, from "totally inactive" at one end to the "totally active" at the other, with four gradations in between. Almost without exception, however political participation was defined, socioeconomic status was not only a significant predictor in a statistical sense, but the differences across classes were large.[17] Among the totally inactive (the lowest category), people were almost six times as likely to be from the bottom third in socioeconomic status as from the top third; among the totally active (the highest category), more than four times as many were from the top third as from the bottom third. In between the extremes of political participation, the trends were unbroken and smooth: The higher the level of participation, the more likely the person was from a high-status background; the lower the level of participation, the more likely the person was from a low-status background.

Voting and Education

What is it about socioeconomic status that leads people to behave so differently? Verba and Nie did not present the breakdowns that permit an answer to that question.[18] For that, we turn to another study, by Raymond Wolfinger and Steven Rosenstone, that used the Current Population Surveys (CPS), conducted by the Census Bureau, to answer questions about voting.[19] The authors asked which of the three components of socioeconomic status—education, income, and occupational status—primarily influences voting. The clear answer was education. A college education raised a person's probability of voting almost 40 percentage points over what it would be if the person had less than five years of education, independent of income or occupational status; postgraduate education raised it even more. Even for people in the top income category (more than $75,000 per year in 1990 dollars) a college education added 34 percentage points to a person's probability of voting. Occupational status per se had an even smaller overall effect than income, and it was ambiguous to boot. For example, with education held constant, sales and clerical workers voted at slightly higher rates than professionals or managers.

Educational attainment correlates not just with voting itself but with political knowledge, interest, and attitudes—in short, with political sophistication.[20] Political sophistication, in turn, correlates with voting.[21] Educated people read more about political issues, and they keep their television sets and radios tuned to the news and public issues programs more than do people with less education. They think about political issues at more abstract levels than do less educated people, and less in terms of concrete, personal benefit. They are more likely to disagree with statements like, "So many people vote in the national election that it doesn't matter much to me whether I vote or not." Or, "It isn't so important to vote when you know your party doesn't have a chance to win."[22] By disagreeing, educated people seem to be saying that they participate in an election even when the only payoff is a sense of having done the right thing, which we see as a mark of civility.

Other scholars who have examined this issue have come to the same conclusion that Wolfinger and Rosenstone demonstrated most decisively: it is predominantly education, rather than income or occupational status, that links voting and socioeconomic status.[23] Some scholars go so far as to conclude that, aside from the major effect of education, voting and socioeconomic status have little to do with each other.[24] This turns the standard theory on its head: Rather than explaining the correlation between education and voting as an effect of socioeconomic status, the evidence says that the correlation between socioeconomic status and voting would more properly be attributed to education.

Turning the explanation on its head may solve a puzzle that Verba and Nie noted.[25] Having shown that political leaders respond to pressure from their constituencies, they wondered why the upper socioeconomic classes participated more in political matters, when those at the bottom were more dependent on the government to solve their problems. If the people who have the most to gain or lose participated the most, then the lower classes would vote more than the middle or upper. Why don't they? The answer is that participation is less a matter of direct benefit than of civility in the sense we are using the word here, and civility is higher among more educated people than among less educated ones.[26]

Some of the more cynical dismissals of American political life are similarly answered. Poor and humble workers, it is sometimes argued, are disenfranchised whether they vote or not, because the government does the bidding of the rich and well placed. It is small wonder, then, that they do not vote, this argument continues. But the evidence shows it is not so much the poor and humble who fail to vote; it is the uneducated. It may be easy to believe that the poor are disenfranchised, but it is less obvious why it should be the uneducated (poor or not). What is the cynic to make of the fact that an underpaid but well-educated shop clerk is more likely to vote than a less educated, rich businessman?

Voting and Cognitive Ability

The link between education and voting is clear. Does it really signify a link between cognitive ability and voting? There is an indirect argument that says yes, described in the notes,[27] but we have been able to find only two studies that tackle the question directly.

The first did not have an actual measure of IQ, only ratings of intelligence by interviewers, based on their impressions after some training. This is a legitimate procedure—rated intelligence is known to correlate with tested intelligence—but the results must be treated as approximate. With that in mind, a multivariate analysis of a national sample in the American National Election study in 1976 showed that, of all the variables, by far the most significant in determining a person's political sophistication were rated intelligence and expressed interest. Interest, however, was itself most tellingly affected by intelligence.[28] The more familiar independent variables—education, income, occupational status, exposure to the media, parental interest in politics—had small or no effects, after rated intelligence was taken into account.

The one study of political involvement that included a test of intelligence was conducted in the San Francisco area in the 1970s. The intelligence test was a truncated one, based on a dozen vocabulary items.[29] About 150 people were interviewed in depth and assessed on political sophistication, which is known to correlate with political participation.[30] The usual background variables—income and education, for example—were also obtained. Educational attainment was, as expected, correlated with the test score. But even this rudimentary intelligence test score predicted political sophistication as well as education did. To Russell Neuman, the study's author, "the evidence supports the idea of an independent cognitive-ability effect" as part of the proved link between socioeconomic status and political participation.[31]

We do not imagine that we have told the entire story of political participation. Age, sex, and ethnic identity are among the individual factors that we have omitted but that political scientists routinely examine against the background of voting laws, regional variations, historical events, and the general political climate of the country. In various periods and to varying degrees, these other factors have been shown to be associated with either the sheer level of political involvement or its character. Older people, for example, are more likely to vote than younger people, up to the age at which the debilities of age intervene; women in the past participated less than men, but the gap has narrowed to the vanishing point (especially for educated men and women); different ethnic groups resonate to different political causes.[32]

Our focus on education and intelligence similarly gives insufficient attention to other personal traits that influence political participation.[33] People vary in their sense of civic duty and in the strength of their party affiliations, apart from their educational or intellectual level; their personal values color their political allegiances and how intensely they are felt. Their personalities are expressed not just in personal life but also in their political actions (or inactions).

The bottom line, then, is not that political participation is simple to describe but that, despite its complexity, so narrow a range of individual factors carries so large a burden of explanation. For example, the zero-order correlations between intelligence and the fourteen political dimensions in the study of high school students described above ranged from .01 to .53, with an average of .22; the average correlation with the youngsters' socioeconomic background was .09.[34] For the sentiment of civic duty—the closest approximation to civility in this particular set of dimensions—the correlation with intelligence was .4. As we cautioned above, this may be an overestimate, but perhaps not by much: The zero-order correlation between scores on a brief vocabulary test and the political sophistication of a sample of adults was .33.[35] The coefficients for rated intelligence in a multivariate analysis of political sophistication were more than twice as large as for any of the other variables examined, which included education, occupation, age, and parental interest in politics.[36]

The coherence of the evidence linking IQ and political participation as a whole cannot be neglected. The continuity of the relationship over the life span gives it a plausibility that no single study can command. The other chapters in Part II have shown that cognitive ability often accounts for the importance of socioeconomic class and underlies much of the variation that is usually attributed to education. It appears that the same holds for political participation.

MIDDLE-CLASS VALUES: DATA FROM THE NLSY

The NLSY does not permit us to extend this discussion directly. None of the questions in the study asks about political participation or knowledge. But as we draw to the close of this long sequence of chapters about IQ and social behavior, we may use the NLSY to take another tack.

For many years, "middle-class values" has been a topic of debate in American public life. Many academic intellectuals hold middle-class values in contempt. They have a better reputation among the public at large, however, where they are seen—rightly, in our view—as ways of behaving that produce social cohesion and order. To use the language of this chapter, middle-class values are related to civility.

Throughout Part II, we have been examining departures from middle-class values: adolescents' dropping out of school, babies born out of wedlock, men dropping out of the labor force or ending up in jail, women going on welfare. Let us now look at the glass as half full instead of half empty, concentrating on the people who are doing everything right by conventional standards. And so, to conclude Part II, we present the Middle Class Values (MCV) Index. It has scores of "Yes" and "No." A man in the NLSY got a "Yes" if by 1990 he had obtained a high school degree (or more), been in the labor force throughout 1989, never been interviewed in jail, and was still married to his first wife. A woman in the NLSY got a "Yes" if she had obtained a high school degree, had never given birth to a baby out of wedlock, had never been interviewed in jail, and was still married to her first husband. People who failed any one of the conditions were scored "No." Never-married people who met all the other conditions except the marital one were excluded from the analysis. We also excluded men who were not eligible for the labor force in 1989 or 1990 because they were physically unable to work or in school.

Note that the index does not demand economic success. A man can earn a "Yes" despite being unemployed if he stays in the labor force. A woman can be on welfare and still earn a "Yes" if she bore her children within marriage. Men and women alike can have incomes below the poverty line and still qualify. We do not require that the couple have children or that the wife forgo a career. The purpose of the MCV Index is to identify among the NLSY population, in their young adulthood when the index was scored, those people who are getting on with their lives in ways that fit the middle-class stereotype: They stuck with school, got married, the man is working or trying to work, the woman has confined her childbearing to marriage, and there is no criminal record (as far as we can tell).

What does this have to do with civility? We propose that even though many others in the sample who did not score "Yes" are also fine citizens, it is this population that forms the spine of the typical American community, filling the seats at the PTA meetings and the pews at church, organizing the Rotary Club fund-raiser, coaching the Little League team, or circulating a petition to put a stop light at a dangerous intersection—and shoveling sidewalks and returning lost wallets. What might IQ have to do with qualifying for this group? As the table shows, about half of the sample earned "Yes" scores. They are markedly con-

Whites and the Middle-Class Values Index	
Cognitive Class	Percentage Who Scored "Yes" as of 1990
I Very bright	74
II Bright	67
III Normal	50
IV Dull	30
V Very dull	16
Overall	51

centrated among the brighter people, with progressively smaller proportions on down through the cognitive classes, to an extremely small 16 percent of the Class Vs qualifying.

Furthermore, as in so many other analyses throughout Part II, cognitive ability, independent of socioeconomic background, has an important causal role to play. Below is the final version of the graphic you have seen so often.

Cognitive Ability and the Middle Class Values Index

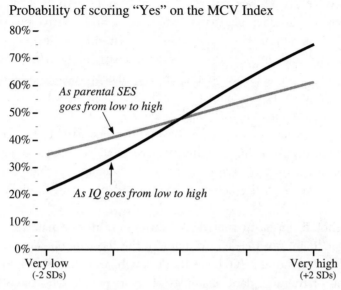

Probability of scoring "Yes" on the MCV Index

As parental SES goes from low to high

As IQ goes from low to high

Very low (-2 SDs)

Very high (+2 SDs)

Note: For computing the plot, age and either SES (for the black curve) or IQ (for the gray curve) were set at their mean values.

As intuition might suggest, "upbringing" in the form of socioeconomic background makes a significant difference. But for the NLSY sample, it was not as significant as intelligence. Even when we conduct our usual analyses with the education subsamples—thereby guaranteeing that everyone meets one of the criteria (finishing high school)—a significant independent role for IQ remains. Its magnitude is diminished for the high school sample but not, curiously, for the college sample. The independent role of socioeconomic background becomes insignificant in these analyses and, in the case of the high-school-only sample, goes the "wrong" way after cognitive ability is taken into account.

Much as we have enjoyed preparing the Middle Class Values Index, we do not intend it to become a new social science benchmark. Its modest goals are to provide a vantage point on correlates of civility in a population of young adults and then to serve as a reminder that the old-fashioned virtues represented through the index are associated with intelligence.

THE DIFFERENCE BETWEEN BEING SMART AND BEING CIVIL

Cognitive ability is a raw material for civility, not the thing itself. Suppose that the task facing a citizen is to vote on an initiative proposing some environmental policy involving (as environmental issues usually do) complex and subtle trade-offs between costs and benefits. Above-average intelligence means that a person is likely to be better read and better able to think through (in a purely technical sense) those trade-offs. On the average, smarter people are more able to understand points of view other than their own. But beyond these contributions of intelligence to citizenship, high intelligence also seems to be associated with an interest in issues of civil concern. It is associated, perhaps surprisingly to some, with the behaviors that we identify with middle-class values.

We should emphasize that vast quantities of this raw material called intelligence are not needed for many of the most fundamental forms of civility and moral behavior. All of us might well pause at this point to think of the abundant examples of smart people who have been conspicuously uncivil. Yet these qualifications notwithstanding, the statistical tendencies remain. A smarter population is more likely to be, and more capable of being made into, a civil citizenry. For a nation predicated on a high level of individual autonomy, this is a fact worth knowing.

PART III

The National Context

Part II was circumscribed, taking on social behaviors one at a time, focusing on causal roles, with the analysis restricted to whites wherever the data permitted. We now turn to the national scene. This means considering all races and ethnic groups, which leads to the most controversial issues we will discuss: ethnic differences in cognitive ability and social behavior, the effects of fertility patterns on the distribution of intelligence, and the overall relationship of low cognitive ability to what has become known as the underclass. As we begin, perhaps a pact is appropriate. The facts about these topics are not only controversial but exceedingly complex. For our part, we will undertake to confront all the tough questions squarely. We ask that you read carefully.

PART III

The National Context

Chapter 13

Ethnic Differences in
Cognitive Ability

Despite the forbidding air that envelops the topic, ethnic differences in cognitive ability are neither surprising nor in doubt. Large human populations differ in many ways, both cultural and biological. It is not surprising that they might differ at least slightly in their cognitive characteristics. That they do is confirmed by the data on ethnic differences in cognitive ability from around the world. One message of this chapter is that such differences are real and have consequences. Another is that the facts are not as alarming as many people seem to fear.

East Asians (e.g., Chinese, Japanese), whether in America or in Asia, typically earn higher scores on intelligence and achievement tests than white Americans. The precise size of their advantage is unclear; estimates range from just a few to ten points. A more certain difference between the races is that East Asians have higher nonverbal intelligence than whites while being equal, or perhaps slightly lower, in verbal intelligence.

The difference in test scores between African-Americans and European-Americans as measured in dozens of reputable studies has converged on approximately a one standard deviation difference for several decades. Translated into centiles, this means that the average white person tests higher than about 84 percent of the population of blacks and that the average black person tests higher than about 16 percent of the population of whites.

The average black and white differ in IQ at every level of socioeconomic status (SES), but they differ more at high levels of SES than at low levels. Attempts to explain the difference in terms of test bias have failed. The tests have approximately equal predictive force for whites and blacks.

In the past few decades, the gap between blacks and whites narrowed by perhaps three IQ points. The narrowing appears to have been mainly caused by a shrinking number of very low scores in the black population rather than

an increasing number of high scores. Improvements in the economic circum-
stances of blacks, in the quality of the schools they attend, in better public
health, and perhaps also diminishing racism may be narrowing the gap.

The debate about whether and how much genes and environment have to
do with ethnic differences remains unresolved. The universality of the con-
trast in nonverbal and verbal skills between East Asians and European whites
suggests, without quite proving, genetic roots. Another line of evidence point-
ing toward a genetic factor in cognitive ethnic differences is that blacks and
whites differ most on the tests that are the best measures of g, or general in-
telligence. On the other hand, the scores on even highly g-loaded tests can be
influenced to some extent by changing environmental factors over the course
of a decade or less. Beyond that, some social scientists have challenged the
premise that intelligence tests have the same meaning for people who live in
different cultural settings or whose forebears had very different histories.

Nothing seems more fearsome to many commentators than the possibility
that ethnic and race differences have any genetic component at all. This be-
lief is a fundamental error. Even if the differences between races were entirely
genetic (which they surely are not), it should make no practical difference in
how individuals deal with each other. The real danger is that the elite wisdom
on ethnic differences—that such differences cannot exist—will shift to oppo-
site and equally unjustified extremes. Open and informed discussion is the one
certain way to protect society from the dangers of one extreme view or the
other.

E thnic differences in measured cognitive ability have been found
since intelligence tests were invented. The battle over the meaning
of these differences is largely responsible for today's controversy over intelligence testing itself. That many readers have turned first to this chapter indicates how sensitive the issue has become.

Our primary purpose is to lay out a set of statements, as precise as the
state of knowledge permits, about what is currently known about the
size, nature, validity, and persistence of ethnic differences on measures
of cognitive ability. A secondary purpose is to try to induce clarity in
ways of thinking about ethnic differences, for discussions about such differences tend to run away with themselves, blending issues of fact, theory, ethics, and public policy that need to be separated.

The first thing to remember is that the differences among individuals are far greater than the differences between groups. If all the ethnic differences in intelligence evaporated overnight, most of the intellectual variation in America would endure. The remaining inequality would still strain the political process, because differences in cognitive ability are problematic even in ethnically homogeneous societies. The chapters in Part II, looking only at whites, should have made that clear. But the politics of cognitive inequality get hotter—sometimes too hot to handle—when they are attached to the politics of ethnicity. We believe that the best way to keep the temperature down is to work through the main facts carefully and methodically. This chapter first reviews the evidence bearing on ethnic differences in cognitive ability, then turns to whether the differences originate in genes or in environments. At the chapter's end, we summarize what this knowledge about ethnic differences means in practical terms.

We frequently use the word *ethnic* rather than *race*, because race is such a difficult concept to employ in the American context.[1] What does it mean to be "black" in America, in racial terms, when the word black (or African-American) can be used for people whose ancestry is more European than African? How are we to classify a person whose parents hail from Panama but whose ancestry is predominantly African? Is he a Latino? A black? The rule we follow here is to classify people according to the way they classify themselves. The studies of "blacks" or "Latinos" or "Asians" who live in America generally denote people who *say* they are black, Latino, or Asian—no more, no less.

Ethnic Nomenclature

We want to call people whatever they prefer to be called, including their preferences for ethnic labels. As we write, however, there are no hard-and-fast rules. People from Latin America wish to be known according to their national origin: Cuban-American, Mexican-American, Puerto Rican, and so forth. *Hispanic* is still the U.S. government's official label, but *Latino* has gained favor in recent years. We use Latino. Opting for common usage and simplicity, we usually use *black* instead of *African-American* and *white* (which always refers to non-Latino whites) instead of *European-American* or *Anglo*. Americans of Asian descent are called *Asian* when the context leaves no possibility of confusion with Asians living in Asia. We shift to the hyphenated versions for everyone when it would avoid such confusions or when, for stylistic reasons, the hyphenated versions seem appropriate.

It would be disingenuous to leave the racial issue at that, however, for race is often on people's minds when they think about IQ. Thus we will eventually comment on cognitive differences among races as they might derive from genetic differences, telling a story that is interesting but still riddled with more questions than answers. This prompts a second point to be understood at the outset: There are differences between races, and they are the rule, not the exception. That assertion may seem controversial to some readers, but it verges on tautology: Races are by definition groups of people who differ in characteristic ways. Intellectual fashion has dictated that all differences must be denied except the absolutely undeniable differences in appearance, but nothing in biology says this should be so. On the contrary, race differences are varied and complex—and they make the human species more adaptable and more interesting.

THE TESTED INTELLIGENCE OF ASIANS, BLACKS, AND WHITES

So much for preliminaries. Answers to commonly asked questions about the ethnic groups in America follow, beginning with the basics and moving into successively more complicated issues. The black-white difference receives by far the most detailed examination because it is the most controversial and has the widest social ramifications. But the most common question we have been asked in recent years has not been about blacks but about Asians, as Americans have watched the spectacular economic success of the Pacific rim nations at a distance and, closer to home, become accustomed to seeing Asian immigrant children collecting top academic honors in America's schools.

Do Asians Have Higher IQs Than Whites?

Probably yes, if *Asian* refers to the Japanese and Chinese (and perhaps also Koreans), whom we will refer to here as East Asians. How much higher is still unclear. Richard Lynn, a leading scholar of racial and ethnic differences, has reviewed the assembled data on overall Asian IQ in two major articles. In his 1991 review of the literature, he put the median IQ for the studies of Chinese living in Hong Kong, Singapore, Taiwan, and China proper at 110; the median IQ for the studies of Japanese living in Japan at 103; and the median for studies of East Asians living in North America at 103.[2] But as Lynn acknowledges, these comparisons are imprecise because the IQs were not corrected for the changes that have been observed over time in national IQ averages. In Lynn's 1987 compilation, where such corrections were made, the medians for both Chinese and Japanese were 103.[3] Mean white American IQ is typically estimated as 101 to 102.[4] Additional studies of Chinese in Hong Kong, conducted by J. W. C. Chan using the Ravens Standard Progressive Matrices, a nonverbal test that is an especially good measure of *g*, found IQ equivalents in the region of 110 for both elementary and secondary students, compared to about 100 for whites in Hong Kong.[5] Another study postdating Lynn's review compared representative samples of South Korean and British 9-year-olds and found an IQ difference of nine points.[6]

The most extensive compilation of East Asian cognitive performance in North America, by Philip Vernon, included no attempt to strike an overall estimate for the current gap between the races, but he did draw conclusions about East Asian–white differences in verbal and nonverbal abilities, which we will describe later in the chapter.[7] In addition to studies of abilities, Vernon compiled extensive data on the schoolwork of East Asians, documenting their superior performance by a variety of measures ranging from grades to the acquisition of the Ph.D. Is this superior performance caused by superior IQ? James Flynn has argued that the real explanation for the success of Asian-Americans is that they are overachievers.[8] He also says that Asian-Americans actually have the same nonverbal intelligence as whites and a fractionally lower verbal intelligence.[9] Richard Lynn disagrees and concludes from the same data used by Flynn that there is an ethnic difference in overall IQ as well.[10]

The NLSY is not much help on this issue. The sample contained only forty-two East Asians (Chinese, Japanese, and Koreans). Their mean IQ was 106, compared to the European-American white mean of 103, consistent with the evidence that East Asians have a higher IQ than whites but based on such a small sample that not much can be made of it.

The indeterminacy of the debate is predictable. The smaller the IQ difference, the more questionable its reality, and this has proved to be the case with the East Asian–white difference. It is difficult enough to find two sets of subjects within a single city who can be compared without problems of interpretation. Can one compare test scores obtained in different years with different tests for students of different ages in different cultural settings, drawn from possibly different socioeconomic populations? One answer is that it can be done through techniques that take advantage of patterns observed over many studies. Lynn in particular has responded to each new critique, in some cases providing new data, in others refining earlier estimates, and always pointing to the striking similarity of the results despite the disparity of the tests and settings.[11] But given the complexities of crossnational comparisons, the issue must eventually be settled by a sufficient body of data obtained from identical tests administered to populations that are comparable except for race.

We have been able to identify three such efforts. In one, samples of American, British, and Japanese students ages 13 to 15 were administered a test of abstract reasoning and spatial relations. The American and British samples had scores within a point of the standardized mean of 100 on both the abstract and spatial relations components of the test; the Japanese adolescents scored 104.5 on the test for abstract reasoning and 114 on the test for spatial relations—a large difference, amounting to a gap similar to the one found by Vernon for Asians in America.[12]

In a second set of studies, 9-year-olds in Japan, Hong Kong, and Britain, drawn from comparable socioeconomic populations, were administered the Ravens Standard Progressive Matrices. The children from Hong Kong averaged 113; from Japan, 110; and from Britain, 100—a gap of well over half a standard deviation between both the Japanese and Hong Kong samples and a British one equated for age and socioeconomic status.[13]

The third set of studies, directed by Harold Stevenson, administered a battery of mental tests to elementary school children in Japan, Taiwan, and Minneapolis, Minnesota. The key difference between this study and the other two was that Stevenson and his colleagues carefully matched the children on socioeconomic and demographic variables.[14] No significant difference in overall IQ was found, and Stevenson and colleagues concluded that "this study offers no support for the argument that there are differences in the general cognitive functioning of Chinese, Japanese, and American children."[15]

Where does this leave us? The parties in the debate are often individually confident, and you will find in their articles many flat statements that an overall East Asian–white IQ difference does, or does not, exist. We will continue to hedge. Harold Stevenson and his colleagues have convinced us that matching subjects by socioeconomic status can reduce the difference to near zero, but he has not convinced us that

Jews, Latinos, and Gender

In the text we focus on three major racial-ethnic groupings—whites, East Asians, and blacks—because they have dominated both the research and contentions regarding intelligence. But whenever the subject of group differences in IQ comes up, three other questions are sure to be asked: Are Jews really smarter than everyone else? Where do Latinos fit in, compared to whites and blacks? What about women versus men?

Jews—specifically, Ashkenazi Jews of European origins—test higher than any other ethnic group.[16] A fair estimate seems to be that Jews in America and Britain have an overall IQ mean somewhere between a half and a full standard deviation above the mean, with the source of the difference concentrated in the verbal component. In the NLSY, ninety-eight whites with IQ scores identified themselves as Jews. The NLSY did not try to ensure representativeness within ethnic groups other than blacks and Latinos, so we cannot be sure that the ninety-eight Jews in the sample are nationally representative. But it is at least worth noting that their mean IQ was .97 standard deviation above the mean of the rest of the population and .84 standard deviation above the mean of whites who identified themselves as Christian. These tests results are matched by analyses of occupational and scientific attainment by Jews, which consistently show their disproportionate level of success, usually by orders of magnitude, in various inventories of scientific and artistic achievement.[17]

The term *Latino* embraces people with highly disparate cultural heritages and a wide range of racial stocks. Many of these groups are known to differ markedly in their social and economic profiles. Add to that the problem of possible language difficulties with the tests, and generalizations about IQ become especially imprecise for Latinos. With that in mind, it may be said that their test results generally fall about half to one standard deviation below the national mean. In the NLSY, the disparity with whites was .93 standard deviation. This may be compared to an overall average difference of .84 standard deviation between whites and Mexican-Americans found in the 1960s on the tests used in the famous Coleman report (described in Chapter 17).[18] We will have more to say about the interpretation of Latino scores with regard to possible language bias in Chapter 14.

When it comes to gender, the consistent story has been that men and women have nearly identical mean IQs but that men have a broader distribution. In the NLSY, for example, women had a mean on the Armed Forces Qualification Test (AFQT) that was .06 standard deviation lower than the male mean and a standard deviation that was .11 narrower. For the Wechsler Intelligence Scale for Children, the average boy tests 1.8 IQ points higher than the average girl, and boys have a standard deviation that is .8 point larger than girls.[19] The larger variation among men means that there are more men than women at either extreme of the IQ distribution.

matching by socioeconomic status is a good idea if one wants to know an estimate of the overall difference between East Asians and whites (we will return to the question of matching by socioeconomic status when we discuss comparisons between blacks and whites). In our judgment, the balance of the evidence supports the proposition that the overall East Asian mean is higher than the white mean. If we had to put a number on it, three IQ points currently most resembles a consensus, tentative though it still is. East Asians have a greater advantage than that in a particular kind of nonverbal intelligence, described later in the chapter.

Do Blacks Score Differently from Whites on Standardized Tests of Cognitive Ability?

If the samples are chosen to be representative of the American population, the answer has been yes for every known test of cognitive ability that meets basic psychometric standards of reliability and validity.[20] The answer is also yes for almost all of the studies in which the black and white samples are matched on some special characteristics—samples of juvenile delinquents, for example, or of graduate students—but there are exceptions. The implication of this effect of selecting the groups to be compared is discussed later in the chapter. Since black-white differences are the ones that strain discourse most severely, we will probe deeply into the evidence and its meaning.

How Large Is the Black-White Difference?

The usual answer to this question is one standard deviation.[21] In discussing IQ tests, for example, the black mean is commonly given as 85, the white mean as 100, and the standard deviation as 15. But the differences observed in any given study seldom conform exactly to one standard deviation. The figure below shows the distribution of the black-white difference (subsequently abbreviated as the "B/W difference") expressed in standard deviations, in the American studies conducted in this century that have reported the IQ means of a black sample and a white sample and meet basic requirements of interpretability as described in the note.[22] A total of 156 studies are represented in the plot, and the mean B/W difference is 1.08 standard deviations, or about sixteen IQ points.[23] The spread of results is substantial, however, reflecting the diversity of the age of the subjects, their geographic loca-

Overview of studies of reporting black-white differences in cognitive test scores, 1918–1990

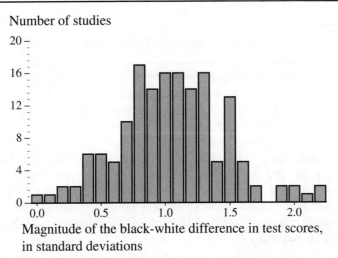

Number of studies

Magnitude of the black-white difference in test scores, in standard deviations

Sources: Shuey 1966; Osborne and McGurk 1982; Sattler 1988; Vincent 1991; Jensen 1985, 1993b.

tion, their background characteristics, the tests themselves, and sampling error.

When we focus on the studies that meet stricter criteria, the range of values for the B/W difference narrows accordingly. The range of results is considerably reduced, for example, for studies that have taken place since 1940 (after testing's most formative period), outside the South (where the largest B/W differences are found), with subjects older than age 6 (after scores have become more stable), using full test batteries from one of the major IQ tests, and with standard deviations reported for that specific test administration. Of the forty-five studies meeting these criteria, all but nine of the B/W differences are clustered between .5 and 1.5 standard deviations. The mean difference was 1.06 standard deviations, and all but eight of the thirty-one reported a B/W difference greater than .8 standard deviation.

Still more rigorous selection criteria do not diminish the size of the gap. For example, with tests given outside the South only after 1960, when people were increasingly sensitized to racial issues, the number of studies is reduced to twenty-four, but the mean difference is 1.10 standard deviations. The NLSY, administered in 1980 to by far the largest

sample (6,502 whites, 3,022 blacks) in a national study, found a difference of 1.21 standard deviations on the AFQT.[24]

Computing the B/W Difference

The simplest way to compute the B/W difference when limited information is available is to take the two means and to compare them using the
standard deviation for the reference population, defined in this case as
whites. This is how the differences in the figure on page 277 showing the
results of 156 studies were computed. When all the data are available, however, as in the case of the NLSY, a more accurate method is available, which
takes into account the standard deviations within each population and the
relative size of the samples. The equation is given in the note.[25] Unless
otherwise specified, all of the subsequent expressions of the B/W differences are based on this method. (For more about the scoring of IQs in the
NLSY, see Appendix 2.)

Answering the question "How large is the difference?" in terms of
standard deviations does not convey an intuitive sense of the size of the
gap. A rough-and-ready way of thinking about the size of the gap is to
recall that one standard deviation above and below the mean cuts off
the 84th and 16th percentiles of a normal distribution. In the case of
the B/W difference of 1.2 standard deviations found in the NLSY, a
person with the black mean was at the 11th percentile of the white distribution, and a person with the white mean was at the 91st percentile
of the black distribution.

A difference of this magnitude should be thought of in several different ways, each with its own important implications. Recall first that the
American black population numbers more than 30 million people. If the
results from the NLSY apply to the total black population as of the 1990s,
around 100,000 blacks fall into Class I of our five cognitive classes, with
IQs of 125 or higher.[26] One hundred thousand people is a lot of people.
It should be no surprise to see (as one does every day) blacks functioning at high levels in every intellectually challenging field.

It is important to understand as well that a difference of 1.2 standard
deviations means considerable overlap in the cognitive ability distribution for blacks and whites, as shown for the NLSY population in the
figure below. For any equal number of blacks and whites, a large pro-

The black and white IQ distributions in the NLSY, Version I

Frequency distributions for populations of equal size

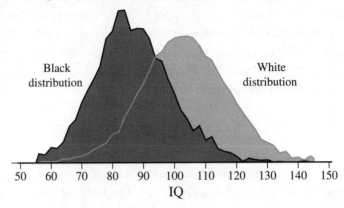

portion have IQs that can be matched up. This is the distribution to keep in mind whenever thinking about individuals.

But an additional complication has to be taken into account: In the United States, there are about six whites for every black. This means that the IQ overlap of the two populations as they actually exist in the United States looks very different from the overlap in the figure just above. The next figure presents the same data from the NLSY when the distributions are shown in proportion to the actual population of young

The black and white IQ distributions in the NLSY, Version II

Frequency distributions proportional to the ethnic composition of the U.S. population

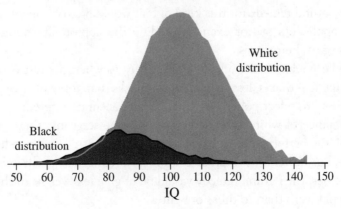

people represented in the NLSY. This figure shows why a B/W difference can be problematic to American society as a whole. At the lower end of the IQ range, there are approximately equal numbers of blacks and whites. But throughout the upper half of the range, the disproportions between the number of whites and blacks at any given IQ level are huge. To the extent that the difference represents an authentic difference in cognitive functioning, the social consequences are potentially huge as well. But is the difference authentic?

Are the Differences in Black and White Scores Attributable to Cultural Bias or Other Artifacts of the Test?

Appendix 5 contains a discussion of the state of knowledge regarding test bias. Here, we shall quickly review the basic findings regarding blacks, without repeating the citations in Appendix 5, which we urge you to read.

EXTERNAL EVIDENCE OF BIAS. Tests are used to predict things—most commonly, to predict performance in school or on the job. Chapter 3 discussed this issue in detail. You will recall that the ability of a test to predict is known as its validity. A test with high validity predicts accurately; a test with poor validity makes many mistakes. Now suppose that a test's validity differs for the members of two groups. To use a concrete example: The SAT is used as a tool in college admissions because it has a certain validity in predicting college performance. If the SAT is biased against blacks, it will *underpredict* their college performance. If tests were biased in this way, blacks as a group would do better in college than the admissions office expected based just on their SATs. It would be as if the test underestimated the "true" SAT score of the blacks, so the natural remedy for this kind of bias would be to compensate the black applicants by, for example, adding the appropriate number of points onto their scores.

Predictive bias can work in another way, as when the test is simply less reliable—that is, less accurate—for blacks than for whites. Suppose a test used to select police sergeants is more accurate in predicting the performance of white candidates who become sergeants than in predicting the performance of black sergeants. It doesn't underpredict for blacks, but rather fails to predict at all (or predicts less accurately). In these cases, the natural remedy would be to give less weight to the test scores of blacks than to those of whites.

The key concept for both types of bias is the same: *A test biased against blacks does not predict black performance in the real world in the same way that it predicts white performance in the real world.* The evidence of bias is *external* in the sense that it shows up in differing validities for blacks and whites. External evidence of bias has been sought in hundreds of studies. It has been evaluated relative to performance in elementary school, in secondary school, in the university, in the armed forces, in unskilled and skilled jobs, in the professions. Overwhelmingly, the evidence is that the major standardized tests used to help make school and job decisions[27] do not underpredict black performance, nor does the expert community find any other general or systematic difference in the predictive accuracy of tests for blacks and whites.[28]

INTERNAL EVIDENCE OF BIAS. Predictive validity is the ultimate criterion for bias, because it involves the proof of the pudding for any test. But although predictive validity is in a technical sense the decisive issue, our impression from talking about this issue with colleagues and friends is that other types of potential bias loom larger in their imaginations: the many things that are put under the umbrella label of "cultural bias."

The most common charges of cultural bias involve the putative cultural loading of items in a test. Here is an SAT analogy item that has become famous as an example of cultural bias:

RUNNER:MARATHON
(A) envoy:embassy
(B) martyr:massacre
(C) oarsman:regatta
(D) referee:tournament
(E) horse:stable

The answer is "oarsman:regatta"—fairly easy if you know what both a marathon and a regatta are, a matter of guesswork otherwise. How would a black youngster from the inner city ever have heard of a regatta? Many view such items as proof that the tests must be biased against people from disadvantaged backgrounds. "Clearly," writes a critic of testing, citing this example, "this item does not measure students' 'aptitude' or logical reasoning ability, but knowledge of upper-middle-class recreational activity."[29] In the language of psychometrics, this is called *internal* evidence of bias, as contrasted with the external evidence of differential prediction.

The hypothesis of bias again lends itself to direct examination. In effect, the SAT critic is saying that culturally loaded items are producing at least some of the B/W difference. Get rid of such items, and the gap will narrow. Is he correct? When we look at the results for items that have answers such as "oarsman:regatta" and the results for items that seem to be empty of any cultural information (repeating a sequence of numbers, for example), are there any differences?[30] Are differences in group test scores concentrated among certain items?

The technical literature is again clear. In study after study of the leading tests, the hypothesis that the B/W difference is caused by questions with cultural content has been contradicted by the facts.[31] Items that the average white test taker finds easy relative to other items, the average black test taker does too; the same is true for items that the average white and black find difficult. Inasmuch as whites and blacks have different overall scores on the average, it follows that a smaller proportion of blacks get right answers for either easy or hard items, but the order of difficulty is virtually the same in each racial group. For groups that have special language considerations—Latinos and American Indians, for example—some internal evidence of bias has been found, unless English is their native language.[32]

Studies comparing blacks and whites on various kinds of IQ tests find that the B/W difference is not created by items that ask about regattas or who wrote *Hamlet*, or any of the other similar examples cited in criticisms of tests. How can this be? The explanation is complicated and goes deep into the reasons why a test item is "good" or "bad" in measuring intelligence. Here, we restrict ourselves to the conclusion: *The B/W difference is wider on items that appear to be culturally neutral than on items that appear to be culturally loaded.* We italicize this point because it is both so well established empirically yet comes as such a surprise to most people who are new to this topic. We will elaborate on this finding later in the chapter. In any case, there is no longer an important technical debate over the conclusion that the cultural content of test items is not the cause of group differences in scores.

"MOTIVATION TO TRY." Suppose that the nature of cultural bias does not lie in predictive validity or in the content of the items but in what might be called "test willingness." A typical black youngster, it is hypothesized, comes to such tests with a mindset different from the white subject's. He is less attuned to testing situations (from one point of view), or less inclined to put up with such nonsense (from another). Perhaps he just doesn't give a damn, since he has no hopes of going to college or otherwise benefiting from a good test score. Perhaps he figures that the test is biased against him anyway, so what's the point. Perhaps he consciously refuses to put out his best effort because of the peer pressures against "acting white" in some inner-city schools.

The studies that have attempted to measure motivation in such situations have generally found that blacks are at least as motivated as whites.[33] But these are not wholly convincing, for why shouldn't the measures of motivation be just as inaccurate as the measures of cognitive ability are alleged to be? Analysis of internal characteristics of the tests once again offers the best leverage in examining this broad hypothesis. Two sets of data seem especially pertinent.

The first involves the *digit span* subtest, part of the widely used Wechsler intelligence tests. It has two forms: *forward digit span*, in which the subject tries to repeat a sequence of numbers in the order read to him, and *backward digit span*, in which the subject tries to repeat the sequence of numbers backward. The test is simple in concept, uses numbers that are familiar to everyone, and calls on no cultural information besides knowing numbers. The digit span is especially informative regarding test motivation not just because of the low cultural loading of the items but because the backward form is twice as g-loaded as the forward form, it is a much better measure of general intelligence. The reason is that reversing the numbers is mentally more demanding than repeating them in the heard order, as readers can determine for themselves by a little self-testing.

The two parts of the subtest have identical content. They occur at the same time during the test. Each subject does both. But in most studies the black-white difference is about twice as great on backward digits as on forward digits.[34] The question arises: How can lack of motivation (or test willingness or any other explanation of that type) explain the difference in performance on the two parts of the same subtest?[35]

A similar question arises from work on reaction time. Several psychometricians, led by Arthur Jensen, have been exploring the underlying nature of g by hypothesizing that neurologic processing speed is implicated, akin to the speed of the microprocessor in a computer.

Smarter people process faster than less smart people. The strategy for testing the hypothesis is to give people extremely simple cognitive tasks—so simple that no conscious thought is involved—and to use precise timing methods to determine how fast different people perform these simple tasks. One commonly used apparatus involves a console with a semicircle of eight lights, each with a button next to it. In the middle of the console is the "home" button. At the beginning of each trial, the subject is depressing the home button with his finger. One of the lights in the semicircle goes on. The subject moves his finger to the button closest to the light, which turns it off. There are more complicated versions of the task (three lights go on, and the subject moves to the one that is farthest from the other two, for example), but none requires much thought, and everybody gets every trial "right." The subject's response speed is broken into two measurements: reaction time (RT), the time it takes the subject to lift his finger from the home button after a target light goes on, and movement time (MT), the time it takes to move the finger from just above the home button to the target button.[36]

Francis Galton in the nineteenth century believed that reaction time is associated with intelligence but could not prove it. He was on the right track after all. In modern studies, reaction time is correlated with the results from full-scale IQ tests; even more specifically, it is correlated with the g factor in IQ tests—in some studies, *only* with the g factor.[37] Movement time is much less correlated with IQ or with g.[38] This makes sense: Most of the cognitive processing has been completed by the time the finger leaves the home button; the rest is mostly a function of small motor skills.

Research on reaction time is doing much to advance our understanding of the biological basis of g. For our purposes here, however, it also offers a test of the motivation hypothesis: The consistent result of many studies is that white reaction time is faster than black reaction time, but black movement time is faster than white movement time.[39] One can imagine an unmotivated subject who thinks the reaction time test is a waste of time and does not try very hard. But the level of motivation, whatever it may be, seems likely to be the same for the measures of RT and MT. The question arises: How can one be unmotivated to do well during one split-second of a test but apparently motivated during the next split-second? Results of this sort argue against easy explanations that appeal to differences in motivation as explanatory of the B/W difference.

UNIFORM BACKGROUND BIAS. Other kinds of bias discussed in Appendix 5 include the possibility that blacks have less access to coaching than whites, less experience with tests (less "testwiseness"), poorer understanding of standard English, and that their performance is affected by white examiners. Each of these hypotheses has been investigated, for many tests, under many conditions. None has been sustained. In short, the testable hypotheses have led toward the conclusion that cognitive ability tests are not biased against blacks. This leaves one final hypothesis regarding cultural bias that does not lend itself to empirical evaluation, at least not directly.

Suppose our society is so steeped in the conditions that produce test bias that people in disadvantaged groups underscore their cognitive abilities on *all* the items on tests, thereby hiding the internal evidence of bias. At the same time and for the same reasons, they underperform in school and on the job in relation to their true abilities, thereby hiding the external evidence. In other words, the tests may be biased against disadvantaged groups, but the traces of bias are invisible because the bias permeates all areas of the group's performance. Accordingly, it would be as useless to look for evidence of test bias as it would be for Einstein's imaginary person traveling near the speed of light to try to determine whether time has slowed. Einstein's traveler has no clock that exists independent of his space-time context. In assessing test bias, we would have no test or criterion measure that exists independent of this culture and its history. This form of bias would pervade everything.

To some readers, the hypothesis will seem so plausible that it is self-evidently correct. Before deciding that this must be the explanation for group differences in test scores, however, a few problems must be overcome. First, the comments about the digit span and reaction time results apply here as well. How can this uniform background bias suppress black reaction time but not the movement time? How can it suppress performance on backward digit span more than forward digit span? Second, the hypothesis implies that many of the performance yardsticks in the society at large are not only biased, they are all so similar in the degree to which they distort the truth—in every occupation, every type of educational institution, every achievement measure, every performance measure—that no differential distortion is picked up by the data. Is this plausible?

It is not good enough to accept without question that a general "background radiation" of bias, uniform and ubiquitous, explains away black and white differences in test scores and performance measures. The hypothesis might, in theory, be true. But given the degree to which everyday experience suggests that the environment confronting blacks in different sectors of American life is not uniformly hostile and given the consistency in results from a wide variety of cognitive measures, assuming that the hypothesis is true represents a considerably longer leap of faith than the much more limited assumption that race prejudice is still a factor in American life. In the matter of test bias, this brings us to the frontier of knowledge.

Are the Differences in Overall Black and White Test Scores Attributable to Differences in Socioeconomic Status?

This question has two different answers depending on how the question is understood, and confusion is rampant. We will take up the two answers and their associated rationales separately:

First version: *If you extract the effects of socioeconomic class, what happens to the overall magnitude of the B/W difference?* Blacks are disproportionately in the lower socioeconomic classes, and socioeconomic class is known to be associated with IQ. Therefore, many people suggest, part of what appears to be an ethnic difference in IQ scores is actually a socioeconomic difference.

The answer to this version of the question is that the size of the gap shrinks when socioeconomic status is statistically extracted. The NLSY gives a result typical of such analyses. The B/W difference in the NLSY is 1.21. In a regression equation in which both race and socioeconomic background are entered, the difference between whites and blacks shrinks to .76 standard deviation.[40] Socioeconomic status explains 37 percent of the original B/W difference. This relationship is in line with the results from many other studies.[41]

The difficulty comes in interpreting what it means to "control" for socioeconomic status. Matching the status of the groups is usually justified on the grounds that the scores people earn are caused to some extent by their socioeconomic status, so if we want to see the "real" or "authentic" difference between them, the contribution of status must be excluded.[42] The trouble is that socioeconomic status is also a *result* of cognitive ability, as people of high and low cognitive ability move to correspondingly high and low places in the socioeconomic continuum. The reason that parents have high or low socioeconomic status is in part a function of their intelligence, and their intelligence also affects the IQ of the children via both genes and environment.

Because of these relationships, "controlling" for socioeconomic status in racial comparisons is guaranteed to reduce IQ differences in the same way that choosing black and white samples from a school for the intellectually gifted is guaranteed to reduce IQ differences (assuming race-blind admissions standards). But the remaining difference is not necessarily more real or authentic than the one we start with. This seems to be a hard point to grasp, judging from the pervasiveness of controlling for socioeconomic status in the sociological literature on ethnic differences. But suppose we were asking whether blacks and whites differed in sprinting speed, and controlled for "varsity status" by examining only athletes on the track teams in Division I colleges. Blacks would probably still sprint faster than whites on the average, but it would be a smaller difference than in the population at large. Is there any sense in which this smaller difference would be a more accurate measure of the racial difference in sprinting ability than the larger difference in the general population? We pose that as an interesting theoretical issue. In terms of numbers, a reasonable rule of thumb is that controlling for socioeconomic status reduces the overall B/W difference by about a third.

Second version: *As blacks move up the socioeconomic ladder, do the differences with whites of similar socioeconomic status diminish?* The first version of the SES/IQ question referred to the overall score of a population of blacks and whites. The second version concentrates on the B/W difference within socioeconomic classes. The rationale goes like this: Blacks score lower on average because they are socioeconomically at a disadvantage in our society. This disadvantage should most seriously handicap the children of blacks in the lower socioeconomic classes, who suffer from greater barriers to education and occupational advancement than do the children of blacks in the middle and upper classes. As blacks advance up the socioeconomic ladder, their children, less exposed to these environmental deficits, will do better and, by extension, close the gap with white children of their class.

This expectation is not borne out by the data. A good way to illustrate this is by using our parental SES index and matching it against the mean IQ score, as shown in the figure below. IQ scores increase with economic status for both races. But as the figure shows, the magnitude of the B/W difference in standard deviations does not decrease. Indeed, it gets larger as people move up from the very bottom of the socioeco-

Black IQ scores go up with socioeconomic status, but the black-white difference does not shrink

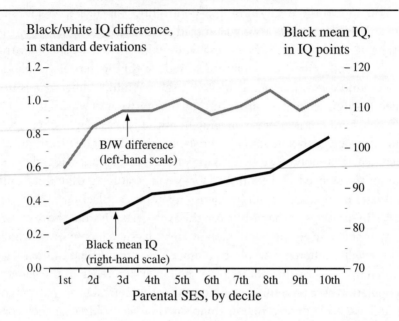

Black/white IQ difference,
in standard deviations

Black mean IQ,
in IQ points

nomic ladder. The pattern shown in the figure is consistent with many other major studies, except that the gap flattens out. In other studies, the gap has continued to increase throughout the range of socioeconomic status.[43]

How Do African-Americans Compare with Blacks in Africa on Cognitive Tests?

This question often arises in the context of black-white comparisons in America, the thought being that the African black population has not been subjected to the historical legacy of American black slavery and discrimination and might therefore have higher scores. Many studies of African students in primary and secondary schools, in both urban and rural areas, have included cognitive ability tests. As in the United States, it has been demonstrated in Africa that the same test items that discriminate best among blacks discriminate best among whites and that the same factors that depress white scores (for example, coming from a rural area) depress black scores. The predictive validity of tests for academic and job performance seems to be about the same. In general, the psychometric properties of the standardized tests are the same for blacks living in Africa as for American blacks.[44]

It has been more difficult to assemble data on the score of the average African black than one would expect, given the extensiveness of the test experience in Africa. In the same review of the literature that permitted the above generalizations, for example—a thirty-page article followed by a bibliography of more than 200 titles—not a single average is reported.[45] One reason for this reluctance to discuss averages is that blacks in Africa, including urbanized blacks with secondary educations, have obtained extremely low scores. Richard Lynn was able to assemble eleven studies in his 1991 review of the literature. He estimated the median black African IQ to be 75, approximately 1.7 standard deviations below the U.S. overall population average, about ten points lower than the current figure for American blacks.[46] Where other data are available, the estimates of the black African IQ fall at least that low and, in some instances, even lower.[47] The IQ of "coloured" students in South Africa—of mixed racial background—has been found to be similar to that of American blacks.[48]

In summary: African blacks are, on average, substantially below African-Americans in intelligence test scores. Psychometrically, there is little reason to think that these results mean anything different about cognitive functioning than they mean in non-African populations. For our purposes, the main point is that the hypothesis about the special circumstances of American blacks depressing their test scores is not substantiated by the African data.

Is the Difference in Black and White Test Scores Diminishing?

The answer is yes with (as usual) some qualifications.

IQ TEST DATA. The most straightforward way to answer the question would be to examine the repeated administrations of the same IQ tests to comparable populations, but large, nationally representative IQ data are not produced every year (or even every decade). The NLSY data are among the most recent for a young adult population, and they have a B/W difference toward the high end of the range. The only post-1980 study reporting black and white adult averages that we have found is the renorming of the Wechsler Adult Intelligence Scale (WAIS-R) in 1981 in which the difference between blacks and a sample of whites (that apparently did not try to discriminate between Latino and Anglo whites) was 1.0 standard deviation.[49]

Recent data on children tell opposite stories. In a review of IQ tests of children conducted since 1980, Ken Vincent of the University of Houston reports results for four normative studies that showed a B/W difference of only seven IQ points for the Ravens Standard Progressive Matrices (SPM) and the Kaufman Assessment Battery for Children (K-ABC).[50] Two other studies involving the Stanford-Binet IV found B/W differences of ten points for children ages 7 to 11 and twelve points for children ages 2 to 6.[51] Qualifications must be attached to these findings. The B/W difference on the K-ABC normative sample has in particular been subjected to reexamination suggesting that the diminished gap largely reflected psychometric and statistical artifacts.[52] Nonetheless, the data on children that Vincent reviews may be read as encouraging. The most impressive of the findings is the comparatively small B/W difference of only seven IQ points on the Ravens SPM administered to 12-year-olds. This finding corresponds to Jensen's 1992 study of black and white children in an upper-middle-class setting in which the difference on the Ravens SPM was similarly below the norm (a deficit corresponding to ten IQ points).[53]

In contrast to Vincent's optimistic conclusions, the NLSY shows a growing rather than a shrinking gap in the next generation of blacks and whites. As discussed in Chapter 15, the B/W difference between NLSY children is currently wider than the B/W difference separating their mothers.

ACADEMIC APTITUDE AND ACHIEVEMENT TESTS. The most extensive evidence of a narrowing black-white gap can be found in longitudinal data from the National Assessment of Educational Progress (NAEP), the American College Testing (ACT) examination, the SAT, a comparison of the 1972 and 1980 national high school surveys, and some state-level achievement test data. We review the NAEP and the SAT here, and others (which tell the same story) in Appendix 5.

The National Assessment of Educational Progress is an ongoing program sponsored by the federal government to monitor the academic achievement of the nation's youth. It began in 1969, periodically testing 9-, 13-, and 17-year-olds in science, mathematics, reading, and writing in nationally representative samples. The table below shows the changes from the first round of testing in 1969–1973 to the data for

Reductions in the Black-White Difference on the National Assessment of Educational Progress

| | White-Black Difference, in Standard Deviations[a] | | Change |
	1969–1973	1990	
9-year-olds			
Science	1.14	.84	−.30
Math	.70	.54	−.16
Reading	.88	.70	−.18
Average	.91	.69	−.21
13-year-olds			
Science	.96	.76	−.20
Math	.92	.54	−.38
Reading	.78	.40	−.38
Average	.89	.57	−.32
17-year-olds			
Science	1.08	.96	−.12
Math	.80	.42	−.38
Reading	1.04	.60	−.44
Average	.97	.66	−.31
Overall average	.92	.64	−.28

Source: National Center for Education Statistics, 1991b.

[a] The computations assume a standard deviation of 50.

1990, expressed in standard deviations. The "Change" column gives the earlier B/W difference minus the later B/W difference, which is negative if the gap is closing. The fourth component of the NAEP, a writing test, was introduced only in 1984, with replications in 1988 and 1990. Unlike all the others, it does not show a narrowing of the white-black gap (.46 SD in both 1984 and 1990) and is not included in the table.

As the table indicates, black progress in narrowing the test score discrepancy with whites has been substantial on all three tests and across all of the age groups. The overall average gap of .92 standard deviation in the 1969–1973 tests had shrunk to .64 standard deviation by 1990. The gap narrowed because black scores rose, not because white scores fell. Altogether, the NAEP provides an encouraging picture.

The first published breakdowns of SAT scores by ethnicity appear for 1976, when the downward trend in SAT scores nationwide after 1963 was nearing its bottom (see Chapter 18). From 1976 to 1993, the white-black gap in SAT scores narrowed from 1.16 to .88 standard deviation in the verbal portion of the test and from 1.27 to .92 standard deviation in the mathematics portion of the test.[54] Comparable narrowing has also brought black and white achievement test scores closer, as presented in Appendix 5. Because the ethnic self-identification of SAT test takers contains some anomalies[55] and because the SAT pool is unrepresentative of the general population, the numbers should be interpreted with caution. But even so, the SAT data indicate a narrowing gap. Black SAT test takers improved substantially more in scores than white SAT test takers, and neither the changes in the pool of test takers nor the well-advertised national decline in SAT scores was responsible, for reasons explained in the notes.[56]

EXPLAINING THE CONVERGENCE. Let us assume that during the past two decades black and white cognitive ability as measured by IQ has in fact converged by an amount that is consistent with the convergence in educational aptitude measures such as the SAT or NAEP—a narrowing of approximately .15 to .25 standard deviation units, or the equivalent of two to three IQ points overall.[57] Why have the scores converged? The answer calls for speculation.

We take for granted that individual variations in cognitive ability depend on both genes and environment (see Chapter 4). In a period as short as twenty years, environmental changes are likely to provide the main reason for the narrowing racial gap in scores.[58] Real and important though the problems of the underclass are, and acknowledging that the underclass is disproportionately black, living conditions have improved for most African-Americans since the 1950s—socially, economically, and educationally.

Consider the schools that blacks attend, for example. Some schools in the inner cities are worse than they were thirty years ago, but proportionately few blacks live in these worst-of-the-worst areas.[59] Throughout the South and in much of the rest of the country, many black children as recently as the 1950s attended ramshackle schools with undertrained teachers and meager teaching materials. Any comparison between the schools that most blacks attend now and the ones they attended in the 1950s favors contemporary schools. Assuming that education affects cognitive capacity, the rising investment in education disproportionately benefits the cognitive levels at the lower end of the socioeconomic spectrum.

The argument can be repeated for public health. If nutrition, shelter, and health care affect intellectual development, then rising standards of living are disproportionately going to show up in rising scores for the economically disadvantaged rather than for the upper classes. For travel and its educational benefits, the argument also applies. Not so long ago, many less advantaged people spent their lives within a few miles of their birthplaces. Today, Americans of nearly all walks of life crowd the interstate roads and the airports. Finally, for that most contemporary form of vicarious travel—the popular media—the leveling is still more dramatic. The modern media can bring the world to everyone in ways that were once open only to the rich.

Because blacks are shifted toward the lower end of the socioeconomic range, such improvements benefit them, on average, more than whites. If the improvements affect cognitive development, the black-white gap should have contracted. Beyond this socioeconomic leveling, there might also have been a leveling due to diminishing racism. The legacy of historic racism may still be taking its toll on cognitive development, but we must allow the possibility that it has lessened, at least for new generations. This too might account for some narrowing of the black-white gap.

LOOKING TO THE FUTURE. The question that remains is whether black and white test scores will continue to converge. If all that separates blacks from whites are environmental differences and if fertility patterns for different socioeconomic groups are comparable, there is no reason why they shouldn't. The process would be very slow, however. If it continues at the pace observed over the last twenty years, then we could expect black and white SAT scores to reach equality sometime in the middle of the twenty-first century, but linear extrapolations over such long periods are not worth much.[60]

If black fertility is loaded more heavily than white fertility toward low-IQ segments of the population, then at some point convergence may be expected to stop, and the gap could even begin to widen again. We take up the fertility issue in Chapter 15. A brief summary statement concerning fertility patterns is that the news is not good. For now, the test score data leave open the possibility that convergence has already stalled. For most of the tests we mentioned, black scores stopped rising in the mid-1980s. On the NAEP, the B/W gap actually increased from 1986 to 1990 in all but one test group (the math test for 17-year-olds). On the SAT, black scores on both verbal and math parts were nearly flat for the five years ending in 1993, after substantial gains in the preceding decade. On the ACT, however, black scores continued to rise after 1986, albeit modestly.[61]

One explanation for the stalled convergence on the NAEP and SAT is that American education stopped improving for everyone, blacks included. This is consistent with the white experience on the SAT, where white scores have also been nearly flat since the mid-1980s. But the logic is suspect. Just because a group at a higher mean stops improving does not imply that a group with a lower mean should also stop improving. On the contrary, pessimists can develop a case that the convergence of black and white SAT scores in the last two decades is symptomatic of what happens when education slows down toward the speed of the slowest ship in the convoy. It may well be that education improves for students at the low end of the distribution but gets worse (or, more optimistically, improves less) for students at the top end.[62] If that is the case, the gap between people at the low and high end of the distribution should narrow, but the narrowing will stop once the educational system completes its readjustment favoring less capable students.

The narrowing black-white gap on the SAT looks consistent with some such explanation.[63] Seen from one perspective, there is good news all along the spectrum of test scores. From 1980 to 1993, the proportion of black test takers who scored in the 700s on the SAT-Verbal increased by 27 percent, for example.[64] But such changes at the high end of the range of test scores mean little, because so small a proportion of all black students were involved.[65] The real source of the black increase of twenty-three points in the average verbal test score from 1980 to 1993 was a rise in the scores at the low end of the range. More than half (51 percent) of the gain occurred because the proportion of black students scoring in the 200s dropped from 42 percent to 30 percent.[66] In contrast, less than 1 percent (0.4 percent) of the gain occurred because of the change in the proportion of black students scoring in the 700s. For the math test, 22 percent of the gain from 1980 to 1993 was accounted for by a drop in students scoring in the 200s; 4 percent of it was accounted for by an increase in students scoring in the 700s.

Pessimists reading these data may think of an analogy with the increases in height that follow from better nutrition: Better nutrition helps raise the height of children whose diets would otherwise have been inadequate, but it does not add anything to the height of those who have been receiving a good diet already.[67] Optimists may use the opposite sort of nutritional analogy: the experience of trying to lose weight. Even a successful diet has its plateaus, when the weight stubbornly stops coming off for a while. A plateau is all that we are seeing in recent test data. Perhaps convergence will resume or even accelerate in the near future.

At the least, the optimists may say that it is too soon to pass judgment, and that seems the safest conclusion. As we reach the end of this discussion of convergence, we can imagine the responses of readers of varying persuasions. Many of you will be wondering why we have felt it necessary to qualify the good news. A smaller number of readers who specialize in mental testing may be wondering why we have given so much prominence to educational achievement trends and a scattering of IQ results that may be psychometrically ephemeral. The answer for everyone is that predicting the future on this issue is little more than guesswork at this point. We urge upon our readers a similar suspension of judgment.

GENETICS, IQ, AND RACE

This brings us to the flashpoint of intelligence as a public topic: the question of genetic differences between the races. Expert opinion, when it is expressed at all, diverges widely. In the 1980s, Mark Snyderman and Stanley Rothman, a psychologist and a political scientist, respectively, sent a questionnaire to a broad sample of 1,020 scholars, mostly academicians, whose specialties give them reason to be knowledgeable about IQ.[68] Among the other questions, they asked, "Which of the following best characterizes your *opinion* of the heritability of the black-white difference in IQ?" (emphasis in the questionnaire item). The answers were divided as follows:

- The difference is entirely due to environmental variation: 15 percent.
- The difference is entirely due to genetic variation: 1 percent.
- The difference is a product of both genetic and environmental variation: 45 percent.

- The data are insufficient to support any reasonable opinion: 24 percent.
- No response: 14 percent.

The responses reveal the degree of uncertainty within the scientific community about where the truth lies. We have considered leaving the genetics issue at that, on grounds that no useful purpose is served by talking about a subject that is so inflammatory, so painful, and so far from resolution. We could have cited any number of expert reassurances that genetic differences among ethnic groups are not worth worrying about. For example, a recently published textbook from which college students around the country are learning about intelligence states unequivocally that "there is no convincing direct or indirect evidence in favor of a genetic hypothesis of racial differences in IQ."[69] Stephen J. Gould, whose *Mismeasure of Man* so successfully cemented the received wisdom about IQ in the media, expresses this view as confidently and more eloquently. "Equality [of the races] is not given a priori," he once wrote in his column for *Natural History* magazine. "It is neither an ethical principle (though equal treatment may be) nor a statement about norms of social action. It just worked out that way. A hundred different and plausible scenarios for human history would have yielded other results (and moral dilemmas) of enormous magnitude. They just didn't happen."[70] He goes on to make three arguments. First, the very concept of race is illegitimate, given the extensiveness of interbreeding and the imprecise nature of most of the traits that people think of as being "racial." Second, the division of races is recent, occurring only in the last tens or perhaps hundreds of thousands of years, limiting the amount of time that groups of humans could have taken separate evolutionary paths. Third, developments in genetics demonstrate that the genetic differences among human beings are minor. "We now know that our usual metaphor of superficiality—skin deep—is literally accurate," Gould writes.[71] He concludes: "Say it five times before breakfast tomorrow; more important, understand it as the center of a network of implication: 'Human equality [i.e., equality among the races] is a contingent fact of history.' "[72]

Our difficulty with this position is not that Gould (or others who make similar arguments) is wrong about the blurred lines between the races, or about how long the races have been separated, or about the number of genes that are racially distinctive. All his facts can be true, and yet people who call themselves Japanese or Xhosa or Caucasians or

Maori can still differ intellectually for genetic reasons. We may call them "ethnic groups" instead of races if we wish—we too are more comfortable with *ethnic*, because of the blurred lines—but some ethnic groups nonetheless differ genetically for sure, otherwise they would not have differing skin colors or hair textures or muscle mass. They also differ intellectually on the average. The question remaining is whether the intellectual differences overlap the genetic differences to any extent.

Our reason for confronting the issue of genetic cognitive differences is not to quarrel with those who deny them. If the question of genetic differences in cognitive ability were something that only professors argued about among themselves, we would happily ignore it here. We cannot do so, first because in the public discussion of genes and intelligence, no burden of proof at all is placed on the innumerable public commentators who claim that racial differences in intelligence are purely environmental. This sometimes leads to a next statement: that the differences are therefore inauthentic and that public policy must be measured against the assumption that there are no genuine cognitive differences between the races.[73] The assumption of genetic cognitive equality among the races has practical consequences that require us to confront the assumption directly.

Second, we have become convinced that the topic of genes, intelligence, and race in the late twentieth century is like the topic of sex in Victorian England. Publicly, there seems to be nothing to talk about. Privately, people are fascinated by it. As the gulf widens between public discussion and private opinion, confusion and error flourish. As it was true of sex then, so it is true of ethnic differences in intelligence now: Taboos breed not only ignorance but misinformation.

The dangers of the misinformation are compounded by the nature of the contemporary discussion of race. Just beneath the surface of American life, people talk about race in ways that bear little resemblance to the politically correct public discussion. Conducted in the workplace, dorm rooms, taverns, and country clubs, by people in every ethnic group, this dialogue is troubled and often accusatory. The underground conversation is not limited to a racist minority. It goes on everywhere, and we believe is increasingly shaped by privately held beliefs about the implications of genetic differences that could not stand open inspection.

The evidence about ethnic differences can be misused, as many people say to us. Some readers may feel that this danger places a moral prohibition against examining the evidence for genetic factors in public. We disagree, in part because we see even greater dangers in the current gulf between public pronouncements and private beliefs. And so, for better or worse, here are the major strands of current thinking about the role of genes in cognitive differences between races.[74]

Heritability and Group Differences

A good place to start is by correcting a common confusion about the role of genes in individuals and in groups. As we discussed in Chapter 4, scholars accept that IQ is substantially heritable, somewhere between 40 and 80 percent, meaning that much of the observed variation in IQ is genetic. And yet this information tells us nothing for sure about the origin of the differences between races in measured intelligence. This point is so basic, and so commonly misunderstood, that it deserves emphasis: *That a trait is genetically transmitted in individuals does not mean that group differences in that trait are also genetic in origin.* Anyone who doubts this assertion may take two handfuls of genetically identical seed corn and plant one handful in Iowa, the other in the Mojave Desert, and let nature (i.e., the environment) take its course.[75] The seeds will grow in Iowa, not in the Mojave, and the result will have nothing to do with genetic differences.

The environment for American blacks has been closer to the Mojave and the environment for American whites has been closer to Iowa. We may apply this general observation to the available data and see where the results lead. Suppose that all the observed ethnic differences in tested intelligence originate in some mysterious environmental differences—mysterious, because we know from material already presented that socioeconomic factors cannot be much of the explanation. We further stipulate that one standard deviation (fifteen IQ points) separates American blacks and whites and that a fifth of a standard deviation (three IQ points) separates East Asians and whites. Finally, we assume that IQ is 60 percent heritable (a middle-ground estimate). Given these parameters, how different would the environments for the three groups have to be in order to explain the observed difference in these scores?

The observed ethnic differences in IQ could be explained solely by the environment if the mean environment of whites is 1.58 standard deviations better than the mean environment of blacks and .32 standard deviation worse than the mean environment for East Asians, when environments are measured along the continuum of their capacity to nurture intelligence.[76] Let's state these conclusions in percentile terms: The *average* environment of blacks would have to be at the 6th percentile of the distribution of environments among whites, and the *average* environment of East Asians would have to be at the 63rd percentile of environments among whites, for the racial differences to be entirely environmental.

Environmental differences of this magnitude and pattern are implausible. Recall further that the B/W difference (in standardized units) is smallest at the lowest socioeconomic levels. Why, if the B/W difference is entirely environmental, should the advantage of the "white" environment compared to the "black" be greater among the better-off and better-educated blacks and whites? We have not been able to think of a plausible reason. An appeal to the effects of racism to explain ethnic differences also requires explaining why environments poisoned by discrimination and racism for some other groups—against the Chinese or the Jews in some regions of America, for example—have left them with higher scores than the national average.

Environmental explanations may successfully circumvent these problems, but the explanations have to be formulated rather than simply assumed. Our initial objective is to warn readers who come to the discussion with firmly held opinions on either side. The heritability of individual differences in IQ does not necessarily mean that ethnic differences are also heritable. But those who think that ethnic differences are readily explained by environmental differences haven't been tough-minded enough about their own argument. At this complex intersection of complex factors, the easy answers are unsatisfactory ones.

Reasons for Thinking that Genetic Differences Might Be Involved

Now we turn to some of the more technical arguments, beginning with those that argue for some genetic component in group differences.

PROFILE DIFFERENCES BETWEEN WHITES AND EAST ASIANS. Races differ not just in average scores but in the profile of intellectual capacities. A full-scale IQ score is the aggregate of many subtests. There are thirteen of them in the Wechsler Intelligence Scale for Children (WISC-R), for example. The most basic division of the subtests is into a verbal IQ and a performance IQ. In white samples, the verbal and performance IQ subscores tend to have about the same mean, because IQ tests have been standardized on predominantly white populations. But individuals can have imbalances between these two IQs. People with high verbal abilities are likely to do well with words and logic. In school they excel in history and literature; in choosing a career to draw on those talents, they tend to choose law or journalism or advertising or politics. In contrast, people with high performance IQs—or, using a more descriptive phrase, "visuospatial abilities"—are likely to do well in the physical and biological sciences, mathematics, engineering, or other subjects that demand mental manipulation in the three physical dimensions or the more numerous dimensions of mathematics.

East Asians living overseas score about the same or slightly lower than whites on verbal IQ and substantially higher on visuospatial IQ. Even in the rare studies that have found overall Japanese or Chinese IQs no higher than white IQs (e.g., the Stevenson study of Japanese, Taiwanese, and Minnesotans mentioned earlier),[77] the discrepancy between verbal and visuospatial IQ persists. For Japanese living in Asia, a 1987 review of the literature demonstrated without much question that the verbal-visuospatial difference persists even in examinations that have been thoroughly adapted to the Japanese language and, indeed, in tests developed by the Japanese themselves.[78] A study of a small sample of Korean infants adopted into white families in Belgium found the familiar elevated visuospatial scores.[79]

This finding has an echo in the United States, where Asian-American students abound in engineering, in medical schools, and in graduate programs in the sciences, but are scarce in law schools and graduate programs in the humanities and social sciences. Most people reflexively assume that this can be explained by language differences. People who did not speak English as their first language or who grew up in households where English was not the language of choice choose professions that are not so dependent on fluent English, we often hear. But the explanation becomes less credible with every passing year. Philip Vernon, after reviewing the evidence on Asian-Americans, concluded that unfamiliarity with the English language and American culture is a plausible explanation only for the results of the early studies. Contemporary studies of Asian-Americans who are thoroughly acculturated also show the typical discrepancy in verbal and visuospatial abilities. American Indians and Inuit similarly score higher visuospatially than verbally;

their ancestors migrated to the Americas from East Asia hundreds of centuries ago.[80] The verbal-visuospatial discrepancy goes deeper than linguistic background.

Vernon's overall appraisal was that the mean Asian-American IQ is about 97 on verbal tests and about 110 on visuospatial tests.[81] Lynn's 1987 review of the IQ literature on East Asians found a median verbal IQ of 98 and a median visuospatial IQ of 106.[82] As of 1993, for Asian-American students who reported that English was the first language they learned (alone or with another language), the Asian-American SAT mean was .21 standard deviation above the national mean on the verbal test and .43 standard deviation above the national mean on the math test. Converted to an IQ metric, this amounts to a 3.3 point elevation of mathematical scores over verbal scores for the high IQ Asian-American population that takes the SAT.[83]

Why do visuospatial abilities develop more than verbal abilities in people of East Asian ancestry in Japan, Hong Kong, Taiwan, mainland China, and other Asian countries and in the United States and elsewhere, despite the differences among the cultures and languages in all those countries? Any simple socioeconomic, cultural, or linguistic explanation is out of the question, given the diversity of living conditions, native languages, educational resources, and cultural practices experienced by Hong Kong Chinese, Japanese in Japan or the United States, Koreans in Korea or Belgium, and Inuit or American Indians. We are not so rash as to assert that the environment or the culture is *wholly* irrelevant to the development of verbal and visuospatial abilities, but the common genetic history of racial East Asians and their North American or European descendants on the one hand, and the racial Europeans and their North American descendants, on the other, cannot plausibly be dismissed as irrelevant.

PROFILE DIFFERENCES BETWEEN WHITES AND BLACKS. Turning now to blacks and whites (using these terms to refer exclusively to Americans), ability profiles have also been important in understanding the nature, and possible genetic component, of group differences. The argument has been developing around what is known as *Spearman's hypothesis*.[84] This hypothesis says that if the B/W difference on test scores reflects a real underlying difference in the general mental ability, g, then the size of the B/W difference will be related to the degree to which the test is saturated with g.[85] In other words, the better a test measures g, the larger the black-white difference will be. Arthur Jensen began to explore this possibility when he looked at the pattern of subtest scores on the WISC-R, taking advantage of the fact that the WISC-R has thirteen subtests, each measuring a somewhat different skill. Converting their statistical procedures into a more easily understood form, here is the logic of what Arthur Jensen and his coauthor, Cyril Reynolds, did.[86]

On average, low-SES whites get lower test scores than high-SES whites. But suppose you were to go through a large set of white test scores from a low-SES and a high-SES group and pull out everyone with an overall IQ score of, say, 105. Now you have identical scores but very different SES groups. The question becomes, What does the pattern of subtest scores look like? The answer is, The same. Once you equalize the overall IQ scores, low-SES and high-SES whites also had close-to-identical mean scores on the individual subtests.

Now do the same exercise with blacks and whites. Again, let us say that you pull all the tests with a full-scale IQ score of exactly 105. Again, you examine the scores on the subtests. But this time the pattern of subtest scores is *not* the same for blacks and whites, even though the subtests add up to the identical overall score.[87] Despite identical overall scores, whites are characteristically stronger than blacks on the subtests involving spatial-perceptual ability, and blacks are characteristically stronger than whites in subtests such as arithmetic and immediate memory, both of which involve retention and retrieval of information.[88] As Jensen and Reynolds note, the pattern of subtest differences between whites and blacks differs sharply from the "no differences" result associated with SES. This directly contradicts the hypothesis that the B/W difference reflects primarily SES differences.[89] What accounts for the different subtest profiles? Jensen and Reynolds proceeded to demonstrate that the results are consistent with Spearman's hypothesis. Whites and blacks differ more on the subtests most highly correlated with *g*, less on those least correlated with *g*.

Since that initial study using the WISC-R, Jensen has been assembling studies that permit further tests of Spearman's hypothesis. He concluded from over a dozen large and representative samples of blacks and whites[90] that "Spearman's hypothesis has been borne out significantly by every study (i.e., 13 out of 13) and no appropriate data set has yet been found that contradicts Spearman's hypothesis."[91] There appears to be no dispute with his summary of the facts. It should be noted that not all group differences behave similarly. For example, deaf children often get lower test scores than hearing children, but the size of the difference is not positively correlated with the test's loading on g.[92] The phenomenon seems peculiarly concentrated in comparisons of ethnic groups.

Jensen's most recent work on Spearman's hypothesis uses reaction time tests instead of traditional mental tests, bypassing many of the usual objections to intelligence test questions. Once again, the more g-loaded the activity is, the larger the B/W difference is, on average.[93] Critics can argue that the entire enterprise is meaningless because g is meaningless, but the hypothesis of a correlation between the magnitude of the g-loading of a test and the magnitude of the black-white difference on that test has been confirmed.[94]

How does the confirmation of Spearman's hypothesis bear on the genetic explanation of ethnic differences? In plain though somewhat imprecise language: The broadest conception of intelligence is embodied in g. Anything other than g is either a narrower cognitive capacity or measurement error. Spearman's hypothesis says in effect that as mental measurement focuses most specifically and reliably on g, the observed black-white mean difference in cognitive ability gets larger.[95] At the same time, g or other broad measures of intelligence typically have relatively high levels of heritability.[96] This does not in itself demand a genetic explanation of the ethnic difference, but by asserting that "the better the test, the greater the ethnic difference," Spearman's hypothesis undercuts many of the environmental explanations of the difference that rely on the proposition (again, simplifying) that the apparent black-white difference is the result of bad tests, not good ones.

Arguments Against a Genetic Explanation

The ubiquitous Arthur Jensen has also published the clearest evidence that the disadvantaged environment of some blacks has depressed their test scores. He found that in black families in rural Georgia, the elder sibling typically has a lower IQ than the younger.[97] The larger the age difference is between the siblings, the larger is the difference in IQ. The implication is that something in the rural Georgia environment was depressing the scores of black children as they grew older.[98] In neither the white families of Georgia, nor white or black families in Berkeley, California, are there comparable signs of a depressive effect of the environment.

But demonstrating that environment can depress cognitive development does not prove that the entire B/W difference is environmental, and in this lies an asymmetry between the contending parties in the debate. Those who argue that genes might be implicated in group differences do not try to argue that genes explain everything. Those who argue against them—Leon Kamin and Richard Lewontin are the most prominent—typically deny that genes have *anything* to do with group differences, a much more ambitious proposition.

CONFRONTING SPEARMAN'S HYPOTHESIS. If one is to make this case against a genetic factor on psychometric grounds, the data supporting Spearman's hypothesis must be confronted. There are two ways to do so: dispute the fact itself or grant the fact but argue that it does not mean what Jensen says it does.

The most searching debate about Spearman's hypothesis was conducted in a journal that publishes both original scholarly works and commentaries on them, *Behavioral and Brain Sciences*, where, in two separate issues in the latter 1980s, thirty-six experts in the relevant fields commented on Jensen's evidence.[99] A number of comments were favorable and provided further support for Jensen's conclusion. Others were critical, for reasons that varied from the philosophical (research into such hurtful issues is not useful) to the highly technical (were Jensen's results the result of varying reliabilities among the tests?). We summarize them in the notes, but the striking feature was that no commentator was able to dispute the empirical claim that the racial gap in cognitive performance scores tends to be larger on tests or activities that draw most on g.[100]

Several years after the exchange on Spearman's hypothesis in *Behavioral and Brain Sciences*, Jan-Eric Gustafsson presented some data finding a considerably smaller correlation than Jensen and others do between g loading and B/W differences on a group of subtests.[101] It is not clear why Gustafsson obtained these atypical results, but, as of this writing, they are still atypical. We have found no others for representative groups of blacks and whites. Our own appraisal of the situation is that Jensen's main contentions regarding Spearman's hypothesis are intact and constitute a major challenge to purely environmental explanations of the B/W difference.

CULTURAL EXPLANATIONS. Another approach has been taken by Jane Mercer, a sociologist and the developer of the System of Multicultural Pluralistic Assessment (SOMPA). Tests are artifacts of a culture, she argues, and a culture may not diffuse equally into every household and community. In a heterogeneous society, subcultures vary in ways that inevitably affect scores on IQ tests. Fewer books in the home means less exposure to the material that a vocabulary subtest measures; the varying ways of socializing children may influence whether a child acquires the skills, or a desire for the skills, that tests test; the "common knowledge" that tests supposedly draw on may not be common in certain households and neighborhoods.

So far, this sounds like a standard argument about cultural bias, and yet Mercer accepts the generalizations that we discussed earlier about internal evidence of bias.[102] She is not claiming that less exposure to books means that blacks score lower on vocabulary questions but do as well as whites on culture-free items. Rather, she argues, the effects of culture are more diffuse. Her argument may be seen as a variant of the "uniform background radiation" hypothesis that we discussed earlier.

Furthermore, she points out, strong correlations between home or community life and IQ scores are readily found. In a study of 180 Latino and 180 non-Latino white elementary school children in Riverside, California, Mercer examined eight sociocultural variables: (1) mother's participation in formal organizations, (2) living in a segregated neighborhood, (3) home language level, (4) socioeconomic status based on occupation and education of head of household, (5) urbanization, (6) mother's achievement values, (7) home ownership, and (8) intact biological family. She then showed that once these sociocultural variables were taken into account, the remaining correlation between ethnic group and IQ among the children fell to near zero.[103]

The problem with this procedure lies in determining what, in fact, these eight variables control for: cultural diffusion, or genetic sources of variation in intelligence as ordinarily understood? Recall that we pointed out earlier that controlling for socioeconomic status typically reduces the B/W difference by about a third. To the extent that parental socioeconomic status is produced by parental IQ, controlling for socioeconomic status controls for parental IQ. One obvious criticism of SOMPA is that it broadens the scope of the control variables to such an extent that the procedure becomes meaningless. After the correlations between the eight sociocultural variables and IQ are, in effect, set to zero, little difference in IQ remains among her ethnic samples. But what does this mean? The obvious possibility is that Mercer has demonstrated only that parents matched on IQ will produce children with similar IQs—not a startling finding.

Mercer points out that the samples differ on the sociocultural variables even after controlling for IQ. The substantial remaining correlations indicate that "important amounts of the variance in sociocultural characteristics [are] unexplained by IQ,"[104] evidence, she says, that they may be treated as substantially independent of IQ.[105] But they are, in fact, not independent of IQ. They remain correlated. Her basic conclusion that "there is no justification for ignoring sociocultural factors when interpreting between-group differences in IQ" seems to us unchallengeable.[106] In the next chapter, we will present other examples of ethnic differences in social behavior that persist after controlling for IQ. But to conclude that genetic differences are ruled out by her analysis is unwarranted, because she cannot demonstrate that a family's sociocultural characteristics are independent of their IQ.[107]

Scholars of Jensen's school point to a number of other difficulties with Mercer's interpretation. When she concludes that cultural diffusion explains the black-white difference, the data she uses show the familiar pattern of Spearman's hypothesis: The more a test loads on *g*, the greater is the B/W difference.[108] Why should cultural diffusion manifest itself in such a patterned way? Her appeal to sociocultural factors does not explain why blacks score lower on backward digit span than forward; why in chronometric tests, black movement time is faster, but reaction time slower, than among whites; or why the B/W difference persists on nonverbal tests such as the Ravens Standard Progressive Matrices. It is also not explained why, if the role of European white cultural diffusion (or the lack of it) is so important in depressing black test performance, it has been so unimportant for Asians.

A number of authors besides Mercer have advanced theories of cultural difference, often treated as part of the "cultural bias" argument but asserting in more sweeping fashion that cultures differ in ways that will be reflected in test scores. In the American context, Wade Boykin is one of the most prominent academic advocates of a distinctive black culture, arguing that nine interrelated dimensions put blacks at odds with the prevailing Eurocentric model. Among them are spirituality (blacks approach life as "essentially vitalistic rather than mechanistic, with the conviction that non-material forces influence people's everyday lives"); a belief in the harmony between humankind and nature; an emphasis on the importance of movement, rhythm, music, and dance "which are taken as central to psychological health"; personal styles that he characterizes as "verve" (high levels of stimulation and energy) and "affect" (emphasis on emotions and expressiveness); and "social time perspective," which he defines as "an orientation in which time is treated as passing through a social space rather than a material one."[109] The notes reference a variety of other authors who have made similar arguments.[110] All, in different ways, purport to explain how large B/W differences in test scores could coexist with equal predictive validity of the test for such things as academic and job performance and yet still not be based on differences in "intelligence," broadly defined, let alone genetic differences.

John Ogbu, a Berkeley anthropologist, has proposed a more specific version of this argument. He suggests that we look at the history of various minority groups to understand the sources of differing levels of intellectual attainment in America. He distinguishes three types of minorities: "autonomous minorities" such as the Amish, Jews, and Mormons, who, while they may be victims of discrimination, are still within the cultural mainstream; "immigrant minorities," such as the Chinese, Filipinos, Japanese, and Koreans within the United States, who moved voluntarily to their new societies and, while they may begin in menial jobs, compare themselves favorably with their peers back in the home country; and, finally, "castelike minorities," such as black Americans, who were involuntary immigrants or otherwise are consigned from birth to a distinctively lower place on the social ladder.[111] Ogbu argues that the differences in test scores are an outcome of this historical distinction, pointing to a number of castes around the world—the untouchables in India, the Buraku in Japan, and Oriental Jews in Israel—that have exhibited comparable problems in educational achievement despite being of the same racial group as the majority.

THE FLYNN EFFECT. Indirect support for the proposition that the observed B/W difference could be the result of environmental factors is provided by the worldwide phenomenon of rising test scores.[112] We call it "the Flynn effect" because of psychologist James Flynn's pivotal role in focusing attention on it, but the phenomenon itself was identified in the 1930s when testers began to notice that IQ scores often rose with every successive year after a test was first standardized. For example, when the Stanford-Binet IQ was restandardized in the mid-1930s, it was observed that individuals earned lower IQs on the new tests than they got on the Stanford-Binet that had been standardized in the mid-1910s; in other words, getting a score of 100 (the population average) was harder to do on the later test.[113] This meant that the average person could answer more items on the old test than the new test. Most of the change has been concentrated in the nonverbal portions of the tests.

The tendency for IQ scores to drift upward as a function of years since standardization has now been substantiated, primarily by Flynn, in many countries and on many IQ tests besides the Stanford-Binet.[114] In some countries, the upward drift since World War II has been as much as a point a year for some spans of years. The national averages have in fact changed by amounts that are comparable to the fifteen or so IQ points separating whites and blacks in America. To put it another way, on the average, whites today may differ in IQ from whites, say, two generations ago as much as whites today differ from blacks today. Given their size and speed, the shifts in time necessarily have been due more to changes in the environment than to changes in the genes.

The question then arises: Couldn't the mean of blacks move 15 points as well through environmental changes? There seems no reason why not—but also no reason to believe that white and Asian means can be made to stand still while the Flynn effect works its magic.

There is a further question to answer: Does a 15-point IQ difference between grandparents and their grandchildren mean that the grandchildren are 15 points *smarter*? Some experts do not believe that the rise is wholly, perhaps not even partly, a rise in intelligence but in the narrower skills involved in intelligence test taking per se;[115] others believe that at least some of rise is in genuine intelligence, perhaps owing to the improvements in public education (by the schools and the media), health care, and nutrition. There is evidence that the rise in scores may be due to a contraction in the distribution of test scores in the population at large, with most of the shrinkage in the bottom half of the distribution.[116] In large-scale studies of the Danish population, virtually all of the upward drift in intelligence test scores is accounted for by the rising performances of the lower half of the distribution.[117] The data we presented earlier on the rise in SAT scores by American blacks are consistent with this story. In general, egalitarian modern societies draw the lower tail of the distribution closer to the mean and thereby raise the average.[118] These findings accord with everyday experience as well. Whether one looks at the worlds of science, literature, politics, or the arts, one does not get the impression that the top of the IQ distribution is filled with more subtle, insightful, or powerful intellects than it was in our grandparents' day.

Whatever we discover about the reasons for the upward drift in the mean of the distribution of test scores, two points are clear. First, a rapid rise in intelligence does not plausibly stretch far into either the past or the future. No one is suggesting, for example, that the IQ of the average American in 1776 was 30 or that it will be 150 a century from now.[119] The rising trend in test scores may already be leveling off in some countries.[120] Second, at any point in time, it is one's position in the distribution that has the most significant implications for social and economic life as we know it and also for the position of one's children.[121]

Flynn suggests that the intergenerational change in IQ has more to do with a shifting link between IQ scores and the underlying trait of intelligence than with a change in intelligence per se.[122] Even so, the instability of test scores across generations should caution against taking the current ethnic differences as etched in stone. There are things we do not yet understand about the relation between IQ and intelligence, which may be relevant for comparisons not just across times but also across cultures and races.

RACIAL ANCESTRY. Just over 100 families with adopted children of white, black, and mixed racial ancestry are being studied in an ongoing analysis of the effects of being raised by white adopting parents of middle or higher social status.[123] This famous transracial adoption study by psychologists Sandra Scarr and Richard Weinberg is the most comprehensive attempt yet to separate the effects of genes and of family environment on the cognitive development of American blacks and whites. The first reports (when the children were about 7 years old) indicated that the black and interracial children had IQs of about 106, well above the national black average or the black average in Minnesota, where the samples were drawn. This result pointed to a considerable impact of the home setting on intelligence. However, a racial and adoptive ordering on IQ existed even in the first follow-up: The mean IQs were 117 for the biological children of white parents, 112 for the white adoptive children, 109 for the adopted children with one black and one white or Asian parent, and 97 for the adopted children with two black parents.[124] Altogether, the data were important and interesting but not decisive regarding the source of the B/W difference. They could most easily have been squared with a theory that the B/W difference has both genetic and environmental elements in it, but, with considerable straining, could perhaps have been stretched to argue for no genetic influence at all.

A follow-up a decade later, with the children in adolescence, does not favor the no-genetics case.[125] The new ordering of IQ means was 109 for the biological children of white parents, 106 for the white adoptive children, 99 for the adopted children with one black parent, and 89 for the adopted children with two black parents.[126] The mean of 89 for adopted children with two black parents was slightly above the national black mean but not above the black mean for the North Central United States. The bottom line is that the gap between the adopted children with two black parents and the adopted children with two white parents was seventeen points, in line with the B/W difference customarily observed. Whatever the environmental impact may have been, it cannot have been large.

Scarr and Weinberg continue to argue that the results are consistent with some form of mixed gene and environmental source of the B/W difference, which seems to us the most plausible conclusion.[127] But whatever the final consensus about the data may be, the debate over the Minnesota transracial adoption study has shifted from an argument about whether the environment explains all or just some of the B/W difference to an argument about whether it explains more than a trivial part of the difference.

Several smaller studies bearing on racial ancestry and IQ were well summarized almost two decades ago by Loehlin, Lindzey, and Spuhler.[129] They found the balance of evidence tipped toward some sort of mixed gene-environment explanation of the B/W difference without saying how much of the difference is genetic and how much environmental.[130] This also echoes the results of Snyderman and Rothman's survey of contemporary specialists.

The German Story

One of the intriguing studies arguing against a large genetic component to IQ differences came about thanks to the Allied occupation of Germany following World War II, when about 4,000 illegitimate children of mixed racial origin were born to German women. A German researcher tracked down 264 children of black servicemen and constructed a comparison group of 83 illegitimate offspring of white occupation troops. The results showed no overall difference in average IQ.[128] The actual IQs of the fathers were unknown, and therefore a variety of selection factors cannot be ruled out. The study is inconclusive but certainly consistent with the suggestion that the B/W difference is largely environmental.

But dissenting voices can be heard in the academic world. For example, a well-known book, *Not in Our Genes*, by geneticist Richard Lewontin and psychologists Steven Rose and Leon Kamin, criticizes anyone who even suggests that there may be a genetic component to the B/W difference or who reads the data as we do, as tipping toward a mixture of genetic and environmental influences.[131] How can they do this? Mostly by emphasizing those aspects of the data that suggest environmental influences, such as the correlations between the adopting parents' IQs or educational levels and the IQs of their black adopted children in the Minnesota study from the first follow-up (the book was published before the second follow-up). But they have nothing to say about the aspects that are consistent with genetic influence, such as the even larger correlations between the educational level of either the biological mothers or fathers and the IQs of their adopted-away black children.[132] Although Lewontin, Rose, and Kamin do not say it in so many words, their argument makes sense if it is directed at the claim that the B/W difference is *entirely* genetic. It does little to elucidate the ongoing scientific inquiry into whether the difference has a genetic component.

We have touched on only the highlights of the arguments on both sides of the genetic issue. One main topic we have left untouched involves the malleability of intelligence, with two extremes of thought: that intelligence is remarkably unmalleable, which undercuts environmental arguments in general and cultural ones in particular, and that intelligence is highly malleable, supporting those same arguments. Because the malleability of intelligence is so critical a policy issue, it deserves a chapter of its own (Chapter 17).

RETHINKING ETHNIC DIFFERENCES

If the reader is now convinced that either the genetic or environmental explanation has won out to the exclusion of the other, we have not done a sufficiently good job of presenting one side or the other. It seems highly likely to us that both genes and the environment have something to do with racial differences. What might the mix be? We are resolutely agnostic on that issue; as far as we can determine, the evidence does not yet justify an estimate.

We are not so naive to think that making such statements will do much good. People find it next to impossible to treat ethnic differences with detachment. That there are understandable reasons for this only increases the need for thinking clearly and with precision about what is and is not important. In particular, we have found that the genetic aspect of ethnic differences has assumed an overwhelming importance. One symptom of this is that while this book was in preparation and regardless of how we described it to anyone who asked, it was assumed that the book's real subject had to be not only ethnic differences in cognitive ability but the genetic source of those differences. It is as if people assumed that we are faced with two alternatives: either (1) the cognitive difference between blacks and whites is genetic, which entails unspoken but dreadful consequences, or (2) the cognitive difference between blacks and whites is environmental, fuzzily equated with some sort of cultural bias in IQ tests, and the difference is therefore temporary and unimportant.

But those are not the only alternatives. They are not even alternatives at all. The major ethnic differences in the United States are not the result of biased tests in the ordinary sense of the term. They may well include some (as yet unknown) genetic component, but nothing suggests that they are entirely genetic. And, most important, it matters little whether the genes are involved at all.

We have already explained why the bias argument does not readily explain the ethnic differences and also why we say that genes may be part of the story. To show why we believe that it makes next to no difference whether genes are part of the reason for the observed differences, a thought experiment may help. Imagine that tomorrow it is discovered that the B/W difference in measured intelligence is entirely genetic in origin. The worst case has come to pass. What difference would this news make in the way that you approach the question of ethnic differences in intelligence? Not someone else but *you.* What has changed for the worse in knowing that the difference is genetic? Here are some hypothetical possibilities.

If it were known that the B/W difference is genetic, would I treat individual blacks differently from the way I would treat them if the differences were environmental? Probably, human nature being what it is, some people would interpret the news as a license for treating all whites as intellectually superior to all blacks. But we hope that putting this possibility down in words makes it obvious how illogical—besides utterly unfounded—such reactions would be. Many blacks would continue to be smarter than many whites. Ethnic differences would continue to be differences in means and distributions; they would continue to be useless, for all practical purposes, when assessing individuals. If you were an employer looking for intellectual talent, an IQ of 120 is an IQ of 120, whether the face is black or white, let alone whether the mean difference in ethnic groups were genetic or environmental. If you were a teacher looking at a classroom of black and white faces, you would have exactly the same information you have now about the probabilities that they would do well or poorly.

If you were a government official in charge of educational expenditures and programs, you would continue to try to improve the education of inner-city blacks, partly out of a belief that everyone should be educated to the limits of his ability, partly out of fairness to the individuals of every degree of ability within that population—but also, let it be emphasized, out of a hardheaded calculation that the net social and economic return of a dollar spent on the elementary and secondary education of a student does not depend on the heritability of a group difference in IQ. More generally: *We cannot think of a legitimate argument why any encounter between individual whites and blacks need be affected by the knowledge that an aggregate ethnic difference in measured intelligence is genetic instead of environmental.*

It is true that employers might under some circumstances find it economically advantageous to use ethnicity as a crude but inexpensive screen to cut down hiring costs (assuming it were not illegal to do so). But this incentive exists already, by virtue of the existence of a difference in observed intelligence regardless of whether the difference is genetic. The *existence* of the difference has many intersections with policy issues. The *source* of the difference has none that we can think of, at least in the short term. Whether it does or not in the long term, we discuss below.

If the differences are genetic, aren't they harder to change than if they are environmental? Another common reaction, this one relies on false assumptions about intelligence. The underlying error is to assume that an environmentally caused deficit is somehow less hard-wired, that it has less impact on "real" capabilities, than does a genetically caused deficit. We have made this point before, but it bears repeating. Some kinds of environmentally induced conditions can be changed (lack of familiarity with television shows for a person without a television set will probably be reduced by purchasing him a television set), but there is no reason to think that intelligence is one of them. To preview a conclusion we will document at length in Chapter 17, an individual's realized intelligence, no matter whether realized through genes or the environment, is not very malleable.

Changing cognitive ability through environmental interventions has proved to be extraordinarily difficult. At best, the examples of special programs that have permanently raised cognitive ability are rare. Perhaps as time goes on we will learn so much about the environment, or so much about how intelligence develops, that effective interventions can be designed. But this is only a hope. Until such advances in social interventions come about, which is unlikely to happen any time soon, it is essential to grasp the point made earlier in the book: A short person who could have been taller had he eaten better as a child is nonetheless really short. The corn planted in the Mojave Desert that could have flourished if it had been planted in Iowa, wasn't planted in Iowa, and there's no way to rescue it when it reaches maturity. Saying that a difference is caused by the environment says nothing about how real it is.

Aren't genetic differences passed down through the generations, while environmental differences are not? Yes and no. Environmentally caused characteristics are by definition not heritable in the narrow technical sense that they do not involve genetic transmission. But nongenetic characteristics can nonetheless run in families. For practical purposes, environments are heritable too. The child who grows up in a punishing environment and thereby is intellectually stunted takes that deficit to the parenting of his children. The learning environment he encountered and the learning environment he provides for his children tend to be similar. The correlation between parents and children is just that: a statistical tendency for these things to be passed down, despite society's attempts to change them, without any necessary genetic component. In trying to break these intergenerational links, even adoption at birth has its limits. Poor prenatal nutrition can stunt cognitive potential in ways that cannot be remedied after birth. Prenatal drug and alcohol abuse can stunt cognitive potential. These traits also run in families and communities and persist for generations, for reasons that have proved difficult to affect.

In sum: If tomorrow you knew beyond a shadow of a doubt that all the cognitive differences between races were 100 percent genetic in origin, nothing of any significance should change. The knowledge would give you no reason to treat individuals differently than if ethnic differences were 100 percent environmental. By the same token, knowing that the differences are 100 percent environmental in origin would not suggest a single program or policy that is not already being tried. It would justify no optimism about the time it will take to narrow the existing gaps. It would not even justify confidence that genetically based differences will not be upon us within a few generations. The impulse to think that environmental sources of difference are less threatening than genetic ones is natural but illusory.

HOW ETHNIC DIFFERENCES FIT INTO THE STORY

In any case, you are *not* going to learn tomorrow that all the cognitive differences between races are 100 percent genetic in origin, because the scientific state of knowledge, unfinished as it is, already gives ample evidence that environment is part of the story. But the evidence eventually may become unequivocal that genes are also part of the story. We are worried that the elite wisdom on this issue, for years almost hysterically in denial about that possibility, will snap too far in the other direction. It is possible to face all the facts on ethnic and race differences in intelligence and not run screaming from the room: That is the essential message.

This chapter is also central to the larger themes of the book, which is why we ask readers who have started with Part III to turn back to the Introduction and begin the long trek. In Part I, we described the formation of a cognitive elite. Given the cognitive differences among ethnic and racial groups, the cognitive elite cannot represent all groups equally, a statement with implications that we will develop in Part IV. In Part II, we described how intelligence is important for understanding the social problems of our time. We limited the discussion to whites to make it easier to think about the evidence without constantly having to worry about racism, cultural bias in the tests, or other extraneous issues.

The material in this chapter lets us proceed. As far as anyone has been able to determine, IQ scores on a properly administered test mean about the same thing for all ethnic groups. A substantial difference in cognitive ability distributions separates whites from blacks, and a smaller one separates East Asians from whites. These differences play out in public and private life. In the rest of Part III, we may now examine the relationship between social problems and IQ on a national scale.

Chapter 14

Ethnic Inequalities in Relation to IQ

Ethnic differences in education, occupations, poverty, unemployment, illegitimacy, crime , and other signs of inequality preoccupy scholars and thoughtful citizens. In this chapter, we examine these differences after cognitive ability is taken into account.

We find that Latinos and whites of similar cognitive ability have similar social behavior and economic outcomes. Some differences remain, and a few are substantial, but the overall pattern is similarity. For blacks and whites, the story is more complicated. On two vital indicators of success—educational attainment and entry into prestigious occupations—the black-white discrepancy reverses. After controlling for IQ, larger numbers of blacks than whites graduate from college and enter the professions. On a third important indicator of success, wages, the black-white difference for year-round workers shrinks from several thousand to a few hundred dollars.

In contrast, the B/W gap in annual family income or in persons below the poverty line narrows after controlling for IQ but still remains sizable. Similarly, differences in unemployment, labor force participation, marriage, and illegitimacy get smaller but remain significant after extracting the effect of IQ. These inequalities must be explained by other factors in American life. Scholars have advanced many such explanations; we will not try to adjudicate among them here, except to suggest that in trying to understand the cultural, social, and economic sources of these differences, understanding how cognitive ability plays into the mix of factors seems indispensable. The role of cognitive ability has seldom been considered in the past. Doing so in future research could clarify issues and focus attention on the factors that are actually producing the more troubling inequalities.

America's pressing social problems are often portrayed in ethnic terms. Does the nation have an unemployment problem? It depends. Among whites in the recession year of 1992, unemployment was under seven percent, but it was fourteen percent among blacks.[1] Poverty? The poverty rate in 1992 for whites was less than twelve percent but thirty-three percent for blacks.[2] Such numbers, and the debate over what they should mean for policy, have been at the center of American social policy since the early 1960s. As Latinos have become a larger portion of the population, the debate has begun to include similar disparities between Latinos and whites.

Such disparities are indisputable. The question is why. Surely history plays a role. Open racism and institutional discrimination of less obvious sorts have been an important part of the historical story for blacks and are relevant to the historical experience of Latinos and Asian-Americans as well. Cultural differences may also be involved. An ethnic group with a strong Roman Catholic heritage, such as Latinos, may behave differently regarding birth control and illegitimacy than one without that background. The tradition of filial respect in the Confucian countries may bear on the behavior of American teenagers of East Asian ancestry when one looks at, for example, delinquency.

Part II showed the impact of cognitive ability on poverty, illegitimacy, crime, and other social problems in America among whites. Chapter 13 showed that the major ethnic groups in America differ, on the average, in cognitive ability. There is accordingly reason to ask what happens to ethnic differences in economic and social behavior when intelligence is held constant. This chapter examines that question.

The NLSY, with its large samples of blacks and Latinos (though not Asians), permits us to address the question directly and in detail. We will show what happens to the ethnic gap on a variety of indicators when IQ is taken into account. To anticipate: In some cases, large ethnic differences disappear altogether, or even reverse, with whites having the disadvantageous outcome compared to blacks and Latinos. In other cases, substantial differences remain, even after the groups are equated not only for cognitive ability but for parental SES and education as well. We do not try to press the analysis further, to find the other reasons why groups may differ socially. The goal of this chapter is to broaden the search for answers after three decades during which scholars have ignored the contribution of IQ to ethnic differences in the main social outcomes of everyday life.

First, we look at the indicators of success that were the focus of Part I, then the indicators of problems that were the focus of Part II.

ETHNIC DIFFERENCES IN EDUCATIONAL AND OCCUPATIONAL SUCCESS

We begin with what should be hailed as a great American success story. Ethnic differences in higher education, occupations, and wages are strikingly diminished after controlling for IQ. Often they vanish. In this sense, America has equalized these central indicators of social success.

Educational Attainment

The conventional view of ethnic differences in education holds that blacks and Latinos still lag far behind, based on comparisons of the percentage of minorities who finish high school, enter college, and earn college degrees. Consider, for example, graduation from high school. As of 1990, 84 percent of whites in the NLSY had gotten a high school diploma, compared to only 73 percent of blacks and 65 percent of Latinos, echoing national statistics.[3] But these percentages are based on everybody, at all levels of intelligence. What were the odds that a black or Latino with an IQ of 103—the average IQ of all high school graduates—completed high school? The answer is that a youngster from either minority group had a *higher* probability of graduating from high school than a white, if all of them had IQs of 103: The odds were 93 percent and 91 percent for blacks and Latinos respectively, compared to 89 percent for whites.[4]

College has similarly opened up to blacks and Latinos. Once again, the raw differentials are large. In national statistics or in the NLSY sample, whites are more than twice as likely to earn college degrees than either blacks or Latinos.[5] The average IQ of all college graduates was, however, about 114. What were the odds that a black or Latino with an IQ of 114 graduated from college? The figure below shows the answers.

All the graphics in this chapter follow the pattern of this one. The top three bars show the probabilities of a particular outcome—college graduation in this case—by ethnic group in the NLSY, given the average age of the sample, which was 29 as of the 1990 interview. In this figure, the top three bars show that a white adult had a 27 percent chance of holding a bachelor's degree, compared to the lower odds for blacks (11 percent) and Latinos (10 percent). The probabilities were computed through a logistic regression analysis.

After controlling for IQ, the probability of graduating from college is about the same for whites and Latinos, higher for blacks

The probability of holding a bachelor's degree

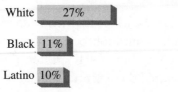

For a person of average age (29) before controlling for IQ

White 27%

Black 11%

Latino 10%

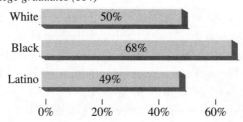

For a person of average age and average IQ for college graduates (114)

White 50%

Black 68%

Latino 49%

0%   20%   40%   60%

The lower set of bars also presents the probabilities by ethnic group, but with one big difference: Now, the equation used to compute the probability assumes that each of these young adults has a certain IQ level. In this case, the computation assumes that everybody has the average IQ of all college graduates in the NLSY—a little over 114. We find that a 29-year-old (in 1990) with an IQ of 114 had a 50 percent chance of having graduated from college if white, 68 percent if black, and 49 percent if Latino. After taking IQ into account, blacks have a better record of earning college degrees than either whites or Latinos. We discuss this black advantage in Chapter 19, when we turn to the effects of affirmative action.

Occupational Status

One of the positive findings about ethnic differences has been that education pays off in occupational status for minorities roughly the same as it does for whites.[6] This was reflected in the NLSY as well: Holding education constant, similar proportions of blacks, Latinos, and whites are found in the various occupational categories.[7]

To what extent does controlling for IQ produce the same result? We know from Chapter 2 that occupations draw from different segments of the cognitive ability distribution. Physicians come from the upper part of the distribution, unskilled laborers from the lower part, and so forth. If one ethnic group has a lower average IQ than another ethnic group, this will be reflected in their occupations, other things equal. What would the occupational distributions of different ethnic groups be after taking cognitive ability into account?

Sociologist Linda Gottfredson has examined this question for blacks and whites.[8] If, for example, black and white males were recruited without discrimination into careers as physicians above a cutoff of an IQ of 112 (which she estimates is a fair approximation to the lower bound for the actual population of physicians), the difference in the qualifying population pools would place the black-white ratio at about .05—about one black doctor for every twenty white ones. According to census data, the actual per capita ratio of black to white male physicians was about .3 in 1980, which is about six black doctors for every twenty white ones. Another example is secondary school teaching, for which a similar calculation implies one black high school teacher for every ten white ones. The actual per capita ratio in 1980 was instead about six black teachers for every ten white ones. In both examples, there are about six times as many blacks in the occupation as there would be if selection by cognitive ability scores were strictly race blind. Gottfredson made these calculations for occupations spanning most of the range of skilled jobs, from physician and engineer at the top end to truck driver and meat cutter at the low end. She concluded that blacks are overrepresented in almost every occupation, but most of all for the high-status occupations like medicine, engineering, and teaching.[9]

We confirm Gottfredson's conclusions with data from the NLSY by going back to the high-IQ occupations we discussed in Chapter 2: lawyers, physicians, dentists, engineers, college teachers, accountants, architects, chemists, computer scientists, mathematicians, natural scientists, and social scientists. Grouping all of these occupations together, what chance did whites, blacks, and Latinos in the NLSY have of entering them? The figure below shows the results.

Before controlling for IQ and using unrounded figures, whites were almost twice as likely to be in high-IQ occupations as blacks and more than half again as likely as Latinos.[10] But after controlling for IQ, the picture reverses. The chance of entering a high-IQ occupation for a

After controlling for IQ, blacks and Latinos have substantially higher probabilities than whites of being in a high-IQ occupation

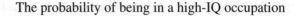

The probability of being in a high-IQ occupation

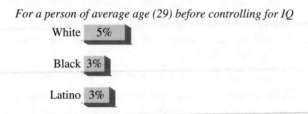

For a person of average age (29) before controlling for IQ

White   5%

Black   3%

Latino   3%

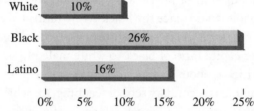

For a person of average age and average IQ for people in high-IQ occupations (117)

White   10%

Black   26%

Latino   16%

0%	5%	10%	15%	20%	25%

black with an IQ of 117 (which was the average IQ of all the people in these occupations in the NLSY sample) was over twice the proportion of whites with the same IQ. Latinos with an IQ of 117 had more than a 50 percent higher chance of entering a high-IQ occupation than whites with the same IQ.[11] This phenomenon applies across a wide range of occupations, as discussed in more detail in Chapter 20.

Wages

We come now to what many people consider the true test of economic equality, dollar income. Two measures of income need to be separated because they speak to different issues. *Wages* provides a direct measure of how much a person gets per unit of time spent on the job. *Annual family income* reflects many other factors as well, being affected by marital status (does the family have two incomes?), nonwage income (from stock dividends to welfare), and the amount of time spent earning wages (did the person have a job for all fifty-two weeks of the year?). We begin with wages, the measure that most directly reflects the current workplace.

As of 1989, white year-round workers (of average age) in the NLSY sample (men and women) made an average of $6,378 more than blacks and $3,963 more than Latinos.[12] The figure below shows what happens controlling for intelligence, this time presenting the results for a year-

After controlling for IQ, ethnic wage differentials shrink from thousands to a few hundred dollars

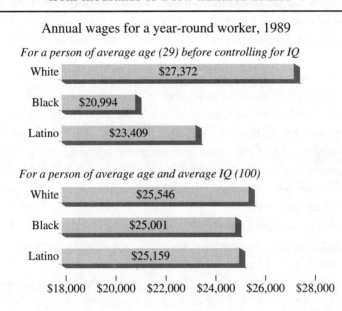

Annual wages for a year-round worker, 1989

For a person of average age (29) before controlling for IQ

White $27,372
Black $20,994
Latino $23,409

For a person of average age and average IQ (100)

White $25,546
Black $25,001
Latino $25,159

$18,000 $20,000 $22,000 $24,000 $26,000 $28,000

round worker with an IQ of 100. The average black who worked year-round was making less than 77 percent of the wage of the average employed white.[13] After controlling for IQ, the average black made 98 percent of the white wage. For Latinos, the ratio after controlling for IQ was also 98 percent of the white wage. Another way to summarize the outcome is that 91 percent of the raw black-white differential in wages and 90 percent of the raw Latino-white differential disappear after controlling for IQ.

These results say that only minor earnings differences separate whites, blacks, and Latinos of equal IQ in the NLSY.[14] Because this finding is so far from what the public commentary assumes, we explore it further. We focus on the situation facing blacks, because the black-white disparities have been at the center of the political debate. Parallel analyses for Latinos and whites generally showed smaller initial income disparities and similar patterns of convergence after controlling for IQ.

Our finding that wage differentials nearly disappear may be a surprise especially in light of the familiar conclusion that wage disparities persist even for blacks and whites with the same education. For example, in the 1992 national data collected by the Bureau of the Census, median earnings of year-round, full-time workers in 1992 were $41,005 for white male graduates with a bachelor's degree and only $31,001 for black males with the same degree.[15] Similar disparities occur all along the educational range. The same pattern is found in the NLSY data. Even after controlling for education, blacks in the NLSY still earned only 80 percent of the white wage, which seems to make a prima facie case for persistent discrimination in the labor market.

Blacks and whites who grow up in similar economic and social circumstances likewise continue to differ in their earning power as adults. This too is true of the NLSY data. Suppose we control for three factors—age, education, and socioeconomic background—that are generally assumed to influence people's wages. The result is that black wages are still only 84 percent of white wages, again suggesting continuing racial discrimination.

And yet controlling just for IQ, ignoring both education and socioeconomic background, raises the average black wage to 98 percent of the white wage and reduces the dollar gap in annual earnings from wages for year-round workers to less than $600. A similar result is given as the bottom row in the following table, this time extracting as well the ef-

Black Wages as a Percentage of White Wages, 1989				
Occupation	Controlling Only for Age	Controlling for Age and Education	Controlling for Age, Education, and Parental SES	Controlling Only for Age and IQ
Professional/technical	87	92	95	102
Managers/administrators	73	72	74	82
Clerical workers	99	97	101	119
Sales workers	74	74	77	89
Craft and kindred workers	81	80	83	96
Transport operatives	88	87	90	108
Other operatives	80	80	84	100
Service workers	92	96	102	119
Unskilled laborers	67	69	72	84
All employed persons	80	82	86	98

fects of different occupational distributions between whites and blacks. The rows above it show what happens when separate wages are computed for different occupational groupings.

The table contains a number of noteworthy particulars, but the most interesting result, which generalizes to every occupational category, is how little difference education makes. A common complaint about wages is that they are artificially affected by credentialism. If credentials are important, then educational differences between blacks and whites should account for much of their income differences. The table, however, shows that knowing the educational level of blacks and whites does little to explain the difference in their wages. Socioeconomic background also fails to explain much of the wage gaps in one occupation after another. That brings us to the final column, in which IQs are controlled while education and socioeconomic background are left to vary as they will. The black-white income differences in most of the occupations shrink considerably. Altogether, the table says that an IQ score is more important—in most cases, much more important—in explaining black-white wage differences than are education and socioeconomic background for every occupational category in it.

Analyzing the results in detail would require much finer breakdowns than the ones presented in the table. Why is there still a meaningful differential in the managers/administrators category after controlling for IQ? Why do blacks earn a large wage premium over whites of equivalent age and IQ in clerical and service jobs? The explanations could have something to do with ethnic factors, but the varieties of jobs within these categories are so wide that the differentials could reflect nothing more than different ethnic distributions in specific jobs (for example, the managers/administrators category includes jobs as different as a top executive at GM and the shift manager of a McDonalds; the service workers category includes both police and busboys). We will not try to conduct those analyses, though we hope others will. At the level represented in the table, it looks as if the job market rewards blacks and whites of equivalent cognitive ability nearly equally in almost every job category.

Although we do not attempt the many analyses that might enrich this basic conclusion, one other factor—gender— is so obvious that we must mention it. When gender is added to the analysis, the black-white differences narrow by one or two additional percentage points for each of the comparisons. In the case of IQ, this means that the racial difference disappears altogether. Controlling for age, IQ, and gender (ignoring education and parental SES), the average wage for year-round black workers in the NLSY sample was 101 percent of the average white wage.

Annual Income and Poverty

We turn from wages to the broader question of annual family income. The overall family income of a 29-year-old in the NLSY (who was not still in school) was $41,558 for whites, compared to only $29,880 for blacks and $35,514 for Latinos. Controlling for cognitive ability shrinks the black-white difference in family income from $11,678 to $2,793, a notable reduction, but not as large as for the wages discussed above: black family income amounted to 93 percent of white family income after controlling for IQ. Meanwhile, mean Latino family income after controlling for IQ was slightly higher than white income (101 percent of the white mean). The persisting gap in family income between blacks and whites is reflected in the poverty data, as the figure below shows. Controlling for IQ shrinks the difference between whites and other ethnic groups substantially but not completely.

Controlling for IQ cuts the poverty differential by 77 percent for blacks and 74 percent for Latinos

The probability of being in poverty

For a person of average age (29) before controlling for IQ

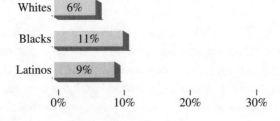

Whites   7%

Blacks   26%

Latinos   18%

For a person of average age and average IQ (100)

Whites   6%

Blacks   11%

Latinos   9%

0%   10%   20%   30%

If commentators and public policy specialists were looking at a 6 percent poverty rate for whites against 11 percent for blacks—the rates for
whites and blacks with IQs of 100 in the lower portion of the graphic—
their conclusions might differ from what they are when they see the unadjusted rates of 7 percent and 26 percent in the upper portion. At the
least, the ethnic disparities would look less grave. But even after controlling for IQ, the black poverty rate remains almost twice as high as
the white rate—still a significant difference.[16] Why does this gap persist, like the gap in total family income, while the gaps in educational
attainment, occupations, and wages did not? The search for an answer
takes us successively further from the things that IQ can explain into
ethnic differences with less well understood roots.[17]

ETHNIC DIFFERENCES ON INDICATORS OF SOCIAL PROBLEMS

Ethnic differences in poverty persist, albeit somewhat reduced, after
controlling for IQ. Let us continue with some of the other signs of social maladjustment that Part II assessed for whites alone, adding ethnic
differences to the analysis. We will not try to cover each of the indicators in those eight chapters (Appendix 6 provides much of that detail),
but it may be instructive to look at a few of the most important ones,
seeing where IQ does, and does not, explain what is happening behind
the scenes.

Unemployment and Labor Force Participation

Black unemployment has been higher than white unemployment for as
long as records have been kept—more than twice as high in 1992, typical of the last twenty years.[18] Once again the NLSY tracks with the national statistics. Restricting the analysis to men who were not enrolled
in school, 21 percent of blacks spent a month or more unemployed in
1989, more than twice the rate of whites (10 percent). The figure for
Latinos was 14 percent. Controlling for cognitive ability reduces these
percentages, but differently for blacks and Latinos. The difference between whites and Latinos disappears altogether, as the figure below
shows; that between whites and blacks narrows but does not disappear.
Black males with an IQ of 100 could expect a 15 percent chance of being unemployed for a month or more as of 1989, compared with an 11
percent chance for whites. Dropping out of the labor force is similarly

After controlling for IQ, the ethnic discrepancy in male unemployment shrinks by more than half for blacks and disappears for Latinos

---

The probability of being unemployed for a month or more

For a person of average age (29) before controlling for IQ

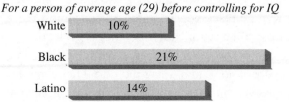

White   10%

Black   21%

Latino   14%

For a person of average age and average IQ (100)

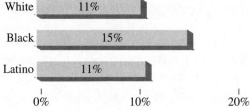

White   11%

Black   15%

Latino   11%

0%   10%   20%

related to IQ. Controlling for IQ shrinks the disparity between blacks and whites by 65 percent and the disparity between Latinos and whites by 73 percent.[19]

Scholars are discussing many possible explanations of the poorer job outcomes for black males, some of which draw on the historical experience of slavery, others on the nature of the urbanizing process following slavery, and still others on the structural shifts in the economy in the 1970s, but ethnic differences in IQ are not often included among the possibilities.[20] Racism and other historical legacies may explain why controlling for IQ does not eliminate differences in unemployment and dropping out of the labor force, but, if so, we would be left with no evident explanation of why such factors are not similarly impeding the equalization of education, occupational selection, or wages, once IQ is taken into account. With the facts in hand, we cannot distinguish between the role of the usual historical factors that people discuss and the possibility of ethnic differences in whatever other personal attributes besides IQ determine a person's ability to do well in the job market. We do not know whether ethnic groups differ on the average in these other ways, let alone why they do so if they do. But to the extent that there are such differences, controlling for IQ will not completely wash out the disparities in unemployment and labor force participation. We will not speculate further along these lines here.

Marriage

Historically, the black-white difference in marriage rates was small until the early 1960s and then widened. By 1991, only 38 percent of black women ages 15 to 44 were married, compared to 58 percent of white women.[21] In using the NLSY, we will limit the analysis to people who had turned 30 by the time of the 1990 interview. Among this group, 78 percent of whites had married before turning 30 compared to only 54 percent of blacks. The white and Latino marriage rates were only a few percentage points apart. When we add cognitive ability to the picture, not much changes. According to the figure below, only 8 percent of the black-white gap disappears after controlling for IQ, leaving a black with an IQ of 100 with a 58 percent chance of having married by his or her thirtieth birthday, compared to a 79 percent chance for a white with the same IQ.

The reasons for this large difference in black and white marriage have been the subject of intense debate that continues as we write. One

Controlling for IQ explains little of the large black-white difference in marriage rates

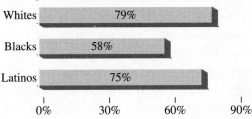

The probability of having married by age 30

For persons age 30 and above before controlling for IQ

Whites 78%

Blacks 54%

Latinos 76%

For persons age 30 and above with average IQ (100)

Whites 79%

Blacks 58%

Latinos 75%

0%   30%   60%   90%

school of thought argues that structural unemployment has reduced the number of marriageable men for black women, but a growing body of information indicates that neither a shortage of black males nor socioeconomic deprivation explains the bulk of the black-white disparity in marriage.[22] As we have just demonstrated, neither does IQ explain much. For reasons that are yet to be fully understood, black America has taken a markedly different stance toward marriage than white and Latino America.

Illegitimacy

A significant difference between blacks and whites in illegitimate births goes back at least to the early part of this century. As with marriage, however, the ethnic gap has changed in the last three decades. In 1960, 24 percent of black children were illegitimate, compared to only 2 percent of white children—a huge proportional difference. But birth within marriage remained the norm for both races. By 1991, the figures on illegitimate births were 68 percent of all births for blacks compared to 39 percent for Latinos and 18 percent for non-Latino whites.[23] The proportional difference had shrunk, but the widening numerical difference between blacks and whites had led to a situation in which births within marriage were no longer the norm for blacks, while they remained the norm (though a deteriorating one) for whites.

The black-white disparity in the NLSY is consistent with the national statistics (although somewhat lower than the latest figures, because it encompasses births from the mid-1970s to 1990). As of the 1990 interview wave, the probabilities that a child of an NLSY woman would be born out of wedlock (controlling for age) were 62 percent for blacks, 23 percent for Latinos, and 12 percent for non-Latino whites. As far as we are able to determine, this disparity cannot be explained away, no matter what variables are entered into the equation. The figure below shows the usual first step, controlling for cognitive ability.

Controlling for IQ reduced the Latino-white difference by 44 percent but the black-white difference by only 20 percent. Nor does it change much when we add the other factors discussed in Chapter 8: socioeconomic background, poverty, coming from a broken home, or education. No matter how the data are sliced, black women in the NLSY (and in every other representative database that we know of) have a much higher proportion of children out of wedlock than either whites or Latinos. As we write, the debate over the ethnic disparity in illegit-

Controlling for IQ narrows the Latino-white difference in illegitimacy but leaves a large gap between blacks and whites

The probability that women bear their children out of wedlock

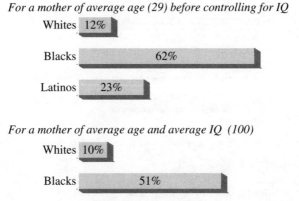

For a mother of average age (29) before controlling for IQ

Whites 12%

Blacks 62%

Latinos 23%

For a mother of average age and average IQ (100)

Whites 10%

Blacks 51%

Latinos 17%

0% 10% 20% 30% 40% 50% 60% 70%

imacy remains as intense and as far from resolution as ever.[24] We can only add that ethnic differences in cognitive ability do not explain much of it either.

Welfare

As of 1991, about 21 percent of black women ages 15 to 44 were on AFDC nationwide, compared to 12 percent of Latino women and 4 percent of white women (including all women, mothers and nonmothers).[25] The NLSY permits us to ask a related question that extends back through time: How many of the NLSY women, ages 26 to 33 as of 1990, had *ever* been on welfare? The answer is that 49 percent of black women and 30 percent of all Latino women had been on welfare at one time or another, compared to 13 percent of white women.[26] The figure shows the effects of controlling for IQ.

Adding cognitive ability explains away much of the disparity in welfare recipiency among blacks, whites, and Latinos. In the case of Latinos, where 84 percent of the difference disappears, the remaining disparity with whites is about three percentage points. The disparity between blacks and whites—30 percent of black women receiving wel-

Controlling for IQ cuts the gap in black-white welfare rates by half and the Latino-white gap by 84 percent

The probability that a woman has ever been on welfare
(all women, mothers and non-mothers)

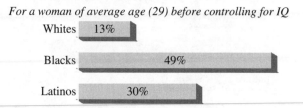

For a woman of average age (29) before controlling for IQ

Whites   13%

Blacks   49%

Latinos   30%

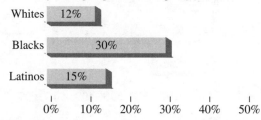

For a woman of average age and average IQ (100)

Whites   12%

Blacks   30%

Latinos   15%

0%   10%   20%   30%   40%   50%

fare, compared to about 12 percent for whites—is still large but only half as large as the difference not adjusted for IQ.

This is as much as we are able to explain away. When we probe further, IQ does not do more to explain the black-white difference. For example, we know that poverty is a crucial factor in determining whether women go on welfare. We therefore explored whether IQ could explain the black-white difference in a particular group of women: those who had had children and had been below the poverty line in the year prior to birth. The results of the analysis are shown in the figure below. Among women who were poor in the year prior to birth, the black-white difference is slightly *larger* after controlling for IQ, not smaller. These data, like those on illegitimacy and marriage, lend support to the suggestion that blacks differ from whites or Latinos in their likelihood of being on welfare for reasons that transcend both poverty and IQ, for reasons that are another subject of continuing debate in the literature.[27]

Low-Birth-Weight Babies

Low birth weight, defined as infants weighing less than 5.5 pounds at birth, is predictive of many subsequent difficulties in the physical, so-

Even among poor mothers, controlling for IQ does not diminish the black-white disparity in welfare recipiency

The probability that a poor mother has ever been on welfare

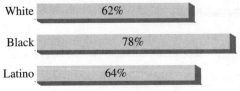

For a poor mother of average age (29) before controlling for IQ

White   62%

Black   78%

Latino   64%

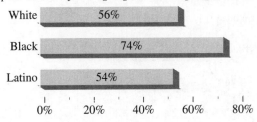

For a poor mother of average age and average IQ (100)

White   56%

Black   74%

Latino   54%

0%   20%   40%   60%   80%

cial, and cognitive development of children. Historically, blacks have had much higher rates of low birth weight than either Latinos or whites. In the most recent reporting year (1991) for national data, almost fourteen percent of all black babies were low birth weight, compared to five percent of white babies and six percent of Latino babies.[28] In our analyses of the NLSY data, we focus on babies who were low birth weight relative to the length of gestation, excluding premature babies who were less than 5.5 pounds but were appropriate for gestational age using the standard pediatric definition.[29] Using unrounded data, the rate of low-birth-weight births for blacks (10 percent) was 2.9 times as high as for whites. The Latino rate was 1.5 times the white rate. The figure shows what happens after controlling for IQ. The black rate, given an IQ of 100, drops from 10 percent to 6 percent, substantially closing the gap with whites.[30] The Latino-white gap remains effectively unchanged.

Children Living in Poverty

In 1992, 47 percent of black children under the age of 18 were living under the poverty line. This extraordinarily high figure was nearly as bad for Latino children, with 40 percent under the poverty line. For

Controlling for IQ cuts the black-white disparity in low-birth-weight babies by half

The probability of giving birth to a low-birth-weight baby

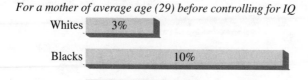

For a mother of average age (29) before controlling for IQ

Whites 3%

Blacks 10%

Latinos 5%

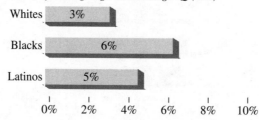

For a mother of average age and average IQ (100)

Whites 3%

Blacks 6%

Latinos 5%

0%   2%   4%   6%   8%   10%

non-Latino whites, the proportion was about 14 percent.[31] In approaching this issue through the NLSY, we concentrated on very young children, identifying those who had lived in families with incomes below the poverty line throughout their first three years of life. The results, before and after controlling for IQ, are shown in the upper figure on the next page. Given a mother with average IQ and average age, the probability that a black child in the NLSY lived in poverty throughout his first three years was only 14 percent, compared to an uncorrected black average of 54 percent. The reduction for Latinos, from 30 percent to 10 percent, was also large. The proportional difference between minorities and whites remains large.[32]

The Child's Home Environment

We now turn to the measure of the home environment, the HOME index, described in Chapter 10. For this and the several other indexes used in the assessment of NLSY children, we follow our practice in Chapter 10, focusing on children at the bottom of each scale, with bottom operationally defined as being in the bottom 10 percent.

The disparities in low HOME index scores between whites and minorities were large (see the lower figure on the next page). It was

Controlling for IQ reduces the discrepancy between minority and white children living in poverty by more than 80 percent

The probability of a child living in poverty for the first three years

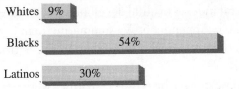

Born to a mother average age (29) before controlling for IQ

Whites 9%

Blacks 54%

Latinos 30%

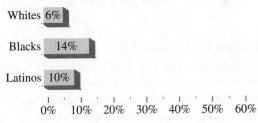

Born to a mother of average age and average IQ (100)

Whites 6%

Blacks 14%

Latinos 10%

0% 10% 20% 30% 40% 50% 60%

Controlling for IQ cuts the ethnic disparity in home environments by half for blacks and more than 60 percent for Latinos

The probability of being in the bottom decile on the HOME index

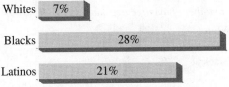

Born to a person of average age (29) before controlling for IQ

Whites 7%

Blacks 28%

Latinos 21%

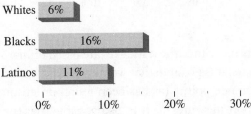

Born to a person of average age and average IQ (100)

Whites 6%

Blacks 16%

Latinos 11%

0% 10% 20% 30%

substantially reduced, by 52 percent for blacks and 64 percent for Latinos, but the black rate remained well over twice the white rate and the Latino rate close to twice the white rate.[33]

Indicators of the Child's Development

Details on the several indexes of child development presented in Chapter 10 may be found in Appendix 6. We summarize them here by showing the proportion of children who showed up in the bottom decile of *any* of the indexes.

As the figure below shows, the ethnic disparities were not great even before controlling for IQ, and they more than disappeared after controlling for IQ. We leave this finding as it stands, but it obviously raises

**Controlling for IQ more than eliminates overall
ethnic differences in the developmental indexes**

The probability that a child was in the bottom decile of
one or more of the developmental indexes

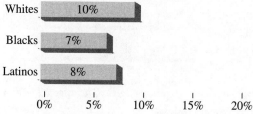

Born to a mother of average age (29) before controlling for IQ

Whites — 10%
Blacks — 13%
Latinos — 13%

Born to a mother of average age and average IQ (100)

Whites — 10%
Blacks — 7%
Latinos — 8%

0%   5%   10%   15%   20%

a number of issues. Since these indexes are based primarily on the mothers' assessments, it is possible that women of different ethnic groups use different reference points (as has been found on ethnic differences in other self-report measures).[34] It is also possible that the results may be taken at face value and that minority children with mothers of similar age and IQ do better on developmental measures than white children, which could have important implications. Filling out this story lies beyond the scope of our work, but we hope it will be taken up by others.[35]

Intellectual Development

We will discuss this topic in more detail in Chapter 15 as we present the effects of differential fertility across ethnic groups. The figure below shows the children of NLSY mothers who scored in the bottom decile on the Peabody Picture Vocabulary Test (PPVT) *based on national norms*, not the bottom decile of children within the NLSY sample. Control-

Based on national norms, high percentages of minority children remain in the bottom decile of IQ after controlling for the mother's IQ

The probability that a child is in the bottom decile of the PPVT
(based on national norms)

Born to a person of average age (29) before controlling for IQ

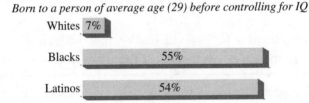

Whites 7%
Blacks 55%
Latinos 54%

Born to a person of average age and average IQ (100)

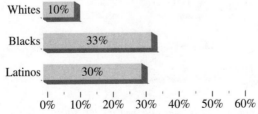

Whites 10%
Blacks 33%
Latinos 30%

0% 10% 20% 30% 40% 50% 60%

ling for the mother's IQ reduces ethnic disparities considerably while once again leaving a broad gap with whites—in this case, roughly an equal gap between whites and both blacks and Latinos. The point that stands out, however, is the extremely large proportion of minority NLSY children who were in the bottom decile of the PPVT—in effect, meaning an IQ of 80 or lower—when national norms are applied. This is one of the reasons for concern about fertility that we discuss in Chapter 15.

Crime

In the national data, blacks are about 3.8 times more likely to be arrested relative to their numbers in the general population than whites (Latino and non-Latino whites are combined in this comparison).[36] Blacks are also disproportionately the victims of crime, especially violent crime. The ratio of black homicide victims to white as of 1990 was 7.7 to 1 for men and 4.8 to 1 for women.[37]

Sociologist Robert Gordon has analyzed black-white differences in crime and concluded that virtually all of the difference in the prevalence of black and white juvenile delinquents is explained by the IQ difference, independent of the effect of socioeconomic status.[38] The only reliable indicator from the NLSY that lets us compare criminal behavior across ethnic groups is the percentage of young men who were ever interviewed while incarcerated.[39] The figure below shows the standard comparison, before and after controlling for cognitive ability. Among white men, the proportion interviewed in a correctional facility after

Controlling for IQ cuts the black-white difference in incarceration by almost three-quarters

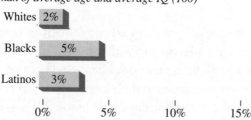

The probability of ever having been interviewed
in a correctional facility

For a man of average age (29) before controlling for IQ

Whites   2%
Blacks   13%
Latinos   6%

For a man of average age and average IQ (100)

Whites   2%
Blacks   5%
Latinos   3%

0%   5%   10%   15%

controlling for age was 2.4 percent; among black men, it was 13.1 percent. This large black-white difference was reduced by almost three-quarters when IQ was taken into account. The relationship of cognitive ability to criminal behavior among whites and blacks appears to be similar.[40] As in the case of other indicators, we are left with a nontrivial black-white difference even after controlling for IQ, but the magnitude of the difference shrinks dramatically.

The Middle Class Values Index

We concluded Part II with the Middle Class Values (MCV) Index, which scores a "yes" for those young adults in the NLSY who were still married to their first spouse, in the labor force if they were men, bearing their children within marriage if they were women, and staying out of jail, and scores a "no" for those who failed any of those criteria. Never-married people who met all the other criteria were excluded. The MCV Index, as unsophisticated as it is, has a serious purpose: It captures a set of behaviors that together typify (though obviously do not define) "solid citizens." Having many such citizens is important for the creation of peaceful and prosperous communities. The figure below shows what

The MCV Index, before and after controlling for IQ

The probability of scoring "yes" on the
Middle Class Values Index

For a person of average age (29) before controlling for IQ

Whites	51%
Blacks	20%
Latinos	31%

For a person of average age and average IQ (100)

Whites	48%
Blacks	32%
Latinos	45%

0%   20%   40%   60%

happens when the MCV Index is applied to different ethnic groups, first adjusting only for age and then controlling for IQ as well. (In interpreting these data, bear in mind that large numbers of people of all ethnicities who did not score "yes" are leading virtuous and productive lives.) The ethnic disparities remain instructive. Before controlling for IQ, large disparities separate both Latinos and blacks from whites. But given average IQ, the Latino-white difference shrank to three percentage points. The difference between blacks and whites and Latinos remains substantial, though only about half as large as it was before controlling for IQ. This outcome is not surprising, given what we have already shown about ethnic differences on the indicators that go into the MCV Index, but it nonetheless points in a summary fashion to a continuing divergence between blacks and the rest of the American population in some basic social and economic behaviors.

A MORE REALISTIC VIEW OF ETHNIC DISPARITIES IN SOCIAL AND ECONOMIC INDICATORS

If one of America's goals is to rid itself of racism and institutional discrimination, then we should welcome the finding that a Latino and white of similar cognitive ability have the same chances of getting a bachelor's degree and working in a white-collar job. A black with the same cognitive ability has an even higher chance than either the Latino or white of having those good things happen. A Latino, black, and white of similar cognitive ability earn annual wages within a few hundred dollars of one another.

Some ethnic differences are not washed away by controlling either for intelligence or for any other variables that we examined. We leave those remaining differences unexplained and look forward to learning from our colleagues where the explanations lie. We urge only that they explore those explanations after they have extracted the role—often the large role—that cognitive ability plays.

Similarly, the evidence presented here should give everyone who writes and talks about ethnic inequalities reason to avoid flamboyant rhetoric about ethnic oppression. Racial and ethnic differences in this country are seen in a new light when cognitive ability is added to the picture. Awareness of these relationships is an essential first step in trying to construct an equitable America.

Chapter 15

The Demography of Intelligence

When people die, they are not replaced one for one by babies who will develop identical IQs. If the new babies grow up to have systematically higher or lower IQs than the people who die, the national distribution of intelligence changes. Mounting evidence indicates that demographic trends are exerting downward pressure on the distribution of cognitive ability in the United States and that the pressures are strong enough to have social consequences.

Throughout the West, modernization has brought falling birth rates. The rates fall faster for educated women than the uneducated. Because education is so closely linked with cognitive ability, this tends to produce a dysgenic effect, or a downward shift in the ability distribution. Furthermore, education leads women to have their babies later—which alone also produces additional dysgenic pressures.

The professional consensus is that the United States has experienced dysgenic pressures throughout either most of the century (the optimists) or all of the century (the pessimists). Women of all races and ethnic groups follow this pattern in similar fashion. There is some evidence that blacks and Latinos are experiencing even more severe dysgenic pressures than whites, which could lead to further divergence between whites and other groups in future generations.

The rules that currently govern immigration provide the other major source of dysgenic pressure. It appears that the mean IQ of immigrants in the 1980s works out to about 95. The low IQ may not be a problem; in the past, immigrants have sometimes shown large increases on such measures. But other evidence indicates that the self-selection process that used to attract the classic American immigrant—brave, hard working, imaginative, self-starting, and often of high IQ—has been changing, and with it the nature of some of the immigrant population.

Putting the pieces together, something worth worrying about is happening to the cognitive capital of the country. Improved health, education, and childhood interventions may hide the demographic effects, but that does not reduce their importance. Whatever good things we can accomplish with changes in the environment would be that much more effective if they did not have to fight a demographic head wind.

So far, we have been treating the distribution of intelligence as a fixed entity. But as the population replenishes itself from generation to generation by birth and immigration, the people who pass from the scene are not going to be replaced, one for one, by other people with the same IQ scores. This is what we mean by the demography of intelligence. The question is not whether demographic processes in and of themselves can have an impact on the distribution of scores—that much is certain—but what and how big the impact is, compared to all the other forces pushing the distribution around. Mounting evidence indicates that demographic trends are exerting downward pressures on the distribution of cognitive ability in the United States and that the pressures are strong enough to have social consequences.

We will refer to this downward pressure as *dysgenesis*, borrowing a term from population biology. However, it is important once again not to be sidetracked by the role of genes versus the role of environment. Children resemble their parents in IQ, for whatever reason, and immigrants and their descendants may not duplicate the distribution of America's resident cognitive ability distribution. If women with low scores are reproducing more rapidly than women with high scores, the distribution of scores will, other things equal, decline, no matter whether the women with the low scores came by them through nature or nurture.[1] More generally, if population growth varies across the range of IQ scores, the next generation will have a different distribution of scores.[2] In trying to foresee changes in American life, what matters is *how* the distribution of intelligence is changing, more than *why*.

Our exploration of this issue will proceed in three stages. First, we will describe the state of knowledge about when and why dysgenesis occurs. Next, we will look at the present state of affairs regarding differential birth rates, differential age of childbearing, and immigration. Finally, we will summarize the shape of the future as best we can discern it and describe the magnitude of the stakes involved.

THE EVOLVING UNDERSTANDING OF DYSGENESIS

The understanding of dysgenesis has been a contest between pessimists and optimists. For many decades when people first began to think systematically about intelligence and reproduction in the late nineteenth century, all was pessimism. The fertility rate in England began to fall in the 1870s, and it did not take long for early students of demography to notice that fertility was declining most markedly at the upper levels of social status, where the people were presumed to be smarter.[3] The larger families were turning up disproportionately in the lower classes. Darwin himself had noted that even within the lower classes, the smaller families had the brighter, the more "prudent," people in them.

All that was needed to conclude that this pattern of reproduction was bad news for the genetic legacy was arithmetic, argued the British scholars around the turn of the twentieth century who wanted to raise the intelligence of the population through a new science that they called eugenics.[4] Their influence crossed the ocean to the United States, where the flood of immigrants from Russia, eastern Europe, and the Mediterranean raised a similar concern. Were those huddled masses bringing to our shores a biological inheritance inconsistent with the American way of life? Some American eugenicists thought so, and they said as much to the Congress when it enacted the Immigration Act of 1924, as we described in the Introduction.[5] Then came scientific enlightenment—the immigrants did not seem to be harming America's genetic legacy a bit—followed by the terrors of nazism and its perversion of eugenics that effectively wiped the idea from public discourse in the West. But at bottom, the Victorian eugenicists and their successors had detected a demographic pattern that seems to arise with great (though not universal) consistency around the world.

For this story, let us turn first to a phenomenon about which there is no serious controversy, the *demographic transition*. Throughout the world, the premodern period is characterized by a balance between high death rates and high birth rates in which the population remains more or less constant. Then modernization brings better hygiene, nutrition, and medicine, and death rates begin to fall. In the early phases of modernization, birth rates remain at their traditional levels, sustained by deeply embedded cultural and social traditions that encourage big families, and population grows swiftly. But culture and tradition eventually give way to the attractions of smaller families and the practical fact that when fewer children die, fewer children need to be born to achieve the same eventual state of affairs. Intrinsic birth rates begin to decline, and eventually the population reaches a slow- or no-growth state.[6]

The falling birth rate is a well known and widely studied feature of the demographic transition. What is less well known, but seems to be true among Western cultures that have passed through the demographic transition, is that declines in lifetime fertility occur disproportionately among educated women and women of higher social status (we will refer to such women as "privileged"), just as the Victorians thought.[7]

Why? One reason is that privileged women lose their reproductive advantage. In premodern times, privileged young women were better nourished, better rested, and had better medical care than the unprivileged. They married earlier and suffered fewer marital disruptions.[8] The net result was that, on average, they ended up with more surviving children than did unprivileged women. As modernization proceeds, these advantages narrow. Another reason is that modern societies provide greater opportunities for privileged women to be something other than full-time mothers. Marriage and reproduction are often deferred for education, for those women who have access to it. On the average, they spend more of their reproductive years in school because they do well in school, because their families support their schooling, or both. Negative correlations between fertility and educational status are likely to be the result.

Even after the school years, motherhood imposes greater cost in lost opportunities on a privileged woman than on an unprivileged one in the contemporary West.[9] A child complicates having a career, and may make a career impossible. Ironically, even monetary costs work against motherhood among privileged women. By our definition, privileged women have more money than deprived women, but for the privileged woman, a child entails expenses that can strain even a high income— from child care for the infant to the cost of moving to an expensive suburb that has a good school system when the child gets older. In planning for a baby—and privileged women tend to plan their babies carefully— such costs are not considered optional but what *must* be spent to raise a child properly. The cost of children is one more reason that privileged women bear few children and postpone the ones they do bear.[10]

Meanwhile, children are likely to impose few opportunity costs on a very poor woman; a "career" is not usually seen as a realistic option. Children continue to have the same attractions that have always led young women to find motherhood intrinsically rewarding. And for women near the poverty line in most countries in the contemporary West, a baby is either free or even profitable, depending on the specific terms of the welfare system in her country.

The Demographic Transition Elsewhere

The generalizations in the text may be stated with confidence about most communities in the West. Elsewhere, there is still much to be learned. Japan has passed through the demographic transition in that overall fertility has dropped, but reproduction has not shifted as markedly toward the lower end of the scale of privilege as in the Western democracies.[11] The reason may be that in Japan, as in other East Asian societies, social obligations that encourage childbearing among the educated may take precedence over the individualistic motives that might otherwise compete with parenthood. Similar considerations may apply to Islamic communities as well, where the demographic transition has been weak. The Mormons offer an American example of a weak demographic transition.[12] An account of the patterns of reproduction must consider cultural, personal, religious, and familial factors, as well as the more obvious social variables, such as the rising levels of education, women's employment, and public health.[13]

Whatever the reasons and whatever the variations from community to community, the reality of the demographic transition in the modern West is indisputable and so, it would seem, is the implication. If reproductive rates are correlated with income and educational levels, which are themselves correlated with intelligence, people with lower intelligence would presumably be outreproducing people with higher intelligence and thereby producing a dysgenic effect.[14] Can we find evidence that dysgenesis is actually happening?

The early studies from the United States, England, France, and Greece all seemed to confirm the reality of dysgenesis.[15] In the 1930s, the eminent psychometrician Raymond Cattell was predicting a loss of 1.0 to 1.5 IQ points per decade,[16] while others were publishing estimated losses of 2 to 4 IQ points per generation.[17] In 1951, another scholar gloomily predicted that "if this trend continues for less than a century,

England and America will be well on the way to becoming nations of near half-wits."[18] The main source of their pessimism was that the average IQ in large families was lower than in smaller families.

Then came a period of optimism. Its harbinger was Frederick Osborn's Eugenic Hypothesis, first stated in 1940, which foresaw a eugenic effect arising from greater equality of social and economic goods and wider availability of birth control.[19] In the late 1940s, data began to come in that seemed to confirm this more sanguine view. Surveys in Scotland found that Scottish school children were getting higher IQs, not lower ones, despite the familiar negative relationship between family size and IQ.[20] Examining this and other new studies, Cattell reconsidered his position, concluding that past estimates might not have adequately investigated the relationship between intelligence and marriage rates, which could have skewed their results.[21]

The new optimism got a boost in 1962 with the publication of "Intelligence and Family Size: A Paradox Resolved," in which the authors, using a large Minnesota sample, showed how it was possible to have both a negative relationship between IQ and family size and, at the same time, to find no dysgenic pattern for IQ.[22] The people who had no children, and whose fertilities were thus omitted from the earlier statistics, the authors suggested, came disproportionately from the lower IQ portion of the population. From the early 1960s through 1980, a series of studies were published showing the same radically changed picture: slowly rising or almost stable intelligence from generation to generation, despite the lower average IQs in the larger families.[23]

The optimism proved to be ephemeral. As scholars examined new data and reexamined the original analyses, they found that the optimistic results turned on factors that were ill understood or ignored at the time the studies were published. First, comparisons between successive generations tested with the same instrument (as in the Scottish studies) were contaminated by the Flynn effect, whereby IQ scores (though not necessarily cognitive ability itself) rise secularly over time (see Chapter 13). Second, the samples used in the most-cited optimistic studies published in the 1960s and 1970s were unrepresentative of the national population. Most of them came from nearly all-white populations of states in the upper Midwest.[24] Two of the important studies published during this period were difficult to interpret because they were based not only on whites but on males (estimating fertility among males poses numerous problems, and male fertility can be quite different from female fertility) and on samples that were restricted to the upper half of the ability distribution, thereby missing what was going on in the lower half.[25]

Apart from these technical problems, however, another feature of the studies yielding optimistic results in the 1960s and 1970s limited their applicability: They were based on the parents of the baby boomers, the children born between 1945 and about 1960. In 1982, demographer Daniel Vining, Jr., opened a new phase of the debate with the publication of his cautiously titled article, "On the Possibility of the Reemergence of a Dysgenic Trend with Respect to Intelligence in American Fertility Differentials."[26] Vining presented data from the National Longitudinal Survey cohorts selected in 1966 and 1968 (the predecessors of the much larger 1979 NLSY sample that we have used so extensively) supporting his hypothesis that people with higher intelligence tend to have fertility rates as high as or higher than anyone else's *in periods of rising fertility* but that in periods of falling birth rates, they tend to have lower fertility rates. The American fertility rate had been falling without a break since the late 1950s, as the baby boom subsided, and Vining suspected that dysgenesis was again underway.

Then two researchers from the University of Texas, Marian Van Court and Frank Bean, finding no evidence for any respite during the baby boom in a nationally representative sample, determined that the childless members of the sample were not disproportionately low IQ at all; on the contrary, they had slightly higher IQs than people with children. Van Court and Bean concluded that the United States had been experiencing an unbroken dysgenic effect since the early years of the century.[27]

Since then, all the news has been bad. Another study of the upper Midwest looked at the fertilities in the mid-1980s of a nearly all-white sample of people in Wisconsin who had been high school seniors as of 1957 and found a dysgenic effect corresponding to about 0.8 IQ point per generation.[28] A 1991 study based on a wholly different approach and using the NLSY suggests that 0.8 per generation may be an underestimate.[29] This study estimated the shifting ethnic makeup of the population, given the differing intrinsic birth rates of the various ethnic groups. Since the main ethnic groups differ in average IQ, a shift in America's ethnic makeup implies a change in the overall average IQ. Even disregarding the impact of differential fertility within ethnic groups, the shifting ethnic makeup by itself would lower the average American IQ by 0.8 point per generation. Since the differential fertility within those ethnic groups is lowering the average score for each group itself (as we show later in the chapter), the 0.8 estimate is a lower bound of the overall population change.

To summarize, there is still uncertainty about whether the United States experienced a brief eugenic interlude after World War II. Van Court and Bean conclude it has been all downhill since the early part of the twentieth century; other researchers are unsure.[30] There is also uncertainty deriving from the Flynn effect. James Flynn has by now convinced everyone that IQ scores rise over time, more or less everywhere they are studied, but there remains little agreement about what that means. For those who believe that the increase in scores represents authentic gains in cognitive ability, the dysgenic effects may be largely swamped by overall gains in the general environment. For those who believe that the increases in scores are primarily due to increased test sophistication without affecting *g*, the Flynn effect is merely a statistical complication that must be taken into account whenever comparing IQ scores from different points in time or across different cultures.

But within the scholarly community, there is little doubt about differential fertility or about whether it is exerting downward pressure on cognitive ability. Further, the scholarly debate of the last fifty years has progressed: The margin of error has narrowed. Scientific progress has helped clarify the dysgenic effects without yet producing a precise calibration of exactly how much the distribution of cognitive ability is declining. This leads to our next topic, the current state of affairs.

DYSGENIC PRESSURES IN AMERICA IN THE EARLY 1990S

Foretelling the future about fertility is a hazardous business, and foretelling it in terms of IQ points per generation is more hazardous still. The unknowns are too many. Will the ranks of career women continue to expand? Or might our granddaughters lead a revival of the traditional family? How will the environmental aspects of cognitive development change (judging from what has happened to SAT scores, it could be for worse as well as better)?[31] Will the Flynn effect continue? Even if it does, what does it mean? No one has any idea how these countervailing forces might play out.

For all these reasons, we do not put much confidence in any specific predictions about what will happen to IQ scores decades from now. But we can say with considerable confidence what is happening right now, and the news is worrisome.[32] There are three major factors to take into account: the number of children born to women at various IQ levels, the age at which they have them, and the cognitive ability of immigrants.

Cognitive Ability and Number of Children

Demographers often take a lifetime fertility of about 2.1 births as the dividing line between having enough children to replenish the parent generation and having too few.[33] Bear that in mind while examining the figure below showing the "completed fertility"—all the babies they have ever had—of American women who had virtually completed their childbearing years in 1992, broken down by their educational attain-

The higher the education, the fewer the babies

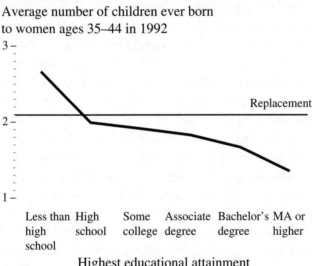

Average number of children ever born
to women ages 35–44 in 1992

Source: Bachu 1993, Table 2.

ment. Overall, college graduates had 1.56 children, one child less than the average for women without a high school diploma. Let us consider the ratio of the two fertilities as a rough index of the degree to which fertility is tipped one way or the other with regard to education. A ratio greater than 1.0 says the tip is toward the lower educational levels. The actual ratio is 1.71, which can be read as 71 percent more births among high school dropouts than among women who graduated from college. At least since the 1950s, the ratio in the United States has been between 1.5 and 1.85.[34]

What does this mean for IQ? We may compute an estimate by using what we know about the mean IQs of the NLSY women who reached various levels of education. Overall, these most recent data on American fertility (based on women ages 35 to 44 in 1992, when the survey was taken) implies that the overall average IQ of American mothers was a little less than 98.[35] This is consistent with the analyses of American fertility that suggest a decline of at least 0.8 point per generation.

This estimate is strengthened by using an altogether different slice of the national picture, based on the birth statistics for virtually all babies born in the United States in a given year, using the data compiled in *Vital Statistics* by the National Center for Health Statistics (NCHS). The most recent data available as we write, for 1991, provide modestly good news: The proportions of children born to better-educated women—and therefore higher-IQ women, on average—have been going up in the last decade. The proportion of babies born to women with sixteen or more years of school (usually indicating a college degree or better) rose from 4.8 percent in 1982 to 5.9 percent in 1991. The proportion of babies born to women with something more than a high school diploma rose from 34.2 percent to 38.2 percent—small changes but in the right direction. The bad news is that the proportion of children born to women with less than a high school education has risen slightly over the last decade, from 22 percent to 24 percent, attributable to an especially steep rise among white women since 1986.

In trying to use the educational information in *Vital Statistics* to estimate the mean IQ of mothers in 1991, it is essential to anticipate the eventual educational attainment of women who had babies while they were still of school age. After doing so, as described in the note,[36] the estimated average IQ of women who gave birth in 1991 was 98. Considering that census data and the *Vital Statistics* data come from different sources and take two different slices of the picture, the similarities are remarkable. The conclusion in both cases is that differential fertility is exerting downward pressure on IQ. At the end of the chapter, we show how much impact changes of this size may have on American society.

What of evidence about dysgenesis in the NLSY itself? As of 1990, the women of the NLSY, ages 25 to 33, still had many childbearing years ahead. Presumably the new births will be weighted toward more highly educated women with higher IQs. Therefore the current mean IQ of the mothers of the NLSY children will rise. Currently, however, it stands at less than 96.[37]

Cognitive Ability and Mother's Age

Population growth depends not just on the total number of children women have but on how old they are when they have them. The effect is dysgenic when a low-IQ group has babies at a younger age than a high-IQ group, even if the total number of children born in each group eventually is the same. Because this conclusion may not be intuitively obvious, think of a simplified example. Suppose that over several generations Group A and Group B average exactly the same number of children, but all the women in Group A always have their babies on their twentieth birthday and all the women in Group B have their children on their thirtieth birthday. The women in group A will produce three generations of children to every two produced by Group B. Something like this has been happening in the United States, as women of lower intelligence have babies younger than women of higher intelligence. The NLSY once again becomes the best source, because it provides age and education along with IQ scores.

The oldest women in the NLSY had reached the age of 33 in 1990, by which time the great majority of first births have taken place.[38] We can thus get a good idea of how age at first birth or average age at all births varies with cognitive ability, recognizing that a small minority of women, mostly highly educated and at the upper portion of the IQ distribution, will eventually nudge those results slightly.[39] We will not try to compensate for these missing data, because the brunt of our argument is that the timing of births has a dysgenic effect. The biases in the data, reported in the table below for women who were 30 or older, tend to *understate* the true magnitude of age differences by IQ.[40]

The average age at first birth was a few months past the 23d birthday. This varied widely, however, by cognitive class. Combining all the ethnic groups in the NLSY, women in the bottom 5 percent of intelligence have their first baby more than seven years younger than women in the top 5 percent. When these figures are computed for the average age for all births (not just the first birth, as in the table), women in the bottom 5 percent have their babies (or all of the ones they have had by their early thirties) at an average of five and a half years earlier. This gap will grow, not shrink, as the NLSY women complete their child-

Age at Childbearing	
Cognitive Class	**Mean Age at First Birth**
I Very bright	27.2
II Bright	25.5
III Normal	23.4
IV Dull	21.0
V Very dull	19.8
Overall average	23.1

bearing years. Even using the current figures, women in the bottom 5 percent of the IQ distribution will have about five generations for every four generations of the top 5 percent. A large and often ignored dysgenic pressure from differences in age at birth is at work.

ETHNIC DIFFERENCES IN FERTILITY

Whatever the ethnic differences in cognitive ability are now, they may change if ethnic groups differ in the extent to which their fertilities are dysgenic or not. In the long run, the vector of demographic trends in intelligence—converging or diverging across ethnic groups—could profoundly affect America's future.

Fertility Rates by Ethnicity

In the 1992 analysis of American fertility using the Current Population Survey (CPS) to which we referred for a national estimate of dysgenesis, women ages 35 to 44 had given birth to an average of 1.94 children: 1.89 for white women, 2.23 for black women, and 2.47 for Latino women.[41] Similar or larger ethnic differences have characterized fertility data for as long as such data have been available, and they have led to a widespread belief that something in black and Latino culture leads them to have larger numbers of children than whites do. We do not dispute that culture can influence family size—the Catholic tradition among Latinos may foster high overall birth rates, for example—but the trends for the three groups are similar once the role of educational level is held constant. Consider the figure below, based on the 1992 CPS study of fertility, again using women in the 35 to 44 age group who have nearly completed their childbearing years.

This figure represents almost total lifetime fertilities, and it tells a simple story. In all three groups of women, more education means lower

Fertility falls as educational level rises in similar fashion for black, white, and Latino women

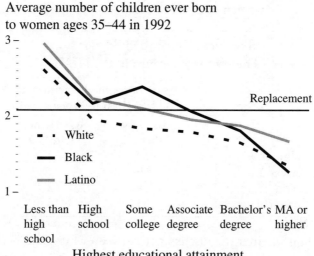

Average number of children ever born
to women ages 35–44 in 1992

Replacement

- - White

— Black

▬ Latino

Less than   High   Some   Associate   Bachelor's MA or
high   school college degree   degree   higher
school

Highest educational attainment

Source: Bachu 1993, Table 2.

fertility. The two minority groups have higher overall fertility, but not by much when education is taken into account. Given the known relationship between IQ and educational attainment, fertility is also falling with rising IQ for each ethnic group. Indeed, if one tries to look into this relationship by assigning IQ equivalents based on the relationship of educational attainment and cognitive ability in the NLSY, it appears that after equating for IQ, black women at a given IQ level may have lower fertility rates than either white or Latino women.[42]

May we then conclude that whites, blacks, and Latinos are on a downhill slope together, neither converging nor diverging in IQ? No, for two reasons. The first is that each ethnic group has different proportions of women at different IQ levels. For example, black women with IQs of 90 and below probably have a fertility rate no higher than that of white women with the same IQs. But even so, only 15 percent of white women in the NLSY fall in the 90-and-below range, compared with 52 percent of black women. The relatively higher fertility rates of women with low IQs therefore have a larger impact on the black population as a whole than on the white. Even if two ethnic groups have equal birth *rates* at a given IQ, one group may have a larger *proportion* of its babies than the other at that IQ. This is illustrated by the next table, which uses the NLSY to see what the next generation looks like so far, when the women of the NLSY had reached the ages of 25 to 33.

	As of 1990, the Percentage of Children Born to Women with:	
	IQs Less than 90	IQs Higher than 110
Whites	19	22
Blacks	69	2
Latinos	64	2
National population	33	15

The Next Generation So Far, for Three Ethnic Groups in the NLSY

Deciding whether the discrepancy between whites and both blacks and Latinos implies an increasing gap in cognitive ability would require extensive modeling involving many assumptions. On the face of it, the discrepancies are so dramatically large that the probability of further divergence seems substantial. Furthermore, insofar as whites have the highest proportion of college-educated women who are delaying child-birth, the gap between whites and the other minorities is more likely to

Delayed Childbearing Across Ethnic Groups

The ages of the women in the NLSY ranged from 25 to 33 as of our last observation of them, meaning that more children remain to be born, a disproportionate number of whom will be born to women at the higher levels of cognitive ability. This prevented us from using the NLSY to make any estimate of the overall dysgenic effect. But the remaining childbearing years are less of a problem when comparing differentials among ethnic groups. The evidence suggests that better-educated women of all ethnic groups postpone childbearing, to similar degrees.[43] Based on this experience, the differentials as they exist among ethnic groups in the 25–33 age cohort will probably remain about the same through the rest of the NLSY women's childbearing years, though the means for each group will probably rise somewhat. Insofar as an artifact exists, it presumably acts to understate the eventual mean for whites, since whites have the largest proportion of women with college and advanced degrees, and therefore presumably the largest group of high-IQ women delaying childbirth.

increase than to diminish as the NLSY women complete their child-bearing years.

Age at Birth by Ethnicity

The second potential source of divergence between ethnic groups lies in the ages at which women are having their children. For NLSY mothers, the average ages when they gave birth as of 1990 (when they were ages 25 to 33) were 24.3 for whites, 23.2 for Latinos, and 22.3 for blacks. Once again, these gaps may be expected to increase as the NLSY women complete their childbearing years. If these age differentials persist over time (and they have been found for as long as the statistics for the different groups have been available), they will produce increasing divergence in the mean cognitive ability of successive generations for the three groups. Evidence from other sources confirms the NLSY, finding an increasing gap between white and nonwhite (primarily black) women in when their reproductive lives begin, and also in their likelihood of remaining childless.[44]

Mothers and Children in the NLSY

As we leave this topic, we may see how these various forces have played out so far in the successive generations of the NLSY. The NLSY has been testing the children of its original subjects, which should eventually provide one of the cleanest estimates of dysgenic trends within ethnic groups. The version of an IQ measure that the NLSY uses is the Peabody Picture Vocabulary Test (PPVT), a highly reliable, g-loaded test that does not require that the child be able to read. It was normed in 1979 with a national sample of 4,200 children to a mean of 100 and a standard deviation of 15.

If we take the NLSY results at face value, American intelligence is plunging. The mean of the entire sample of NLSY children tested in 1986 and 1988 is only 92, more than half a standard deviation below the national mean. We cannot take these results at face value, however. The NLSY's sampling weights make the results "representative of the children of a nationally representative sample of women" who were of certain age ranges in the years the tests were given—which is subtly but importantly different from being a representative sample of American children.[45] But although it is not possible to interpret the overall children's mean with any confidence, it is possible to compare the children of women in different ethnic groups. The results for children at least six years old and their mothers, shown in the table below, indicate that the gap between the children is larger than the gap separating the mothers,

Ethnic Differences in Test Scores in Two Generations		
Ethnic Comparison	Gap Separating the Mothers in IQ Points	Gap Separating the Children in IQ Points
White-black	13.2	17.5
White-Latino	12.2	14.1

by more than 4 points in the case of blacks and whites, by almost two points in the case of whites and Latinos. There are technical reasons to hedge on any more specific interpretation of these data.[46] We may at least say that the results point in a worrisome direction.

Pulling these different views of the situation together, the data reveal demographic pressures for further ethnic divergence in IQ. We will not hazard a guess about the magnitude of ethnic divergence or its speed. Within another decade, assuming that the NLSY continues its testing program, guesses will not be necessary. When large numbers of the NLSY women approach the end of their childbearing years and their children have been tested after reaching an age when IQ scores are stable, we not only will be able to answer whether and how much ethnic groups diverged for that generation of Americans but be able to pin down answers to many of the other questions about dysgenic effects nationwide.

IMMIGRATION

Immigration is an even older American trip wire for impassioned debate than differential fertility, and the disputes continue to the present day.[49] The reason is not hard to find: America has more people flowing into it than any other country. About half of the world's migrants resettling in new countries are coming to America as we write.[50] The people already living here have always viewed this influx of newcomers with

Regression to the Mean to the Rescue?

Those who dismiss the importance of dysgenic trends have mistakenly latched onto the statistical phenomenon known as regression to the mean as a magic cure-all. The editorial page of the *New York Times*, no less, is on record with an assurance to its readers that because of regression to the mean, each successive generation of children of below-average IQ women will get closer to the average and therefore black and white scores will tend to converge.[47] Alas, it doesn't work that way. The results on the PPVT provide a concrete illustration.

Suppose that we recalculate the gap between the three ethnic groups in two successive generations, this time expressing them in terms of standard deviations based on the mothers' and childrens' own standard deviations, not on their place within the national distribution (as in the preceding table).

Regression to the Mean and Ethnic Differences in Test Scores in Two Generations

Ethnic Comparison	Gap Separating the Mothers in SDs	Gap Separating the Children in SDs
White-black	1.17	1.17
White-Latino	1.05	.93

Calculated in this way and shown in the table above, the gap between white and Latino children has shrunk somewhat compared to the gap separating their mothers. The gap between white and black children has at least grown no larger.[48] Why can we obtain this result and still show a growing gap in IQ points between the ethnic groups? The answer is that "mean" referred to in "regression to the mean" is *the population's own mean*. White children of dull white women will, on average, be closer to the mean for whites in *their* generation than their mothers were in *their* generation. A parallel statement applies to black children of dull black women. But this does not necessarily imply that the IQ scores of black and white children must be closer to each other than their mothers' IQ scores were. It is a slippery concept. Some people find it is helpful to remember that regression to the mean works both ways: If you start with a population of dull children and then find the IQs of their parents, you will find that the parents were closer to the mean (on average) than their children. Regression to the mean is a statistical phenomenon, not a biological one.

complicated reactions ranging from pride to alarm. John Higham and others have traced the crests and troughs of nativism and xenophobia, often laced with open racism, in our history.[51]

Recently the debate over immigration has intensified, as the large influx of immigrants in the 1980s, legal and illegal, has reopened all the old arguments. Those who favor open immigration policies point to the adaptability of earlier immigrant populations and their contribution to America's greatness, and remind us that the dire warnings of earlier anti-immigrationists were usually unfounded.[52] Anti-immigrationists instead emphasize the concentration within some immigrant groups of people who commit crimes, fail to work, drop out of school, and go on public assistance. They see limits in the American capacity for assimilating people from alien cultures and for finding productive work for them.[53]

It seems apparent that there are costs and benefits to any immigration policy and that no extreme view, pro or con, is likely to be correct. Beyond that truism, it is apparent that the normative "American" will undergo at least as large a change in the twenty-first century as he has since the original settlement. The nearly 100 percent of immigrants from northern and western Europe in the original settlement gave way to increasing fractions from Africa and from southern and eastern Europe throughout the nineteenth century, thence to a large majority from Asia and Latin America today. America was remade several times over by its immigrants before, and we trust the process will continue. By 2080, according to a typical estimate, America's population will be less than 50 percent non-Latino white, 15 percent black, 25 percent Latino, and over 10 percent Asian and other.[54] Multiculturalism of some sort is certain. Whether it will be a functioning multiculturalism or an unraveling one is the main question about immigration, and not one we can answer.

Our first objective is simply to bring to people's attention that the question is important. Legal immigration in the 1980s contributed 29 percent of the United States' net population increase, much more than at any earlier period in the postwar era.[55] If illegal immigration could be included, the figure would be significantly higher. Immigration does indeed make a difference to the future of the national distribution of intelligence. It may not make as much difference as births in terms of raw numbers, but there is also this consideration: Whereas policy can have only long-term effects on the cognitive distribution of births, it can have large immediate effects on the nature of the immigrant population.

There are few, if any, other domains where public policy could so directly mold the cognitive shape of things to come. Meanwhile, the nation's political ground rules have yet to accept that the intelligence of immigrants is a legitimate topic for policymakers to think about.

Ethnicity and IQ as They Apply to Immigration

In trying to estimate an envelope of what the effects on the cognitive distribution might be, a useful first step is to assume that immigrants to the United States have the mean IQ that has generally been found among persons of that ethnic group, then apply those numbers to the actual distribution of immigrants by ethnicity. Keeping in mind that we are hoping to do no more than establish a range of possibilities, we will begin by following Richard Lynn's computations based on a review of the international data and assign means of 105 to East Asians, 91 to Pacific populations, 84 to blacks, and 100 to whites.[56] We assign 91 to Latinos. We know of no data for Middle East or South Asian populations that permit even a rough estimate. They and an unclassifiable "other" component in the immigration statistics constitute about 11 percent of immigrants and are omitted from the analysis. The ethnic ancestry of legal immigrants in the 1980s breaks down as follows:[57]

Latino	41%
East and Southeast Asian	21%
Non-Latino white	11%
Black	9%
Filipino	7%
Middle East, South Asian, other	11%

Applying the assigned IQ means to this breakdown, the mean IQ of immigrants in the 1980s works out to about 95—essentially unchanged from the 1960s and the 1970s (when the same procedure yields estimates of 96 and 95 respectively). As the proportion of non-Latino whites dropped from 46 percent of immigrants in the 1960s to 11 percent in the 1990s, the percentage of East and Southeast Asians rose from 6 percent to 21 percent, two counterbalancing trends regarding IQ.

Modifying the estimates of ethnic IQs does not make much difference. Some would argue that the East Asian mean is too high. Suppose we drop it to 100. Some would argue that the Latino mean is too low. Suppose we increase it to 94. We could shift the black estimate up or down by large amounts without affecting the overall mean very far. Fiddling with the numbers moves the overall estimated mean by only about a point or two for defensible sets of values. The basic statement is that about 57 percent of legal immigrants in the 1980s came from ethnic groups that have scores significantly below the white average, and in consequence the IQ mean for all immigrants is likely to be below 100.

How about the idea that people who are willing to pack up and move to a strange place in search of a better life are self-selected for desirable qualities such as initiative, determination, energy, and perhaps intelligence as well? Given this plausible expectation, why not assume that the mean for immigrants is significantly *higher* than average for their ethnic groups? Here, the NLSY provides a snapshot of the effects on the distribution of intelligence of the people coming across our borders, insofar as we may compare the IQs of those who were born abroad with those who were born in the United States.

Overall, the IQ of NLSY members who were born abroad was .4 standard deviation lower than the mean of those who were born in the United States, putting the average immigrant for this cohort at about the 34th centile of the native-born population. A breakdown of these results by ethnic groups reveals that different groups are making different contributions to this result. White immigrants have scores that put them a bit above the mean for the native-born American population (though somewhat lower than the mean for native-born American whites). Foreign-born blacks score about five IQ points higher than native-born blacks, for reasons we do not know. Latino immigrants have mean scores more than seven points lower than native-born Latinos and more than a standard deviation below the overall national native-born mean. The NLSY gives no information on the large immigrant population from the countries of East Asia and Vietnam, who might be significantly boosting the immigrant mean.

Even considered simply as cognitive test scores, these results must be interpreted very cautiously. Immigrants typically earn higher scores on tests as they become acculturated, even on tests designed to be "culture fair."[58] The extremely large gap between native-born and foreign-born Latino students seems likely to reflect additional effects of poor English. We do not know if this rise with acculturation is enough to counterbalance the overall .4 standard deviation disadvantage of a sample born elsewhere. Nonetheless, keeping all of these qualifications in mind, the kernel of evidence that must also be acknowledged is that Latino and black immigrants are, at least in the short run, putting some downward pressure on the distribution of intelligence.

Self-Selection Past and Present

Many readers will find these results counterintuitive—the concept of the high-achieving immigrant is deeply ingrained in Americans' view of our country—but a few moments reflection, plus some additional data, may make the results more understandable.[59]

Think back to the immigrant at the turn of the century. America was the Land of Opportunity—but that was all. There were no guarantees, no safety nets. One way or another, an immigrant had to make it on his own. Add to that the wrench of tearing himself and family away from a place where his people might have lived for centuries, the terrors of having to learn a new language and culture, often the prospect of working at jobs he had never tried before, a dozen other reasons for apprehension, and the United States had going for it a crackerjack self-selection mechanism for attracting immigrants who were brave, hard-working, imaginative, self-starting—and probably smart. Immigration can still select for those qualities, but it does not have to. Someone who comes here because his cousin offers him a job, a free airplane ticket, and a place to stay is *not* necessarily self-selected for those qualities. On the contrary, immigrating to America can be for that person a much easier option than staying where he is.

Economists have made considerable progress in understanding how the different types of immigration (and all the ones in between) have played out in practice. To begin with, it has been demonstrated beyond much doubt that immigrants as a whole have more steeply rising earnings than American natives of equal age and measured skills and that, after a relatively short adaptation period of ten to fifteen years, immigrants of equal age and education earn as much as natives.[60] Here is empirical support for the proposition that immigrants taken as a whole are indeed self-selected for qualities that lead to economic success, and one might expect cognitive ability to be among them.

But the experience of different immigrants at different times has varied drastically. Economist George Borjas has systematized the conditions under which immigrants will be self-selected from the upper and lower tails of the ability distribution. Suppose, he says, that you are living in a foreign country, considering whether to emigrate to America. Presumably a major consideration is your potential income in the United

States versus your income if you stay put. Borjas proposes that this calculation interacts with a person's earning potential. It makes sense for
high-ability people to emigrate when they can reasonably think that
they are being underrewarded in their home country, relative to their
ability, and that the United States rewards the same level of ability more
generously. It makes sense for low-ability people to emigrate when they
can reasonably think that the United States not only pays better for the
same work but protects them against poor labor market outcomes (in
comparison to their birth country) with welfare payments and other en-
titlements.[61] In other words, the United States may be expected to draw
high-ability workers from countries that have more extensive welfare
states and less income inequality than the United States (such as Western Europe), and will draw low-ability workers from countries that have
less extensive welfare states and higher income inequality (such as the
poorer countries of the Third World).

Borjas used census data from 1970 and 1980 to examine the experience of immigrants from forty-one countries. In his analysis, he holds
constant the individual immigrant's schooling, age, marital status,
health, and the metropolitan area where the immigrant settled. By holding completed schooling constant, Borjas also factored out some of the
influence of cognitive ability. But the educational systems in the non-
European countries of origin (where we will focus our attention) are
much less efficient at identifying talent than the American educational
system; many bright immigrants have little formal education. We may
think of the unmeasured residual that Borjas did not hold constant as a
cluster of personal and cultural qualities, among which is some role for
cognitive ability. With this in mind, the Borjas data reveal two important findings.

In the 1960s and 1970s, America became much more of a welfare
state. Consistent with that, the earnings potential of the Latino immigrant group fell substantially from 1955 through 1980. Among the non-
European countries, three of the four steepest declines in earnings
potential were among immigrant groups from Colombia, the Dominican Republic, and Mexico, all large contributors to the Latin American
immigrant population. Many of the other countries were not included
in Borjas's forty-one countries, so we do not know whether they followed
the same pattern. Among the Latin American and Latino-Caribbean
nations, only the immigrant groups from Cuba, Brazil, and Panama had

improving potential by Borjas's measures. The 1980 Mexican wave of immigrants had an earnings potential about 15 percent lower than the wave that arrived in 1955. For the Dominican Republic and Colombia, the earnings potential of the 1980 wave was more than 30 percent lower than those who came in 1955, a decline that remains *after* holding education, marital status, age, and location constant.[62]

Similarly, the success of the early waves of West Indian blacks seems unlikely to repeat itself. In his book *Ethnic America*, Thomas Sowell described the successes of West Indian black immigrants, starting from early in the twentieth century, noting among other things that, by 1969, second-generation West Indian blacks had a higher mean income than whites.[63] His account has since become widely cited as evidence for everything from the inherent equality of black and white earning ability to the merits of unrestricted immigration. The Borjas data include three of the major contributors of black immigrants from that region: Jamaica, Haiti, and Trinidad/Tobago. The earnings potential of the immigrant cohorts from these countries in 1970 ranged from 31 to 34 percent less than American natives (after holding education, marital status, age, and location constant).[64] In 1980, the earnings potential from the most recent immigrant waves from these three countries ranged from 26 to 52 percent less than American natives. Immigrants from all three countries are on an extremely slow route to income equality, with Jamaicans and Haitians lagging behind everyone except the lowest-ranking Latin American countries. Borjas's study did not include immigrants from any countries in sub-Saharan Africa.

The results for European immigrants were also consistent with the theory. Borjas's overall appraisal of the data is worth quoting in full:

> The empirical analysis of the earnings of immigrants from 41 different countries using the 1970 and 1980 censuses shows that there are strong country-specific fixed effects in the (labor market) quality of foreign-born persons. In particular, persons from Western European countries do quite well in the United States, and their cohorts have exhibited a general *increase* in earnings (relative to their measured skills) over the postwar period. On the other hand, persons from less developed countries do not perform well in the U.S. labor market and their cohorts have exhibited a general *decrease* in earnings (relative to their measured skills) over the postwar period.[65]

These analyses should not obscure the energy and ability that we often see among immigrants, whether they are staffing the checkout counter at the corner convenience store or teaching classes in the nation's most advanced research centers. The observations of everyday life and the statistical generalizations we have just presented can both be true at the same time, however.

HOW IMPORTANT IS DYSGENIC PRESSURE?

Putting the pieces together—higher fertility and a faster generational cycle among the less intelligent and an immigrant population that is probably somewhat below the native-born average—the case is strong that something worth worrying about is happening to the cognitive capital of the country. How big is the effect? If we were to try to put it in terms of IQ points per generation, the usual metric for such analyses, it would be nearly impossible to make the total come out to less than one point per generation. It might be twice that. But we hope we have emphasized the complications enough to show why such estimates are only marginally useful. Even if an estimate is realistic regarding the current situation, it is impossible to predict how long it may be correct or when and how it may change. It may shrink or grow or remain stable. Demographers disagree about many things, but not that the further into the future we try to look, the more likely our forecasts are to be wrong.

This leads to the last issue that must be considered before it is fruitful to talk about specific demographic policies. So what if the mean IQ is dropping by a point or two per generation? One reason to worry is that the drop may be enlarging ethnic differences in cognitive ability at a time when the nation badly needs narrowing differences. Another reason to worry is that when the mean shifts a little, the size of the tails of the distribution changes a lot. For example, assuming a normal distribution, a three-point drop at the average would reduce the proportion of the population with IQs above 120 (currently the top decile) by 31 percent and the proportion with IQs above 135 (currently the top 1 percent) by 42 percent. The proportion of the population with IQs below 80 (currently the bottom decile) would rise by 41 percent and the proportion with IQs below 65 (currently the bottom 1 percent) would rise by 68 percent. Given the predictive power of IQ scores, particularly in the extremes of the distribution, changes this large would profoundly alter many aspects of American life, none that we can think of to the good.

Suppose we select a subsample of the NLSY, different in only one respect from the complete sample: We randomly delete persons who have a mean IQ of more than 97, until we reach a sample that has a mean IQ of 97—a mere three points below the mean of the full sample.[66]

How different do the crucial social outcomes look? For some behaviors, not much changes. Marriage rates do not change. With a three-point decline at the average, divorce, unemployment, and dropout from the labor force rise only marginally. But the overall poverty rate rises by 11 percent and the proportion of children living in poverty throughout the first three years of their lives rises by 13 percent. The proportion of children born to single mothers rises by 8 percent. The proportion of men interviewed in jail rises by 13 percent. The proportion of children living with nonparental custodians, of women ever on welfare, and of people dropping out of high school all rise by 14 percent. The proportion of young men prevented from working by health problems increases by 18 percent.

This exercise assumed that everything else but IQ remained constant. In the real world, things would no doubt be more complicated. A cascade of secondary effects may make social conditions worse than we suggest or perhaps not so bad. But the overall point is that an apparently minor shift in IQ could produce important social outcomes. Three points in IQ seem to be nothing (and indeed, they *are* nothing in terms of understanding an individual's ability), but a population with an IQ mean that has slipped three points is likely to be importantly worse off. Furthermore, a three-point slide in the near-term future is well within the realm of possibility. The social phenomena that have been so worrisome for the past few decades may in some degree already reflect an ongoing dysgenic effect. It is worth worrying about, and worth trying to do something about.

At the same time, it is not impossible to imagine more hopeful prospects. After all, IQ scores are rising with the Flynn effect. The nation can spend more money more effectively on childhood interventions and improved education. Won't these tend to keep this three-point fall and its consequences from actually happening? They may, but whatever good things we can accomplish with changes in the environment would be that much more effective if they did not have to

---

How Would We Know That IQ Has Been Falling?

Can the United States really have been experiencing falling IQ? Would not we be able to see the consequences? Maybe we have. In 1938, Raymond Cattell, one of most illustrious psychometricians of his age, wrote an article for the *British Journal of Psychology*, "Some Changes in Social life in a Community with a Falling Intelligence Quotient."[67] The article was eerily prescient.

In education, Cattell predicted that academic standards would fall and the curriculum would shift toward less abstract subjects. He foresaw an increase in "delinquency against society"—crime and willful dependency (for example, having a child without being able to care for it) would be in this category. He was not sure whether this would lead to a slackening of moral codes or attempts at tighter government control over individual behavior. The response could go either way, he wrote.

He predicted that a complex modern society with a falling IQ would have to compensate people at the low end of IQ by a "systematized relaxation of moral standards, permitting more direct instinctive satisfactions."[68] In particular, he saw an expanding role for what he called "fantasy compensations." He saw the novel and the cinema as the contemporary means for satisfying it, but he added that "we have probably not seen the end of its development or begun to appreciate its damaging effects on 'reality thinking' habits concerned in other spheres of life"—a prediction hard to fault as one watches the use of TV in today's world and imagines the use of virtual reality helmets in tomorrow's.[69]

Turning to political and social life, he expected to see "the development of a larger 'social problem group' or at least of a group supported, supervised and patronized by extensive state social welfare work." This, he foresaw, would be "inimical to that human solidarity and potential equality of prestige which is essential to democracy."[70]

---

fight a demographic head wind. Perhaps, for example, making the environment better could keep the average IQ at 100, instead of falling to 97 because of the demographic pressures. But the same improved environment could raise the average to 103, if the demographic pressures would cease.

Suppose that downward pressure from demography stopped and maybe modestly turned around in the other direction—nothing dramatic, no eugenic surges in babies by high-IQ women or draconian measures to stop low-IQ women from having babies, just enough of a shift so that the winds were at least heading in the right direction. Then improvements in education and childhood interventions need not struggle to keep us from falling behind; they could bring real progress. Once again, we cannot predict exactly what *would* happen if the mean IQ rose to 103, for example, but we can describe what *does* happen to the statistics when the NLSY sample is altered so that its subjects have a mean of 103.[71]

For starters, the poverty rate falls by 25 percent. So does the proportion of males ever interviewed in jail. High school dropouts fall by 28 percent. Children living without their parents fall by 20 percent. Welfare recipiency, both temporary and chronic, falls by 18 percent. Children born out of wedlock drop by 15 percent. The incidence of low-weight births drops by 12 percent. Children in the bottom decile of home environments drop by 13 percent. Children who live in poverty for the first three years of their lives drop by 20 percent.

The stories of falling and rising IQ are not mirror images of each other, in part for technical reasons explained in the note and partly because the effects of above- and below-average IQ are often asymmetrical.[72] Once again, we must note that the real world is more complex than in our simplified exercise. But the basic implication is hard to dispute: With a rising average, the changes are positive rather than negative.

Consider the poverty rate for people in the NLSY as of 1989, for example. It stood at 11.0 percent.[73] The same sample, depleted of above-97 IQ people until the mean was 97, has a poverty rate of 12.2 percent. The same sample, depleted of below-103 IQ people until the mean was 103, has a poverty rate of 8.3 percent. This represents a swing of almost four percentage points—more than a third of the actual 1989 poverty problem as represented by the full NLSY sample. Suppose we cast this discussion in terms of the "swing." The figure below contains the indicators that show the biggest swing.

A swing from an average IQ of 97 to 103 in the NLSY reduces the proportion of people who never get a high school education by 43 percent, of persons below the poverty line by 36 percent, of children living in foster care or with nonparental relatives by 38 percent, of women ever on welfare by 31 percent. The list goes on, and shows substantial reductions for other indicators discussed in Part II that we have not included in the figure.

The nation is at a fork in the road. It will be moving somewhere within this range of possibilities in the decades to come. It is easy to un-

The swing in social problems that can result
from small shifts in the mean IQ of a population

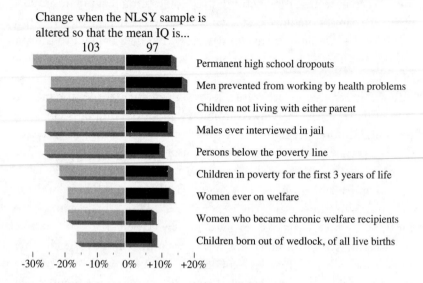

Change when the NLSY sample is
altered so that the mean IQ is...

103   97

Permanent high school dropouts

Men prevented from working by health problems

Children not living with either parent

Males ever interviewed in jail

Persons below the poverty line

Children in poverty for the first 3 years of life

Women ever on welfare

Women who became chronic welfare recipients

Children born out of wedlock, of all live births

-30%   -20%   -10%   0%   +10%   +20%

derstand the historical and social reasons why nobody wants to talk about the demography of intelligence. Our purpose has been to point out that the stakes are large and that continuing to pretend that there's nothing worth thinking about is as reckless as it is foolish. In Part IV, we offer some policies to point the country toward a brighter demographic future.

Chapter 16

Social Behavior and the Prevalence of Low Cognitive Ability

In this chapter, the question is not whether low cognitive ability causes social problems but the prevalence of low cognitive ability among people who have those problems. It is an important distinction. Causal relationships are complex and hard to establish definitely. The measure of prevalence is more straightforward. For most of the worst social problems of our time, the people who have the problem are heavily concentrated in the lower portion of the cognitive ability distribution. Any practical solution must therefore be capable of succeeding with such people.

This chapter brings together the social behaviors we covered in Part II from a new vantage point. The earlier chapters showed that low cognitive ability raises the risk of living in conditions or behaving in ways that society hopes to change. Now the question concerns prevalence: To what extent does low cognitive ability describe the people thus afflicted? The distinction is more familiar in the medical context. High cholesterol may be a risk factor for heart disease, but most people with heart disease may or may not have high cholesterol. If most people who have heart attacks do not have high cholesterol, then lowering the cholesterol of those with high levels will not do much to reduce the frequency of heart attacks in the population at large. Similarly, to the extent that low cognitive ability is prevalent among people who have the problems we hope to solve, policies that are effective for people with low scores should be sought.

The entire NLSY sample, including the Asian-Americans, American Indians, and other ethnic groups that have hitherto been excluded, are used here. The proportions presented in this chapter are representative of America's national population for an age cohort that was 26 to 33 as of 1990.

POVERTY

In 1989, the official national statistics revealed that 11.1 percent of persons ages 25 to 34 years old were poor in that year, virtually identical with the 10.9 percent below the poverty line in the NLSY sample ages 25 to 33. So while the NLSY cannot give us a precise figure for overall national poverty, there is no reason to think that the results from it are misleading for young adults. This is in preface to the sobering figure that follows.

**Forty-eight percent of the poor in 1989 came
from the bottom 20 percent in intelligence**

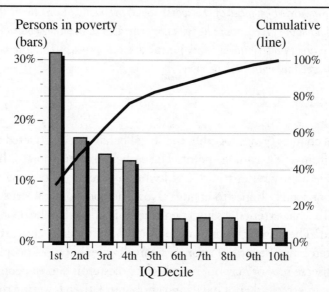

This graph uses conventions that we follow throughout the chapter: The headline gives the percentage of the population in question (in this instance, the poor) in the bottom 20 percent of IQ, and the scale is the same for each graph. The bars show the percentage of the poor population who come from each decile, marked by the scale on the left. If cognitive ability were irrelevant to poverty, the bars would be of equal height, each at just 10 percent. Adding up the percentages in each bar from left to right gives the cumulative percentage, shown by the black line and the right-hand scale. For example, the first two deciles add up to 48 percent; therefore the black line crosses the 48 percent mark at the second bar. The cumulative scale is a way of showing what proportion of poor people fall below any given decile. For example, in the case of poverty, almost 80 percent of poor people are in or below the fourth decile. If cognitive ability were irrelevant, the line would be a straight diagonal from lower left to the upper right.

In terms of IQ points, the cognitive ability deciles in the figure above, as in all the others in the chapter, correspond to the scores in the table below. The bottom two deciles cut off IQ 87 and below and the top two

IQ Equivalents for the Deciles		
Decile	Range	Median
1st	Under 81	74
2d	81–87	84
3d	87–92	90
4th	92–96	94
5th	96–100	98
6th	100–104	102
7th	104–108	106
8th	108–113	110
9th	113–119	116
10th	Above 119	126

deciles cut off IQ 113 and above. It may also be useful to recall that most college graduates and almost everyone with a professional degree fall in the ninth and tenth deciles.

The figure tells us forcefully that poverty is concentrated among those with low cognitive ability. The mean IQ of people below the poverty line was 88. A third of them came from the very bottom decile; they had IQs under 81. Eighty-two percent had below-average IQs.

HIGH SCHOOL DROPOUTS

It will come as no surprise to find that most high school dropouts have low intelligence. The figure below shows the results for persons who

Two-thirds of high school dropouts came from the bottom 20 percent in intelligence

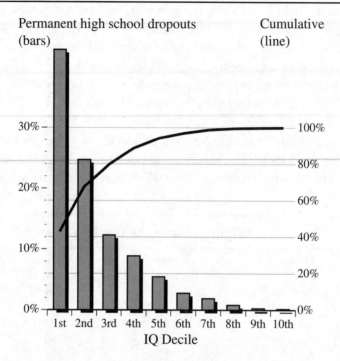

Permanent high school dropouts
(bars)

Cumulative
(line)

dropped out of school and did not subsequently obtain a GED. Overall, 94 percent of those who permanently dropped out of school were below average in IQ. As we noted in Chapter 6, this disproportion is not materially affected by analyses limited to persons who took the intelligence test before they dropped out, so it cannot be explained by the effects of a lack of schooling on their IQs.

Those who drop out of school and later return to get their GED are markedly below the mean of those who finish high school in the normal way, but they are not as severely skewed toward the bottom end of the distribution. Twenty-five percent are in the bottom two IQ deciles, and 69 percent are in the bottom half of the distribution.

MEN AND WORK

The Employed

Year-round employment has only a minor association with cognitive ability. The figure below, based on men who worked fifty-two weeks in 1989, makes this point plainly. We italicize it because, although it is consistent with the analysis presented for whites in Chapter 7, we want to emphasize that the same result applies across ethnic groups.

Seventeen percent of the men who worked year round in 1989 were in the bottom 20 percent of intelligence

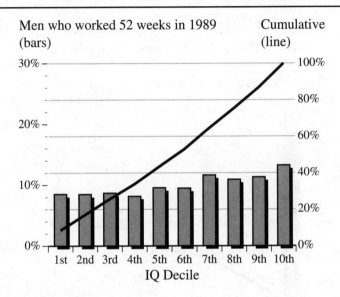

Men who worked 52 weeks in 1989 (bars)   Cumulative (line)

By and large, men who were employed throughout 1982 were spread across the full range of IQs, with only a minor elevation for those in the top four deciles. The mean IQ of year-round workers was 102. Those with low IQ have a statistically tougher time in many ways, but they contribute very nearly their full share to the population of men employed year round, an important fact to remember as a counterweight to most of the other findings in this chapter.

Nonworkers

The prototypical member of the underclass in the public imagination is a young male hanging out on the streets, never working. This amounted to very few men. Only 2.2 percent of NLSY men not in school and not prevented from working because of health problems failed to work at least a week in 1989. But among these 2.2 percent, low cognitive ability predominated. The figure below, limited to civilian men out of school and not physically prevented from working, combines those who said they were unemployed and those who said they had dropped out of the labor force; their common denominator is that they reported zero weeks of working for 1989. The mean IQ of men who did not work at all was 84. Fifty percent were in the bottom decile. Eighty-four percent were below average.

Sixty-four percent of able-bodied men who did not work in 1989 were in the bottom 20 percent of intelligence

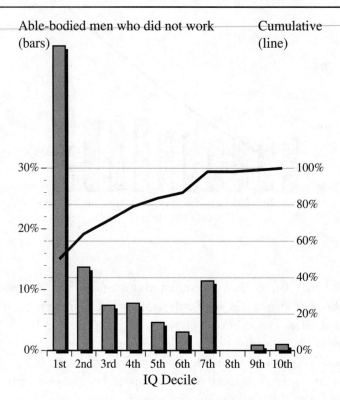

Unemployment

Now we turn to the men not represented in either of the two figures above: men who worked at least some time during 1989 but were out of work for more than four weeks. There was somewhat more unemployment among the lower deciles of IQ, as the figure below shows, but, as the almost straight diagonal line shows, the relationship was not strong.

Twenty-nine percent of able-bodied men who were temporarily out of work in 1989 were in the bottom 20 percent of intelligence

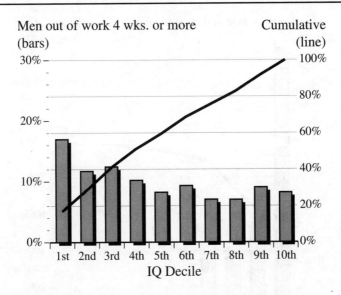

For these men, the mean IQ was 97, three points below average. If we were to add another graph, for men who were out of work for six months but not the full year, it would show a stronger relationship, about halfway between the graph just above and the earlier graph for men who were out of the labor force all year. The general principle is that the longer the period of unemployment, the more prevalent is low IQ. Short-term unemployment is not conspicuously characterized by low IQ; long-term unemployment is.

MEN AND CRIME

The next figure contains the breakdown of the IQs of men in the NLSY who were interviewed in a correctional facility, showing that they had committed at least one offense serious enough to get them locked up. The mean IQ of men who were ever interviewed in a correctional facility was 84. Forty-five percent were concentrated in the bottom decile of cognitive ability. Ninety-three percent of the men were somewhere in the bottom half of the cognitive ability distribution. This high prevalence of low IQ among offenders is consistent with other estimates in the literature, as summarized in Chapter 11.

Sixty-two percent of men ever interviewed in jail or prison came from the bottom 20 percent of intelligence

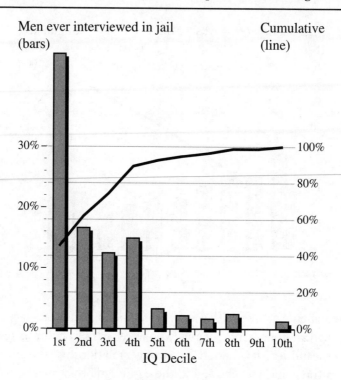

Men ever interviewed in jail (bars)

Cumulative (line)

IQ Decile

WOMEN AND WELFARE

We start with women who have ever received welfare. The data are shown in the figure below. Overall, the mean IQ of women who ever received welfare was 89. About 85 percent of them were below average in IQ, and fewer than 4 percent had IQs in the top two deciles.

For chronic welfare recipients, defined as women who had received welfare for at least five years by 1990, the cognitive distribution was even lower.[1] As the figure shows, 57 percent of chronic welfare mothers were in the bottom two deciles of IQ, 88 percent were in the bottom half of the distribution, and their mean IQ was 86. Just as low IQ was increasingly prevalent as the level of male unemployment increased, so also is low IQ more prevalent among mothers as their dependency on welfare rises.

**Forty-five percent of women who ever received welfare
are in the bottom 20 percent of intelligence**

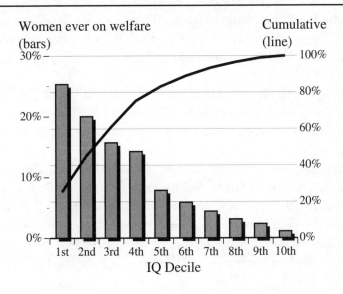

**Fifty-seven percent of chronic welfare recipients
are in the bottom 20 percent of intelligence**

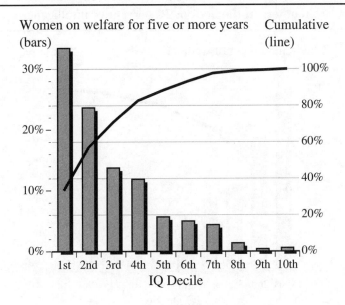

OUTCOMES FOR CHILDREN

In this section, we describe the prevalence of low IQ among the mothers of children with various problems. That is, we are presenting an answer to the question, "If I am trying to deal with a certain problem regarding the children of young adults, what can I assume about the intelligence of their mothers?"

We begin with the overriding fact that, as of 1990, the NLSY mothers as a group were markedly below average in IQ. Their mean IQ was 95.7. Fourteen percent of NLSY children were born to mothers in the bottom decile of IQ; 27 percent to mothers in the bottom two deciles; 62 percent to mothers in the bottom half of the distribution. Thus, for example, a problem involving NLSY children will "ordinarily" show that 62 percent of the children have mothers with below-average IQ. As will be clear, the observed proportions of low-IQ mothers are often considerably elevated above that expectation.[2] But these benchmark figures must be kept in mind when interpreting all the analyses involving children.

Illegitimacy

We start with the children who are born to unmarried women (see the figure below). The mean IQ of mothers of children born out of wedlock

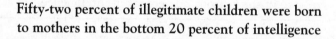

Fifty-two percent of illegitimate children were born to mothers in the bottom 20 percent of intelligence

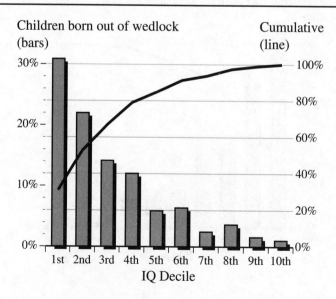

Children born out of wedlock (bars)

Cumulative (line)

IQ Decile

was 87.[3] Of all illegitimate children in the NLSY sample, almost one out of three was born to a mother in the bottom 10 percent of the intelligence distribution, with an IQ under 81, and 85 percent were born to women in the bottom half of the cognitive ability distribution.

Restricting the analysis to those children who are most at risk, these percentages, already extreme, become even more bunched at the lower end of the distribution. Consider children who fit the archetype of the child at risk: born to a poor, single, teenage girl (with poverty measured in the year prior to giving birth). Almost two out of three (64 percent) of such children were born to women in the bottom 20 percent of the cognitive ability distribution. Ninety-five percent of them were born to women in the bottom half.

Other Forms of Single Parenthood

The figure below shows the proportion of NLSY children born to a married couple but living (in 1990) with just their mothers because of divorce or separation. First, a caution: The profile we are about to present

Thirty-one percent of children living with divorced or separated mothers had mothers with IQs in the bottom 20 percent of intelligence

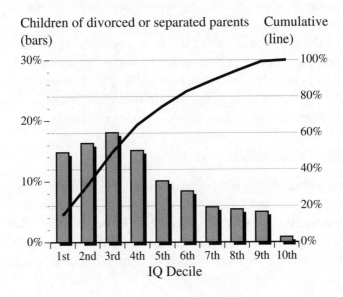

Children of divorced or separated parents (bars)   Cumulative (line)

IQ Decile

may change in the future because so many of the expected divorces among the NLSY sample have not yet occurred. For women who had ever been married in the 25 to 33 age range as of 1990, we may, however, ask: Among their children who were living in mother-only families as of 1990, what is the distribution of the mother's intelligence?

Divorced and separated mothers averaged an IQ of 93.[4] More than half of all children living with their divorced or separated mothers in the NLSY were born to women in the bottom 30 percent of the IQ distribution. Seventy-six percent were born to women in the bottom half of the distribution. Remember that there is no confounding with illegitimacy; all children born out of wedlock are excluded from this sample. The prevailing notion that separation and divorce are so endemic that they affect everyone more or less equally is wrong as regards cognitive ability, at least in this age group.

Perhaps the differences will even out to some extent in the long run. Brighter women get married and have their children later. In the NLSY sample, their marriages have had less time to break up than those for women lower in the distribution. Only time will tell whether and how much the distribution in the graph above will change in the years to come. At this point, the skew is notable and clear.

Pulling together the data on illegitimacy and other forms of single parenthood, here are a few key points:

- Within the bottom two deciles of intelligence, illegitimacy is more common than divorce or separation as the source of single parenthood.
- Beginning with the third decile, divorce and separation become an equal or predominant source of single parenthood.
- The bottom half of the cognitive ability distribution accounts for 82 percent of all children in single-parent homes (combining illegitimacy with divorce or separation) as of 1990.

Low-Birth-Weight Babies

Among whites, the chances of having a low-birth-weight baby were associated with IQ, not socioeconomic background, when both variables were taken into account (Chapter 10). The prevalence of low-birth-weight babies among women in the bottom half of the distribution persists when the entire NLSY sample is considered (the figure below).

**Forty-five percent of low-birth-weight babies had
mothers in the bottom 20 percent of intelligence**

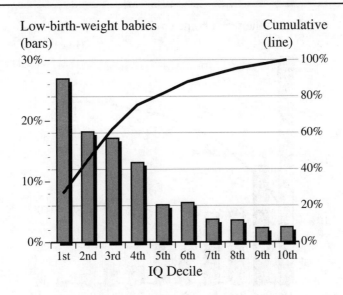

Mothers with low-birth-weight babies averaged an IQ of 89. Almost three out of four (74 percent) mothers were in the bottom half of the IQ distribution.

Deprived Home Environments

Chapter 10 discussed the HOME inventory, a measure combining many indicators of both emotional support (for example, disciplinary style) and cognitive stimulation (for example, reading to the child). Here, we examine children whose HOME scores put them in the bottom 10 percent of environments (using national norms for the HOME inventory).

The mean IQ of mothers of children in the worst home environments was 86. Three out of eight had IQs below 81; 86 percent had IQs below 100. The figure below combines the results for children in all age groups. There were some age differences, however: Generally, the concentration of the worst environments among mothers with low cognitive ability got worse as the children got older. For children ages 3 to 5 who were in the worst home environments, 59 percent had mothers with IQs in the bottom two deciles. For children 6 and older, the figure was 65 percent.

**Fifty-six percent of all children from bottom decile in home environ-
ment were born to mothers in the bottom 20 percent of intelligence**

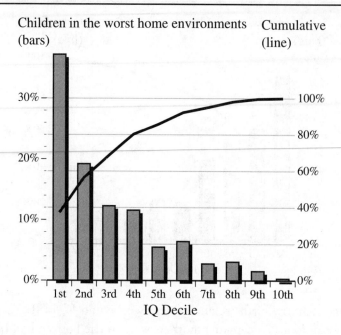

Children in Poverty

The proportion of children living in poverty is one of the most frequently cited statistics in public policy debates and one of the most powerful appeals to action. In considering what actions might be taken, and
what will and won't work, keep the following figure in mind. It shows
the distribution of maternal cognitive ability among children who spent
their first three years below the poverty line. Mothers whose children
lived in poverty throughout their first three years averaged an IQ of 84.
Forty-one percent had mothers in the very bottom decile in cognitive
ability. In all, 93 percent were born to women in the bottom half of the
IQ distribution. Of all the social problems examined in this chapter,
poverty among children is preeminently a problem associated with low
IQ—in this case, low IQ among the mothers.

Developmental Problems Among Children

The prevalence of developmental problems among children is skewed
toward the lower half of the IQ distribution. Rather than present graphs
for each of them, the table below summarizes a consistent situation. See

Sixty-three percent of children who lived in poverty throughout the first three years had mothers in the bottom 20 percent of intelligence

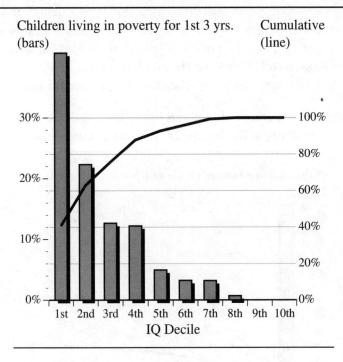

Children living in poverty for 1st 3 yrs. (bars)   Cumulative (line)

IQ Decile

Prevalence of Low IQ Among Mothers of Children with Developmental Problems			
Children in the Worst Decile on:	Percentage of These Children with Mothers in Bottom:		Mean IQ of Mothers
	20% of IQ	50% of IQ	
Friendliness index, 12–23 mos.	49	82	88
Difficulty index, 12–23 mos.	40	71	91
Motor and social development index, birth–47 mos.	38	67	93
Behavioral problems index, children ages 4–11 yrs.	42	78	90

Chapter 10 for a description of the indexes. Low IQ is prevalent among the mothers of children with each of these developmental problems, but none shows as strong a concentration as the developmental indicator we consider the most important for eventual social adjustment: the child's own IQ. The figure below is limited to the cognitive ability of children ages 6 and older when they took the test.

Seventy-two percent of children in the bottom decile of IQ had mothers in the bottom 20 percent of intelligence

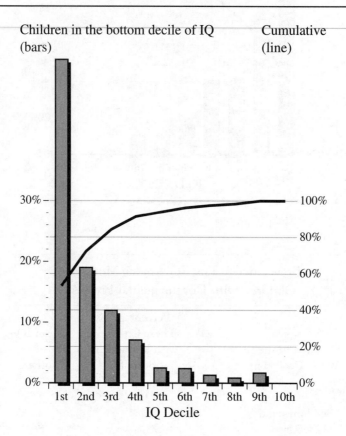

The mean IQ of mothers of children who scored in the bottom decile of a childhood intelligence test was 81.[5] Overall, 94 percent of these children had mothers with IQs under 100. The extreme concentration of low IQ among the children of low-IQ mothers is no surprise. That it is predictable does not make the future any brighter for these children.

CONCLUDING REMARKS

Let us conclude on a brighter note, after so unrelenting a tally of problems. You will recall from Chapter 12 that we developed a Middle Class Values Index. To qualify for a score of "yes," an NLSY person had to be married to his or her first spouse, in the labor force (if a man), bearing children within wedlock (if a woman), and never have been interviewed in jail. How did the NLSY sample break down by IQ? The results are set out in the figure.

Ten percent of people scoring "yes" on the Middle Class Values Index were in the bottom 20 percent of intelligence

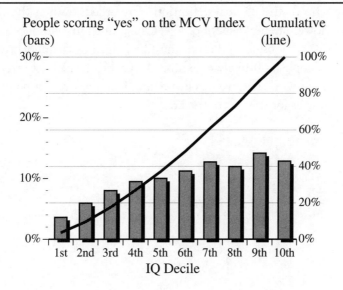

The mean IQ of those who scored "yes" was 104. Those in the bottom two deciles contributed only about 10 percent, half of their proportional share. Those in the bottom half of the cognitive distribution contributed 37 percent. As in the case of year-round employment, the skew toward those in the upper half of the cognitive ability distribution is not extreme. This reminds us again more generally that most people in the lower half of the cognitive distribution are employed, out of poverty, not on welfare, married when they have their babies, providing a nurturing environment for their children, and obeying the law.

We must add another reminder, however. There is a natural tendency to review these figures and conclude that we are really looking at the consequences of social and economic disadvantage, not intelligence. But in Part II, we showed that for virtually all of the indicators reviewed in this chapter, controlling for socioeconomic status does not get rid of the independent impact of IQ. On the contrary, controlling for IQ often gets rid of the independent impact of socioeconomic status. We have not tried to present the replications of those analyses for all ethnic groups combined, but they tell the same story.

The lesson of this chapter is that large proportions of the people who exhibit the behaviors and problems that dominate the nation's social policy agenda have limited cognitive ability. Often they are near the definition for mental retardation (though the NLSY sample screened out people who fit the clinical definition of retarded). When the nation seeks to lower unemployment or lower the crime rate or induce welfare mothers to get jobs, the solutions must be judged by their effectiveness with the people most likely to exhibit the problem: the least intelligent people. And with that, we reach the practical questions of policy that will occupy us for the rest of the book.

PART IV

Living Together

Our analysis provides few clear and decisive solutions to the major domestic issues of the day. But, at the same time, there is no major domestic issue for which the news we bring is irrelevant.

Do we want to persuade poor single teenagers not to have babies? The knowledge that 95 percent of poor teenage women who have babies are also below average in intelligence should prompt skepticism about strategies that rely on abstract and far-sighted calculations of self-interest. Do we favor job training programs for chronically unemployed men? Any program is going to fail unless it is designed for a target population half of which has IQs below 80. Do we wish to reduce income inequality? If so, we need to understand how the market for cognitive ability drives the process. Do we aspire to a "world class" educational system for America? Before deciding what is wrong with the current system, we had better think hard about how cognitive ability and education are linked. Part IV tries to lay out some of these connections.

Chapter 17 summarizes what we know about direct efforts to increase cognitive ability by altering the social and physical environment in which people develop and live. Such efforts may succeed eventually, but so far the record is spotty.

Chapter 18 reviews the American educational experience of the past few decades. It has been more successful with the average and below-average student than many people think, we conclude, but has neglected the gifted minority who will greatly affect how well America does in the twenty-first century.

In Chapters 19 and 20, the focus shifts to affirmative action policies in education and in the workplace. Our society has dedicated itself to coping with a particular sort of inequality, trying to equalize outcomes for various groups. The country has retreated from older principles of individual equality before the law and has adopted policies that treat people as members of groups. Our contribution (we hope) is to calibrate the policy choices associated with affirmative action, to make costs and benefits clearer than they usually are.

The final two chapters look to the future. In Chapter 21, we sound a tocsin. Predictions are always chancy, and ours are especially glum, but we think that cognitive stratification may be taking the country down dangerous paths. Chapter 22 follows up with our conception of a liberal and just society, in light of the story that the rest of the book has told. The result is a personal statement of how we believe America can face up to inequality in the 21st century and remain uniquely America.

Chapter 17

Raising Cognitive Ability

Raising intelligence significantly, consistently, and affordably would circum-vent many of the problems that we have described. Furthermore, the needed environmental improvements—better nutrition, stimulating environments for preschool children, good schools thereafter—seem obvious. But raising intel-ligence is not easy.

Nutrition may offer one of the more promising approaches. Height and weight have increased markedly with better nutrition. The rising IQs in many countries suggest that better nutrition may be increasing intelligence too. Con-trolled studies have made some progress in uncovering a link between improved nutrition and elevated cognitive ability as well, but it remains unproved and not well understood.

Formal schooling offers little hope of narrowing cognitive inequality on a large scale in developed countries, because so much of its potential contribu-tion has already been realized with the advent of universal twelve-year sys-tems. Special programs to improve intelligence within the school have had minor and probably temporary effects on intelligence. There is more to be gained from educational research to find new methods of instruction than from more interventions of the type already tried.

Preschool has borne many of the recent hopes for improving intelligence. However, Head Start, the largest program, does not improve cognitive func-tioning. More intensive, hence more costly, preschool programs may raise in-telligence, but both the size and the reality of the improvements are in dispute.

The one intervention that works consistently is adoption at birth from a bad family environment to a good one. The average gains in childhood IQ associ-ated with adoption are in the region of six points—not spectacular but not neg-ligible either.

Taken together, the story of attempts to raise intelligence is one of high hopes, flamboyant claims, and disappointing results. For the foreseeable fu-ture, the problems of low cognitive ability are not going to be solved by out-side interventions to make children smarter.

Can people become smarter if they are given the right kind of help? If raising intelligence is possible, then the material in Parts II and III constitutes a clarion call for programs to do so. Social problems are highly concentrated among people at the bottom of the cognitive distribution; those problems become much less prevalent as IQ increases even modestly; and the history of increases in IQ suggests that they occur most readily at the bottom of the distribution. Why not mount a major national effort to produce such increases? It does not appear on its face to be an impossible task. Even the highest estimates of heritability leave 20 to 30 percent of cognitive ability to be shaped by the environment. Some researchers continue to argue that the right proportion is 50 to 60 percent. In either case, eliminating the disadvantages that afflict people in poor surroundings should increase their cognitive functioning.[1]

Upon first consideration, the ways to eliminate those disadvantages seem obvious. Many children of low-income parents grow up in terrible home environments, with little stimulation or nurturing. Surely, it would seem, intelligence would rise if these children were placed in day care environments where professionals provided that stimulation and nurturing. Schools in poor neighborhoods are often run down and chaotic. Isn't it clear that increasing the investment in schools would pay off in higher scores?

Limitless possibilities for improving intelligence environmentally wait to be uncovered by science: improved educational methods, diets, treatments for disease, prenatal care, educational media, and even medicines to make one smarter. In principle, intelligence can be raised environmentally to unknown limits.

Yet the more one knows about the evidence, the harder it is to be optimistic about prospects in the near future for raising the scores of the people who are most disadvantaged by their low scores. For one thing, it is hard to find new ways to use existing resources that are not already being done. The nurturing of the young—including the cognitive nurturing—is one of the central purposes of human society. That, after all, is what families mainly do. Very high proportions of children already get prenatal care, nutrition, home environments, and classroom environments that are good enough to leave little room for measurable improvement. The grim stories about childhood deprivation involve a small proportion of children. And when it comes to helping that small proportion of children, the results seldom approach expectations. We may be deeply and properly dissatisfied with the nurturing of American intelligence, but finding solutions that are affordable, politically tolerable, and not already being tried is another matter altogether.

In this chapter, we move through a succession of topics. First we consider the effects of nutrition. We then discuss a sequence of successively more targeted, intense social interventions: education in general, preschool interventions, intensive support for children at risk for retardation, and the most extreme form of social intervention, adoption at birth. We close with our thoughts on what society's experiences with these interventions should mean for policy in the future.

NUTRITION

Most of us have been urged by a parent or grandparent to eat the "brain food," which seemed invariably to be the most unpalatable thing on the table. This idea of a connection between diet and intelligence has an ancient history going back to *mens sana in corpora sano*.[2] In the twentieth century, the plausibility of a connection has been reinforced by the fact that people in affluent countries are larger than their ancestors were, presumably in part because they are eating better. IQ scores, too, have been rising during approximately the same period—the Flynn effect described in Chapter 13. These coincident changes do not prove that better eating makes for smarter people, but count as circumstantial evidence.

For a while, however, scientific research seemed to have weakened the case for any link between nutrition and IQ. The most damaging blow was a study of over 100,000 Dutch men who were born around a time of intense famine in several Dutch cities near the end of World War II.[3] Nineteen years later, the men took intelligence tests as part of the qualification for national military service, and it occurred to scholars to compare the ones who were born in the depths of the famine to those born just before and just after it. Many pregnant women miscarried during the famine, but their surviving sons scored no lower in intelligence than the men born to mothers who had little or no exposure to famine. But as important as this study was, some scientists were not entirely convinced by its negative findings. The Dutch famine was relatively brief—three months or so—and limited to the pre- and perinatal period of the men's lives. And while the mothers were indeed starving for calories, their deficiencies in vitamins, minerals, and other dietary elements were perhaps too brief to take a toll.[4]

Another approach to the impact of nutrition on cognitive ability is to see whether enriched diets can raise scores. A breakthrough study done in Great Britain in the late 1980s concluded that the answer was yes.[5] David Benton and Gwilym Roberts gave a sample of thirty Welsh 12- to 13-year-old children vitamin and mineral supplements for eight months and compared their test scores with an equal number of their schoolmates getting nonnutritive placebos. The Welsh children were not known to be malnourished, but those getting the supplement gained eight points more in their nonverbal intelligence test scores than those getting the placebo, a large and statistically significant improvement. Verbal scores showed no differential improvement.[6]

A recent American confirmation of the Welsh results gave over 600 eighth and tenth graders in several California schools daily pills for thirteen weeks.[7] The pills contained either half the recommended daily allowances (RDA) of a wide assortment of vitamins and minerals, precisely the RDA, twice the RDA, or a placebo. The vitamin and mineral supplement raised scores on most of the nonverbal subtests of a standard intelligence test.[8] The verbal intelligence test scores again failed to register any benefit, but that is consistent with the Flynn effect: The rising average intelligence scores of nations seem primarily to be on nonverbal tests.

The net average benefit for pills providing one RDA was about four points in nonverbal intelligence in the California study. But this average gain comprised many youngsters who did not benefit at all, mixed with some whose gains exceeded fifteen points. The children who did not benefit were presumably already getting the vitamins and minerals they needed for developing their nonverbal scores in their regular diets. But this is just a hypothesis at present. It remains to be shown whether the gain from vitamins or minerals can be associated with preexisting food deficiencies, let alone which particular dietary ingredients, in what amounts, produce the gains.[9] Youngsters getting exactly the RDA had the largest gain in scores; those taking either more or less of the supplement benefited less, if at all.[10] This is not only puzzling but worrisome. Could it mean that excessive dosages of vitamins and/or minerals harm intellectual functioning? There is no evidence that it does, but at the least, it reinforces the prudence of doing more research before going overboard for vitamin and mineral supplements.

Other Physiological Influences on IQ. Or Are They? Two Further Examples

---

The physiological environment seems to be associated with IQ in other ways. For example, some studies (but not all) have found a small decline in IQ of each successive child born to a given woman, even after holding overall family size constant.[12] Is this a matter of the social environment within the family, which changes as new children enter it, or the physiological environment in the uterus, which is both older on average and has a longer history of childbirth with each successive pregnancy? The answer is unclear, and both views have been advanced. But, whichever it is, this would be a genuine environmental effect on intelligence, since the rolls of the genetic dice for the successive offspring of a given mother and father are independent as far as anyone knows.

Another environmental and possibly physiological influence on IQ is suggested by data from twins. Among identical twins, the one with the higher IQ is likely to have been heavier at birth.[13] This is part of a more general finding that higher weights at birth are associated with higher IQs in childhood, but the identical twin data decisively prove that the correlation between birth weight and later intelligence has an environmental element, since identical twins are genetic clones.[14] It is less certain that there are no social factors here: People may treat twin babies differently if one is plumper than the other. Training mothers in how to be more attentive to their low-birth-weight babies seems, in fact, to raise later IQ, at least up to the age of 7.[15]

This caution is reinforced by the inconsistency of the nutritional effect on IQ. Many studies that seem to be well-conducted variations of the successful ones have failed to demonstrate any effect on IQ at all.[11] The reasonable middle ground at this point is to conclude that providing children with the recommended daily allowance of vitamins is a good idea for many reasons and might also have a helpful effect on IQ.

RAISING IQ THROUGH BETTER EDUCATION

The almost reflexive reaction of most people when they hear about the below-average test scores among children in the bottom of the socioeconomic distribution is that of course they have low scores because they have gotten poor educations. Improve the schools, it is assumed, and the scores will rise.

There are a number of problems with this assumption. One basic error is to assume that new educational opportunities that successfully raise the average will also reduce *differences* in cognitive ability. Consider trying to raise the cognitive level by putting a public library in a community that does not have one. Adding the library could increase the average intellectual level, but it may also spread out the range of scores by adding points to the IQs of the library users, who are likely to have been at the upper end of the distribution to begin with. The literature on such "aptitude-treatment interactions" is large and complex.[16] For example, providing computer assistance to a group of elementary school children learning arithmetic increased the gap between good and bad students;[17] a similar effect was observed when computers were used to teach reading;[18] the educational television program, "Sesame Street" increased the gap in academic performances between children from high- and low-status homes.[19] These results do not mean that such interventions are useless for the students at the bottom, but one must be careful to understand what is and is not being improved: The performance of those at the bottom might improve, but they could end up even further behind their brighter classmates.

A second broad difficulty with relying on improvements in education is that although they make some difference in IQ, the size of the effect is small. This conclusion is supported by evidence from both natural variation in education and planned educational experiments.

Looking at Natural Variation

Parents buying new houses often pick the neighborhood according to the reputation of the local schools. Affluent parents may spend tens of thousands of dollars to put their children through private schools. Tell parents that the quality of the schools doesn't matter, and they will unanimously, and rightly, ignore you, for differences in schools do matter in many important ways. But in affecting IQ, they do not matter nearly as much as most people think.

This conclusion was first and most famously reached by a study that was expected to demonstrate just the opposite. The study arose out of a mandate of the Civil Rights Act of 1964 to examine how minority groups are affected by educational inequalities. The result was a huge national survey, with a sample that eventually numbered 645,000 students, led by the eminent sociologist James S. Coleman. His researchers measured school quality by such objective variables as credentials of the teachers, educational expenditures per pupil, and the age and quality of school facilities.

Because the schools that most minority children attended were measurably subpar in facilities and staff, it was assumed that the minority children fortunate enough to attend better schools would also show improved cognitive functioning. But the report, issued in July 1966, announced that it had failed to find any benefit to the cognitive abilities of children in public primary or secondary schools that could be credited to better school quality.[20] The usual ways in which schools tried to improve their effectiveness were not likely to reduce the cognitive differences among individual children or those between ethnic groups.

The Coleman report's gloomy conclusions were moderated in subsequent analyses that found some evidence for marginal benefits of school quality on intellectual development.[21] Coleman himself later concluded that parochial schools generally do a better job of developing the cognitive abilities of their students than public schools, which pointed to at least some factor in schooling that might be exploited to improve intelligence.[22] Yet the basic conclusion of the report has stood the test of time and criticism: Variations in teacher credentials, per pupil expenditures, and the other objective factors in public schools do not account for much of the variation in the cognitive abilities of American school children.[23]

The several hundred thousand children assessed in the Coleman study had not been subjects in educational experiments. They were just students in several thousand local schools. The schools varied in quality, as they inevitably will.[24] Some schools, usually in prosperous urban or suburban districts, got (and still get) more money, more teachers with better qualifications, newer school buildings, and the like. Poorer or rural districts usually made (and make) do with less. The Coleman report, in other words, is one of a species of educational research that draws on *natural variation*—variation that is occurring spontaneously rather than by design.

Looking at the effects of natural variation has advantages as a research strategy. One is that this kind of research does not require new investments of time and money to intervene in schools. The intervening has already been done at someone else's expense. The disadvantage of such studies is that the variation is often narrow—an example of the restriction of range problem that we described in Part I. If almost all classes have, say, between twenty-five and thirty-five children in them, then looking at natural variation cannot reveal what would happen in classes with five or ten children in them. The Coleman report did not prove that educational reform is always futile, but that, on the whole, America had already achieved enough objective equalization in its schools by 1964 so that it was hard to pick up any effects of unequal school quality. The Coleman report tells us that the cognitive ability differences among individuals and groups alike on a national scale cannot be reduced much by further attempts to equalize the kinds of bricks-and-mortar factors and teacher credentials that school boards and taxpayers most often concern themselves with.

Aside from the issue of school quality is the question of whether simply going to school makes any difference to one's intelligence. The answer is self-evidently yes. Going to school and learning how to read and write, manipulate numbers, find out about one's culture and about the discoveries of science are going to raise scores on IQ tests compared to not going to school. But although it is obvious that schooling itself fosters intelligence, it is far less obvious how much of the intellectual variation around us can be attributed to differences in the amount of schooling people get. If large numbers of people were getting no schooling at all, there would be cognitive disadvantages on a grand scale that could be blamed on a lack of formal education. But in modern countries, natural variation does not span so wide a range.

An example of a study that had enough natural variation in it to find an effect of schooling was done in Sweden a half-century ago.[25] IQ tests were given in 1938 to a representative sample of several hundred 10-year-old boys in public and private schools in a Swedish city. Ten years later, the boys were tested again as part of an induction examination for national military service. In addition to the two IQ scores, the boys' home and family backgrounds and the total years of schooling were available for analysis.

The average subject in the study had completed only eight years of schooling, which means that many of them had completed fewer. Fewer than 10 percent of them had finished high school, and still fewer had gone on to university. Compared to present-day Sweden or America, the men experienced a wide range of years in school. Even so, the main determiner by far of IQ at the age of 20 was the IQ at the age of 10, by a factor of more than five times as important as years of schooling.[26] On the other hand, schooling *was* a significant though much weaker predictor, after holding IQ at age 10 and family background constant.

Since there was some beneficial effect of schooling, the results of the study were properly used to argue that additional years of school would pay off in higher scores.

We can infer from the Swedish study that some of the Flynn effect around the world is explained by the upward equalization of schooling, but a by-product is that schooling in and of itself no longer predicts adult intelligence as strongly, assuming it did so when many people were not getting much schooling.[27] The more uniform a country's schooling is, the more correlated the adult IQ is with childhood IQ.

The average American now gets more than three extra years of schooling compared to the time when the earliest intelligence tests were given. To be sure, years spent in school still varies in America, and it is presumably still contributing to variation in cognitive abilities.[28] But given how small the effect was in the Sweden of the 1930s and 1940s, it is unlikely to be large in America today, given the enormous compression of educational variation in America during the twentieth century (see Chapters 1 and 6). Nevertheless, we accept the basic premise that variation in the amount of schooling accounts for some portion of the observed variation in cognitive ability. Besides not knowing how large this remaining effect is, it is hard to estimate how much more would be gained on the average by further equalization of years of schooling. Gains reaped at the bottom of the cognitive ability distribution may be paid for by losses at the top, a process we discuss in the next chapter.

School differences can nonetheless be important. If a child is near the top of the intelligence distribution to begin with, the school can make a major difference in whether that intellectual talent is actually realized, a topic we consider in the next chapter. Or if a child has specific learning disabilities, access to the latest pedagogical techniques and technology may make a major difference. There doubtless are, in addition, pockets in America's vast educational realm where schools are uncommonly good or uncommonly poor, in which the children are benefiting or suffering cognitively. By definition, however, these are unusual cases, not likely to show up in national data on intelligence.

This discussion has not meant to imply that the fostering of cognitive ability is the only result we want from schools. The civility, let alone the safety, of the environment may vary widely from school to school. Skillful teachers may make learning more interesting. They may infuse children with a love of learning to some extent. These are effects worth worrying about, but they do not alter the fundamental message that the data convey: Equalizing the amount or objective quality of schooling in America cannot be counted on to equalize cognitive ability much.

Compensatory Education

Just a year prior to the Coleman report, the U.S. Congress passed the Elementary and Secondary Education Act (ESEA) of 1965, thereby opening a massive and continuing effort to improve the education of disadvantaged students that continues to this day. In the first fiscal year, grants for educationally deprived children under Title I of the ESEA went from zero to $3 billion, rose to $4 billion in the next year, and have remained there, or higher, ever since. Expenditures in fiscal 1992 were at an all-time high of $5.6 billion (all figures are in 1990 dollars).[29]

Sponsors of Title I assumed that these programs would narrow the gap in cognitive functioning between disadvantaged children and other students. To prove this, the act also funded an aggressive, ongoing evaluation effort, resulting over the years in a mounting stack of reports. In the mid-1970s, the National Institute of Education (NIE) commissioned a synthesis of the results. Reviewing all the federal studies from 1965 to 1975, researchers found no evidence that students in compensatory education programs closed the gap with their more able peers. Some plausible data suggested that "students in compensatory programs tend to fall behind other students, but not as fast as if they had received no compensatory instructions," an outcome that the institute treated as evidence of success.[30] The greatest support in the various studies was for a simpler "no effect" conclusion: The gap was about as great after compensatory education as before.[31] No evidence whatsoever supported a conclusion that compensatory education narrowed the achievement gap.

More optimistically, supporters of compensatory education can call upon the evidence of converging black-white test scores that we described in Chapter 13 as indirect evidence that *something* positive has been happening in elementary and secondary education for minorities. As we described, improvement has been the largest at the bottom of the IQ distribution, which in turn points toward compensatory programs as a possible cause. But direct evidence of the link remains elusive. In recent years, compensatory programs have set more modest goals, for themselves.[32] Now, they focus on teaching specific academic skills or problem solving, not expecting improvements in overall academic achievement or general intelligence.[33]

Stories Too Good to Be True

Accounts of phenomenal success stories in education—the inner-city school that suddenly excels as the result of a new program or a new teacher—are a perennial fixture of American journalism. Are they true? If the question is whether an inspirational teacher or some new program has the capacity to make an important difference in students' lives, then the answer is surely yes. But claims for long-term academic improvement, let alone increases in cognitive functioning, typically fade as soon as hard questions begin to be asked. A case in point is Chicago's Marva Collins, who gained national attention with claims that her shoestring-budget inner-city school, launched in 1975, was turning out students who blew the top off standardized tests and were heading to the best universities. Between the ages of 5 and 10, she claimed, her pupils, deemed "unteachable" in regular schools, were reading Plato, Aristotle, Chaucer, Shakespeare, and Tolstoy, according to stories in the popular media. According to other newspaper reports, she was asked by both Presidents Reagan and Clinton to become secretary of education. She continues to train large numbers of teachers in her methods.[34] Are her celebrated anecdotes borne out by data? We do not know. Despite years of publicity about Marva Collins, we can find no hard evidence.[35]

More generally, the large test score increases in local schools that are widely and routinely reported by the media have been plagued by fraud. In several schools in and around Washington, D.C., for example, the *Washington Post* reported that gains in test performance were found to be due to improper coaching on the tests by school employees or by allowing extra time for students to complete the tests.[36] A story in the *Los Angeles Times* told of various methods of cheating on standardized tests, including the replacing of wrong answers with right ones by teachers and staff, in at least fifty elementary public schools statewide.[37] The *New York Times* wrote about a public school principal who had been caught tampering with student test scores for years.[38] These specific instances seem to be part of a widespread problem.[39]

Raising IQ Among the School-Aged: Converging Results from Two Divergent Tries

The question remains: Is there any evidence that cognitive ability as measured by IQ tests can be increased by special interventions after children reach school age? We have some reason for thinking the answer is a highly qualified yes, and some basis for estimating how much, from two sources of evidence drawn from strikingly different contexts.

The first is one of the largest controlled experiments attempting explicitly to raise the intelligence of school-age children. It occurred in Venezuela, where in 1979 the incoming president named to his cabinet a Minister of State for the Development of Human Intelligence.[40] The new minister was convinced that a nation's average intellectual level was fundamental to its well-being, and he set out to see what could be done to raise the IQ of Venezuelan school children. The result was Project Intelligence, designed over four years by a team of Venezuelan and American psychologists, educators, and other specialists. In the fifth year, 900 youngsters in seventh grade in a poor district of a Venezuelan provincial city were randomly divided into experimental and control groups.[41] Those in the experimental group were taught approximately sixty forty-five-minute lessons in addition to their regular curriculum during the year and were cognitively tested before, during, and after the year. The students in the control group were tested at the same intervals, without receiving any of the additional instruction. The special lessons involved instruction in the kinds of intellectual activities that turn up on intelligence tests—visuospatial and verbal reasoning, vocabulary and word analogies—in addition to lessons in inventive thinking.[42] At the end of the year, the youngsters in the experimental group, compared to the controls, had gained a net of more than 0.4 standard deviation on a conventional intelligence test and a net gain of just over 0.1 standard deviation on a culture-fair intelligence test—in other words, a net gain in the range between 1.6 and 6.5 IQ points. There was no chance to see if the gain faded out or was reflected in the rest of the students' academic performance, nor can we even guess how much a second or third year of lessons would have accomplished.

The second source of evidence comes from the unsystematic but massive attempt to raise intelligence that goes on in the innumerable commercial coaching services promising to raise SAT scores. Few people think of the prep courses in that way. On the surface, it is all about getting into the college of your choice. But raising an SAT is just like raising an IQ if the SAT is an intelligence test and, however adroitly the current officials of the College Board and the admissions officers in universities try to avoid saying so, the SAT is partly an intelligence test.[43]

Can the SAT be coached? Yes, but it is not easy. Everyone who looks into this topic immediately hears about students who gained 100, 150, or 200 points on the SAT after a few hours of coaching. The tales may even be true, but they need to be averaged with the tales that don't get told about the scores that improve by only a few points—and the scores that drop—after spending a few dozen hours and hundreds of dollars on a coaching course. Scholars have by now largely sorted out the reality behind the sales pitches. After a furious debate about the issue in the late 1970s and early 1980s, the best evidence indicates that the coaching programs which can offer convincing scientific backing for their claims consist not of a few hours of practice but of lengthy training, comparable to going to school full time.[44] In the best of these analyses, Samuel Messick and Ann Jungeblut reviewed the published studies on coaching for the SAT, eliminated the ones that were methodologically unsound, and estimated in a regression analysis the point gain for a given number of hours spent studying for the test.[45] Their estimate of the effect of spending thirty hours on either the verbal or math test in a coaching course (including homework) was an average of sixteen points on the verbal SAT and twenty-five points for the math SAT. Larger investments in time earn larger payoffs with diminishing returns. For example, 100 hours of studying for either test earns an average twenty-four points on the verbal SAT and thirty-nine points on the math SAT. The next figure summarizes the results of their analysis.

Studying really does help, but consider what is involved. Sixty hours

The diminishing returns to coaching for the SAT

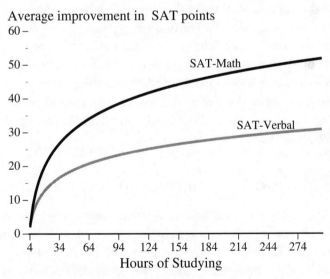

Source: Messick and Jungeblut 1981, Figs. 1, 3.

of work is not a trivial investment of time, but it buys (on average) only forty-one points on the combined Verbal and Math SATs—typically not enough to make much difference if a student is trying to impress an admissions committee. Even 300 hours—and now we are talking about two additional hours for 150 school days—can be expected to reap only seventy additional points on the combined score. And at 300 hours (150 for each test), the student is already at the flat part of the curve. Double the investment to 600 hours, and the expected gain is only fifteen more points.

Although intended for utterly different purposes, the benefits of the Venezuelan program and of SAT coaching schools are remarkably similar. The sixty lessons of the Venezuelan course, representing forty-five hours of study, added between .1 and .4 standard deviation on various intelligence tests. From the figure on SAT coaching, we estimate that 45 hours of studying adds about .16 standard deviation to the Verbal score and about .23 standard deviation to the Math score.[46]

These increases in test scores represent a mix of coaching effects— "cramming" is the process, with a quite temporary effect, that you may remember from school days—and perhaps an authentic increase in intelligence. We also are looking at short-term results here and must keep in mind that whenever test score follow-ups have been available (see the next section), the gains fade out. The net result is that any plausible estimate of the long-term increase in real cognitive ability must be small, and it is possible to make the case that it approaches zero.

Taken together, the negative findings about the effects of natural variation in schools, the findings of no effect except maybe to slow the falling-behind process in the evaluations of compensatory education, and the results of the Venezuelan and SAT coaching efforts all point to the same conclusion: As of now, the goal of raising intelligence among school-age children more than modestly, and doing so consistently and affordably, remains out of reach.

HEAD START AND ITS SOMETIMES DISTANT RELATIVES

During the 1970s when scholars were getting used to the disappointing results of programs for school-age children, they were also coming to a consensus that IQ becomes hard to budge at about the time children go to school. Longitudinal studies found that individual differences in IQ stabilized at approximately age 6.[47] Meanwhile, developmental psychologists found that the year-to-year correlations in mental test performance were close to zero in the first few years of life and then rose to asymptotic levels by age 6.[48] These findings conformed with the intuitive notion that, in the poet's words, "as the twig is bent the tree's inclined."[49] Any intervention designed to increase intelligence (or change any other basic characteristics of the child) must start early, and the earlier the better.[50] Here, we will characterize the more notable attempts to help children through preschool interventions and summarize the expert consensus about them.

Preschool Programs for Disadvantaged Children in General

HEAD START. One of the oldest, largest, and most enduring of the contemporary programs designed to foster intellectual development came about as the result of the Economic Opportunity Act of 1964, the opening salvo of Lyndon Johnson's War on Poverty. A year later, the mandated executive agency, the Office of Economic Opportunity, launched Project Head Start, a program intended to break the cycle of poverty by targeting preschool children in poor families.[51] Designed initially as a summer program, it was quickly converted into a year-long program providing classes for raising preschoolers' intelligence and communication skills, giving their families medical, dental, and psychological services, encouraging parental involvement and training, and enriching the children's diets.[52] Very soon, thousands of Head Start centers employing tens of thousands of workers were annually spending hundreds of millions of dollars at first, then billions, on hundreds of thousands of children and their families.

The earliest returns on Head Start were exhilarating. A few months spent by preschoolers in the first summer program seemed to be producing incredible IQ gains—as much as ten points.[53] The head of the Office of Economic Opportunity[54] reported the gains to Congress in the spring of 1966, and the program was expanded. By then, however, experts were noticing the dreaded "fade-out," the gradual convergence in test scores of the children who participated in the program with comparable children who had not. To shorten a long story, every serious attempt to assess the impact of Head Start on intelligence has found fade-out.[55] Cognitive benefits that can often be picked up in the first grade of school are usually gone by the third grade. By sixth grade, they have vanished entirely in aggregate statistics.

Head Start programs, administered locally, vary greatly in quality. Perhaps, some have suggested, the good programs are raising intelligence, but their impact is diluted to invisibility in national statistics.[56] That remains possible, but it becomes ever less probable as time passes without any clear evidence for it emerging. To this point, no lasting improvements in intelligence have ever been statistically validated with *any* Head Start program. Many of the commentators who praise Head Start value its family counseling and public health benefits, while granting that it does not raise the intelligence of the children.[57]

One response to the disappointment of Head Start has been to redefine its goals. Instead of raising intelligence, contemporary advocates say it reduces long-term school failure, crime, and illegitimacy and improves employability.[58] These delayed benefits are called sleeper effects, and they are what presumably justify the frequent public assertions that "a dollar spent on Head Start earns three dollars in the future," or words to that effect.[59] But even these claims do not survive scrutiny. The evidence for sleeper effects, such as it is, almost never comes from Head Start programs themselves but from more intensive and expensive preschool interventions.[60]

PERRY PRESCHOOL. The study invoked most often as evidence that Head Start works is known as the Perry Preschool Program. David Weikart and his associates have drawn enormous media attention for their study of 123 black children (divided into experimental and control groups) from the inner city in Ypsilanti, Michigan, whose IQs measured between 70 and 85 when they were recruited in the early 1960s at the age of 3 or 4.[61] Fifty-eight children in the program received cognitive instruction five half-days[62] a week in a highly enriched preschool setting for one or two years, and their homes were visited by teachers weekly for further instruction of parents and children. The teacher-to-child ratio was high (about one to five), and most of the teachers had a master's degree in appropriate child development and social work fields. Perry Preschool resembled the average Head Start program as a Ferrari resembles the family sedan.

The fifty-eight children in the experimental group were compared with another sixty-five who served as the control group. By the end of their one or two years in the program, the children who went to preschool were scoring eleven points higher in IQ than the control group. But by the end of the second grade, they were just marginally ahead of the control group. By the end of the fourth grade, no significant difference in IQ remained.[63] Fadeout again.

Although this intensive attempt to raise intelligence failed to produce lasting IQ gains, the Ypsilanti group believes it has found evidence for a higher likelihood of high school graduation and some post–high school education, higher employment rates and literacy scores, lower arrest rates and fewer years spent in special education classes as a result of the year or two in preschool. The effects are small and some of them fall short of statistical significance.[64] They hardly justify investing billions of dollars in run-of-the-mill Head Start programs.

OTHER LONGITUDINAL STUDIES OF PRESCHOOL PROGRAMS. One problem faced by anyone who tries to summarize this literature is just like that faced by people trying to formulate public policy. With hundreds of studies making thousands of claims, what can be concluded? We are fortunate to have the benefit of the efforts of a group of social scientists known as the Consortium for Longitudinal Studies. Initially conceived by a Cornell professor, Irving Lazar, the consortium has pulled together the results of eleven studies of preschool education (including the Perry Preschool Project), chosen because they represent the best available scientifically.[65] None of them was a Head Start program, but a few were elaborations of Head Start, upgraded and structured to lend themselves to evaluation, as Head Start programs rarely do. The next figure summarizes the cognitive outcomes in the preschool studies that the consortium deemed suitable for follow-up IQ analysis. The reported changes control for pretest IQ score, mother's education, sex, number of siblings, and father presence.

Soon after completing one of these high-quality experimental preschool programs, the average child registers a net gain in IQ of more than seven IQ points, almost half a standard deviation. The gain shrinks to four to five points in the first two years after the program, and to about three points in the third year.[66] The consortium also collected later follow-up data that led the researchers to conclude that "the effect of early education on intelligence test scores was not permanent."[67]

Intensive Interventions for Children at Risk of Mental Retardation

The preschool programs we have just described were targeted at disadvantaged children in general. Now we turn to two studies that are more intensive than even the ones analyzed by the consortium and deal with

IQ gains attributable to the Consortium preschool projects

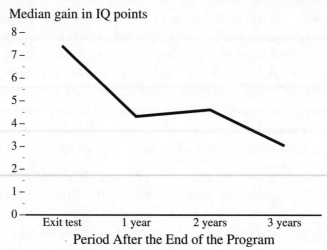

Median gain in IQ points

Source: Lazar and Darlington 1982, Table 15.

children who are considered to be at high risk of mental retardation, based on their mothers' low IQs and socioeconomic deprivation.

A case can be made for expecting interventions to be especially effective for these children, since their environments are so poor that they are unlikely to have had any of the benefits that a good program would provide. Moreover, if the studies have control groups and are reasonably well documented, there is at least a hope of deciding whether the programs succeeded in forestalling the emergence of retardation. We will briefly characterize the two studies approximating these conditions that have received the most scientific and media attention.

THE ABECEDARIAN PROJECT. The Carolina Abecedarian Project started in the early 1970s, under the guidance of Craig Ramey and his associates, then at the University of North Carolina.[68] Through various social agencies, they located pregnant women whose children would be at high risk for retardation. As the babies were born, the ones with obvious neurologic disorders were excluded from the study, but the remainder were assigned to two groups, presumably randomly. In all, there were four cohorts of experimental and control children. Both groups of babies and their families received a variety of medical and social work services, but one group of babies (the "experimentals") went into a day care program. The program started when the babies were just over a month old, and it provided care for six to eight hours a day, five days a week, fifty weeks a year, emphasizing cognitive enrichment activities with teacher-to-child ratios of one to three for infants and one to four to one to six in later years, until the children reached the age of 5. It also included enriched nutrition and medical attention until the infants were 18 months old.[69] The Abecedarian Project is the apotheosis of the day care approach. This is extremely useful from a methodological perspective: Even if the nation cannot afford to supply the same services to the entire national population of children who qualified for the Abecedarian Project, it serves as a way of defining the outer limit of what day care can accomplish given the current state of the art.

At the end of the fifth year, the children receiving the day care outscored those who did not by half a standard deviation on an intelligence test. At last report, the children were 12 years old and were still doing better intellectually than the controls. Combining all the cohorts, only 28 percent of the experimental children had repeated a grade, compared to 55 percent of the control children. Only 13 percent of the experimental children had IQs of less than 85, compared to 44 percent of the control children.[70]

This would be unequivocal good news, except for charges that the two groups were not comparable in their intellectual prospects at birth. Ignoring the more technical issues, the major stumbling block to deciding what the Abecedarian Project has accomplished is that the experimental children had already outscored the controls on cognitive performance tests by at least as large a margin (in standard score units) by the age of 1 or 2 years, and perhaps even by 6 months, as they had after nearly five years of intensive day care.[71] There are two main explanations for this anomaly. Perhaps the intervention had achieved all its effects in the first months or the first year of the project (which, if true, would have important policy implications). Or perhaps the experimental and control groups were different to begin with (the sample sizes for any of the experimental or control groups was no larger than fifteen and as small as nine, so random selection with such small numbers gives no guarantee that the experimental and control groups will be equivalent). To make things still more uncertain, test scores for children younger than 3 years are poor predictors of later intelligence test scores, and test results for infants at the age of 3 or 6 months are extremely unreliable. It would therefore be difficult in any case to assess the random placement from early test scores. The debate over the results is ongoing and unresolved as we write.

THE MILWAUKEE PROJECT. The Abecedarian Project was inspired by an earlier attempt to forestall mental retardation in a population of children who were at high risk. The famous Milwaukee Project started in 1966 under the supervision of Richard Heber, a professor at the University of Wisconsin (Madison) who had been research director of President John F. Kennedy's panel on mental retardation at the beginning of the decade. Healthy babies of poor black mothers with IQs below 75 were almost, but not quite, randomly assigned to no day care at all or day care starting at 3 months and continuing until they went to school. The day care lasted all day, five days a week, all year. The families of the babies selected for day care received a variety of additional services and health care. The mothers were paid for participation, received training in parenting and job skills, and their other young children received free child care. Only thirty-five children are considered to have completed the study, seventeen receiving the special attention and the remainder serving as controls.

Soon after the Milwaukee project began, reports of enormous net gains in IQ (more than 25 points) started appearing in the popular media and in psychology textbooks.[72] However, there was a dearth of publication that allowed experts to evaluate the project. The few technical items that appeared raised more questions than they answered.[73] It was not until 1988 that another Wisconsin professor associated with the work, Howard Garber, published an interpretable analysis of what had been done in the Milwaukee Project and what was found.[74]

By the age of 12 to 14 years, the children who had been in the program were scoring about ten points higher in IQ than the controls. Compared to other early interventions, this is a notably large difference. But this increase was not accompanied by increases in school performance compared to the control group. Experimental and control groups were both one to two years retarded in reading and math skills by the time they reached fourth grade; their academic averages and their achievement scores were similar, and they were similarly rated by their teachers for academic competence. From such findings, psychologists Charles Locurto and Arthur Jensen have concluded that the program's substantial and enduring gain in IQ has been produced by coaching the children so well on taking intelligence tests that their scores no longer measure intelligence or *g* very well.[75] Time will tell whether a more hopeful conclusion can be drawn.

In summary, the two experiments contain some promising leads. But it is not obvious where to go from here, for they differed in possibly important ways. The Abecedarian Project evaluated day care; the Milwaukee Project provided numerous interventions besides day care, including parental payment and training. It is hard to tell whether the former found enduring IQ benefits, given the very early divergence in test scores for experimental and control groups, but some academic benefits; the latter found an enduring IQ gain, but has not yet shown comparable intellectual gains in school work. It may be relevant that the Abecedarian mothers had higher IQs than the Milwaukee mothers, so the children may not have been at equal risk for retardation.

Reading this history of interventions, you may have noticed a curious parallelism: In the media, the good news is trumpeted as if there were no ambiguity; in the technical journals, the good news is viewed with deep suspicion and discounted. Are the scholars as excessively nitpicking as the journalists are credulous? Here is the difficult-to-discuss problem that overhangs the interpretation of these results: The people who run these programs want them to succeed. This is hardly a criticism. People who are spending their lives trying to help disadvantaged children ought to be passionately committed to their success. But it is hard for them to turn around and be dispassionate about the question, "How well are we doing?" Often the raw data from these programs are not easily accessible to outside scholars. Not infrequently, when such data finally are made available, they reveal a different and less positive way of viewing the successful results than the one that had previously been published.

Consensus has thus been hard to reach, but progress is being made. In our account, we have avoided dwelling on technical problems that, though perhaps valid, would modify the results only at the margin. When we have alluded to uncertainties and methodological difficulties, we have restricted ourselves to clear potential problems, which, if true, seriously weaken the basis for claiming success. In other words, we have tried to avoid nitpicking. The fact is that we and everyone else are far from knowing whether, let alone how, any of these projects have increased intelligence. We write this pessimistic conclusion knowing how many ostensibly successful projects will be cited as plain and indisputable evidence that we are willfully refusing to see the light.

CHANGING THE ENVIRONMENT AT BIRTH

There is one sure way to transform a child's environment beneficially: adoption out of a bad environment into a good one. If adoption occurs at birth, it is at least possible that the potential effects of postnatal environmental disadvantage could be wiped out altogether.[76] The specific question now is: How many points does being raised in a good adoptive home add to an IQ score?

Children are not put up for adoption for the edification of social theorists. There are no controlled experiments on the effects of adoption. Adoption usually means trouble in the biological family; trouble usually lands on families nonrandomly and unaccountably, making it hard to extract clear, generalizable data. The most famous studies were mostly done decades ago, when the social and financial incentives for adoption were different from today's. Legalized contraception and abortion, too,

---

When Environment Is Decisive

Lest anyone doubt that environment matters in the development of intelligence, consider the rare and bizarre cases in which a child is hidden away in a locked room by a demented adult or breaks free of human contact altogether and runs wild. From the even rarer cases that are investigated and told with care and accuracy, we know that if the isolation from human society lasts for years, rather than for just months, the children are intellectually stunted for life.[77] Such was, for example, the experience of the "Wild Boy of Aveyron," discovered in southern France soon after the Revolution and the establishment of the first French Republic, like an invitation to confirm Rousseau's vision of the noble savage. The 12- or 13-year-old boy had been found running naked in the woods, mute, wild, and evidently out of contact with humanity for most of his life. But, as it turned out, neither he, nor the others like him that we know about, resemble Rousseau's noble savage in the least. Most of them never learn to speak properly or to become independent adults. They rarely learn to meet even the lowest standards of personal hygiene or conduct. They seem unable to become fully human despite heroic efforts to restore them to society. From these rare cases we can draw a hopeful conclusion: If the ordinary human environment is so essential for bestowing human intelligence, we should be able to create extraordinary environments to raise it further.[78]

have altered the pool of subjects for adoption studies. Both the environmental and genetic legacies of children put up for adoption have surely changed over the years, but it is impossible to know exactly in what ways and how much. In short, although data are abundant and we will draw some broad conclusions, this is an area in which solid estimates are unlikely to be found.

As a group, adopted children do not score as high as the biological children of their adopting parents.[79] The deficit may be as large as seven to ten IQ points. It's not completely clear what this deficit means. One hypothesis is that the adopted children's genes hold them back; another is that there is an intellectually depressing effect of adoption itself, or that being placed in adopting homes not immediately after birth (as only some of them are), but only after several months or years, loses the benefit of the nurturing their adopting parents would have provided earlier in their lives.

At the same time, researchers think it very likely that adopted children earn higher scores than they would have had if they been raised by their biological parents, because the adopting home environment is likely to be better than the one their biological parents would have provided. If so, this would be a genuine effect of the home environment. How large is the effect? Charles Locurto, reviewing the evidence and striking an average, concludes that it is about six points.[80] As a consensus figure, that seems about right to us. However, a consensus figure is not what we want, as Locurto recognizes. It does not identify how wide a gap separates the environments provided by adopting homes and the homes in which the children would have been reared had they not been adopted. We seek a comparison of the IQs of children growing up in homes of a known low socioeconomic status and genetically comparable children reared in homes of a known high socioeconomic status. What would the increment in IQ look like then?

Two approximations to an ideal adoption study, albeit with very small samples, have recently been done in France.[81] In one, Michel Schiff and his colleagues searched French records for children abandoned in infancy, born to working-class (unskilled) parents, who were adopted into upper-class homes. Only thirty-two children met the study's criteria. In childhood, their average IQ was 107. To understand what this means, two further comparisons are in order. First, the adopted children scored eight points lower on average than their schoolmates, presumably from comparable upper-class homes. This confirms the usual finding with adopted children. But, second, they scored twelve points higher than twenty of their full or half-siblings who were reared at least for a time by a biological parent or grandparent in lower-class surroundings.[82] This study provides a rare chance to estimate roughly where the adoptees would have been had they remained in their original homes.

A second French study compared four small groups of adopted children, reared in either high- or low-SES homes, and the biological offspring of high- or low-SES parents. Thus one could ask, albeit with only a handful of children,[83] what happens when children born to low-SES parents are adopted into a high-SES home or when children born to high-SES parents are adopted into low-SES homes; and so on. In this study as well, the switch from low to high status in the home environment produced a twelve-point benefit in IQ.[84] Such findings, of course, implicate the home environment as a factor in the development of cognitive ability. We cannot be sure how much, because we do not know exactly how far down the SES ladder the children came from, or how far up the ladder they were moved into their adoptive homes. If the twelve-point shift is produced by a small shift in environment (e.g., a child of a truck driver adopted by the family of a bank clerk), it gives a great deal of hope for the effects of adoption; if it was produced only by a huge shift in the environment (e.g., the child of a chronically unemployed illiterate adopted by the Rothschilds), not so much hope. In general, the more important the environment is in shaping cognitive ability, the larger the impact a given change in environment has on IQ.

To see what the policy implications might be, let us suppose that low- and high-SES homes in the French studies represented the 10th and 90th centiles in the quality of the home environment, respectively. If that were the case, what might be accomplished by moving children from very deprived homes (at the 2d centile, to make the example concrete) to very advantaged ones (98th centile)? The results of the French study imply that such a shift in home environment would produce a benefit of almost twenty IQ points.[85]

A swing of twenty points is considerable and seems to open up the possibility of large gains in intelligence to be had by equalizing homes "upward," by appropriating for more families whatever nurturing things go on in the homes of the top 1 or 2 percent in socioeconomic status.[86] The problem, obviously, is that no one knows how to equalize environments upward on so grand a scale, particularly since so much of what goes on in the nurturing of children is associated with the personality and behavior of the parent, not material wealth. This brings us to a variety of policy issues that it is now time to discuss more explicitly.

A POLICY AGENDA

Research

Nothing is more predictable than that researchers will conclude that what is most needed is more research. In this case, however, the usually predictable is a little less so.

Certain kinds of research are *not* needed. Next to nothing is to be learned about how to raise IQ by more evaluations of Head Start, or even by replicating much better programs such as Perry Preschool or Abecedarian. The main lesson to be learned from these better programs has already been learned: It is tough to alter the environment for the development of general intellectual ability by anything short of adoption at birth. By now, researchers know enough to be confident that the next demonstration program is not going to be the magic bullet, because they have already demonstrated beyond dispute that the "environment" is an unimaginably complex melange of influences and inputs for all the child's waking hours (and perhaps some sleeping hours too). No meaningful proportion of that melange can reasonably be expected to be shaped by *any* outside intervention into the child's social environment, even one that lasts eight hours a day, using the repertoire of techniques now available. To have a large effect, we need new knowledge about cognitive development.

New knowledge is likely to come from sharply focused investigations into the development of cognitive ability, conducted in an atmosphere that imposes no constraints on the researchers other than to seek and find useful knowledge within commonly accepted ethical constraints. The most promising leads may come from insights into the physiological basis of intelligence rather than from the cultural or educational variables that have been customary in educational research. Long-term funding, buffers against bureaucratic meddling, readiness to fund research on the hardest questions, if they are brought forward by the inner logic of the science, and not just the politically correct questions: This is what is needed, and what today's research programs seldom provide. With that set of caveats on the table, more research is indeed at the top of our policy agenda. Because intelligence is less than completely heritable, we can assume that, some day, it will be possible to raise the intelligence of children through environmental interventions. But new knowledge is required. Scientific research is the only way to get it.

Nutrition

Advocating that all children receive good nutrition does not come under the heading of daring new ideas. We advocate it nonetheless. Especially if the inconsistent but suggestive results about the effects of vitamin and mineral supplements on cognitive functioning are borne out, it would be worth considering such supplements as part of school and preschool lunch programs.

Investment in Schooling

When quantum changes are made in education—moving from no education to an elementary education, or from 6 years of schooling to 12—then broad gains can occur, but the United States has in most respects passed this stage. Additional attempts to raise IQ through special accelerated courses have modest effects: short-term gains of two to four IQ points after extensive training. Long-term gains are less clear and likely to be smaller. In short, the school is not a promising place to try to raise intelligence or to reduce intellectual differences, given the constraints on school budgets and the state of educational science.

General Purpose Preschool Programs

Much is already known about what can be accomplished by ordinarily good preschool interventions—"ordinarily good" meaning that a few modestly trained adults who enjoy being with children watch over a few dozen children in a pleasant atmosphere. It is hard to know how many Head Start programs reach this standard. But a vast amount of research tells us that even ordinarily good Head Starts do not affect cognitive functioning much if at all. There is no reason to think that any realistically improved version of Head Start, with its thousands of centers and millions of participants, can add much to cognitive functioning. Even the claims for long-term benefits of Head Start on social behavior are unsubstantiated.

Such findings do not invalidate Head Start's value as a few hours' daily refuge for small children who need it. But the debate over Head Start should move away from frivolous claims about how many dollars it will save in the long run, none of which stands up to examination, and focus instead on the degree to which it is actually serving the laudable and more fundamental function of rescuing small children from unsuitable, joyless, and dangerous environments.

Highly Targeted Preschool Programs

The nation cannot conceivably implement a Milwaukee Project or Abecedarian Project for all disadvantaged children. It is not just the dollar costs that put such ambitions out of reach (though they do) but the impossibility of staffing them. With teacher-to-child ratios ranging as high as one to three and staff-to-child ratios even higher, these programs come close to calling for a trained person per eligible child.

But should such programs be mounted for the extremes—the children far out in the left-hand tail of home environments? We are not talking about children who are just poor or just living in bad neighborhoods, but children who are at high risk of mental retardation in an awful environment, with parents who function at a very low cognitive level. Should such children be enrolled, within a few weeks of birth, in a full-time day care setting until they begin kindergarten?

The decision cannot be justified purely on grounds of cognitive benefits, judging from what has come out of the Milwaukee and Abecedarian projects. On the other hand, the evidence about improvements in social adjustment from the Perry Preschool Project may be relevant, if they stand up to further critical scrutiny. If they do, then highly intensive preschool programs have an important role to play in socializing children from highly disadvantaged backgrounds. Such results are not as hopeful as they are sometimes portrayed, but they may be substantial. Earlier, we said that the cost-benefit claims for Head Start could not withstand examination. For programs that achieve results comparable to those claimed for Perry Preschool, perhaps they could.[87] But even this limited endorsement is applicable only to the small fraction of the population that is both at substantial risk for mental retardation and living in the worst conditions. Comparatively few children typically classified as "disadvantaged" fall in that category.

Adoption

Adoption at birth from bad environments into good environments raises cognitive functioning, especially in childhood and by amounts that are not well established. In general, the worse the home that would have been provided by the biological parents and the better the adoptive home, the greater is the cognitive benefit of adoption. Adoption at birth seems to produce positive noncognitive effects as well. In terms of government budgets, adoption is cheap; the new parents bear all the costs of twenty-four-hour-a-day care for eighteen years or so. The supply of eager and qualified adoptive parents for infants is large, even for infants with special needs.

If adoption is one of the only affordable and successful ways known to improve the life chances of disadvantaged children appreciably, why has it been so ignored in congressional debate and presidential proposals? Why do current adoption practices make it so difficult for would-be parents and needy infants to match up? Why are cross-racial adoptions so often restricted or even banned? All these questions have political and social answers that would take us far outside our territory. But let it be said plainly: Anyone seeking an inexpensive way to do some good for an expandable number of the most disadvantaged infants should look at adoption.

The tough question about adoption involves the way the adoption decision is made. Governments should not be able to force parents to give up their children for any except the most compelling of reasons. Right now, the government already has the power (varying by state), based on evidence of neglect and abuse, which we do not advocate expanding. Instead, we want to return to the state of affairs that prevailed until the 1960s, when children born to single women—where much of the problem of child neglect and abuse originates—were more likely to be given up for adoption at birth. This was, in our view, a better state of affairs than we have now. Some recommendations for turning back this particular clock are in Chapter 22.

Realism

An inexpensive, reliable method of raising IQ is not available. The wish that it were is understandable, and to pursue the development of such methods is worthwhile. But to think that the available repertoire of social interventions can do the job if only the nation spends more money on them is illusory. No one yet knows how to raise low IQs substantially on a national level. We need to look elsewhere for solutions to the problems that the earlier chapters have described.

Chapter 18

The Leveling of American Education

Most people think that American public education is in terrible shape, and any number of allegations seem to confirm it. But a search of the data does not reveal that the typical American school child in the past would have done any better on tests of academic skills. An American youth with average IQ is probably better prepared academically now than ever before. The problem with American education is confined mainly to one group of students, the cognitively gifted. Among the most gifted students, SAT scores started falling in the mid-1960s, and the verbal scores have not recovered since.

One reason is that disadvantaged students have been "in" and gifted students "out" for thirty years. Even in the 1990s, only one-tenth of 1 percent of all the federal funds spent on elementary and secondary education go to programs for the gifted. Because success was measured in terms of how well the average and below-average children performed, American education was dumbed down: Textbooks were made easier, and requirements for courses, homework, and graduation were relaxed. These measures may have worked as intended for the average and below-average students, but they let the gifted get away without ever developing their potential.

In thinking about policy, the first step is to realize where we are. In a universal education system, many students will fall short of basic academic competence. Most American parents say they are already satisfied with their local school. The average student has little incentive to work hard in high school. Getting into most colleges is easy, and achievement in high school does not pay off in higher wages or better jobs for those who do not go to college. On a brighter note, realism also leads one to expect that modest improvements in the education of average students will continue as they have throughout the century except for the aberrational period from the mid-1960s to mid-1970s.

In trying to build on this natural improvement, the federal government should support greater flexibility for parents to send their children to schools of their choosing, whether through vouchers, tax credits, or choice within the public schools. Federal scholarships should reward academic performance. Some federal funds now so exclusively focused on the disadvantaged should be reallocated to programs for the gifted.

We urge primarily not a set of new laws but a change of heart within the ranks of educators. Until the latter half of this century, it was taken for granted that one of the chief purposes of education was to educate the gifted—not because they deserved it through their own merit but because, for better or worse, the future of society was so dependent on them. It was further understood that this education must aim for more than technical facility. It must be an education that fosters wisdom and virtue through the ideal of the "educated man." Little will change until educators once again embrace this aspect of their vocation.

The education of the young is something that all human societies are committed to do. They can do it well or poorly. Many billions of dollars are already available for education in America. Can we spend them more wisely and produce better results? Our corner of the topic is how cognitive ability fits into the picture.

It seems self-evident: Education is what intelligence is most obviously good for. One ideal of American education is to educate everyone to his or her potential. The students with the most capacity to absorb education should get the most of it—most in years, breadth, depth, and challenge. But what should be self-evident is not. For thirty years, IQ has been out of fashion among American educators, and the idea that people with the most capacity to be educated should become the most educated sounds dangerously elitist.

It needs to be said openly: The people who run the United States—create its jobs, expand its technologies, cure its sick, teach in its universities, administer its cultural and political and legal institutions—are drawn mainly from a thin layer of cognitive ability at the top. (Remember—just the top 1 percent of the American population consists of 2.5 million people.) It matters enormously not just that the people in the top few centiles of ability get to college (almost all of them do, as we described in Chapter 1) or even that many of them go to elite colleges but that they are educated *well*. One theme of this chapter is that since the 1960s, while a cognitive elite has become increasingly segregated from the rest of the country, the quality of the education they receive has been degraded. They continue to win positions, money, prestige, and success in competition with their less gifted fellow citizens, but they are less well educated in the ways that make smart children into wise adults.

Letting people develop to their fullest potential is not the only important goal of public education. Since the founding of the republic, thoughtful Americans have recognized that an educated citizenry is vital to its survival. This chapter therefore examines how well our country fares in educating the average student—not the one who is likely to occupy a place among the cognitive elite but the one most representative of the typical American. We find that the average American youngster is probably doing better on tests of academic skills than ever before. We will try to understand why a sense of crisis nevertheless surrounds American education despite this unexpected good news.

We begin with quantitative evidence that shows the general outline of these trends and their connection to each other. Then we switch to observations of the kind that do not lend themselves to survey results or regression equations but that we believe to be justified by everyday experience in our schools and colleges.

TRENDS IN EDUCATION I: THE AVERAGE STUDENT

A few years ago, the *Wall Street Journal* devoted its op-ed page to a reproduction of an examination administered by Jersey City High School in 1885.[1] It consisted of questions such as the following:

Find the product of $3 + 4x + 5x^2 - 6x^3$ and $4 - 5x - 6x^2$.

Write a sentence containing a noun used as an attribute, a verb in the perfect tense potential mood, and a proper adjective.

Name three events of 1777. Which was the most important and why?

The test was not for high school graduation (which would be impressive enough) but for *admission* to Jersey City High School. Fifteen-year-olds were supposed to know the answers to these questions. Of course, not many people went to high school in 1885. But could even the cream of the 15-year-olds in Jersey City's middle schools pass that exam today? It seems unlikely.

Bits of national memorabilia like this reinforce an impression that is nearly universal in this country: American elementary and secondary education used to be better. The 1983 report by the Department of Education, *A Nation at Risk*, said so most famously, concluding that "we have, in effect, been committing an act of unthinking, unilateral educational disarmament."[2] Its chairman concluded flatly that "for the first time in the history of our country, the educational skills of one generation will not surpass, will not equal, will not even approach, those of their parents."[3]

We begin by affirming the conventional wisdom in one respect: The academic performance of the average American student looks awful at first glance. Consider illiteracy, for example. Some authorities claim that a third of the population is functionally illiterate.[4] No one really knows—when does "literacy" begin?—but no matter where the precise figure lies, the proportion is large. As of 1990, 16 percent of the 17-year-olds still in school were below the level called "intermediate" in the National Assessment of Educational Progress (NAEP) reading test—in effect, below the threshold for dealing with moderately complex written material.[5] Then one must consider that more than 20 percent of 17-year-olds had already dropped out of school and were not part of the sample,[6] bringing us somewhere above 20 percent of the population who cannot use reading as a flexible tool of daily life.

There is a profusion of horror stories in other subjects. Fewer than one in three American 17-year-olds in a nationally representative sample could place the Civil War within the correct half-century of its actual occurrence.[7] Fewer than 60 percent of American 17-year-olds could correctly answer the item, "A hockey team won five of its 20 games. What percent of the games did it win?"[8] More than 60 percent of adults in their early twenties cannot synthesize the main argument of a newspaper article.[9] Forty-four percent of adult Americans cannot understand "help wanted" ads well enough to match their qualifications with the job requirements. Twenty-two percent cannot address a letter well enough to make sure the post office can deliver it.[10]

Critics of American education also point to international comparisons. Between the early 1960s and the end of the 1980s, six major international studies compared mathematical competence, science knowledge, or both, across countries.[11] The National Center for Education Statistics has conveniently assembled all of the results for the first five studies in a series of twenty-two tables showing the United

States' ranking for each scale. The results for the industrialized coun-tries are easily summarized: In seven of the twenty-two tables, the United States is at the very bottom; in eight others, within two coun-tries of the bottom; in four of the remaining seven, in the bottom half.[12] The most recent study, conducted in 1991, found that the United States continued to rank near the bottom on every test of every age group for the math tests and near the middle on the science tests.[13]

International comparisons need to be interpreted cautiously.[14] But the most common defense for America's poor showing is losing credi-bility. For years, educators excused America's performance as the price America pays for retaining such a high proportion of its students into high school. But Japan has had as high a retention rate for years, and recently many European nations, including some that continue to outscore us on the international tests, have caught up as well.[15]

The picture is surely depressing. But as we look back to the idealized America of the earlier part of the century, can we catch sight of Amer-ican school children who, on average, would have done any better on such measures than the youngsters of today? A growing number of ed-ucational researchers are arguing that the answer is no.[16] With qualifi-cations that the chapter will explain, we associate ourselves with their findings. *According to every longitudinal measure that we have been able to find, there is no evidence that the preparation of the average American youth is worse in the 1990s than it has ever been.* Considerable evidence suggests that, on the contrary, education for the average youth has improved steadily throughout the twentieth century except for a period of decline in the late 1960s and early 1970s (which justified to some degree the alarming conclusions of the early 1980s) but from which the educational system has already fully recovered. How can we get away with these statements that seem so contrary to what everyone knows? We do it by means of that innocuous word, "average."

During the first half of the twentieth century, education for the average American young person improved steadily, partly because the average American young person spent more time in school than previously (Chapter 6). But much other evidence, marshaled convincingly by economist John Bishop, indicates a steady, long-term improvement in what Bishop calls "general intellectual achievement" that extended from the earliest data at the turn of the century into the 1960s.[17] Even if we discount some of these results as reflections of the Flynn effect,[18] it is impossible to interpret the data from 1900 to 1950 as showing anything other than some improvement. Then in the mid-1960s began a period of decline, as manifested most notably by the fall in SAT scores. Many people are under the impression that the decline was deep and permanent for the entire population of students. In reality, the decline for the *average* student was modest and recovery was quick. We know this first through the NAEP, begun in 1969, which we discussed with regard to ethnic differences in Chapter 13.[19] When the first NAEP tests were given, the SAT score decline was in its fifth year and would continue for most of the next decade. The SAT is generally for a population concentrated at the upper end of the cognitive ability distribution, whereas the NAEP is for a nationally representative sample. While the scores for the population taking the SAT were still declining, the trendlines of the NAEP results were flat. The differences between the earliest NAEP scores in reading, science, and math (which date from 1969 to 1973, depending on the test) and the scores in 1990 are a matter of a few points and small fractions of a standard deviation, and scores often went up rather than down over that period.[20]

SAT scores had started declining in 1964, but the NAEP goes back only to 1969. To reach back further for nationally representative data, we turn first to five almost completely unpublicized studies, known collectively as the national norm studies, conducted by the Educational Testing Service (ETS) in 1955, 1960, 1966, 1974, and 1983. In these tests, a short version of the SAT (the Preliminary Scholastic Aptitude Test, or PSAT) was administered to a nationally representative sample of American high school juniors. The results are summarized in the table below, adjusted so as to represent the mean score that *all* American ju-

---

What SAT Score Decline? The Results of the National Norm Studies, 1955–1983

Year	Verbal Mean	Math Mean
1955	348	417
1960	374	410
1966	383	395
1974	368	402
1983	376	411

Sources: Cole 1955; Chandler and Schrader 1966; Katz and others 1970; Jackson and Schrader 1976; Braun, Centra, and King 1987.

niors would have received on the SAT had they stayed in school for their senior years and had they taken the SAT.

These results say that American eleventh graders as of 1983 were, as a whole, roughly as well prepared in both verbal and math skills as they had been when the college-bound SAT scores were at their peak in 1963, and noticeably stronger in their verbal skills than they had been in the first norm study in 1955. The decline in verbal scores between the 1966 and 1974 tests was 15 points—only about .14 standard deviation. About half of that had been recovered by the 1983 test.[21]

A third source is the Iowa Test of Educational Development (ITED), a well-validated test, equated for stability from year to year, that has been administered to virtually a 100 percent sample of Iowa's high school students for fifty years. What may one learn from rural, white Iowa? For examining trends in educational outcomes over time, quite a bit. Iowa's sample of students provides socioeconomic variance—even Iowa has single-parent families and welfare recipients. Paradoxically, Iowa's atypical racial homogeneity (the population was more than 97 percent non-Latino white throughout the period we are discussing) is an advantage for a longitudinal analysis by sidestepping the difficulties of analyzing trends for populations that are changing in their ethnic composition. In examining Iowa's test scores over time, we may not be able to make judgments about how the education of minorities has changed but we have a good view of what happened over the last several decades for the white population.

Test scores for high school students in Iowa increased from the early 1940s to the mid-1960s, dropped sharply from 1966 to 1978, but then rebounded, as shown in the figure below. We show the ninth-grade scores, which have been least affected by changes in dropout rates during the last fifty years. They show a steep rise through 1965 and an equally steep rise after 1977, reaching new heights from 1983 onward.[22] The improvement has been substantial—on the order of half a standard deviation since the mid-1970s, and about .2 standard deviation above the previous high in 1965. The increase of 5.3 points from 1942 to 1992 may be interpreted as approaching one standard deviation.

Evidence from other, independent sources is consistent with the story told by the national norm studies and the Iowa data. Project TALENT, the huge study of high school students undertaken in 1960, readministered its reading comprehension test in 1970 to another sample and found that a nationally representative sample of eleventh graders had

A half-century of Iowa tests: Improvement as the norm, the slump as a twelve-year aberration

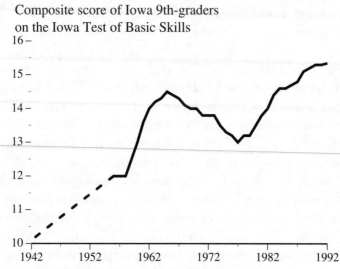

Composite score of Iowa 9th-graders
on the Iowa Test of Basic Skills

Source: Iowa Testing Program, University of Iowa.

gained slightly over its counterpart of 1960, during the same decade that saw the steepest decline in the SAT. Other data on state tests in Virginia, New York, Texas, and California, summarized by the Congressional Budget Office in its study of trends in educational achievement, cannot match the time range of the Iowa or SAT norm data, but, within their limits, they are generally consistent with the picture we have sketched.[23] Even the international assessments are consistent. The United States had some of its worst results in the first international assessment, conducted in the early to mid-1960s when American SAT scores were near their peak.[24] Since then, the national American averages have been, on balance, rising and the deficit in international comparisons shrinking.

Taken as a whole, the data from representative samples of high school students describe an American educational system that was probably improving from the beginning of the century into the mid-1960s, underwent a decline into the mid-1970s—steep or shallow, depending on the study—and rebounded thereafter. Conservatively, average high school students seem to be as well prepared in math and verbal skills as they were in the 1950s. They may be better prepared than they have ever been. If U.S. academic skills are deficient in comparison with other nations, they have been comparatively so for a long time and are probably better than they were.

TRENDS IN EDUCATION II: COLLEGE STUDENTS

Having questioned the widespread belief that high school education today is worse on average than it used to be, we now reverse course and offer some reasons for thinking that it has gotten worse for one specific group of students: the pool of youths in the top 10 to 20 percent of the cognitive ability distribution who are prime college material. To make this case, we will focus on the best-known educational trend, the decline in SAT scores. Visually, the story is told by what must be the most frequently published trendlines in American educational circles, as shown below.[25]

The steep drop from 1963 to 1980 is no minor statistical fluctuation. Taken at face value, it tells of an extraordinarily large downward shift in academic aptitude—almost half a standard deviation on the Verbal,

Forty-one years of SAT scores

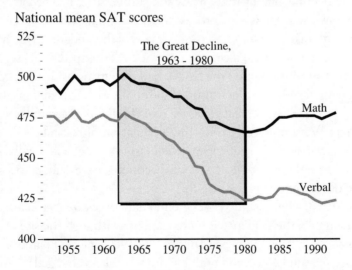

Source: The College Board. Scores for 1952–1969 are based on all tests administered during the year; 1970–1993 on the most recent test taken by seniors.

almost a third of a standard deviation on the Math.[26] And yet we have just finished demonstrating that this large change is not reflected in the aggregate national data for high school students. Which students, then, account for the SAT decline? We try to answer that question in the next few paragraphs, as we work our way through the most common explanation of the decline. To anticipate our conclusion, the standard explanation does not stand up to the data. We are left with compelling evidence of a genuine decline in the intellectual resources of our brightest youngsters.

The most familiar explanation of the great decline is that the SAT was "democratized" during the 1960s and 1970s. The pool of people taking the test expanded dramatically, it is said, bringing in students from disadvantaged backgrounds who never used to consider going to college. This was a good thing, people agree, but it also meant that test scores went down—a natural consequence of breaking down the old elites. The real problem is not falling SAT scores but the inferior education for the disadvantaged that leads them to have lower test scores, according to the standard account.[27]

This common view is mistaken. To make this case requires delving into the details of the SAT and its population.[28] To summarize a complex story: During the 1950s and into the early 1960s, the SAT pool expanded dramatically, but scores remained steady. In the mid-1960s, scores started to decline, but, by then, many state universities had become less selective in their admissions process, often dropping the requirement that students take SATs, and, as a result, many of the students in the middle level of the pool who formerly took the SAT stopped doing so. Focusing on the whites taking the SAT (thereby putting aside the effects of the changing ethnic composition of the pool), we find that *throughout most of the white SAT score decline, the white SAT pool was shrinking, not expanding.* We surmise that the white population of test takers during this period was probably getting more exclusive socioeconomically, not less. It is virtually impossible that it was becoming more democratized in any socioeconomic sense.

After 1976, when detailed background data on white test takers become available, the evidence is quite explicit. Although the size of the pool once again began to expand during the 1980s, neither parental income nor parental education of the white test takers changed.[29] After factoring in the effects of changes in the gender of the pool and changes in the difficulty of the SAT, we conclude that the aggregate real decline from 1963 to 1976 among whites taking the SAT was on the order of thirty-four to forty-four points on the Verbal and fifteen to twenty-five points on the Math. From 1976 to 1993, the real white losses were no more than a few additional points on the Verbal. On the Math, white scores improved about three or four points in real terms after changes in the pool are taken into account. Or in other words, when everything is considered, there is reason to conclude that the size of the drop in the SAT as shown in that familiar, unsophisticated graphic with which we opened the discussion is for practical purposes the same size and shape as the real change in the academic preparation of white college-bound SAT test takers. Neither race, class, parental education, composition of the pool, nor gender can explain this decline of forty-odd points on the Verbal score and twenty-odd points on the Math for the white SAT-taking population during the 1960s and 1970s. For whatever reasons, during the 1960s America stopped doing as well intellectually by the core of students who go to college.

Rather than democratization, the decline was more probably due to leveling down, or mediocritization: a downward trend of the educational skills of America's academically most promising youngsters toward those of the average student. The net drop in verbal skills was especially large, much larger than net drop in math skills. It affected even those students with the highest levels of cognitive ability.

Does this drop represent a fall in realized intelligence as well as a drop in the quality of academic training? We assume that it does to some extent but are unwilling to try to estimate how much of which. The SAT score decline does underscore a frustrating, perverse reality: However hard it may be to raise IQ among the less talented with discrete interventions, as described in Chapter 17, it may be within the capability of an educational system—probably with the complicity of broader social trends—to put a ceiling on, or actually dampen, the realized intelligence of those with high potential.[30]

TRENDS IN EDUCATION III: THE BRIGHTEST OF THE BRIGHTEST

One more piece of the puzzle needs to be put in place. The SAT population constitutes a sort of broad elite, encompassing but not limited to the upper quartile of the annual national pool of cognitive ability. What has been happening to the scores of the narrow elite, the most gifted students—roughly, those with combined scores of 1400 and more—who are most likely to fill the nation's best graduate and professional schools? They have gone down in the Verbal test and up in the Math.

The case for a drop in the Verbal scores among the brightest can be made without subtle analysis. In 1972, 17,560 college-bound seniors scored 700 or higher on the SAT-Verbal. In 1993, only 10,407 scored 700 or higher on the Verbal—a drop of 41 percent in the raw number of students scoring 700 and over, despite the larger raw number of students taking the test in 1993 compared to 1972.[31] Dilution of the pool (even if it were as real as legend has it) could not account for smaller raw numbers of high-scoring students. But we may make the case more systematically.

The higher the ability level, the higher the proportion of students who take the SAT. At the 700 level and beyond, the proportion approaches 100 percent and has probably been so since the early 1960s (see Chapter 1). That is, almost all 17-year-olds who *would* score above 700 if they took the SAT do in fact take the SAT at some point in their high school career, either because of their own ambitions, their parents', or the urging of their teachers and guidance counselors. It is therefore possible to think about the students who score in the 700s on the SAT as a proportion of all 17-year-olds, not just as a proportion of the SAT pool. We cannot carry the story back further than 1967 but the results are nonetheless provocative, as shown in the next figure.[32]

The good news is that the mathematics score of the top echelon of American students has risen steeply since hitting its low point in 1981. Given all the attention devoted to problems in American education, this finding is worth lingering over for a moment. In a period of just twelve years, from 1981 to 1993, the proportion of 17-year-olds scoring over 700 on the SAT-Math test increased by 143 percent. This dramatic improvement during the 1980s is not explainable by any artifact that we can identify, such as having easier Math SAT questions.[33] Nor is it due to the superior math performance of Asian-American students and their increase as a proportion of the SAT population. Asian-Americans are still such a small minority (only 8 percent of test takers in 1992) that their accomplishments cannot account for much of the national improvement. The upward bounce in the Math SAT from 1981 through 1992 was a robust 104 percent among whites.[34]

Now let us turn to the less happy story about the SAT-Verbal. The proportion of students attaining 700 or higher on the SAT fell sharply

Among the most gifted students, there is good news about math, bad news about verbal

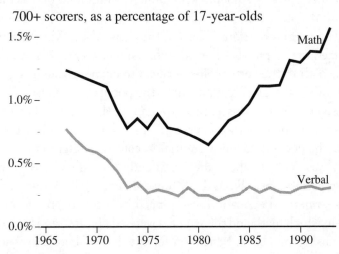

700+ scorers, as a percentage of 17-year-olds

Source: The College Board.

from 1967 to the mid-1970s. Furthermore, SAT scores as of 1967 had been dropping for four years before that, so we start from a situation in which the verbal skills of America's most gifted students dropped precipitously from the early 1960s to the early 1970s. Unlike the Math scores, however, the Verbal scores did not rebound significantly. Nor may one take much comfort from the comparatively shallow slope of the decline as it is depicted in the figure. The proportional size of the drop was large, from about eight students per 1,000 17-year-olds in 1967 to three per 1,000 in 1993, a drop of about 60 percent.[35] The other major source of data about highly talented students, the Graduate Record Examination, parallels the story for the students scoring 700 or above on the SAT.[36]

AN EXPLANATION: DUMBING DOWN

How might these disparate and sometimes contradictory trends be tied together?

One important part of the story begins with the 1950s. Why didn't the scores fall, though the proportion of students taking the SAT went from a few percent to almost a third of the high school population in little more than a decade? The answer is that the growing numbers of SAT takers were not students with progressively lower levels of academic ability but able students who formerly did not go on to college or went to the state university (and didn't take the SAT) and now were broadening their horizons. This was the post–World War II era that we described in Chapter 1, when educational meritocracy was on the rise. As the path to the better colleges began to open for youngsters outside the traditional socioeconomic elites, the population of test takers grew explosively. During this period, we can safely assume that the pool opened up to new socioeconomic groups, but it occurred with no dilution of the pool's academic potential, because the reservoir of academic ability was deep. Then, as the 1950s ended, another factor worked to sustain performance: From the *Sputnik* scare in 1957 through the early 1960s, American education was gripped by a get-tough reform movement in which math and the sciences were emphasized and high schools were raising standards. Education for the college bound probably improved during this period.

Softened Standards

Then came the mid-1960s and a decade of decline. What happened to education during this period has been described by many observers, and we will not recount it here in detail or place blame.[37] The simple and no longer controversial truth is that educational standards declined, along with other momentous changes in American society during that decade.

The educational change is epitomized by the title for this section. "Dumbing down" has become a term of art for the process by which the vocabulary in a textbook is deliberately simplified. We use it in a broader sense. One of the chief effects of the educational reforms of the 1960s was to dumb down elementary and secondary education as a whole, making just about everything easier for the average student and easing the demands on the gifted student.

The dumbing down of textbooks permeated the textbook market, as publishers and authors strove to satisfy school boards, which routinely applied "readability" formulas to the books they were considering.[38] Thomas Sowell has described a typical example of this process, in which the words *spectacle* and *admired* were deleted from a textbook because they were deemed too difficult for high school students. Sowell compares such timidity to the McGuffey's *Readers*, the staple text of nineteenth-century children in one-room schoolhouses, pointing out that the *Third Reader* used words such as *species, dialogue, heath,* and *benighted*—intended for 8-year-olds.[39]

Dumbing down also occurred in the high school's college track. More electives were permitted, and the requirements for credits in science, mathematics, and literature were relaxed. There were exceptions, such as the high-quality Advanced Placement courses offered in a minority of high schools, taken by about 1 percent of American students.[40] But the broader result was that the number of courses in the core disciplines declined. Educational specialists agree that grades inflated—it took less work, and less homework, to earn good grades[41]—and that less homework was done.[42]

In this context, it comes as no surprise that SAT scores declined even among the diminishing proportion of high school seniors who took the SAT during the last half of the 1960s. Indeed, it was not just students who took the SAT who suffered during that period. For a time, educational preparation got worse for everyone, as reflected in the Iowa data and the SAT national norm studies, not just for the college-bound tracks. But why was the size of the drop smaller and the rebound quicker and more complete for the population as a whole than for the SAT population? And why, in the SAT population, do we observe such a large difference between Math, where decline was small and the recovery substantial, and Verbal, where the decline was large with no apparent recovery at all? Why were these contradictory trends most pronounced for the most gifted students?

Competing Agendas

Our explanation is consistent with the facts as we understand them, but we should emphasize that our explanation is interpretive as well. It goes like this:

Since the late 1970s, the public dissatisfaction about the state of American elementary and secondary education has produced some changes. From 1982 to 1987, for example, the proportion of high school graduates who completed a solid program of four years of English, three of social sciences, three of the hard sciences, and three of math more than doubled.[43] The average course loads in all the academic areas went up, most dramatically in foreign languages but with sizable gains in science and math as well.[44] Many people wanted higher standards in their schools, and the schools tried to respond.

But other pressures were (and are) put on the schools, and they created a gulf between what happened to courses in mathematics and to courses in every other academic field. If a school, trying to have higher standards in math, began to require a basic calculus course for its college prep students, there were limits to the amount of fudging that could be done with the course content. Somehow a core of analytic techniques in calculus had to be part of the course. There was no way around it. Furthermore, there is a well-established standard for deciding whether calculus has been learned: Can the student solve calculus problems?

Another feature of math skills at the high school level is that they can be increased independent of the student's development in other intellectual skills. A student may learn to manipulate quadratic equations even if he is given not a glimmer of how formal logic might relate to expository prose or to the use of evidence in civics class. It is good that math scores have risen, but it remains true that raising math standards can be routinized in ways that cannot be applied to the rest of the curriculum.

How, for example, does one decide that the standards for an English literature course have been "raised"? In the old days, it wouldn't have been seen as a difficult question. Standards would be raised if the students were required to read a larger number of the Great Books (no one would have had much quarrel about what they were) or if students were required to write longer term papers, subject to stricter grading on argumentation and documentation. But since the late 1960s, such straightforward ways of looking at standards in the humanities, social sciences, and even the physical sciences were corrupted, in the sense that the standards of each discipline were subordinated to other considerations. Chief among these other considerations were multiculturalism in the curriculum, the need to minimize racial differences in performance measures, and enthusiasm for fostering self-esteem independent of performance.[45] We assume that a politically compromised curriculum is less likely to sharpen the verbal skills of students than one that hews to standards of intellectual rigor and quality. We make these observations without belittling the issues that have been at center stage in American secondary education. But if the question is why the downhill slide in verbal skills has not reversed, here is one possible explanation: The agendas that have had the most influence on curricula are generally antagonistic to traditional criteria of rigor and excellence.

These influences come together when textbooks are selected by large school systems. A school board runs no risk whatsoever of angry historians picketing their offices. They run grave risks of pickets (and of being voted out of office) if a textbook offends one of the many interest groups that scrutinize possible choices. Publishers know the market and take steps to make sure that their products will sell.

There are doubtless other culprits that help explain the difference between the recovery in math scores and the failure to recover in verbal scores. Television, rather than the printed page, became the primary medium for getting news and recreation at home after mid-century, and that process was also reaching full flower in the 1960s. Telephones displaced letter writing as the medium for long-range communication. Such trends are hostile to traditional definitions of excellence in verbal skills. The simple hypothesis of this story is that these pressures existed across the curriculum and in society at large but that math skills were less susceptible to them. (Math skills may instead have been getting a boost from the accessibility of computers, calculators, and other high-tech gadgetry.) When parents demanded higher standards, their schools introduced higher standards in the math curriculum that really were higher, and higher standards in the humanities and social sciences that really were not.

The same dynamics provide a hypothesis for explaining why the rebound was more complete for the nation's overall student population than for the SAT population. A textbook that is dumbed down is in fact helpful to the mediocre student. A recent study of six textbooks over a twelve-year period demonstrated that they had indeed been simplified, and students performed significantly better on the current, dumbed-down texts.[46] Subjects that were traditionally not included in the curriculum for the lower end of the distribution—for example, exposure to serious literature—have now been so simplified as to be accessible to almost all.

The same dumbed-down textbook can quite easily have a depressing effect on the talented student's development. And while the textbooks were being simplified, subjects that would push the best students to their limits, such as the classical languages, were all but dropped. Offered this diluted curriculum, talented students do not necessarily take the initiative to stretch themselves. Plenty of students with high IQs will happily choose to write about *The Hobbit* instead of *Pride and Prejudice* for their term paper if that option is given to them. Few of even the most brilliant youngsters tackle the *Aeneid* on their own.

The Neglect of the Gifted

Another factor in the declining capabilities of America's brightest students is that the decline occurred when, in policy circles, disadvantaged students were "in" and gifted students were "out." When the first significant aid went to secondary education at the end of the Eisenhower years, it was for the brightest students who might become scientists or engineers. In 1965, with the passage of the Elementary and Secondary Education Act of 1965 (ESEA), the funding priority turned 180 degrees, and it has remained anchored in the new position ever since. As of 1993, the ESEA authorized forty-six programs with budgets that added up to $8.6 billion. Most of these programs are specifically designated for students in low-income areas and students with special educational needs. Even the programs that might apply to any sort of student (improvements in science and mathematics education, for example) often are worded in ways that give preference to students from low-income areas. Another set of programs are for support services. And, finally, there are programs designated for the gifted and talented. This is the way that the $8.6 billion budget broke out for fiscal 1993:[47]

Programs for the disadvantaged	92.2%
Programs that might benefit any student	5.6%
Support and administration of ESEA programs	2.1%
Programs for the gifted	0.1%

This breakdown omits other federal programs with large budgets aimed at the education of the disadvantaged—more than $2 billion for Head Start (funded by the Department of Health and Human Services, not the Department of Education), more than $3 billion for job training programs, plus a scattering of others.[48]

Theoretically, programs targeted at disadvantaged students could also be programs for the cognitively gifted among the socioeconomically disadvantaged. But that's not the way it has worked. *Disadvantaged* as used by three decades of administrators and school boards using ESEA funds has consistently meant not just students who are poor or living in an inner-city neighborhood but students who exhibit learning problems. Programs for the intellectually gifted but otherwise disadvantaged attract little support and, occasionally, hostility. A case in point is Banneker High School in Washington, D.C., a special academic high school in the middle of the black northeast section of the city, established by a former superintendent of schools with the school board's reluctant permission in 1981.

The establishment of Banneker High followed a proud tradition in Washington, where once-elite Dunbar High had turned out many of the nation's black leaders. But throughout the 1980s, Banneker was underfunded and repeatedly threatened with closure. Banneker was "elitest," said an influential school board member, a luxury for parents who "had their children in private school and can no longer afford it and bring them back to essentially a private school at the public expense."[49] Banneker's "elitest" admissions policy? Applicants had to write an essay, be interviewed, be in the top 18 percent of their class, and read and compute *at grade level*—a broad conception of "elitest" indeed. Throughout it all, teachers competed to teach at Banneker and students competed to attend. Banneker placed large proportions of its graduates in college and had no significant problems with discipline, drugs, crime, or the other ills of contemporary urban schools.[50] And yet, as we write, Banneker continues to be barely tolerated by the school system. Banneker's story has numerous counterparts in other urban centers. Funds for the economically and socially disadvantaged have meant, for practical purposes, funds concentrated on the cognitively disadvantaged as well.

A POLICY AGENDA

What are the implications for policy? The pros and cons of the specific reforms on the table—national achievement tests, national curricula, school choice, vouchers, tuition tax credits, apprenticeship programs, restoration of the neighborhood school, minimum competency tests, ability grouping, and a host of others—involve nuts-and-bolts issues that are better argued out in detail, on their merits, in works that are specifically devoted to them. We also leave for other settings a discussion of the enormous potential of new technologies, from the personal computer to laser disks to the information superhighway, to enrich and broaden educational resources. Here we concentrate on certain strategic implications about educational reform that flow from our account—first, regarding attempts to upgrade American education as a whole, and then regarding the education of the gifted.

Realism About the Limits of General Improvements in Education

We begin with the first and most widely accepted conclusion: The extent and quality of learning for American students in general is low—lower than in most other industrialized countries but also (it would seem) low by basic standards of what a person of ordinary ability ought to learn. Before jumping into any particular set of solutions, however, policymakers need to be more realistic about what can be done to improve the education of students in a heterogeneous, nontotalitarian country. Specifically, critics of American education must come to terms with the reality that *in a universal education system, many students will not reach the level of education that most people view as basic.* Consider again the example of functional illiteracy mentioned earlier: that over 20 percent of 17-year-olds are below the intermediate reading level on the NAEP, meaning that they are marginal readers or worse. This is usually considered a failure of American education, and perhaps it is. But most of these nonreaders come from the bottom of the cognitive ability distribution. How well *should* they be able to read after a proper education, given the economic, technological, and political constraints on any system of mass education?

The United States has not yet completed the first half-century of human history in which universal secondary education became a goal. It was not until 1963 that the dropout rate fell below 30 percent of all 17-year-olds. Already we have seen improving performance in academic tests for the average student as educational opportunities have spread across the population. At about the same time, educators—and educational critics—stopped thinking hard or openly about variation in intellectual abilities. It is time to reopen the issue. What constitutes educational success for persons at various points along the cognitive ability distribution? The aspirations of educational reformers should be accompanied by a realistic and systematic assessment of where the room for improvement lies, taking the cognitive distribution into account.

Some critics blame students who do not work hard enough, rather than schools that fail to teach, for the shortcomings of American education. One hears repeatedly about students as couch potatoes. The average American student, it is said, takes the easy way out compared not only to the fabled Japanese but to children in countries such as Norway, the Netherlands, Ireland, and Italy.[51] The obvious policy implication is to do something to make students work harder. Lengthen the school year. Lengthen the school day. Require homework every night. Toughen the grading.[52] The proposals fill the air. We think many of them are good ideas. But the closer one looks at the reasons why students do not work harder, the less it seems that they are to blame.

First, *most American parents do not want drastic increases in the academic work load.* Some of the evidence for this lies in quantitative survey data. In Harold Stevenson's landmark cross-national study of Chinese, Japanese, and American education, 91 percent of American parents said their school is doing an "excellent or good job," compared to only half that proportion of Taiwanese or Japanese parents.[53] It has become a truism in survey research: Americans tell interviewers that American education in general is going to the dogs, then in the next breath give high marks to their children's own school.[54] In surveys, many American parents are either apathetic about school or hostile toward more homework and tougher grading.[55] In this climate, more demanding standards cannot easily be imposed from above.

But if you live near a public school, you need not search the technical journals to verify the point. Visit the school and talk to any teacher about the last half-dozen parents who have complained to him. For every parent who visits the principal to tell him that Johnny isn't getting enough homework are several who visit to complain Johnny is being overworked. Parents who are upset about inflated grades seldom make a teacher's life miserable. Parents who are upset about their child's low grade do.

Parents *do* want orderly classrooms, no weapons, no violence, no drugs, and other safeguards for their children that many schools, especially in large cities, no longer provide. These urgent needs are fueling much of the shift into private schools and political backing for the "school choice" movement. But the average parent seems unprepared to support genuinely stiffer academic standards.

A second point is that *the average American student has little incentive to work harder than he already does in high school.* Economist John Bishop has taken the lead in making this case, emphasizing two points.[56] Bishop first observes that a demanding high school curriculum is not necessary for admission to most colleges. For most college-bound students, finding the money is harder than amassing the necessary high school record. And it's their parents who typically need to find the money. Why bother to take tough courses? This is true even of talented students applying to selective schools; only a handful of schools at the summit routinely turn away students with SATs in the 1200s and up (see Chapter 1). A student who tests reasonably well (he knows this by the time he gets to high school) and doesn't have his sights set on the likes of Yale does not have to be too careful about which courses to take as long as his grades are decent. Only youngsters who aspire to colleges that usually take students with higher scores than their own have a strong incentive to study hard—and however common this situation may seem at the school attended by the children of most of our readers, it describes a minuscule proportion of the national high school population.

Bishop also shows that achievement in high school does not pay off in higher wages or better jobs. Many employers assume that the high school diploma no longer means much more than that the student warmed a seat for twelve years. Others are willing to look at high school transcripts as part of the hiring process, but though schools are legally obligated to respond to requests for transcripts, hardly any transcripts ever reach the employer, and those that do usually arrive so late that they are useless.[57] Using the NLSY, Bishop found that better test scores in science, language arts, and math were associated with *lower* wages and employment among young men in the first ten years after high school.[58] Students, like everybody else, respond to what's in it for them. There's close to nothing in it for them in working hard in high school. Ergo, they do not work hard in high school.

How might policy changes reconnect high school performance with payoffs after graduation? For students not continuing to college, Bishop recommends a variety of measures to certify competencies, to make transcripts understandable and available to employers, and to build up data banks, national or regional (private, not federal), to enable youths to send their "competency profile" to potential employers.[59]

Such programs may work if employers of high school graduates had a shortage of competent workers applying for jobs. Some pilot projects are underway that should tell how much such data banks are needed and used.[60] But in thinking about linking up performance in high school with the job market, here is a dose of realism: When it comes to predicting job productivity in most common jobs, an employer who routinely trains new employees in specific job skills anyway hasn't much reason to care about whether the applicant got an A or a C in high school English or, for that matter, how well the applicant did in high school vocational courses, except perhaps as a rough measure of how bright and conscientious the applicant is. On the average, and assuming no legal restrictions on testing, an employer can get a better idea of how well a job applicant will perform in job training by giving him an inexpensive twelve-minute intelligence test than by anything that the high school can tell the employer about the applicant's academic record.[61] This puts sharp limits on how interested employers will be high school performance.

As far as colleges are concerned, what incentive do they have to raise admissions requirements if it means fewer students? During and just after the baby boom years, private colleges added many students to their rosters and now face an oversupply of places for a shrinking market. Few prefer to go out of business rather than take students with modest credentials. Public universities make their admissions policies in response to political pressures that generally push them toward more inclusiveness, not less. When neither buyer nor seller profits from higher standards, why would standards rise?

Realism About How Federal Reforms Will Work in the American Context

In ways that few people want to acknowledge, America does not want its schools to take a large leap in what they demand of youngsters. Our conclusion is that if parents, students, and employers do not broadly support a significantly more demanding educational system, it's not going to happen. Nonetheless, a variety of sensible reforms are on the table— more homework, a longer school year, and the like. Why don't we at least recommend that the federal government mandate these good things? On this question, the experience of the 1960s and 1970s serves as an object lesson for today.

Educational reformers in the 1960s and 1970s were confident that *their* ideas were good things to do. They were impatient with the conservatism of local school districts. They turned to a responsive White House, Congress, and Supreme Court, achieved many of their objectives, and thereby contributed to a historic shift in American education. On balance, the turn was for the worse as far as academic excellence was concerned, but that doesn't mean the ideas were bad in themselves. Ideas such as more racial integration in the schools, more attention to the needs of disadvantaged students, and more equitable treatment of students in disciplinary matters do not seem less obviously "good" to us than ideals such as more homework and a longer school year. It was not the core ideas that were at fault (in most instances) but some basic problems that go with reforming American education at a national level.

We characterize the situation as follows: Slow improvement seems to have been a natural part of twentieth-century American education until the 1960s. This slow improvement had great inertia, in the sense that a slow-moving freight train has inertia. It is very difficult for an outside force to accelerate the freight train but comparatively easy for an outside force to derail it. In the United States, the federal government tends to be an outside force, more often derailing than pushing along, for reasons that are peculiarly American.

In countries such as France and Germany, with more homogeneous populations and more authoritarian and unapologetically elitest educational traditions, the national government can get away with centralized school systems that educate their brightest youth well. In the United States, it cannot. Federal standards, federal rules, and federal curricula, were they to be established, would inevitably be watered down and educational goals would be compromised with social and political ones. The federal government responds to pushes from all sides and gets equally nervous about affirming the genius of either *Huck Finn* or Charles Darwin. Powerful teachers' organizations will not tolerate certification tests that flunk large numbers of teachers. Organizations that represent minority groups will not tolerate national educational standards that cause large numbers of minority children to flunk. These are political facts of life that will not change soon, no matter who is in the White House.

With America's immense diversity and its tradition of local control, Washington is the wrong place to look for either energy or wisdom on educational reform. In our view, any natural impulse toward educational improvement will be best nourished by letting the internal forces—the motivations of parents for their children and teachers for a satisfying career—have their head. We will state our recommendation in broad terms:

The federal government should actively support programs that enable all parents, not just affluent ones, to choose the school that their children attend. Current movements to provide increased parental choice in schools are a hopeful sign, whether it be choice within the public school system, vouchers, or tuition tax credits. Without being any more specific than that, we urge that increased parental choice extend to private as well as public schools, and to religious private schools as well as secular ones.

Will increased parental choice help, given the modest academic goals that many parents have for their children? There are reasons for thinking it will. First, the learning that goes on in a school depends on the school environment as well as on its curriculum. Here, the great majority of parents and teachers stand on common ground. Orderly classrooms and well-enforced codes of behavior do not need to be mandated but simply permitted; parents, teachers, and administrators alike will see to it, if the control they once had over their schools is returned to them. To have America's children, poor as well as rich, once again attending safe, orderly schools would be no small achievement and would likely foster more learning than the often chaotic public schools do now.

Gifted youngsters would also benefit by restoring local control. While most parents do not want an authentically tougher education for their children, some do, and they tend to be concentrated among the parents of the brightest. Policy should make it as easy as possible for them to match up with classes that satisfy their ambitions.

To the extent that the government succeeds in this first goal, the others that we have in mind become less important. But as long as the current situation prevails, in which federal money and the conditions surrounding it play a major role in shaping public education, we recommend two other measures:

A federal prize scholarship program. This is one instance in which a specific, federal program could do some good in restoring educational excellence. As the law stands, federal scholarships and loan assistance are awarded almost exclusively on the basis of financial need, leaving the administration of standards to the colleges that admit and teach the students. That program may continue as is, but Congress should add a second program, not contingent on financial need but awarded competitively—for example, a flat one-time award of $20,000 to the 25,000 students in the country earning the top scores on standardized tests of academic achievement, over and above whatever scholarship assistance the student was receiving from other sources. How much would such "American Scholars" (the Congress might call them) cost? Five hundred million dollars a year—an amount equivalent to a rounding error in the national budget but one that would dramatically transform the signal that the federal government sends about the value it places on academic excellence.[62]

Reallocate some portion of existing elementary and secondary school fed-

eral aid away from programs for the disadvantaged to programs for the gifted. The objective is to make sure that public school systems have roughly the same capability to provide for students at the high end of the distribution as they have for helping students at the low end. A collateral part of this reform should be to rescind any federal regulations or grant requirements that might discourage local school systems from experimenting with or supporting programs for the gifted. At present, there is an overwhelming tilt toward enriching the education of children from the low end of the cognitive ability distribution. We propose more of a balance across the cognitive ability distribution.

Restoring the Concept of the Educated Man

Why should the federal government shift money from programs for the disadvantaged to programs for the gifted, when we know that a large portion of the gifted come from privileged families? Why not just support programs for the gifted who happen to come from poor families as well? In Part I, we went to some lengths to describe the dangers of a cognitive elite. And yet here we call for steps that could easily increase the segregation of the gifted from everyone else. Won't programs for the gifted further isolate them?

The answers to such questions have nothing to do with social justice but much to do with the welfare of the nation, including the ultimate welfare of the disadvantaged.

The first point echoes a continuing theme of this book: To be intellectually gifted is indeed a gift. Nobody "deserves" it. The monetary and social rewards that accrue to being intellectually gifted are growing all the time, for reasons that are easily condemned as being unfair. Never mind, we are saying. These gifted youngsters are important not because they are more virtuous or deserving but because our society's future depends on them. The one clear and enduring failure of contemporary American education is at the high end of the cognitive ability distribution.

Ideally we would like to see the most gifted children receive a demanding education *and* attend school side by side with a wide range of children, learning firsthand how the rest of the world lives. But that option is no more available now than it was during the attempts to force the racial integration of urban schools in the 1960s and 1970s. The nation's elementary and secondary schools are highly segregated by socioeconomic status, they will tend to become more so in the future, and the forces pushing these trends are so powerful, stemming from the deeply rooted causes that we described in Part I, that they can be reversed only by a level of state coercion that would be a cure far deadlier than the disease.

Most gifted students are going to grow up segregated from the rest of society no matter what. They will then go to the elite colleges no matter what, move into successful careers no matter what, and eventually lead the institutions of this country no matter what. Therefore, the nation had better do its damnedest to make them as *wise* as it can. If they cannot grow up knowing how the rest of the world lives, they can at least grow up with a proper humility about their capacity to reinvent the world de novo and thoughtfully aware of their intellectual, cultural, and ethical heritage. They should be taught their responsibilities as citizens of a broader society.

The educational deficit that worries us is symbolized by the drop in verbal skills on the SAT. What we call verbal skills encompass, among other things, the ability to think about difficult problems: to analyze, pick apart, disaggregate, synthesize, and ultimately to understand. It has seldom been more apparent how important it is that the people who count in business, law, politics, and our universities know how to think about their problems in complex, rigorous modes and how important it is that they bring to their thinking depth of judgment and, in the language of Aristotle, the habit of virtue. This kind of wisdom—for wisdom is what we need more of—does not come naturally with a high IQ. It has to be added through education, and education of a particular kind.

We are not talking about generalized higher standards. Rather, we are thinking of the classical idea of the "educated man"—which we will amend to "educated person"—in which to be educated meant first of all to master a core body of material and skills. The idea is not wedded to the specific curriculum that made an educated man in the nineteenth-century British public school or in the Greek lyceum. But it is wedded to the idea of certain high intellectual goals. For example, to be an educated person meant being able to write competently and argue logically. Therefore, children were taught the inner logic of grammar and syntax because that kind of attention to detail was believed to carry over to greater precision of thinking. They were expected to learn Aristotle's catalog of fallacies, because educators understood that the ability to assess an argument in everyday life was honed by mastering the formal elements of logic. Ethics and theology were part of the curriculum, to teach and to refine virtue. We will not try to prescribe how a contemporary curriculum might be revised to achieve the same ends, beyond a few essentials: To be an educated person must mean to have mastered a core of history, literature, arts, ethics, and the sciences and, in the process of learning those disciplines, to have been trained to weigh, analyze, and evaluate according to exacting standards. This process must begin in elementary school and must continue through the university.

Our proposal will sound, and is, elitist, but only in the sense that, after exposing students to the best the world's intellectual heritage has to offer and challenging them to achieve whatever level of excellence they are capable of, just a minority of students has the potential to become "an educated person" as we are using the term. It is not within everyone's ability to understand the world's intellectual heritage at the same level, any more than everyone who enters college can expect to be a theoretical physicist by trying hard enough. *At every stage of learning, some people reach their limits.* This is not a controversial statement when it applies to the highest levels of learning. Readers who kept taking mathematics as long as they could stand it know that at some point they hit the wall, and studying hard was no longer enough.

The nation has been unwilling to accept in recent decades that the same phenomenon of individual limitation applies at every level of education. Given the constraints of time and educational resources, some students cannot be taught statistical theory; a smaller fraction of students cannot be taught the role of mercantilism in European history; for even a smaller fraction, writing a coherent essay may be out of reach. Each level of accomplishment deserves respect on its own merits, but the ideal of the educated person is in itself an ideal that must be embraced openly. By abandoning it, America has been falling short both in educating its most gifted and in inculcating, across the entire cognitive distribution, the values we would want in an educated citizenry.

But what do we want to *do*? What courses should be required of educated persons? Do we want to have separate schools for the gifted and average student? Tracking systems? A national Great Books curriculum?

We will say it again: Different parents will want to make different choices for their children. We are not wise enough—and neither are any of our colleagues wise enough, nor is the federal government wise enough—to prescribe for them what is best for their children. The goal of developing educated persons, like the goal of improving American

---

Educated, Not Credentialed

If we have not already made it plain, let us state explicitly that we are proposing a traditional ideal of education, not glorifying academic credentials. To be an educated person as we use the term will ordinarily entail getting a degree, but that is incidental. Credentialism—unnecessarily limiting access to jobs to people with certain licenses and degrees—is part of the problem, not a solution. Because academic credentials are so overvalued, America shies away from accepting that many people have academic limitations—hence, the dumbing down that holds back the brightest youngsters.

---

education in general, will best be served by letting parents and local communities make those choices.

But parents and communities must turn to educators to implement their hopes for their children, and here is the problem: Too few *educators* are comfortable with the idea of the educated person. A century ago the notion of an educated person was an expression of a shared understanding, not of legal requirements. That understanding arose because people were at ease with intellectual standards, with rigor, with a recognition that people differ in their capacities. The criterion for being an educated person did not have to be compromised to include the supposition that everyone could meet it. The concept of the educated person has been out of fashion with the people who run elementary and secondary schools and, for that matter, with too many of the people who run universities.

Our policy goal? That educators who read these words change their minds. It is a reform that is at once impossible to legislate but requires no money at all. It a reform that would not jeopardize the educational advances of the average student. All that we ask is that educational leaders rededicate themselves to the duty that was once at the heart of their calling, to demand much from those fortunate students to whom much has been given.

Chapter 19

Affirmative Action in Higher Education

Affirmative action on the campus needs, at last, to be discussed as it is actually practiced, not as the rhetoric portrays it. Our own efforts to assemble data on a secretive process lead us to conclude that affirmative action as it is practiced cannot survive public scrutiny.

The edge given to minority applicants to college and graduate school is not a nod in their favor in the case of a close call but an extremely large advantage that puts black and Latino candidates in a separate admissions competition. On elite campuses, the average black freshman is in the region of the 10th to 15th percentile of the distribution of cognitive ability among white freshman. Nationwide, the gap seems to be at least that large, perhaps larger. The gap does not diminish in graduate school. If anything, it may be larger.

In the world of college admissions, Asians are a conspicuously unprotected minority. At the elite schools, they suffer a modest penalty, with the average Asian freshman being at about the 60th percentile of the white cognitive ability distribution. Our data from state universities are too sparse to draw conclusions. In all the available cases, the difference between white and Asian distributions is small (either plus or minus) compared to the large differences separating blacks and Latinos from whites.

The edge given to minority candidates could be more easily defended if the competition were between disadvantaged minority youths and privileged white youths. But nearly as large a cognitive difference separates disadvantaged black freshmen from disadvantaged white freshmen. Still more difficult to defend, blacks from affluent socioeconomic backgrounds are given a substantial edge over disadvantaged whites.

There is no question that affirmative action has "worked," in the sense that it has put more blacks and Latinos on college campuses than would otherwise have been there. But this success must be measured against costs. When students look around them, they see that blacks and Latinos constitute small pro-

447

portions of the student population but high proportions of the students doing poorly in school. The psychological consequences of this disparity may be part of the explanation for the increasing racial animosity and the high black dropout rates that have troubled American campuses. In society at large, a college degree does not have the same meaning for a minority graduate and a white one, with consequences that reverberate in the workplace and continue throughout life.

It is time to return to the original intentions of affirmative action: to cast a wider net, to give preference to members of disadvantaged groups, whatever their skin color, when qualifications are similar. Such a change would accord more closely with the logic underlying affirmative action, with the needs of today's students of all ethnic groups, and with progress toward a healthy multiracial society.

W e come to national policies that require people to treat groups differently under the law. Affirmative action began to be woven into American employment and educational practices in the 1960s as universities and employers intensified their recruiting of blacks—initially on their own, then in compliance with a widening body of court decisions and laws. By the early 1970s, affirmative action had been expanded beyond blacks to include women, Latinos, and the disabled. It also became more aggressive. Targets, guidelines, and de facto quotas[1] evolved as universities and employers discovered that the equality of outcome that people sought was not to be had from traditional recruiting methods. As it became more aggressive, affirmative action became correspondingly more controversial.

Affirmative action creates antagonism partly because it affects the distribution of scarce goods—university places, scholarships, job offers, and promotions—that people prize. But it is also problematic for reasons that reach into deeply held beliefs—most fundamentally, beliefs about the ideal of equal opportunity versus the reality of the historical experience of certain groups, preeminently blacks, in this country. As the rhetoric heats up, the arguments about affirmative action become blurred. Affirmative action raises different questions in different contexts. What, people ask, are the proper goals of affirmative action, the proper methods? Which groups are to be benefited? What are the costs of affirmative action, and who should bear them? Is affirmative action a temporary expedient to correct past wrongs, or must the American ideal of individualism be permanently modified for the collective needs of members of certain groups?

Affirmative action is part of this book because it has been based on the explicit assumption that ethnic groups do not differ in the abilities that contribute to success in school and the workplace—or, at any rate, there are no differences that cannot be made up with a few remedial courses or a few months on the job. Much of this book has been given over to the many ways in which that assumption is wrong. The implications have to be discussed, and that is the purpose of this chapter and the next, augmented by an appendix on the evolution of affirmative action regulations (Appendix 7). Together, these materials constitute a longer discussion than we devote to any other policy issue, for two reasons. First, we are making a case that contradicts a received wisdom embedded in an intellectual consensus, federal legislation, and Supreme Court jurisprudence. If the task is to be attempted at all, it must be done thoroughly. Second, we believe affirmative action to be one of the most far-reaching domestic issues of our time—not measured in its immediate effects, but in its deep and pervasive impact on America's understanding of what is just and unjust, how a pluralist society should be organized, and what America is supposed to stand for.

In this chapter, the topic is the college campus. In Chapter 20, we discuss affirmative action in the workplace. In both chapters, we provide data as available on Asians and Latinos, but the analysis centers on blacks, as has the debate over affirmative action.

THE "EDGE" IN AFFIRMATIVE ACTION

People may agree that they want affirmative action in higher education until they say more precisely what they mean by it. Then they may disagree. But whatever the argument, it would help to have some data about how colleges and universities have translated the universal desire for greater fairness in university education into affirmative action programs. Our first goal is to inform the debate with such data.

At first glance, ours may seem an odd objective, for certain kinds of data about affirmative action are abundant. Universities and businesses keep detailed numbers about the numbers of minorities who apply and are accepted. But data about the core mechanism of affirmative action—

the magnitudes of the values assigned to group membership—are not part of the public debate.

This ignorance about practice was revealed in 1991 by a law student at Georgetown University, Timothy Maguire, who had been hired to file student records.[2] He surreptitiously compiled the entrance statistics for a sample of applicants to Georgetown's law school and then published the results of his research in the law school's student newspaper. He revealed that the mean on the Law School Aptitude Test (LSAT) differed by a large margin for accepted black and white students.

In the storm that ensued, the dean of the law school ordered copies of the newspaper to be confiscated and black student groups called for Maguire's expulsion. Hardly anyone would acknowledge that Maguire's numbers even raised a legitimate issue. "Incomplete and distorted information about minority qualifications for admission into the Law Center renew the long-standing and intellectually dishonest myth that they are less qualified than their white counterparts to compete in school, perform on the job or receive a promotion," wrote the authors of an op-ed article in the *Washington Post*,[3] and that seemed to be the prevailing attitude. The numerical magnitude of the edge given to members of certain groups—the value assigned to the state of being black, Latino, female, or physically disabled—was not considered relevant.

Such edges are inherent in the process. In as neutral and precise language as we can devise: Perfectly practiced, the traditional American ideal of equal opportunity means using exclusively individual measures, applied uniformly, to choose some people over others. Perfectly practiced, affirmative action means assigning a premium, an edge, to group membership in addition to the individual measures before making a final assessment that chooses some people over others.

The size of the premium assigned to group membership—an ethnic premium when it is applied to affirmative action for favored ethnic groups—is important in trying to judge whether affirmative action in principle is working. This knowledge should be useful not only (or even primarily) for deciding whether one is "for" or "against" affirmative action in the abstract. It should be especially useful for the proponents of affirmative action. Given that one is in favor of affirmative action, how may it be practiced in a way that conforms with one's overall notions of what is fair and appropriate? If one opposes affirmative action in principle, how much is it deforming behavior in practice?

It is not obvious precisely where questions of fact trail into questions of philosophy, but we will attempt to stay on the factual side of the line at first. A bit of philosophical speculation is reserved for the end of the chapter. We first examine evidence on the magnitude of the ethnic premium from individual colleges and universities, then from professional schools. We then recast the NLSY data in terms of the rationale underlying affirmative action. We conclude that the size of the premium is unreasonably large, producing differences in academic talent across campus ethnic groups so gaping that they are in no one's best interest. We further argue that the current practice is out of keeping with the rationale for affirmative action.

The Magnitude of the Edge in Undergraduate Schools

We have obtained SAT data on classes entering twenty-six of the nation's top colleges and universities. In 1975, most of the nation's elite private colleges and universities formed the Consortium on Financing Higher Education (COFHE), which, among other things, compiles and shares information on the students at member institutions, including their SAT scores. We have obtained these data for the classes entering in 1991 and 1992.[4] They include sixteen out of the twenty top-rated private universities and five of the top ten private colleges, as ranked in *U.S. News and World Report* for 1993.[5] The figure below shows the difference in the sum of the average Verbal and Math SAT scores between whites and two minorities, blacks and Asians, for the classes in the COFHE schools that matriculated in the fall of 1992. In addition, the figure includes data on the University of Virginia and the University of California at Berkeley in 1988.[6]

The difference between black and white scores was less than 100 points at only one school, Harvard. It exceeded 200 points at nine schools, reaching its highest at Berkeley (288 points). Overall, the median difference between the white mean and the black mean was 180 SAT points, or, conservatively estimated, about 1.3 standard deviations.[7] This would put the average black at about the 10th percentile of white students. In all but four schools, Asians were within 6 points of the white mean or above it, with a median SAT 30 points above the local white average, working out to about .2 standard deviations. Or in other words, the average Asian was at about the 60th percentile of the white distribution. This combination means that blacks and Asians have even less overlap than blacks and whites at most schools, with the

At selective schools, the median black edge was 180 SAT points, while Asians faced a median penalty of 30 points

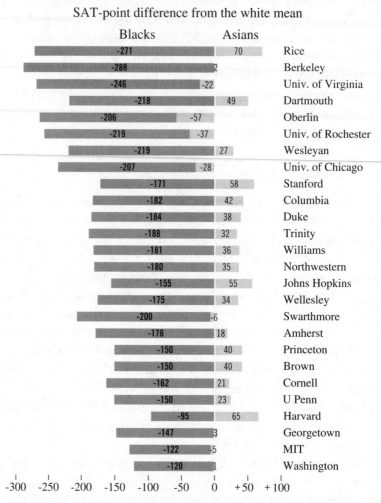

SAT-point difference from the white mean

	Blacks	Asians	
	-271	70	Rice
	-288	2	Berkeley
	-246	-22	Univ. of Virginia
	-218	49	Dartmouth
	-206	-57	Oberlin
	-219	-37	Univ. of Rochester
	-219	27	Wesleyan
	-207	-28	Univ. of Chicago
	-171	58	Stanford
	-182	42	Columbia
	-184	38	Duke
	-188	32	Trinity
	-181	36	Williams
	-180	35	Northwestern
	-155	55	Johns Hopkins
	-175	34	Wellesley
	-200	-6	Swarthmore
	-178	18	Amherst
	-150	40	Princeton
	-150	40	Brown
	-162	21	Cornell
	-150	23	U Penn
	-95	65	Harvard
	-147	3	Georgetown
	-122	-5	MIT
	-120	1	Washington

-300 -250 -200 -150 -100 -50 0 +50 +100

Sources: Consortium on Financing Higher Education 1992; Sarich 1990 (for Berkeley); L. Feinberg, "Black freshman enrollment rises 46% at U-Va," *Washington Post,* Dec. 26, 1988, p. C1 (for University of Virginia).

median black at the 5th to 7th percentile of the distribution of Asian students. Data for Latinos (not shown in the figure) put them between blacks and whites, with a median of 129 points below the white mean, or about .9 standard deviation below the white mean in the typical case. The average Latino is therefore at about the 20th percentile of the distribution of white students.[8]

The ordering of black, Latino, white, and Asian is similar to that reported for IQ and SAT scores in Chapter 13. In other words, elite universities are race norming (though it is doubtful they think of it that way), carrying with them into their student populations the ethnic differences in cognitive distributions observed in the population at large.

We would prefer to have a sample of nonelite state universities represented in our data, but such numbers are closely guarded.[9] The only data we have obtained come from the University of California at Davis, for 1979. The black-white difference then was 271 SAT points, and the Latino-white difference 211 points.[10] The Asian mean at Davis was, atypically, 54 points *below* the white mean, the largest such difference we have found.

The data from the University of Virginia and the two University of California campuses suggest that the gap between minorities and whites among freshmen at state universities may be larger than at the elite private schools. It is only a suggestion, given the limited data, but it also

---

Are Asians the Victims of Reverse Discrimination?

Complaints that Asian-American applicants were being subjected to reverse discrimination led eventually to a full-scale inquiry in the late 1980s by the federal Office for Civil Rights. Harvard, which was examined closely, was able to show that the SAT penalty of their Asian admitted students was accounted for by the smaller number of alumni children and athletes in the pool, and eventually got a clean bill of health, but the controversy remains at many other institutions.[11] Brown responded to a report from its Asian-American Students Association by admitting the existence of "an extremely serious situation" and called for "immediate remedial measures."[12] At Berkeley, Stanford, Princeton, and other elite schools, special committees have investigated the issue, issuing reports that tend to exonerate their colleges of actual reverse discrimination but acknowledge shortcomings in keeping up with the revolution in Asian applicants.[13]

The underlying source of tension remains: Asians are an ethnic minority, many of whom, or whose parents, came to the United States under circumstances of extreme deprivation. Many suffered from racial prejudice. Whether or not they are treated differently from whites by elite universities, Asians are indisputably treated differently from every other nonwhite ethnic minority. University officials everywhere have been reluctant to confront this issue forthrightly.

makes sense: Places like Harvard, Stanford, Yale, and MIT get first pick. Because the raw numbers of high-scoring black and Latino students are so small, the top schools dig deep into the thin layer of minority students at the top of the SAT distribution. In 1993, for example, only 129 blacks and 234 Latinos nationwide had SAT-Verbal scores in the 700s—and these represented all-time highs—compared to 7,114 whites. Even highly rated state institutions such as the University of California's Berkeley campus and the University of Virginia lose many of these most talented minority students to the elite private schools while continuing to get many of the top scorers in the larger white pool. Such are the mathematics of competition for a scarce good, borne out by the limited university data available, which show the three state universities with three of the four largest black-white gaps in SATs.

The Law of Supply and Demand in Minority Recruiting

Affirmative action has produced intense competition for the top black and Latino students. In the spring of 1992, Harvard reported that its "yield" of black students abruptly declined from the year before. The Harvard report suggested that the decline was due at least in part to the large financial incentives being offered to blacks by other colleges. One such black student, it was reported, received a straight grant of $85,000, plus $10,000 in annual travel budgets, from one of Harvard's competitors in minority recruiting.[14] An article in the *New York Times* provided more instances of a practice that increasingly includes the kind of enticements—full scholarships even for families with ample financial resources, free trips to visit the campus, recruiting visits, and promotional activities—that used to be reserved for star high school athletes. "As a result, a number of college officials privately accuse each other of 'stealing' black students," the *Times* reporter noted.[15]

The differences do not seem to have changed a great deal between the 1970s and the 1990s. The best longitudinal data from Berkeley illustrate a perverse effect of a strong affirmative action policy: The more aggressive the recruitment of minorities, the higher the average ability of the *nonminority* students. From 1978 to 1988, the combined SATs of blacks at Berkeley rose by 101 points, a major improvement in the academic quality of black students at Berkeley. But the competition for the allotment of white slots became ever more intense. The result was that the SAT scores for Berkeley whites rose too, and the gap between black and white students at Berkeley did not close but widened.[16] Meanwhile, the unprotected minority, Asians, also were competing for a restricted allotment of slots. Their mean scores rose more than any other group's, and by a large margin, going from far below the white mean to slightly above it. In just eleven years, the Asian mean at Berkeley soared by 189 points.

The summary statement about affirmative action in undergraduate institutions is that being either a black or a Latino is worth a great deal in the admissions process at every undergraduate school for which we have data. Even the smallest known black-white difference (95 points at Harvard) represents close to a standard deviation for Harvard undergraduates. The gap in most colleges is so large that the black and white student bodies have little overlap. The situation is less extreme for Latino students but still severe. Asian students appear to suffer a penalty for being Asian, albeit a small one on the average. We have seen no data that would dispute this picture. If such data exist, perhaps this presentation will encourage their publication.

The Magnitude of the Edge in Graduate Schools

LAW SCHOOLS. Timothy Maguire's findings about the Georgetown Law Center were consistent with more systematic evidence. The table below shows the national Law School Aptitude Test (LSAT) results for 1992 for registered first-year law students. For blacks, overlap with the white incoming law students was small; only 7 percent had scores above the white mean. The overall Latino-white difference was 1 standard deviation. It was markedly larger for Puerto Ricans (−2.0 SDs) than for

Affirmative Action Weights: The Law School Aptitude Test	
Ethnic Group	**Difference from White Mean, in SDs**
Asian/Pacific	−.32
Blacks	−1.49
Latinos	−1.01

Source: Barnes and Carr 1993.

Mexican-Americans (−.8) or "other" Latinos (−.7). The overall Asian mean corresponds to the 38th percentile on the white distribution, evidence of modest affirmative action on behalf of Asian applicants in the law schools.

The table above is for the national population of first-year law students. To assess the effects of affirmative action, it would be preferable to have data from individual law schools. At upper reaches of the LSAT distribution, from which the elite law schools drew most of their students, there was even less overlap between whites and blacks than in the SAT pool. More than 1,100 registered white law students had scores of 170 or higher on a scale going from 120 to 180, compared to three blacks. At ten highly selective law schools for which individual data were reported in a 1977 report by the Law School Admissions Council, the smallest black-white difference in LSAT scores (expressed in terms of the white distribution) at any of the ten schools was 2.4 standard deviations, the largest was 3.6 standard deviations, and the average difference for the ten schools was 2.9 standard deviations, meaning that the average black was in the bottom 1 percent of the white distribution.[17]

MEDICAL SCHOOLS. Medical students repeat the familiar pattern, as shown for the national population of matriculated first-year students in 1992 in the table below. In the national pool, the black-white gap is

---

Affirmative Action Weights:
The Medical College Admissions Test

Ethnic Group	Difference from the White Mean, in SDs		
	Biological Sciences	Physical Sciences	Verbal Reasoning
Blacks	−1.36	−1.26	−1.40
"Other under-represented minorities"[a]	−.75	−.84	−.84
"Other"[b]	+.04	+.15	−.45

Source: Division of Educational Research and Assessment 1993, pp. 59–63.

[a] "Other under-represented minorities" consists of American Indian/Alaskan natives, Mexican-American/Chicanos, and mainland Puerto Ricans.

[b] Asian/Pacific, commonwealth Puerto Ricans, and Latinos not otherwise classified.

about the same as in the law schools, with the average entering black medical student at the 8th to 10th percentile of the white distribution, depending on which subtest of the Medical College Admissions Test (MCAT) we consider. The gap between whites and "other underrepresented minorities" is a bit smaller than the Latino-white gap in law school, with the average student in this group standing at the 20th to 23d percentile of the white distribution. The "other" category—mostly Asian—had higher scores than whites on the physical sciences and (fractionally) on biological sciences, standing, respectively, at the 56th and 52d percentiles of the white distribution, while scoring lower in verbal reasoning (32d percentile).

As in the case of law schools, the black medical student pool is even more severely depleted at the top end of the range than it is in undergraduate schools, with important implications for the gap in the elite schools. In none of the three subtests did more than 19 blacks score in the 12 to 15 range (on a scale that goes from 1 to 15), compared to 1,146, 1,469, and 853 whites (for the biological sciences, physical sciences, and verbal reasoning tests, respectively).[18] In practical terms, several of the elite schools can fill their entire class with white students in the top range, but only the one or two most elite schools can hope to have a significant number of black students without producing extremely large black-white differences, comparable to those reported for elite law schools.

Other studies have published data on medical school admissions, expressed in terms of the odds of being accepted to medical school for different minorities. All tell similar stories to ours.[19]

GRADUATE SCHOOLS IN THE ARTS AND SCIENCES. Applicants to graduate schools other than law and medicine typically take the Graduate Record Examination (GRE), comprising verbal, quantitative, and analytical subtests. The reports of GRE scores do not distinguish between persons who take the test and persons who actually register in a graduate school, so they are less useful than the LSAT or MCAT in trying to understand the scope and magnitude of affirmative action in those schools. Nonetheless, the results, in the table below, look familiar. The magnitudes of the ethnic differences on the individual subtests of the GRE (in 1987–1988, the most recent year for which we were given data) were somewhat smaller than for the professional schools, putting blacks at the 10th to 12th percentile of the white distribution, depending on the subtest. Asians were (as usual) higher than whites on the quantitative and lower on the verbal. Adding up all three subtest means, Asians were a few points higher than whites.

Applicants to Graduate Schools			
	Difference from the White Mean, in SDs		
Ethnic Group	**Verbal**	**Quantitative**	**Analytical**
Asian/Pacific	−.37	+.52	−.15
Blacks	−1.20	−1.19	−1.29
Latino	−.74	−.46	−.54

Source: Wah and Robinson, 1990, Table 2.2.

The summary statement is that the ethnic gaps in objective test scores observed in undergraduate institutions are matched, and perhaps exceeded, in graduate and professional schools. If data become available from individual schools, this question can be answered definitively.

AFFIRMATIVE ACTION AS PART OF THE ADMISSIONS PROCESS

The data we have just summarized should restrain casual assertions that the differences among the blacks, Latinos, Asians, and whites who go to college are not worth worrying about. The differences we have described are large by any definition. But do these data give us any leverage on the question of whether affirmative action as it is currently practiced is good or bad? For an answer, we begin by inquiring into the logic of affirmative action and then examine whether the patterns of racial and socioeconomic differences observed in the NLSY make sense in terms of that logic.

The Logic of College Admissions

On the campus, affirmative action is not at odds with the normal admissions process. College admission is not, has never been, nor is there reason to think it should be, a competition based purely on academic merit. The nonacademic ends can be legitimate and important. No admissions policy can serve all good ends equally, because the ends are often inconsistent with one another. The admissions process is a juggling act, and affirmative action fits squarely in a long tradition. Our understanding of the legitimate role of affirmative action, which owes much to Robert Klitgaard's discussion of the same topic, will be categorized under the headings of "institutional benefit," "social utility," and "just deserts."[20]

INSTITUTIONAL BENEFIT. One of the goals of any admissions process is to serve the institution's own interests. Why do many colleges give some preference to students from faraway states? To children of alumni?[21] To all-state linebackers or concert pianists? Some of the answers involve the good of the institution as a whole. A student from Montana can add diversity to a college in Connecticut; a good football team can strengthen a college's sense of community and perhaps encourage alumni generosity. Black and Latino students admitted under affirmative action can enrich a campus by adding to its diversity.

The institution also has interests beyond daily campus life. Admitting the children of its faculty and of its most generous alumni may add little that is distinctive to the student body, for example, but their parents make a big difference to the health and quality of the institution, and keeping them happy is important. Beyond the college gates is society at large. Universities cannot disregard what the broader community thinks of them, and so they must be sensitive to the currents of their time. The political pressure (let alone the legal requirement) for some level of affirmative action in the universities has been irresistible.

These institutional interests are valid and significant but unsatisfactory as the entire rationale for affirmative action, for there are too many ways in which affirmative action has self-evident drawbacks. If it is admissible to augment the presence of some racial or ethnic minorities solely because they serve the interests of the university, is it not also appropriate to limit the presence of minorities for the same reason? It is a relevant question, for, while limits for Jews may be largely behind us, limits for Asians may be upon us. Furthermore, one cannot avoid the problem by arguing that it is appropriate to have floors for certain groups but inappropriate to have ceilings for others. Making more room for one group must reduce the room for others. Instinctively, one wishes for morally stronger justifications for affirmative action than institutional interests. Two are available.

SOCIAL UTILITY. Consider the case of the crown prince of a large kingdom who also happens to be a young man of pedestrian intelligence and indifferent character. He applies to a competitive American university—Princeton, we shall say. Should Princeton admit him in preference to the many brighter and more virtuous students whose applications flood the admissions office? The social utility criterion may say yes, for this young man is eventually going to influence the lives of the millions of people in his own country. He may be drawn into issues that could affect international peace and prosperity. Princeton makes a contribution to human happiness if it can help the crown prince develop into a thoughtful and humane adult.

The same kind of calculation bedevils professional schools in choosing among men and women. For example, if it is empirically true that women are more likely than men to leave a profession, there is an authentic question of resources to be considered when selecting who shall be trained in that profession. Given that the good called a medical education is severely limited, how important is the ethical nudge in the direction of using scarce resources efficiently? Conversely, how important is it to get women into these professions so that, in the future, it will be easier for more of them to pursue such careers?

Suppose now that it is again Princeton choosing between two candidates, one black and one white. Both are from affluent professional families, so socioeconomic disadvantage is not an issue. The white has higher test scores and (just to make the case still plainer) more glowing references than the black candidate. Both plan to become attorneys. In some sense, the white candidate "deserves" admission more. But who is going to provide more social "value-added"? Adding one more white attorney to the ranks of prominent attorneys, or adding one more black one? Princeton could reasonably choose the black candidate on grounds that only by expanding the size of the next generation of minority lawyers, physicians, businessmen, and professors can society attain racial equality at the higher socioeconomic and professional levels. Only when equality is reached at those higher levels will minority youths routinely aspire to such careers. And, the argument continues, only when the aspirations for success and their fulfillment are thus equalized will we reach the kind of real racial equality that will eventually show up in test scores as well as everything else.

For now, let us ignore whether affirmative action will in fact have these good effects and concentrate instead on the logic of the argument. The same logic can justify not only choosing a member of a minority over a white, it can justify choosing a member of one minority over another. For example, a case may be made for systematically favoring blacks over Asians on the social utility criterion—based not on calculations that African slaves faced greater oppression in the past than the Chinese brought to build the railroads but on the proposition that the opportunities for a degree may be more valuably distributed to African Americans instead of Asian Americans, given the contemporary state of affairs in American society. Indeed, early in this century, when colleges were discriminating against Jews, the reasons given, when they were given at all, were a mixture of institutional self-interest and social utility.[22]

Once again, however, the rationale for affirmative action is not fully satisfactory. Looking back to the time when the numbers of Jews or women on a campus were strictly limited, most people feel uncomfortable with the rationales, however dispassionately accurate they might have seemed at the time. They are uncomfortable partly because of the injustice, which brings us to the final criterion that should be part of the admissions process.

JUST DESERTS. Beyond institutional benefit and social utility, college admissions may recognize what might be called "just deserts." As the director of admissions to Columbia College expressed it, "One has to take into account how well one has done with the environment [an applicant has] been handed."[23] The applicant who overcame poverty, cultural disadvantages, an unsettled home life, a prolonged illness, or a chronic disability to do as well as he did in high school will get a tip from most admissions committees, even if he is not doing as well academically as the applicants usually accepted. This tip for the disadvantaged does not seem unfair.

This is the intuitive rationale of affirmative action for blacks, who were demonstrably the victims of legal oppression, enforced by the state, from the founding of the colonies through the middle of this century, and of pervasive social discrimination that still persists to some degree.

To give blacks an edge because they are black accords with this sense of justice. At an elaborated level, there is a widespread impression that the underrepresentation of blacks and Latinos (and perhaps other groups, such as American Indians) in elite schools is an effect of racial or ethnic injustice, properly corrected by affirmative action in university admissions. If it were not for the racism in our society, the groups would be proportionally represented, some believe. A still more elaborated version of the argument is that the very approach to learning, reasoning, and argumentation in universities is itself racist, so that the predictors of university performance, such as SAT or IQ scores, are therefore racist too. Affirmative action redresses the built-in racism in the admissions process and the curriculum.[24]

Two Common But Invalid Arguments Regarding Affirmative Action

We have reviewed the rationales for affirmative action without even mentioning the two most commonly made points: first, that the real difference in academic ability between minority and white candidates is much smaller than the difference as measured by test scores, and, second, that gradations in ability do not count for much after a certain threshold of ability has been met.

This first point is based on allegations of cultural bias in the tests, covered in Chapter 13 and Appendix 5. As readers will by now be aware, much research argues strongly against it. The second point, often expressed by university officials with the words "everyone we admit can do the work," is true in the limited sense that students with comparatively low levels of ability can get passing grades. It is not correct in any broader sense. Higher scores predict better academic performance throughout the range of scores. There is no reason to think that a threshold exists above which differences in tested ability have little effect on the quality of the student body, student performance, and the nature of student interactions.[25]

So there are three coherent rationales for concluding that it is just, as well as institutionally and socially useful, to admit minority students from specific minority groups even if they are somewhat less qualified than the other candidates who would be admitted. The rationales are not even controversial. Few of the opponents of affirmative action are prepared to argue that universities should ignore any of these criteria altogether in making admissions decisions. With that issue behind us, the question becomes whether affirmative action as it is being practiced is doing what its advocates want it to do. Does it serve worthwhile purposes for the institutions themselves, for students, for society at large, or for a commonly shared sense of justice?

A Scheme for Comparing Rationales with Practice

We will set the problem first with hypothetical applicants to college, divided into four categories, then we will insert the actual cognitive ability scores of the college students in those categories. The four categories are represented in the 2 × 2 table below, where "low" and "high" refer to the full range of cultural and economic advantages and disadvantages.

		WHITE	
		Low	High
	High	(3) Scarsdale Appalachia	(4) Scarsdale Scarsdale
MINORITY			
	Low	(2) South Bronx Appalachia	(1) South Bronx Scarsdale

A Framework for Thinking about the Magnitude of Preference That Should Be Given to a Minority Candidate

"Scarsdale" denotes any applicant from an upscale family. "South Bronx" denotes a disadvantaged minority youth, and "Appalachia" denotes a disadvantaged white youth. Each cell in the table corresponds to a pair of applicants—a white and a minority—from either high or low socioeconomic and cultural circumstances. Starting at the lower right and going clockwise around the table, the categories are: (1) a minority applicant from a disadvantaged background and a white from a privileged background; (2) a minority and a white applicant, both from disadvantaged backgrounds; (3) a minority applicant from a privileged background and a white from a disadvantaged background, and (4) a minority and a white applicant, both from privileged backgrounds.

Imagine you are on the admissions committee and choosing between two candidates. Assume that all the nonacademic qualifications besides race are fully specified by high and low status for this pair of candidates and that the IQ is the only measure of academic ability being considered. (In other words, let us disregard grades, extracurricular activities, athletics, alumni parents, and other factors.) You are trying to decide whether to admit the minority applicant or the white applicant. How big a difference in IQ are you willing to accept in each cell and still pick the minority candidate over the white candidate? Let us consider each cell in turn, starting with the situation in which the minority might be expected to get the largest premium to the one in which the premium arguably should go to the white.

CELL 1: THE SOUTH BRONX MINORITY VERSUS THE SCARSDALE WHITE. The largest weight obviously belongs in the cell in which the minority student is disadvantaged and the white student is advantaged. Considerations of just deserts argue that it is not fair to equate the test scores of the youngster who has gotten the finest education money and status can buy with the test scores of the youngster who has struggled through poor schools and a terrible neighborhood. Considerations of social utility argue that it is desirable to have more minority students getting good college educations, so that society may alter the effects of past discrimination and provide a basis for an eventually color-blind society in the future. We assign ++ to this cell to indicate a large preference for the minority candidate. A relatively large deficit in the minority applicant's test score may properly be overlooked.

CELL 4: THE SCARSDALE MINORITY VERSUS THE SCARSDALE WHITE. If a college is choosing between two students in the high-high cell, both from Scarsdale with college-educated parents and family incomes in six figures, the social utility criteria say that there is a rationale for picking the minority youth even if his test scores are somewhat lower. But doing so would violate just deserts when the white student has higher test scores and is in every other way equal to the minority student. Which criterion should win out? There is no way to say for sure. Our own view is that, as personally hurtful as this injustice may be to the individual white person involved, it is relatively minor in the grand scheme of things. The privileged white youth, with strong credentials and parents who can pay for college, will get into a good college someplace. We therefore assign a + to this cell to signify some ethnic premium to the minority candidate but less than in the first instance.

CELL 2: THE SOUTH BRONX MINORITY VERSUS THE APPALACHIAN WHITE. Now imagine a minority student from the South Bronx and a white student from an impoverished Appalachian community. The families of both students are at the wrong end of the scale of advantage. Which one should get the nod in a close call? The white has just as much or nearly as much "social utility" going for him as the black does. American society will benefit from educating youngsters from disadvantaged white backgrounds, too. Both have a claim based on just deserts. America likes to think that people can work their way up from the bottom, and Appalachia is the bottom no less than the South Bronx. Perhaps there is some residual premium associated with being black, based on the supposition that just being black puts one at a greater disadvantage than a white in the "all else equal" case—a more persuasive point when applied to blacks from the South Bronx than when applied to blacks from Scarsdale. We assign ≈0 to this cell, indicating that the appropriate ethnic premium for the minority student is not much greater than zero (other things being equal) and is certainly smaller than in the Scarsdale-Scarsdale case.

CELL 3: THE SCARSDALE MINORITY VERSUS THE APPALACHIAN WHITE. Now we are comparing the privileged minority student with the disadvantaged white student. Where one comes out on the scale of social utility depends on how one values the competing goals to be served. It seems hard to justify a social utility value that nets out in favor of the minority youth, however. (Yes, there is social utility in adding a minority to the ranks of successful attorneys, even if he comes from an affluent background, but there is also social utility in vindicating the American dream for poor whites and in adding a representative of disadvantaged white America to the ranks of successful attorneys.) Something close to zero seems to be the appropriate expected value on the social utility measure, and the white youth should get a plus on the just deserts argument. If the choice is between a poor white youngster from an awful environment and an affluent minority youngster who has gone to fine schools, and if the poor white has somewhat lower test scores than the affluent minority, it is appropriate to give the poor white at least a modest premium. We thus enter – into this cell, to reflect the fact the white youth gets the nod in a close call.

The filled-in table is shown below. We may argue about how large an ethnic premium, expressed in IQ, should be tolerated in each cell, but

---

A Rationale for Thinking About the Preference Given to a Minority Candidate

	WHITE	
	Low SES	High SES
MINORITY High SES	(3) −	(4) +
Low SES	(2) ≈0	(1) ++

---

the ranking of the premiums seems hard to dispute. With this in mind, we are ready to examine how affirmative action in the NLSY sample squared with this view of the appropriate discrepancies.[26]

Rationale vs. Practice

To fill in the table with data, we divided NLSY students who went to four-year institutions into those in the upper and lower halves of socioeconomic background, using the socioeconomic status index described in Appendix 2. (We also conducted the analysis with more extreme definitions of privilege and disadvantage.)[27] We then selected the subsample of whites and blacks who had attended the same schools, and computed the mean IQ for the upper and lower halves of socioeconomic status for these matched pairs, statistically controlling for institution. Sample sizes of these matched pairs ranged from 72 for the cell in the top left to 504 for the cell in the lower right. The filled-in table below shows the difference between the white and black IQ scores in standard deviations.[28]

Let us try to put these numbers in terms of the choices facing an admissions officer. He has two folders on the desk, representing the lower left-hand cell of the table. The two applicants differ in cognitive ability by 1.17 standard deviations, and both are socioeconomically disadvantaged. More specifically (incorporating information about the means not shown in the table), one student is almost exactly average in cognitive ability for such college students, at the 49th percentile of the distribution; the other is at the 12th percentile. Is it appropriate to treat the choice as a toss-up if the student at the 12th percentile happens to

The Actual Magnitude of the Preference Given to Black Candidates

	WHITE SES	
	Below average	Above average
BLACK SES Above average	+.58 (–)	+.91 (+)
Below average	+1.17 (≈0)	+1.25 (++)

be black?[29] The typical admissions officer has, in effect, been treating two such applicants as a toss-up.

We put the question in that way to try to encourage thinking about a subject that is not much thought about. How big an edge is appropriate? In a properly run system of affirmative action, should the average disadvantaged black and average disadvantaged white who got to a given college differ by so large a margin?

Consider the next pair of folders, with two applicants from privileged backgrounds (the upper right-hand cell). One is at the 57th centile of college students, the other at the 23d centile, corresponding to almost a standard deviation difference. Is it reasonable to choose each with equal likelihood if the one at the 23d centile is black, as the typical admissions officer now does?

How might one justify the upper left cell, representing the privileged black versus the disadvantaged white, where the edge given to the black candidate should be no greater than zero under any plausible rationale for affirmative action (or so we argue), and probably should be less than zero? A disadvantaged white youth with cognitive ability at the 36th centile of college youths now has the same chance of being admitted as a privileged black youth at the 17th centile.

Finally, consider the lower right cell, the one that most closely fits the image of affirmative action, in which a privileged white is competing with a disadvantaged black. The logic of affirmative action implies a substantial difference in the qualifications of two youths fitting this description who have an equal chance of being admitted. Is the difference actually observed—between a white at the 57th percentile of college students and one at the 12th percentile—a reasonable one? In IQ terms, this is a difference of almost nineteen points.

We do not suppose that admissions officers have these folders side by side as they make their decisions. In fact, given the pressures on admissions committees, the determining factor for admission is often the sheer numbers of minority applicants. If the percentage of minorities in the incoming freshman class goes up, that is considered good. If the percentage goes down, that is considered bad. To make the numbers come out right, the admissions committee feels pressed to dig deeper into the pool of available applicants if necessary. They do not want to admit unqualified minority candidates, nor do they want to prefer advantaged minority applicants over disadvantaged whites. But these questions arise, if they arise at all, only after the more pressing matter of minority representation is attended to. The goal is to have "enough" blacks and other minorities in the incoming class. Meanwhile, white applicants are judged in competition with other white candidates, using the many criteria that have always been applied.

The main purpose of the exercise we have just conducted is to suggest that admissions committees should be permitted to behave a little more like our imaginary one than they are at present, given the pressures from higher levels in the university. If university officials think that these data are not adequate for the purposes we have used them, or if they think that we have misrepresented the affirmative action process, there is an easy remedy. Universities across the country have in their admissions files all the data needed for definitive analyses of the relationship of ethnicity, socioeconomic disadvantage, and academic ability—test data, grade data, parental background data in profusion—for students who were accepted and students who were rejected, students who enrolled and students who did not. At many schools, the data are already in computer files, ready for analysis. They may readily be made available to scholars without compromising confidentiality. Our proposition is that affirmative action as it is currently practiced in America's universities has lost touch with any reasonable understanding of the logic and purposes of affirmative action. It is easy to put this proposition to the test.

THE SUCCESS OF AFFIRMATIVE ACTION IN THE UNIVERSITIES

The success of affirmative action in the university is indisputable, in the sense that a consciously designed public policy, backed by the enthusi-

astic cooperation of universities, drastically increased the number of minority students who attend and graduate from college. The magnitude of the success during the first flush of affirmative action is apparent in the figure below, which shows the result for black enrollments.[30]

When aggressive affirmative action began, black college enrollment surged for a decade

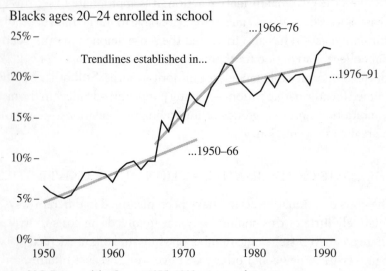

Source: U.S. Bureau of the Census 1975, 1993, various editions.

In 1967, black enrollment of 20–24-year-olds suddenly shot up, and continued to rise steeply through the mid-1970s. White enrollment experienced no comparable surge during that period. The most plausible cause of the surge is the aggressive affirmative action that began in the mid-1960s. On the other hand, this figure previews a problem we will discuss at more length in the next chapter: Whatever initial impetus was provided by affirmative action, it soon lost momentum. Black enrollment in the early 1990s was higher than the trendline from 1950 to 1966 would have predicted, but some sort of evening-out process seems to have set in as well. Black enrollment dropped during the late 1970s, recovered modestly during the early and mid-1980s, then in-

creased sharply at the end of the decade. The level of black college enrollment as of the early 1990s is higher than at any other time in history.

Furthermore, the enrollment of blacks rose not only to equality but to more than equality with whites of comparable socioeconomic background and intelligence. As we showed in Chapter 14, the proportion of blacks obtaining college degrees substantially exceeds that of whites, after controlling for IQ. As we have just finished documenting at length, the opportunity for college is also more open to blacks than to whites with equivalent test scores.

Given the goals of affirmative action, it is appropriate to see this increase as a success. We assume as well (we have found no hard data) that affirmative action has also increased the sense among minority youths that college is an option for them and increased the number of college-educated minority role models for minority youths. Still other benefits claimed for affirmative action—helping jump-start advances in the next generation of minority groups or improving race relations—are yet in the realm of speculation.

THE COSTS OF AFFIRMATIVE ACTION IN THE UNIVERSITIES

The costs of affirmative action have been measured in different ways.[31] Relatively little of this commentary has involved the costs to whites. There are such costs—some number of white students are denied places at universities they could otherwise have won, because of affirmative action.[32] But most of the concern about affirmative action comes down to this question: How much harm is done to minority self-esteem, to white perceptions of minorities, and ultimately to ethnic relations by a system that puts academically less able minority students side by side with students who are more able? There are no hard-and-fast answers, but at least we can discuss the magnitude of the problem from the student's eye view and from the vantage point of the general population.

The Student's Eye View of Minority and White Cognitive Ability

Getting to know students from different backgrounds is a proper part of a college education. But given the differences in the cognitive abilities of the students in different groups, diversity has other consequences. To the extent that the groups have different scores, both perceptions and grades will track with them. Consider once again the probability of

reaching college for students at different levels of cognitive ability. Comparatively small proportions of students with low intelligence get to college, no matter what their race. But the student on the ground does not see the entire population of students with IQs in the bottom quartile (let us say). Rather, the only people in the bottom quartile whom he sees are the ones who reached college.

To see just how different these perspectives can be, let us take first the extreme "above the battle" view of racial tensions that might be caused by affirmative action. The argument goes as follows:

> *Yes, there is a racial discrepancy in test scores, though one should interpret those differences cautiously no matter what the evidence on cultural bias may be. But in reality we are talking about small numbers and small differences. In the NLSY data, blacks in the bottom quartile of cognitive ability who reach four-year colleges amount to less than 4 percent of the youths on those campuses, while whites amount to almost 2 percent. Can anyone seriously think that this trivial difference can be a major problem?*

The answer seems as if it is self-evidently no. But now we switch to the view from ground level: from the vantage point of the college student who attends classes, listens to fellow students talk in class, observes what is going on in the library and the labs, and gossips with friends about other students. Let us imagine three observations of the kind that students commonly make in the normal course of campus life: the racial mix of the entire student population, the students who stand out because they seem to be especially out of place in a university, and the students who stand out because they seem to be especially smart.

We will operationalize this student's campus view by looking at the NLSY subjects who attended a four-year university (excluding historically black schools), focusing on those with IQs that put them in the top and bottom 10 percent of such students. The figure below displays what our hypothetical student sees. It shows students by IQ, but a figure that contained the same breakdown by college grades (unavailable in the NLSY) would show roughly the same pattern. Backed up by the many studies that have examined the relationship between cognitive test scores (especially SAT scores) and performance in college: Cognitive test scores generally *overpredict* college grade point average (GPA) for both blacks and Latinos, in comparison to whites.[33] If anything, a figure showing students with the top and bottom 10 percent of GPAs would show an even greater ethnic discrepancy in college performance

The student's eye view of cognitive ability

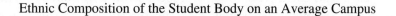

Ethnic Composition of the Student Body on an Average Campus

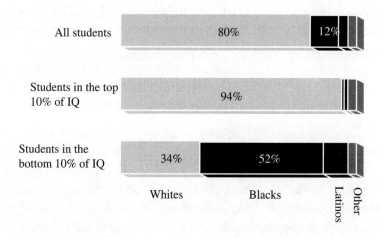

between whites and blacks or Latinos than the discrepancy in IQs in-dicates.[34] Similarly, the data from individual colleges that opened the chapter suggest that this aggregate national picture would look no bet-ter, and might well look worse, in a school-by-school portrait.

Such large differences in performance are obvious to all, including other students. The problem, and a major cost of affirmative action, is that while blacks in the NLSY constituted only 12 percent of those who went to college, they were 52 percent of the students in the bottom 10 percent in cognitive ability and an almost invisibly small proportion of the top 10 percent. The statistical difference that was trivial in the view from above the battle has become a large racial discrepancy at ground level. Meanwhile the imbalance between Latinos' representation in the campus population and in the bottom 10 percent of intelligence is less obvious, while the "other" category (a combination of Asians, Pacific ethnic groups, and American Indians) is proportionately represented in the top and bottom (as a conglomerate—if we split them up, most of those in the top are Asian). We suggest that the figure presented above is important in trying to understand some of the most difficult racial problems besetting America's universities.

RACIAL ANIMOSITY. Racial clashes on campuses began to surface in the early 1980s and apparently have been growing since then, with the great bulk of the difficulties between whites and blacks.[35] A plausible expla-

nation is that whites resent blacks, who are in fact getting a large edge in the admissions process and often in scholarship assistance and many of whom, as whites look around their own campus and others, "don't belong there" academically. Some whites begin to act out these resentments. Blacks perceive the same disproportions and resentments, then conclude that the college environment is hostile to them.

We will not pursue this line of argument. Rather, we refer our readers to a growing literature by black scholars who have couched it in the context of their own experience.[36] It is plain that affirmative action fosters differences in the distribution of academic ability across races in the communities on college campuses. Students are not imagining these differences.

BLACK DROPOUT RATES. The high black dropout rates from college are also easier to understand in the light of the figure above. Typically, the black dropout rate from universities in the last decade has run at about twice the white rate.[37] This was also true of the NLSY. Of all those who ever entered a four-year institution, 63 percent of whites had gotten a bachelor's degree by 1990 (when the youngest reached 26) compared to only 34 percent of blacks. But the discrepancy is not mysterious. The first and dominant explanation of higher black dropout rates is cognitive ability. Controlling for age and IQ, the black and white dropout rates converge. Given the average IQ of those who entered four-year institutions (about 110), the expected probability that a youth entering a four-year college would graduate was 59 percent for blacks and 61 percent for whites, a trivial difference.[38]

But whereas cognitive ability explains most of the difference in dropout rates, it may not explain everything. In particular, the NLSY data reflect the overall experience of blacks and whites, ignoring the experience at specific colleges as we described it earlier. Let us consider MIT, for which dropout rates by race have also been reported. In 1985, the average SAT-Math score for a black male accepted at MIT was 659, a score that put him above the 90th percentile of all students taking the SAT but below the 25th centile of all students at MIT.[39] The dropout rate for black students at MIT in the mid-1980s was 24 percent, compared to 14 percent for whites.[40] Even if the average MIT black freshman in 1985 could indeed do the work there in some objective sense, getting discouraged about one's capacity to compete in an environment may be another cost of affirmative action, a phenomenon that has been described anecdotally by a number of observers, black and white alike.[41]

The Population's Eye View of People with College Degrees

The other vantage point to take into account is the view of the public toward minority and white college graduates. The college degree—what it is and where you got it—packs a lot of information in today's America, not just as a credential that employers evaluate in hiring but as a broad social signal. One may lament this (people ought to be judged on their own merits, not by where they went to school), but it also has a positive side. Historically, that little sentence, "I have a [solid degree] from [a well-regarded university]," jolted you loose from any number of stereotypes that the person you encountered might have had of you. The reason it did so was that a well-regarded college had a certain set of standards, and its graduates presumably met those standards. No matter what one's view is of "credentialing" in theory, the greatest beneficiaries of credentialing are those who are subject to negative stereotypes. One of the great losses of preferential affirmative action has been to dilute the effects of the university credential for some minorities. Today the same degree from the same university is perceived differently if you have a black face or a white one. This is not a misguided prejudice that will be changed if only people are given more accurate information about how affirmative action really works. On the contrary, more accurate information about how affirmative action really works confirms such perceptions.

This unhappy reality is unnecessary. There is no reason that minority graduates from any given college have to be any different from white college graduates in their ability or accomplishments. Restoring the value of the credential is easy: Use uniform procedures for selecting, grading, and granting degrees to undergraduates. Some difference in the cognitive distributions among college graduates would still remain, because even if individual schools were to treat applicants and students without regard to race, we could expect some cognitive difference in the national distributions of graduates (since a group with disproportionately fewer high-scoring students would probably gravitate to less competitive schools; they would graduate, but nonetheless have lower mean ability). But within schools, the group differences could be as close to zero as the institution chooses to get. America's universities are instead perpetuating in the ranks of their graduates the same gap in cognitive ability that separates blacks and Latinos from whites in the general population. As we saw in the data on law and medical schools, there is no reason to think that the gap shrinks as people move further up the educational ladder, and some reason to think it continues to grow.

Some will argue the gap in ability is an acceptable price to pay for the other good things that are supposed to be accomplished by aggressive affirmative action. Our judgment, in contrast, is that in trying to build a society where ethnicity no longer matters in the important events in life, it is crucially important that society's prestigious labels have the same or as close to the same meaning as possible for different ethnic groups. In the case of one of these key labels—the educational degree—policymakers, aided and abetted by the universities, have prevented this from happening.

We will trace some of the consequences in the next chapter, when we turn to affirmative action in the workplace and present at more length our assessment of how the double standard embedded in affirmative action affects society. For now, we will observe only that the seeds of the consequences in the workplace and beyond are sown in colleges and universities. To anticipate our larger conclusion, affirmative action as it is being practiced is a grave error.

A POLICY AGENDA

We urge that affirmative action in the universities be radically modified, returning to the original conception. Universities should cast a wide net in seeking applicants, making special efforts to seek talent wherever it lives—in the black South Bronx, Latino Los Angeles, and white Appalachia alike. In the case of two candidates who are fairly closely matched otherwise, universities should give the nod to the applicant from the disadvantaged background. This original sense of affirmative action seems to us to have been not only reasonable and fair but wise.

What does "closely matched" mean in terms of test scores? We have no firm rules, but as a guideline, admissions officers might aim for an admissions policy such that no identifiable group (such as a racial minority) has a mean that is more than half a standard deviation below the rest of the student body.[42] This guideline is by no means demanding. In effect, it asks only that the average minority student is at the 30th centile of the white distribution. Perhaps experience would prove that this is not closely matched enough. But at least let us move toward that standard and see how it works. The present situation, with black students averaging well over a full standard deviation below the white mean, sometimes approaching two standard deviations, is so far out of line with any plausible rationale that universities today cannot publish the data on their admitted students and hope to persuade the public (or specialists in education) that their policies are reasonable.

Would an end to aggressive affirmative action mean that minorities who can profit from a genuine college education will find the door of opportunity closed to them? There is no reason to think so. On the contrary, we urge that people examine more closely an ignored, brief era in American university life—from the mid-1950s to the mid-1960s. Simultaneously, the civil rights movement was gaining momentum, white upper-middle-class America was having its consciousness raised on the subject of racial discrimination, and color-blindness was actively taken as the ideal. At many colleges during that era, applicants were forbidden to enclose a photograph and instructed to avoid any information in the essay that might help identify their race or religion. Whether admissions committees were truly innocent of this information is another question, but the intent was clear, and so was the result: Racial differences in qualifications during that time were minor, or so it appeared to both of us at the time.

What were campus race relations like then? What were the attitudes of the black students toward achievement? What was the performance of black students relative to the predictions that might have been made based on their high school performance? What were the dropout rates of blacks relative to whites in the same institution? What were the subsequent careers of black students from that era? How do black students from that era, looking back, assess the pluses and minuses of the current state of affairs versus their experience?

We must put such topics as questions because that era has been ignored. We suggest this possibility: American universities once approached the ideal in their handling of race on the campus, and there is no reason why they could not do so again.

Fewer blacks would be at Berkeley or Yale if there were no affirmative action. But admitting half as many black students to Yale does not mean that the rejected ones will not go to college; it just means that they will not go to Yale. For some individuals who are not chosen, this will be a loss, for others a blessing, but it is a far different choice from "college" versus "no college." It is not even clear how much the goals of diversity would be adversely affected for the system as a whole. If affirmative action in its present form were ended, the schools at the very top would have smaller numbers of blacks and some other minorities on their campuses, but many other schools in the next echelons would add those students, even as they lost some of their former students to schools further down the line. And at every level of school, the gap in cognitive ability between minorities and whites would shrink.

Ending affirmative action as it is currently practiced will surely have other effects. Affirmative action does in fact bring a significant number of minority students onto campuses who would not otherwise be there. Perhaps the overall percentage of some minorities who attend college would drop. But their white counterparts at the same level of ability and similar socioeconomic background are not in college now. To what extent is a society fair when people of similar ability and background are treated as differently as they are now? In 1964, the answer would have been unambiguous: Such a society is manifestly unfair. The logic was right then, and right now.

Chapter 20

Affirmative Action in the Workplace

Employers want to hire the best workers; employment tests are one of the best and cheapest selection tools at their disposal. Since affirmative action began in the early 1960s, and especially since a landmark decision by the Supreme Court in 1971, employers have been tightly constrained in the use they may make of tests. The most common solution is for employers to use them but to hire enough protected minorities to protect themselves from prosecution and lawsuits under the job discrimination rules.

The rules that constrain employers were developed by Congress and the Supreme Court based on the assumptions that tests of general cognitive ability are not a good way of picking employees, that the best tests are ones that measure specific job skills, that tests are biased against blacks and other minorities, and that all groups have equal distributions of cognitive ability. These assumptions are empirically incorrect. Paradoxically, job hiring and promotion procedures that are truly fair and unbiased will produce the racial disparities that public policy tries to prevent.

Have the job discrimination regulations worked? The scholarly consensus is that they had some impact, on some kinds of jobs, in some settings, during the 1960s and into the 1970s, but have not had the decisive impact that is commonly asserted in political rhetoric. It also appears, however, that since the early 1960s blacks have been overrepresented in white collar and professional occupations relative to the number of candidates in the IQ range from which these jobs are usually filled, suggesting that the effects of affirmative action policy may be greater than usually thought.

The successes of affirmative action have been much more extensively studied than the costs. One of the most understudied areas of this topic is job performance. The scattered data suggest that aggressive affirmative action does produce large racial discrepancies in job performance in a given workplace. It is time that this important area be explored systematically.

479

In coming to grips with policy, a few hard truths have to be accepted. First, there are no good ways to implement current job discrimination law without incurring costs in economic efficiency and fairness to both employers and employees. Second, after controlling for IQ, it is hard to demonstrate that the United States still suffers from a major problem of racial discrimination in occupations and pay.

As we did for affirmative action in higher education, we present the case for returning to the original conception of affirmative action. This means scrapping the existing edifice of job discrimination law. We think the benefits to productivity and to fairness of ending the antidiscrimination laws are substantial. But our larger reason is that this nation does not have the option of ethnic balkanization.

Affirmative action in the workplace arose at the same time that it did in the universities but with important differences. One difference is that in the workplace, the government and the courts have been the main activists, forcing businesses into a variety of involuntary practices, whereas universities and colleges largely create their own policies regarding student selection. Affirmative action policies in the workplace have been more a matter of evolution than of coherent policymaking. (Appendix 7 traces this evolution.) Universities and colleges occasionally run afoul of affirmative action laws in their hiring and promotion decisions, but in student admissions they are usually far ahead of what has been legally required of them.

A second important difference is that almost everyone has a personal stake, and can see what is going on, in the workplace, unlike on campus. In colleges, the applicant who does not get in because he was displaced by an affirmative action admission never knows exactly why he was rejected. In many workplaces, individuals can identify others who are hired, fired, and promoted under the aegis of affirmative action, and they tend to have strong opinions about the merits of each case. In many workplaces, affirmative action decisions regarding a few people can affect the daily life of tens or hundreds of people who work with them and under them. College and university admission decisions have less obvious immediate effects. These may be some of the reasons that few, if any, points of friction in American society have been rubbed so raw as where affirmative action operates in the workplace. The topic inflames relations between white elites (who generally favor the policies) and white workers (many of whom feel victimized by them), between ethnic groups, between the sexes, and between many citizens and their government.

The chapter is organized around several factual questions regarding affirmative action in the workplace. We start with the facts because they are pivotal to the arguments about affirmative action yet are often overlooked or misconstrued. First, what are America's affirmative action policies? Second, do they make sense, given the relevant data? Third, what difference have they made? After reviewing the data on these issues, we turn to some broader questions that the facts raise but cannot altogether resolve. How should we think about the economic costs of affirmative action in the workplace? Assuming that just about everyone wants employment to be fair, what should "fairness" mean in the labor market?

Throughout, we concentrate on the situation regarding blacks. Affirmative action has expanded to embrace many other groups, but this policy came about because of an urgently felt national desire to redress the plight of blacks, and the focal point of tension, intellectual and social, has been affirmative action for blacks ever since. Many of the points we make about that story apply with modifications to other groups as well. Our policy recommendations also apply generally.

THE FEDERAL GOVERNMENT'S REQUIREMENTS FOR AFFIRMATIVE ACTION IN THE WORKPLACE

People apply for jobs. The employer hires some and not others. Later the employer promotes some and not others. An employer who appears to have based hiring or promotion decisions on the person's being white (or one of the other outlawed reasons) is in violation of the law. A pure heart and good faith are not enough. If a rejected applicant or an unpromoted employee brings a complaint, an employer must be able to prove that the hiring and promotion processes meet legal definitions of fairness.

For some positions, employers may post job requirements and demonstrate that the hired or promoted employees had the best qualifications. But many jobs do not lend themselves to such case-by-case selection. In these cases, how does the employer demonstrate that the chosen employees have been selected without illegal discrimination? The obvious answer (or so it seemed in the beginning) is to use an objective job test and hire applicants with the highest scores. Testing has therefore been at the center of the history of employment discrimination law, as it has played out from the Civil Rights Act of 1964 to the Civil Rights Act of 1991. Here are some features of the prevailing situation facing employers, with variations and an interlude described in the appendix, since the Supreme Court's landmark *Griggs v. Duke Power Co.* decision in 1971:

If an employer uses a test in the employment process and the results of that test lead to different results for different protected groups (mainly blacks, Latinos, and women) that employer faces the prospect of lawsuits, fines, and damages that could cost the company millions—perhaps tens of millions—of dollars. Employers can protect themselves in three ways.

First, they may decline to use tests. Nevertheless, they will still be vulnerable if their alternative hiring process has disparate impact (the legal phrase) on the hiring of different groups.

Second, they can try to construct a test that has an urgent economic justification and a manifest, direct relationship with the skills required by the job. A general ability test is always unacceptable. Usually off-the-shelf tests of any kind will also be found unacceptable until they are validated for the particular job in question

Third, an employer may meet the 80 percent rule. Created as part of federal guidelines issued in 1978, the 80 percent rule says in effect that people in the protected groups have to be hired or promoted at 80 percent or more of the rate enjoyed by the group with the highest rate of success in being hired or promoted. Here is how it works in practice: Suppose that the Acme Corporation uses a test for all its job applicants. Let us say that 225 white males apply and 90 are hired. This hiring rate of 40 percent is the benchmark against which the hiring of other groups is measured. All other groups must be hired at a rate no lower than 80 percent of the 40 percent hiring rate of white males, which comes to 32 percent. If 150 white women apply and 50 are hired—33 percent—Acme meets the hiring rate for women. Suppose that 100 Latinos apply and 25 are hired. Now Acme is vulnerable to discrimination suits by the rejected Latino applicants because its hiring rate for Latinos is 25 percent, not 32 percent. It should hire at least seven more Latinos, bringing the Latino percentage up to the needed 32.[1]

Note that we have said nothing about how the test was used or even what the comparative scores were. With the 80 percent rule, those considerations are irrelevant. It makes no difference if the rejected male applicants had scores that were twice those of the successful women applicants: All that matters is the bottom line: the 80 percent criterion. Less than 80 percent, and Acme is in trouble; more than 80 percent, and the government will probably leave Acme alone. Just "probably," however. The 80 percent rule is a guideline, not a law, and there is no guarantee that meeting it will head off litigation.[2]

SOME FALSE FACTUAL ASSUMPTIONS BEHIND EMPLOYMENT TESTING POLICY

Federal affirmative action policy toward employment testing is laden with assumptions not about fairness but about what is true as a factual matter. Specifically, Congress and the Supreme Court developed federal job discrimination policy on the assumptions that (1) tests of general cognitive ability are not a good way of picking employees, (2) the best tests are ones that measure specific job skills, (3) tests are biased against blacks and other minorities, and (4) all groups have equal distributions of cognitive ability.

To varying degrees, these assumptions were defensible when they were first voiced in the 1960s. Ethnic differences in test scores were known to exist, but many experts at that time still thought they reflected test bias, or that the differences would melt away as educational opportunity for minorities improved. The predictive validity of tests for job performance was poorly understood. But however understandable these views were in the 1960s, public policy over the next twenty years suffered from an increasingly severe case of psychometric lag. To summarize the by-now solidly established empirical situation described in Chapters 3 and 13:

- Cognitive ability has an economically important relationship to job productivity that applies across the range of jobs and the range of abilities.
- Cognitive ability tests are often the single most predictive method of picking employees—more predictive than grades, education, or a job interview.
- The predictive power of tests derives almost completely from their measure of general cognitive ability, not measures of job-specific skills.

- Cognitive ability tests either are not biased against blacks as predictors of job performance, or in some cases are biased in favor of blacks.
- Different ethnic groups have substantially different distributions of cognitive ability that are not explainable by cultural bias and not easily altered by remedial steps.

What *is* true regarding jobs, IQ, and group differences in cognitive ability is the opposite of what the courts, the Congress, and many others have supposed the truth to be. The dilemma is that job hiring and promotion procedures that are truly fair and unbiased in the sense in which everyone used those terms in 1964 will produce the ethnic and group disparities that public policy so vigorously tries to prevent. The most valid hiring tests may have the largest disparate impact. As a first step in coming to terms with affirmative action—however one balances the many other factors that make affirmative action desirable or undesirable—the government should scrap the invalid scientific assumptions that undergird policy and express policy in terms that are empirically defensible.

This step need not mean scrapping affirmative action. It means only discarding rhetoric about testing and affirmative action ("tests aren't valid for minorities," "tests of general ability don't predict anything worth knowing about job performance") that are not true and instead defending affirmative action on whatever grounds can be authentically defended. Some progress has been made on this front. The Hartigan Committee's report on the General Aptitude Test Battery[3] was a step in the right direction, for example, acknowledging many of the key facts about tests while continuing to defend affirmative action (though the basis for their defense is in itself open to technical debate). A few other proponents of strong affirmative action are becoming more forthright about what they are really promoting—not just equal opportunity but equal employment outcomes despite unequal job performance.[4] But these are exceptions to a general public discussion of affirmative action that relies on inaccurate and to some degree dishonest representations of the state of knowledge about tests, employment, and competition among protected and unprotected groups.

HAS AFFIRMATIVE ACTION WORKED?

The scholarly debate over the effects of antidiscrimination legislation in the workplace has been lively, and this is a good time to summarize where that debate stands. The answers are complicated, but scholars have done much better than the public commentators on this score.

Version I: Ignoring Cognitive Ability

According to official statistics, wages for blacks have risen since the 1960s and more blacks have entered prestigious occupations. Most people take for granted that these changes have happened to some important degree because of antidiscrimination laws. But what may seem obvious at first glance is not obvious upon further inspection. "Two decades of research have failed to produce professional consensus on the contribution of federal government civil rights activity to the economic progress of black Americans," wrote economists James Heckman and Brook Payner in 1989,[5] and the situation has clarified only marginally since then. The nature of the problem facing the analysts is illustrated by the figure below for two categories of white-collar jobs that affirma-

The uncertain effects of affirmative action in the workplace

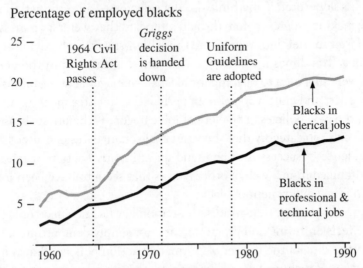

Sources: Bureau of Labor Statistics 1983, 1989; U.S. Department of Labor 1991. Figures prior to 1973, reported for "blacks and others," are adjusted pro-rata to the black-only population.

tive action was supposed to open up for blacks.[6] The vertical lines demarcate three landmarks in antidiscrimination law: the passage of the Civil Rights Act of 1964 that outlawed job discrimination, the *Griggs* decision that put increased pressure on employers to hire the right number of minorities even if they were using consistent hiring practices, and adoption of the Uniform Guidelines on Employee Selection Procedures that established the 80 percent guideline (all described further in Appendix 7).

To see why the analysts have a complicated task, consider clerical jobs (the gray line in the figure). The story here seems obvious: From 1959 until the passage of the Civil Rights Act, improvement was slow. Immediately after the act came a sudden increase in the percentage of employed blacks who held clerical jobs; thereafter the percentage continued rising but at a slower rate. Furthermore, the gap between black and white percentages for these jobs (not shown in this graph) also closed—again, faster for a while after 1964 than before. We might conclude that the Civil Rights Act itself was effective but that the two subsequent landmarks in affirmative action policy were not, at least for these jobs.

Now follow the black line in the above figure, representing professional and technical jobs. Its slope before 1964 was certainly no lower than its slope after; if anything, the slope decreased after the act. Blacks were making progress before the act; afterward they weren't progressing any faster in their movement into these high-status, high-paying occupations. Trendlines for other job categories, not shown in the graph, that were supposed to open up for blacks—managerial and administrative, sales, and craft workers—similarly fail to register much of a gain from the new policies. The clerical job category is the unusual case; it is the *only* job category that shows a visible change in slope after 1964. If evidence of success is to be found for affirmative action, it must be disentangled from a web of other factors that seem to have been influencing the employment of blacks.[7]

This is not to say that antidiscrimination law had no effect, only that the effects on hiring and promotion are not simply demonstrated. Our understanding of the impact of affirmative action policies, drawn from a number of technical assessments that have not taken cognitive ability into account, may be summarized as follows:[8]

- Affirmative action policies had the expected effect in public bureaucracies. Police and firefighters are the most conspicuous examples, but affirmative action also has demonstrably increased the proportion of minorities throughout government bureaucracies, from the federal level on down.[9] At the federal level, the strongest effects are at the clerical level and below. In cities with large minority populations, the effects are spread across a broader range of government positions, with de facto quotas up to the highest levels.

- Among private companies, affirmative action has had some effects, particularly in the South and among companies that do business with the federal government. Some unknown fraction of the increase in black employment by companies with government contracts is balanced off by compensating declines in companies without them.

- In private industry in the South (where much of the most demonstrable progress in private industry has been made), a complicated mix of forces seems to have been at work: partly the Civil Rights Act of 1964 and its aftermath, partly the repeal of Jim Crow laws restricting job entry into certain industries, partly a broader breakdown of racial segregation, legal and otherwise.[10]

- Whatever effects affirmative action may have had during the 1960s and 1970s, they had become too small to measure by the 1980s and will probably continue to be small in the future, largely for economic reasons.

- The behavior of employers has certainly been affected by job discrimination law. Every large company must maintain a bureaucracy to monitor compliance with federal regulations and to defend against (or, commonly, settle out of court) lawsuits alleging discrimination. The amounts of time, money, and resources devoted to compliance are substantial.

In short, federal antidiscrimination efforts writ large—embracing all the disparate events following on the rise of the civil rights movement in the mid-1950s—probably had a significant impact on black economic progress. Job discrimination law in particular probably had a smaller but significant effect for some blacks in some settings. No serious student of the topic argues that job discrimination law had the decisive impact that is commonly attributed to it in political rhetoric.

Version II: When Cognitive Ability Is Taken into Account

We now pose a question of affirmative action that has not been asked in the literature we just reviewed: How do the observed differences between blacks and whites in occupations and wages compare to those that would be predicted from the observed black-white difference in the distribution of cognitive ability? We presented the summary answer as of the end of the 1980s in Chapter 14, when we showed that, after controlling for IQ, a higher proportion of blacks than whites in the NLSY are in the professions and that wages for blacks and whites are essentially equal. Neither education nor socioeconomic background, accounted as well as IQ for the differences in jobs or wages between blacks and whites.

These findings may bear on the question of the impact of affirmative action in the workplace. To see why, let us examine the mean IQs for NLSY members in different job categories as of 1990, as shown in the table below. In all job categories, from highest to lowest in skill, employers are hiring blacks who differ from whites in those jobs by one or more standard deviations in IQ. Part of the reason may be that employers hire blacks and whites of differing cognitive ability because of

---

The Black-White IQ Difference by Job Category, 1990

Job Category	Mean White IQ	Black-White Difference, in Standard Deviations
Professions	114	1.3
Managerial	108	1.1
Technical	113	1.5
Sales	106	1.4
Clerical	104	1.1
Protective services	103	1.4
Other service jobs	97	1.4
Craft	99	1.1
Low-skill labor	96	1.1

the pressures brought on them by government policies regarding the representation of minority groups. Without such pressures and in a race-blind labor market, blacks and whites should be equal in those traits that best predict performance on the job. From the kinds of data reviewed in Chapter 3, we know that cognitive ability is such a trait—the more so, the greater the skills are involved in the job. Consequently, we should expect the IQ gap between whites and blacks to be the narrowest for high-skill jobs if hiring is race blind.

We may draw this conclusion without knowing whether an employer administers cognitive tests to job candidates or even thinks consciously about cognitive ability when hiring. The relationship of cognitive ability to job productivity exists independent of the existence of test scores, and all hiring practices that succeed in choosing productive workers will tend to select employees with only small group differences in intelligence for occupations in which IQ is most important. The table above shows no such narrowing for the cognitively demanding jobs. If anything the gap widens toward the top of the table.

The most plausible explanation for the large gap toward the top of the table is that employers are using dual standards for black and white job applicants. Moreover, we venture the hypothesis that employers are using dual standards at least in part because someone or something (the government or an aversion to harmful publicity) is making them do so—hence our conclusion that affirmative action is probably having a more substantial impact on hiring practices than the standard analyses indicate.

This also leads to a reinterpretation of the graph on page 485 for clerical and professional and technical jobs. We pointed out that the trendlines for black employees did not get steeper, with the single exception of clerical jobs, after the Civil Rights Act was passed. Now we are suggesting an alternative perspective: The fact that the trendlines continued to go up as long as they did is in itself evidence of the impact of affirmative action. Without affirmative action, the trendlines would have leveled off sooner, perhaps at the point at which blacks and whites of equal IQ had equal chances of employment in high-status jobs. In the next figure, we adjust the hiring proportions for the known difference in IQ between whites and blacks.[11] For professional and technical jobs, the assumption is that employees are normally drawn from people with

IQs of 98 or higher; for clerical jobs, the assumption is that they are drawn from within the range of 86 to 123.[12] The results are shown in the figure below.

A revised view of equal employment opportunity after correcting for ethnic differences in the IQ distributions

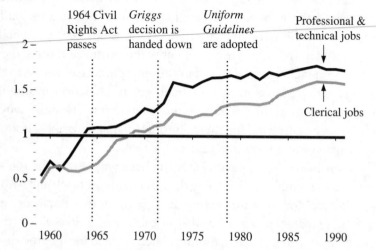

Source: Bureau of Labor Statistics 1983, 1989; U.S. Department of Labor 1991.

[a] The ratio represents blacks employed in a given occupational grouping expressed as a percentage of eligible blacks, divided by the whites employed in the same occupational grouping expressed as a percentage of eligible whites. The number of eligibles is determined by the size of the working-age population in that race who fall within the IQ range for that occupation, as calculated from a table of normal probabilities. The assumptions for computing the ratio are: (1) the IQ range for professional and technical jobs is 98 and higher; (2) the IQ range for clerical jobs is 86–123; (3) IQ is normally distributed with a mean of 85 for blacks and 100 for nonblacks, with a standard deviation of 15 for both groups.

What "should" the lines look like? If the assumptions in drawing them were accurate, then both lines should have risen to 1 (to signify that blacks and whites in the same IQ range are hired at the same rate) after the antidiscrimination laws were passed and then hovered near 1 thereafter. Anything above 1.0 signifies a higher likelihood for blacks of being hired, once IQ is held constant; below 1.0, the opposite is true. The proportion of blacks in professional and technical jobs rose above 1 in the early 1960s, flattened after the Civil Rights Act of 1964, took another steep jump after *Griggs*, and then settled into a gradual rise through the late 1980s. For clerical jobs, progress after 1964 led to parity in the late 1960s. The relative proportion of blacks in clerical jobs then continued to increase at a slower but more nearly linear pace since then. In both categories of employment, blacks have been hired at higher rates than whites of equal IQ since the late 1960s, and the upward trend lasted at least until the late 1980s.

Since these job categories do not have precisely defined IQ ranges, it may be asked what would happen if the assumptions were changed. Some of the alternatives we tried are described in the note to this paragraph. The short answer is that the picture stays essentially the same within any reasonable range of assumptions. The overall conclusion is that blacks have for some years had more people working in both clerical jobs and professional and technical jobs than would ordinarily be expected, given the IQ range from which those jobs are usually filled.[13]

The figure above uses broad guidelines about the IQ range from which certain jobs are held and applies them to national data about occupations. For a narrower focus, the NLSY supplies data about specific individuals, their occupations, and IQs.[14] In 1990, using the same definition of "professional and technical occupations," and after controlling for IQ (set at 113, the mean IQ for whites in such occupations), the proportion of blacks in the NLSY employed in professional and technical occupations was 1.5 times the proportion for whites, compared to the ratio of 1.7 shown for 1990 in the graph. For clerical jobs, after controlling for age and IQ (with IQ set at 103, the mean value for whites holding clerical jobs), a black in the NLSY was 1.9 times more likely than a white to be employed in a clerical job, compared to the figure of 1.6 for 1990 as shown in the graph.[15] The conclusion drawn from national statistics is thus confirmed by the individual data in the NLSY.

Several points may be drawn from this exercise. First, it highlights the reality and magnitude of the discrimination suffered by blacks prior to the civil rights movement. As recently as 1959, the employment of blacks in clerical and professional and technical jobs was only half the proportion that would have been expected from recruitment to those jobs based on IQ alone. Decennial census data (not to mention living memory) tell us that this underrepresentation was still more severe in the 1950s and 1940s.[16] There was a clear and large racial deficit to be made up.

Second, the exercise shows how rapidly changes were made in the 1960s and early 1970s. If cognitive ability is taken into account, the underrepresentation of blacks in professional and technical jobs was gone by 1964, prior to the Civil Rights Act. This closing of the occupational gap between blacks and whites, obscured by trendlines that do not compensate for IQ differences, argues that something besides antidiscrimination legislation was already afoot in America, making the job market less stacked against blacks.

Third, by the end of the 1960s, the job market had pressed beyond the point of parity for blacks and whites, again after cognitive ability is taken into account. One might argue that this merely proves that IQ is not so important for job productivity after all—except that a large literature, already summarized, demonstrates beyond much doubt that IQ is as predictive of job performance for blacks as for whites.[17] We can only surmise that the reason for attaining such high levels of black representation, particularly in the occupations that most strongly correlate with IQ, includes the impact of affirmative action policies. To that extent, if these affirmative action policies were changed, black employment in these occupations would fall. Would this be a return to unfairness? We will return to this hard question after considering the costs of affirmative action for job performance.

THE COSTS OF AFFIRMATIVE ACTION: JOB PERFORMANCE

Inasmuch as cognitive ability is related to job performance and as minority workers are entering professions with lower ability distributions than whites, is there evidence of lower average performance for minority workers than for whites? Of all the many kinds of double-speak associated with affirmative action, this question points to one of the most egregious. Private complaints about the incompetent affirmative-action hiree are much more common than scholarly examination of the issue. We may nonetheless present several cases bearing on job performance, all telling similar stories for different occupations, using different kinds of data.

Teacher Competency Examinations

The nationwide enthusiasm for teacher competency examinations in the 1980s resulted in teacher testing programs in virtually all states by the end of the decade.[18] These competency tests are seldom job performance tests as such, but rather a test of basic knowledge of reading, writing, and mathematics. Even so, teachers who score higher on the tests have greater success with their students.[19] The competency exams seem to have had some generally beneficial effects, though the cutoffs are low by the usual standards of what we expect teachers to know.[20] The pass rates for whites typically exceed 80 percent and sometimes 90 percent. Whatever your profession may be, think about the meaning of a test that would "pass" aspirants to the profession who perform in the bottom 20 percent. But having so low a cutoff for whites sharpens the evidence of the disparity in black and white qualifications, as shown in the following table.

Typical Results of State Teacher Competency Examinations

	Pass Rate		Implied
	Whites	**Blacks**	**Difference in SDs[a]**
California, 1983–1991	80%	35%	1.2
Pennsylvania, 1989	93	68	1.0
New York, 1987	83	36	1.3
Georgia, 1978–1986	87	40	1.4

Sources: H. Collins, "Minority groups are still lagging on teacher exam," *Philadelphia Inquirer*, Aug. 5, 1989, p. B1; T. Spofford, "Teacher test called biased," *Albany Times Union*, Nov. 20, 1987, p. A1; B. Davila, "State's teacher test biased against minorities, lawsuit contends," *Sacramento Bee*, Sept. 24, 1992, p. B8; "Minority teachers," *Richmond News Leader*, May 16, 1989, p. A14.

[a] Assumes a normal distribution and equal standard deviations in both groups.

These are not cognitive ability scores or scores that are being used to select people for further education but the scores achieved by people who are heading into the nation's classrooms. According to the institutions that have graduated these applicants for teacher certification (in some cases, the scores are for teachers already on the job), all of them have met the requirements for a college degree, and they presumably can read, write, and do basic math. The scores are on tests that make no pretense to seek excellence but to weed out the most obviously unsuited.[21] With differences ranging upwards of 1 standard deviation, the inescapable conclusion is that a large gap separates black and white teachers in basic skills.[22]

The Compensating Skills Fallacy

One of the most common arguments about the current practice of affirmative action might be called the compensating skills fallacy. It is commonly applied to any profession under discussion, but teachers provide an especially good example. The argument goes like this:

There are many skills and qualities that go into being a good teacher besides test scores. The ability to inspire confidence, to create an eagerness to learn, to listen to children are all part of the wide repertoire of skills that go into being a good teacher that have nothing to do with the traits measured by a cognitive ability or academic skills test.

The statement itself is correct. Most professions involve a number of important nonintellectual attributes. The fallacy lies in assuming that people who have lower cognitive test scores will, on average, be better endowed in these other areas than people with higher scores.

Suppose that the teacher competency exams consisted of several parts, each of which measured one of these nonintellectual skills. It would be possible to defend hiring teachers with marginal grades on the intellectual skills *if* these teachers were hired from the top of the list on the tests of the other qualities. But the way affirmative action programs actually work, these other qualities are not tested or compared. The minority candidate with the best score on the test of intellectual qualities is selected. As for the other qualities, not measured by the test, there is no reason to assume that they are any higher than average.[23]

A Journalist's Account of the Washington, D.C., Police Force

Because affirmative action has been practiced most aggressively in public employment—police, firefighters, social welfare agencies, departments of motor vehicles, and the like—they are logical places to look if indeed job performance has been compromised.[24] The Washington, D.C., Police Department is a case in point, as described by journalist Tucker Carlson.[25]

In the mid-1970s, the Washington, D.C., Police Department installed a residency requirement for police. Washington's white population is densely concentrated among white-collar and professional groups, with no significant white working-class neighborhoods. The residency requirement thereby severely restricted the pool of potential white applicants. By 1982, 40 percent of the candidates who took the police admissions test failed it, and the department was having a hard time filling positions. A new test was introduced in 1985, normed to favor minority applicants. Standards in the police academy were lowered to the point at which not one student flunked out of the training course in 1983 (despite the lower cognitive ability of the candidates being admitted). In 1988, the academy abolished its final comprehensive pencil-and-paper examination after 40 percent of graduating recruits failed it. The former head of the Fraternal Order of Police and a veteran of twenty-two years on the force reported that, at about that time, he began hearing "about people at the academy who could not read or write."[26] A former academy instructor says that "I saw people who were practically illiterate. I've seen people diagnosed as borderline retarded graduate from the police academy."[27]

This degradation of intellectual requirements translates into police performance on the street. For example, the paperwork that follows an arrest has been a bane of police everywhere for many years, but when police can do the work, it is mainly an inconvenience, not a barrier. An officer who *cannot* do the paperwork or who finds that it pushes the limits of his abilities may forgo making arrests in marginal cases. The arrests that are made are often botched. Between 1986 and 1990, about a third of all the murder cases brought to the U.S. attorney's office in the District were dismissed, historically an unusually high rate, often because the prosecutors were unable to make sense of the arrest reports.

The basic features of Carlson's account are confirmed by a variety of other journalistic accounts, most conspicuously a 1993 investigative series by the *Washington Post* on police performance.[28] Two facts about the Washington Police Department seem clear: Recruitment and training standards deteriorated markedly in recent decades, and the performance of the department, once considered a national model, has also deteriorated badly.

Washington is not unique. In Miami in 1985, the police department was rocked by the discovery and seizure of hundreds of pounds of cocaine hidden by police officers working in cahoots with smugglers. We have the results of the intense self-examination that resulted. The main conclusion was that this crime, as well as the many others that were straining community-police relations at the time, could be traced in part to the relaxation of hiring standards mandated by affirmative action regulations. Almost 90 percent of the officers who were dismissed or suspended within a few years of the initiation of aggressive affirmative action policies at the beginning of the 1980s were officers with marginal qualifications, hired because of those policies.[29]

Such stories are common among people who have worked in, or been a client of, organizations that practice aggressive affirmative action, and the link they ascribe to affirmative action is usually explicit and emphatic.[30] There is a great deal of smoke emanating from such accounts. We urge that people start checking out whether there is any fire.

A Scholarly Analysis of an Affirmative Action Program for Blue-Collar Jobs

Economist Eugene Silberberg systematically compared the experience of blacks who were admitted to craft unions (electricians, plumbers, and pipefitters) in Seattle at the end of the 1970s under a court order and whites who were admitted under ordinary selection procedures at the same time.[31] Silberberg assembled data on performance in apprentice school, on-the-job ratings, and educational background, then was given access to a variety of job performance measures over an eighteen-month follow-up period: hours worked, number of employees who quit, jobs turned down, failures to respond to a dispatch, and being listed by an employer as not eligible for rehire. The table below shows the combined differences, expressed in standard deviations, for the pipefitters and plumbers.

Job Performance of Black Affirmative Action Plumbers and Pipefitters Compared to White Regular Hirees

	Black-White Difference in SDs
Job performance measures	
Quits or no rehire	+.6
Termination for cause	+.5
Nonresponse to job call	+.6
Hours worked	−.9
IQ-related measures	
GPA in apprentice school	−1.3
GPA in on-the-job training	−.8

Source: Silberberg 1985, Table 2.

Note: The table combines data on apprentices and journeyman for both crafts using weighted standard deviations.

Comparing the blacks admitted under the court order with whites admitted under the ordinary procedures at the same time, the blacks quit at more than six times the rate for whites, were terminated for cause at more than three times the rate for whites, and did not respond to a job dispatch at more than six times the rate for whites. Similar results were obtained for the electricians. The results track closely with the larger literature on IQ and job productivity. The differences in the job performance measures are what might be expected from the discussion in Chapter 3. Furthermore, the size of the difference in job performance is economically important. Silberberg discusses the possibility that the differences are themselves a result of bias among the dispatchers and supervisors. Given the procedures for assigning jobs in the Seattle unions, he concludes that it is extremely difficult to explain away the differences in such terms.[32]

Having reviewed the less than plentiful data at hand about ethnic differences in job performance, we are reminded of a passage by Andrew Hacker, one of the stoutly "pro" voices in the affirmative action debate:

A favorite question of affirmative action's opponents is whether you would want to be operated on by a surgeon who had been admitted to medical school under a racial dispensation. As it happens, few posing this kind of question have any knowledge of what makes for surgical skill. In fact, there are no known correlations between good grades or high scores and subsequent success with a scalpel. If we mean to debate this subject seriously, we should rely on hard data rather than scare tactics.[33]

We cannot agree with Hacker's characterization of the state of knowledge, but we enthusiastically subscribe to his concluding sentence. By all means, let people on all sides of this issue assemble hard data. The purpose of the foregoing examples is to make two points: (1) the scattered evidence about job performance and affirmative action—indirect and direct, soft and hard—suggests large and pervasive effects, and (2) there is no excuse for not having many more hard-data studies of the type that Silberberg conducted. Job performance is important, it is measurable, and the issue of affirmative action and its effects on job performance has been on many people's minds for years. Many corporations routinely conduct studies of job performance and have databases that could be reanalyzed to assess the effects of affirmative action on job performance.

The request we make of Hacker and other proponents of affirmative action is that they join us in encouraging such work. Confident that group differences in job performance are not an important problem, they can try to prove their case. Our own conclusion is that they cannot do so. If this is so, the debate about affirmative action must shift to another level: How much degradation of job performance is acceptable in pursuit of the other goals of affirmative action? And that in turn brings us to first questions. What, after all, is the nation trying to accomplish with affirmative action in the workplace? What are the right measures of success?

A POLICY AGENDA

In thinking about affirmative action in the workplace, more than psychometric realities or efficiency in the workplace must be considered. To avoid misunderstanding, this is a good time to lay out our perspective on these other matters.

- As of the 1950s, minorities, especially blacks, in many parts of the country were systematically and unjustly excluded from entering skilled and professional occupations of all kinds.
- At least since the 1950s, changes in white attitudes, as expressed in the civil rights movement and in myriad other events in race

relations, the removal of Jim Crow restrictions in the South, and affirmative action requirements opened up opportunities for minorities. Progress was made.

- In the 1990s, racial hostility continues to be a significant problem in American life.
- Affirmative action has an internally consistent rationale even if it is at odds with the maximum efficiency in hiring productive workers.

This last remark calls for some elaboration. Suppose, for the sake of argument, that we are sure that a history of unfair discrimination has handicapped some people so that they fare less well in the job market than they otherwise would. Their handicaps may handicap their descendants, so that past unfairness is propagated indefinitely into the future, unless we do something about it. A properly constructed affirmative action policy may then be temporarily less efficient but more efficient in the long run. If it achieves long-run efficiency by breaking the cycle of past discrimination, it is arguably fair. And even if the long run is indefinitely far off, many people are willing to pay some price in lost productivity for a large enough gain in group equality.

Or suppose that we knew that the inequality in employment that we observe arises for reasons we consider inherently unfair. Perhaps blacks are, for example, not being hired to be shop clerks in neighborhoods because the customers (or the other workers) are bigoted.[34] It may be efficient to hire fewer clerks who will be discriminated against, but it is not fair. Many people would be willing, again, to lose some efficiency in return for greater equality.

In short, we sympathize with some of the imaginable reasons for affirmative action in the workplace and are under no illusions about the ways in which perceptions of racial differences still affect employers' hiring decisions. But affirmative action does not mean just wanting good things. It means specific and often substantial constraints on the employer's ability to make use of the most qualified people. What should we make of such policies as of the 1990s?

Trying to Reconcile Ethnic Equity and Competitive Fairness

It is possible for an advocate of current affirmative action policies to concede all the factual points we have made in this discussion and still be in favor of continuing and even stronger affirmative action policies.

For such advocates, it makes no difference if the tests are reliable and valid predictors of job performance. If a disadvantaged group performs at a lower level, to these advocates, it is self-evidently society's fault, and government must take whatever steps are necessary to bring the disadvantaged group up to the level of other groups, ensuring equal employment and income in the meantime. Sometimes this argument is couched specifically in terms of the black experience in the United States, sometimes as part of a broader argument for an egalitarian agenda.[35]

Our dispute with the egalitarian position has to be carried out on ethical and philosophical grounds, for there is nothing much to argue about in the facts. Briefly, we differ with the contemporary advocates of continued quotalike hiring requirements on two counts.

First, we adhere to the 1964 view of what constitutes fairness, exemplified by Hubert Humphrey, who, in fighting for passage of the Civil Rights Act of 1964, declared that it "does not limit the employer's freedom to hire, fire, promote, or demote for any reason—or for no reasons—so long as his action is not based on race," and then volunteered to eat the bill in public if he were wrong about what the new law would do.[36] Like the senator, we reject equality of outcome as an appropriate goal. Equality of opportunity is the test most consistent with the vision of the Congress that enacted the law in 1964, and for that matter with the vision that animated the Constitution. The appropriate goal is a job market in which people are not favored or held back simply because of their race. Nothing in nature or knowledge, however, says that all groups should be equally successful in every walk of life. This may be "unfair" in the same sense that life is unfair, but it need not mean that human beings are treating one another unfairly.

Consider the convenient and appropriate case of athletic performance. By the standard of proportional equality, there are "too many" black players in the National Basketball Association compared to the number of white players. No one thinks this is unjust. When professional tennis equalized the purses for male and women champions, it did not also require the men and women to play against other, because everyone recognized that all the top men would almost always beat all of the top women. If men and women players were ranked in a single list, would there be "too many" males among the top 100 tennis players in the world? Any particular disproportion *may* be unfair, but it may not. It may be less obvious why there are disproportions in other pursuits, hence harder to tell whether they are fair, but the principle is the same, and simple: If the quality of performance fairly differs among individuals, it may fairly differ among groups.[37] If a disproportion is fair, then "correcting" it—making it proportional—may produce unfairness along with equal representation. We believe that is what has happened in the case of current forms of affirmative action. People who bring equal qualifications to a job should have an equal shot at being hired, and affirmative action regulations, originally intended to promote precisely that goal, now impede it.

Second, the debate will be healthier if those who want private businesses to support social objectives openly acknowledge that such support does in fact entail costs in efficiency and productivity, hence the benefits that flow from greater efficiency and higher productivity—including a stronger economy for American society as a whole.[38] Nor are the costs in productivity unique to private businesses. When a police department hires people who become less effective police officers than those it could have hired, the department loses some of its capability to provide law enforcement. Affirmative action can cost something in government services every bit as much as in the productivity of a private business.

We do not require equal outcomes, but we do want fair treatment. What policy alternatives might be employed to bring about this state of affairs in hiring and promotion? Before exploring four alternatives, let us say clearly that the worst alternative, the one we do not discuss further, is what we are now doing: not raising the question at all and proceeding as if there are easy and costless ways to achieving fairness.

Alternative I: Creating Tests That Are Legal Under the Current Requirements

In theory, employers could construct job-specific tests that meet the Supreme Court's (and now the Congress's) definition of fairness. It would be expensive, and the tests would seldom (if ever) be more predictive than a general test of cognitive ability. But it is feasible. The difficulty is that predictiveness comes primarily from the tests' measure of g. Therefore, although they cannot be faulted under the other legal requirements, they will nonetheless be thrown out because of disparate impact. This is what has happened most famously at New York City's Police Department, which for more than a decade has been spending large amounts of money trying to create a sergeant's examination. Each successive version has met strict standards of job specificity and freedom from demonstrable cultural bias, but large ethnic disparities have persisted.[39] The disparities themselves invalidate the test, and a new version must be prepared. The police department has even used a videobased test, on grounds that any form of paper-and-pencil test must necessarily discriminate against minorities.

The case of the New York Police Department is one example of many.[40] In practice, no test that produces disparate results has been able to withstand challenge. The lesson of the last two decades is that ethnic bias in a job test need not be proved. It need only be alleged. This has been most consistently the case for public employment—police, firefighters, sanitation workers, teachers, administrative staff—where political constituencies can most easily bring pressure to bear.

Alternative II: Choosing Among Applicants with Equal Education

Ordinarily a fair way to ease the existing affirmative action requirement would be to permit employers to narrow the pool of qualified applicants by using education as a screen. Thus, for example, the 80 percent rule (see the definition on page 482) could be calculated on the basis of applicants who met a minimum educational level, not all applicants. But affirmative action at the university level (Chapter 19) prevents this solution from working, because the same degree may not have the same meaning for blacks, Latinos, and whites in terms of cognitive ability. We showed this for the bachelor's degree in the preceding chapter. But employers who try to make finer discriminations are no better off. In the NLSY, the black-white differences for every educational level, from high school diploma to Ph.D, are large, with the smallest being a difference of 1.2 standard deviations.[41]

Nor does it help to differentiate by major area of study. In the NLSY, a black and a white with a bachelor's degree in engineering, math, or a hard science—majors that would apparently be least susceptible to double standards—were nonetheless separated by 1.1 standard deviations in IQ. Differences for other common majors (behavioral and social sciences, fine arts, education, or business) ranged from 1.4 to 1.6 standard deviations. For Latinos, the gap was smallest for engineering, math, or a hard science (.7 standard deviation) and ranged from .9 to 1.3 standard deviations for the others.

The educational credential used to be an effective way for a person from a deprived background to stand on an equal footing with other job applicants. It is still so treated that way in political rhetoric. The reality facing employers is that, given the aggressive affirmative action that universities have employed over the last three decades, educational credentials can no longer be used to compare the intellectual qualifications of black, Latino, and white job candidates.

Alternative III: Race Norming

An employer who hires large numbers of people cannot very well get along without using a test, but at the same time probably cannot devise a test that will pass muster with the government. So it will have to test applicants knowing that the test will produce unacceptably large group differences between whites and blacks, then comply with the 80 percent rule by hiring additional applicants from the protected minorities.

The simplest way to do this is to employ a pass-fail cutoff. Everyone above the cutoff is deemed qualified for the job, and then the employer uses other methods to choose among the candidates, making sure that the end result meets the 80 percent rule. This is a common solution and requires only that the cutoff be low enough that a sufficient number of protected candidates get into the final group of candidates.[42] But the pass-fail cutoff throws away a great deal of valuable information. Suppose that after complying with the 80 percent rule, the employer ends up with six new white employees out of twenty whites who applied and two out of seven black applicants. Why just take any six whites who scored above the cutoff? Why not instead take the whites with the top six scores? Similarly, why not take the top-scoring two blacks?

This is called top-down hiring. If the test has high validity, if the group differences are large, and if there are many applicants, it is much more efficient than a cutoff.[43] But there is a difficulty with this method. By deciding in advance on the number of whites and blacks who will be hired and then picking the top-scoring candidates, the employer is using quotas, which is illegal (even before the 1991 Civil Rights Act, an employer who used explicit quotas was vulnerable to legal action).

One way to get around this difficulty is to use race norming. The raw scores are converted into percentiles based on the distribution of scores within each group: a white applicant receives a percentile score based on the distribution of white scores; a black applicant's score represents his percentile within the black distribution; and so on. Then the employer makes hiring decisions on the basis of these race-normed percentiles. Starting in the late 1970s, the U.S. Department of Labor began promoting this solution, offering such race-normed scores for the General Aptitude Test Battery (the GATB, described in Chapter 3).[44]

By the early 1980s, race norming had became a common solution to the employer's dilemma. To see how race norming works, we may use the example of the popular Wonderlic Personnel Test, a highly g-loaded paper-and-pencil test that takes just twelve minutes. In its test manual in use during the 1980s, the Wonderlic company gave precise instructions for what it called "percentile selection"—its term for race norming—along with an "Ethnic Conversion Table." Suppose that five candidates—white, black, Latino, Asian, and American Indian—all got the Wonderlic's mean score of 22 prior to any adjustment for group distributions. Using the Ethnic Conversion Table, the personnel office would then assign those five candidates, all of whom had identical scores, to the 45th percentile (for the white), 80th percentile (for the black), 75th percentile (for the Latino), 55th percentile (for the Asian), and 60th percentile (for the American Indian), and those scores would thereafter be treated as the "real" scores.[45] An employer could then hire from the top down using these adjusted scores and expect to end up with ratios of employees that would avoid triggering the Uniform Guidelines.

In 1986, the U.S. Department of Justice challenged race norming on the grounds that it was an unlawful and unconstitutional violation of the rights of people who were neither black nor Latino. In our example, a black with a score of 80 would indeed have a much better chance of being hired than a white with a score of 45, though both had the same score on an unbiased, valid test. The Departments of Justice and Labor adjudicated their differences, agreeing to study the method further. Race norming had few defenders in public, where its unfairness seemed palpable. In the Civil Rights Act of 1991, race norming was banned for any employer subject to federal regulation. For now, this experiment in affirmative action policy—ironically, by far the most efficient from a productivity standpoint and even the "fairest," insofar as the highest scorers at least won out in competition with members of their own group—has been suspended.

Alternative IV: Returning to the Original Conception of Affirmative Action

We are dissatisfied with all of the foregoing alternatives and are broadly critical of the way in which the well-intentioned effort to end employment discrimination has played out. We therefore close by urging consideration of this proposition: *If tomorrow all job discrimination regulations based on group proportions were rescinded, the United States would have a job market that is ethically fairer, more conducive to racial harmony, and economically more productive, than the one we have now.* We cannot prove that the proposition is true (just as no one can prove that it is not), but here are two reasons for taking it seriously.

The first is public approval of the old concept of fairness. Preferential affirmative action has been a favorite cause of intellectuals, journalists, and liberal politicians, but it has never been rooted in broad public support. Instead, according to polls taken in the 1970s and 1980s, most Americans favor hiring by ability test scores over preferential hiring for protected groups. At the same time, they approve of having the government offer a helping hand—for example, by offering free courses to people to help them do better on ability tests used for employment. A clear majority of blacks similarly favor ability test scores over preferential hiring.[46] A return to policies based on evenhandedness for individuals (not for groups) seems sure to attract enthusiastic and broad public support.

The second reason is the potential for good faith. Our fundamental recommendation for the workplace resembles the one we offered for higher education: get rid of preferential affirmative action and return to the original conception of casting a wider net and leaning over backward to make sure that all minority applicants have a fair shot at the job or the promotion. To the extent that the government has a role to play, it is to ensure equality of opportunity, not of outcome. Once again, we anticipate that the main objection will be that ending affirmative action as now practiced will take us back to the bad old days. As we come to the end of our long wrestle with the new American Dilemma known as affirmative action, let us expand on our reasons for our optimism that the United States can do without it very well.

Try this thought experiment on yourself. If all antidiscrimination law were rescinded tomorrow, would you (if you are an employer) hire whites in preference to blacks or Latinos? Would you (if you are an employee) begin looking for workplaces where you did not have to work with blacks or Latinos? Would you (if you are a customer) seek out stores and services that did not have black or Latino personnel? We put the issue that way to expose a strange dissonance among Americans. We are confident that the answer to all of those questions by virtually all of the white readers of this book is an emphatic, deeply felt "no." May we even suggest that many of you would feel much happier about what you were doing if, as an employer, you spent your time concentrating on whether a minority applicant was the right person for the job rather than worrying about whether the applicant was likely to sue you if you turned him down; that, as an employee, you would find it a blessed relief to work in an office with black or Latino colleagues where it could be taken for granted by everyone that the personnel office had hired all of you using the same yardstick; that, as a consumer of services, you wish you could choose a surgeon who happens to be an ethnic minority, because you could be confident that his degree meant the same thing for everyone who received it.

We have no doubt that all of the above statements are true for the vast majority of our readers, and yet many people are convinced that the population as a whole would take advantage of the situation if affirmative action were ended. Talk about it with your friends, and you will find it to be a commonplace not limited to yourself. Although they too are authentically committed to treating people fairly regardless of race, color, or creed, they worry that massive bigotry still exists and will bring back the bad old days as soon as the heavy hand of the government regulation is lifted from them. By odd happenstance, the people one knows personally are much more fair-minded than the people one doesn't know personally.

Is this really true? That bigotry still exists is incontestable. But that does not mean that bigotry would prevail in the American job market as of the end of the twentieth century if the vast machinery of antidiscrimination law did not exist. Much of what we have presented in this chapter about occupational gains by blacks in the years before and after 1964 suggests the opposite. The civil rights movement authentically raised white awareness of the oppression and exploitation of blacks in the job market. The trendlines in both white behavior and black outcomes began to move in the right direction, gathering speed. The civil rights legislation came along at the same time and probably tweaked the slopes of those trendlines in some instances. But the great truth about the 1960s was not that the nation finally enacted the civil rights laws but that the American people were finally and inexorably moving in the right direction anyway. We are asking that you consider seriously the proposition that it is feasible to remove antidiscrimination law, replacing it with vigorous enforcement of the time-honored American principle that all citizens are equal before the law.

As in the case of college admissions, some economic and occupational reshuffling would occur. Some minorities would fail to get jobs that they get now. If, for example, the Washington Police Department returns to a policy of hiring the best-qualified candidates, a smaller proportion of those new police would be black. Wherever else standards have been lowered to increase the number of minorities in a workplace, the number of minorities in those positions in that workplace would probably diminish. On the other hand, the quality of the Washington police force is likely to improve, which will be of tangible benefit to the hundreds of thousands of blacks who live in that city. Minorities in all walks of life will have lifted from them the post-1964 form of second-class citizenship that affirmative action has imposed on them.

Much of the reshuffling that may be expected will not be bad even for those who are reshuffled. As matters stand, newly hired minority executives in corporations often enjoy short-term benefits (higher pay and status at the front end than new graduates could ordinarily expect) but a career dead end. Blacks in companies that do business with the federal government are routinely used in highly visible positions as evidence of affirmative action compliance and diverted from the more pedestrian but ultimately more beneficial apprenticeship positions that the white employees have no choice but to serve. Minority business-people are channeled into the minority set-aside game, learning how to serve as fronts for contracts that are actually carried out by whites, instead of running the business itself. Affirmative action has deformed many aspects of American life, not least in twisting the ways in which minorities must try to get ahead.

We will not try to estimate what the effects of doing away with job discrimination legislation would be for business productivity. The effects would vary widely by industry and location in any case, from trivial to substantial. Nor will we spend much time talking about the benefits for whites, except to say that these benefits should be counted. It is easy for highly educated whites with many options to look benignly on affirmative action. It has little effect on their job prospects. For a young white man with fewer advantages who has wanted to be a fire-fighter all his life and is passed over in favor of a less-qualified minority or female candidate, the costs loom larger. To dismiss his disappointment and the hardships worked on him just because his skin is white and his sex is male is a peculiarly common—and cruel—reaction of people who burst with indignation at every other kind of injustice.

Whatever their precise amounts, the benefits to productivity and to fairness of ending the antidiscrimination laws are substantial. But our largest reason for wanting to scrap job discrimination law is our belief that the system of affirmative action, in education and the workplace alike, is leaking a poison into the American soul. This nation does not have the option of ethnic balkanization. The increasing proportions of ethnic minorities—Latino, East Asian, South Asian, African, East European—make it more imperative, not less, that we return to the melting pot as metaphor and color blindness as the ideal. Individualism is not only America's heritage. It must be its future.

Chapter 21

The Way We Are Headed

In this penultimate chapter we speculate about the impact of cognitive stratification on American life and government. Predicting the course of society is chancy, but certain tendencies seem strong enough to worry about:

- An increasingly isolated cognitive elite.
- A merging of the cognitive elite with the affluent.
- A deteriorating quality of life for people at the bottom end of the cognitive ability distribution.

Unchecked, these trends will lead the U.S. toward something resembling a caste society, with the underclass mired ever more firmly at the bottom and the cognitive elite ever more firmly anchored at the top, restructuring the rules of society so that it becomes harder and harder for them to lose. Among the other casualties of this process would be American civil society as we have known it. Like other apocalyptic visions, this one is pessimistic, perhaps too much so. On the other hand, there is much to be pessimistic about.

RECAPITULATION: THE INVISIBLE MIGRATION

As we described in Part I, the cognitive elite refers to people in the top percentiles of cognitive ability who, over the course of the American twentieth century, have been part of a vast but nearly invisible migration. The migration does not reveal itself in masses of humanity crossing frontiers but in countless bits of data about the movement of individuals across the levels of society. Like all other great migrations, this one too will transform both the place people left and the place they go.

At the beginning of the century, the great majority of people in the top 5 or 10 percent of the intelligence distribution were not college educated, often not even high school educated, and they lived their lives scattered almost indistinguishably among the rest of the population. Their interests were just as variegated. Many were small businessmen or farmers, sharing the political outlook of those groups. Many worked on assembly lines or as skilled craftsmen. The top of the cognitive ability distribution probably included leaders of the labor movement and of community organizations. Among the smart women, a few had professional careers of their own, but most of them kept house, reared children, and were often the organizing forces of their religious and social communities.

People from the top of the cognitive ability distribution lived next door to people who were not so smart, with whose children their own children went to school. They socialized with, went to church with, and married people less bright than themselves as a matter of course. This was not an egalitarian utopia that we are trying to recall. On the contrary, communities were stratified by wealth, religion, class, ethnic background, and race. The stratifications may have been stark, even bitter, but people were not stratified by cognitive ability.

As the century progressed, the historical mix of intellectual abilities at all levels of American society thinned as intelligence rose to the top. The upper end of the cognitive ability distribution has been increasingly channeled into higher education, especially the top colleges and professional schools, thence into high-IQ occupations and senior managerial positions, as Part I detailed. The upshot is that the scattered brightest of the early twentieth century have congregated, forming a new class.

Membership in this new class, the cognitive elite, is gained by high IQ; neither social background, nor ethnicity, nor lack of money will bar the way. But once in the club, usually by age eighteen, members begin to share much else as well. Among other things, they will come to run much of the country's business. In the private sector, the cognitive elite dominates the ranks of CEOs and the top echelon of corporate executives. Smart people have no doubt always had the advantage in commerce and industry, but their advantage has grown as the barriers against the "wrong" nationalities, ethnicities, religions, or socioeconomic origins have been dismantled. Meanwhile, the leaders in medicine, law, science, print journalism, television, the film and publishing industries, and the foundation world come largely from the cognitive elite. Almost all of the leading figures in academia are part of it. In Washington, the top echelons of federal officialdom, special interest groups, think tanks, and the rest of Washington's satellite institutions draw heavily from the cognitive elite. At the municipal level, the local business and political movers are often members of the cognitive elite.

GIVING MERITOCRACY ITS DUE

Part I mostly described a success story—success for the people lucky enough to be part of the cognitive elite but also a success for the nation as a whole. Before turning to the dark side, we should be explicit about the good things that flow from the invisible migration.

Chief among them is the triumph of an American ideal. Americans believe that each person should be able to go as far as talent and hard work will take him, and much of what we have described is the realization of that conviction, for people with high IQs. The breadth of the change was made possible by twentieth-century technology, which expanded the need for people with high IQs by orders of magnitude. But the process itself has been a classic example of people free to respond to opportunity and of an economic system that created opportunities in abundance.

Life has been increasingly good for the cognitive elite, as it has displaced the socioeconomic elites of earlier times. We showed in Part I the increasing financial rewards for brains, but money is only a part of the cornucopia. In the far-from-idyllic past when most of the people at the top of the cognitive distribution were farmers, housewives, workers, and shop owners, many of them were also frustrated, aware that they had capabilities that were not being used. The graph on page 56 that traced the steep rise in high-IQ jobs over the course of the century was to some important extent a picture of people moving from unsatisfying jobs to lucrative and interesting ones.

Technology has not just created more jobs for the cognitive elite but revolutionized the way they may be done. Modern transportation has expanded the realm in which people work. Beyond that, physical separation is becoming irrelevant. A scientist passionately devoted to the study of a certain protein or an investment analyst following a market can be in daily electronic conversation with people throughout the world who share the same passion, passing drafts of work back and forth, calling up data files, doing analyses that would have required a mainframe computer and a covey of assistants only a few years ago—all while sitting alone at a computer, which need not be in an office, but can as easily be in a beach house overlooking the ocean. Across the occupational domain of those who work primarily with their minds, the explosion of computer and communications technologies has liberated and expanded creativity, productivity, and personal freedom. There may be some costs of this physical isolation, but many people are happier and more fulfilled as a result of the reach of modern technology.

For the nation as a whole, the invisible migration has surely brought benefits as well. We cannot measure the gains precisely, but they are the inevitable side effect of greater efficiency in identifying intellectual talent and channeling it into high-IQ occupations. Compared to 1900 or even 1950, America in the 1990s is getting more productivity out of its stock of human capital, and this presumably translates into more jobs, gains in GNP, and other effects that produce more wealth for the society at large.

So what's the problem? The old stratifications are fading, erased by a greater reliance on what people often call merit. Millions of people have benefited from the changes—including us. Would we prefer less of a meritocracy? Put that way, no—but "no" for larger reasons as well. The invisible migration is in many ways an expression of what America is all about.

ISOLATION WITHIN THE COGNITIVE ELITE

What worries us first about the emerging cognitive elite is its coalescence into a class that views American society increasingly through a lens of its own. In *The End of Equality*, which analyzes the stratification of American society from a vantage point different from ours, social critic Mickey Kaus describes the isolation we have in mind. He identifies it broadly with the decline of "the public sphere."[1] The end of the military draft, the social segregation of the school system, and the divisive effects of the underclass are among his suspects, and each has doubtless played an important role independent (to some degree) of the effects of the cognitive stratification that we described in Part I. Thinking about the way these forces had affected his own life, Kaus remarked: "I entered a good Ivy League college in 1969. I doubt I've had a friend or regular social acquaintance since who scored less than an 1100 on his or her SAT boards."[2]

Kaus is probably right. The reason why this is a problem is captured by a remark attributed to the *New Yorker*'s one-time movie critic Pauline Kael following Richard Nixon's landslide victory in the presidential election of 1972: "Nixon can't have won; no one I know voted for him."[3] When the members of the cognitive elite (of whatever political convictions) hang out with each other, often exclusively with each other, they find it hard to understand what ordinary people think.

The problem is not simply that smart people rise to the top more efficiently these days. If the only quality that CEOs of major corporations and movie directors and the White House inner circle had in common were their raw intelligence, things would not be so much different now than they have always been, for to some degree the most successful have always been drawn disproportionately from the most intelligent. But the invisible migration of the twentieth century has done much more than let the most intellectually able succeed more easily. It has also segregated them and socialized them. The members of the cognitive elite are likely to have gone to the same kinds of schools, live in similar neighborhoods, go to the same kinds of theaters and restaurants, read the same magazines and newspapers, watch the same television programs, even drive the same makes of cars.

They also tend to be ignorant of the same things. They watch far less commercial television than the average American. Their movie-going tends to be highly selective. They seldom read the national tabloids that have the nation's largest circulation figures or listen to the talk radio that has become a major form of national communication for other parts of America. This does not mean that the cognitive elite spend their lives at the ballet and reading Proust. Theirs is not a high culture, but it is distinctive enough to set them off from the rest of the country in many important ways.

The isolation of the cognitive elite is by no means complete, but the statistical tendencies are strong, and the same advances in transportation and communication that are so enhancing the professional lives of the cognitive elite will make their isolation from the rest of the public that much greater. As their common ground with the rest of society decreases, their coalescence as a new class increases. The traditional separations between the business world, the entertainment world, the university intellectuals, and government are being replaced by an axis of bright people that runs through society. They already sense their kinship across these spheres of interest. This too will increase with time.

THE COALITION OF THE COGNITIVE ELITE AND THE AFFLUENT

The trends we have described would not constitute a threat to the republic if the government still played the same role in civic life that it played through the Eisenhower administration. As recently as 1960, it did not make a lot of political difference what the cognitive elite thought, because its power to impose those values on the rest of America was limited. In most of the matters that counted—the way the schools were run, keeping order in the public square, opening a business or running it—the nation remained decentralized. The still inchoate cognitive elite in 1960 may have had ideas about how it wanted to move the world but, like Archimedes, it lacked a place to stand.

We need not become embroiled here in a debate about whether the centralization of authority since 1960 (or 1933, for those who take a longer view) was right or wrong. We may all agree as a statement of fact that such centralization occurred, through legislation, Supreme Court decisions, and accretions of executive authority in every domain of daily life. With it came something that did not exist before: a place for the cognitive elite to stand. With the end of the historic limits on the federal reach, everything was up for grabs. If one political group could get enough votes on the Supreme Court, it could move the Constitution toward its goals. If it could get enough votes in Congress, it could do similarly with legislation.

Through the 1960s, 1970s, and 1980s, the battle veered back and forth, with groups identifiably "liberal" and "conservative" bloodying each other's noses in accustomed ways. But in the Bush and Clinton administrations, the old lines began to blur. One may analyze these trends conventionally in terms of the evolution of party politics. The rise of the New Democrats and the breakup of the Reagan coalition are the conventional way of looking at the evolution. We think something else is happening as well, with potential dangers: the converging interests of the cognitive elite with the larger population of affluent Americans.

For most of the century, intellectuals and the affluent have been antagonists. Intellectuals have been identified with the economic left and the cultural avant-garde, while the affluent have been identified with big business and cultural conservatism. These comfortable categories have become muddled in recent years, as faculty at the top universities put together salaries, consulting fees, speeches, and royalties that garner them six-figure incomes while the *New York Review of Books* shows up in the mailbox of young corporate lawyers. The very bright have become much more uniformly affluent than they used to be while, at the same time, the universe of affluent people has become more densely populated by the very bright, as Part I described. Not surprisingly, the interests of affluence and the cognitive elite have begun to blend.

This melding has its limits, particularly when the affluent person is not part of the cognitive elite. The high-IQ Stanford professor with the best-selling book and the ordinary-IQ fellow who makes the same income with his small chain of shoe stores are hardly allies on everything. But in looking ahead to alliances and social trends, it is still useful to think in terms of their increasing commonalities because, as any good economist or politician will point out, there are theoretical interests and practical interests. The Stanford professor's best-selling book may be a diatribe against the punitive criminal justice system, but that doesn't mean that he doesn't vote with his feet to move to a safe neighborhood. Or his book may be a withering attack on outdated family norms, but that doesn't mean that he isn't acting like an old-fashioned father in looking after the interests of his children—and if that means sending his children to a lily-white private school so that they get a good education, so be it. Meanwhile, the man with the chain of shoe stores may be politically to the right of the Stanford professor, but he is looking for the same safe neighborhood and the same good schools for his children. And even if he is more likely to vote Republican than the professor, he is unlikely to be the rugged individualist of yore. On the contrary, he is likely to have become quite comfortable with the idea that government is there to be used. He and the professor may not be so far apart at all on how they want to live their own personal lives and how government might serve those joint and important interests.

Consider the sheer size of this emerging coalition and how quickly the affluent class as a whole (not just the cognitive elite) is growing. What is "affluence"? The median answer in 1992 when the Roper Organization asked people how much annual income they would need "to fulfill all your dreams" was $82,100, which indicates where affluence is thought to start by most Americans.[4] For purposes of this exercise, we will define affluence as beginning at an annual family income of $100,000 in 1990 dollars, about three times the median family income. By that definition, more than one out of twenty American families is affluent, roughly double what it was a decade earlier.[5] Furthermore, this growth has accompanied stagnant real income for the average family. Here is the last of the many graphs we have asked you to examine in this book. In some ways, it is more loaded with social implications than any that have come before.

In the 1970s, economic growth began to enlarge the affluent class

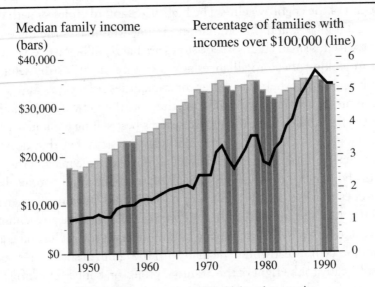

The shaded years are ones in which real per capita
GNP dropped. All figures are based on 1990 dollars.

Sources: Median family income: U.S. Bureau of the Census 1991, Table B-4, supplemented with U.S. Bureau of the Census 1993, Table B-11. For families with incomes over $100,000, data from 1967–1990 are taken from U.S. Bureau of the Census 1991, Table B-3; U.S. Bureau of the Census, 1993, Table B-6. Figures for 1947–1964 are estimated from U.S. Bureau of the Census 1975, Series G 269-282, adjusted for differences in definition of the family.

The graph illustrates the reason for the intense recent interest in American income inequality. From the end of World War II until the early 1970s, average family income rose. Then in 1973, median family income hit a peak. Part of the reason for the subsequent lack of progress has been the declining real wages for many categories of blue-collar jobs, described in Chapter 4. Part of the reason has been the decline in two-parent families (economic progress continued, though modestly, for families consisting of married couples). In any case, the average American family has been stuck at about the same place economically for more than twenty years.

For the affluent, the story diverges sharply. Until the early 1970s, the proportion of families with $100,000 in 1990 purchasing power increased slowly and in tandem with the growth in median family income. But after progress for the average family stalled, it continued for the affluent. The steepest gains occurred during the 1980s, and Ronald Reagan's policies of the 1980s are commonly thought to be an important force (in praise or blame) for increasing the number of affluent. But economists know that there is a difficulty with this explanation, as you will see when you compare the 1970s with the 1980s. The rising proportion of families with incomes of more than $100,000 since the early 1970s does not seem to be a function of any particular political party or policy, except insofar as those policies encourage an expanding economy. It has gone with gains in real per capita GNP (indicated by the unshaded bars in the graphic) whether those gains occurred under Richard Nixon, Jimmy Carter, Ronald Reagan, or George Bush.[6] There is no reason to think that this trend will be much different under Bill Clinton or his successors, if the economy grows. The net result is that the affluent will constitute a major portion of the population in the relatively near future, and they will increasingly be constituted of the most talented.

Try to envision what will happen when 10 or 20 percent of the population has enough income to bypass the social institutions they don't like in ways that only the top 1 percent used to be able to do. Robert Reich has called it the "secession of the successful."[7] The current symbol of this phenomenon is the gated community, secure behind its walls and guard posts, but many other signs are visible. The fax, modem, and Federal Express have already made the U.S. Postal Service nearly irrelevant to the way that the affluent communicate, for example. A more portentous development is the private court system that businesses are beginning to create. Or the mass exodus from public schools among those living in cities, if they can afford it. Or the proliferation of private security forces for companies, apartment houses, schools, malls, and anywhere else where people with money want to be safe.

Try to envision what will happen to the political process. Even as of the early 1990s, the affluent class is no longer a thin layer of rich people but a political bloc to be reckoned with. Speaking in round numbers (for the precise definitions of both groups are arbitrary), a coalition of the cognitive elite and the affluent class now represents something well in excess of 5 percent of families and, because of their much higher than average voting rates, somewhere in the vicinity of 10 to 15 percent of the voters.[8] The political clout of this group extends well beyond its mere voting size because of its financial contributions to campaigns and because this group contributes a large proportion of local political organizers. The combined weight of the cognitive elite and the affluent is already considerable. But we asked you to envision tomorrow, not today. Do you think that the rich in America already have too much power? Or do you think the intellectuals already have too much power? We are suggesting that a "yes" to both questions is probably right. And if you think the power of these groups is too great now, just watch what happens as their outlooks and interests converge.

Cynical readers will be asking what else is new. The privileged have always used the law to their advantage. Our own analysis is hardly novel; it is taken straight from a book of essays written more than two centuries ago, *The Federalist*. People are not naturally angelic but self-interested—else, as Publius pointed out, governments would not be necessary in the first place. Politically, people form factions to pursue their common ends. Give them access to government power to further those ends, and they will take advantage of it. The only modest additions we make to these ancient truths are two propositions: First, as of the 1990s, the constitutional restraints on how a faction may use government to further its ends have loosened. Second, an unprecedented coalition of the smart and the rich will take advantage of this new latitude in new ways.

FACING REALITY ABOUT THE UNDERCLASS

What new ways? There are many possibilities, but the central ones all involve the underclass. We fear that a new kind of conservatism is becoming the dominant ideology of the affluent—not in the social tradition of an Edmund Burke or in the economic tradition of an Adam Smith but "conservatism" along Latin American lines, where to be conservative has often meant doing whatever is necessary to preserve the mansions on the hills from the menace of the slums below. In the case of the United States, the threat comes from an underclass that has been with American society for some years but has been the subject of unrealistic analysis and ineffectual, often counterproductive policy. The new coalition is already afraid of the underclass. In the next few decades, it is going to have a lot more to be afraid of. Now is the time to bring together from many chapters throughout the book the implications of cognitive stratification for the underclass.

The Fate of Children

Statistically, it is not good for children to be born either to a single mother or a married couple of low cognitive ability. But the greatest problems afflict children unlucky enough to be born to and reared by unmarried mothers who are below average in intelligence—about 20 percent of children currently being born.[9] They tend to do badly, socially and economically. They tend to have low cognitive ability themselves. They suffer disproportionately from behavioral problems. They will be disproportionately represented in prisons. They are less likely to marry than others and will themselves produce large proportions of the children born to single women of low intelligence.

Attempts to compensate for cognitive disadvantage at birth have shown how extraordinarily hard it is to do. Many readers no doubt find the plight of children to be among the most compelling arguments for government activism, as we do. But inadequate nutrition, physical abuse, emotional neglect, lack of intellectual stimulation, a chaotic home environment—all the things that worry us when we think about the welfare of children—are very difficult to improve from outside the home when the single mother is incompetent. Incompetent mothers are highly concentrated among the least intelligent, and their numbers are growing. In Chapter 15, we discussed differential fertility—a bloodless term—and suggested that the nation is experiencing dysgenic pressure—another bloodless term. In the metric of human suffering, increasing numbers of children are born into the conditions we most deplore and the conditions that government is most helpless to affect.

What happens to the child of low intelligence who survives childhood and reaches adulthood trying to do his best to be a productive citizen? Out of the many problems we have just sketched, this is the one we choose to italicize: *All of the problems that these children experience will become worse rather than better as they grow older, for the labor market they will confront a few decades down the road is going to be much harder for them to cope with than the labor market is now.* There will still be jobs for low-skill labor, mostly with service businesses and private households, but the natural wage for those jobs will be low. Attempts to increase their wage artificially (by raising the minimum wage, for example, or mandating job benefits) may backfire by making alternatives to human labor more affordable and, in many cases, by making the jobs disappear altogether. People in the bottom quartile of intelligence are becoming not just increasingly expendable in economic terms; they will sometime in the not-too-distant future become a net drag. In economic terms and barring a profound change in direction for our society, many people will be unable to perform that function so basic to human dignity: putting more into the world than they take out.

Perhaps a revolution in teaching technology will drastically increase the productivity returns to education for people in the lowest quartile of intelligence, overturning our pessimistic forecast. But there are no harbingers of any such revolution as we write. And unless such a revolution occurs, all the fine rhetoric about "investing in human capital" to "make America competitive in the twenty-first century" is not going to be able to overturn this reality: For many people, there is nothing they can learn that will repay the cost of the teaching.

The Emerging White Underclass

The dry tinder for the formation of an underclass community is a large number of births to single women of low intelligence in a concentrated spatial area. Sometime in the next few decades it seems likely that American whites will reach the point of conflagration. The proportion of white illegitimate births (including Latinos) reached 22 percent in 1991.[10] There is nothing about being Caucasian that must slow down the process. Britain, where the white illegitimacy ratio, which was much lower than the American white ratio as recently as 1979, hit 32 percent in 1992 with no signs of slowing down.

When 22 percent of all births are to single women, the proportion in low-income communities is perhaps twice that. In the NLSY, 43 percent of all births to white women who were below the poverty line were illegitimate, compared to 7 percent for all white women anywhere above the poverty line.[11] In the nation at large, we know from the 1992 Census Bureau study of fertility that women with college degrees contribute only 4 percent of white illegitimate babies, while women with a high school education or less contribute 82 percent. Women with family incomes of $75,000 or more contribute 1 percent of white illegitimate babies, while women with family incomes under $20,000 contribute 69 percent.[12] White illegitimacy is overwhelmingly a lower-class phenomenon.

In the past, whites have not had an "underclass" as such, because the whites who might qualify have been too scattered among the working class. Instead, white communities in America had a few streets on the outskirts of town inhabited by the people who couldn't seem to cope and skid rows of unattached white men in large cities, but these scatterings were seldom large enough to make up a neighborhood. An underclass needs a critical mass, and white America has not had one. But if the overall white illegitimacy ratio is 22 percent—probably somewhere in the 40 percent range in low-income communities—and rising fast, the question arises: At what point is critical mass reached? How much illegitimacy can a community tolerate? Nobody knows, but the historical fact is that the trendlines on black crime, dropout from the labor force, and illegitimacy all shifted sharply upward as the overall black illegitimacy ratio passed 25 percent and the rate in low-income black communities moved past 50 percent.

We need not rely on the analogy with the black experience. White illegitimacy is also overwhelmingly a lower-cognitive-class phenomenon, as we detailed in Chapter 8. Three-quarters of all white illegitimate births are to women below average in IQ, and 45 percent are to women with IQs under 90.[13] These women are poorly equipped for the labor market, often poorly equipped to be mothers, and there is no reason to think that the outcomes for their children will be any better than the outcomes have been for black children. Meanwhile, as never-married mothers grow in numbers, the dynamics of the public housing market (where they will probably continue to be welcome) and the private housing market (where they will not) will foster increasing concentrations of whites with high unemployment, high crime, high illegitimacy, and low cognitive ability, creating communities that look very much like the inner-city neighborhoods that people now tend to associate with minorities.

The white cognitive elite is unlikely to greet this development sympathetically. On the contrary, much of white resentment and fear of the black underclass has been softened by the complicated mixture of white guilt and paternalism that has often led white elites to excuse behavior in blacks that they would not excuse in whites. This does not mean that white elites will abandon the white underclass, but it does suggest that the means of dealing with their needs are likely to be brusque.

Spatial Concentration, Low Cognitive Ability, and Underclass Behavior

As the patience of whites for other whites wears thin, the black inner city will simultaneously be getting worse rather than better. Various scholars, led by William Julius Wilson, have described the outmigration of the ablest blacks that has left the inner city without its former leaders and role models.[14] Given a mean black IQ of about 85 and the link between socioeconomic status and IQ within ethnic populations, the implication is that the black inner city has a population with a mean IQ somewhere in the low 80s at best, with a correspondingly small tail in the above-average range.[15]

What is the minimum level of cognitive resources necessary to sustain a community at any given level of social and economic complexity? For sustaining a village of a few hundred people in a premodern society, the minimum average level is probably quite modest. What is it for sustaining a modern community? The question is of enormous practical significance yet remains innocent of any empirical investigation whatsoever. Perhaps the crucial feature is the average cognitive ability. Perhaps it is the size of the cadre of high-ability people. Perhaps it is the weight of the population at low end of the distribution. No one knows. Whatever the details, a prima facie case exists that the cognitive resources in the contemporary inner city have fallen below the minimum level. What looked like a rising tide of social problems a generation ago has come to look more like a fundamental breakdown in social organization.

One may look for signs that these communities are about to recover. The crack cocaine epidemic of the 1980s has ebbed, for example, although crack is cheaper than ever, as the savage effects of the drug became evident to younger brothers and sisters. Black grass-roots efforts to restore the family and combat crime have increased in recent years. But counterpoised against these forces working on behalf of regeneration within the inner city is a powerful force working against it: A large majority of the next generation of blacks in the inner city is growing up without fathers and with limited cognitive ability. The numbers continue to increase. The outmigration of the able continues.

While we can see how these trends *might* be reversed, which we describe in the next and final chapter, let us consider the prospect we face if they do not. This brings us to the denouement of our prognosis.

THE COMING OF THE CUSTODIAL STATE

When a society reaches a certain overall level of affluence, the haves begin to feel sympathy toward, if not guilt about, the condition of the have-nots. Thus dawns the welfare state—the attempt to raise the poor and the needy out of their plight. In what direction does the social welfare system evolve when a coalition of the cognitive elite and the affluent continues to accept the main tenets of the welfare state but are increasingly frightened of and hostile toward the recipients of help? When the coalition is prepared to spend money but has lost faith that remedial social programs work? The most likely consequence in our view is that the cognitive elite, with its commanding position, will implement an expanded welfare state for the underclass that also keeps it out from underfoot. Our label for this outcome is the custodial state.[16] Should it come to pass, here is a scenario:

Over the next decades, it will become broadly accepted by the cognitive elite that the people we now refer to as the underclass are in that condition through no fault of their own but because of inherent shortcomings about which little can be done. Politicians and intellectuals alike will become much more open about the role of dysfunctional behavior in the underclass, accepting that addiction, violence, unavailability for work, child abuse, and family disorganization will keep most members of the underclass from fending for themselves. It will be agreed that the underclass cannot be trusted to use cash wisely. Therefore policy will consist of greater benefits, but these will be primarily in the form of services rather than cash. Furthermore, there will be new restrictions. Specifically, these consequences are plausible:

Child care in the inner city will become primarily the responsibility of the state. Infants will get better nutrition because they will be spending their days in day care centers from infancy. Children will get balanced diets because they will be eating breakfast, lunch, and perhaps supper at school. Day care centers and schools for elementary students will edge closer toward comprehensive care facilities, whose staff will try to provide not only education and medical care but to train children in hygiene, sexual socialization, socialization to the world of work, and other functions that the parents are deemed incapable of providing.

The homeless will vanish. One of the safer predictions is that sometime in the near future, the cognitive elite will join the broad public sentiment in favor of reasserting control over public spaces. It will become easier to consign mentally incompetent adults to custodial care. Perhaps the clinically borderline cases that now constitute a high proportion of the homeless will be required to reside in shelters, more elaborately equipped and staffed than most homeless shelters are today. Police will be returned their authority to roust people and enforce laws prohibiting disorderly conduct.

Strict policing and custodial responses to crime will become more acceptable and widespread. This issue could play out in several ways. The crime rate in affluent suburbs may be low enough to keep the pressure for reform low. But events in the early 1990s suggest that fear of crime is rising, and support for strict law enforcement is increasing.

One possibility is that a variety of old police practices—especially the stop-and-frisk—will quietly come back into use in new guises. New prisons will continue to be built, and the cells already available will be used more efficiently to incarcerate dangerous offenders (for example, by eliminating mandatory sentences for certain drug offenses and by incarcerating less serious offenders in camps rather than prisons). Technology will provide new options for segregating and containing criminals, as the electronic bracelets now being used to enforce house arrest (or perhaps "neighborhood arrest") become more flexible and foolproof. Another possibility is that support will grow for a national system of identification cards, coded with personal information including criminal record. The possibilities for police surveillance and control of behavior are expanding rapidly. Until recently, the cognitive elite has predominantly opposed the use of such technology. In a few years, we predict, it will not.

The underclass will become even more concentrated spatially than it is today. The expanded network of day care centers, homeless shelters, public housing, and other services will always be located in the poorest part of the inner city, which means that anyone who wants access to them will have to live there. Political support for such measures as relocation of people from the inner city to the suburbs, never strong to begin with, will wither altogether. The gaping cultural gap between the habits of the underclass and the habits of the rest of society, far more impassable than a simple economic gap between poor and not poor or the racial gap of black and white, will make it increasingly difficult for children who have grown up in the inner city to function in the larger society even when they want to.

The underclass will grow. During the 1980s, scholars found evidence that the size of the underclass was no longer expanding.[17] But even as they wrote, the welfare rolls, which had moved within a narrow range since the late 1970s, began to surge again. The government will try yet another round of the customary social programs—sex education, job training, parenting training, and the like—and they will be as ineffectual this round as they were in the 1960s and 1970s.[18] Meanwhile, many low-income parents who try to do all the right things and pass their values on to their children will be increasingly unable to do so. They cannot propagate their norms in the face of a local culture in which illegitimacy, welfare, crime, and drugs are commonplace, and there is nothing magically invulnerable about them or their children. Some of the reforms we have described will be improvements—crime might actually drop in the inner city as well as in the other parts of town, for example—but the main effect will be to make it harder for the children in these solid and conventional working-class families to emulate their parents. Marriage, steady employment, and responsible behavior of many kinds will fall among the next generation, and some portion of the working class will become members of the underclass. Few children of those already in the underclass will escape.

Social budgets and measures for social control will become still more centralized. The growing numbers of illegitimate children born to poor women will have multiplier effects on social welfare budgets—directly and through increased indirect costs generated in the educational and law enforcement systems. As states become overwhelmed, the current cost sharing between the states and federal government will shift toward the federal budget. The mounting costs will also generate intense political pressure on Washington to *do* something. Unable to bring itself to do away with the welfare edifice—for by that time it will be assumed that social chaos will follow any radical cutback—the government will continue to try to engineer behavior through new programs and regulations. As time goes on and hostility toward the welfare-dependent increases, those policies are likely to become authoritarian and rely increasingly on custodial care.

Racism will reemerge in a new and more virulent form. The tension between what the white elite is supposed to think and what it is actually thinking about race will reach something close to a breaking point. This pessimistic prognosis must be contemplated: When the break comes, the result, as so often happens when cognitive dissonance is resolved, will be an overreaction in the other direction. Instead of the candor and realism about race that is so urgently needed, the nation will be faced with racial divisiveness and hostility that is as great as, or greater, than America experienced before the civil rights movement. We realize how outlandish it seems to predict that educated and influential Americans, who have been so puritanical about racial conversation, will openly revert to racism. We would not go so far as to say it is probable. It is, however, more than just possible. If it were to happen, all the scenarios for the custodial state would be more unpleasant—more vicious—than anyone can now imagine.

In short, by *custodial state*, we have in mind a high-tech and more lavish version of the Indian reservation for some substantial minority of the nation's population, while the rest of America tries to go about its business. In its less benign forms, the solutions will become more and more totalitarian. Benign or otherwise, "going about its business" in the old sense will not be possible. It is difficult to imagine the United States preserving its heritage of individualism, equal rights before the law, free people running their own lives, once it is accepted that a significant part of the population must be made permanent wards of the state.

Extrapolating from current trends, we project that the policies of custodialism will be not only tolerated but actively supported by a consensus of the cognitive elite. To some extent, we are not even really projecting but reporting. The main difference between the position of the cognitive elite that we portray here and the one that exists today is to some extent nothing more than the distinction between tacit and explicit.

If we wish to avoid this prospect for the future, we cannot count on the natural course of events to make things come out right. Now is the time to think hard about how a society in which a cognitive elite dominates and in which below-average cognitive ability is increasingly a handicap can also be a society that makes good on the fundamental promise of the American tradition: the opportunity for everyone, not just the lucky ones, to live a satisfying life. That is the task to which we now turn.

Chapter 22

A Place for Everyone

How should policy deal with the twin realities that people differ in intelligence for reasons that are not their fault, and that intelligence has a powerful bearing on how well people do in life?

The answer of the twentieth century has been that government should create the equality of condition that society has neglected to produce on its own. The assumption that egalitarianism is the proper ideal, however difficult it may be to achieve in practice, suffuses contemporary political theory. Socialism, communism, social democracy, and America's welfare state have been different ways of moving toward the egalitarian ideal. The phrase *social justice* has become virtually a synonym for economic and social equality.

Until now, these political movements have focused on the evils of systems in producing inequality. Human beings are potentially pretty much the same, the dominant political doctrine has argued, except for the inequalities produced by society. These same thinkers have generally rejected, often vitriolically, arguments that individual differences such as intelligence are to blame. But there is no reason why they could not shift ground. In many ways, the material in this book is tailor-made for their case. If it's not someone's fault that he is less intelligent than others, why should he be penalized in his income and social status?

We could respond with a defense of income differences. For example, it is justified to pay the high-IQ businessman and engineer more than the low-IQ ditch digger, producing income inequality, because that's the only way to make the economy grow and produce more wealth in which the ditch digger can share. We could grant that it is a matter not of just deserts but of economic pragmatism about how to produce compensating benefits for the least advantaged members of society.[1]

Such arguments make sense to us, as far as they go. After the experience of the twentieth century, it is hard to imagine that anyone still disagrees with them. But there are other issues, transcending the efficiency of an economy. Our central concern since we began writing this book is how people might live together harmoniously despite fundamental individual differences. The answer lies outside economics.

The initial purpose of this chapter is to present for your consideration another way of thinking about equality and inequality. It represents an older intellectual tradition than social democracy or even socialism. In our view, it is also a wiser tradition, more attuned to the way in which individuals go about living satisfying lives and to the ways in which societies thrive. The more specific policy conclusions to which we then turn cannot be explained apart from this underpinning.

THINKING ABOUT EQUALITY AS AN IDEAL

For thousands of years, great political thinkers of East and West tried to harmonize human differences. For Confucius, society was like his conception of a family—extensions of a ruling father and obedient sons, devoted husbands and faithful wives, benign masters and loyal servants. People were defined by their place, whether in the family or the community. So too for the ancient Greek and Roman philosophers: place was all. All the great religious traditions define a place for everyone, if not on earth then in heaven.

Society was to be ruled by the virtuous and wise few. The everyday business of the community fell to the less worthy multitude, with the most menial chores left to the slaves. Neither the Greek democrats nor the Roman republicans believed that "all men are created equal." Nor did the great Hindu thinkers of the Asian subcontinent, where one's work defined one's caste, which in turn circumscribed every other aspect of life. The ancients accepted the basic premise that people differ fundamentally and importantly and searched for ways in which people could contentedly serve the community (or the monarch or the tyrant or the gods), rather than themselves, despite their differences. Philosophers argued about obligations and duties, what they are and on whom they fall.

In our historical era, political philosophers have argued instead about rights. They do so because they are trying to solve a different problem. The great transformation from a search for duties and obligations to a search for rights may be dated with Thomas Hobbes, writing in the mid-

1600s about a principle whereby all people, not just the rich and well born, might have equal rights to liberty.[2] Everyone, said Hobbes, is entitled to as much liberty in gratifying his desires as he is willing to allow others in gratifying theirs.[3] People differ, acknowledged Hobbes, but they do not differ so much that they may justifiably be deprived of liberty by differing amounts. In the modern view that Hobbes helped shape, individuals freely accept constraints on their own behavior in exchange for ridding themselves of the dangers of living in perfect freedom, hence perfect anarchy.[4] The constraints constitute lawful government.

Hobbes believed that the only alternatives for human society are, in effect, anarchy or absolute monarchy. Given those alternatives, said Hobbes, a rational person would choose a monarch to ensure the equality of political rights, rather than take his chances with perfect freedom. His successor in English political thought, John Locke, did not accept the Hobbesian choice between despotism and anarchy. He conceived of people in a state of nature as being in "a *State* also of *Equality*, wherein all the Power and Jurisdiction is reciprocal, no one having more than another,"[5] and sought to preserve that condition in actual societies through a strictly limited government. What Locke propounded is especially pertinent here because it was his theory that the American Founders brought into reality.

But with Locke also arose a confusion, which has grown steadily with passing time. For most contemporary Americans who are aware of Locke at all, he is identified with the idea of man as tabula rasa, a blank slate on which experience writes. Without experience, Locke is often believed to have said, individuals are both equal and empty, a blank slate to be written upon by the environment. Many contemporary libertarians who draw their inspiration from Locke are hostile to the possibility of genetic differences in intelligence because of their conviction that equal rights apply only if in fact people at birth are tabulae rasae. With that in mind, consider these remarks about human intelligence from Locke's *An Essay on Human Understanding*:

> Now that there is such a difference between men in respect of their understandings, I think nobody who has had any conversation with his neighbors will question. . . . Which great difference in men's intellectuals, whether it rises from any defect in the organs of the body particularly adapted to thinking, or in the dullness or untractableness of those faculties for want of use, or, as some think, in the natural dif-

ferences of men's souls themselves; or some or all of these together, it matters not here to examine. Only this is evident, that there is a difference of degrees in men's understandings, apprehensions, and reasonings, to so great a latitude that one may, without doing injury to mankind, affirm that there is a greater distance between some men and others in this respect, than between some men and some beasts.[6]

Locke is strikingly indifferent to the source of cognitive differences and strikingly harsh in his judgment about their size. But that does not mean he believed people to have different rights. They are equal in rights, Locke proclaimed, though they be unequal in everything else. Those rights, however, are negative rights (to impose contemporary terminology): They give all human beings the right *not* to have certain things done to them by the state or by other human beings, not the right *to* anything, except freedom of action.

This way of putting it is out of tune with the modern sensibility. The original concept of equal rights is said to be meaningless cant, outmoded; taking equal rights seriously, it is thought, requires enforcing equal outcomes. The prevailing political attitude is so dismissive toward the older conception of equal rights that it is difficult to think of serious public treatments of it; the Founders just didn't think hard enough about that problem, it seems to be assumed. If he were alive today, some eminent political scientists have argued, Thomas Jefferson would surely be a social democrat or at least a New Deal Democrat.[7] We are asking that you consider the alternative: that the Founders were fully aware of how unequal people are, that they did not try to explain away natural inequalities, and that they nonetheless thought the best way for people to live together was under a system of equal rights.

The Founders wrote frankly about the inequality of men. For Thomas Jefferson, it was obvious that they were especially unequal in virtue and intelligence. He was thankful for a "natural aristocracy" that could counterbalance the deficiencies of the others, an "aristocracy of virtue and talent, which Nature has wisely provided for the direction of the interests of society."[8] It was, he once wrote, "the most precious gift of nature," and he thought that the best government was one that most efficiently brought the natural aristocracy to high positions.[9]

Jefferson saw the consequences of inequalities of ability radiating throughout the institutions of society. The main purpose of education, he believed, was to prepare the natural aristocracy to govern, and he did not mince words. The "best geniuses" should be "raked from the rubbish annually" by competitive grading and examinations, sent on to the next educational stage, and finally called to public life.[10] But if the author of the Declaration of Independence was by today's standards unrepentantly elitist, he was nonetheless a democrat in his belief that the natural aristocracy was "scattered with equal hand through all [of society's] conditions,"[11] and in his confidence that the electorate had the good sense to choose them. "Leave to the citizens the free election and separation of the *aristoi* from the pseudo-*aristoi*," he advised. "In general, they will elect the real good and wise."[12] For Madison, the "great republican principle" was that the common people would have the public-spiritedness and the information necessary to choose "men of virtue and wisdom" to govern them.[13] For both Jefferson and Madison, *political* equality was both right and workable. They would have been amazed by the notion that humans are equal in any other sense.

Nor were Jefferson's and Madison's views a reflection of their southern heritage. John Adams, that quintessential Yankee, agreed that "natural aristocracy is a fact essential to be considered in the institution of government"—or, as he put it in another instance, "I believe there is as much in the breed of men as there is in that of horses."[14] He was not as optimistic as Jefferson and Madison, for he was keenly aware that intelligence does not necessarily go with virtue, and he was fearful that Jefferson's natural aristocracy would within a few generations have cemented its descendants' positions into that of a ruling caste. But he did not doubt that the reality of human inequalities was of central political importance.[15]

The other Founders, including Hamilton and Washington, ruminated in the same vein about the inequality of men and the political implications of that inequality. In doing so, they were following an ancient tradition. Political philosophers have always begun from the understanding that good policy must be in accordance with what is good for human beings, and that what is good for humans must be based on an understanding of how they are similar and how they differ. Aristotle put it earliest and perhaps best: "All men believe that justice means equality in some sense. . . . The question we must keep in mind is, equality or inequality in what sort of thing."[16]

The Founders saw that making a stable and just government was difficult precisely *because* men were unequal in every respect except their right to advance their own interests. Men had "different and unequal faculties of acquiring property," Madison reflected in *The Federalist*.[17] This diversity was the very reason why rights of property were so important and why "the protection of those faculties is the first object of Government." But the diversity was also the defect of populist democracy, because the unequal distribution of property to which it led was "the most common and durable source of factions." And faction, he argued, was the great danger that the Constitution sought above all to confine and tame. The task of government was to set unequal persons into a system of laws and procedures that would, as nearly as possible, equalize their rights while allowing their differences to express themselves. The result would not necessarily be serene or quiet, but it would be just. It might even work.

In reminding you of these views of the men who founded America, we are not appealing to their historical eminence, but to their wisdom. We think they were right. Let us stop using words like *factions* and *faculties* and *aristoi* and state in our own words, briefly and explicitly, how and why we think they were right in ways that apply today.

The egalitarian ideal of contemporary political theory underestimates the importance of the differences that separate human beings. It fails to come to grips with human variation. It overestimates the ability of political interventions to shape human character and capacities. The systems of government that are necessary to carry out the egalitarian agenda ignore the forces that the Founders described in *The Federalist*, which lead inherently and inevitably to tyranny, throughout history and across cultures. These defects in the egalitarian tradition are reflected in political experience, where the failure of the communist bloc to construct happy societies is palpably apparent and the ultimate fate of even the more benign egalitarian model in Scandinavia is coming into question.

The perversions of the egalitarian ideal that began with the French Revolution and have been so plentiful in the twentieth century are not accidents of history or produced by technical errors in implementation. Something more inevitable is at work. People who are free to behave differently from one another in the important affairs of daily life inevitably generate the social and economic inequalities that egalitarianism seeks to suppress. That, we believe, is as close to an immutable law as the uncertainties of sociology permit. To reduce inequality of condition, the state must impose greater and greater uniformity. Perhaps that is as close to an immutable law as political science permits. In T. H. White's version of the Arthurian legend, *The Once and Future King*,

Merlyn transforms young Arthur into an ant as part of his education in governance. In this guise, Arthur approaches the entrance to the ant colony, where over the entrance are written the words, EVERYTHING NOT FORBIDDEN IS COMPULSORY.[18] Such, in our view, is where the logic of the egalitarian ideal ultimately leads. It is appropriate in the ant colony or the beehive but not for human beings. Egalitarian tyrannies, whether of the Jacobite or the Leninist variety, are worse than inhumane. They are inhuman.

The same atmosphere prevails on a smaller scale wherever "equality" comes to serve as the basis for a diffuse moral outlook. Consider the many small tyrannies in America's contemporary universities, where it has become objectionable to say that some people are superior to other people in any way that is relevant to life in society. Nor is this outlook confined to judgments about people. In art, literature, ethics, and cultural norms, differences are not to be judged. Such relativism has become the moral high ground for many modern commentators on life and culture.

Even the existence of differences must be discussed gingerly, when they are human differences. As soon as the differences are associated with membership in a group, censorship arises. In this book, we have trod on one of those most sensitive areas by talking about ethnic differences, but there are many others. In what respects do men differ from women? Young differ from old? Heterosexuals from homosexuals? The permissible answers, often even the permissible questions, are sharply circumscribed. The moral outlook that has become associated with equality has spawned a vocabulary of its own. Discrimination, once a useful word with a praiseworthy meaning, is now almost always used in a pejorative sense. Racism, sexism, ageism, elitism—all are in common parlance, and their meanings continue to spread, blotting up more and more semantic territory.

The ideology of equality has done some good. For example, it is not possible as a practical matter to be an identifiable racist or sexist and still hold public office. But most of its effects are bad. Given the power of contemporary news media to imprint a nationwide image overnight, mainstream political figures have found that their allegiance to the rhetoric of equality must extend very far indeed, for a single careless remark can irretrievably damage or even end a public career. In everyday life, the ideology of equality censors and straitjackets everything from pedagogy to humor. The ideology of equality has stunted the range of moral dialogue to triviality. In daily life—conversations, the lessons taught in public schools, the kinds of screenplays or newspaper feature stories that people choose to write—the moral ascendancy of equality has made it difficult to use concepts such as virtue, excellence, beauty and—above all—truth.

Within the realm of government, small versions of the "everything not forbidden is compulsory" mentality may be seen everywhere. The informal old American principle governing personal behavior was that you could do whatever you wanted as long you didn't force anyone else to go along with you and as long as you let the other fellow go about his affairs with equal freedom. The stopping point was defined by the useful adage, "Your freedom to swing your arm stops where my nose begins."[19] In laws great and small, this principle has been perverted beyond recognition, as the notions of what constitutes "where my nose begins" stretch far out into space. The practice of affirmative action has been a classic example of the "everything not forbidden is compulsory" mentality, as the idea of forbidding people to discriminate by race mutated into the idea of compelling everyone to help produce equal outcomes by race. In tort law, the destruction of the concept of negligence grew out of an explicitly egalitarian view of the purpose of liability—not to redress individual victims for acts of irresponsibility but to redistribute goods more equitably.[20] In personal life, the idea of forbidding people from interfering with members of other groups (blacks, homosexuals, women) as they went about their lives has been extended to the idea of compelling people to "treat them the same." It is a mark of how far things have gone that many people no longer can see the distinction between "not interfering" and "treating the same."

Our views on all of these issues are decidedly traditional. We think that rights are embedded in our freedom to act, not in the obligations we may impose on others to act; that equality of rights is crucial while equality of outcome is not; that concepts such as virtue, excellence, beauty, and truth should be reintroduced into moral discourse. We are comfortable with the idea that some things are better than others—not just according to our subjective point of view but according to enduring standards of merit and inferiority—and at the same time reject the thought that we (or anyone else) should have the right to impose those standards. We are enthusiastic about diversity—the rich, unending diversity that free human beings generate as a matter of course, not the imposed diversity of group quotas.

And so we come to this final chapter, discussing the broadest policy implications of all that has gone before. We bring to our recommendations a predisposition, believing that the original American conceptions of human equality and the pursuit of happiness still offer the wisest guidance for thinking about how to run today's America. These have been some of our reasons why.

LETTING PEOPLE FIND VALUED PLACES IN SOCIETY

With these thoughts on the table, let us return to the question that opened the chapter: *How should policy deal with the twin realities that people differ in intelligence for reasons that are not their fault and that intelligence has a powerful bearing on how well people do in life?* The answer turns us back to the ancient concern with place.

The Goal and a Definition

The broadest goal is a society in which people throughout the functional range of intelligence can find, and feel they have found, a valued place for themselves. For "valued place," we offer a pragmatic definition: *You occupy a valued place if other people would miss you if you were gone.* The fact that you would be missed *means* that you were valued. Both the quality and quantity of valued places are important. Most people hope to find a soulmate for life, and that means someone who would "miss you" in the widest and most intense way. The definition captures the reason why children are so important in defining a valued place. But besides the quality of the valuing, quantity too is important. If a single person would miss you and no one else, you have a fragile hold on your place in society, no matter how much that one person cares for you. To have many different people who would miss you, in many different parts of your life and at many levels of intensity, is a hallmark of a person whose place is well and thoroughly valued. One way of thinking about policy options is to ask whether they aid or obstruct this goal of creating valued places.

Finding Valued Places

The great bulk of the American population is amply equipped, in their cognitive resources and in other personal characteristics, to find valued places in society. We must emphasize that, because for hundreds of pages we have focused on people at the two tails of the bell curve. Now is a good time to recall the people in the broad part of the curve, between the extremes. In figure after figure throughout Chapter 16, the pattern was consistent: The prevalence of the social maladies we reviewed was strikingly concentrated in the bottom IQ deciles. By the time people were even approaching average IQ, the percentages of people who were poor, had babies out of wedlock, provided poor environments for their children, or exhibited any other problem constituted small percentages of the population. Translated into the themes we are about to introduce, the evidence throughout this book supports the proposition that most people by far have enough intelligence for getting on with the business of life. We believe the policies we advocate will benefit them as well, by creating a generally richer and more vital society, but it should be made explicit: Our solutions assume that the average American is an asset, not part of the problem.

Finding Valued Places If You Aren't Very Smart: The Traditional Context

Nonetheless, millions of Americans have levels of cognitive ability low enough to make their lives statistically much more difficult than life is for most other people. How may policy help or obstruct them as they go about their lives? Our thesis is that it used to be easier for people who are low in ability to find a valued place than it is now.

In a simpler America, being comparatively low in the qualities measured by IQ did not necessarily affect the ability to find a valued niche in society. Many such people worked on farms. When farms were small, technology was limited to the horse-drawn plow and a few hand tools, and the same subsistence crops were grown year after year. People who would score 80 or 90 on an IQ test could be competent farmworkers, not conspicuously distinguished from most other people in wealth, home, neighborhood, or status in the community. Much the same could be said of a wide variety of skilled and unskilled trades. Even an unskilled laborer who was noticeably lower on the economic scale was part of a community in which many others with many levels of ability lived close to him, literally and socially. Inevitably, with technological advances, the niches for the less intelligent have shrunk.

As for the most intimate affiliations—marriage and children—there formerly was little difference between people of varying abilities: To be married meant to be responsible for each other, and for the children of that marriage, in unqualified and uncompromising ways that the entire community held to be of the highest importance. Those who met those responsibilities had a valued place in the community by definition. Those who failed conspicuously in those responsibilities were outcasts by definition. Meeting the responsibilities of marriage and parenthood did not take a lot of money and did not take high intelligence. The community provided clear and understandable incentives for doing what needed to be done.

Urban communities were somewhat different from small towns in these respects but not unrecognizably so. The top socioeconomic layer moved off to its own part of town, but this left a broad range of people living together in the rest of a city's neighborhoods, and the social functioning of those neighborhoods shared many characteristics with small towns. The responsibilities of marriage and children were as clearly defined in urban neighborhoods as in rural ones, and success and failure in those responsibilities were as visibly rewarded and punished.

As for the other ways in which people found valued places for themselves, urban neighborhoods teemed with useful things to do. Anyone who wanted to have a place in the community could find one in the local school boards, churches, union halls, garden clubs, and benevolent associations of one sort or another. The city government provided the police who walked the local beat. It ran the courthouse and public hospital downtown, and perhaps an orphanage and a home for the aged, but otherwise the neighborhood had to do for itself just about everything that needed doing to keep the social contract operative and daily life on an even keel. Someone who was mentally a bit dull might not be chosen to head up the parish clothing drive but was certainly eligible to help out. And these were just the organized aspects of community life. The unorganized web of interactions was even more extensive and provided still more ways in which people of all abilities, including those without much intelligence, could fit in.

It is not necessary to idealize old-fashioned neighborhoods or old-fashioned families to accept the description we have just given. All sorts of human problems, from wretched marriages to neighborhood feuds and human misery of every other sort, could be found. Poverty was rampant (recall from Chapter 5 that more than half of the population prior to War II was in poverty by today's definition). Even so, when the responsibilities of marriage and parenthood were clear and uncompromising and when the stuff of community life had to be carried out by the neighborhood or it wouldn't get done, society was full of accessible valued places for people of a broad range of abilities.

Finding Valued Places If You Aren't Very Smart: The Contemporary Context

Out of the myriad things that have changed since the beginning of the century, two overlapping phenomena have most affected people with modest abilities: It has become harder to make a living to support the valued roles of spouse, parent, and neighbor, and functions have been stripped from one main source of valued place, the neighborhood.

THE ECONOMIC ARGUMENT. The cognitive elite has pulled away from the rest of the population economically, becoming more prosperous even as real wages in the rest of the economy stagnated or fell. The divergence has been most conspicuous in the lowest-skilled jobs. From their high point in 1973, the median earnings of full-time workers in general nonfarm labor had fallen by 36 percent by 1990, far more than for any other category.[21] A strong back isn't worth what it used to be. Workers in those occupations have been demoralized. They have lost their valued place in the workplace.

So far, we agree that economics plays an important role in taking valued places in the workplace from those with low cognitive ability. But the argument typically widens, asserting that economic change also explains why people in low-skill occupations experience the loss of other valued places evidenced by falling marriage rates and rising illegitimacy: Men in low-skill jobs no longer make enough money to support a family, it is said. This common argument is too simplistic. In constant dollars, the income of a full-time, year-round male worker in general nonfarm labor in 1991 was at the level of his counterpart in 1958, when the norm was still one income per family, marriage rates were as high as ever, and illegitimacy was a fraction of its current levels. We may look back still further: The low-skill laborer in 1991 made about twice the real income of his counterpart in 1920, a year when no one thought to question whether a laborer could support a family.[22] Economics is relevant in understanding how it has become harder for people of modest abilities to find a valued place, and solutions should take economics into account. But economics is not decisive.

STRIPPING FUNCTIONS FROM THE NEIGHBORHOOD. Communities are rich and vital places to the extent that they engage their members in the stuff of life—birth, death, raising children, making a living, helping friends, singing in the local choir or playing on the softball team, coping with problems, setting examples, welcoming, chastising, celebrating, reconciling, and negotiating.[23]

If there is one theme on which observers from both left and right recently sound very much alike, it is that something vital and important has drained out of American communities.[24] Most adults need something to do with their lives other than going to work, and that something consists of being stitched into a fabric of family and community. In the preceding chapter, we alluded to the federal domination of public policy that has augmented the cognitive elite's political leverage during the last thirty years. The same process has had the collateral effect of stripping the neighborhood of much of the stuff of life. For what seemed like sufficient reasons at the time, Congress and presidents have deemed it necessary to remove more and more functions from the neighborhood. The entire social welfare system, services and cash payments alike, may be viewed in that light. Certain tasks—such as caring for the poor, for example—were deemed to be too difficult or too poorly performed by the spontaneous efforts of neighborhoods and voluntary organizations, and hence were transferred. The states have joined in this process. Whether federal and state policymakers were right to think that neighborhoods had failed and that the centralized government has done better is still a subject of debate, as is the net effect of the transfers, but the transfers did indeed occur and they stripped neighborhoods of traditional functions.[25]

The cognitive elite may not detect the declining vitality in the local community. For many of them, the house is important—its size, location, view, grounds. They may want the right kind of address and the right kind of neighbors. But their lives are centered outside a geographic community; their professional associates and friends may be scattered over miles of suburbs, or for that matter across the nation and the world. For large segments of American society, however, the geographic neighborhood is the major potential resource for infusing life with much of its meaning. Even the cognitive elite needs local communities, if not for itself, then for those of its children who happen not to land at the top of the cognitive ability distribution. The massive transfer of functions from the locality to the government has stripped neighborhoods of their traditional shared tasks. Instead, we have neighborhoods that are merely localities, not communities of people tending to their communal affairs. Valued places in a neighborhood are created only to the extent that the people in a neighborhood have valued tasks to do.

People who have never lived in such a neighborhood—and as time goes on this includes more and more of the cognitive elite and the affluent in general—often find this hard to believe. It is another case of the isolation we discussed in Chapter 21: They may read about such communities in books, but surely they no longer exist in real life. But they do. Thumb through a few weeks' issues of the newspaper from any small town, and you will find an America that is still replete with fund-raising suppers for the local child who has cancer, drives to collect food and clothing for a family that has suffered a reverse, and even barn raisings. They may exist as well (though they are less well documented) in urban working-class neighborhoods that have managed to retain their identity. It is through such activities that much of the real good for the disadvantaged is accomplished. Beyond that, they have a crucial role, so hard to see from a Washington office, of creating ways for people of a wide level of incomes and abilities to play a part. It creates ways for them to be known—not just as a name but as a helpful fellow, a useful person to know, the woman you can always count on. It creates ways in which you would be missed if you were gone.

Thus arises our first general policy prescription: *A wide range of social functions should be restored to the neighborhood when possible and otherwise to the municipality.* The reason for doing so, in the context of this book, is not to save money, not even because such services will be provided more humanely and efficiently by neighborhoods (though we believe that generally to be the case), but because this is one of the best ways to multiply the valued places that people can fill. As the chapter continues, we will offer some other possibilities for accomplishing this and collateral objectives. But before arguing about how it is to be done, we hope that there can be wide agreement on the importance of the goal: In a decent postindustrial society, neighborhoods shall not have lost their importance as a source of human satisfactions and as a generator of valued places that all sorts of people can fill. Government policy can do much to foster the vitality of neighborhoods by trying to do less for them.

SIMPLIFYING RULES

The thesis of this section may be summarized quickly: As of the end of the twentieth century, the United States is run by rules that are congenial to people with high IQs and that make life more difficult for everyone else. This is true in the areas of criminal justice, marriage and divorce, welfare and tax policy, and business law, among others. It is true of rules that have been intended to help ordinary people—rules that govern schooling, medical practice, the labeling of goods, to pick some examples. It has happened not because the cognitive elite consciously usurped the writing of the rules but because of the cognitive stratification described throughout the book. The trend has affected not just those at the low end of the cognitive distribution but just about everybody who is not part of the cognitive and economic elites.

The systems have been created, bit by bit, over decades, by people who think that complicated, sophisticated operationalizations of fairness, justice, and right and wrong are ethically superior to simple, black-and-white versions. The cognitive elite may not be satisfied with these systems as they stand at any given point, but however they may reform them, the systems are sure to become more complex. Additionally, complex systems are precisely the ones that give the cognitive elite the greatest competitive advantage. Deciphering complexity is one of the things that cognitive ability is most directly good for.

We have in mind two ways in which the rules generated by the cognitive elite are making life more difficult for everyone else. Each requires somewhat more detailed explanation.

Making It Easier to Make a Living

First come all the rules that make life more difficult for people who are trying to navigate everyday life. In looking for examples, the 1040 income tax form is such an easy target that it need only be mentioned to make the point. But the same complications and confusions apply to a single woman with children seeking government assistance or a person who is trying to open a dry-cleaning shop. As the cognitive elite busily goes about making the world a better place, it is not so important to them that they are complicating ordinary lives. It's not so complicated to *them*.

The same burden of complications that are only a nuisance to people who are smart are much more of a barrier to people who are not. In many cases, such barriers effectively block off avenues for people who are not cognitively equipped to struggle through the bureaucracy. In other cases, they reduce the margin of success so much that they make the difference between success and failure. "Sweat equity," though the phrase itself has been recently coined, is as distinctively an American concept as "equality before the law" and "liberty." You could get ahead by plain hard work. No one would stand in your way. Today that is no longer true. American society has erected barriers to individual sweat equity, by saying, in effect, "Only people who are good at navigating complex rules need apply." Anyone who has tried to open or run a small business in recent years can supply evidence of how formidable those barriers have become.

Credentialism is a closely related problem. It goes all the way up the cognitive range—the Ph.D. is often referred to as "the union card" by graduate students who want to become college professors—but it is especially irksome and obstructive for occupations further down the ladder. Increasingly, occupations must be licensed, whether the service involves barbering or taking care of neighborhood children. The theory is persuasive—do you want someone taking care of your child who is not qualified?—but the practice typically means jumping through bureaucratic hoops that have little to do with one's ability to do the job. The rise of licensing is both a symptom and a cause of diminishing personal ties, along with the mutual trust that goes with those ties. The licensing may have some small capacity to filter out the least competent, but the benefits are often outweighed by the costs of the increased bureaucratization.

Enough examples. American society is rife with them. In many ways, life is more complicated than it used to be, and there's nothing to be done about it. But as the cognitive elite has come to power, it has trailed in its wake a detritus of complexities as well, individually minor, that together have reshaped society so that the average person has a much tougher time running his own life. Our policy recommendation is to stop it and strip away the nonsense. Consider the costs of complexity itself. Return to the assumption that in America the government has no business getting in people's way except for the most compelling reasons, with "compelling" required to meet a stiff definition.

Making It Easier to Live a Virtuous Life

We start with the supposition that almost everyone is capable of being a morally autonomous human being most of the time and given suitable circumstances. Political scientist James Q. Wilson has put this case eloquently in *The Moral Sense,* calling on a wide range of social science findings to support an old but lately unfashionable truth: Human beings in general are capable of deciding between right and wrong.[26] This does not mean, however, that everyone is capable of deciding between right and wrong with the same sophistication and nuances. The difference between people of low cognitive ability and the rest of society may be put in terms of a metaphor: Everyone has a moral compass, but some of those compasses are more susceptible to magnetic storms than others. First, consider crime, then marriage.

CRIME. Imagine living in a society where the rules about crime are simple and the consequences are equally simple. "Crime" consists of a few obviously wrong acts: assault, rape, murder, robbery, theft, trespass, destruction of another's property, fraud. Someone who commits a crime is probably caught—and almost certainly punished. The punishment almost certainly hurts (it is meaningful). Punishment follows arrest quickly, within a matter of days or weeks. The members of the society subscribe to the underlying codes of conduct with enthusiasm and near unanimity. They teach and enforce them whenever appropriate. Living in such a world, the moral compass shows simple, easily understood directions. North is north, south is south, right is right, wrong is wrong.

Now imagine that all the rules are made more complicated. The number of acts defined as crimes has multiplied, so that many things that are crimes are not nearly as obviously "wrong" as something like robbery or assault. The link between moral transgression and committing crime is made harder to understand. Fewer crimes lead to an arrest. Fewer arrests lead to prosecution. Many times, the prosecutions are not for something the accused person did but for an offense that the defense lawyer and the prosecutor agreed upon. Many times, people who are prosecuted are let off, though everyone (including the accused) acknowledges that the person was guilty. When people are convicted, the consequences have no apparent connection to how much harm they have done. These events are typically spread out over months and sometimes years. To top it all off, even the "wrongness" of the basic crimes is called into question. In the society at large (and translated onto the television and movie screens), it is commonly argued that robbery, for example, is not always wrong if it is in a good cause (stealing medicine to save a dying wife) or if it is in response to some external condition (exploitation, racism, etc.). At every level, it becomes fashionable to point out the complexities of moral decisions, and all the ways in which things that might seem "wrong" at first glance are really "right" when properly analyzed.

The two worlds we have described are not far removed from the contrast between the criminal justice system in the United States as recently as the 1950s and that system as of the 1990s. We are arguing that a person with comparatively low intelligence, whose time horizon is short and ability to balance many competing and complex incentives is low, has much more difficulty following a moral compass in the 1990s than he would have in the 1950s. Put aside your feelings about whether these changes in the criminal justice system represent progress. Simply consider them as a magnetic storm—as a set of changes that make the needle pointing to right and wrong waver erratically if you happen to be looking at the criminal justice system from the perspective of a person who is not especially bright. People of limited intelligence can lead moral lives in a society that is run on the basis of "Thou shalt not steal." They find it much harder to lead moral lives in a society that is run on the basis of "Thou shalt not steal unless there is a really good reason to."[27]

The policy prescription is that the criminal justice system should be made *simpler*. The meaning of criminal offenses used to be clear and objective, and so were the consequences. It is worth trying to make them so again.

MARRIAGE. It has become much more difficult for a person of low cognitive ability to figure out why marriage is a good thing, and, once in a marriage, more difficult to figure out why one should stick with it through bad times. The magnetic storm has swept through from many directions.

The sexual revolution is the most obvious culprit. The old bargain from the man's point of view—get married, because that's the only way you're going to be able to sleep with the lady—was the kind of incentive that did not require a lot of intellect to process and had an all-powerful effect on behavior. Restoring it is not feasible by any (reasonable) policy we can think of

But the state has interfered as well to make it more difficult for people with little intelligence to do that thing—find a compatible partner and get married—that constitutes the most accessible and richest of all valued places. Marriage fills a vital role in people's lives to the extent that it is hallowed as an institution and as a relationship unlike any other. Marriage is satisfying to the extent that society validates these propositions: "Yes, you may have a baby outside marriage if you choose; but it isn't the same." "Yes, you may live with someone without marrying, but it isn't the same." "Yes, you may say that you are committed to someone without marrying, but it isn't the same."

Once sex was no longer playing as important a role in the decision to marry, it was essential that these other unique attributes of marriage be highlighted and reinforced. But the opposite has happened. Repeatedly, the prerogatives and responsibilities that used to be limited to marriage have spilled over into nonmarital relationships, whether it is the rights and responsibilities of an unmarried father, medical coverage for same-sex partners, or palimony cases. Once the law says, "Well, in a legal sense, living together *is* the same," what is the point of getting married?

For most people, there are still answers to that question. Even given the diminished legal stature of marriage, marriage continues to have unique value. But to see those values takes forethought about the long-term differences between living together and being married, sensitivity to many intangibles, and an appreciation of second-hand and third-hand consequences. As Chapter 8's evidence about marriage rates implies, people low on the intelligence distribution are less likely to think through those issues than others.

Our policy prescription in this instance is to return marriage to its formerly unique legal status. If you are married, you take on obligations. If you are not married, you don't. In particular, we urge that marriage once again become the sole legal institution through which rights and responsibilities regarding children are exercised. If you are an unmarried mother, you have no legal basis for demanding that the father of the child provide support. If you are an unmarried father, you have no legal standing regarding the child—not even a right to see the child, let alone any basis honored by society for claiming he or she is "yours" or that you are a "father."

We do not expect such changes miraculously to resuscitate marriage in the lowest cognitive classes, but they are a step in the return to a simpler valuation of it. A family is unique and highly desirable. To start one, you have to get married. The role of the state in restoring the rewards of marriage is to validate once again the rewards that marriage naturally carries with it.

More General Implications for Policy

Crime and marriage are only examples of a general principle: Modern American society can be simplified. No law of nature says that the increasing complexity of technology must be matched by a new complexity in the way the nation is governed. The increasing complexity of technology follows from the functions it serves. The increasing complexity of government does not. Often the complexities introduced by technology require highly sophisticated *analysis* before good law and regulation can be developed. But as a rule of thumb, the more sophisticated the analysis, the simpler the policies can be. Policy is usually complicated because it has been built incrementally through a political process, not because it has needed to become more complicated. The time has come to make simplification a top priority in reforming policy—not for a handful of regulations but across the board.

More broadly, we urge that it is possible once again to make a core of common law, combined with the original concepts of negligence and liability in tort law, the mechanism for running society—easily understood by all and a basis for the straightforward lessons that parents at all levels of cognitive ability above the lowest can teach their children about how to behave as they grow up. We readily acknowledge that modernity requires some amplifications of this simple mechanism, but the nation needs to think through those amplifications from the legal equivalent of zero-based budgeting. As matters stand, the legal edifice has become a labyrinth that only the rich and the smart can navigate.

BLANKS UNFILLED

We have presented what we believe needs to be done. We also understand that a common response will be incredulity, for different readers will interpret the long chapters that have come before as a manifesto for completely different kinds of policy initiatives. Specifically, two lines of argument are likely to follow from this book. To some, we will have made a case for increased income redistribution. To others, we will have made a case for steps to manipulate the fertility of people with high and low IQs. We will be pleased if the book leads to a vigorous discussion of these issues, but we have just a few words to say about them here.

Dealing with Income

Ever since most people quit believing that a person's income on earth reflects God's judgment of his worth, it has been argued that income distributions are inherently unfair; most wealthy people do not "deserve" their wealth nor the poor their poverty. That being the case, it is appropriate for societies to take from the rich and give to the poor. The statistical relationship we have documented between low cognitive ability and income is more evidence that the world is not fair.

But it is not news that the world is unfair. You knew before reading this book that income differences arise from many arbitrary causes, sociological and psychological, besides differences in intelligence. All of them are reflected in correlations of varying sizes, which mean all of them are riddled with exceptions. This complicates solutions. Whenever individual cases are examined, differences in circumstances will be found that *do* reflect the individual's fault or merit. The data in this book support old arguments for supplementing the income of the poor without giving any new guidance for how to do it.

The evidence about cognitive ability causes us to be sympathetic to the straightforward proposition that "trying hard" ought to be rewarded. Our prescription, borrowing from the case made by political scientist David Ellwood, is that people who work full time should not be too poor to have a decent standard of living, even if the kinds of work they can do are not highly valued in the marketplace.[28] We do not put this as a principle of government for all countries—getting everybody out of poverty is not an option in most of the world—but it is appropriate for rich countries to try to do.

How? There is no economically perfect alternative. Any government supplement of wages produces negative effects of many kinds. Such defects are not the results of bad policy design but inherent. The least damaging strategies are the simplest ones, which do not try to oversee or manipulate the labor market behavior of low-income people, but rather augment their earned income up to a floor. The earned income tax credit, already in place, seems to be a generally good strategy, albeit with the unavoidable drawbacks of any income supplement.[29]

We will not try to elaborate on these arguments here. We leave the income issue with this: As America enters the twenty-first century, it is inconceivable that it will return to a laissez-faire system regarding income. Some sort of redistribution is here to stay. The question is how to redistribute in ways that increase the chances for people at the bottom of society to take control of their lives, to be engaged meaningfully in their communities, and to find valued places for themselves. Cash supplements need not compete with that goal, whereas the social welfare system that the nation has developed in the twentieth century most definitely does. We should be looking for ways to replace the latter with the former.

Dealing with Demography

Of all the uncomfortable topics we have explored, a pair of the most uncomfortable ones are that a society with a higher mean IQ is also likely to be a society with fewer social ills and brighter economic prospects, and that the most efficient way to raise the IQ of a society is for smarter women to have higher birth rates than duller women. Instead, America is going in the opposite direction, and the implication is a future America with more social ills and gloomier economic prospects. These conclusions follow directly from the evidence we have presented at such length, and yet we have so far been silent on what to do about it.

We are silent partly because we are as apprehensive as most other people about what might happen when a government decides to social-engineer who has babies and who doesn't. We can imagine no recommendation for using the government to manipulate fertility that does not have dangers. But this highlights the problem: The United States already has policies that inadvertently social-engineer who has babies, and it is encouraging the wrong women. *If the United States did as much to encourage high-IQ women to have babies as it now does to encourage low-IQ women, it would rightly be described as engaging in aggressive manipulation of fertility.* The technically precise description of America's fertility policy is that it subsidizes births among poor women, who are also disproportionately at the low end of the intelligence distribution. We urge generally that these policies, represented by the extensive network of cash and services for low-income women who have babies, be ended.

The government should stop subsidizing births to anyone, rich or poor. The other generic recommendation, as close to harmless as any government program we can imagine, is to make it easy for women to make good on their prior decision not to get pregnant by making available birth control mechanisms that are increasingly flexible, foolproof, inexpensive, and safe.

The other demographic factor we discussed in Chapter 15 was immigration and the evidence that recent waves of immigrants are, on the average, less successful and probably less able, than earlier waves. There is no reason to assume that the hazards associated with low cognitive ability in America are somehow circumvented by having been born abroad or having parents or grandparents who were. An immigrant population with low cognitive ability will—again, on the average—have trouble not only in finding good work but have trouble in school, at home, and with the law.

This is not the place, nor are we the people, to try to rewrite immigration law. But we believe that the main purpose of immigration law should be to serve America's interests. It should be among the goals of public policy to shift the flow of immigrants away from those admitted under the nepotistic rules (which broadly encourage the reunification of relatives) and toward those admitted under competency rules, already established in immigration law—not to the total exclusion of nepotistic and humanitarian criteria but a shift. Perhaps our central thought about immigration is that present policy assumes an indifference to the individual characteristics of immigrants that no society can indefinitely maintain without danger.

CONCLUSION

Hundreds of pages ago, in the Preface, we reflected on the question that we have been asked so often, "What good can come from writing this book?" We have tried to answer it in many ways.

Our first answer has been implicit, scattered in material throughout the book. For thirty years, vast changes in American life have been instituted by the federal government to deal with social problems. We have tried to point out what a small segment of the population accounts for such a large proportion of those problems. To the extent that the problems of this small segment are susceptible to social-engineering solutions at all, they should be highly targeted. The vast majority of Americans can run their own lives just fine, and policy should above all be constructed so that it permits them to do so.

Our second answer, also implicit, has been that just about any policy in any area—education, employment, welfare, criminal justice, or the care of children—can profit if its designers ask how the policy accords with the wide variation in cognitive ability. Policies may fail not because they are inherently flawed but because they do not make allowances for how much people vary. There are hundreds of ways to frame bits and pieces of public policy so that they are based on a realistic appraisal of the responses they will get not from people who think like Rhodes scholars but people who think in simpler ways.

Our third answer has gone to specific issues in raising the cognitive functioning of the disadvantaged (Chapter 17) and in improving education for all (Chapter 18). Part of our answer has been cautionary: Much of public policy toward the disadvantaged starts from the premise that interventions can make up for genetic or environmental disadvantages, and that premise is overly optimistic. Part of our answer has been positive: Much can and should be done to improve education, especially for those who have the greatest potential.

Our fourth answer has been that group differences in cognitive ability, so desperately denied for so long, can best be handled—can *only* be handled—by a return to individualism. A person should not be judged as a member of a group but as an individual. With that cornerstone of the American doctrine once again in place, group differences can take their appropriately insignificant place in affecting American life. But until that cornerstone is once again in place, the anger, the hurt, and the animosities will continue to grow.

In this closing chapter, we have focused on another aspect of what makes America special. This most individualistic of nations contains one of the friendliest, most eager to oblige, neighborly peoples in all the world. Visitors to America from Tocqueville on down have observed it. As a by-product of this generosity and civic mindedness, America has had a genius for making valued places, for people of all kinds of abilities, given only that they played by a few basic rules.

Once we as a nation absorbed people of different cultures, abilities, incomes, and temperaments into communities that worked. The nation was good at it precisely because of, not in spite of, the freedom that

American individuals and communities enjoyed. Have there been exceptions to that generalization? Yes, predominantly involving race, and the nation rightly moved to rid itself of the enforced discrimination that lay behind those exceptions. Is the generalization nonetheless justified? Overwhelmingly so, in our judgment. Reducing that freedom has enervated our national genius for finding valued places for everyone; the genius will not be revitalized until the freedom is restored.

Cognitive partitioning will continue. It cannot be stopped, because the forces driving it cannot be stopped. But America can choose to preserve a society in which every citizen has access to the central satisfactions of life. Its people can, through an interweaving of choice and responsibility, create valued places for themselves in their worlds. They can live in communities—urban or rural—where being a good parent, a good neighbor, and a good friend will give their lives purpose and meaning. They can weave the most crucial safety nets together, so that their mistakes and misfortunes are mitigated and withstood with a little help from their friends.

All of these good things are available now to those who are smart enough or rich enough—if they can exploit the complex rules to their advantage, buy their way out of the social institutions that no longer function, and have access to the rich human interconnections that are growing, not diminishing, for the cognitively fortunate. We are calling upon our readers, so heavily concentrated among those who fit that description, to recognize the ways in which public policy has come to deny those good things to those who are not smart enough and rich enough.

At the heart of our thought is the quest for human dignity. The central measure of success for this government, as for any other, is to permit people to live lives of dignity—not to *give* them dignity, for that is not in any government's power, but to make it accessible to all. That is one way of thinking about what the Founders had in mind when they proclaimed, as a truth self-evident, that all men are created equal. That is what we have in mind when we talk about valued places for everyone.

Inequality of endowments, including intelligence, is a reality. Trying to pretend that inequality does not really exist has led to disaster. Trying to eradicate inequality with artificially manufactured outcomes has led to disaster. It is time for America once again to try living with inequality, as life is lived: understanding that each human being has strengths and weaknesses, qualities we admire and qualities we do not admire, competencies and incompetences, assets and debits; that the success of each human life is not measured externally but internally; that of all the rewards we can confer on each other, the most precious is a place as a valued fellow citizen.

Appendix 1

Statistics for People Who Are Sure They Can't Learn Statistics

The short explanations of standard deviation (page 44), correlation (page 67), and regression (page 122) should be satisfactory for people who are at home with math but never took a statistics course. The longer explanations in this appendix are for people who would like to understand what *distribution*, *standard deviation*, *correlation*, and *regression* mean, but who are not at home with math.

DISTRIBUTIONS AND STANDARD DEVIATIONS

Why Do We Need "Standard Deviation"?

Every day, formally or informally, people make comparisons—among people, among apples and oranges, among dairy cows or egg-laying hens, among the screws being coughed out by a screw machine. The standard deviation is a measure of how spread out the things being compared are. "This egg is a lot bigger than average," a chicken farmer might say. The standard deviation is a way of saying precisely what "a lot" means.

What Is a Frequency Distribution?

To get a clear idea of what a frequency distribution is, imagine yourself back in your high school gym, with all the boys in the senior class in the school gym assembled before you (including both sexes would complicate matters, and the point of this discussion is to keep things simple). Line up these boys from left to right in order of height.

Now you have a long line going from shortest to tallest. As you look along the line you will see that only few boys are conspicuously short and tall. Most are in the middle, and a lot of them seem identical in height. Is there any way to get a better idea of how this pattern looks?

Tape a series of cards to the floor in a straight line from left to right, with "60 inches and shorter" written on the one at the far left, "80 inches and taller" on the card at the far right, and cards in 1-inch increments in between. Tell everyone to stand behind the card that corresponds to his height.

Someone loops a rope over the rafters and pulls you up in the air so you can look straight down on the tops of the heads of your classmates standing in their single files behind the height labels. The figure below shows what you see: a frequency distribution.[1] What good is it? Look-

The raw material of a frequency distribution

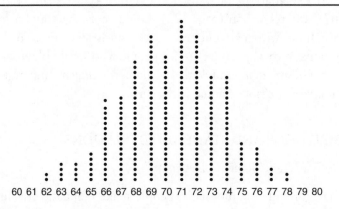

ing at your high school classmates standing around in a mob, you can tell very little about their height. Looking at those same classmates arranged into a frequency distribution, you can tell a lot, quickly and memorably.

How Is the Distribution Related to the Standard Deviation?

We still lack a convenient way of expressing where people are in that distribution. What does it mean to say that two different students are, say, 6 inches different in height. How "big" is a 6-inch difference? That brings us back to the standard deviation.

When it comes to high school students, you have a good idea of how big a 6-inch difference is. But what does a 6-inch difference mean if you are talking about the height of elephants? About the height of cats? It depends. And the things it depends on are the average height and how much height varies among the things you are measuring. A *standard de-*

viation gives you a way of taking both the average and that variability into ac-count, so that "6 inches" can be expressed in a way that means the same thing for high school students relative to other high school students, elephants rela-tive to other elephants, and cats relative to other cats.

How Do You Compute a Standard Deviation?

Suppose that your high school class consisted of just two people who were 66 inches and 70 inches. Obviously, the average is 68 inches. Just as obviously, one person is 2 inches shorter than average, one person is 2 inches taller than average. The standard deviation is a kind of aver-age of the differences from the mean—2 inches, in this example. Sup-pose you add two more people to the class, one who is 64 inches and the other who is 72 inches. The mean hasn't changed (the two new people balance each other off exactly). But the newcomers are each 4 inches different from the average height of 68 inches, so the standard devia-tion, which measures the spread, has gotten bigger as well. Now two people are 4 inches different from the average and two people are 2 inches different from the average. That adds up to a total 12 inches, di-vided among four persons. The simple average of these differences from the mean is 3 inches (12 ÷ 4), which is almost (but not quite) what the standard deviation is. To be precise, the standard deviation is calculated by squaring the deviations from the mean, then summing them, then finding their average, then taking the square root of the result. In this example, two people are 4 inches from the mean and two are 2 inches from the mean. The sum of the squared deviations is 40 (16 + 16 + 4 + 4). Their average is 10 (40 ÷ 4). And the square root of 10 is 3.16, which is the standard deviation for this example. The technical reasons for using the standard deviation instead of the simple average of the de-viations from the mean are not necessary to go into, except that, in nor-mal distributions, the standard deviation has wonderfully convenient properties. If you are looking for a short, easy way to think of a standard deviation, view it as the average difference from the mean.

As an example of how a standard deviation can be used to compare apples and oranges, suppose we are comparing the Olympic women's gymnastics team and NBA basketball teams. You see a woman who is 5 feet 6 inches and a man who is 7 feet. You know from watching gym-nastics on television that 5 feet 6 inches is tall for a woman gymnast, and 7 feet is tall even for a basketball player. But you want to do better than a general impression. Just *how* unusual is the woman, compared to the average gymnast on the U.S. women's team, and how unusual is the man, compared to the average basketball player on the U.S. men's team?

We gather data on height among all the women gymnasts, and determine that the mean is 5 feet 1 inches with a standard deviation (SD) of 2 inches. For the men basketball players, we find that the mean is 6 feet 6 inches and the SD is 4 inches. Thus the woman who is 5 feet 6 inches is 2.5 standard deviations taller than the average; the 7-foot man is only 1.5 standard deviations taller than the average. These numbers—2.5 for the woman and 1.5 for the man—are called *standard scores* in statistical jargon. Now we have an explicit numerical way to compare how different the two people are from their respective averages, and we have a basis for concluding that the woman who is 5 feet 6 inches is a lot taller relative to other female Olympic gymnasts than a 7-foot man is relative to other NBA basketball players.

How Much More Different? Enter the Normal Distribution

Even before coming to this book, most readers had heard the phrases *normal distribution* or *bell-shaped curve*, or, as in our title, *bell curve*. They refer to a common way that natural phenomena arrange themselves approximately. (The true normal distribution is a mathematical abstraction, never perfectly observed in nature.) If you look again at the distribution of high school boys that opened the discussion, you will see the makings of a bell curve. If we added several thousand more boys to it, the kinks and irregularities would smooth out, and it would actually get very close to a normal distribution. A perfect one is in the figure below.

A perfect bell curve

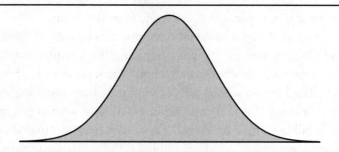

It makes sense that most things will be arranged in bell-shaped curves. Extremes tend to be rarer than the average. If that sounds like a tautology, it is only because bell curves are so common. Consider height again. Seven feet is "extreme" for humans. But if human height were distributed so that equal proportions of people were 5 feet, 6 feet, and 7 feet tall, the extreme would not be rarer than the average. It just so happens that the world hardly ever works that way.

Bell curves (or close approximations to them) are not only common in nature; they have a close mathematical affinity to the meaning of the standard deviation. In any true normal distribution, no matter whether the elements are the heights of basketball players, the diameters of screw heads, or the milk production of cows, 68.27 percent of all the cases fall in the interval between 1 standard deviation above the mean and 1 standard deviation below it. It is worth pausing a moment over this link between a relatively simple measure of spread in a distribution and the way things in everyday life vary, for it is one of nature's more remarkable uniformities.

In its mathematical form, the normal distribution extends to infinity in both directions, never quite reaching the horizontal axis. But for practical purposes, when we are talking about populations of people, a normal distribution is about 6 standard deviations wide. The next figure shows how the bell curve looks, cut up into six regions, each marked

A bell curve cut into standard deviations

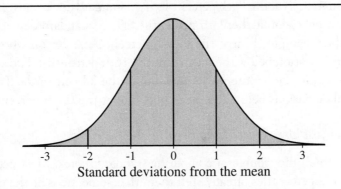

Standard deviations from the mean

by a standard deviation unit. The range within ± 3 standard deviation units includes 99.7 percent of a population that is distributed normally.

We can squeeze the axis and make it look narrow, or stretch it out and make it look wide, as shown in the following figure. Appearances notwithstanding, the mathematical shape is not really changing. The

Standard deviations cut off the same portions of the population for any normal distribution

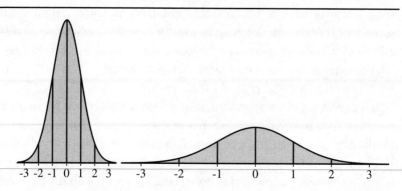

standard deviation continues to chop off proportionately the same size chunks of the distribution in each case. And therein lies its value. The standard deviation has the same meaning no matter whether the distribution is tall and skinny or short and wide.

Furthermore, there are some simple characteristics about these scores that make them especially valuable. As you can see by looking at the figures above, it makes intuitive sense to think of a 1 standard deviation difference as "large," a 2 standard deviation difference as "very large," and a 3 standard deviation difference as "huge." This is an easy metric to remember. Specifically, a person who is 1 standard deviation above the mean in IQ is at the 84th percentile. Two standard deviations above the mean puts him at the 98th percentile. Three standard deviations above the mean puts him at the 99.9th percentile. A person who is 1 standard deviation below the mean is at the 16th percentile. Two standard deviations below the mean puts him at the 2d percentile. Three standard deviations below the mean puts him at the 0.1th percentile.

Why Not Just Use Percentiles to Begin With?

Why go to all the trouble of computing standard scores? Most people understand percentiles already. Tell them that someone is at the 84th percentile, and they know right away what you mean. Tell them that he's at the 99th percentile, and they know what that means. Aren't we just introducing an unnecessary complication by talking about "standard scores"?

Thinking in terms of percentiles is convenient and has its legitimate uses. We often speak in terms of percentiles—or centiles—in the text. But they can also be highly misleading, because they are artificially compressed at the tails of the distributions. It is a longer way from, say, the 98th centile to the 99th than from the 50th to the 51st. In a true normal distribution, the distance from the 99th centile to the 100th (or, similarly, from the 1st to the 0th) is infinite.

Consider two people who are at the 50th and 55th centiles in height. Using the NLSY as our estimate of the national American distribution of height, their actual height difference is only half an inch.[2] Consider another two people who are at the 94th and 99th centiles on height—the identical gap in terms of centiles. Their height difference is 3.1 inches, six times the height difference of those at the 50th and 55th centiles. The further out on the tail of the distribution you move, the more misleading centiles become.

Standard scores reflect these real differences much more accurately than do centiles. The people at the 50th and 55th centiles, only half an inch apart in real height, have standard scores of 0 and .13. Compare that difference of .13 standard deviation to the standard scores of those at the 94th and 99th centiles: 1.55 and 2.33, respectively. In standard scores, their difference—which is .78 standard deviation—is six times as large, reflecting the six-fold difference in inches.

The same logic applies to intelligence test scores, and it explains why they should be analyzed in terms of standard scores, not centiles. There is a lot of difference between people at the 1st centile and the 5th, or between those at the 95th and the 99th, much more than those at the 48th and the 52d. If you doubt this, ask a university teacher to compare the classroom performance of students with an SAT-Verbal of 600 and those with an SAT-Verbal of 800. Both are in the 99th centile of all 18-year-olds—but what a difference in verbal ability![3]

CORRELATION AND REGRESSION

We now need to consider dealing with the relationships between two or more distributions—which is, after all, what scientists usually want to do. How, for example, is the temperature of a gas related to its volume? The answer is Boyle's Law, which you learned in high school science. In social science, the relationships between variables are less clear cut and harder to unearth. We may, for example, be interested in wealth as a variable, but how shall wealth be measured? Yearly income? Yearly income averaged over a period of years? The value of one's savings or possessions? And wealth, compared to many of the other things social science would like to understand, is easy, reducible as it is to dollars and cents.

But beyond the problem of measurement, social science must cope with sheer complexity. Our physical scientist colleagues may not agree, but we believe it is harder to do science on human affairs than on inanimate objects—so hard, in fact, that many people consider it impossible. We do not believe it is impossible, but it is rare that any human or social relationship can be fully captured in terms of a single pair of variables, such as that between the temperature and volume of a gas. In social science, multiple relationships are the rule, not the exception.

For both of these reasons, the relations between social science variables are typically less than perfect. They are often weak and uncertain. But they are nevertheless real, and, with the right methods, they can be rigorously examined.

Correlation and regression, used so often in the text, are the primary ways to quantify weak, uncertain relationships. For that reason, the advances in correlational and regression analysis since the late nineteenth century have provided the impetus to social science. To understand what this kind of analysis is, we need to introduce the idea of a scatter diagram.

Scatter Diagrams

We left your male high school classmates lined up by height, with you looking down from the rafters. Now imagine another row of cards, laid out along the floor at a right angle to the ones for height. This set of cards has weights in pounds on them. Start with 90 pounds for the class shrimp, and in 10-pound increments, continue to add cards until you reach 250 pounds to make room for the class giant. Now ask your classmates to find the point on the floor that corresponds to both their height and weight (perhaps they'll insist on a grid of intersecting lines extending from the two rows of cards). When the traffic on the gym floor ceases, you will see something like the figure below. This is a scatter diagram. Some sort of relationship between height and weight is immediately obvious. The heaviest boys tend to be the tallest, the lightest ones the shortest, and most of them are intermediate in both height and weight. Equally obvious are the deviations from the trend that link height and weight. The stocky boys appear as points above the mass,

A scatter diagram

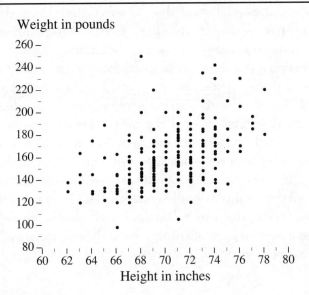

Weight in pounds

Height in inches

the skinny ones as points below it. What we need now is some way to quantify both the trend and the exceptions.

Correlations and *regressions* accomplish this in different ways. But before we go on to discuss these terms, be reassured that they are simple. Look at the scatter diagram. You can see by the dots that as height increases, so does weight, in an irregular way. Take a pencil (literally or imaginarily) and draw a straight, sloping line through the dots in a way that seems to you to best reflect this upward-sloping trend. Now continue to read, and see how well you have intuitively produced the result of a correlation coefficient and a regression coefficient.

The Correlation Coefficient

Modern statistics provides more than one method for measuring correlation, but we confine ourselves to the one that is most important in both use and generality: the Pearson product-moment correlation coefficient (named after Karl Pearson, the English mathematician and biometrician). To get at this coefficient, let us first replot the graph of the class, replacing inches and pounds with standard scores. The variables are now expressed in general terms. Remember: *Any* set of measurements can be transformed similarly.

The next step on our way to the correlation coefficient is to apply a formula (here dispensed with) that, in effect, finds the best possible straight line passing through the cloud of points—the mathematically "best" version of the line you just drew by intuition.

What makes it the "best"? Any line is going to be "wrong" for most of the points. For example, look at the weights of the boys who are 64 inches tall. Any sloping straight line is going to cross somewhere in the middle of those weights and may not cross any of the dots exactly. For boys 64 inches tall, you want the line to cross at the point where the total amount of the error is as small as possible. Taken over all the boys at all the heights, you want a straight line that makes the sum of all the errors for all the heights as small as possible. This "best fit" is shown in the new version of the scatter diagram below, where both height and weight are expressed in standard scores and the mathematical best-fitting line has been superimposed.

The "best-fit" line for a scatter diagram

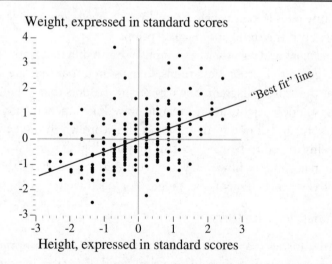

Weight, expressed in standard scores

Height, expressed in standard scores

This scatter diagram has (partly by serendipity) many lessons to teach about how statistics relate to the real world. Here are a few of the main ones:

1. *Notice the many exceptions.* There is a statistically substantial relationship between height and weight, but, visually, the exceptions

seem to dominate. So too with virtually all statistical relationships in the social sciences, most of which are much weaker than this one.

2. *Linear relationships don't always seem to fit very well.* The best-fit line looks as if it is too shallow. Look at the tall boys, and see how consistently it underpredicts how much they weigh. Given the information in the diagram, this might be an optical illusion—many of the dots in the dense part of the range are on top of each other, as it were, and thus it is impossible to grasp visually how the errors are adding up—but it could also be that the relationship between height and weight is not linear.

3. *Small samples have individual anomalies.* Before we jump to the conclusion that the straight line is not a good representation of the relationship, remember that the sample consists of only 250 boys. An anomaly of this particular small sample is that one of the boys in the sample of 250 weighed 250 pounds. Eighteen-year-old boys are very rarely that heavy, judging from the entire NLSY sample, fewer than one per 1,000. And yet one of those rarities happened to be picked up in a sample of 250. That's the way samples work.

4. *But small samples are also surprisingly accurate, despite their individual anomalies.* The relationship between height and weight shown by the sample of 250 18-year-old males is identical to the third decimal place with the relationship among all 6,068 males in the NLSY sample.[4] This is closer than we have any right to expect, but other random samples of only 250 generally produce correlations that are within a few hundredths of the one produced by the larger sample. (There are mathematics for figuring out what "generally" and "within a few hundredths" mean, but we needn't worry about them here.)

Bearing these basics in mind, let us go back to the sloping line in the figure above. Out of mathematical necessity, we know several things about it. First, it must pass through the intersection of the zeros (which, in standard scores, correspond to the averages) for both height and weight. Second, the line would have had exactly the same slope had height been the vertical axis and weight the horizontal one. Finally, and most significant, the slope of the best-fitting line cannot be steeper than 1.0. The steepest possible best-fitting line, in other words, is one along which one unit of change in height is exactly matched by one unit of change in weight, clearly not the case in these data. Real data in the social sciences never yield a slope that steep.

In the picture, the line goes uphill to the right, but for other pairs of variables, it could go downhill. Consider a scatter diagram for, say, educational level and fertility by the age of 30. Women with more education tend to have fewer babies when they are young, compared to women with less education, as we discuss in Chapters 8 and 15. The cloud of points would decline from left to right, just the reverse of the cloud in the picture above. The downhill slope of the best-fitting line would be expressed as a negative number, but, again, it could be no steeper than −1.0.

We focus on the slope of the best-fitting line because it *is* the correlation coefficient—in this case, equal to .50, which is quite large by the standards of variables used by social scientists. The closer it gets to ± 1.0, the stronger is the linear relationship between the standardized variables (the variables expressed as standard scores). When the two variables are mutually independent, the best-fitting line is horizontal; hence its slope is 0. Anything other than 0 signifies a relationship, albeit possibly a very weak one.

Whatever the correlation coefficient of a pair of variables is, squaring it yields another notable number. Squaring .50, for example, gives .25. The significance of the squared correlation is that it tells how much the variation in weight would decrease if we could make everyone the same height, or vice versa. If all the boys in the class were the same height, the variation in their weights would decline by 25 percent. Perhaps, if you have been compelled to be around social scientists, you have heard the phrase "explains the variance," as in, for example, "Education explains 20 percent of the variance in income." That figure comes from the squared correlation.

In general, the squared correlation is a measure of the mutual redundancy in a pair of variables. If they are highly correlated, they are highly redundant in the sense that knowing the value of one of them places a narrow range of possibilities for the value of the other. If they are uncorrelated or only slightly correlated, knowing the value of one tells us nothing or little about the value of the other.[5]

Regression Coefficients

Correlation assesses the strength of a relationship between variables. But we may want to know more about a relationship than merely its strength. We may want to know what it is. We may want to know how much of an increase in weight, for example, we should anticipate if we compare 66-inch boys with 73-inch boys. Such questions arise naturally if we are trying to explain a particular variable (e.g., annual income) in terms of the effects of another variable (e.g., educational level). How much income is another year of schooling worth? is just the sort of question that social scientists are always trying to answer.

The standard method for answering it is regression analysis, which has an intimate mathematical association with correlational analysis. If we had left the scatter diagram with its original axes—inches and pounds—instead of standardizing them, the slope of the best-fitting line would have been a regression coefficient, rather than a correlation coefficient. The figure below shows the scatter diagram with nonstandardized axes.

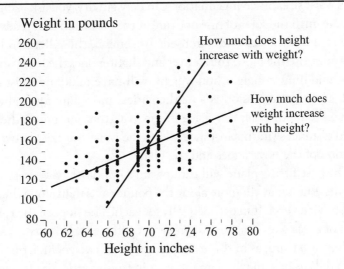

What a regression coefficient is telling you

Why are there two lines? Recall that the best-fitting line is the one that minimizes the aggregated distances between the data points and the line. For standardized measurements, it makes no difference whether the distances are measured along the pounds axis or the inches axis; for unstandardized measurements, it may make a difference. Hence we may get two lines, depending on which axis was used to fit the line. The two lines, which always intersect at the average values for the two variables, answer different questions. One answers the question we first posed: How much of a difference in pounds is associated with a given difference in inches (i.e., the regression of weight on height). The other one tells us how much of a difference in inches is associated with a given difference in pounds (i.e., the regression of height on weight).

Multiple Regression

Multiple regression analysis is the main way that social science deals with the multiple relationships that are the rule in social science. To get a fix on multiple regression, let us return to the high school gym for the last time. Your classmates are still scattered about the floor. Now imagine a pole, erected at the intersection of 60 inches and 90 pounds, marked in inches from 18 inches to 50 inches. For some inscrutable reason, you would like to know the impact of both height and weight on a boy's waist size. Since imagination can defy gravity, you ask each boy to levitate until the soles of his shoes are at the elevation that reads on the pole at the waist size of his trousers. In general, the taller and heavier boys must rise the most, the shorter and slighter ones the least, and most boys, middling in height and weight, will have middling waist sizes as well. Multiple regression is a mathematical procedure for finding that plane, slicing through the space in the gym, that minimizes the aggregated distances (in this instance, along the waist size axis) between the bottoms of the boys' shoes and the plane.

The best-fitting plane will tilt upward toward heavy weights and tall heights. But it may tilt more along the pounds axis than along the inches axis, or vice versa. It may tilt equally for each. The slope of the tilt along each of these axes is again a regression coefficient. With two variables predicting a third, as in this example, there are two coefficients. One of them tells us how much of an increase in trouser waist size is associated with a given increase in weight, holding height constant; the other, how much of an increase in trouser waist size is associated with a given increase in height, holding weight constant.

With two variables predicting a third, we reach the limit of visual imagination. But the principle of multiple regression can be extended to any number of variables. Income, for example, may be related not just to education but also to age, family background, IQ, personality, business conditions, region of the country, and so on. The mathematical procedures will yield coefficients for each of them, indicating again how much of a change in income can be anticipated for a given change in any particular variable, with all the others held constant.

Logistic Regression

The text frequently resorts to a method of analysis called *logistic regression*. Here, we need only say what the method is for rather than what it is. Many of the variables we discuss are such things as being unemployed or not, being married or not, being a parent or not, and so on. Because they are measured in two values—corresponding to yes and no—they are called binary variables. Logistic regression is an adaptation of ordinary regression analysis tailored to the case of binary variables. (It can also be used for variables with larger numbers of discrete values.) It tells us how much change there is in the probability of being unemployed, married, and so forth, given a unit change in any given variable, holding all other variables in the analysis constant.

Appendix 2

Technical Issues Regarding the National Longitudinal Survey of Youth

This appendix provides details about the variables used in the text and about other technical issues associated with the NLSY.[1] Colleagues who wish to recreate analyses will need additional information, which may be obtained from the authors.[2]

SURVEY YEAR, CONSTANT DOLLARS, AND SAMPLE WEIGHTS

Our use of the NLSY extends through the 1990 survey year.[3]

All dollar figures are expressed in 1990 dollars, using the consumer price index inflators as reported in the 1992 edition of *Statistical Abstract of the United States*, Table 737.

Sample weights were employed in all analyses in the main text. We do not so note in each instance, to simplify the description. In computing scores that were based on the 11,878 subjects who had valid scores on the Armed Forces Qualification Test (AFQT), we used the sampling weights specifically assigned for the AFQT population. For analyses based on the NLSY subjects' status as of a given year (usually 1990), we used the sampling weights for that survey year. For analyses in which the children of NLSY women were the unit of analysis, the child's sampling weights were used rather than the mother's.

To make interpretation of the statistical significance easier, we replicated all the analyses in Part II using just the unweighted cross-sectional sample of whites, as reported in Appendix 4.

SCORING OF THE ARMED FORCES QUALIFICATION TEST (AFQT)

The AFQT is a combination of highly g-loaded subtests from the Armed Services Vocational Aptitude Battery (ASVAB) that serves as the armed services' measure of cognitive ability, described in detail in Appendix 3. Until 1989, the AFQT consisted the summed raw scores of the ASVAB's arithmetic reasoning, word knowledge, and paragraph comprehension subtests, plus half of the score on numerical operations subtest. In 1989, the armed forces decided to rescore the AFQT so that it consisted of the word knowledge, paragraph comprehension, arithmetic reasoning, and mathematics knowledge subtests. The reason for the change was to avoid the numerical operations subtest, which was both less highly g-loaded than the mathematics knowledge subtest and sensitive to small discrepancies in the time given to subjects when administering the test (numerical operations is a speeded test in which the subject completes as many arithmetic problems as possible within a time limit).

A draft of *The Bell Curve* was well underway when we became aware of the 1989 scoring scheme. We completed a full draft using the 1980 scoring system but decided that the revised scoring system was psychometrically superior to the old one and therefore replicated all of the analyses using the 1989 version.

Scholars who wish to replicate our analyses should note that the 1989 AFQT score as reported in the NLSY database is *not* the one used in the text. The NLSY's variable is rounded to the nearest whole centile and based on the 18- to 23-year-old subset of the NLSY sample. We recomputed the AFQT from scratch using the raw subtest scores, and the population mean and standard deviation used in producing the across-ages AFQT score was based on all 11,878 subjects, not just those ages 18 to 23.[4] This measure is useful for multivariate analyses in which age is also entered as an independent variable but should not be used (and is never used in the text) as a representation of an individual subject's cognitive ability because of age-related differences in test scores (see discussion below).

Age

AFQT scores in the NLSY sample rose by an average of .07 standard deviations per year. The simplest explanation for this is that the AFQT was designed by the military for a population of recruits who would be taking the test in their late teens, and younger subjects in the NLSY sample got lower scores for the same reason that high school freshmen get lower SAT scores than high school seniors. However, a cohort effect could also be at work, whereby (because of educational or broad environmental reasons) youths born in the first half of the 1960s had lower realized cognitive ability than youths born in the last half of the 1950s. There is no empirical way of telling which reason really explains the age-related differences in the AFQT or what the mix of reasons might be. The age-related increase is not perfectly linear (it levels off in the top two years) but close enough that the age problem is best handled in the multivariate analyses by entering the subject's birthdate as an independent variable (all the NLSY sample took the AFQT within a few months of each other in late 1980).

For all analyses *except* the multivariate regression analyses, we use age-equated scores. These were produced by using the sample weight as a frequency, then preparing separate distributions by birth year, expressed in centiles.[5] Each subject's rank in that population (mathematically, the "population" is the sum of the sample weights for that birth year) was divided by the population to obtain the centile where that subject fell within his birth year cohort.[6]

That AFQT scores vary according to education raises an additional issue: To what extent is the AFQT a measure of cognitive ability, and not just length and quality of education? We explore this issue at length in Appendix 3.

Skew

The distribution of the AFQT in either of its versions is skewed so that the high scores tend to be more closely bunched than the low scores. To put it roughly, the most intelligent people who take the test have less of an opportunity to get a high score than the least intelligent people have to get a low score. One effect is to limit artificially the maximum size of a standardized score. It is artificial because the AFQT does in fact discriminate reasonably well at the high end of the scale. For example, only 22 youths out of 11,878 in the NLSY with valid AFQT scores earned perfect scores on the subtests, representing 0.253 percent of the national population of their age (using sampling weights). In a test with a normal distribution, those youths would have had a standardized score of 2.80. But given the skew in the NLSY, it is impossible for anyone to have a standardized score higher than 1.66. The standard deviation for a high-scoring group is similarly squeezed.

A certain amount of skew is not a concern for many kinds of analysis. For the analyses in *The Bell Curve*, however, the difference between two groups is often expressed in terms of standard deviations, and the size of that difference was likely to be affected by skew.

We therefore computed standardized scores corrected for skew, first by computing the centile scores for the NLSY population, using sample weights as always, then assigning to each subject the standardized score corresponding to that centile in a normal distribution. We did this for both the old and new versions of the AFQT. Following armed forces' convention, all scores greater or smaller than 3 standard deviations from the mean were set at 3 standard deviations (this affected only a small number of scores at the low end of the distribution).

The effects of correcting for skew were noticeable when expressing differences between groups. For example, for the most sensitive group comparison, between ethnic groups, the results are shown in the following table. As always when full information about means, standard

Comparison of Two Versions of The AFQT, Uncorrected and Corrected for Skew

Version of the AFQT	Corrected for Skew?	Black Mean	SD	Latino Mean	SD	White Mean	SD	Black/ White Difference	Latino/ White Differences
Pre-1989	No	−.97	.91	−.67	1.01	.24	.88	1.36	1.02
	Yes	−.90	.81	−.64	.93	.23	.92	1.25	.94
1989 revision	No	−.93	.87	−.67	.98	.23	.90	1.30	.99
	Yes	−.88	.83	−.64	.94	.22	.92	1.21	.93

deviations, and sample sizes is available, the group differences are computed using the weighted average of the groups' standard deviations. The equation is given in note 25 for Chapter 13. The primary effect of the skew was to squeeze the standard deviation of the higher-scoring group (whites) and, in comparison, elongate the standard deviation of the lower scoring groups. Correcting for skew thus shrank both the black-white and Latino-white differences. The same phenomenon affected all comparisons involving subgroups with markedly different

AFQT means. All standardized AFQT scores, for both the regression analyses and the age-equated scores, are therefore corrected for skew. In other words, each represents the standardized score in a normal distribution that corresponds to the (unrounded) centile score of the subject in the observed distribution.

The effects of the different scoring methods on ethnic differences raise a larger question that we should answer directly: How would the results presented in this book be different if we had used the 1980 version of the AFQT instead of the 1989 version? If we had not corrected for skew instead of correcting for skew? For most analyses, the answer is that the results are unaffected. But it may also be said that whenever

---

Why Not Just Use Centiles?

One way of avoiding the skew problem is to leave the AFQT scores in centiles. This was unsatisfactory, however, for we knew from collateral data that much of the important role of IQ occurs at the tails of the distribution. Using centiles throws away information about the tails. (See Appendix 1 on the normal distribution.)

---

differences were found, the scoring procedure we used tended to produce smaller relationships between IQ and the indicators, and smaller ethnic differences, than the alternatives. We did not compute every analysis by each of the four scoring permutations, but we did replicate all of the analyses using the two extremes (1980 version uncorrected for skew and the 1989 version corrected for skew). In no instance did the 1989 version corrected for skew—the version reported in the text—yield significant findings that were not also found when using the 1980 uncorrected version. In terms of the relationships explored in this book, the 1989 version corrected for skew is the most conservative of the alternatives.

THE SOCIOECONOMIC STATUS INDEX

The SES index was created with the variables that are commonly used in developing measures of socioeconomic status: education, income, and occupation. Since the purpose of the index was to measure the socioeconomic environment in which the NLSY youth was raised, the specific variables employed referred to the parents' status: total net family income, mother's education, father's education, and an index of occupational status of the adults living with the subject at the age of 14. The population for the computation was limited to the 11,878 NLSY subjects with valid AFQT scores. In more detail:

Mother's education and father's education were based on years of education, converted to standardized scores.

Family income was based on the averaged total net family income for 1978 and 1979, in constant dollars, when figures for both years were available. If income for only one of the two years was reported, that year was used. Family income was excluded if the subject was a Schedule C interviewee (the reported income for the year in question referred to his or her own income, not to the parental household's income). The dollar figure was expressed as a logarithm before being standardized. This procedure, customary when working with income data, has the effect of discounting extremely high values of income and permitting greater discrimination among lower incomes. A minimum standardized value of −4 was set for incomes of less than $1,000 (all figures are in 1990 dollars).

Parental occupation was coded with a modified version of the Duncan socioeconomic index, grouping the Duncan values (which go from 1 to 100) into deciles. A value of -1 was assigned to persons out of the labor force altogether. It was assumed that the family's socioeconomic status is predominantly determined by the higher of the two occupations held by two parents. Thus the occupational variable was based on the higher of the two ratings of the two parents. The increment in socioeconomic status represented by both parents holding high-status occupations is indirectly reflected in the higher income and in the two educational variables. The eleven values in the modified Duncan scale were standardized.

The reliability of the four-indicator index (Cronbach's α) is .76. The correlations among the components of the index are shown in the table. The four variables were summed and averaged. If only a subset of variables had valid scores, that subset was summed and averaged. By far the most common missing variable was family income, since many of the NLSY youths were already living in independent households as of

Correlations of Indicators in the Socioeconomic Status Index

	Mother's Education	Father's Education	Parental Occupation
Father's education	.63	—	
Parental occupation	.47	.55	—
Family income	.36	.40	.47

the beginning of the survey, and hence were reporting their own income, not parental income. Overall, data were available on all four indicators for 7,447 subjects, for three on an additional 3,612, on two for 679, and on one for 138. Two subjects with valid scores on the AFQT had no information available on any of the four indicators. For use in the regression analyses, the SES index scores were set to a mean of 0 and a standard deviation of 1.

EDUCATIONAL ATTAINMENT

Highest Grade Completed.

The NLSY creates a variable each year for "highest grade completed," incorporating information from several questions.[7] For analyses based on the occurrence of an event (e.g., the birth of a child), the value of "highest grade completed" for the contemporaneous survey year is used. For all other analyses, the 1990 value for "highest grade completed" is used. Values run from 0 through 20.

Highest Degree Ever Received

In the 1988–1990 surveys, the NLSY asked respondents to report the highest degree they had ever received. The possible responses were: high school diploma, associate degree, bachelor of arts, bachelor of science, master's, Ph.D., professional degree (law, medicine, dentistry), and "other." These self-reported degrees were sometimes questionable, especially when the degree did not correspond to the number of years of education (e.g., a bachelor's degree for someone who also reported only fourteen years of education). To eliminate the most egregiously suspicious cases, we made adjustments. For those who reported their highest degree as being a high school diploma, we required at least eleven reported years of completed education. For degrees beyond the high school diploma, we required that the report of the highest grade completed be within at least one year of the normal number of years required to obtain that degree. Specifically, the minimum number of years of completed years of education required to use a reported degree were thirteen for the Associate's degree, fifteen for a bachelor's degree, sixteen for a master's degree, and 18 for a Ph.D., law degree, or medical degree.

We also employed the NLSY's variables to discriminate between those whose terminal degree was a high school diploma versus a GED. We excluded the 190 persons whose degree was listed as "other," after trying fruitlessly to come up with a satisfactory means of estimating what the "other" meant from collateral educational data.

The "high school" and "college graduate" samples used throughout Part II are designed to isolate populations with homogeneous educational experiences as of the 1990 survey year. The high school sample is defined as those who reported twelve years of completed education and a high school diploma received through the normal process (i.e., excluding GEDs) as the highest attained degree. The college graduate sample is defined as all those who reported sixteen years of completed education and a B.A. or B.S. as the highest attained degree.

Transition to College

In Chapter 1, we used the NLSY to determine the percentage of students in various IQ groupings who went directly to college. We limited the analysis to students who obtained a high school diploma between January 1980 and July 1982, meaning that all subjects had taken the AFQT prior to attending college. The analysis thus also reflects the experience of those who obtain their high school diploma via the normal route (comparable to the analyses from the 1960s and 1920s, which are also reported in the same figure). A subject is classified as attending college in the year following graduation if he reported having enrolled in college at any point in the calendar year following the date of graduation.

MARITAL AND FERTILITY VARIABLES

All variables relating to marital history and childbearing employed the NLSY's synthesis as contained in the 1990 Fertility File of the NLSY.

BIRTH WEIGHT

The most commonly reported measure of a problematic birth weight is "low birth weight," defined as no more than 5.5 pounds. In its raw form, however, low birth weight is limited as a measure because it is confounded with prematurity. A baby born five weeks prematurely will probably weigh less than 5.5 pounds and yet be a fully developed, healthy child for gestational age, with excellent prospects. Conversely, a child carried to term but weighing slightly more than the cutoff of 5.5 pounds is (given parents of average stature) small for its gestational age. We therefore created a variable expressing the baby's birth weight as a ratio of the weight for fetuses at the 50th centile for that gestational age, using the Colorado Intrauterine Growth Charts as the basis for the computation. If a baby weighed less than 5.5 pounds but the ratio was equal to or greater than 1, that case was excluded from the analysis. All uses of this variable in Chapters 10 and 13 are based on a sample that is exclusively white (Latino or non-Latino) or black, thereby sidestepping the complications that would be introduced by the populations of smaller stature, such as East Asians. We further excluded cases reporting gestational ages of less than twenty-six weeks, reports of pregnancies that lasted more than forty-four weeks or birth weights in excess of thirteen pounds, and one remarkable case in which a mother reported gestation of twenty-six weeks and a birth weight of more than twelve pounds.

Appendix 3

Technical Issues Regarding the Armed Forces Qualification Test as a Measure of IQ

Throughout *The Bell Curve*, we use the Armed Forces Qualification Test (AFQT) as a measure of IQ. This appendix discusses a variety of related issues that may help readers interpret the meaning of the analyses presented in the full text.

DOES THE AFQT MEASURE THE SAME THING THAT IQ TESTS MEASURE?

The AFQT is a paper-and-pencil test designed for youths who have reached their late teens. In effect, it assumes exposure to an ordinary high school education (or the opportunity to get one). This kind of restriction is shared by any IQ test, all of which are designed for certain groups.

The AFQT as scored by the armed forces is not age referenced. The armed forces have no need to do so, because the overwhelming majority of recruits taking the test are 18 and 19 years old. In contrast, the NLSY sample varied from 14 to 23 years old when they took the test. Therefore, as discussed in Appendix 3, all analyses in the book take age into account through one of two methods: entering age as an independent variable in the multivariate analyses, and, for all descriptive statistics, age referencing the AFQT score by expressing it in terms of the mean and standard deviation for each year's birth cohort. In this appendix, we will uniformly use the age-referenced version for analyses based on the NLSY.

Is a set of age-referenced AFQT scores appropriately treated as IQ scores? We approach this issue from two perspectives. First, we examine the internal psychometric properties of the AFQT and show that the AFQT is one of the most highly g-loaded mental tests in current use. It seems to do what a good IQ test is supposed to do—tap into a general factor rather than specific bits of learning or skill—as well as or better than its competitors. Second, we examine the correlation between the AFQT and other IQ tests, and show that the AFQT is more highly correlated with a wide range of other mental tests than those other mental tests are with each other. On both counts, the AFQT qualifies not just as an IQ test, but one of the better ones psychometrically.

Psychometric Characteristics of the ASVAB

Let us begin by considering the larger test from which the AFQT is computed, the ASVAB (Armed Services Vocational Aptitude Battery), taken every year by between a half million and a million young adults who are applying for entry into one of the armed services. The ASVAB has ten subtests, spanning a range from test items that could appear equally well on standard tests of intelligence to items testing knowledge of automobile repair and electronics.[1] Scores on the subtests determine whether the applicant will be accepted by his chosen branch of service; for those accepted, the scores are later used for the placement of enlisted personnel into military occupations. How well or poorly a person performs in military occupational training schools, and also how well he does on the job, can therefore be evaluated against the scores earned on a battery of standardized tests.

The ten subtests of ASVAB can be paired off into forty-five correlations. Of the forty-five, the three highest correlations in a large study of enlisted personnel were between Word Knowledge and General Science, Word Knowledge and Paragraph Completion, and, highest of all, between Mathematics Knowledge and Arithmetic Reasoning.[2] Correlations above .8, as these were, are in the range observed between different IQ tests, which are frankly constructed to measure the same attribute. To see them arising between tests of such different subject matter should alert us to some deeper level of mental functioning. The three lowest correlations, none lower than .22, were between Coding Speed and Mechanical Comprehension, Numerical Operations and Auto/Shop Information, and, lowest of all, between Coding Speed and Automobile/Shop Information. Between those extremes, there were rather large correlations between Paragraph Completion and General

Science and between Word Knowledge and Electronics Information but only moderate correlations between Electronics Information and Coding Speed and between Mathematics Knowledge and Automobile/Shop Information. Thirty-six of the forty-five correlations were above .5.

Psychometrics approaches a table of correlations with one or another of its methods for factor analysis. Factor analysis (or other mathematical procedures that go under other names) extracts the factors[3] that account for the observed pattern of subtest scores. The basic idea is that scores on any pair of tests are correlated to the extent that the tests measure something in common: If they test traits in common, they are correlated, and if not, not. Factor analysis tells how many different underlying factors are necessary to account for the observed correlations between them. If, for example, the subtest scores were totally uncorrelated, it would take ten independent and equally significant factors, one for each subtest by itself. With each test drawing on its own unique factor, the forty-five correlations would all be zeros. At the other extreme, if the subtests measured precisely the same thing down to the very smallest detail, then all the correlations among scores on the subtests could be explained by a single factor—that thing which all the subtests precisely measured—and the correlations would all be ones. Neither extreme describes the actuality, but for measures of intellectual performance, one large factor comes closer than many small ones. This is not the place to dwell on mathematical details except to note that, contrary to claims in nontechnical works,[4] the conclusions we draw about general intelligence do not depend on the particular method of analysis used.[5]

For the ASVAB, 64 percent of the variance among the ten subtest scores is accounted for by a single factor, *g*. A second factor accounts for another 13 percent. With three inferred factors, 82 percent of the variance is accounted for.[6] The intercorrelations indicate that people do vary importantly in some single, underlying trait and that those variations affect how they do on every test. Nor is the predominance of *g* a fortuitous result of the particular subtests in ASVAB. The air force's aptitude test for prospective officers, the AFOQT (Air Force Officer Qualifying Test) similarly has *g* as its major source of individual variation.[7] Indeed, all broad-gauged test batteries of cognitive ability have *g* as their major source of variation among the scores people get.[8]

The naive theory assumes that when scores on two subtests are correlated, it is because of overlapping content. But it is impossible to make sense of the varying correlations between the subtests in terms of overlapping content. Consider again the correlation between Arithmetic Reasoning and Mathematical Knowledge, which is the highest of all. It may seem to rest simply on a knowledge of mathematics and arithmetic. However, the score on Numerical Operations is less correlated with either of those two tests than the two are with each other. Content provides no clue as to why. Arithmetic Reasoning has only word problems on it; Mathematical Knowledge applies the basic methods of algebra and geometry; and Numerical Operations is an arithmetic test. Why are scores on algebra and geometry more similar to those on word problems than to those on arithmetic? Such variations in the correlations between the subtests arise, in fact, less from common content than from how much they draw on the underlying ability we call g. The varying correlations between the subtests preclude explaining g away as, for example, simply a matter of test-taking ability or test-taking experience, which should affect all tests more or less equally. We try to make some of these ideas visible in the figure below.

The relation of the ASVAB subtests to each other and to g

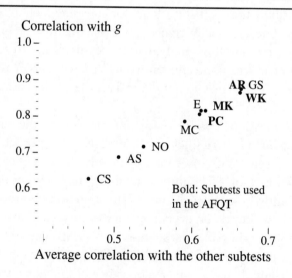

For each subtest on ASVAB, we averaged the nine correlations with each of the other subtests, and that average correlation defines the horizontal axis. The vertical axis is a measure, for each subtest, of the correlation between the score and *g*.[9] The two-letter codes identify the subtests. At the top is General Science (GS), closely followed by Word Knowledge (WK), and Arithmetical Reasoning (AR), for which the scores are highly correlated with *g* and have the highest average correlations with all the subtests. Another three subtests— Mathematics Knowledge (MK), Paragraph Comprehension (PC), and Electronics Information (EI)—are just slightly below the top cluster in both respects. At the bottom are Coding Speed (CS), Automobile/Shop Information (AS), Numerical Operations (NO), and Mechanical Comprehension (MC), subtests that correlate, on the average, the least with other subtests and are also the least correlated with *g* (although still substantially correlated in their own right). The bottom group includes the two speeded subtests, CS and NO, thereby refuting another common misunderstanding about *g*, which is that it refers to mental speed and little more. Virtually without exception, the more dependent a subtest score is on *g*, the higher is its average correlation with the other subtests. This is the pattern that betrays what *g* means—a broad mental capacity that permeates performance on anything that challenges people cognitively. A rough rule of thumb is that items or tests that require mental complexity draw more on *g* than items that do not—the difference, for example, between simply repeating a string of numbers after hearing them once, which does not much test *g*, and repeating them in reverse order, which does.[10]

The four subtests used in the 1989 scoring version of the AFQT (the one used throughout the text) and their *g* loadings are Word Knowledge (.87), Paragraph Comprehension (.81), Arithmetic Reasoning (.87), and Mathematics Knowledge (.82).[11] The AFQT is thus one of the most highly *g*-loaded tests in use. By way of comparison, the factor loadings for the eleven subtests of the Wechsler Adult Intelligence Scale (WAIS) range from .63 to .83, with a median of .69.[12] Whereas the first factor, *g*, accounts for over 70 percent of the variance in the AFQT, it accounts for only 53 percent in the WAIS.

Correlations of the AFQT with Other IQ Tests

Our second approach to the question, Is the AFQT an IQ test? is to ask how the AFQT correlates with other well-known standardized mental tests (see the table below). We can do so by making use of the high school transcript survey conducted by the NLSY in 1979. In addition to gathering information about grades, the survey picked up any other IQ test that the student had taken within the school system. The data usually included both the test score and the percentile rank, based on national norms. In accordance with the recommendation of the NLSY *User's Manual*, we use percentiles throughout.[13]

Correlations of the AFQT with Other IQ Tests in The NLSY		
	Sample	**Correlation with the AFQT**
California Test of Mental Maturity	356	.81
Coop School and College Ability Test	121	.90
Differential Atitude Test	443	.81
Henmon Nelson Test of Mental Maturity	152	.71
Kuhlmann-Anderson Intelligence Test	36	.80
Lorge-Thorndike Intelligence Test	170	.72
Otis-Lennnon Mental Ability Test	530	.81

The magnitudes of the correlations between the AFQT (using the age-referenced percentile scores) and classic IQ tests are as high as or higher than the observed correlations of the classic IQ tests with each other. For example, the best-known adult test, the WAIS, is known to correlate (using the median correlation with various studies, and not correcting for restriction of range in the samples) with the Stanford-Binet at .77, with the Ravens Standard Progressive Matrices at .72, the SRA Non-verbal test at .81, the Peabody Picture Vocabulary Test at .83, and the Otis at .78.[14] The table below summarizes the intercorrelations of IQ tests, based on the comparisons assembled by Arthur Jensen as of 1980, and adding a line for the AFQT comparisons from the NLSY. The AFQT compares favorably with the other major IQ tests by this measure, which in turn is consistent with the high g-loading of the AFQT.

Correlations of the Major IQ Tests with Other Standardized Mental Tests

	Median Correlation with Other Mental Tests
AFQT (age-referenced, 1989 scoring)	.81
Wechsler-Bellevue I	.73
Wechsler Adult Intelligence Scale (WAIS)	.77
Wechsler Intelligence Scale for Children	.64
Stanford-Binet	.71

Source: Jensen 1980, Table 8.5, and author's analysis of the NLSY.

HOW SENSITIVE ARE THE RESULTS TO THE ASSUMPTION THAT IQ IS NORMALLY DISTRIBUTED?

Any good test designed to measure a complex ability (whether a test of cognitive ability or carpentry ability) will have several characteristics that common sense says are desirable: a large number of items, a wide range of difficulty among the items, no marked gaps in the difficulty of the items, a variety of types of items, and items that have some relationship to each other (i.e., are to some degree measuring the same thing).[15] Empirically, tests with these characteristics, administered to a representative sample of those for whom the test is intended, will yield scores that are spread out in a fashion resembling a normal distribution, or a bell curve. In this sense, tests of mental ability are not designed to produce normally distributed scores; that's just what happens, the same way that height is normally distributed without anyone planning it.

It is also true, however, that tests are usually scored and standardized under the assumption that intelligence is normally distributed, and this has led to allegations that psychometricians have bamboozled people into accepting that intelligence is normally distributed, when in fact it may just be an artifact of the way they choose to measure intelligence. For a response to such allegations, Chapter 4 of Arthur Jensen's *Bias in Mental Testing* (New York: Free Press, 1980) remains the best discussion we have seen.

For purposes of assessing the analyses in this book, it may help readers to know the extent to which any assumptions about the distribution of AFQT scores might have affected the results, especially since we rescored the AFQT to correct for skew (see Appendix 2). The descriptive statistics showing the breakdown of each variable by cognitive class, presented in each chapter of Part II, address that issue. Assignment to cognitive classes was based on the subject's rank within the distribution, and these ranks are invariant no matter what the normality of the distribution might be. Ranks were also unaffected by the correction for skew.

The descriptive statistics in the text were bivariate. To examine this issue in a multivariate framework, we replicated the analyses of Part II substituting a set of nominal variables, denoting the cognitive classes, for the continuous AFQT measure. That is, the regression treated "membership in Class I" as a nominal variable, just as it would treat "married" or "Latino" as a nominal characteristic—and similarly for the other four cognitive classes, also entered as nominal variables (See Appendix 4 for a discussion of how to interpret the coefficients for nominal variables as created by the software used in these analyses, JMP 3.0). Below, we show the results for the opening analysis of Part II (Chapter 5), the probability of being in poverty.

Comparison of results when AFQT is treated as a continuous, normally distributed variable and when it is treated as a set of nominal categories based on groupings by centile

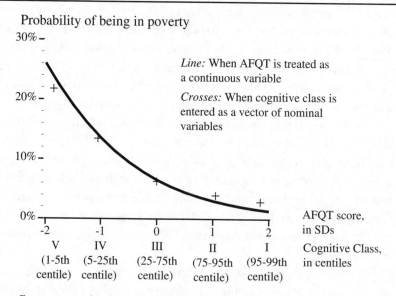

Probability of being in poverty

Line: When AFQT is treated as a continuous variable

Crosses: When cognitive class is entered as a vector of nominal variables

AFQT score, in SDs

Cognitive Class, in centiles

V	IV	III	II	I
(1-5th centile)	(5-25th centile)	(25-75th centile)	(75-95th centile)	(95-99th centile)

Note: For computing the plot, age and SES were set at their mean values.

The results of the logistic regression analysis using the normally distributed AFQT score follow:

Whole–Model Test

Source	DF	–LogLikelihood	ChiSquare	Prob>ChiSq
Model	3	477222.0	954443.9	0.000000
Error	4488	4587166.7		
C Total	4491	5064388.7		

RSquare (U)	0.0942	
Observations	4,492	

Parameter Estimates

Term	Estimate	Std Error	ChiSquare	Prob>ChiSq
Intercept	−2.6579692	0.0009826	.	0.0000
zAFQT89	−0.8177031	0.0012228	447179	0.0000
zSES	−0.2744971	0.0011661	55416	0.0000
zAge	−0.0482156	0.0009187	2754.1	0.0000

These are the results using the categorization into cognitive classes by centile:

Whole–Model Test

Source	DF	–LogLikelihood	ChiSquare	Prob>ChiSq
Model	6	383494.7	766989.4	0.000000
Error	4485	4680894.0		
C Total	4491	5064388.7		

RSquare (U)	0.0757	
Observations	4,492	

Parameter Estimates

Term	Estimate	Std Error	ChiSquare	Prob>ChiSq
Intercept	−2.5097718	0.0015823	.	0.0000
CogClas.[1-5]	−1.0067168	0.0050693	39439	0.0000
CogClas.[2-5]	−0.6803606	0.0025486	71265	0.0000
CogClas.[3-5]	−0.1905042	0.0018498	10606	0.0000
CogClas.[4-5]	0.64764109	0.0021336	92138	0.0000
zSES	−0.3902981	0.0011276	119800	0.0000
zAge	−0.1605992	0.000907	31350	0.0000

We repeated these comparisons for a broad sampling of the outcome variables discussed in Part II. The results for poverty were typical. When the results for the two expressions of IQ do not correspond (e.g., the relationship of mother's IQ to low birth weight, as discussed in Chapter 10), the lack of correspondence also showed up in the bivariate table showing the breakdown by cognitive class. Or to put it another way, the results presented in the text using IQ as a continuous, normally distributed variable are produced as well when IQ is treated as a set of categories. Any exceptions to that may be identified through the bivariate tables based on cognitive class.

RELATIONSHIP OF THE AFQT SCORE TO EDUCATION AND PARENTAL SES

The relationship of an IQ test score to education and socioeconomic background is a constant and to some extent unresolvable source of controversy. It is known that the environment (including exposure to education) affects realized cognitive ability. To that extent, it is conceptually appropriate that parental SES and years of education show an independent causal effect on IQ. On the other hand, an IQ test score is supposed to represent cognitive ability and to have an independent reality of its own; in other words, it should not simply be a proxy measure of either parental SES or years of education. The following discussion elaborates on the statistical relationship of both parental SES and years of education to the AFQT score.

The Socioeconomic Status Index and the AFQT Score.

The SES index consists of four indicators as described in Appendix 2: mother's and father's years of education, the occupational status of the parent with the higher-status job, and the parents' total family income in 1979–1980. The correlations of the index and its four constituent variables with the AFQT are in the table below.

Intercorrelations of the AFQT and the Indicators in the Socioeconomic Status Index	
	AFQT
Mother's education	.43
Father's education	.46
Occupational status	.43
Family income	.38
SES Index	.55

The correlation of AFQT with the SES index itself is .55, consistent with other investigations of this topic.[16]

There are three broad interpretations of these correlations:

1. *Test bias.* IQ tests scores are artificially high for persons from high-status backgrounds because the tests are biased in favor of people from high-status homes.
2. *Environmental advantage.* IQ tends to be genuinely higher for children from high-status homes, because they enjoy a more favorable environment for realizing their cognitive ability than do children from low-status homes.
3. *Genetic advantage.* IQ tends to be genuinely higher for children from high-status homes because they enjoy a more favorable genetic background (parental SES is a proxy measure for parental IQ).

The first explanation is discussed in Appendix 5. The other two explanations have been discussed at various points in the text (principally Chapter 4's discussion of heritability, Chapter 10's discussion of parenting styles, and Chapter 17's discussion of adoption). To summarize those discussions, being brought up in a conspicuously high-status or low-status family from birth probably has a significant effect on IQ, independent of the genetic endowment of the parents. The magnitude of this effect is uncertain. Studies of adoption suggest that the average is in the region of six IQ points, given the difference in the environments provided by adopting and natural parents. Outside interventions to augment the environment have had only an inconsistent and uncertain effect, although it remains possible that larger effects might be possible for children from extremely deprived environments. In terms of the topic of this appendix, the flexibility of the AFQT score, the AFQT was given at ages 14–23, when the effect of socioeconomic background on IQ had already played whatever independent role it might have.

Years of Education and the AFQT Score

For the AFQT as for other IQ tests, scores vary directly with educational attainment, leaving aside for the moment the magnitude of reciprocal cause and effect. But to what extent could we expect that, if we managed to keep low-scoring students in school for another year or two, their AFQT scores would have risen appreciably?

Chapter 17 laid out the general answer from a large body of research: Systematic attempts to raise IQ through education (exemplified by the Venezuelan experiment and the analyses of SAT coaching) can indeed have an effect on the order of .2 standard deviation, or three IQ points. As far as anyone can tell, there are diminishing marginal benefits of this kind of coaching (taking three intensive SAT coaching programs in succession will raise a score by less than three times the original increment).

We may explore the issue more directly by making use of the other IQ scores obtained for members of the NLSY. Given scores that were obtained several years earlier than the AFQT score, to what extent do the intervening years of education appear to have elevated the AFQT?

Underlying the discussion is a simple model:

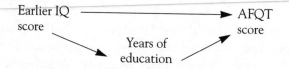

The earlier IQ score affects both years of education and is a measure of the same thing that AFQT measures. Meanwhile, the years of education add something (we hypothesize) to the AFQT score that would not otherwise have been added.

Actually testing the model means bringing in several complications, however. The elapsed time between the earlier IQ test and the AFQT test presumably affects the relationships. So does the age of the subject (a subject who took the test at age 22 had a much different "chance" to add years of education than did a subject who took the test at age 18, for example). The age at which the earlier IQ test was taken is also relevant, since IQ test scores are known to become more stable at around the age of 6. But the main point of the exercise may be illustrated straightforwardly. We will leave the elaboration to our colleagues.

The database consists of all NLSY students who had an earlier IQ test score, as reported in the table on page 596, plus students with valid Stanford-Binet and WISC scores (too few to report separately). We report the results for two models in the table below, with the AFQT score as the dependent variable in both cases. In the first model, the explanatory variables are the earlier IQ score, age at the first test, elapsed years between the two tests, and type of test (entered as a vector of dummy variables). In the second model, we add years of education as an independent variable. An additional year of education is associated with a gain of 2.3 centiles per year, in line with other analyses of the effects of

The Independent Effect of Education on AFQT Scores as Inferred from Earlier IQ Tests

Dependent variable: AFQT percentile score

Independent Variables	Model 1		Model 2	
	Coefficient	Std. Error	Coefficient	Std. Error
Intercept	12.303	1.653	−6.783	2.443
Earlier IQ percentile score	.787	.016	.753	.015
Elapsed years between tests	−.316	.166	−1.005	.173
Years of education	—	—	2.280	.221
Type of test (entered as a vector of nominal variables, coefficients not shown.)				
No. of observations	1,408		1,408	
R^2 (Adjusted)	.659		.681	

education on IQ.[17] What happens if the dependent variable is expressed in standardized scores rather than percentiles? In that case (using the same independent variables), the independent effect of education is to increase the AFQT score by .07 standard deviation, or the equivalent of about one IQ point per year—also in line with other analyses.

We caution against interpreting these coefficients literally across the entire educational range. Whereas it may be reasonable to think about IQ gains for six additional years of education when comparing subjects who had no schooling versus those who reached sixth grade, or even comparing those who dropped out in sixth grade and those who remained through high school, interpreting these coefficients becomes problematic when moving into post–high school education.

The negative coefficient for "elapsed years between tests" in the table above is worth mentioning. Suppose that the true independent relationship between years of education and AFQT is negatively accelerated—that is, the causal importance of the elementary grades in developing a person's IQ is greater than the causal role of, say, graduate school. If so, then the more years of separation between tests, the lower would be the true value of the dependent variable, AFQT, compared to the predicted value in a linear regression, because people with many years of separation between tests in the sample are, on average, getting less incremental benefit of years of education than the sample with just a few years of separation. The observed results are consistent with this hypothesis.

Appendix 4

Regression Analyses from Part II

This appendix presents the logistic regressions for the figures in Chapters 5 through 12. In the text, the figures are based on regressions that use the entire white sample in the NLSY and are calculated using sample weights. We use the entire sample and weights to take advantage of the NLSY's supplemental sample of low-income whites; in our judgment, doing so provides the best available estimates of the relationships we discuss. But interpreting standard errors and statistical significance is greatly complicated when using sample weights. In the regression results that follow, we therefore restrict the analyses to the nationally representative cross-sectional sample of whites. This procedure not only enables direct interpretation of the standard errors but also provides the raw material for interested readers to see how much difference there is between the results from the entire white sample and the cross-sectional sample (which you may do by computing the probabilities for the cross-sectional sample and comparing them to the ones shown in the text figures). We have done so ourselves and can report that the differences are so small that they are seldom visually evident.

By "whites," we mean all NLSY subjects who were identified as "non-black, non-Hispanic" in the NLSY's racial/ethnic cohort screening (variable R2147, in the NLSY's documentation), deleting those who identified themselves as being of American Indian, Asian, or Pacific descent in the "first or only racial/ethnic origin" item (R96).

In the text, we do not refer to the usual measure of goodness of fit for multiple regressions, R^2, but they are presented here for the cross-sectional analyses. As the ratio of the explained sum of squares to the total sum of squares, R^2 is in this instance the square of the correlation between the set of independent variables and the dependent variable expressed as the logarithm of the odds ratio. Inasmuch as the values of R^2 range widely in the tables to follow, some mention of them is warranted.

The size of R^2 tells something about the strength of the logistic relationship between the dependent variable and the set of independent variables, but it also depends on the composition of the sample, as do correlation coefficients in general. Even an inherently strong relationship can result in low values of R^2 if the data points are bunched in various ways, and relatively noisy relationships can result in high values if the sample includes disproportionate numbers of outliers. For example, one of the smallest R^2 in the following analyses, only 0.17, is for white men out of the labor force for four weeks or more in 1989. Apart from the distributional properties of the data that produce this low R^2, a rough common-sense meaning to keep in mind is that the vast majority of NLSY white men were in the labor force even though they had low IQs or deprived socioeconomic backgrounds. But the parameter for zAFQT in that same equation is significant beyond the .001 level and large enough to make a big difference in the probability that a white male would be out of the labor force. This illustrates why we therefore consider the regression coefficients themselves (and their associated p values) to suit our analytic purposes better than R^2, and that is why those are the ones we relied on in the text.

The standard independent variables, described in Appendix 2, are zAFQT89, the 1989 scoring of the AFQT; zSES, the socioeconomic background of the NLSY subjects; and zAge, based on the age of the NLSY subjects as of December 31, 1990. All are expressed as standard scores with a mean of 0 and a standard deviation of 1.

All dependent variables are binary. The coefficients are parameter estimates when the dependent variable = "yes." The linear logistic model has the form

$$\text{logit}(p) = \log(p/(1-p)) = \alpha + \beta'\mathbf{x}$$

where α is the intercept parameter and β is the vector of slope parameters for a vector of independent variables $\mathbf{x}$. Take as an example the first set of results presented subsequently, involving poverty. Suppose you want to know the probability that a person is under the poverty line in 1989 (Poverty = "Yes"), stipulating that the person in question has an IQ (zAFQT) 1.5 standard deviations below the mean, socioeconomic background (zSES) .3 standard deviation above the mean, and is exactly of mean age. Using the parameters in the basic analysis for poverty rounded to four decimal places, and a computationally convenient re-expression of p, the probability is computed as follows:

$$\text{logit}(p) = -2.6487 + (-.8376 \times -1.5) + (-.3301 \times 3) + (-.0238 \times 0) = -1.4913$$
$$p = e^{-1.4913}/(1+e^{-1.4913})$$
$$p = .1837$$

The probability we set out to compute is 18.37 percent.

"The High School Sample" consists of those who received a high school diploma through the normal route (not a GED) and reported exactly twelve years of education as of the 1990 interview.

"The College Sample" consists of those who completed a bachelor's degree and reported exactly sixteen years of education as of the 1990 interview.

The software used for the analyses is JMP Version 3, by SAS Institute Inc. JMP treats nominal independent variables differently from other major software packages such as SAS and SPSS. In those packages, a parameter for a nominal variable represents the difference between that level of the nominal variable and an omitted level serving as a reference group. In JMP, a parameter represents the difference of a given level from the average over all levels of the nominal variable. The implied parameter for the remaining level is the negative sum of the other levels (i.e., the parameters sum to zero over all the effect levels). For example, suppose Race were being used as a nominal variable, with categories of Black, Latino, and White. In the JMP printout, the coefficients would appear as

Race[Black-White] x_1
Race[Latino-White] x_2

The order is determined by the alphabetical order of the categories. In this case, the coefficient x_1 applies to blacks, x_2 to Latinos. The implied White coefficient is $-1*(x_1 + x_2)$. In the case of a binary independent variable such as Sex, the printout would show a single line

Sex[Female-Male] x_1

which applies to females. The coefficient for Male equals $-x_1$.

CHAPTER 5: POVERTY

DEPENDENT VARIABLE: Under the official poverty line in 1989.

SAMPLE RESTRICTIONS: Excludes those who reported they were out of the labor force because they were in school in either the 1989 or 1990 interviews.

Basic Analysis:

Whole–Model Test

Source	DF	–LogLikelihood	ChiSquare	Prob>ChiSq
Model	3	90.94009	181.8802	0.000000
Error	3363	784.40179		
C Total	3366	875.34188		
		RSquare (U)	0.1039	
		Observations	3367	

Parameter Estimates

Term	Estimate	Std Error	ChiSquare	Prob>ChiSq
Intercept	−2.6487288	0.0768803	1187	0.0000
zAFQT89	−0.8376338	0.0935061	80.25	0.0000
zSES	−0.3300720	0.0900996	13.42	0.0002
zAge	−0.0238375	0.0723735	0.11	0.7419

The High School Sample:

Whole–Model Test

Source	DF	–LogLikelihood	ChiSquare	Prob>ChiSq
Model	3	22.01811	44.03622	0.000000
Error	1232	325.26939		
C Total	1235	347.28750		
		RSquare (U)	0.0634	
		Observations	1236	

Parameter Estimates

Term	Estimate	Std Error	ChiSquare	Prob>ChiSq
Intercept	−2.7237775	0.1290286	445.63	0.0000
zAFQT89	−0.8267293	0.1627358	25.81	0.0000
zSES	−0.3619703	0.1499855	5.82	0.0158
zAge	+0.1049227	0.1094603	0.92	0.3378

The College Sample: Omitted. Only six persons in the cross-sectional College Sample were in poverty.

For Mothers Married as of the 1989 Interview:

Whole–Model Test

Source	DF	–LogLikelihood	ChiSquare	Prob>ChiSq
Model	3	17.14553	34.29106	0.000000
Error	786	179.84999		
C Total	789	196.99552		
		RSquare (U)	0.0870	
		Observations	790	

Parameter Estimates

Term	Estimate	Std Error	ChiSquare	Prob>ChiSq
Intercept	−2.7732817	0.1646023	283.87	0.0000
zAFQT89	−0.6437797	0.2140132	9.05	0.0026
zSES	−0.3910629	0.2020317	3.75	0.0529
zAge	−0.3338674	0.1587605	4.42	0.0355

For Mothers Who Were Separated, Divorced, or Never Married as of the 1989 Interview:

Whole–Model Test

Source	DF	−LogLikelihood	ChiSquare	Prob>ChiSq
Model	3	8.07114	16.14228	0.001060
Error	211	135.77658		
C Total	214	143.84772		
	RSquare (U)		0.0561	
	Observations		215	

Parameter Estimates

Term	Estimate	Std Error	ChiSquare	Prob>ChiSq
Intercept	−0.7449132	0.1713794	18.89	0.0000
zAFQT89	−0.6722121	0.2277019	8.72	0.0032
zSES	−0.1597461	0.1952709	0.67	0.4133
zAge	−0.1524315	0.1530986	0.99	0.3194

CHAPTER 6: SCHOOLING

DEPENDENT VARIABLE: Permanently dropped out of high school.
SAMPLE RESTRICTIONS: Excludes those who obtained a GED.

Basic Analysis:

Whole–Model Test

Source	DF	−LogLikelihood	ChiSquare	Prob>ChiSq
Model	3	393.8978	787.7956	0.000000
Error	3568	779.9904		
C Total	3571	1173.8882		
	RSquare (U)		0.3355	
	Observations		3572	

Parameter Estimates

Term	Estimate	Std Error	ChiSquare	Prob>ChiSq
Intercept	−2.85322606	0.0939659	922.00	0.0000
zAFQT89	−1.72295934	0.1028145	280.83	0.0000
zSES	−0.64776232	0.0896658	52.19	0.0000
zAge	+0.05695640	0.0688286	0.68	0.4079

Basic Analysis, Adding an Interaction Term for zAFQT and zSES:

Whole–Model Test

Source	DF	–LogLikelihood	ChiSquare	Prob>ChiSq
Model	4	399.9876	799.9751	0.000000
Error	3567	773.9006		
C Total	3571	1173.8882		
	RSquare (U)		0.3407	
	Observations		3572	

Parameter Estimates

Term	Estimate	Std Error	ChiSquare	Prob>ChiSq
Intercept	−2.9143231	0.1029462	801.41	0.0000
zAFQT89	−1.8937642	0.1188518	253.89	0.0000
zSES	−0.9402389	0.1250634	56.52	0.0000
zAge	+0.0522667	0.0682755	0.59	0.4440
zAFQT89*zSES	−0.4133224	0.1187879	12.11	0.0005

DEPENDENT VARIABLE: Received a GED instead of a high school diploma.

SAMPLE RESTRICTIONS: Excludes those who obtained neither a high school diploma nor a GED.

Basic Analysis:

Whole–Model Test

Source	DF	–LogLikelihood	ChiSquare	Prob>ChiSq
Model	3	72.06475	144.1295	0.000000
Error	3490	915.28145		
C Total	3493	987.34620		
	RSquare (U)		0.0730	
	Observations		3494	

Parameter Estimates

Term	Estimate	Std Error	ChiSquare	Prob>ChiSq
Intercept	−2.3548461	0.0653867	1297	0.0000
zAFQT89	−0.4325254	0.0851185	25.82	0.0000
zSES	−0.6082151	0.0837515	52.74	0.0000
zAge	−0.0416441	0.0662445	0.40	0.5296

DEPENDENT VARIABLE: Received a bachelor's degree.

SAMPLE RESTRICTIONS: Excludes those who had less than a bachelor's degree and were in postsecondary education in either the 1989 or 1990 interview.

Basic Analysis:

Whole–Model Test

Source	DF	–LogLikelihood	ChiSquare	Prob>ChiSq
Model	3	807.9072	1615.814	0.000000
Error	3817	1364.3417		
C Total	3820	2172.2489		
	RSquare (U)		0.3719	
	Observations		3821	

Parameter Estimates

Term	Estimate	Std Error	ChiSquare	Prob>ChiSq
Intercept	−2.41992250	0.0786991	945.50	0.0000
zAFQT89	+1.80771403	0.0795537	516.34	0.0000
zSES	+1.04818417	0.0690372	230.52	0.0000
zAge	−0.29777760	0.0516373	33.25	0.0000

CHAPTER 7: UNEMPLOYMENT, IDLENESS, AND INJURY

DEPENDENT VARIABLE: Out of the labor force for four weeks or more in 1989.

SAMPLE RESTRICTIONS: Civilian males who did not respond "unable to work" or "in school" to the question on labor force participation in the 1989 or 1990 interview.

Basic Analysis:

Whole–Model Test

Source	DF	–LogLikelihood	ChiSquare	Prob>ChiSq
Model	3	9.44293	18.88586	0.000289
Error	1682	548.25144		
C Total	1685	557.69437		
	RSquare (U)		0.0169	
	Observations		1686	

Parameter Estimates

Term	Estimate	Std Error	ChiSquare	Prob>ChiSq
Intercept	−2.20264085	0.0868001	643.94	0.0000
zAFQT89	−0.36246881	0.0992802	13.33	0.0003
zSES	+0.21788340	0.1075722	4.10	0.0428
zAge	−0.12815393	0.0864018	2.20	0.1380

The High School Sample:

Whole–Model Test

Source	DF	–LogLikelihood	ChiSquare	Prob>ChiSq
Model	3	4.45831	8.916625	0.030420
Error	617	156.98046		
C Total	620	161.43878		
	RSquare (U)		0.0276	
	Observations		621	

Parameter Estimates

Term	Estimate	Std Error	ChiSquare	Prob>ChiSq
Intercept	−2.69780012	0.1767563	232.95	0.0000
zAFQT89	−0.42151253	0.2264362	3.47	0.0627
zSES	+0.56489480	0.230053	6.03	0.0141
zAge	−0.14556950	0.1672623	0.76	0.3841

The College Sample:

Whole–Model Test

Source	DF	–LogLikelihood	ChiSquare	Prob>ChiSq
Model	3	6.794337	13.58867	0.003522
Error	264	56.536860		
C Total	267	63.331196		
		RSquare (U)	0.1073	
		Observations	268	

Parameter Estimates

Term	Estimate	Std Error	ChiSquare	Prob>ChiSq
Intercept	−3.12957075	0.6081769	26.48	0.0000
zAFQT89	−0.84324247	0.4526768	3.47	0.0625
zSES	+0.94514750	0.3875388	5.95	0.0147
zAge	−0.46061574	0.299044	2.37	0.1235

DEPENDENT VARIABLE: Unemployed for four weeks or more in 1989.

SAMPLE RESTRICTIONS: Civilian males who did not respond "unable to work" or "in school" to the question on labor force participation in the 1989 or 1990 interview and were in the labor force throughout 1989.

Basic Analysis:

Whole–Model Test

Source	DF	–LogLikelihood	ChiSquare	Prob>ChiSq
Model	3	11.30841	22.61682	0.000049
Error	1393	348.71511		
C Total	1396	360.02353		
		RSquare (U)	0.0314	
		Observations	1397	

Parameter Estimates

Term	Estimate	Std Error	ChiSquare	Prob>ChiSq
Intercept	−2.53577016	0.1076083	555.30	0.0000
zAFQT89	−0.49486463	0.1298967	14.51	0.0001
zSES	−0.02534849	0.1383889	0.03	0.8547
zAge	−0.02181428	0.1108396	0.04	0.8440

The High School Sample:

Whole–Model Test

Source	DF	–LogLikelihood	ChiSquare	Prob>ChiSq
Model	3	1.86533	3.730657	0.292056
Error	533	140.49123		
C Total	536	142.35656		
		RSquare (U)	0.0131	
		Observations	537	

Parameter Estimates

Term	Estimate	Std Error	ChiSquare	Prob>ChiSq
Intercept	−2.59878187	0.1766146	216.51	0.0000
zAFQT89	−0.39353140	0.2368752	2.76	0.0966
zSES	+0.13951940	0.2353179	0.35	0.5532
zAge	−0.10510566	0.1762471	0.36	0.5509

The College Sample:

Whole–Model Test

Source	DF	−LogLikelihood	ChiSquare	Prob>ChiSq
Model	3	3.570096	7.140193	0.067561
Error	224	40.506133		
C Total	227	44.076230		
		RSquare (U)	0.0810	
		Observations	228	

Parameter Estimates

Term	Estimate	Std Error	ChiSquare	Prob>ChiSq
Intercept	−3.1686886	0.7276735	18.96	0.0000
zAFQT89	−0.9196886	0.5641635	2.66	0.1031
zSES	+1.0039255	0.5015717	4.01	0.0453
zAge	+0.2941965	0.3311174	0.79	0.3743

CHAPTER 8: FAMILY MATTERS

DEPENDENT VARIABLE: Ever married before the age of 30.
SAMPLE RESTRICTIONS: Persons who turned thirty by the 1990 interview.

Basic Analysis:

Whole–Model Test

Source	DF	−LogLikelihood	ChiSquare	Prob>ChiSq
Model	3	6.43345	12.8669	0.004933
Error	1630	839.76747		
C Total	1633	846.20092		
		RSquare (U)	0.0076	
		Observations	1634	

Parameter Estimates

Term	Estimate	Std Error	ChiSquare	Prob>ChiSq
Intercept	+1.19841361	0.128902	86.44	0.0000
zAFQT89	−0.0473587	0.0757854	0.39	0.5320
zSES	−0.1905526	0.0786307	5.87	0.0154
zAge	+0.20403379	0.1290545	2.50	0.1139

The High School Sample:

Whole–Model Test

Source	DF	–LogLikelihood	ChiSquare	Prob>ChiSq
Model	3	6.92871	13.857	0.003106
Error	601	259.40296		
C Total	604	266.33168		
	RSquare (U)		0.0260	
	Observations		605	

Parameter Estimates

Term	Estimate	Std Error	ChiSquare	Prob>ChiSq
Intercept	+1.41494853	0.2342703	36.48	0.0000
zAFQT89	+0.51424443	0.1598383	10.35	0.0013
zSES	−0.1128845	0.1582799	.51	0.4757
zAge	+0.36827169	0.2422543	2.31	0.1285

The College Sample:

Whole–Model Test

Source	DF	–LogLikelihood	ChiSquare	Prob>ChiSq
Model	3	0.17181	0.343616	0.951627
Error	233	145.35748		
C Total	236	145.52929		
	RSquare (U)		0.0012	
	Observations		237	

Parameter Estimates

Term	Estimate	Std Error	ChiSquare	Prob>ChiSq
Intercept	+0.71372375	0.3946174	3.27	0.0705
zAFQT89	+0.05013859	0.2237528	0.05	0.8227
zSES	+0.0968295	0.1833680	0.28	0.5975
zAge	−0.0177807	0.2950863	0.00	0.9520

DEPENDENT VARIABLE: Divorced within the first five years of marriage.
SAMPLE RESTRICTIONS: Persons married prior to January 1, 1986.

Basic Analysis, Adding Date of First Marriage (MarDate1):

Whole–Model Test

Source	DF	–LogLikelihood	ChiSquare	Prob>ChiSq
Model	4	21.8881	43.77626	0.000000
Error	2026	991.3719		
C Total	2030	1013.2600		
	RSquare (U)		0.0216	
	Observations		2031	

Parameter Estimates

Term	Estimate	Std Error	ChiSquare	Prob>ChiSq
Intercept	+5.70860970	1.9858067	8.26	0.0040
zAFQT89	−0.35734009	0.0781258	20.92	0.0000

Term	Estimate	Std Error	ChiSquare	Prob>ChiSq
zSES	+0.22195410	0.0787612	7.94	0.0048
zAge	−0.17766944	0.0741478	5.74	0.0166
MarDate1	−0.08677335	0.0243113	12.74	0.0004

The High School Sample, Adding Date of First Marriage (MarDate1):

Whole–Model Test

Source	DF	−LogLikelihood	ChiSquare	Prob>ChiSq
Model	4	3.54304	7.086073	0.131409
Error	870	428.70643		
C Total	874	432.24947		
		RSquare (U)	0.0082	
		Observations	875	

Parameter Estimates

Term	Estimate	Std Error	ChiSquare	Prob>ChiSq
Intercept	+5.4451395	3.1286887	3.03	0.0818
zAFQT89	−0.0379171	0.1348129	0.08	0.7785
zSES	+0.2206925	0.1288222	2.93	0.0867
zAge	−0.1078057	0.1146773	0.88	0.3472
MarDate1	−0.0839950	0.0383236	4.80	0.0284

The College Sample, Adding Date of First Marriage (MarDate1):

Whole–Model Test

Source	DF	−LogLikelihood	ChiSquare	Prob>ChiSq
Model	4	5.548154	11.09631	0.025503
Error	204	48.414468		
C Total	208	53.962623		
		RSquare (U)	0.1028	
		Observations	209	

Parameter Estimates

Term	Estimate	Std Error	ChiSquare	Prob>ChiSq
Intercept	+32.392875	13.508886	5.75	0.0165
zAFQT89	−0.75619367	0.4502182	2.82	0.0930
zSES	−0.07354619	0.3588816	0.04	0.8376
zAge	−0.55875424	0.4046911	1.91	0.1674
MarDate1	−0.41113710	0.1629791	6.36	0.0116

Basic analysis, Adding Parental Living Arrangements at Age 14 (Adult14):

Whole–Model Test

Source	DF	−LogLikelihood	ChiSquare	Prob>ChiSq
Model	6	16.7457	33.49136	0.000008
Error	2022	994.6771		
C Total	2028	1011.4228		
		RSquare (U)	0.0166	
		Observations	2029	

Parameter Estimates

Term	Estimate	Std Error	ChiSquare	Prob>ChiSq
Intercept	−1.2952650	0.1066175	147.59	0.0000
zAFQT89	−0.3925580	0.0774209	25.71	0.0000
zSES	+0.1910425	0.0783345	5.95	0.0147
zAge	−0.0278086	0.0617722	0.20	0.6526
Adult14 [2 Bio-UnmarMom]	−0.1472662	0.117616	1.57	0.2105
Adult14 [Bio/Step-UnmarMom]	+0.0621918	0.1601525	0.15	0.6978
Adult14 [Other-UnmarMom]	−0.0872024	0.2553089	0.12	0.7327

DEPENDENT VARIABLE: First birth out of wedlock.
SAMPLE RESTRICTIONS: Women with at least one child.

Basic Analysis:

Whole–Model Test

Source	DF	−LogLikelihood	ChiSquare	Prob>ChiSq
Model	3	39.86862	79.73723	0.000000
Error	1217	461.90618		
C Total	1220	501.77480		
		RSquare (U)	0.0795	
		Observations	1221	

Parameter Estimates

Term	Estimate	Std Error	ChiSquare	Prob>ChiSq
Intercept	−1.9432320	0.0938185	429.01	0.0000
zAFQT89	−0.6537960	0.1239489	27.82	0.0000
zSES	−0.3052597	0.1189878	6.58	0.0103
zAge	−0.2405246	0.0902516	7.10	0.0077

The High School Sample:

Whole–Model Test

Source	DF	−LogLikelihood	ChiSquare	Prob>ChiSq
Model	3	15.09449	30.18898	0.000001
Error	512	187.89956		
C Total	515	202.99405		
		RSquare (U)	0.0744	
		Observations	516	

Parameter Estimates

Term	Estimate	Std Error	ChiSquare	Prob>ChiSq
Intercept	−2.1890354	0.1658602	174.19	0.0000
zAFQT89	−0.7846895	0.2142378	13.42	0.0002
zSES	−0.2428727	0.2165927	1.26	0.2621
zAge	−0.4145066	0.1447961	8.20	0.0042

The College Sample:

Whole–Model Test

Source	DF	–LogLikelihood	ChiSquare	Prob>ChiSq
Model	3	1.1299340	2.259868	0.520253
Error	112	4.6193334		
C Total	115	5.7492674		
	RSquare (U)		0.1965	
	Observations		116	

Parameter Estimates

Term	Estimate	Std Error	ChiSquare	Prob>ChiSq
Intercept	−6.37685240	3.9705049	2.58	0.1083
zAFQT89	−0.31644570	1.9844225	0.03	0.8733
zSES	−0.72608390	1.5248314	0.23	0.6340
zAge	+2.58214793	2.8423709	0.83	0.3636

Basic analysis, Adding Living Arrangements with Adults at Age 14 (Adult14):

Whole–Model Test

Source	DF	–LogLikelihood	ChiSquare	Prob>ChiSq
Model	6	46.62389	93.24777	0.000000
Error	1214	455.15091		
C Total	1220	501.77480		
	RSquare (U)		0.0929	
	Observations		1221	

Parameter Estimates

Term	Estimate	Std Error	ChiSquare	Prob>ChiSq
Intercept	−1.8260275	0.1541482	140.33	0.0000
zAFQT89	−0.6620720	0.1259903	27.61	0.0000
zSES	−0.2460336	0.1221771	4.06	0.0440
zAge	−0.2109268	0.0909302	5.38	0.0204
Adult14 [2 Bio-UnmarMom]	−0.2816545	0.1634249	2.97	0.0848
Adult14 [Bio/Step-UnmarMom]	+0.2928507	0.206926	2.00	0.1570
Adult14 [Other-UnmarMom]	−0.4991684	0.3593261	1.93	0.1648

Basic analysis, Adding Presence of Biological Parents at Age 14 (14Bio):

Whole–Model Test

Source	DF	–LogLikelihood	ChiSquare	Prob>ChiSq
Model	6	47.56391	95.12783	0.000000
Error	1214	454.21088		
C Total	1220	501.77480		
	RSquare (U)		0.0948	
	Observations		1221	

Parameter Estimates

Term	Estimate	Std Error	ChiSquare	Prob>ChiSq
Intercept	−2.0199123	0.2037839	98.25	0.0000
zAFQT89	−0.6567746	0.1250691	27.58	0.0000
zSES	−0.2479794	0.1214895	4.17	0.0412
zAge	−0.2037178	0.0910296	5.01	0.0252
14Bio [MomOnly-PopOnly]	+0.6528652	0.2233927	8.54	0.0035
14Bio [Mom/Pop-PopOnly]	−0.0862208	0.2102335	0.17	0.6817
14Bio[Neither-PopOnly]	−0.2371231	0.4150982	0.33	0.5678

Basic Analysis, Adding Poverty Status in the Calendar Year Prior to Birth (PreBirthPov):

Whole–Model Test

Source	DF	−LogLikelihood	ChiSquare	Prob>ChiSq
Model	4	63.21118	126.4224	0.000000
Error	956	292.73717		
C Total	960	355.94835		
		RSquare (U)	0.1776	
		Observations	961	

Parameter Estimates

Term	Estimate	Std Error	ChiSquare	Prob>ChiSq
Intercept	−1.6785743	0.1460018	132.18	0.0000
zAFQT89	−0.6300049	0.1665952	14.30	0.0002
zSES	−0.1828877	0.1513393	1.46	0.2269
zAge	−0.4759393	0.127232	13.99	0.0002
PreBirthPov [No-Yes]	−0.8178684	0.1266496	41.70	0.0000

Basic Analysis, Restricted to Women Below the Poverty Line in the Calendar Year Prior to Birth:

Whole–Model Test

Source	DF	−LogLikelihood	ChiSquare	Prob>ChiSq
Model	3	3.005867	6.011735	0.111041
Error	95	65.003329		
C Total	98	68.009196		
		RSquare (U)	0.0442	
		Observations	99	

Parameter Estimates

Term	Estimate	Std Error	ChiSquare	Prob>ChiSq
Intercept	−0.65306390	0.2901964	5.06	0.0244
zAFQT89	−0.76887410	0.3453889	4.96	0.0260
zSES	+0.17993445	0.2589166	0.48	0.4871
zAge	−0.13622880	0.2289764	0.35	0.5519

CHAPTER 9: WELFARE DEPENDENCY

DEPENDENT VARIABLE: On welfare by the first calendar year after the birth of the child.

SAMPLE RESTRICTIONS: Women with at least one child born prior to January 1, 1989.

Basic Analysis, Adding Poverty Status in the Year Prior to Birth (PreBirth-Pov) and Marital Status at the Time of the Birth (BStatus):

Whole–Model Test

Source	DF	–LogLikelihood	ChiSquare	Prob>ChiSq
Model	5	100.37993	200.7599	0.000000
Error	833	221.75844		
C Total	838	322.13837		
	RSquare (U)		0.3116	
	Observations		839	

Parameter Estimates

Term	Estimate	Std Error	ChiSquare	Prob>ChiSq
Intercept	−1.03594055	0.1713324	36.56	0.0000
zAFQT89	−0.57972844	0.1892548	9.38	0.0022
zSES	−0.06130137	0.1746782	0.12	0.7256
zAge	−0.11269946	0.1457313	0.60	0.4393
PreBirthPov				
[No-Yes]	−0.89960808	0.1446041	38.70	0.0000
BStatus				
[Illegit-Legit]	+1.05258560	0.1352006	60.61	0.0000

The High School Sample, Adding Poverty Status in the Year Prior to Birth (PreBirthPov) and Marital Status at the Time of the Birth (BStatus):

Whole–Model Test

Source	DF	–LogLikelihood	ChiSquare	Prob>ChiSq
Model	5	29.28354	58.56707	0.000000
Error	384	108.14153		
C Total	389	137.42507		
	RSquare (U)		0.2131	
	Observations		390	

Parameter Estimates

Term	Estimate	Std Error	ChiSquare	Prob>ChiSq
Intercept	−1.44234110	0.2659616	29.41	0.0000
zAFQT89	−0.60735910	0.3004261	4.09	0.0432
zSES	+0.12094082	0.3096641	0.15	0.6961
zAge	−0.24139690	0.2089849	1.33	0.2481

PreBirthPov

[No-Yes]	−0.67898980	0.223275	9.25	0.0024
BStatus				
[Illegit-Legit]	+0.80812194	0.2058033	15.42	0.0001

The College Sample: Omitted. Included no women who had received Aid to Families with Dependent Children (AFDC) within a year after the birth.

DEPENDENT VARIABLE: On welfare for at least five years versus women with no welfare experience at all.

SAMPLE RESTRICTIONS: Women with at least one child born prior to January 1, 1986. For women scored as "no welfare," child born after December 31, 1977 and complete data on welfare receipt from 1978 to 1986.

Basic Analysis, Adding Poverty Status in the Year Prior to Birth (PreBirthPov) and Marital Status at the Time of the Birth (BStatus):

Whole–Model Test

Source	DF	−LogLikelihood	ChiSquare	Prob>ChiSq
Model	5	44.82635	89.65269	0.000000
Error	493	96.90156		
C Total	498	141.72790		
		RSquare (U)	0.3163	
		Observations	499	

Parameter Estimates

Term	Estimate	Std Error	ChiSquare	Prob>ChiSq
Intercept	−1.5840878	0.2826002	31.42	0.0000
zAFQT89	−0.5506878	0.2950687	3.48	0.0620
zSES	−0.4921959	0.2779368	3.14	0.0766
zAge	−0.1094338	0.2276355	0.23	0.6307
PreBirthPov				
[No-Yes]	−0.7636358	0.2336359	10.68	0.0011
BStatus				
[Illegit-Legit]	+1.1951879	0.205013	33.99	0.0000

The High School Sample, Adding Poverty Status in the Year Prior to Birth (PreBirthPov) and Marital Status at the Time of the Birth (BStatus):

Whole–Model Test

Source	DF	−LogLikelihood	ChiSquare	Prob>ChiSq
Model	5	13.898589	27.79718	0.000040
Error	251	48.695997		
C Total	256	62.594585		
		RSquare (U)	0.2220	
		Observations	257	

Parameter Estimates

Term	Estimate	Std Error	ChiSquare	Prob>ChiSq
Intercept	−1.7786656	0.3901684	20.78	0.0000
zAFQT89	−0.2301309	0.4429317	0.27	0.6034
zSES	−0.3131157	0.4832739	0.42	0.5170
zAge	−0.0377430	0.3173131	0.01	0.9053
PreBirthPov [No-Yes]	−0.6891978	0.3355851	4.22	0.0400
BStatus [Illegit-Legit]	+1.1068557	0.307595	12.95	0.0003

The College Sample: Omitted. The cross-sectional College Sample included no women who were on chronic welfare within a year after the birth.

CHAPTER 10: PARENTING

DEPENDENT VARIABLE: Did the mother smoke during pregnancy?
SAMPLE RESTRICTIONS: None.

Basic Analysis:

Whole–Model Test

Source	DF	−LogLikelihood	ChiSquare	Prob>ChiSq
Model	3	84.6762	169.3523	0.000000
Error	2338	1443.8251		
C Total	2341	1528.5013		
		RSquare (U)	0.0554	
		Observations	2342	

Parameter Estimates

Term	Estimate	Std Error	ChiSquare	Prob>ChiSq
Intercept	−0.65729780	0.0465003	199.81	0.0000
zAFQT89	−0.63479220	0.0645408	96.74	0.0000
zSES	−0.13376440	0.0604787	4.89	0.0270
zAge	+0.09727632	0.0484283	4.03	0.0446

DEPENDENT VARIABLE: Low birth weight (weight less than 5.5 pounds at birth).

SAMPLE RESTRICTIONS: Excludes premature babies whose weight was less than 5.5 lbs. but was appropriate for gestational age.

Basic Analysis:

Whole–Model Test

Source	DF	−LogLikelihood	ChiSquare	Prob>ChiSq
Model	3	6.55199	13.10397	0.004417
Error	2273	349.79375		
C Total	2276	356.34574		
		RSquare (U)	0.0184	
		Observations	2277	

Parameter Estimates

Term	Estimate	Std Error	ChiSquare	Prob>ChiSq
Intercept	−3.40600010	0.1270004	719.25	0.0000
zAFQT89	−0.44308170	0.1496847	8.76	0.0031
zSES	+0.03312669	0.1492929	0.05	0.8244
zAge	+0.26896236	0.1226929	4.81	0.0284

Basic Analysis, Adding Poverty Status in the Year Prior to Birth (PreBirth-Pov):

Whole–Model Test

Source	DF	−LogLikelihood	ChiSquare	Prob>ChiSq
Model	4	9.09299	18.18599	0.001135
Error	1859	298.98002		
C Total	1863	308.07301		
		RSquare (U)	0.0295	
		Observations	1864	

Parameter Estimates

Term	Estimate	Std Error	ChiSquare	Prob>ChiSq
Intercept	−3.12509860	0.16455	360.69	0.0000
zAFQT89	−0.45583800	0.1674174	7.41	0.0065
zSES	+0.02995737	0.1628609	0.03	0.8541
zAge	+0.34292817	0.1342861	6.52	0.0107
PreBirthPov [No-Yes]	−0.28644950	0.15725	3.32	0.0685

Basic Analysis, Adding Mother's Age at Birth (AgeBirth):

Whole–Model Test

Source	DF	−LogLikelihood	ChiSquare	Prob>ChiSq
Model	4	6.77955	13.55909	0.008844
Error	2272	349.56619		
C Total	2276	356.34574		
		RSquare (U)	0.0190	
		Observations	2277	

Parameter Estimates

Term	Estimate	Std Error	ChiSquare	Prob>ChiSq
Intercept	−3.90965790	0.7617514	26.34	0.0000
zAFQT89	−0.46251520	0.1522804	9.22	0.0024
zSES	+0.01584480	0.1517047	0.01	0.9168
zAge	+0.25360789	0.1252257	4.10	0.0428
AgeBirth	+0.02095854	0.0311104	0.45	0.5005

The High School Sample:
Whole–Model Test

Source	DF	–LogLikelihood	ChiSquare	Prob>ChiSq
Model	3	1.96999	3.93998	0.268019
Error	944	179.09080		
C Total	947	181.06079		
	RSquare (U)		0.0109	
	Observations		948	

Parameter Estimates:

Term	Estimate	Std Error	ChiSquare	Prob>ChiSq
Intercept	−3.1278597	0.1778908	309.16	0.0000
zAFQT89	−0.3560319	0.2387034	2.22	0.1358
zSES	+0.0653651	0.2379847	0.08	0.7836
zAge	+0.2490558	0.1681270	2.19	0.1385

The College Sample: Omitted. The cross-sectional College Sample included only four low-birth-weight babies.

DEPENDENT VARIABLE: The child's mother was under the poverty line throughout the child's first three years of life.

SAMPLE RESTRICTIONS: Includes children born from January 1, 1978 through December 31, 1987, with complete data on poverty for the first three years of the child's life, beginning with the calendar year of birth. Comparison group consists of children of mothers who were not in poverty in any of those years.

Basic Analysis:
Whole–Model Test

Source	DF	–LogLikelihood	ChiSquare	Prob>ChiSq
Model	3	79.84242	159.6848	0.000000
Error	1054	246.63029		
C Total	1057	326.47271		
	RSquare (U)		0.2446	
	Observations		1058	

Parameter Estimates

Term	Estimate	Std Error	ChiSquare	Prob>ChiSq
Intercept	−2.9319316	0.1679177	304.87	0.0000
zAFQT89	−1.1608860	0.1893877	37.57	0.0000
zSES	−1.0386253	0.1734586	35.85	0.0000
zAge	−0.1837537	0.1320334	1.94	0.1640

Basic Analysis, Adding Poverty Status in the Year Prior to Birth (PreBirthPov):

Whole–Model Test

Source	DF	–LogLikelihood	ChiSquare	Prob>ChiSq
Model	4	133.38437	266.7687	0.000000
Error	967	161.88379		
C Total	971	295.26816		
		RSquare (U)	0.4517	
		Observations	972	

Parameter Estimates

Term	Estimate	Std Error	ChiSquare	Prob>ChiSq
Intercept	−1.9685017	0.2117444	86.43	0.0000
zAFQT89	−1.0772447	0.2375948	20.56	0.0000
zSES	−0.8977385	0.2215879	16.41	0.0001
zAge	+0.0117316	0.1681889	0.00	0.9444
PreBirthPov [No-Yes]	−1.7345986	0.1635206	112.53	0.0000

The High School Sample, Adding Poverty Status in the Year Prior to Birth (PreBirthPov):

Whole–Model Test

Source	DF	–LogLikelihood	ChiSquare	Prob>ChiSq
Model	4	133.38437	266.7687	0.000000
Error	967	161.88379		
C Total	971	295.26816		
		RSquare (U)	0.4517	
		Observations	972	

Parameter Estimates

Term	Estimate	Std Error	ChiSquare	Prob>ChiSq
Intercept	−1.9685017	0.2117444	86.43	0.0000
zAFQT89	−1.0772447	0.2375948	20.56	0.0000
zSES	−0.8977385	0.2215879	16.41	0.0001
zAge	+0.0117316	0.1681889	0.00	0.9444
PreBirthPov [No-Yes]	−1.7345986	0.1635206	112.53	0.0000

The College Sample: Omitted. The cross-sectional College Sample included only one child whose mother was beneath the poverty line throughout the first three years.

DEPENDENT VARIABLE: The child's HOME index score was in the bottom decile.

SAMPLE RESTRICTIONS: None.

Additional control variables: Test year (TestYr, nominal: 1986, 1988, or 1990) and the child's age category for scoring the HOME index (HomeAgeCat, nominal, in years: 0/2, 3/5, 6+).

Basic Analysis:

Whole–Model Test

Source	DF	–LogLikelihood	ChiSquare	Prob>ChiSq
Model	7	88.9225	177.8451	0.000000
Error	5114	1190.6267		
C Total	5121	1279.5492		
	RSquare (U)		0.0695	
	Observations		5122	

Parameter Estimates

Term	Estimate	Std Error	ChiSquare	Prob>ChiSq
Intercept	−2.8430001	0.0687859	1708.3	0.0000
zAFQT89	−0.6710186	0.0765998	76.74	0.0000
zSES	−0.2383458	0.0800828	8.86	0.0029
zAge	−0.1428139	0.062902	5.15	0.0232
TestYr [86-90]	+0.0128625	0.0858087	0.02	0.8808
TestYr [88-90]	−0.0414196	0.0798373	0.27	0.6039
HomeAgeCat [0/2-6+]	+0.3225819	0.081541	15.65	0.0001
HomeAgeCat [3/5-6+]	−0.1338273	0.0852061	2.47	0.1163

Basic Analysis, Adding Poverty Status in the Year Before the HOME Index was Scored (PreTYPov):

Whole–Model Test

Source	DF	–LogLikelihood	ChiSquare	Prob>ChiSq
Model	8	116.4719	232.9438	0.000000
Error	4655	1049.6688		
C Total	4663	1166.1407		
	RSquare (U)		0.0999	
	Observations		4664	

Parameter Estimates

Term	Estimate	Std Error	ChiSquare	Prob>ChiSq
Intercept	−2.5413180	0.0768882	1092.4	0.0000
zAFQT89	−0.5717052	0.0847651	45.49	0.0000
zSES	−0.1646842	0.0848268	3.77	0.0522
zAge	−0.0836204	0.0673282	1.54	0.2142
TestYr [86-90]	Unstable +0.0068172	0.0900515	0.01	0.9397
TestYr [88-90]	−0.0538353	0.0851491	0.40	0.5272
HomeAge Cat[0/2-6+]	+0.3100371	0.0867081	12.79	0.0003

HomeAge				
Cat[3/5-6+]	−0.0968535	0.0892661	1.18	0.2779
PreTYPov				
[No-Yes]	−0.5366001	0.0664395	65.23	0.0000

Basic Analysis, Adding AFDC Status in the Year Before the HOME Index Was Scored (PreTYADC):

Whole–Model Test

Source	DF	−LogLikelihood	ChiSquare	Prob>ChiSq
Model	8	120.4866	240.9733	0.000000
Error	5101	1150.3749		
C Total	5109	1270.8615		
	RSquare (U)		0.0948	
	Observations		5110	

Parameter Estimates

Term	Estimate	Std Error	ChiSquare	Prob>ChiSq
Intercept	−2.4639335	0.0797203	955.26	0.0000
zAFQT89	−0.5835098	0.078223	55.65	0.0000
zSES	−0.1973545	0.0813485	5.89	0.0153
zAge	−0.0908713	0.0644499	1.99	0.1586
TestYr[86–90]	−0.0105341	0.0872339	0.01	0.9039
TestYr[88-90]	−0.0232495	0.0811592	0.08	0.7745
HomeAge				
Cat[0/2-6+]	+0.3429802	0.0829005	17.12	0.0000
HomeAge				
Cat[3/5-6+]	−0.1348740	0.0863764	2.44	0.1184
PreTYADC				
[No-Yes]	−0.5572417	0.0680104	67.13	0.0000

Basic Analysis, Adding Both Poverty and AFDC Status in the Year Before the HOME Index was Scored (PreTYPov, PreTYADC):

Whole–Model Test

Source	DF	−LogLikelihood	ChiSquare	Prob>ChiSq
Model	9	127.1525	254.3049	0.000000
Error	4654	1038.9883		
C Total	4663	1166.1407		
	RSquare (U)		0.1090	
	Observations		4664	

Parameter Estimates

Term	Estimate	Std Error	ChiSquare	Prob>ChiSq
Intercept	−2.3642864	0.0832843	805.89	0.0000
zAFQT89	−0.5452068	0.0849779	41.16	0.0000
zSES	−0.1657978	0.0852414	3.78	0.0518
zAge	−0.0664416	0.0679088	0.96	0.3279

TestYr[86-90]	Unstable	+0.0029083	0.0904431	0.00
0.9743				
TestYr[88-90]	−0.0455863	0.0856239	0.28	0.5944
HomeAge				
Cat[0/2–6+]	+0.3145455	0.087279	12.99	0.0003
HomeAge				
Cat[3/5-6+]	−0.1002522	0.0896764	1.25	0.2636
PreTYADC				
[No-Yes]	−0.3806916	0.0809799	22.10	0.0000
PreTYPov				
[No-Yes]	−0.3774093	0.0762828	24.48	0.0000

The High School Sample:

Whole–Model Test

Source	DF	−LogLikelihood	ChiSquare	Prob>ChiSq
Model	7	26.90513	53.81026	0.000000
Error	2282	526.92206		
C Total	2289	553.82719		
	RSquare (U)		0.0486	
	Observations		2290	

Parameter Estimates

Term	Estimate	Std Error	ChiSquare	Prob>ChiSq
Intercept	−2.9071274	0.1079507	725.23	0.0000
zAFQT89	−0.5655610	0.1331445	18.04	0.0000
zSES	−0.3731384	0.1355456	7.58	0.0059
zAge	−0.1569221	0.0964674	2.65	0.1038
TestYr[86-90]	+0.0755310	0.1295874	0.34	0.5600
TestYr[88-90]	−0.1487970	0.1239539	1.44	0.2300
HomeAge				
Cat[0/2-6+]	+0.3159089	0.1236104	6.53	0.0106
HomeAge				
Cat[3/5-6+]	−0.0254850	0.1242055	0.04	0.8374

The College Sample: Omitted. The cross-sectional sample included only five cases of children in the bottom decile on the HOME index.

DEPENDENT VARIABLE: The child was in the bottom decile on any of the four developmental indicators (friendliness index, difficulty index, motor and social development index, and behavioral problems index).

SAMPLE RESTRICTIONS: None.

ADDITIONAL CONTROL VARIABLES: Test year (TestYr, nominal: 1986, 1988, or 1990).

Basic Analysis:

Whole–Model Test

Source	DF	–LogLikelihood	ChiSquare	Prob>ChiSq
Model	5	35.5004	71.00086	0.000000
Error	4885	1534.3911		
C Total	4890	1569.8915		
		RSquare (U)	0.0226	
		Observations	4891	

Parameter Estimates

Term	Estimate	Std Error	ChiSquare	Prob>ChiSq
Intercept	−2.2678463	0.0523382	1877.5	0.0000
zAFQT89	−0.3374850	0.0666453	25.64	0.0000
zSES	−0.1454605	0.0662047	4.83	0.0280
zAge	−0.0406925	0.0531744	0.59	0.4441
TestYr[86-90]	+0.1789367	0.0698843	6.56	0.0105
TestYr[88-90]	−0.0070670	0.0677961	0.01	0.9170

Basic Analysis, Adding Poverty Status and Welfare Status in the Year Prior to Testing (PreTYPov, PreTYADC) and Whether the Child was Born out of Wedlock (BStatus):

Whole–Model Test

Source	DF	–LogLikelihood	ChiSquare	Prob>ChiSq
Model	8	42.9933	85.98651	0.000000
Error	4329	1350.0000		
C Total	4337	1392.9933		
		RSquare (U)	0.0309	
		Observations	4338	

Parameter Estimates

Term	Estimate	Std Error	ChiSquare	Prob>ChiSq
Intercept	−2.00631470	0.0860525	543.59	0.0000
zAFQT89	−0.25174490	0.075657	11.07	0.0009
zSES	−0.13270420	0.0708367	3.51	0.0610
zAge	+0.01726122	0.0575776	0.09	0.7643
TestYr[86-90]	+0.18566228	0.0735475	6.37	0.0116
TestYr[88-90]	+0.01877328	0.072493	0.07	0.7957
PreTYADC [Yes-No]	+0.13056720	0.0820003	2.54	0.1113
PreTYPov [Yes-No]	+0.24199190	0.0714256	11.48	0.0007
BStatus [Illegit-Legit]	+0.01707707	0.0764089	0.05	0.8231

The High School Sample:

Whole–Model Test

Source	DF	–LogLikelihood	ChiSquare	Prob>ChiSq
Model	5	13.59824	27.19647	0.000052
Error	2181	704.58153		
C Total	2186	718.17976		
	RSquare (U)		0.0189	
	Observations		2187	

Parameter Estimates

Term	Estimate	Std Error	ChiSquare	Prob>ChiSq
Intercept	−2.3178135	0.0834745	770.99	0.0000
zAFQT89	−0.3193097	0.1100786	8.41	0.0037
zSES	−0.3161019	0.1113263	8.06	0.0045
zAge	+0.0231487	0.0778738	0.09	0.7663
TestYr[86-90]	+0.1566625	0.1029997	2.31	0.1283
TestYr[88-90]	+0.0136187	0.0996255	0.02	0.8913

The College Sample:

Whole–Model Test

Source	DF	–LogLikelihood	ChiSquare	Prob>ChiSq
Model	5	5.166097	10.33219	0.066352
Error	346	74.395923		
C Total	351	79.562020		
	RSquare (U)		0.0649	
	Observations		352	

Parameter Estimates

Term	Estimate	Std Error	ChiSquare	Prob>ChiSq
Intercept	−3.0081530	0.530244	32.18	0.0000
zAFQT89	+0.78938018	0.3581312	4.86	0.0275
zSES	−0.80898430	0.3371107	5.76	0.0164
zAge	Unstable	+0.01498142	0.2822683	0.00 0.9577
TestYr[86-90]	+0.41149788	0.3719686	1.22	0.2686
TestYr[88-90]	−0.34603300	0.3626176	0.91	0.3399

DEPENDENT VARIABLE: The child was in the bottom decile on the Peabody Picture Vocabulary Test (PPVT).

SAMPLE RESTRICTIONS: Includes only children tested at age 6 and older.

ADDITIONAL CONTROL VARIABLES: Test year (TestYr, nominal: 1986, 1988, or 1990) and age at which the child was tested (continuous, in months. $m = 107.0$, $s = 27.1$)

Basic Analysis:

Whole–Model Test

Source	DF	–LogLikelihood	ChiSquare	Prob>ChiSq
Model	6	24.69587	49.39173	0.000000
Error	640	186.29121		
C Total	646	210.98708		
		RSquare (U)	0.1170	
		Observations	647	

Parameter Estimates

Term	Estimate	Std Error	ChiSquare	Prob>ChiSq
Intercept	−2.21570603	0.8589707	6.65	0.0099
zAFQT89	−1.11994138	0.1950498	32.97	0.0000
zSES	−0.08185312	0.1820132	0.20	0.6529
zAge	−0.02769682	0.1856376	0.02	0.8814
PPVTAge	−0.00466266	0.0077779	0.36	0.5489
TestYr[86-90]	−0.16528217	0.2424523	0.46	0.4954
TestYr[88-90]	−0.07970146	0.2250145	0.13	0.7232

Basic Analysis Adding Poverty Status in the Year Prior to the PPVT (PreTYPov) and the HOME Index Score Expressed in Standard Scores (zHOME):

Whole–Model Test

Source	DF	–LogLikelihood	ChiSquare	Prob>ChiSq
Model	8	17.72094	35.44187	0.000022
Error	582	153.59135		
C Total	590	171.31229		
		RSquare (U)	0.1034	
		Observations	591	

Parameter Estimates

Term	Estimate	Std Error	ChiSquare	Prob>ChiSq
Intercept	−2.1291342	0.9565224	4.95	0.0260
zAFQT89	−1.0337219	0.2205373	21.97	0.0000
zSES	−0.0861738	0.2093703	0.17	0.6806
zAge	+0.0296014	0.2145926	0.02	0.8903
TestYr[86-90]	−0.2286597	0.2683805	0.73	0.3942
TestYr[88-90]	−0.0483017	0.2526343	0.04	0.8484
PPVTAge	−0.0067930	0.0085395	0.63	0.4263
zHOME	−0.1945375	0.1842224	1.12	0.2910
PreTYPov [No-Yes]	+0.0903504	0.2016689	0.20	0.6541

The High School Sample:
Whole–Model Test

Source	DF	–LogLikelihood	ChiSquare	Prob>ChiSq
Model	6	7.225514	14.45103	0.024984
Error	254	68.236589		
C Total	260	75.462103		
	RSquare (U)		0.0958	
	Observations		261	

Parameter Estimates

Term	Estimate	Std Error	ChiSquare	Prob>ChiSq
Intercept	−0.2705795	1.4383055	0.04	0.8508
zAFQT89	−0.9296387	0.3952333	5.53	0.0187
zSES	−0.0918753	0.3493501	0.07	0.7926
zAge	+0.9267613	0.4137423	5.02	0.0251
TestYr[86-90]	−1.0895230	0.4214316	6.68	0.0097
TestYr[88-90]	+0.3167489	0.3591565	0.78	0.3778
PPVTAge	−0.0287800	0.0132748	4.70	0.0302

The College Sample: Omitted. No cases of a child age 6 or older in the bottom decile on the PPVT in the cross-sectional sample.

Women with Less Than a High School Education:
Whole–Model Test

Source	DF	–LogLikelihood	ChiSquare	Prob>ChiSq
Model	6	6.239129	12.47826	0.052111
Error	139	70.537266		
C Total	145	76.776395		
	RSquare (U)		0.0813	
	Observations		146	

Parameter Estimates

Term	Estimate	Std Error	ChiSquare	Prob>ChiSq
Intercept	−3.6384326	1.460085	6.21	0.0127
zAFQT89	−0.8396200	0.3093784	7.37	0.0066
zSES	+0.0090359	0.2914784	0.00	0.9753
zAge	−0.4386216	0.3016201	2.11	0.1459
TestYr[86-90]	+0.3771342	0.3759239	1.01	0.3158
TestYr[88-90]	−0.4974755	0.3638669	1.87	0.1716
PPVTAge	+0.0133480	0.011851	1.27	0.2600

CHAPTER 11: CRIME

DEPENDENT VARIABLE: The subject was in the top decile on an index of self-reported crime.

SAMPLE RESTRICTIONS: Includes only men.

Basic Analysis:

Whole–Model Test

Source	DF	–LogLikelihood	ChiSquare	Prob>ChiSq
Model	3	10.02735	20.05469	0.000165
Error	2004	649.74218		
C Total	2007	659.76953		
		RSquare (U)	0.0152	
		Observations	2008	

Parameter Estimates

Term	Estimate	Std Error	ChiSquare	Prob>ChiSq
Intercept	−2.22005314	0.0807852	755.20	0.0000
zAFQT89	−0.26980189	0.0902397	8.94	0.0028
zSES	+0.13972790	0.0979853	2.03	0.1539
zAge	−0.20372081	0.080365	6.43	0.0112

The High School Sample:

Whole–Model Test

Source	DF	–LogLikelihood	ChiSquare	Prob>ChiSq
Model	3	4.28228	8.564558	0.035677
Error	661	201.83770		
C Total	664	206.11998		
		RSquare (U)	0.0208	
		Observations	665	

Parameter Estimates

Term	Estimate	Std Error	ChiSquare	Prob>ChiSq
Intercept	−2.35032467	0.1445857	264.24	0.0000
zAFQT89	+0.2120838	0.2006406	1.12	0.2905
zSES	+0.3653400	0.1981511	3.40	0.0652
zAge	−0.26122639	0.1457019	3.21	0.0730

The College Sample:

Whole–Model Test

Source	DF	–LogLikelihood	ChiSquare	Prob>ChiSq
Model	3	2.959829	5.919657	0.115585
Error	276	46.577870		
C Total	279	49.537698		
		RSquare (U)	0.0597	
		Observations	280	

Parameter Estimates

Term	Estimate	Std Error	ChiSquare	Prob>ChiSq
Intercept	−3.33070801	0.7047663	22.33	0.0000
zAFQT89	−0.63468357	0.5194501	1.49	0.2218
zSES	+0.80027390	0.4591207	3.04	0.0813
zAge	+0.39913230	0.306701	1.69	0.1931

DEPENDENT VARIABLE: The subject was interviewed in a correctional facility in one or more interviews from 1979 to 1990.

SAMPLE RESTRICTIONS: Includes only men.

Basic Analysis:

Whole–Model Test

Source	DF	−LogLikelihood	ChiSquare	Prob>ChiSq
Model	3	23.31444	46.62887	0.000000
Error	1941	219.90125		
C Total	1944	243.21569		
	RSquare (U)		0.0959	
	Observations		1945	

Parameter Estimates

Term	Estimate	Std Error	ChiSquare	Prob>ChiSq
Intercept	−3.77716689	0.1717938	483.41	0.0000
zAFQT89	−0.89666260	0.1753619	26.14	0.0000
zSES	−0.15554116	0.1806149	0.74	0.3891
zAge	+0.0782992	0.1468634	0.28	0.5939

The High School Sample:

Whole–Model Test

Source	DF	−LogLikelihood	ChiSquare	Prob>ChiSq
Model	3	4.058464	8.116928	0.043656
Error	712	39.850585		
C Total	715	43.909049		
	RSquare (U)		0.0924	
	Observations		716	

Parameter Estimates

Term	Estimate	Std Error	ChiSquare	Prob>ChiSq
Intercept	−4.96578763	0.4806319	106.75	0.0000
zAFQT89	−1.07006679	0.443121	5.83	0.0157
zSES	−0.16211965	0.4642977	0.12	0.7270
zAge	+0.46727190	0.367754	1.61	0.2039

The College Sample: Omitted. No one in the cross-sectional College Sample was ever interviewed in jail.

CHAPTER 12: CIVILITY AND CITIZENSHIP

DEPENDENT VARIABLE: Did the subject score "yes" on the Middle Class
Values Index?

SAMPLE RESTRICTIONS: Excludes never-married persons who met all the
other conditions of the index and men who were physically unable
to work or not in the labor force because they were attending school.

Basic Analysis:

Whole–Model Test

Source	DF	–LogLikelihood	ChiSquare	Prob>ChiSq
Model	3	161.7136	323.4273	0.000000
Error	3025	1937.4328		
C Total	3028	2099.1465		
		RSquare (U)	0.0770	
		Observations	3029	

Parameter Estimates

Term	Estimate	Std Error	ChiSquare	Prob>ChiSq
Intercept	−0.06385330	0.038934	2.69	0.1010
zAFQT89	+0.63250551	0.0528176	143.41	0.0000
zSES	+0.24495537	0.0520624	22.14	0.0000
zAge	+0.00663732	0.0401929	0.03	0.8688

The High School Sample:

Whole–Model Test

Source	DF	–LogLikelihood	ChiSquare	Prob>ChiSq
Model	3	3.00926	6.018528	0.110712
Error	1158	781.85686		
C Total	1161	784.86612		
		RSquare (U)	0.0038	
		Observations	1162	

Parameter Estimates

Term	Estimate	Std Error	ChiSquare	Prob>ChiSq
Intercept	+0.39447706	0.0611821	41.57	0.0000
zAFQT89	+0.16814512	0.0931181	3.26	0.0710
zSES	−0.17993040	0.0903402	3.97	0.0464
zAge	+0.01887678	0.0621776	0.09	0.7614

The College Sample:

Whole–Model Test

Source	DF	–LogLikelihood	ChiSquare	Prob>ChiSq
Model	3	3.26859	6.537177	0.088208
Error	398	200.09145		
C Total	401	203.36004		
	RSquare (U)		0.0161	
	Observations		402	

Parameter Estimates

Term	Estimate	Std Error	ChiSquare	Prob>ChiSq
Intercept	+0.99516202	0.2386798	17.38	0.0000
zAFQT89	+0.39251349	0.1988073	3.90	0.0483
zSES	+0.03692158	0.168585	0.05	0.8266
zAge	+0.13876137	0.1336384	1.08	0.2991

Appendix 5

Supplemental Material for Chapter 13

Three issues raised in Chapter 13 are elaborated here: a more detailed discussion of cultural bias, more evidence for the narrowing of the black-white difference in cognitive ability, and the broader argument for racial differences advanced by Philippe Rushton.

MORE ON TEST BIAS

In Chapter 13, we reported that the scientific evidence demonstrates overwhelmingly that standardized tests of cognitive ability are not biased against blacks. Here, we elaborate on the reasoning and evidence that lead to that conclusion.

More on External Evidence of Bias: Predictive Validity

Everyday commentary on test bias usually starts with the observation that members of various ethnic (or socioeconomic) groups have different average scores and leaps to the assumption that a group difference is prima facie evidence of bias. But a moment's thought should convince anyone that this is not necessarily so. A group difference is, in and of itself, evidence of test bias only if we have some reason for assuming that an unbiased test would find no average difference between the groups. What might such a reason be? We cast the answer in terms of whites and blacks, since that is the context for most charges of test bias. Inasmuch as the context also usually involves a criticism of the use of the test in selection of persons for school or job, the most pertinent reason for assuming equality in the absence of test bias would be that we have other data showing that a randomly selected black and white with the same test score have different outcomes. This is what the text refers to as external evidence of bias.

If for example, blacks do better in school than whites after choosing blacks and whites with equal test scores, we could say that the test was biased against blacks in academic prediction. Similarly, if they do better on the job after choosing blacks and whites with equal test scores, the test could be considered biased against blacks for predicting work performance. This way of demonstrating bias is tantamount to showing that the regression of outcomes on scores differs for the two groups. On a test biased against blacks, the regression intercept would be higher for blacks than whites, as illustrated in the graphic below. Test scores un-

When a test is biased because it systematically underpredicts one group's performance

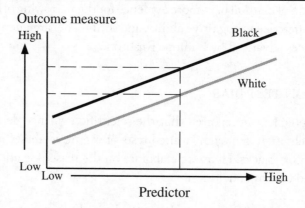

der these conditions would underestimate, or "underpredict," the performance outcome of blacks. A randomly selected black and white with the same IQ (shown by the vertical broken line) would not have equal outcomes; the black would outperform the white (as shown by the horizontal broken lines). The test is therefore biased against blacks. On an unbiased test, the two regression lines would converge because they would have the same intercept (the point at which the regression line crosses the vertical axis).

But the graphic above captures only one of the many possible manifestations of predictive bias. Suppose, for example, a test was less valid for blacks than for whites.[1] In regression terms, this would translate into a smaller coefficient (slope in these graphics), which could, in turn, be associated either with or without a difference in the intercept. The next figure illustrates a few hypothetical possibilities.

All three black lines have the same low coefficient; they vary only

When a test is biased because it is a less valid predictor of performance for one group than another

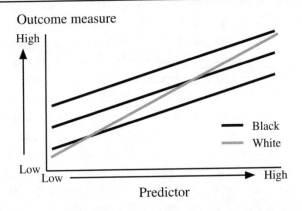

in their intercepts. The gray line, representing whites, has a higher coefficient (therefore, the line is steeper). Begin with the lowest of the three black lines. Only at the very lowest predictor scores do blacks score higher than whites on the outcome measure. As the score on the predictor increases, whites with equivalent predictor scores have higher outcome scores. Here, the test bias is against whites, not blacks. For the intermediate black line, we would pick up evidence for test bias against blacks in the low range of test scores and bias against whites in the high range. The top black line, with the highest of the three intercepts, would accord with bias against blacks throughout the range, but diminishing in magnitude the higher the score.

Readers will quickly grasp that test scores can predict outcomes differently for members of different groups and that such differences may justify claims of test bias. So what are the facts? Do we see anything like the first of the two graphics in the data—a clear difference in intercepts, to the disadvantage of blacks taking the test? Or is the picture cloudier— a mixture of intercept and coefficient differences, yielding one sort of bias or another in different ranges of the test scores? When questions about data come up, cloudier and murkier is usually a safe bet. So let us start with the most relevant conclusion, and one about which there is virtual unanimity among students of the subject of predictive bias in testing: *No one has found statistically reliable evidence of predictive bias against blacks, of the sort illustrated in the first graphic, in large, representative samples of blacks and whites, where cognitive ability tests are the predictor variable for educational achievement or job performance.* In the notes, we list some of the larger aggregations of data and comprehensive analyses substantiating this conclusion.[2] We have found no modern, empirically based survey of the literature on test bias arguing that tests are predictively biased against blacks, although we have looked for them.

When we turn to the hundreds of smaller studies that have accumulated in the literature, we find examples of varying regression coefficients and intercepts, and predictive validities. This is a fundamental reason for focusing on syntheses of the literature. Smaller or unrepresentative individual studies may occasionally find test bias because of the statistical distortions that plague them. There are, for example, sampling and measurement errors, errors of recording, transcribing, and computing data, restrictions of range in both the predictor and outcome measurements, and predictor or outcome scales that are less valid than they might have been.[3] Given all the distorting sources of variation, lack of agreement across studies is the rule.

But even taken down to so fine a level, the case against predictive bias against blacks remains overwhelming. As late as 1984, Arthur Jensen was able to proclaim that "I have not come across a bona fide example of the opposite finding [of a test that underpredicts black performance]."[4] Jensen's every finding regarding racial differences in IQ is routinely subjected to intense scrutiny by his critics, but no one has contradicted this one. We are not absolutely sure that our literature review has identified every study since 1984, but our search revealed no examples to counter Jensen's generalization.[5]

Insofar as the many individual studies show a pattern at all, it points to overprediction for blacks. More simply, this body of evidence suggests that IQ tests are biased in favor of blacks, not against them. The single most massive set of data bearing on this issue is the national sample of more than 645,000 school children conducted by sociologist James Coleman and his associates for their landmark examination of the American educational system in the mid-1960s. Coleman's survey included a standardized test of verbal and nonverbal IQ, using the kinds of items that characterize the classic IQ test and are commonly thought to be culturally biased against blacks: picture vocabulary, sentence completion, analogies, and the like. The Coleman survey also included educational achievement measures of reading level and math level that are thought to be straightforward measures of what the student has learned. If IQ items are culturally biased against blacks, it could be predicted that a black student would do better on the achievement measures than the putative IQ measure would lead one to expect (this is the rationale behind the current popularity of steps to modify the SAT so that it focuses less on aptitude and more on measures of what has been learned). But the opposite occurred. Overall, black IQ scores overpredicted black academic achievement by .26 standard deviations.[6]

One inference that might be drawn from this finding is that black children were for some reason not taking as much from school as their ability would permit, or that black children went to worse schools than white children, or any of several other interpretations. But whatever the explanation might be, the results directly contradict the hypothesis that IQ tests give an unfairly low estimate of black academic performance.

A second major source of data suggesting that standardized tests overpredict black performance is the SAT. Colleges commonly compare the performance of freshmen, measured by grade point average, against the expectations of their performance as predicted by SAT scores. A literature review of studies that broke down these data by ethnic group revealed that SAT scores overpredicted freshman grades for blacks in fourteen of fifteen studies, by a median of .20 standard deviation.[7] In five additional studies where the ethnic classification was "minority" rather than specifically "black," the SAT score overpredicted college performance in all five cases, by a median of .40 standard deviation.[8]

For job performance, the most thorough analysis is provided by the Hartigan Report, assessing the relationship between the General Aptitude Test Battery (GATB) and job performance measures. Out of seventy-two studies that were assembled for review, the white intercept was higher than the black intercept in sixty of them—that is, the GATB overpredicted black performance in sixty out of the seventy-two studies.[9] Of the twenty studies in which the intercepts were statistically significantly different (at the .01 level), the white intercept was greater than the black intercept in all twenty cases.[10]

These findings about overprediction apply to the ordinary outcome measures of academic and job performance. But it should also be noted that "overprediction" can be a misleading concept when it is applied to outcome measures for which the predictor (IQ, in our continuing example) has very low validity. Inasmuch as blacks and whites differ on average in their scores on some outcome that is not linked to the predictor, the more biased it will be against whites. Consider the next figure, constructed on the assumption that the predictor is nearly invalid and that the two groups differ on average in their outcome levels.

A predictor with low validity may seem to be biased against whites
if there is a substantial difference in the outcome measure

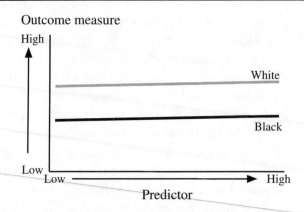

This situation is relevant to some of the outcome measures discussed in Chapter 14, such as short-term male unemployment, where the black and white means are quite different, but IQ has little relationship to short-term unemployment for either whites or blacks. This figure was constructed assuming only that there are factors influencing outcomes that are not captured by the predictor, hence its low validity, resulting in the low slope of the parallel regression lines.[11] The intercepts differ, expressing the generally higher level of performance by whites compared to blacks that is unexplained by the predictor variable. If we knew what the missing predictive factors are, we could include them in the predictor, and the intercept difference would vanish—and so would the implication that the newly constituted predictor is biased against whites. What such results seem to be telling us is, first, that IQ tests are not predictively biased against blacks but, second, that IQ tests alone do not explain the observed black-white differences in outcomes. It therefore often looks as if the IQ test is biased against whites.

More on Internal Evidence of Bias: Item Analysis

Laymen are often skeptical that IQ test items could measure anything as deep as intelligence. Knowing the answers seems to them to depend less on intelligence than on having been exposed to certain kinds of cultural or historical information. It is usually a short step from here to the conclusion that the tests must be biased. Pundits of varying sorts reinforce this intuition about test item bias, claiming that the middle- and upper-class white culture infuses test items even after vigorous efforts to expunge it.

The data confirming Spearman's hypothesis, which we discussed at some length in Chapter 13, provide the most convincing conceptual refutation of this allegation by providing an alternative explanation that has been borne out by many studies: the items on which blacks and whites differ most widely are not those with the most esoteric cultural content, but the ones that best measure the general intelligence factor, *g*.[12] But many other studies have directly asked whether the cultural content of items is associated with the magnitude of the black–white difference, which we review here.

One of the earliest of the studies, a 1951 doctoral thesis at Catholic University, proceeded on the assumption that some test items are more dependent on exposure to culture than others.[13] Frank McGurk, the study's author, consequently had large numbers of independent judges rate many test items for their cultural loading. On exploratory tests, he was able to establish each item's general difficulty, which is defined simply as the proportion of a population that gets the item wrong. He could therefore identify pairs of items, one highly loaded with cultural information and the other not highly loaded but of equal difficulty. Now, finally, the crucial evaluation could be made with a sample of black and white high school students matched for schooling and socioeconomic background. The black-white gap, he discovered, was about twice as large on items rated as *low* in cultural loading as on items rated as high in cultural loading. Consider, for example, a pair of equally difficult test items. The one that is culturally loaded is probably difficult because it draws on esoteric knowledge; the other item is probably difficult because it calls on complex cognitive processing—*g*. McGurk's results undermined the proposition that access to esoteric knowledge was to blame for the black-white difference.

Another approach in the pursuit of test-item bias is based on which items blacks and whites find hard or easy. Conceptually, this is much like McGurk's approach, except that it does not require us to have items rated by experts, a subjective procedure that some might find suspect. Instead, if the cultural influence matters and if blacks and whites have access to different cultural backgrounds, then items that pick up these cultural differences should split the two groups. Items drawing on cultural knowledge more available to whites than to blacks should be, on average, relatively easier for whites than for blacks. Items lacking this tip for whites or items with a tip for blacks should not be differentially easier for whites and may be easier for blacks.

This idea is tested by ranking the items on a test separately for whites and for blacks, in order of difficulty. That is, the easiest item for whites is the one with the highest proportion of correct answers among whites; the next easiest item for whites is the one with the second highest proportion of correct answers for whites; and so on. Now repeat the procedure using the blacks' proportions of correct answers. This will result in two sets of rank orders for all the items. The rank-order correlation between them is a measure of the test-item bias hypothesis: The larger the correlation is, the less support the hypothesis finds. Alternatively, the proportions of correct responses within each group are transformed into standard scores and then correlated by some other measure of correlation, such as the Pearson product-moment coefficient.

Either way, the result is clear. Relative item difficulties are essentially the same for both races (by sex). That is, blacks and whites of the same sex come close to finding the same item the easiest, the same item next easiest, all the way down to the hardest item.[14] When the rank order of difficulty differs across races, the differences tend to be small and unsystematic. Rank order correlations above .95 are not uncommon for the items on the Wechsler and Stanford-Binet tests, which are, in fact, the tests that provide most of the anecdotal material for arguing that test items are biased. Pearson correlations are often somewhat lower but typically still above .8. Moreover, when items do vary in difficulty across races, most of the variation is eliminated by taking mental age into account. Since blacks and whites of the same chronological age differ on average in mental age, allowing a compensating lag in chronological age will neutralize the contribution of mental age. Compare, say, the item difficulties for 10-year-old blacks with that for 9-year-old or 8-year-old whites. When this is done, the correlations in difficulty almost all rise into the .9 range and above.[15]

Because "item bias" ordinarily defined has failed to materialize, the concept has been extended to encompass item characteristics that are intertwined with the underlying rationale for thinking that an item measures g. For example, one researcher has found that the black-white gap is diminished for items that call for the subject to identify the one false response, compared to items requiring the subject to identify the one correct response.[16] Is this a matter of bias, or a matter of how well the two types of items tap the construct called intelligence? This in turn brings us full circle to Spearman's hypothesis discussed in Chapter 13, which offers an interpretative framework for explaining such differences.

More on Other Potential Sources of Bias

We turn now to one of the least precisely but most commonly argued reasons for thinking that tests are biased: Tests are a sort of game, and, as in most games, it helps to have played the testing game, it helps to get coaching, and it helps to be playing on the home field. Privileged groups get more practice and coaching than underprivileged groups. They have a home-court advantage; the tests are given in familiar environments, administered by familiar kinds of people. A major part of the racial differences in test scores may be attributed to these differences. In this discussion, we begin with coaching and practice, then turn to some of the other ways in which the testing situation might influence scores.

PRACTICE AND COACHING. For IQ tests, coaching and practice are not a significant issue because coaching and practice effects exist only under conditions that virtually never apply. To get a sizable practice effect for an IQ test, it is necessary to use subjects who have *never* taken an IQ-like test, administer the *identical* test twice, and do so *quickly* (preferably within a few weeks).[17] If the subjects fail to meet any of those conditions, the chances of finding a practice effect are small, and the size of any effect, if one is found, will be just a few points. Coaching effects are even harder to obtain. We are unable to identify any IQ data in any study, large or small, in which the results are compromised because the IQ scores of part of the sample have been obtained after this kind of experience. That's not the way that IQ tests have been administered anywhere to any significant sample at any time during the history of IQ testing—except to the samples used to assess practice and coaching effects, and sometimes to the subjects of intensive remedial programs such as those discussed in Chapter 17.

The story regarding practice and coaching for such tests as the Scholastic Aptitude Test (SAT), the Law School Admissions Test (LSAT), and the Medical College Admissions Test (MCAT) is much more contentious than the story about IQ. Many people do take these tests more than once, many people practice for them, and many people get extensive coaching. Moreover, these tests are supposed to be "coachable," insofar as they measure the verbal, reasoning, and analytic skills that a good education is supposed to enhance, and prolonged exposure to such coaching should produce better scores. Or to put it another way, two students with the same IQ should be able to get different LSAT and MCAT scores if one student has taken more appropriate courses and studied harder than the other student. That SAT scores declined by almost half a standard deviation from 1964 to 1980 strongly suggests that something coachable—or "negatively coachable" in this example—is being measured. In Chapter 17, we discuss the effects of coaching for the SAT, which are real but also smaller and harder to obtain than the widely advertised claims of the coaching industry.

The belief that coaching might explain part of the black-white gap often rests on a notion that, on the average, blacks receive less of the practice and coaching that might have elevated their scores than does the average white. We have already undermined this notion by showing that the tests are biased against blacks neither predictively nor in terms of particular item difficulties. There is, however, a literature that bears more directly on this idea, by looking for an interaction effect between practice or coaching and race.

If practice and coaching explain any portion of a group difference in scores in the population as a whole, then it necessarily follows that representative samples of those groups who are equally well practiced and well coached will show a smaller difference than is observed in the population at large. It is not enough that practice or coaching raises the mean score of the lower-scoring group; it must raise its mean score *more than* it raises the score of the higher-scoring group.

Several studies have investigated whether this is found for blacks and whites. In a well-designed study, representative samples of blacks and whites are randomly divided into two groups. The experimental black and white groups receive identical coaching (or practice), and the control groups receive no treatment at all. At the end of the experiment, the investigator has four different sets of results: test scores for coached blacks, uncoached blacks, coached whites, and uncoached whites. These results may be analyzed in three basic ways: One may compare blacks overall with whites overall, which will reveal the *main effect of race*; or the coached samples overall with the uncoached samples overall, which will reveal the *main effect of the coaching*; or the way in which the effects of coaching vary according to the race of the persons being coached, known as the *interaction effect*.

One study found a statistically significant differential response to practice, but not to direct instruction, on a reasoning test, between black and white college students.[18] The differential advantage of practice for blacks compared to whites was about an eighth of the overall black-white gap on this test. Other studies have failed to find even this much of a differential response, or they have found differential responses in the opposite direction, tending to increase the black-white gap after practice.[19] Taking the evidence as a whole, any differential coaching and practice effects by race (or socioeconomic status) is at most sporadic and small. If such a differential effect exists, it is too small to be replicated reliably. The scattered evidence of a differential effect is about as supportive of a white advantage from coaching as of a black advantage.

EXAMINER EFFECTS AND OTHER SITUATIONAL VARIABLES. Is it possible that disadvantaged groups come to the test with greater anxiety than confident middle-class students, and this mental state depresses their scores? That, when a black student takes a bus across town to an unfamiliar neighborhood and goes into a testing room filled with white students and overseen by a white test supervisor, this situation has an intimidating effect on performance? What about the time limits on tests? Might these have more pronounced effects on disadvantaged students than on test-wise middle-class students? All are plausible questions, but the answer to each is the same: Investigations to date give no reason to believe that such considerations explain a nontrivial portion of the group differences in scores.

The race of the examiner has been the subject of numerous studies. Of those with adequate experimental designs, most have showed nonsignificant effects; of the rest, the evidence is as strong that the presence of a white examiner *reduces* overall black-white difference as that a white examiner exacerbates the difference.[20] Examinations of the results of time pressures fail to demonstrate either that blacks do better in untimed than in timed tests or that the test-taking "personal tempo" of blacks is different from that of whites.[21] Test anxiety has been investigated extensively but, as in so many other aspects of this discussion, the relationship tends to be the opposite of the expected one: To the extent that test anxiety affects performance at all, it seems to help slightly. Only a few studies have specifically addressed black-white differences in test anxiety; they have shown either nonsignificant results, or that the white subjects were slightly more anxious than the black subjects.[22]

"BLACK ENGLISH." Language looms larger. It is well established that the students from many different cultural backgrounds for whom English is a second language tend to score better on the nonverbal part of the test than a verbal component given in English.[23] Whereas this imbalance may be independent of language for East Asians (Japanese in Japan have superior nonverbal scores even taking verbal test batteries designed in Japanese), it is also manifest among Latinos, who do not otherwise exhibit the characteristic East Asian verbal-nonverbal pattern. This suggests that students who are taking the test in a second language suffer some decrement of their scores.

It has been a small step from this to hypothesize that, for practical purposes, many blacks are taking the test in a "second language," with their first language being the dialect known as "black English," ubiquitous in the black inner city and used to some extent by blacks of broader socioeconomic backgrounds. Researchers have approached the issue in several ways. First, the evidence indicates that black children who use black English understand standard English at least as well.[24] A more direct test came in the 1970s, when L. C. Quay had the Stanford-Binet translated into black dialect and tested several samples with both the original and the revised version. The studies produced no evidence that black students in any of the various test groups benefited (the differences in scores from the two tests generally amounted to less than one IQ point).[25] But the most powerful data suggesting that language does not explain the black-white difference is provided by the evidence for Spearman's hypothesis presented in Chapter 13: If language were the problem, then blacks would be at the greatest disadvantage on test items that rely on a knowledge of standard English and be at the least disadvantage on test items that use no language at all. As we discuss with regard to Spearman's hypothesis in Chapter 13, this expectation is contradicted by a large and consistent body of work. Black populations generally do relatively better on test items that are less saturated with *g* and relatively worse on items more saturated with *g*, whether the items are verbal or nonverbal.

The Continuing Debate

Allegations that standardized tests are culturally biased still appear, and presumably this account will fuel additional ones. What about all the articles appearing in many quarters making these claims? They make up a varied lot, but typically consist of allegations that ignore the data. A particularly striking example was a long article entitled "IQ and Standard English," which appeared in a technical journal and attributed the black-white IQ test differences to language difficulties. The article was followed by four responses, plus by a counterstatement by the author. Neither the original article nor any of the responses cited any of the data discussed above.[26] The debate was carried on entirely on the basis of argumentation about the extent to which black culture is more orally based than white culture. This readiness to theorize about what might be true about black-white differences in test scores while ignoring the pertinent data is common.

Other articles, cited in the note, have discussed a variety of ways in which culture interacts with human functioning, intellectual and otherwise.[27] The movement surrounding Howard Gardner's concept of multiple intelligences (see the Introduction) is only the best known of these new ways of talking about intelligence. But these discussions do not try to argue with the two core statements that we have made: In the major standardized tests, test items function in the same way for both blacks and whites, and the tests results are similarly predictive for blacks and whites, tending to overpredict black performance rather than underpredict it.

In the popular media, the persistence of belief in cultural bias, we think, is based on a misapprehension. To many people, proof that tests are unbiased seems tantamount to proof that the black-white gap reflects genetic differences in intelligence. Since they reject the possibility that genetic differences could be involved, the tests *must* be biased. One of the major purposes of Chapter 13 is to discredit both the notion that real differences in intelligence must be genetically founded and the assumption that a role for genes must have horrific consequences.

IS THE BLACK-WHITE DIFFERENCE IN COGNITIVE ABILITY SHRINKING?

The text discusses the evidence for converging black and white test scores on the NAEP (National Assessment of Education Progress) and the SAT. Here, we summarize other sources of data about the two ethnic populations.

National High School Studies, 1972 and 1980

In 1972 and 1980, the federal government sponsored large-sample studies intended to provide reliable national estimates of the high school population. As part of both studies, tests measuring vocabulary, reading, and mathematics were administered to all participants. Although not technically IQ tests, all three had high *g* loadings. Furthermore, the tests were virtually identical for the two test administrations,[28] and the study procedures in 1980 were deliberately constructed to maximize the comparability of the two samples. In 1982, the sophomores from the 1980 sample were tested as seniors. The table below summarizes the results for the three test years by ethnic group. The black-white difference diminished on two of the three tests, but all of the shrinkage came about because white scores fell, not because black scores rose. Indeed, black scores also fell on all three tests but (except in the case of vocabulary), by less than the reduction in white scores.

Black-White Difference for High School Seniors in 1972, 1980, and 1982		
White-Black Difference, in SDs		
1972	1980	1982
Vocabulary 1.00	.87	1.02
Reading .99	.85	.78
Math 1.09	.91	.86

Source: Rock et al. 1985, Appendixes B,C, E.

College Board Achievement Tests

THE SAT. In Chapter 13, we noted that the overall black-white gap in SAT scores had narrowed between 1976 and 1993, from 1.16 to .88 standard deviation in the verbal portion of the test and from 1.27 to .92 standard deviation in the mathematics portion of the test.[29] More detailed breakdowns are available for the period 1980 to 1991, as shown in the table below. The trend is consistently positive, with narrowing

Reductions in the Black-White Difference on the Scholastic Aptitude and Achievement Tests, 1980–1991

	White-Black Difference, in SDs		
	1980	1991	Change
SAT-Verbal	1.09	.87	−.22
Reading subscore	.93	.83	−.10
Vocabulary subscore	1.09	.83	−.26
SAT-Math	1.10	.90	−.20
Test of standard written English	1.11	.89	−.22
Achievement tests			
Overall average	.83	.78	−.05
English Composition	.73	.71	−.02
Literature	.86	.76	−.10
American History	.69	.69	.00
European History	.81	.56	−.25
Math I	.75	.75	.00
Math II	.98	.83	−.15
Biology	.77	.68	−.09
Chemistry	.69	.74	+.05
Physics	.84	.74	−.10
French	.33	.18	−.15
German	.64	.27	−.37
Latin	.66	.25	−.41
Spanish	.50	.35	−.15

Source: The College Board's annual summaries of test scores by ethnicity.

black-white differences of at least .1 standard deviation units on the tests for Literature. European History, Math II, Physics, French, German, Latin, and Spanish. The average shrinkage of the gap is .05 standard deviation unit. From further analyses, we conclude that the narrowing is not entirely explained away by changes in the representativeness of the black and white samples of test takers or by declining white scores.

To interpret the changes in scores on achievement tests, which are taken by small proportions of the SAT test takers, we used the mean that the College Board provides on the SAT Verbal and Math scores for each achievement test population in each year. The question we asked was: For a given achievement test, how did the place of the average test taker on his race's cognitive ability distribution change from 1980 to

1991? For example, the average white taking the Literature achieve-ment test in 1980 had an SAT Verbal score that put him at the 80th percentile of white testees; in 1991, he was at the 85th percentile. Mean-while, the average black taking the Literature achievement test in 1980 had an SAT Verbal score that put him at the 88th percentile of all black SAT testees; in 1991, he was still at the 88th percentile of the black dis-tribution. The difference between blacks and whites on the Literature achievement test narrowed during that period, but, given where the blacks and whites were relative to the white and black SAT distribu-tions, it seems unlikely that the narrowing was caused by changes in the self-selection that artificially raised black scores relative to whites. Ten of the thirteen achievement tests fit this pattern. In only three cases (European History, Physics, and German) did changes in the SAT Math or Verbal scores indicate that the black pool had become differentially more selective. Only in the case of German was this difference large enough to account plausibly for much of the black improvement rela-tive to whites.

THE ACT. The College Board's major competitor in the college en-trance examination business is the American College Testing program, which has also shown decreasing differences between black and white students who take the test, as summarized in the table below. Reduc-

Black-White Difference in the ACT, 1970–1991			
	White-Black Difference, in SDs		
	1970	1991	Change
English	1.14	.83	−.31
Math	.86	.77	−.09
Science	.97	.91	−.06
Composite	1.12	.96	−.16

Source: ACT 1991, Tables 1 4; Congressional Budget Office 1986, Fig. E-2.

tions in the gap occurred in all the subtests between 1970 and 1991, with by far the largest reduction on the English subtest. The magnitude of the overall change in the composite is about half the size of the re-duction observed in the black-white difference on the SAT. Like the SAT population, the ACT's population of black test takers has been increasing, suggesting that the increases in scores are not the result of a more selective test-taking population.

THE GRADUATE RECORD EXAMINATION (GRE). The GRE is the equivalent of the SAT for admission to graduate school in the arts and sciences. Not many people in any cohort take the GRE, so the sample is obviously highly self-selected and atypical of the population. In 1988, for example, the number of white GRE test takers represented only 5.6 percent of the 22-year-old white population; black test takers represented 2.3 percent of its 22-year-old population. On the other hand, the proportions in 1988 were about the same as they were in 1979. The self-selection process has remained fairly steady over the years, so it is worth at least mentioning the results, as shown in the table below. The GRE

Black-White Difference in the GRE, 1979–1988			
	White-Black Difference, in SDs		
	1979	1988	Change
Verbal	1.25	1.13	−.12
Math	1.28	1.13	−.15
Analytical	1.46	1.21	−.25

Source: Graduate Record Examination Board.

gap narrowed only slightly less than that for the SAT. Another positive note is that the narrowing was achieved because black scores rose more than white scores, not because white scores were falling.

These results from national tests are echoed in state-level data from Texas and North Carolina, as reported in the Congressional Budget Office's survey of trends in educational achievement.[30] Overall, the evidence seems clear beyond a reasonable doubt: On college entrance tests and national tests of educational proficiency, the gap between whites and blacks remained large into the early 1990s, but it had been narrowing in the preceding decade or two. The optimist may argue that the trend will continue indefinitely if improvements in the environment and education for American blacks can be continued. The pessimist may note that there seems to have been little narrowing since the mid-1980s, as we observed in the text for Chapter 13, and that the black-white IQ gap in the NLSY seems to be widening rather narrowing in the next generation, as we discussed in Chapter 15.

RUSHTON ON RACE DIFFERENCES AND REPRODUCTIVE STRATEGIES

Controversy unprecedented even for the contentious subject of racial differences has erupted around the work of J. Philippe Rushton, a developmental psychologist at the University of Western Ontario. Rushton argues that the differences in the average intelligence test scores among East Asians, blacks, and whites are not only primarily genetic but part of a complex of racial differences that includes such variables as brain size,[31] genital size, rate of sexual maturation, length of the menstrual cycle, frequency of sexual intercourse, gamete production, sexual hormone levels, the tendency to produce dizygotic twins, marital stability, infant mortality, altruism, law abidingness, and mental health. For each variable, Rushton has concluded, the three races—Mongoloids, Caucasoids, and Negroids—fall in a certain order, with the average Caucasoid in the middle and the other two races on one side or the other. The ordering of the races, he further argues, has an evolutionary basis; hence these ordered racial differences must involve genes.

To reach his conclusion, Rushton starts with the well-established observation in biology that species vary in their reproductive strategies. Some species produce many offspring (per parent) of which only a small fraction survive; others produce small numbers of offspring with relatively high survival rates. The involvement of parents in their offsprings' health and development (which biologists call "parental investment") tends to be high for species having few offspring and high survival rates and low for those employing the other strategy (many offspring and low survival rates). Many other species differences are concomitant with this fundamental one, according to standard biological doctrine.

Rushton's thesis is that this standard biological principle may be applied within our own species. Rushton acknowledges that human beings are as a species far out along the continuum of low reproduction, high offspring survival, and high parental investment, but he argues that the ordering of the races on the many variables he has identified can be explained as the result of evolutionary differences in how far out the races are. According to Rushton, the average Mongoloid is toward one end of the continuum of reproductive strategies—the few offspring, high survival, and high parental investment end—the average Negroid is shifted toward the other end, and the average Caucasoid is in the middle.

Rushton paints with a broad brush, focusing on the major racial categories rather than the dozens of more finely drawn reproductively isolated human populations that might test his theory more conclusively. But beyond that, his thesis raises numerous questions—moral, pragmatic, and scientific. Many critics attack the theory on scientific, not just moral, grounds. They question whether Rushton has really shown that the races are consistently ordered in the way he says they are, or whether a biological theory that was meant to explain species differences can be properly applied to groups within a single species, or whether the evidence for genetic influences on his variables stands up. Rushton has responded to his critics with increasingly detailed and convincing empirical reports of the race differences in some of the traits on his list, and he cites preeminent biological authority for his use of the concept of reproductive strategies. He has strengthened the case for consistently ordered race differences, at least for some of the variables he discusses, since his first formulation of the theory in 1985. Nevertheless, the theory remains a long way from confirmation.

We cannot at present say who is more nearly right as a matter of science, Rushton or his critics.[32] However, Rushton's work is not that of a crackpot or a bigot, as many of his critics are given to charging. Nor are we sympathetic with Rushton's academic colleagues or the politicians in Ontario who have called for his peremptory dismissal from a tenured professorship. Setting aside whether his work is timely or worthwhile— a judgment we are loath to make under any circumstances—it is plainly science. He is not alone in seeking an evolutionary explanation of the observed differences among the races.[33] As science, there is nothing wrong with Rushton's work in principle; we expect that time will tell whether it is right or wrong in fact.

Appendix 6

Regression Analyses from Chapter 14

This appendix presents the regression analyses underlying the presentation in Chapter 14.

The results in Chapter 14 and in this appendix are based on separate regressions for each of the three ethnic groups in question (black, Latino, and white). This procedure was chosen in preference to a single regression entering ethnicity as a nominal variable so that the relationships would not be constrained to a single slope. The regressions used the entire NLSY sample, with exclusions as noted for specific analyses, applying 1990 sample weights.

LOGISTIC REGRESSIONS

All the indicators in Chapter 14 except for those involving income are binary variables, and the mode of analysis is logistic regression. The interpretation of logistic regressions is discussed in Appendix 4.

The data tables use short labels for the indicators. The full description of each indicator and associated characteristics of the analysis are shown in Table 1.

Table 2 first summarizes the results, by ethnic group, for four sets of regressions: when age (zAge) is the only independent variable, when age and IQ (zAFQT) are independent variables, when age and parental SES (zSES) are independent variables, and when all three are entered as independent variables. Three basic questions are then examined:

1. How much do ethnic differences change when IQ is taken into account?
2. How much do ethnic differences change when parental SES is taken into account?
3. What are the comparative roles of IQ and parental SES?

Table 1 Description of Indicators Used for Logistic Regression Analyses in Chapter 14

Short label	Description	Comments
High school dropout	Probability that an NLSY subject: Dropped out of high school before obtaining a diploma	Includes persons who dropped out and later obtained a GED
Bachelor's degree	Obtained a bachelor's degree or higher	Excludes persons enrolled as an undergraduate in 1990
High-IQ occupation	Was employed in a high-IQ occupation as of 1990	Excludes persons enrolled in college or graduate school in 1990
In poverty	Had family income below the poverty line in 1989	Excludes persons not working because of school 1989 or 1990
Unemployed 1 mo. (men)	Was unemployed for 4 weeks or more in 1989 (men only)	Excludes persons not working because of school 1989 or 1990
Married by 30	Was married before the age of 30	Excludes persons under 30 as of the 1990 interview; age is omitted as a control variable
Ever on welfare (all women)	Had ever been on welfare (all women, including nonmothers)	
Ever on welfare (poor mothers)	Had ever been on welfare (mothers in poverty year before birth)	
Ever in jail (men)	Was ever interviewed in jail (men only)	
"Yes" on MCV index	Scored "Yes" on the Middle Class Values index	Excludes single persons who met other conditions of the MCV
Born out of wedlock	Probability that a child of a NLSY woman: Was born out of wedlock	
Low birth weight	Was low birth weight (less than 5.5 lbs.)	Excludes premature babies under 5.5 lbs whose weight was appropriate for gestational age
In poverty 1st 3 years.	Lived in poverty during the first three years of life	
Ever in nonparental care	Ever lived in foster care or with nonparental relatives	
Worst decile:	Scored in the worst decile of the:	
HOME index	HOME index	Test year and child's age category entered as control variables
Friendliness index	Friendliness index (12–23 mos.)	Test year entered as an additional control variable
Difficulty index	Difficulty index (12–23 mos.)	Test year entered as an additional control variable
Motor & Social Dev. index	Motor & Social Dev. index (0–4 yrs.)	Test year and child's age category entered as control variables
Behavioral Problems index	Behavioral Problems index (4–12 yrs.)	Test year and child's age category entered as control variables
Any developmental index	At least one of the developmental indexes	
PPVT (IQ)	Peabody Picture Vocabulary Test (6 yrs. & older)	Test year and child's test age entered as control variables

646

Because zAge, zAFQT, and zSES are all expressed as standard scores with mean of zero and standard deviation of 1, the intercept for the equation (abbreviated *Int.* in the tables) represents the expected value when those variables are set at their respective means. The coefficients for zAFQT and zSES are given so that you may examine the slopes associated with them.

The summary columns (Table 3) show the computed probabilities of the dependent variable when the independent variables are set at their means.

Income Analyses

Following the tables showing the logistic regressions, we present the detailed results of the ordinary least squares regressions used to estimate differences in income by ethnicity (Table 4). Because education is such an important causal factor in income, we show analyses in which years of education (as of the 1990 interview) replaces IQ as an independent variable.

The first set of models shows the parameters for wages of full-time, year-round workers by ethnic group. The sample for this analysis consisted of all persons in the NLSY who reported working for fifty-two weeks in 1989, had a reported wage greater than 0 (a handful of apparently self-employed persons who reported working fifty-two weeks reported no income), had an identified occupation, and had valid scores for IQ, parental SES, and educational level as of 1990. The second set of models shows the parameters for total family income from all sources. The sample for this analysis includes all persons with valid scores on the independent variables, excluding only those who reported being out of the labor force in 1989 or 1990 because of enrollment in school.

Table 5 shows the results when IQ, parental SES, and education are all entered as independent variables. Education is expressed as the highest degree attained as of 1990 (no high school diploma, high school diploma, associate degree, bachelor's degree, professional degree).

Table 6 shows the analysis of wages by ethnicity and occupational grouping based on the subject's occupation in the 1990 interview (the variable labeled "Occ90"), using the 1970 U.S. Census Occupational Classification System. The software used for these analyses, JMP 3.0, treats nominal variables differently from the convention in many other regression packages. See the introduction to Appendix 4 for details and an example.

Table 2 Coefficients for Logistic Regression Analysis in Chapter 14

| Independent Variables | Controlling for Age (zAge) | | | Controlling for Age and IQ (zAge, zAFQT) | | | | | | Controlling for Age and Parental SES (zAge, zSES) | | | | | |
Indicator	White Int.	Black Int.	Latino Int.	White Int.	White IQ	Black Int.	Black IQ	Latino Int.	Latino IQ	White Int.	White SES	Black Int.	Black SES	Latino Int.	Latino SES
Sample: NLSY subjects															
High school dropout	-2.271	-1.598	-1.080	-2.943	-1.995	-3.676	-1.722	-3.046	-2.031	-2.503	-1.266	-2.245	-.734	-1.949	-.654
Bachelor's degree	-1.018	-2.089	-2.223	-2.004	2.127	-1.078	1.943	-1.927	1.987	-1.644	1.524	-1.665	1.058	-1.634	.908
High-IQ occupation	-2.871	-3.550	-3.335	-3.909	1.532	-2.997	1.705	-3.206	1.379	-3.410	1.036	-3.373	1.194	-2.892	.736
In poverty	-2.560	-1.066	-1.512	-2.671	-.957	-2.128	-1.046	-2.274	-.898	-2.607	-.661	-1.571	-.623	-2.201	-.528
Unemployed 1 mo. (men)	-2.714	-1.352	-1.819	-2.127	-.318	-1.706	-.315	-2.079	-.409	-2.139	-.189	-1.648	-.350	-2.026	-.213
Married by 30	—			1.336	-.193	.311	.122	1.070	-.116	1.329	-.036	1.88	-.238	1.132	.001
Ever on welfare (all women)	-1.911	-.053	-.856	-1.994	-1.191	-.853	-.902	-1.737	-1.060	-1.922	-.907	-.494	-.605	-1.493	-.528
Ever on welfare (poor mothers)	.487	1.287	.592	.250	-.387	1.066	-.186	.169	-.314	.442	-.021	1.363	.083	.223	-.203
Ever in jail (men)	-3.697	-1.895	-2.800	-3.917	-1.067	-3.015	-.954	-3.421	-.657	-3.758	-.727	-2.154	-.314	-3.131	-.229
"Yes" on MCV index	.026	-1.362	-.824	-.061	.727	-.744	.720	-.220	.962	-.045	.555	-1.040	.467	-.442	.355
Sample: Children of NLSY mothers															
Born out of wedlock	-2.008	.504	-1.190	-2.153	-.774	.030	-.479	-1.594	-.359	-2.103	-.622	.262	-.278	-1.506	-.191
Low birth weight	-3.326	-2.191	-2.888	-3.378	-.387	-2.668	-.428	-3.004	-.128	-3.335	-.168	-2.214	-.013	-2.877	.002
In poverty 1st 3 yrs.	-2.287	.151	-.856	-2.693	-1.608	-1.799	-2.036	-2.239	-1.554	-2.860	-1.608	-.862	-1.189	-1.901	-.752
Ever in nonparental care	-5.288	-3.405	-4.369	-5.321	-.454	-3.548	-.165	-4.257	.048	-5.258	-.207	-3.314	.074	-4.503	-.143
Worst decile: HOME index	-2.578	-.960	-1.317	-2.816	-.768	-1.653	-.647	-2.118	-.703	-2.747	-.588	-1.451	-.523	-1.867	-.347
Friendliness index	-2.824	-1.032	-1.872	-2.911	-.707	-1.745	-.713	-3.062	-1.168	-2.882	-.557	-1.117	-.118	-2.418	-.414
Difficulty index	-2.508	-1.272	-2.115	-2.484	-.344	-1.922	-.664	-3.249	-1.110	.000	-.341	-1.520	-.336	-2.748	-.458
Motor & Social Dev. index	-2.626	-2.300	-2.054	-2.619	-.426	-3.100	-.756	-2.540	-.492	-2.614	-.366	-2.597	-.344	-2.543	-.348
Behavioral Problems index	-1.958	-2.052	-2.066	-2.067	-.368	-2.894	-.700	-2.560	-.412	-2.039	-.269	-2.234	-.191	-2.360	-.173
Any developmental index	-2.193	-1.888	-1.935	-2.239	-.401	-2.620	-.651	-2.471	-.494	-2.226	-.326	-2.055	-.187	-2.298	-.244
PPVT (IQ)	-2.575	.202	.139	-2.224	-.968	-.693	-.942	-.831	-1.260	-2.603	-.546	-.148	-.547	-.187	-.691

Table 2 (Cont'd) Coefficients for Logistic Regression Analysis in Chapter 14

Independent Variables									
				Controlling for Age, IQ, and Parental SES (Independent variables: zAge, zAFQT, zSES)					
	White			Black			Latino		
Indicator	Int.	IQ	SES	Int.	IQ	SES	Int.	IQ	SES
Sample: NLSY subjects									
High school dropout	-2.961	-1.705	-.626	-3.930	-1.612	-.424	-3.170	-1.944	-.160
Bachelor's degree	-2.360	1.854	1.047	-.971	1.718	.611	-1.797	1.827	.242
High-IQ occupation	-4.065	1.356	.487	-2.987	1.382	6.90	-3.136	1.287	.133
In poverty	-2.658	-.818	-.274	-2.279	-.904	-.368	-2.489	-.752	-.273
Unemployed 1 mo. (men)	-2.124	-.305	-.027	-1.809	-.214	-.281	-2.119	-.373	-.060
Married by 30	1.354	-.102	-.187	.282	.167	-.099	1.126	-.161	.073
Ever on welfare (all women)	-1.983	-.932	-.516	-.967	-.725	-.377	-1.930	-.910	-.266
Ever on welfare (poor mothers)	.258	-.445	.116	1.175	-.235	.146	.000	-.235	-.169
Ever in jail (men)	-3.933	-.949	-.234	-3.034	-.939	-.048	-3.388	-.683	.049
"Yes" on MCV index	-.083	.597	.274	-.672	.614	.248	-.221	.963	-.002
Sample: Children of NLSY mothers									
Born out of wedlock	-2.178	-.614	-.344	-.034	-.414	-.149	-1.661	-.307	-.086
Low birth weight	-3.378	-.406	.039	-2.608	-.487	.142	-2.957	-.168	.064
In poverty 1st 3 yrs.	-3.009	-1.141	-1.198	-2.142	-1.725	-.737	-2.618	-1.316	-.420
Ever in nonparental care	-5.321	-.471	.034	-3.489	-.225	.146	-4.432	.171	-.203
Worst decile: HOME index	-2.857	-.628	-.312	-1.870	-.501	-.392	-2.238	-.616	-.149
Friendliness index	-2.926	-.552	-.301	-1.717	-.745	.078	-3.075	-1.157	-.017
Difficulty index	-2.493	-.223	-.237	-1.998	-.590	-.188	-3.326	-1.046	-.097
Motor & Social Dev. index	-2.620	-.323	-.220	-3.169	-.700	-.145	-2.721	-.352	-.227
Behavioral Problems index	-2.101	-.300	-.159	-2.893	-.700	.000	-2.597	-.387	-.044
Any developmental index	-2.256	-.310	-.191	-2.618	-.652	.002	-2.547	-.436	-.097
PPVT (IQ)	-2.258	-.875	-.220	-.845	-.837	-.374	-.949	-1.062	-.344

649

Table 3 Expected Probabilities for Logistic Regression Analyses in Chapter 14

Indicator	When Age Is Average (zAge = 0)			When Age and IQ Are Average (zAge = 0, zAFQT = 0)			When Age and Parental SES Are Average (zAge = 0, zSES = 0)			When Age, IQ, and Parental SES are Average (zAge = 0, zAFQT = 0, zSES = 0)		
	White	Black	Latino	White	Black	Latino	White	Black	Latino	White	Black	Latino
Sample: NLSY subjects												
High school dropout	9.4%	16.8%	25.4%	5.0%	2.5%	4.5%	7.6%	9.6%	12.5%	4.9%	1.9%	4.0%
Bachelor's degree	26.5	11.0	9.8	11.9	25.4	12.7	16.2	15.9	16.3	8.6	27.5	14.2
High-IQ occupation	5.4	2.8	3.4	2.0	4.8	3.9	3.2	3.3	5.3	1.7	4.8	4.2
In poverty	7.2	25.6	18.1	6.5	10.6	9.3	6.9	17.2	10.0	6.5	9.3	7.7
Unemployed 1 mo. (men)	10.2	20.6	14.0	10.7	15.4	11.1	10.5	16.1	11.7	10.7	14.1	10.7
Married by 30	77.7	54.2	76.1	79.2	57.7	74.5	79.1	54.7	75.6	79.5	57.0	75.5
Ever on welfare (all women)	12.9	48.7	29.8	12.0	29.9	15.0	12.8	37.9	18.3	12.1	27.5	12.7
Ever on welfare (poor mothers)	61.9	78.4	64.4	56.2	74.4	54.2	60.9	79.6	55.6	56.4	76.4	50.0
Ever in jail (men)	2.4	13.1	5.7	2.0	4.7	3.2	2.3	10.4	4.2	1.9	4.6	3.3
"Yes" on MCV index	50.6	20.4	30.5	48.5	32.2	44.5	48.9	26.1	39.1	47.9	33.8	44.5
Sample: Children of NLSY mothers												
Born out of wedlock	11.8	62.3	23.3	10.4	50.7	16.9	10.9	56.5	18.2	10.2	49.2	16.0
Low birth weight	3.5	10.1	5.3	3.3	6.5	4.7	3.4	9.9	5.3	3.3	6.9	4.9
In poverty 1st 3 yrs.	9.2	53.8	29.8	6.3	14.2	9.6	5.4	29.7	13.0	4.7	10.5	6.8
Ever in nonparental care	0.5	3.2	1.3	0.5	2.8	1.4	0.5	3.5	1.1	0.5	3.0	1.2
Worst decile: HOME index	7.1	27.7	21.1	5.6	16.1	10.7	6.0	19.0	13.4	5.4	13.4	9.6
Friendliness index	5.6	26.3	13.3	5.2	14.9	4.5	5.3	24.7	8.2	5.1	15.2	4.4
Difficulty index	7.5	21.9	10.8	7.7	12.8	3.7	50.0	17.9	6.0	7.6	11.9	3.5
Motor & Social Dev. index	6.7	9.1	11.4	6.8	4.3	7.3	6.8	6.9	7.3	6.8	4.0	6.2
Behavioral Problems index	12.4	11.4	11.2	11.2	5.2	7.2	11.5	9.7	8.6	10.9	5.3	6.9
Any developmental index	10.0	13.1	12.6	9.6	6.8	7.8	9.7	11.4	9.1	9.5	6.8	7.3
PPVT (IQ)	7.1	55.0	53.5	9.8	33.3	30.3	6.9	46.3	45.3	9.5	30.0	27.9

Table 4 Income Analyses in Chapter 14 (in 1990 dollars)

Independent Variables	Model I (zAge)			Model II (zAge, zAFQT)			Model III (zAge, zAFQT, zSES)			Model IV (zAge, zEduc90)			Model V (zAge, zEduc90, zSES)		
	White	Black	Latino	White	Black	Latino	White	Black	Latino	White	Black	Latino	White	Black	Latino
Dependent variable: Annual wages for full-time year-round workers, 1989															
Intercept	27,372	20,994	23,409	25,546	25,001	25,159	25,329	25,339	26,002	26,292	20,962	24,092	26,048	21,841	25,687
Age	2,814	1,354	2,163	1,968	861	1,896	2,057	949	2,144	2,636	1,333	2,188	2,632	1,377	2,463
IQ				5,660	5,454	4,018	4,850	4,875	3,162						
Parental SES							1,753	1,420	1,352				1,341	1,626	2,000
Education as of 1990										5,395	4,794	2,755	4,790	4,140	1,934
Dependent variable: Total family income, 1989[a]															
Intercept	41,558	29,880	35,514	39,225	36,432	39,689	38,623	37,723	41,051	40,194	30,511	37,565	39,453	33,841	40,009
Age	3,326	1,576	3,628	2,049	805	2,709	2,354	888	3,010	2,921	1,415	3,553	2,963	1,294	3,788
IQ				8,332	8,590	8,870	5,936	5,804	7,488						
Parental SES							5,097	5,817	2,223				4,217	6,022	3,109
Education as of 1990										8,313	7,933	7,764	6,394	5,346	6,360
Minority income as a percentage of white income															
Annual wages		76.7%	85.5%		97.9%	98.5%		100.0%	102.7%		79.7%	91.6%		83.8%	98.6%
Family income		71.9%	85.5%		92.9%	101.2%		97.7%	106.3%		75.9%	93.5%		85.8%	101.4%

[a] For persons not out of labor force because of school in 1989 or 1990.

Table 5 Income Analyses in Chapter 14 (in 1990 dollars), by Degree Attained

Dependent Variable:	*Annual Wages for Full-Time, Year-Round Workers, 1989*			*Total Family Income*[a]		
Independent Variables	**White**	**Black**	**Latino**	**White**	**Black**	**Latino**
Intercept	26,994	27,048	26,474	40,813	38,050	41,271
Age	2,338	787	2,207	2,583	946	3,091
IQ	3,082	3,802	2,507	3,025	4,247	4,136
Parental SES	914	840	1,248	3,648	5,191	2,042
Highest degree attained						
Less than high school	−4,992	−3,688	−1,588	−9,743	−4,181	−9,461
GED	−2,622	−3,950	−3,039	−5,202	−4,159	−7,683
High school diploma	−2,602	−3,944	−1,151	−2,789	−2,817	−1,269
Bachelor's degree	3,329	734	2,938	4,286	4,362	10,506
Graduate degree	6,887	10,848	2,840	13,448	6,795	7,907
Minority income as a percentage of white income		100.2%	98.1%		93.2%	101.1%

[a] For persons not out of labor force because of school in 1989 or 1990.

Sample sizes for the different occupations analyzed in Table 6 below are as follow:

	White	**Black**	**Latino**
Professional/technical	605	143	129
Managers/administrators	462	110	103
Clerical workers	473	260	172
Sales workers	163	34	30
Craft and kindred workers	370	113	106
Transport operatives	95	55	40
Other operatives	231	143	67
Service workers	289	218	95
Unskilled laborers	98	78	40
Farmworkers	22	4	12

Because of the small numbers of farmworkers, that category is omitted from the table. Note, however, that farmworkers were included in the actual regression equation; hence the coefficients for the nominal occupation categories will not sum to zero.

Table 6 Income Analyses in Chapter 14 (in 1990 dollars)

Dependent variable: Annual wages for year-round, full-time workers, 1989.

Independent Variables	Model I (zAge, Occ90)			Model II (zAge, zAFQT)			Model III (zAge, zAFQT, zSES)			Model IV (zAge, zEduc90)			Model V (zAge, zEduc90, zSES)		
	White	Black	Latino	White	Black	Latino	White	Black	Latino	White	Black	Latino	White	Black	Latino
Regression coefficients															
Intercept	26,060	20,764	22,131	25,397	24,874	23,999	25,264	25,259	24,914	26,156	21,413	23,028	25,988	22,240	24,608
Age	2,478	1,256	2,176	1,819	830	1,860	1,877	902	2,080	2,374	1,255	2,126	2,371	1,296	2,338
IQ				4,672	4,788	3,347	4,152	4,362	2,567						
Parental SES							1,333	1,247	1,307				1,029	1,519	1,771
Education as of 1990										4,908	3,878	2,350	4,484	3,354	1,697
Occupation in 1990															
Professional/technical	6,127	7,397	6,464	2,295	3,469	3,730	2,008	3,147	3,657	637	3,150	3,808	562	2,905	3,584
Managers/administrators	8,353	4,200	4,578	7,036	1,793	3,002	6,865	1,694	2,781	6,764	2,188	3,786	6,656	2,078	3,208
Clerical workers	-5,950	-768	-2,147	-6,350	-2,250	-2,351	-6,345	-2,349	-2,504	-6,000	-1,857	-2,470	-6,026	-1,991	-2,652
Sales workers	7,033	3,782	-2,466	5,032	2,140	-3,668	4,608	1,766	-4,213	4,806	1,508	-3,426	4,449	1,182	-4,285
Craft and kindred workers	1,176	1,369	3,908	2,085	1,432	4,294	2,289	1,551	4,195	3,078	1,946	4,633	3,149	2,020	4,420
Transport operatives	612	2,833	3,743	2,016	4,690	3,621	2,210	4,759	3,349	2,564	3,468	4,384	2,665	3,665	3,798
Other operatives	-3,315	-2,463	-3,051	-1,645	-1,044	-1,538	-1,364	-970	-1,358	-1,318	-1,548	-2,052	-1,130	-1,427	-1,608
Service workers	-7,666	-3,845	-1,813	-6,979	-2,949	-1,134	-6,962	-2,817	-1,109	-7,421	-3,442	-1,569	-7,370	-3,238	-1,388
Unskilled laborers	-1,428	-4,254	682	487	-3,194	1,381	439	-3,111	1,597	660	-3,007	1,987	607	-2,959	2,138
Fitted annual wage given mean values for the variables in the model															
Professional/technical	32,187	28,161	28,595	27,692	28,343	27,729	27,272	28,406	28,571	26,793	24,563	26,836	26,550	25,145	28,192
Managers/administrators	34,413	24,964	26,709	32,433	26,667	27,001	32,129	26,953	27,695	32,920	23,601	26,814	32,644	24,318	27,816
Clerical workers	20,110	19,996	19,984	19,047	22,624	21,648	18,919	22,910	22,410	20,156	19,556	20,558	19,962	20,249	21,956
Sales workers	33,093	24,546	19,665	30,429	27,014	20,331	29,872	27,025	20,701	30,962	22,921	19,592	30,487	23,422	20,323
Craft and kindred workers	27,236	22,133	26,039	27,482	26,306	28,293	27,553	26,810	29,109	29,234	23,359	27,661	29,137	24,260	29,028
Transport operatives	26,672	23,597	25,874	27,413	29,564	27,620	27,474	30,018	28,263	28,720	24,881	27,412	28,653	25,905	28,406
Other operatives	22,745	18,301	19,080	23,752	23,830	22,461	23,900	24,289	23,556	24,836	19,865	20,976	24,858	20,813	23,000
Service workers	18,394	16,919	20,318	18,418	21,925	22,865	18,302	22,442	23,805	18,735	17,971	21,459	18,618	19,002	23,220
Unskilled laborers	24,632	16,510	22,813	25,884	21,680	25,380	25,703	22,148	26,511	26,816	18,406	25,015	26,595	19,281	26,746

Appendix 7

The Evolution of Affirmative Action in the Workplace

Much of the current debate about affirmative action in employment takes place in ignorance of the original objectives of affirmative action and the ways in which antidiscrimination law has evolved. Because we believe that returning to the original intention of affirmative action is a key to progress in social policy on many fronts and because our recommendation seems so radical in the prevailing context, this appendix presents a full discussion of the nature of the original objectives and the evolution as it pertains specifically to employment tests.

Affirmative action in the workplace, as distinguished from the broader and older civil rights movement, starts with Title VII of the Civil Rights Act of 1964. Title VII laid down principles of fair employment practice as regards race, religion, national origin, and sex, and it created the Equal Employment Opportunities Commission (EEOC) to administer and promote them. Besides Title VII (as amended over the years), affirmative action in the workplace comprises subsequent acts of Congress (and state legislatures), presidential executive orders, rulings by the EEOC and other branches of government, and landmark court cases. The basic intent of all of this energetic policymaking has been to make workplaces fairer to people from oppressed or mistreated groups.

As desirable as that goal may seem to just about anyone, a clear notion either of what it means or how to accomplish it does not emerge from the documents of this enormous (and spreading) battleground of law, regulation, litigation, and commentary. The good news is that many issues of fair employment practice need not concern us here.[1] But we cannot avoid looking at how Title VII (and its elaborations) dealt with the use of ability tests in the selection or promotion of employees. Although the tests are given to individuals, the groups of which they are a part may average high or low compared to the population as a whole; as it happens, some of the groups who average low are protected from "unfair employment practices" by Title VII. Hence the government gets into the business of regulating employment testing.

The ramifications of even the narrow issue of employment test regulation have ranged so far and wide that employment testing has become a new specialty in the creation and practice of law and in government regulation undreamed of by the Founders. Thousands, perhaps millions, of legislative and bureaucratic man hours have been lavished on it. Thousands of cases have been argued in court.[2] Doubtless many more cases have not been argued, as the specter of legal action has shaped innumerable decisions in corporate offices and boardrooms. The stance of the government and the courts has increasingly been to distrust tests that produce group differences, as if they presume that, in the absence of illegal discrimination, the groups should be equal.

THE EVOLUTION OF TITLE VII

Title VII of the 1964 Act specifically did *not* prohibit the use of employment tests, provided that the tests were not "designed, intended or used" to discriminate against people because of their race, color, religion, sex, or national origin. It said nothing about group differences, although it was clear in 1964 that ability tests would result in disproportionately fewer high scores for at least some of the groups of people protected from discrimination by the act. Some of the act's proponents believed that some of the group differences in test scores were being used as a pretext for unfair discrimination; for that reason the act included a proviso regarding the tests. The hope was that Title VII would promptly eradicate this unfair use of tests. It was left to the EEOC to come up with the means of doing so.

In 1966, the EEOC formulated the first of a series of guidelines. An employment test, it ruled, had to have a proven power to measure a person's "ability to perform a particular job or class of jobs."[3] It was not enough, said the guideline, that the test be drawn up by professional testers; it also had to have some practical import—some "job relatedness," in the evolving jargon of the field. Why this particular guideline? The answer is that staff for the newly launched EEOC had quickly become convinced that some employers were, as anticipated, hiding behind the credentials of professional testers to use ability tests that had little bearing on job performance, and that they were doing so to discriminate against blacks.[4] The guideline was an attempt to pierce the veneer of professional respectability and thereby correct this violation of law and principle, as the EEOC saw it.

The criterion of job relatedness did not resolve the uneasiness about testing for the EEOC. Ability testing for employment had, after all, become an issue under Title VII because various groups of people get different average scores. This was the heart of the matter, and new guidelines laid down in 1970 addressed it frontally. For the first time, EEOC guidelines mentioned the issue of disproportionate success of different groups on any given test.[5] When a test "adversely affects" (more jargon, along with "disparate impact" or "adverse impact") members of a protected group, said the new guidelines, it had to be shown not only that the test really did predict job performance but that the prediction was strong enough to make a significant economic difference and that no nondiscriminatory alternative was available. An employer, the reasoning went, may have abandoned older and cruder forms of deliberately discriminatory treatment of workers or job applicants (often called "disparate treatment") but still be violating the intent of the law by using a needlessly discriminatory test. Disparate impact, in other words, was to be the red flag that set the EEOC in motion.

GRIGGS AND AFTERWARD

Soon after, the U.S. Supreme Court entered the fray. Applicants for certain desirable jobs at the Duke Power Company had been required to have a high school diploma or to earn ability test scores above a cutoff. Fewer blacks were getting over these hurdles than whites; a suit found its way to the Supreme Court. The Court's decision in *Griggs* v. *Duke Power Co.*,[6] was instantly recognized as a turning point in the march of affirmative action in the workplace.[7] The Supreme Court struck down the use of either the tests or the educational requirement, because the company was unable to satisfy the Court that either a diploma or a high score on a test had any bearing on the jobs the applicants were being hired for.[8]

Duke Power Co.'s defense was, among other things, that it was trying to raise the general intellectual level of its work force by imposing educational or ability test score requirements. In the Court's unanimous decision (which reversed contrary opinions in both the federal district and circuit courts), Chief Justice Warren Burger approved unstintingly of the EEOC's guidelines: Adverse impact placed a burden of proof on employers to show not just that they were not intentionally discriminating against the protected groups but that their testing procedures could be justified economically, *and* that no other available hiring procedure is equally useful but less discriminatory. Said the Court, good (i.e., nondiscriminatory) intentions do not excuse tests "that operate as 'built-in headwinds' for minority groups and are unrelated to measuring job capability."[9] There must be both "business necessity" and a "manifest relationship" between the test and the job, as the EEOC had ruled. Employers were being told to be wary of off-the-shelf tests of general ability; if they wanted to use a test at all, they would be well advised to write them for the specific job at hand and to do their own validation studies.

Ordinarily there is some presumption that people will obey guidelines proposed by a federal agency like EEOC, but not doing so does not violate the law. Indeed, in the legislative record, Congress was assured that the EEOC had no enforcement powers. However, the Court in *Griggs* said that the EEOC guidelines deserve "great deference,"[10] which endowed them with authority verging on the power of law itself. This laying on of the hands of legality is one reason that *Griggs* has become the landmark case it has turned out to be, for only a defiant or reckless employer would disregard guidelines that the Court embraced so enthusiastically. Beyond that, however, *Griggs* transformed the very conception of affirmative action in the workplace.

The Court grounded its decision in the 1964 Civil Rights Act itself, although the act said nothing about job relatedness, adverse impact, or the lack of alternative hiring criteria. The act did, however, say that a test must not be "designed, intended or used" to discriminate against people in the protected minority groups. Like the EEOC, the Court considered job relatedness and adverse impact to be reasonable translations of Title VII's principles into practice. But it can be argued that job relatedness and disparate impact per se go well beyond Title VII, because a test may have disparate impact and not be specifically related to the particular job being filled without the employer's having designed, intended, or used it for discriminatory purposes.[11]

The issue hinges on whether each of the three terms—"designed, intended or used"—must signify discriminatory intent (i.e., the guilty mind usually required in cases of liability) or only the first two. The first two terms—"designed, intended"—clearly imply discriminatory intent. Must the third? No, said the Supreme Court, "used" need not. And if it need not, then an employer is violating Title VII even if he is not guilty of discriminatory intent, so long as the test has disparate impact and has not been proved, to the Court's satisfaction, to be job related.[12]

After two decades in force, the Court's interpretation may seem correct to many readers, but both the legislative record and the wording of Title VII belie it.[13] Proponents of Title VII, on the floor of Congress and elsewhere, repeatedly assured the opposition that tests administered without discriminatory intent, however adverse their effects, were not being challenged, let alone banned.[14] For example, in a memorandum submitted by Senator Clifford Case, one of Title VII's leading advocates during the legislative debates, we find the following assurance: "No court could read Title VII as requiring an employer to lower or change the occupational qualifications he sets for his employees simply because fewer Negroes than whites are able to meet them."[15] Senator Hubert Humphrey, as we noted in Chapter 20, also assured fellow legislators that Title VII would never be used to impose percentage hiring requirements (disparate impact criteria) on employers.

A year later, in the Equal Employment Opportunity Act of 1972, Congress spoke for the third branch of government, allying itself with the Court and the EEOC. It disapproved of mere "'paper' credentials" (such as cognitive ability test scores) that are of "questionable value." It warned that such credentials burdened people who were "socioeconomically or educationally disadvantaged" with "artificial qualifications."[16] When it first enacted Title VII in 1964, Congress on the whole trusted general ability tests to serve the purpose of predicting worker quality; by 1972, Congress, echoing *Griggs*, had become far more skeptical of the predictive power of those tests and suspicious that they were a pretext for illegal discrimination.[17] In the words of one legal scholar, "The central rationale of the Court's decision in *Griggs* . . . was based on an assumption that those of different races are inherently equal in ability and intelligence, and on a deep skepticism about the utility of devices traditionally used to select among applicants for employment."[18]

With all three branches of government pushing in the same general direction, affirmative action policies evolved toward greater reliance on disparate impact as the touchstone of illegality rather than on discriminatory intent or disparate treatment. As in *Griggs*, the Supreme Court in 1975, in *Albemarle Paper Co. v. Moody*,[19] considered a case in which an employer used intelligence tests (among other criteria) to select workers for well-paying jobs. Once again, black applicants, who earned lower scores than white applicants, brought suit.[20] The Court reaffirmed the general outlines of *Griggs*, but in filling out details, it provided three steps to follow in proving that an employment test was in violation of Title VII (as amended). First, the Court said, a complaining party must show disparate impact. This involved a statistical proof that those who were hired or promoted on the basis of the test included significantly fewer members of a protected group than random selection from the applicant pool would have produced. Given this proof of disparate impact, the burden of proof shifts to the employer, who must now prove that scores on the test have a proven and vital relationship to the *specific* job they were hired for. The criterion expressed in *Griggs*, "business necessity," was carried forward into *Albemarle*. If the employer passes this hurdle, the complaining party can offer evidence that the employer could have used a different hiring procedure, one that was as effective in selecting workers but without the disparate impact. If this can be shown, then, the Court ruled, the employer has been shown to have discriminated illegally by failing to have used the alternative procedure.[21]

Other federal authorities besides the EEOC were monitoring and promoting affirmative action in the workplace. In the mid-1970s, as inconsistencies began to crop up, pressure built up for coordinating as broad a slice of the federal involvement in affirmative action as possible. After some false starts, the Uniform Guidelines on Employee Selection Procedures were adopted in 1978 by EEOC, the Civil Service Commission (later called the Office of Personnel Management), the Department of Justice, the Department of the Treasury, and the Department of Labor.[22] At this writing, they are still in force. The Court's decisions in *Griggs* and *Albemarle* set the broader framework for the Uniform Guidelines, but further details were elaborated, in some respects increasing the pressure on employers using tests. For example, the Uniform Guidelines held—in contrast to the Court in *Albemarle*—that the *employer* has a responsibility for seeking less discriminatory selection procedures, a rather different matter from giving a complaining party the opportunity to do so, as the Court had decreed.

VALIDATING EMPLOYMENT TESTS

The Uniform Guidelines attempt to define a unified approach to affirmative action in the workplace, but practices still vary, and there continue to be new laws and new interpretations by courts. But they come as close to a policy consensus as anything does. They also reveal the underlying assumptions about the facts. On the matter of test validation, the Guidelines espouse the stringent "business necessity" requirement held in *Griggs* and *Albemarle*. They provide detailed requirements for validating tests. Without submerging our readers more deeply in technical minutiae than seems appropriate here, let us say that the Uniform Guidelines lean sharply toward criteria that would be hard and expensive for employers to meet, even when cheaper or easier methods almost certainly would have been more effective.[23] General ability tests, readily available and widely standardized, are rarely acceptable to the EEOC or the courts, unless the employer goes through the difficult, if not impossible, and, psychometrically speaking, needless, process of re-standardization of an established test. To validate a test, an employer needs a measure of performance. The government typically rejects measures of training performance and supervisor ratings. As Chapter 3 detailed, both training scores and supervisor ratings may be suitable measures of performance, and they are relatively easy to obtain. The measures usually required by the government are all but impossible to obtain, especially for job candidates who are not hired.

Despite an air of rigor and precision in discussing validation, neither the EEOC nor any other branch of government involved in administering affirmative action policies has shown any interest in evaluating just how predictive of worker performance the stringent and costly validation procedures it demands are, or whether there is any gain in predictive power when they are used. The thrust continues to be, as it has been from the beginning, to increase the numbers hired or promoted from the protected groups, based on the underlying assumption that, except for discrimination or the legacy of past discrimination, the protected groups should be equally represented across the occupational spectrum.

DISPARATE IMPACT

According to the Guidelines, an employer that comes under their jurisdiction can expect to be required to validate a test—that is, to prove its business necessity—if there is disparate impact. And, the Guidelines further say, disparate impact is assumed if selecting employees by the test violates the 80 percent rule, explained in Chapter 20. As helpful as it may be to employers and regulators to have a fixed standard for disparate impact, the 80 percent rule is psychometrically unsound because it sets a fixed standard. Given two groups with differing average scores and a cutoff for hiring or promotion, the ratio of those selected from the lower group to those selected from the higher group, *given a fair hiring process*, shrinks as the cutoff rises.

Suppose that you are an employer faced with two groups that are of equal size in the applicant pool. The higher group averages one standard deviation above the lower on an IQ test, but the distribution of scores for each group is normal and has the same variability. The eighty percent rule fixes the ratio at eighty hired from the lower group (if it is protected by affirmative action) per hundred hired from the higher group. But if you want to establish a minimum IQ of 100 as the cutoff point for hiring workers, only slightly more than thirty applicants from the lower group would be selected for every hundred from the higher. Suppose that you need a work force with above-average IQs, so you raise the cutoff to an IQ score of 110. In that case, a fair hiring process could be expected to select only twenty of the lower group for each hundred selected from the upper group. If you need a work force with a minimum IQ of 120, the ratio drops to about ten from the lower per hundred from the higher. The ratio will continue to shrink indefinitely as the cutoff moves upward. In other words, applying the 80 percent rule has drastically different effects for an employer hiring people for janitorial jobs compared to an employer hiring lawyers or accountants. Even if one is in favor of the concept of avoiding "disparate impact," the 80 percent rule is an extremely unrealistic way of doing so.

A REVERSAL IN THE AFFIRMATIVE ACTION TREND LINE, OR A BLIP?

The Supreme Court in 1989 backed off from its most demanding requirements for employment testing. In *Wards Cove Packing Co., Inc. v. Atonio*,[24] it softened the obligation on the employer in justifying disparate impact of a test. "Business necessity," the Court said, is an unreasonably stringent criterion, virtually impossible for most ordinary businesses to meet. The result of so extreme a requirement, warned the Court, would be "a host of evils."[25] It was, the Court now said, enough to show that the test serves legitimate business goals. It looked as if the Duke Power Co.'s defense in *Griggs*—to improve the general intellectual quality of its employees—would have met this new standard. Soon thereafter, however, Congress retaliated. The Civil Rights Act of 1991 repudiated *Wards Cove* and returned to the standards of *Griggs* and *Albemarle*—to business necessity, job relatedness, and disparate impact as those earlier decisions had defined it. Once again, employers evidently must satisfy a criterion for employment testing that the Court, two years before, judged to be impossibly demanding. The new law is fraught with ambiguity and will doubtless send lawyers, their clients, and courts back to work to figure out what it requires.[26] But the best guess is that the trendline had blipped, not reversed.

Notes

Abbreviations

DES.   National Center for Education Statistics, *Digest of Education Statistics*. Published annually, Washington, D.C.: Government Printing Office.

NLSY. National Longitudinal Survey of Youth. Center for Human Resource Research, Ohio State University, Columbus, Ohio.

SAUS. U.S. Bureau of the Census. *Statistical Abstract of the United States*. Published annually, Washington, D.C.: Government Printing Office. For each cite in the text, we have added the year of the edition and table numbers to the abbreviation; e.g., *DES*, 19xx, Table xx"

Introduction

1. Galton 1869.
2. Forrest 1974.
3. For a brief history of testing from Galton on, see Herrnstein and Boring 1965.
4. In China, civil service examinations that functioned de facto as intelligence tests—though overweighted with pure memory questions—had been in use for more than a thousand years.
5. Spearman 1904.
6. Galton 1888; Stigler 1986.
7. A correlation matrix is the set of all pairs of correlations. For example, in a 20-item test, each item will have 19 unique correlations with the other items, and the total matrix will contain 190 unique correlations (of Item 1 with Item 2, Item 1 with Item 3, etc.).
8. We are glossing over many complexities, including the effects of varying reliabilities for the items or tests. Spearman understood, and took account of, the contribution of reliability variations.
9. *Buck v. Bell*, 1927.
10. This was Harry Laughlin, whose story is told in Kevles 1985.
11. Brigham 1923; Kevles 1985.
12. The stories have been most influentially told by Fallows 1980; Gould 1981; Kamin 1974.
13. Snyderman and Herrnstein 1983.
14. Snyderman and Herrnstein 1983.

15. Lippmann 1922 p. 10.
16. Lippmann, 1923 p. 46.
17. Snyderman and Herrnstein 1983.
18. Maier and Schneirla 1935.
19. Skinner 1938.
20. Skinner 1953; Skinner 1971.
21. Jensen 1969.
22. Hirsch 1975, p. 3.
23. Pearson 1992.
24. Herrnstein 1971.
25. *Griggs et al. v. Duke Power Co.*, 1971.
26. Quoted in Jensen 1980, p. 13.
27. Elliott 1987.
28. Kamin 1974, p. 3.
29. O. Gillie. 1976. Crucial data faked by eminent psychologist. *Sunday Times* (London), Oct. 24, pp. 1–2.
30. Joynson 1989; Fletcher 1991.
31. Bouchard et al. 1990.
32. Gould 1981.
33. Gould 1981, pp. 27–28.
34. Snyderman and Rothman 1988.
35. Binet himself had died by the time Piaget arrived at the Sorbonne in 1919, but the work on intelligence testing was being carried forward by his collaborator on the first Binet test, Thèophile Simon (see Piaget 1952).
36. Sternberg 1988, p. 8.
37. Sternberg 1985, p. 18.
38. Block and Dworkin 1974.
39. Gardner 1983, pp. 60–61. Emphasis in the original.
40. Gardner 1983, p. 278.
41. Gardner 1983, p. xi. Emphasis in original.
42. Gardner 1983, p. 17. In fact, Gardner's claim about the arbitrariness of factor analysis is incorrect.
43. Gardner 1983, pp. xi–xii.
44. Gardner 1983, p. 17.
45. Although some of the accomplishments of mental calculators remain inexplicable, much has been learned about how they are done. See Jensen 1990; O'Connor and Hermelin 1987.
46. Ceci and Liker 1986.
47. An accurate and highly readable summary of the major points is Seligman 1992. For those who are prepared to dig deeper, Jensen 1980 remains an authoritative statement on most of the basic issues despite the passage of time since it was published.

Introduction to Part I

1. Reuning 1988.
2. Robert Laird Collier, quoted in Manchester 1983, p. 79.

Chapter 1

1. Bender 1960, p. 2.
2. The national SAT-V in 1952 was 476, a little more than a standard deviation lower than the Harvard mean. Perhaps the average Harvard student was much farther ahead of the national average than the text suggests because the national SAT-taking population was so selective, representing only 6.8 percent of high school graduates. But one of the oddities of the 1950s, discussed in more detail in Chapter 18, is that the SAT means remained constant through the decade and into 1963, even as the size of the test-taking population mushroomed. By 1963, when SAT scores hit their all-time high in the post-1952 period, the test-taking population had grown to 47.9 percent of all high school graduates. Thus there is reason to think that the comparison is about the same as the one that would have been produced by a much larger number of test takers in 1952.
3. Bender 1960, p. 4.
4. In the 1920s, fewer than 30 percent of all young people graduated from high school, and the differences between the cognitive ability of graduates and nongraduates were small, as discussed in Chapter 6. Something between 60 and 75 percent of the 18-year-olds in the top IQ quartile never even made it into the calculations shown in the figure on page 34. From the early 1960s on, 70 percent of the nation's youth have graduated from high school, and we know that the difference between the ability of those who do and do not graduate has been large. More concretely, of a nationally representative sample of youth who were administered a highly regarded psychometric test in 1980 when they were 15 and 16 years old, 95 percent of those who scored in the top quartile subsequently graduated from high school, and another 4 percent eventually got a general equivalency diploma. The test was the Armed Forces Qualification Test, and the sample was the 1964 birth cohort of the National Longitudinal Survey of Youth (NLSY), discussed in detail in the introduction to Part II. The figure for the proportion entering colleges is based on the NLSY cohorts and students entering colleges over 1981–1983.
5. The top IQ quartile of the NLSY that first attended college in 1981–1983 was split as follows: 21 percent did not continue to college in the first year after graduation, 18 percent went to a two-year college, and 61 percent attended a four-year college.
6. O'Brien 1928. These percentages are based on high school graduates,

which accounts for the high percentages of students shown as going to college in the 1920s. If the estimates had been based on the proportion of the 18-year-olds who have been graduating from high school since the 1970s, those proportions would have been much smaller. The shape of the curve, however, would be essentially unchanged (because the IQ distribution of students who did not complete high school was so close to the distribution of those who did; see Finch 1946).

7. Another excellent database from the same period, a nationally representative sample tested with the Preliminary SAT in 1960 and followed up a year later, confirms results from Project TALENT, a large, nationally representative sample of high school youths taken in 1960 (Seibel 1962). Among those who scored in the bottom quartile, for example, only 11 percent went to college; of those in the top quartile, 79 percent went to college; of those in the top 5 percent, more than 95 percent went to college.

8. These data are taken from Project TALENT in 1960.

9. From the NLSY, described in the introduction to Part II.

10. The test was Form A of the Otis. Brigham 1932, Table XVIII, p. 336.

11. The schools are Brown, Bryn Mawr, Columbia, Harvard, Mount Holyoke, Princeton, Radcliffe, Smith, University of Pennsylvania (with separate means for men and women), Vassar, Wellesley, Williams, and Yale.

12. Learned and Wood 1938.

13. Not including the University of Pennsylvania, one of the elite schools.

14. Between the earliest SAT and 1964, the SAT had divided into a verbal and a math score. It is a moot question whether the modern overall SAT or the verbal SAT is more comparable to the original SAT. In the comparisons being made here, we rely on the Educational Testing Service norm studies, which enable us to place an SAT value on the *national* 18-year-old cohort, not just the cohort who takes the test. We explain the norm studies in Chapter 18.

15. This is not the usual SAT distribution, which is ordinarily restricted to college-bound seniors, but rather shows the distribution for a nationally representative sample of all high school seniors, based on the norm studies mentioned in note 14. It is restricted to persons still in high school and does not include the 34 percent of 18-year-olds who were not.

16. We know how high the scores were for many schools as of the early 1960s. We know Harvard's scores in the early 1950s. We can further be confident that no school was much more selective than Harvard as of 1952 (with the possible exception of science students going to Cal Tech and MIT). Therefore means for virtually all of the other schools as of 1952 had to be near or below Harvard's, and the dramatic changes for the other elite schools had to be occurring in the same comparatively brief period of time concentrated in the 1950s.

17. Bender 1960, p. 6.
18. This percentage is derived from 1960 data reported by Bender 1960, p. 15, regarding the median family income of candidates who applied for scholarship aid, were denied, but came to Harvard anyway. Total costs at Harvard in 1960 represented 21 percent of that median.
19. The families for whom a year at Harvard represented less than 20 percent of their income constituted approximately 5.8 percent of families in 1950 and 5.5 percent of families in 1950. Estimated from U.S. Bureau of the Census 1975, G-1-15.
20. The faculty's views were expressed in Faculty of Arts and Sciences 1960.
21. Bender 1960, p. 31.
22. For an analysis of the ascriptive qualities that Harvard continued to use for admissions choices in the 1980s, see Karen 1991.
23. The increase in applications to Harvard had been just as rapid from 1952 to 1958, when the size of the birth cohorts was virtually constant, as in 1959 and 1960, when they started to increase.
24. For an analysis of forces driving more recent increases in applications, see Clotfelter 1990 and Cook and Frank 1992.
25. Cook and Frank 1992.
26. Harvard, MIT, Princeton, Stanford, and Cal Tech were in the top seven in all three decades. Columbia and Chicago were the other two in the 1960s, Yale and Cornell in the 1970s and 1980s. Cook and Frank 1992, Table 3.
27. Cook and Frank 1992, Table 4. The list of "most competitive" consists of the thirty-three schools named by *Barron's* in its 1980 list. The Cook and Frank analysis generally suggests that the concentration of top students in a few schools may have plateaued during the 1970s, then resumed again in the 1980s.
28. *U.S. News & World Report*, October 15, 1990, pp. 116–134. It is not necessary to insist that this ranking is precisely accurate. It is enough that it includes all the schools that most people would name if they were asked to list the nation's top schools, and the method for arriving at the list of fifty seems reasonable.
29. The College Board ethnic and race breakdowns for 1991, available by request from the College Board. There is also reason to believe that an extremely high proportion of high school students in each senior class who have the potential to score in the high 600s and the 700s on the SAT actually take the test. See Murray and Herrnstein 1992.
30. See Chapter 18 for where the SAT population resides in the national context.
31. These represent normal distributions based on estimates drawn from the Learned data that the mean IQ of Pennsylvania graduates in 1930 was ap-

proximately two-thirds of a standard deviation above the mean (the mean of incoming freshmen was .48 SDs above the mean), and from the Brigham data that the graduates of the Ivy League and Seven Sisters were approximately 1.25 SDs above the mean (they were 1.1 SDs above the mean as freshmen, and the Ivy League graduated extremely high proportions of the incoming students).

32. The distributions for the main groups are based on the NLSY, for youths who came of college age from 1981 to 1983 and have been followed through the 1990 interview wave. The top dozen universities are those ranked 1 through 12 in the *U.S. News & World Report* survey for 1990. *U.S. News & World Report*, October 15, 1990, pp. 116–134. The analysis is based on published distribution of SAT-Verbal scores, which is the more highly *g*-loaded of the SAT subtests. The estimated verbal mean (weighted by size of the freshman class) for these twenty schools, based on their published SAT distributions, is 633. The estimated mean for graduates is 650 (dropout rates for these schools are comparatively low but highly concentrated among those with the lowest entering scores). This compares with a national SAT-Verbal norm estimated at 376 with an SD of 102 (Braun, Centra, and King, 1987, Appendix B). The distribution in the figure on page 46 converts the SAT data to standardized scores. The implicit assumption is that AFQT (Armed Forces Qualification Test, an intelligence test discussed in Appendix 3) and SAT-Verbal measure the same thing, which is surely wrong to some degree. Both tests are highly *g*-loaded, however, and it is reasonable to conclude that youths who have a mean 2.5 SDs above the mean on the SAT would have means somewhere close to that on a full-fledged mental test.

33. We have defined these as the first twelve of the listed universities in the *U.S. News & World Report* listing for 1990. They are (in the order of their ranking) Harvard, Stanford, Yale, Princeton, Cal Tech, MIT, Duke, Dartmouth, Cornell, Columbia, University of Chicago, and Brown.

34. The probabilities are based on the proportions of people entering these categories in the 1980s, which means that they become progressively too generous for older readers (when the proportion of people getting college degrees was smaller). But this is a technicality; the odds are already so tiny that they are for practical purposes unaffected by further restrictions. The figure for college degrees reflects the final educational attainment of members of the NLSY, who were born in 1957 through 1964, as of 1990 (when the youngest was 25), as a weighted proportion of the NLSY population. The figure for Ph.D., law, and medical degrees is based on the number of degrees awarded over 1980–1989 expressed as a proportion of the population age 26 in each of those years. The figure for graduates of the dozen elite schools is based on the number of undergraduate degrees awarded by

these institutions in 1989 (the figure has varied little for many years), expressed as a proportion of the population age 22 in 1989 (incidentally, the smallest cohort since the mid-1970s.)

35. Based on the median percentages for those score intervals among those schools.

Chapter 2

1. Herrnstein 1973.
2. For a one-source discussion of IQs and occupations, see Matarazzo 1972, Chap. 7. Also see Jencks et al. 1972 and Sewell and Hauser 1975 for comprehensive analyses of particular sets of data. The literature is large and extends back to the early part of the century. For earlier studies, see, for example, Bingham 1937; Clark and Gist 1938; Fryer 1922; Pond 1933; Stewart 1947; Terman 1942. For more recent estimates of minimum scores for a wide variety of occupations, see E. F. Wonderlic & Associates 1983; U.S. Department of Labor 1970.
3. Jencks et al. 1972.
4. Fallows 1985.
5. The Fels Longitudinal Study; see McCall 1977.
6. The correlation was a sizable .5–.6, on a scale that goes from −1 to +1. See Chapter 3 and Appendix 1 for a fuller explanation of what the correlation coefficient means. Job status for the boys was about equally well predicted by childhood IQ as by their completed educational levels; for the girls, job status was *more* correlated with childhood IQ than with educational attainment. In another study, adult intelligence was also more highly correlated with occupational status than with educational attainment (see Duncan 1968). But this may make a somewhat different point, inasmuch as adult intelligence may itself be affected by educational attainment, in contrast to the IQ one chalks up at age 7 or 8 years. In yet another study, based on Swedish data, adult income (as distinguished from occupational status) was less strongly dependent on childhood IQ (age 10) than on eventual educational attainment (T. Husen's data presented in Griliches 1970), although being strongly dependent on both. Other analyses come up with different assessments of the underlying relationships (e.g., Bowles and Gintis 1976; Jencks 1979). Not surprisingly, the empirical picture, being extremely diverse and rich, has lent itself to myriad formal analyses, which we will make no attempt to review. In Chapters 3 and 4, we present our interpretation of the link between individual ability and occupation. We also discuss some of the evident exceptions to these findings.
7. Many of the major studies (e.g., Duncan 1968; Jencks et al. 1972; McCall 1977; Sewell and Hauser 1975) include variables describing familial so-

cioeconomic status, which prove to be somewhat predictive of a person's own status.

8. For a fuller discussion of both the explanation and the controversy, see Herrnstein 1973.

9. Teasdale, Sorenson, and Owen 1984.

10. The authors of the study offered as an explanation for this pattern of results the well-established pattern of resemblances among relatives in IQ, presumably owing to the genes that natural siblings share and that adoptive siblings do not share. It could, of course, be traits of personality rather than of intellect that tie a family's occupational destinies together. However, the small body of evidence bearing on personality traits finds them to be distinctly weaker predictors of job status than is IQ. Another study, of over 1,000 pairs of Norwegian twins, supported the conclusion that the resemblance in job status among close relatives is largely explained by their similarity in IQ and that genes play a significant role in this similarity. See Tambs et al. 1989.

11. For some of the most detailed distributional data, see Stewart 1947, Table 1.

12. Matarazzo 1972, p. 177.

13. Specific cognitive strengths also vary by occupation, with engineers tending to score higher on analytic and quantitative sections of the Graduate Record Exams, while English professors do better on the verbal portions (e.g., Wah and Robinson 1990, Figure 2.2).

14. With a mean of 100 and SD of 15, an IQ score of 120 cuts off the 91st percentile of a normal distribution. But the IQ distribution tends to be skewed so that it is fat on the right tail. To say that 120 cuts off the top tenth is only approximate but close enough for our purposes.

15. The procedure we used to create the figure on page 56 yielded an estimate of 23.2 percent of the top IQ decile in high-IQ occupations in 1990. Of the top IQ decile in the NLSY as of 1990, when they ranged in age from 25 to 32, 22.2 percent of the top decile were employed in the dozen high-IQ occupations. The analysis excludes those who were still enrolled in school in 1990 and those who were in the military (because their occupation within the military was unknown). The NLSY figure is an underestimate (compared to the national estimate) in that those who are still students will disproportionately enter high-IQ professions. On the other hand, the NLSY would be likely to exceed the national data in the figure insofar as the entire NLSY age cohort is of working age, without retirees. One other comment on possible distortions over time: It might be hypothesized that, since 1900, the mean has dropped and distribution has spread, as more and more people have entered those professions. The plausibility of the hypothesis is arguable; indeed, there are reasons for hypoth-

esizing that the opposite has occurred (for the same reasons educational stratification has raised the IQ of students at the elite colleges). But it would not materially affect the plot in the figure on page 56 even if true, because the numbers of people in those professions were so small in the early decades of the century. It may also be noted that in the NLSY data, 46 percent of all job slots in the high-IQ occupations were held by people in the top decile, again matching our conjecture about the IQ scores within the occupations.

16. Terman and Oden 1947.

17. The NLSY cannot answer that question, because even a sample of 11,878 (the number that took the AFQT) is too small to yield adequate sample sizes for analyzing subgroups in the top tenth of the top percentile.

18. There are not that many people with IQs of 120+ left over, after the known concentrations of them in the high IQ occupations are taken into account.

19. The literature is extensive. The studies used for this discussion, in addition to those cited specifically, include Bendix 1949; Macmahon and Millett 1939; Pierson 1969; Stanley, Mann, and Doig 1967; Sturdivant and Adler 1976; Vance 1966; Warner and Abegglen 1955.

20. Newcomer 1955, Table 24, p. 68.

21. Clews 1908, pp. 27, 37, quoted in Newcomer 1955, p. 66.

22. The data are drawn from Newcomer 1955.

23. Burck 1976. The *Fortune* survey was designed to yield data comparable with those in Newcomer 1955.

24. The ostensible decline in college degrees after 1950 is explained by college graduates' going on to get additional educational credentials. For another study of educational attainment of CEOs that shows the same pattern, see Priest 1982.

25. U.S. Bureau of the Census 1992, Tables 18, 615, and U.S. Department of Labor 1991, Table 22.

26. Excluding accountants, who were already counted in the high-IQ professions.

27. Matarazzo 1972, Table 7.3, p. 178.

Chapter 3

1. Bok 1985b. In another setting, again discussing the SAT, he wrote, "Such tests are only modestly correlated with subsequent academic success and give no reliable indication of achievement in later life" (Bok 1985a, p. 15).

2. The correlation of IQ with income in a restricted population such as Harvard graduates could be negative when people toward the top of the IQ distribution are disproportionately drawn into academia, where they make

a decent living but seldom much more than that, while students with IQs of "only" 120 and 130 will more often go into the business world, where they may get rich.
3. See Chapter 19; Dunnette 1976; Ghiselli 1973.
4. Technically, a correlation coefficient is a ratio, with the covariation of the two variables in the numerator and the product of the separate standard deviations of the two variables in the denominator. The formula for computing a Pearson product moment correlation r (the kind that we will be using throughout) is:

$$\frac{\sum (X - \bar{X})(Y - \bar{Y})}{\sqrt{\left[\sum (X - \bar{X})^2\right]\left[\sum (Y - \bar{Y})^2\right]}}$$

where X and Y refer to the actual values for each case and $\bar{X}$ and $\bar{Y}$ refer to the mean values of the X and Y, respectively.
5. We limited the sample to families making less than $100,000, so as to avoid some distracting technical issues that arise when analyzing income across the entire spectrum (e.g., the appropriateness of using logged values rather than raw values). The results from the 1 percent sample are in line with the statistics produced when the analysis is repeated for the entire national sample: a correlation of .31 and an increment of $2,700 per year of additional education. Income data are for 1989, expressed in 1990 dollars.
6. An important distinction: The underlying relationship persists in a sample with restricted range, but the restriction of range makes the relationship harder to identify (i.e., the correlation coefficient is attenuated, sometimes to near zero).

Forgetting about restriction of range produces fallacious reasoning that is remarkably common, even among academics who are presumably familiar with the problem. For example, psychologist David McClelland, writing at the height of the anti-IQ era in 1973, argued against any relationship between career success and IQ, pointing out that whereas college graduates got better jobs than nongraduates, the academic records of graduates did not correlate with job success, even though college grades correlate with IQ. He added, anecdotally, that he recalled his own college class—Wesleyan University, a top-rated small college—and was convinced that the eight best and eight worst students in his class had not done much differently in their subsequent careers (McClelland 1973). This kind of argument is also common in everyday life, as in the advice offered by friends during the course of writing this book. There was, for example, our friend the nuclear physicist, who prefaced his remarks by saying, "I don't think I'm any smarter than the average nuclear physicist . . ." Or an engineer friend, a key figure in the *Apollo* lunar landing program, who insisted that this IQ business is much overemphasized. He had been a C student in college and would not have even graduated, except that he managed to pull himself together in his senior year. His conclusion was that motivation was important, not IQ. Did he happen to know what his IQ was? Sure, he replied. It was 146. He was right, insofar as motivation can make the difference between being a first-rate rocket scientist and a mediocre one—if you start with an IQ of 146. But the population with a score of 146 (or above) represents something less than 0.2 percent of the population. Similarly, correlations of IQ and job success among college graduates suffer from restriction of range. The more selective the group is, the greater the restriction, which is why Derek Bok may plausibly (if not quite accurately) have claimed that SAT scores have "no correlation at all with what you do in the rest of your life" if he was talking about Harvard students.

7. E.g., Fallows 1985.

8. See Chapter 20 for more detail.

9. *Griggs* v. *Duke Power*, 401 U.S. 424 (1971).

10. The doctrine has been built into the U.S. Employment and Training Service's General Aptitude Test Battery (GATB), into the federal civil service's Professional and Administrative Career Examination (PACE), and into the military's Armed Services Vocational Aptitude Battery (ASVAB). Bartholet 1982; Braun 1992; Gifford 1989; Kelman 1991; Seymour 1988. For a survey of test instruments and their use, see Friedman and Williams 1982.

11. For a recent review of the expert community as a whole, see Schmidt and Ones 1992.

12. Hartigan and Wigdor 1989 and Schmidt and Hunter 1991 represent the two ends of the range of expert opinion.

13. For a sampling of the new methods, see Bangert-Drowns 1986; Glass 1976; Glass, McGaw, and Smith 1981; Hunter and Schmidt 1990. Meta-analytic strategies had been tried for decades prior to the 1970s, but it was after the advent of powerful computers and statistical software that many of the techniques became practicable.

14. Hartigan and Wigdor 1989; Hunter and Schmidt 1990; Schmidt and Hunter 1981.

15. We have used the terms *job productivity* or *job performance* or *performance ratings* without explaining what they mean or how they are measured. On the other hand, all of us have a sense of what job productivity is like—we are confident that we know who are the better and worse secretaries, managers, and colleagues among those with whom we work closely. But how is this knowledge to be captured in objective measures? Ratings by supervisors or peers? Samples of work in the various tasks that a job demands? Tests

of job knowledge? Job tenure or promotion? Direct cost accounting of workers' output? There is no way to answer such a question decisively, for people may legitimately disagree about what it is about a worker's performance that is most worth predicting. As a practical matter, ratings by supervisors, being the most readily obtained and the least intrusive in the workplace, have dominated the literature (Hunter 1986). But it is natural to wonder whether supervisor ratings, besides being easy to get, truly measure how well workers perform rather than, say, how they get along with the boss or how they look (Guion 1983).

To get a better fix on what the various measures of performance mean, it is useful to evaluate a number of studies that have included measures of cognitive ability, supervisor ratings, samples of work, and tests of job knowledge. Work samples are usually obtained by setting up stations for workers to do the various tasks required by their jobs and having their work evaluated in some reasonably objective way. Different occupations lend themselves more or less plausibly to this kind of simulated performance. The same is true of written or oral tests of job knowledge.

One of the field's leaders, John Hunter, has examined the correlational structure that relates these different ways of looking at job performance to each other and to an intelligence test score (Hunter 1983, 1986). In a study of 1,800 workers, Hunter found a strong direct link between intelligence and job knowledge and a much smaller direct one between intelligence and performance in work sample tasks. By direct we mean that the variables predict each other without taking any other variable into account. The small direct link between intelligence and work sample was augmented by a large indirect link, via job knowledge: a person's intelligence predicted his knowledge of the job, and his knowledge in turn predicted his work sample. The correlation (after the usual statistical corrections) between intelligence and job knowledge was .8; between intelligence and work sample it was .75. The indirect link between intelligence and work sample, via job knowledge, was larger by half than the direct one (Hunter 1986).

The correlation between intelligence and supervisor ratings in Hunter's analysis was .47. Upon analysis, Hunter found that the primary reason is that brighter workers know more about their jobs, and supervisors respond favorably to their knowledge. A comparable analysis of approximately 1,500 military personnel in four specialties produced the same basic finding (Hunter 1986). This may seem a weakness of the supervisor rating measure, but is it really? How much workers know about their jobs correlates, on the one hand, with their intelligence and, on the other, with both how they do on direct tests of their work and how they are rated by their supervisors. A worker's intelligence influences how much he learns about the job, and job knowledge contributes to proficiency. The knowledge also influences the impression the worker makes on a supervisor rating more than the work as measured by a work sample test (which, of course, the supervisor may never see in the ordinary course of business). Using supervisor rating as a measure of proficiency is thereby justified, without having to claim that the rating directly measures proficiency.

Hunter found that work samples are more dependent on intelligence and job knowledge than are supervisor ratings. Supervisor ratings, which are so predominant in this literature, may, in other words, underestimate how important intelligence is for proficiency. Recent research suggests that supervisor ratings in fact do underestimate the correlation between intelligence and productivity (Becker and Huselid 1992). But we should acknowledge again that none of the measures of proficiency—work samples, supervisor ratings, or job knowledge tests—is free of the taint of artificiality, let alone arbitrariness. Supervisor ratings may be biased in many ways; a test of job knowledge is a test, not a job; and even a worker going from one work station to another under the watchful eye of an industrial psychologist may be revealing something other than everyday competence. It has been suggested that the various contrived measures of workers tell us more about maximum performance than they do about typical, day-to-day proficiency (Guion 1983). We therefore advise that the quantitative estimates we present here (or that can be found in the technical literature at large) be considered only tentative and suggestive.

16. The average validity of .4 is obtained after standard statistical corrections of various sorts. The two most important of these are a correction for test unreliability or measurement error and a correction for restriction of range among the workers in any occupation. All of the validities in this section of the chapter are similarly corrected, unless otherwise noted.

17. Ghiselli 1966, 1973; Hunter and Hunter 1984, Table 1.

18. Hunter 1980; Hunter and Hunter 1984.

19. Where available, ratings by peers, tests of job knowledge, and actual work samples often come close to ability measures as predictors of job performance (Hunter and Hunter 1984). But aptitude tests have the practical advantage that they can be administered relatively inexpensively to large numbers of applicants, and they do not depend on applicants' having been on the job for any length of time.

20. E. F. Wonderlic & Associates 1983; Hunter 1989. These validities, which are even higher than the ones presented in the table on page 74 are for training success rather than for measures of job performance and are more directly comparable with the column for training success in the GATB

studies than the column for job proficiency. Regarding job performance, one major study evaluated the performance of about 1,500 air force enlisted men and women working in eight military specialties, chosen to be representative of military specialties in the air force. Performance was variously measured: by defining a set of tasks involved in each job, then training a group of evaluators to assess those specific tasks; by interviews of the personnel on technical aspects of their jobs; by supervisor ratings after training the supervisors; and combinations of methods. The average correlation between AFQT score and a hands-on job performance measure was .40, with the highest among the precision measurement equipment specialists and the avionics communications specialists and the lowest among the air traffic control operators and the air crew life support specialists. Insofar as the jobs were restricted to those held by enlisted men, the distribution of jobs was somewhat skewed toward the lower end of the skill range. We do not have an available estimate of the validity of the AFQT over all military jobs.

21. Hartigan and Wigdor 1989.
22. It is one of the chronically frustrating experiences when reading scientific results: Two sets of experts, supposedly using comparable data, come out with markedly different conclusions, and the reasons for the differences are buried in technical and opaque language. How is it possible for a layperson to decide who is right? The different estimates of mean validity of the GATB—.45 according to Hunter, Schmidt, and some others; .25 according to the Hartigan committee—is an instructive case in point.

    Sometimes the differences really are technical and opaque. For example, the Hartigan committee based its estimate on the assumption that the reliability of supervisor ratings was higher than other studies assumed—.8 instead of .6 (Hartigan and Wigdor 1989, p. 170). By assuming a higher reliability, the committee's correction for measurement error was smaller than Hunter's. Deciding between the Hartigan committee's use of .8 as the reliability of supervisor ratings instead of the .6 used by Hunter is impossible for anyone who is not intimately familiar with a large and scattered literature on that topic, and even then the choice remains a matter of judgment. But the Hartigan committee's decision not to correct for restriction of range, which makes the largest difference in their estimates of the overall validity, is based on a much different kind of disagreement. Here, a layperson is as qualified to decide as an expert, for this is a disagreement about what question is being answered.

    John Hunter and others assumed that for any job the applicant pool is the entire U.S. work force. That is, they sought an answer to the question, "What is the relationship between job performance and intelligence for the work force at large?" The Hartigan committee objected to their assumption on grounds that, in practice, the applicant pool for any particular job is not the entire U.S. work force but people who have a chance to get the job. As they accurately noted, "People gravitate to jobs for which they are potentially suited" (Hartigan and Wigdor 1989, p. 166).

But embedded in the committee's objection to Hunter's estimates is a tacit switch in the question that the analysis is supposed to answer. The Hartigan committee sought an answer to the question, "Among those people who apply for such-and-such a position, what is the relationship between intelligence and job performance?" If one's objective is not to discourage people who weigh only 250 pounds from applying for jobs as tackles in the NFL, to return to our analogy, then the Hartigan committee's question is the appropriate one. Of course, by minimizing the validity of weight, a large number of 150-pound lineman may apply for the jobs. Thus our reasons for concluding that the assumption used by Hunter and Schmidt (among others), that restriction of range calculations should be based on the entire work force, is self-evidently the appropriate choice if one wants to know the overall relationship of IQ to job performance and its economic consequences.

23. The ASVAB comprises ten subtests: General Science, Arithmetic Reasoning, Word Knowledge, Paragraph Comprehension, Numerical Operations, Coding Speed, Auto/Shop Information, Mathematics Knowledge, Mechanical Comprehension, and Electronics Information. Only Numerical Operations and Coding Speed are highly speeded; the other eight are nonspeeded "power" tests. All the armed services use the four MAGE composites, for Mechanical, Administrative, General, and Electronics specialties, each of which includes three or four subtests in a particular weighting. These composites are supposed to predict a recruit's trainability for the particular specialty. The AFQT is yet another composite from the ASVAB, selected so as to measure g efficiently. See Appendix 3.

24. About 80 percent of the sample had graduated from high school and had no further civilian schooling, fewer than 1 percent had failed to graduate from high school, and fewer than 2 percent had graduated from college; the remainder had some post–high school civilian schooling short of a college degree. The modal person in the sample was a white male between 19 and 20 years old, but the sample also included thousands of women and people from all American ethnic groups; their ages ranged from a minimum of 17 to almost 15 percent above 23 years (see Ree and Earles 1990b). Other studies, using educationally heterogeneous samples, have in fact shown that, holding AFQT constant, high school graduates are more likely to avoid disciplinary action, to be recommended for reenlistment, and to be promoted to higher rank than nongraduates (Office of the Assistant Secretary of Defense 1980). Current enlistment policies reflect the inde-

pendent predictiveness of education, in that of two applicants with equal AFQT score, the high school graduate is selected over the nongraduate if only one is to be accepted.

25. In fact, there may be some upward bias in these correlations, inasmuch as they were not cross validated to exclude capitalization on chance.

26. What does it mean to "account for the observed variation"? Think of it in this way: A group of recruits finishes its training course; their grades vary. How much less would they have varied had they entered the course with the same level of *g*? This may seem like a hypothetical question, but it is answered simply by squaring the correlation between the recruits' level of *g* and their final grades. In general, given any two variables, the degree to which variation in either is explained (or accounted for, in statistical lingo) by the other variable is obtained by squaring the correlation between them. For example, a perfect correlation of 1 between two variables means that each of the variables fully explains the observed variations in the other. When two variables are perfectly correlated, they are also perfectly redundant since if we know the value of one of them, we also know the value of the other without having to measure it. Hence, 1 squared is 1.0 or 100 percent. A correlation of .5 means that each variable explains, or accounts for, 25 percent of the observed variation in the other; a correlation of 0 means that neither variable accounts for any of the observed variation in the other.

In the Ree and Earles study, over all eighty-nine occupational schools, the average value of this square correlation was 58 percent (which corresponds to a correlation of .76). *g*, in other words, accounted for almost 60 percent of the observed variation in school grades in the average military course, once the results were corrected for range restriction. Even without a correction for range restriction, *g* accounted for over 20 percent of the variance in school grades on the average (corresponding to a correlation of .45).

27. Welsh, Watson, and Ree 1990.

28. Jones 1988. A similar analysis was performed for job performance but, because of the expense of obtaining special performance measures, with a much smaller sample (1,545) spread across just eight enlisted job specialties (Ree and Earles 1991). The correlations with *g* in this study did not reach the extraordinarily high levels of predictiveness as for school grades, and the other cognitive factors were relatively more important for job performance than for school grades—points to which we shall return. But combining the results with the previously cited job performance study of air force personnel (Office of the Assistant Secretary of Defense for Force Management and Personnel 1989), the job predictiveness of AFQT for the specialties is correlated above .9 with the job predictiveness of *g*. Using the

highest of the various correlations between job performance measures and g, the product-moment correlation is .97 and the Spearman rank-order correlation is .93. In other words, in predicting job performance, at least for these jobs and these performance tests, the validity of an AFQT score is virtually entirely explained by how well it measures g, per se.

29. Thorndike 1986. The comparison is between the predictiveness of the first factor extracted by factor analysis of the five cognitive subtests of GATB versus the regression-weighted subtest scores themselves, for cross-validating samples of at least fifty workers in each of the twenty-eight occupations.

30. Hawk 1986; Jensen 1980, 1986; Linn 1986.

31. For the linear relationship of cognitive ability, see Schmidt, Ones, and Hunter 1992. For the nonlinear relationship of job experiences see Blankenship and Taylor 1938; Ghiselli and Brown 1947; Taylor and Smith 1956.

32. Hawk 1970; Hunter and Schmidt 1982.

33. Humphreys 1968, 1973; Wilson 1983.

34. See p. 66.

35. Butler and McCauley 1987.

36. McDaniel, Schmidt, and Hunter 1986.

37. Schmidt et al. 1988.

38. Maier and Hiatt 1985.

39. This story echoes the mixed findings for the learning of simple tasks in the psychological laboratory. Depending on which measures are used to predict performance and which tasks are being predicted, one can expect either to see convergence of performance with practice, or no convergence, or even divergence under some circumstances. See Ackermann 1987.

40. Schmidt et al. 1988. No data have yet tested the possibility that productivity diverges (the advantage enjoyed by the smarter employee increases with experience) in very-high-complexity jobs.

41. See also Schmidt et al. 1984.

42. See the discussion in note 15.

43. Burke and Frederick 1984; Hunter and Schmidt 1982; Hunter, Schmidt, and Judiesch 1990; Schmidt and Hunter 1983; Weekley et al. 1985. In the technical literature, the standard deviation of productivity measured in dollars is represented as SD_y and has generally been estimated to average, over many different occupations, .4 times the average wage for the job. The corresponding figure as a proportion of the value of the average worker output is .2. Methods for estimating these distributions are discussed in the cited references, but they include such techniques as supervisor ratings of the dollar costs of replacing workers at various points in the distribution of workers, cost accounting of worker product, and scores on proficiency tests and at work sample stations.

44. Becker and Huselid 1992.
45. The more contemporary estimate would place this value at about $16,000 rather than $8,000. All the other dollar estimates of the benefits of testing mentioned in this section could similarly be doubled.
46. Hunter, Schmidt, and Judiesch 1990.
47. We use rounds numbers to make the calculations easy to follow, but these are in fact close to the current medians.
48. Hunter, Schmidt, and Judiesch 1990.
49. $25,000 \times .15 = 3,750$; $100,000 \times .5 = 50,000$; $50,000/3,750 = 13.33$.
50. $100,000 \times .5 \times .6 = 30,000$; $25,000 \times .15 \times .2 = 750$.
51. There is another point illustrated by this exercise. Recall that a validity (correlation) "explains" only the amount of variance equal to its square; hence a validity of .4 explains only 16 percent of the variance, and this offers a temptation to dismiss the importance of intelligence as being of negligible economic consequences. And yet when we calculated the gains to be realized from an ability test that is less than perfectly valid as a predictor of proficiency, we multiplied the gain from a perfect test by the validity, not by the square of the validity. When trying to estimate how much of the value of a perfect selection procedure is captured by an imperfect substitute, the validity of the imperfect test is equal to the proportion of the value that is captured by it. A test with a validity of .4 captures 40 percent of the value that would be realized from a perfect test, even though it explains only 16 percent of the variance. Readers interested in the mathematical proof, which was first derived in the 1940s, will find it in Hunter and Schmidt 1982.
52. Two of the classic discussions of the conditions under which testing pays off are Brogden 1949 and Cronbach and Gleser 1965.
53. These correlations cover the empirical range in two senses. First, they bracket the values found in the technical literature dealing with the predictiveness of intelligence. Second, they bracket the various occupations, as described by Hunter, Schmidt, and their colleagues. More complex jobs have higher correlations between intelligence and proficiency, but almost all common occupations fall in the range between .2 and .6. The graphs assume normality of the predictor and outcome variables and a linear relation between them. None of these assumptions needs to be strictly met in order for the figure to give at least an approximately correct account of the relationships, nor are there any known deviations from normality or linearity that would materially alter the account.
54. We estimate the percentile values by assuming that proficiencies are normally distributed.
55. Hunter and Hunter 1984; Schmidt, Mack, and Hunter 1984.
56. Hartigan and Wigdor 1989; Hunter and Hunter 1984.

57. The data for the following description come from Herrnstein, Belke, and Taylor 1990.
58. Hunter 1979.
59. Murphy 1986.

Chapter 4

1. Juhn, Murphy, and Pierce 1990; Katz and Murphy 1900.
2. Twenty-three percent for sixteen or more years of education versus 11 percent for twelve or fewer years, according to Katz and Murphy 1990.
3. Freeman 1976.
4. The wage decline in the 1970s for highly educated workers and in the 1980s for less educated workers could conceivably have been due to declines in the quality of college education in the earlier period and in primary and high school education in the later period or in corresponding changes in the skills of people at those levels of education, as reflected, for example, in the decline of SAT scores (Bishop 1989). Economists assessing this hypothesis have concluded that it could not have played a major role (see Blackburn, Bloom, and Freeman 1990; Juhn, Murphy, and Pierce 1990; Katz and Murphy 1990).
5. The dramatic growth of female work force participation would necessitate complex modeling to address for the labor force as a whole the question here dealt with just for men.
6. Comparing men with sixteen or more years in school to those with fewer than twelve years gives a 26.8 percent differential and to those with twelve years in school gives 29.8. Since each category is being compared to its own baseline, this calculation understates the size of the change in actual real wages.
7. In a slightly different approach to the data, Kevin Murphy and Finis Welch, restricting the analysis to white workers, also found that more education had a shrinking wage benefit from 1963 to 1979, followed by a steeply rising benefit, but only for new workers. For experienced workers, the wage benefit for education did not decline during the earlier period, then rose more modestly thereafter. Work experience, in other words, dampened the wage benefit for education from the 1970s to the 1980s (Murphy and Welch 1989. See also Murphy and Welch 1993a, 1993b).
8. That intelligence is confounded with educational attainment is hardly a new idea. See Arrow 1973; Herrnstein 1973; Jencks et al. 1972; Sewell and Hauser 1975.
9. Juhn, Murphy, and Pierce 1990; Katz and Murphy 1990.
10. Public employment shielded workers, especially female workers, from the rising wage premium for education in the 1980s and the rising premium

for unmeasured individual characteristics, presumably including intelligence. In the upper half of the wage distribution for highly educated workers, the ratio of federal to private wages declined from 1979 to 1988, even after corrections for race, age, and region of the country (Cutler and Katz 1991). The decline was especially large for women, perhaps because educated women were finding relatively more lucrative alternatives outside the government. For less educated workers in the lower half of the wage distribution, the ratio of federal to private wages rose during that interval, again especially for women. For state and local (as distinguished from federal) public employees, the rise in the ratio of public to private wages for less educated workers was larger still.

11. "Residual" in the regression analysis sense. After accounting for the effects of education, experience, gender, and their various interactions, a certain amount of real wage variance remains unexplained. This is the residual that has been growing.

12. Juhn, Murphy, and Pierce, 1990; Katz and Murphy 1990; Levy and Murnane 1992.

13. Juhn, Murphy, and Pierce 1990.

14. Diligence, or conscientiousness, is one noncognitive trait that appears to earn a wage premium (Schmidt and Ones 1992). Drive, ambition, and sociability have been examined by Filer (1981). None of these has been as well established as cognitive ability, nor do they appear to be as significant in their economic effects.

15. Blackburn and Neumark 1991.

16. Blackburn and Neumark 1991. This study used the National Longitudinal Survey of Youth (NLSY), a database described in the introduction to Part II.

17. Lest we convey the false impression that we are suggesting that education per se is immaterial, once intelligence is taken account of, we note two ingenious studies by economists Joshua Angrist and Alan Krueger (Angrist and Krueger 1991a, 1991b). They examined wages in relation to schooling for school dropouts born at different times of year and for people with varying draft lottery numbers. Dropouts in many states must remain in school until the end of the academic year in which they reach a given age. For people who want to drop out as soon as possible, those born in, say, October will spend a year in school more than those born in January. Likewise, during the Vietnam era, people whose only reason for staying in school was to avoid the draft would get more schooling if they had low lottery numbers, making them more likely to be drafted, than if they had high numbers. In both populations, the extra schooling showed a wage benefit later on. These findings show effects of education above and beyond personal traits like intelligence, if we assume that intelligence is uncorrelated

with the month in which one is born or the lottery number. In fact, human births are moderately seasonal, and the seasonality differs across races, ethnic groups, and socioeconomic status, which may mean that births are seasonal with respect to average intelligence (Lam and Miron 1991). No such complication confounds the study using lottery numbers. Even so, the generality of these findings for populations other than school dropouts and for people who stayed in school only to avoid being drafted remains to be established.

18. Again from the NLSY. The sample chosen for this particular analysis was at least 30 years old, had been out of school for at least a year, and had worked fifty-two weeks in 1989 (from Top Decile Analysis). The median (as distinguished from the mean) difference in annual wages and salaries was much smaller: $3,000. A bulge of very-high-income individuals in these occupations among those with high IQs explains the gap between the mean and the median. For example, in these occupations, among those in the top decile of IQ, the 97.5th percentile of annual income was over $180,000; for those not in the top IQ decile, the corresponding income was $62,186.

19. The *median* wage for each occupation is the wage that has as many wages above it as below it in the distribution of wages in the occupation. A median expresses an average that is relatively insensitive to extreme values at either end.

20. A high IQ is also worth extra income outside the high-IQ occupations as we defined them. The wages and salaries of people not in the high-IQ occupations but with an IQ in the top 10 percent earned over $11,000 more in 1989 (again in 1990 dollars) than those with IQs below the top decile. The median family income of those in the top IQ decile who did not enter the high-IQ professions was $49,000, putting them at the 72d percentile of family incomes.

21. Solon 1992; Zimmerman 1992. Women are not usually included in these studies because of the analytic complications arising in the recent dramatic changes in their work force participation. The correlation is even higher if the predictor of the son's income is the family income rather than just the father's (Solon 1992). These estimates of the correlation between father and son income represent a new finding. Until recently, specialists mostly agreed that income was not a strong family trait, certainly not like the family chin or the baldness that passes on from generation to generation, and not even as enduring as the family nest egg. They had concluded that the correlation between fathers and sons in income was between .1 and .2—very low. Expert opinion has, however, been changing. The older estimates of the correlation between fathers' and sons' incomes, it turns out, were plagued by two familiar problems that artificially depress corre-

lation coefficients. First, the populations used for gathering the estimates were unrepresentative. One large study, for example, used only high school graduates, which no doubt restricted the range of IQ scores (Sewell and Hauser 1975). Another problem has been measurement error—in the case of intergenerational comparisons of income, measurement error introduced by basing the analysis on a single year's income. Averaging income over a few years reduces this source of error. Now, using the nationally representative, longitudinal data in the National Longitudinal Survey (NLS) and the Panel Study of Income Dynamics (PSID), economists have found the correlations of .4 to .5 reported in the text.

22. Solon 1992. For comparable estimates for Great Britain, see Atkinson, Maynard, and Trinder 1983.

23. U.S. Bureau of the Census 1991b, Table 32.

24. Herrnstein 1973, pp. 197–198.

25. For reviews of the literature as of 1980, see Bouchard 1981; Plomin and DeFries 1980. For more recent analyses, on which we base the upper bound estimate of 80 percent, see Bouchard et al. 1990; Pedersen et al. 1992.

26. Plomin and Loehlin 1989.

27. The proper statistical measure of variation is the standard deviation squared, which is called the variance.

28. Heritability is a concept in quantitative genetics; for a good textbook, see Falconer 1989.

29. Social scientists will recognize the heritability question as being akin to the general statistical model of variance analysis.

30. Plomin and Loehlin 1989.

31. Bouchard et al. 1990.

32. Estimating heritabilities from any relationship other than for identical twins is inherently more uncertain because the modeling is more complex, involving the estimation of additional sources of genetic variation, such as assortative mating (about which more below) and genetic dominance and epistasis. See Falconer 1989.

33. For a broad survey of all kinds of data published before 1981, set into several statistical models, the best fitting of which gave .51 as the estimate of IQ heritability, see Chipuer, Rovine, and Plomin 1990. Most of the data are from Western countries, but a recent analysis of Japanese data, based on a comparison of identical and fraternal twin correlations in IQ, yields a heritability estimate of .58 (Lynn and Hattori 1990).

34. The extraordinary discrepancy between what the experts say in their technical publications on this subject and what the media say the experts say is well described in Snyderman and Rothman 1988.

35. Cyphers et al. 1989; Pedersen et al. 1992.

36. Cyphers et al. 1989; Pedersen et al. 1992.

37. Based primarily on a large study of Swedish identical and fraternal twins followed into late adulthood (Pedersen et al. 1992).
38. Plomin and Bergeman 1987; Rowe and Plomin 1981.
39. IQ is not the only trait with a biological component that varies across socioeconomic strata. Height, head size, blood type, age at menarche, susceptibility to various congenital diseases, and so on are some of the other traits for which there is evidence of social class differences even in racially homogeneous societies (for review, see Mascie-Taylor 1990).
40. The standard deviation squared times the heritability gives variance due just to genes; the square root of that number is the standard deviation of IQ in a world of perfectly uniform environments: $\sqrt{(15^2 \times .6)} = 11.6$ A heritability of .4 would reduce the standard deviation from the normative value of 15 to 9.5; with a heritability of .8., it would be reduced to 13.4.
41. If we take the heritability of IQ to be .6, then the swing in IQ is 24 points for two children with identical genes, but growing up in circumstances that are at, say, the 10th and the 90th centile in their capacity to foster intelligence, a very large swing indeed. A less extreme swing from the 40th to the 60th centile in environmental conditions would move the average IQ only 4.75 points. In a normal distribution, the distance from the 10th to the 90th percentile is about 2.5 standard deviation units; from the 40th to the 60th percentile, it is about .5 standard deviation units. If the heritability is .8, instead of .6, then the swing from the 10th to the 90th percentile would be worth 17 IQ points, from the 40th to the 60th, 3.4 IQ points.
42. Burgess and Wallin 1943.
43. Spuhler 1968.
44. Jensen 1978. This estimate may be high for a variety of technical reasons that are still being explored, but apparently not a lot too high. For more, see DeFries et al. 1979; Mascie-Taylor 1989; Mascie-Taylor and Vandenberg 1988; Price and Vandenberg 1980; Watkins and Meredith 1981. In the 1980s, some researchers argued that data from Hawaii indicated a falling level of assortative mating for IQ, which they attributed to increased social mobility and greater access to higher education (Ahern, Johnson, and Cole 1983; Johnson, Ahern, and Cole 1980; Johnson, Nagoshi, and Ahern 1987). But the evidence seems to be limited to Hawaii. Other recent data from Norway and Virginia, not to mention the national census data developed by Mare and discussed in the text, fail to confirm the Hawaii data (Heath et al. 1985, 1987). When intelligence and educational level are statistically pulled apart, the assortative mating for education, net of intelligence, is stronger than that for intelligence, net of educational level (Neale and McArdle 1990; Phillips et al. 1988).
45. For a discussion of regression to the mean, see Chapter 15. The calcula-

tion in the text assumes a correlation of +.8 between the average child's IQ and the midpoint of the parental IQs, consistent with a heritability of .6 and a family environment effect of .2. The estimate of average IQs in 1930 is explained in Chapter 1. The estimate for the class of 1964 (who were freshmen in 1960) is based on Harvard SAT-Verbal scores compared to the Educational Testing Service's national norm study conducted in 1960, which indicates that the mean verbal score for entering Harvard freshmen was 2.9 SDs above the mean of all high school seniors—and, by implication, considerably higher than that for the entire 18-year old cohort (which includes the high school dropouts; Seibel 1962, Bender 1960). If we estimate the correlation between the SAT-Verbal and IQ as +.65 (from Donlon 1984), the estimated mean IQ of Harvard freshmen as of 1960 was about 130, from which the estimate of children's IQ has been calculated.

46. With a parent-child correlation of .8, 64 percent of the variance is accounted for, 36 percent not accounted for. The square root of .36, which is .6, times 15, is the standard deviation of the distribution of IQ scores of the children of these parents. This gives a value of 9, from which the percentages in the text are estimated.

47. Operationally, Mare compared marriage among people with sixteen or more years of schooling with those who had fewer than sixteen years of schooling (Mare 1991, p. 23). For additional evidence of increasing educational homogamy in the 1970s and 1980s, see Qian and Preston 1993.

48. Oppenheimer, 1988.

49. *DES* 1992, Tables 160, 168.

50. Buss 1987. For evidence that this phenomenon is well underway, see Qian and Preston 1993.

51. In the NLSY, whose members graduated from high school in the period 1976–1983, 59.3 percent had obtained a bachelor's or higher degree by 1990. In the "High School and Beyond" study conducted by the Department of Education, only 44 percent of 1980 high school graduates who were in the top quartile of ability had obtained a B.A. or B.S. by 1986 (Eagle 1988a, Table 3).

52. See Chapter 1.

53. Authors' analysis of the NLSY.

54. Authors' analysis of the NLSY.

55. *SAUS* 1991, Table 17.

Introduction to Part II

1. Sussman and Steinmetz 1987. This is still a valuable source of information about myriad aspects of family life, mainly in America.

2. For example, in the last ten years, out of hundreds of articles and research notes, the preeminent economics journal, *American Economic Review*, has published just a handful of articles that call upon IQ as a way of understanding such problems. The most conspicuous exceptions are Bishop 1989; Boissiere et al. 1985; Levin 1989; Silberberg 1985; Smith 1984.

3. The criterion for eligibility was that they be ages 14 to 21 on January 1, 1979, which meant that some of them had turned 22 by the time the first interview occurred.

4. Details of the Department of Defense enlistment tests, the ASVAB, are also given in Appendix 3.

5. The test battery was administered to small groups by trained test personnel. That each NLSY subject was paid $50 to take the test helped ensure a positive attitude toward the experience.

6. See Appendix 3 for more on the test and its *g* loading, and the Introduction for a discussion of *g* itself.

7. Raw AFQT scores in the NLSY sample rose with age throughout the age cohorts who were still in their teens when they took the test. The simplest explanation is that the AFQT was designed by the military for a population of recruits who would be taking the test in their late teens, and younger youths in the NLSY sample got lower scores for the same reason that high school freshmen get lower SAT scores than high school seniors. However, a cohort effect could also be at work, whereby (because of educational or broad environmental reasons) youths born in the first half of the 1960s had lower realized cognitive ability than youths born in the last half of the 1950s. There is no empirical way of telling which reason explains the age-related differences in the AFQT or what the mix of reasons might be. This uncertainty is readily handled in the multivariate analyses by entering the subject's birthdate as an independent variable (all the NLSY sample took the AFQT within a few months of each other in late 1980). When we present descriptive statistics, we use age-equated centiles.

8. We assigned the NLSY youths to a cognitive class on the basis of their age-equated centile scores. We use the class divisions as a way to communicate the data in an easily understood form. It should be remembered, however, that all of the statistical analyses are based on the actual test scores of each individual in the NLSY.

9. Regression analysis is only remotely related to the regression to the mean referred to earlier. See Appendix 1.

10. Age, too, is always part of the analytic package, a necessity given the nature of the NLSY sample (see note 7).

11. The white sample for the NLSY was chosen by first selecting all who were categorized by the interview screener as nonblack and non-Hispanic. From

this group, we excluded all youths who identified their own ethnicity as Asian, Pacific, American Indian, African, or Hispanic.

Chapter 5

1. Ross et al. 1987. The authors used the sample tapes for the 1940 and 1950 census to calculate the figures for 1939 and 1949, antedating the beginning of the annual poverty statistics in 1959. The numbers represent total money income, including government transfers. The figure for 1939 is extrapolated, since the 1939 census did not include data on income other than earnings. It assumes that the ratio of poverty based on earnings to poverty based on total income in 1949 (.761) also applied in 1939, when 68.1 percent of the population had earnings that put them below the poverty line. Since government transfers increased somewhat in the intervening decade, the resulting figure for 1939 should be considered a lower bound.

    It may be asked if the high poverty percentage in 1939 was an artifact of the Great Depression. The numbers are inexact, but the answer is no. The poverty rate prior to the Depression—defined by the contemporary poverty line—was higher yet. (See Murray 1988b, pp. 72–73).

2. See the introduction to Part II for more on the distinction between independent and dependent variables.

3. Jensen 1980, p. 281.

4. The observed stability of tests for children up to 10 years of age is reasonably well approximated by the formula,

$$r_{12} = \sqrt{\left(r_{11} \times r_{22}\right)} \times \sqrt{\frac{CA_1}{CA_2}}$$

    where r_{11} and r_{22} are the reliabilities of the tests on occasions 1 and 2, CA_1 and CA_2 are the subject's chronological age on occasions 1 and 2, and r_{12} is the correlation between a test taken and retaken at ages CA_1 and CA_2. See Bloom 1964 for a full discussion.

5. After age 10, the correlation of test scores will usually fall between the product of the reliabilities of the two tests and the square root of their product. Thus, for example, the correlation of two measures of IQ after age 10 when both tests had reliabilities of .9 may be expected to fall between .81 and .9. Since the best IQ tests have reliabilities in excess of .9, this is tantamount to saying that the stability of scores is quite high. Following are some sample reliabilities as reported in the publisher's test manuals. WISC = .95, WAIS = .97, Wonderlic Personnel Test = .95. The reliabilities of

some of the major standardized achievement tests are also extremely high. For example: ACT = .95, SAT = 90+, California Achievement Tests = .90–.95, Iowa Test of Basic Skills Composite = .98–.99. For a longer list of reliabilities and an accessible discussion of both reliability and stability, see Jensen 1980, Chap. 7.

6. Is there reason to think that, had the test been administered earlier, at age 7 or 8, the results would have turned out differently? The answer, with some reservations, is no. We would observe the normal level of fluctuation in tests administered at ages 7 and 20, with some individuals scoring higher and some lower as they grow up. The correlations between a person's IQ obtained at age 7 and social behavior in adulthood would support the same qualitative conclusions as those based on an IQ obtained at age 20. The correlations using the younger scores would be smaller, because they measure the adult trait of intelligence less reliably than a score obtained later in life. See Appendix 3 for a discussion of changes in IQ among the members of the NLSY sample.

7. Himmelfarb 1984.

8. E.g., Ryan 1971.

9. For a few words about regression analysis, see the Introduction to Part II and Appendix 1. In fewer words still, this is a method for assessing the independent impact of each of a set of independent variables on a dependent variable. The specific form used here is called *logistic* regression analysis, the appropriate method for binary dependent variables, such as yes-no or female-male or married-unmarried.

10. We eliminate students to avoid misleading ourselves with, for example, third-year law students who have low incomes in 1989 but are soon to be making high incomes.

11. Note a distinction: Age has an important independent effect on income (income trajectories are highly sensitive to age), but not on the yes-no question of whether a person lives above the poverty line. It is also worth noting that age in the NLSY is restricted in range because the sample was all born within a few years of each other.

12. The imaginary person is sexless.

13. We refrain from precise numerical estimates of how much more important IQ is than socioeconomic background, for two reasons. First, they are not essential to the point of this discussion. Second, doing so would get us into problems of measurement and measurement error that would needlessly complicate the text. It seems sufficient for our purpose to note that IQ has a greater impact on the likelihood of being poor than socioeconomic background, as those variables are usually measured.

14. The 1991 poverty rate for persons 15 and over was 11.9 percent, compared

to 22.4 percent for children under 15. U.S. Bureau of the Census, 1992, Table 1.

15. For an analysis of the demographic reasons and some measurement issues, see Smith 1989.

16. U.S. Bureau of the Census 1992, Table C, p. xiv.

17. U.S. Bureau of the Census 1992, Table C, p. xiv.

18. Eggebeen and Lichter 1991; Smith 1989.

19. Given childless white men and women of average age, socioeconomic background, and IQ, the expected poverty rates are only 1.6 percentage points apart and are exceedingly low in both cases: 3.1 and 4.7 percent, respectively.

20. The relationships of IQ to poverty were statistically significant beyond the .01 level for both married and unmarried women. Our policy throughout the book is not routinely to report significance statistics, but at the same time not to present any relationship as being substantively significant unless we know that it also is statistically significant.

21. An entire draft of the book was written using a different measure of IQ. As described in Appendix 3, the armed forces changed the scoring system for the AFQT in 1989. The first draft was written using the old version. After discussing the merits of the old and new measures at length, we decided to switch to the new one, because, for arcane reasons, it is psychometrically superior. The substantive effects of this change on the conclusions in the book are, as far as we can tell, effectively nil. All of the analyses have also been repeated with two versions of the SES index, and many of them with three. Again, the three versions yielded substantively indistinguishable results. But each of the successive versions of the SES index was, in our judgment, a theoretically more satisfying and statistically more robust way of capturing the construct of "socioeconomic status."

Regarding the specific analysis of the role of gender and marital status in mediating the relationship between IQ and poverty: Originally, the analysis (and the graphic included in the text on page 138) was based on married/unmarried, men/women. Then we looked more closely at women and their various marital situations, then at those marital situations for women with children. All of the poverty analyses were conducted with two measures of poverty: the official definition (represented in this book), and a definition based on cash income obtained from sources other than government transfers. We decided to present the results using the official definition to avoid an extra layer of explanation, but we have the comfort of knowing that the interpretation fits both definitions, except for a few nuances that are not important enough to warrant a place in this concise an account. We have conducted some of these analyses for age-restricted samples, to see if things change for older cohorts in ways that are not captured by using age as an independent variable in the regression equation. Throughout all of these regression analyses, we were also looking at cross-tabulations and frequency distributions to try to see what gnomes might be lurking in the regression coefficients. Finally, we duplicated all of the analyses you see with and without sample weights, to ensure that there were no marked, mysterious differences in the two sets of results. There were undoubtedly other iterations and variations that we have forgotten over the last four years.

None of this will be surprising to our colleagues, for the process we have described is SOP for social scientists engaged in complex analyses. But for nonspecialists, the story is worth remembering. It should make you more skeptical, insofar as you understand that such enterprises are not as elegant and preordained as authors (including us) sometimes make it sound. But the story can also give you some additional confidence, insofar as, when you find yourself wondering whether we considered such-and-such an alternative way of looking at the data, the chances are fairly good that we did.

22. In passing, it just isn't so for blacks either. The independent roles of poverty and socioeconomic status are almost exactly the same for blacks in the NLSY as for whites. See Chapter 14.

Chapter 6

1. Kronick and Hargis 1990.
2. For a discussion of definitional issues in measuring the dropout rate, see Kominski 1990.
3. Most people get their high school degrees or equivalences later than at the age of 17, so the figure on page 144 implicitly overestimates the proportion of dropouts in the population as a whole, at least for recent times. In 1985, the U.S. Government Accounting Office estimated that 13 percent of the population between the ages of 16 and 24 could be characterized as school dropouts, which amounted to 4.3 million people (cited by Hahn and Lefkowitz 1987; Kronick and Hargis 1990). Dropout rates in some locales may differ markedly from the national averages. In Boston, for example, dropping out of the public schools (as distinguished from losses due to transferring out of the school system) has recently risen above 45 percent (Camayd-Freixas and Horst 1987).
4. In 1990, the percentage of persons ages 25 to 29 who had completed four years of high school or more was 85.7 percent, higher than the plotted "graduation ratio," which is based on 17-year-olds (National Center for Education 1992, Table 8).
5. Quoted in Clignet 1974, p. 38. See Chapter 22 for additional discussion.
6. Tildsley 1936, p. 89.

7. These numbers represent an unweighted mean of the six studies of ninth graders and the nine studies of students who were either seniors or graduates. When sample sizes are taken into account, the (weighted) means for the two groups are 104.2 and 105.5 (Finch 1946, Table I, pp. 28–29). This may understate the degree of difference between the dropout and the high school senior. Other studies indicate that within any given school, a statistical relationship existed between IQ and the likelihood of finishing high school. In urban areas, the size of the correlation itself could be substantial. In one of the best such studies, Lorge found for the city of New York in the 1930s that the correlation of IQ with highest completed grade was +.66 (Lorge 1942). Some of the individual studies of specific high schools conducted during that period reviewed by Finch also showed larger differences. But those studies tended to be subject to a number of technical errors. Even giving substantial weight to them, the difference between the mean IQ of the high school dropout and youths who made it to the senior year during the 1920s was considerably less than half a standard deviation (7.5 IQ points). Perhaps children who dropped out before the ninth grade had somewhat lower IQs, so that the overall difference between diploma holders and dropouts was larger than the difference between ninth graders and twelfth graders. The data on this issue for the first half of the century are fragmentary, however.

8. If a third dropped out between ninth grade and twelfth grade, their average IQ must have been 101, compared to 107 for the seniors and graduates; if half dropped out, it must have been 103. Assuming a population average of 100, this implies that those who dropped out prior to ninth grade had still lower scores than those who dropped out afterward.

9. Iowa State Department of Public Instruction, 1965.

10. Dillon 1949, quoted in Jensen 1980, p. 334.

11. Based on a comparison of the academic aptitude scores of the ninth graders in the sample who had and had not graduated from high school five years later. The IQ equivalents are computed from a graduate-dropout gap of 1.14 standard deviations (SDs) for boys and 1.00 SDs for girls, or approximately 1.05 SDs overall (Wise et al. 1977, Table A-3). In the late 1960s, the Youth in Transition study found a difference of about .8 SDs on the vocabulary subtest of the GATB and the Gates Reading Tests between dropouts and nondropouts, consistent with a 1 SD difference on a full-scale battery of tests (reconstructed from Table 6-1, p. 100, and Tables C-3-7 and C-3-8 in Bachman et al. 1971).

12. Looking at these numbers, some readers will be wondering how much these dropout figures represent cause and how much effect. After all, wouldn't a person who stayed through high school and then took the IQ test have got-

ten a higher score by virtue of staying in high school? This question of cause and effect may be raised with all of the topics using the NLSY, but it is most obvious for school dropout. But while age has an effect on AFQT scores and is always taken into account (either through age-equated scores in the descriptive statistics or by entering age as an independent variable in the regression analyses), there is no reason to think that presence in school is decisive. The simplest way to document this is by replicating the analyses for a restricted sample of youths who were age 16 and under when they took the test, thereby excluding almost all of the members of the sample who might create these artifacts. Having done so for all of the results reported in this chapter, we may report that it makes no difference in terms of interpretations. We will not present all of these duplicate results, but an example will illustrate.

Using the full sample of whites, the mean IQs, expressed in standard scores, of those who completed high school via the normal route, those who got a high school equivalency, and those who dropped out permanently were +.37, −.14, and −.94 respectively. For whites who took the AFQT before they were age 17, the comparable means were +.34, −.04, and −.95. The main effect of using the age-restricted sample is drastically to reduce sample sizes, which we judged to be an unnecessary sacrifice. The NLSY data are consistent with other investigations of this issue (e.g., Husén and Tuijnman 1991). Continued schooling makes a modest contribution to intellectual capital but not enough to make much difference in the basic relationships linking IQ to other outcomes. Chapter 17 specifically discusses the impact of schooling on IQ, and Appendix 3 elaborates on the relationship of schooling to IQ in the NLSY.

13. Other data confirm this general picture. In the High School and Beyond national sample conducted by the Department of Education in 1980, it was found that those in the lowest quartile on the cognitive ability test dropped out at a rate of 26.5 percent, compared to 14.7 percent, 7.8 percent, and 3.2 percent in the next three quartiles, respectively (Barro and Kolstad 1987, Table 6.1, p. 46). Similar results have been found in other recent studies of dropouts and cognitive ability (e.g., Alexander et al. 1985; Hill 1979). Comparable rates of dropping out across the IQ categories and across categories defined by vocabulary test scores were also found in the earlier Youth in Transition study, based on approximately 2,000 men selected to be representative of the national population in the tenth grade in 1967 (Bachman et al. 1971). For an estimate of the loss in cognitive ability that may be attributed to dropout itself, see Alexander et al. 1985.

14. The General Educational Development exam is administered by the American Council on Education.

15. Cameron and Heckman 1992.

16. *DES* 1991, Tables 95, 97. In the NLSY, 9.5 percent of those classified as having a high school education got their certification through the GED.

17. As depicted in, for example, Coles 1967, in his work on certain impoverished populations. The relative roles of socioeconomic background and IQ found in the NLSY are roughly comparable to those found for the Youth in Transition study based on students in the late 1960s, though the method of presentation in that study does not lend itself to a precise comparison (Bachman et al. 1971, Chap. 4–6).

18. In passing, it may be noted that these results hold true for blacks as well. Of the blacks in the NLSY who permanently dropped out of school, none was in the top quartile of IQ. Only nine-tenths of 1 percent of black permanent dropouts were in the top half of IQ and the bottom half of SES. See Chapter 14 as well.

19. In a logistic regression, with all independent variables expressed as standard scores, the coefficients for IQ, SES, Age, and the SES × IQ interaction term were 1.91, .98, −.06, and .32, respectively. The intercept was 2.81. The interaction term was significant at the .005 level, and r^2 = .38. The equation is predicting "true" for a binary variable denoting high school graduation (with permanent dropout as the "false" state).

20. Press accounts of the GED population suggest that the typical youngster in it had trouble with the routine of ordinary school and comes from uncommonly deprived family circumstances (e.g., Marriot 1993).

21. Matarazzo 1972, pp. 178–180.

22. The percentages were 68 and 23, respectively.

Chapter 7

1. The figure on page 156 also echoes some of the large macroeconomic forces that we did discuss in preceding chapters. To some extent, the pool of "16–19-year-olds not in school" has changed as high schools have retained more students longer and colleges have recruited larger numbers of the brightest into college. As the pool has changed, so perhaps has the employability of its members. The greater employment problems shown by the figure also fit in with the discussion about earnings in Chapter 4 and the way in which income has stagnated or fallen for those without college educations. For concise reviews of the empirical literature on labor supply and unemployment, see Heckman 1993; Topel 1993. Studies focused on young disadvantaged men include Wolpin 1992; Cogan 1982; Bluestone and Harrison 1988; Cohen 1973; Holzer 1986. There is, of course, a large literature devoted explicitly to blacks. See Chapters 14 and 20.

2. We conducted parallel analyses with a sample based on the most recent year of observation (back to 1984), which enabled us to include data on some men who were being followed earlier but subsequently disappeared from the NLSY sample. The purpose was to compensate for a potential source of attrition bias, on the assumption that men who disappeared from the NLSY sample might be weighted to some degree toward those with the fewest connections to a fixed address and (by the same token) to the labor market. The results obtained by this method were substantively indistinguishable from the ones reported.

3. We replicated all of the analyses using the actual number of weeks out of the labor force as the dependent variable instead of a binary yes-no measure of whether any time was spent out of the labor force. The relative roles of the independent variables were the same as in the reported analyses, with similar comparative magnitudes as well as the same signs and levels of statistical significance. The relationship, such as it is, does not seem to be concentrated among the children of the very wealthy.

4. A more fine-grained examination of the data reveals that absence from the labor force and job disabilities is extraordinarily concentrated within a limited set of the lowest-status jobs. Using a well-known index of job prestige, the Duncan index, 46 percent of the reports of job limitations and 63 percent of those who reported being prevented from working (but who were still listing an occupation) came from jobs scored 1 to 19 on the Duncan scale, which ranges from 1 to 100. A total of 975 white men in the NLSY listed such a job as their occupation in 1990. The five most common jobs in this range, accounting for 35 percent of the total, were truck driver, automobile mechanic, construction laborer, carpenter, and janitor. Another 299 white males working in blue-collar jobs scored 20 to 29 on the Duncan scale. The five most common jobs in this range, accounting for 37 percent of the total, were welder, heavy equipment mechanic, other mechanic and repairman, brick mason, and farmer. Another 158 white males were working in blue-collar jobs scored 30 to 39 on the scale. The five most common jobs in this range, accounting for 47 percent of the total, were delivery man, plumber and pipefitter, machinist, sheet metal worker, and fireman.

Looking over these jobs, it is not readily apparent that the lowest-rated jobs in terms of prestige are also the physically most dangerous or demanding. Construction work fits that description in the lowest category, but so does fireman, sheet metal worker, and others in the higher categories. Meanwhile, some of jobs in the lowest category (e.g., truck driver, janitor) are not self-evidently more dangerous or physically demanding than some jobs in the higher categories. Or to put it another way: If a third party were given these fifteen job titles and told to rank them in terms of potential accidents and the importance of physical fitness, it is unlikely that the list would also be rank-ordered according to the job prestige index or even that the rank ordering would have much of a positive correlation with the job prestige index.

Instead, the index was created based on the pay and training that the jobs entail—both of which would tend to give higher ratings to cognitively more demanding jobs. And so indeed it works out. Here are the mean IQ scores of white males in blue-collar jobs, subdivided by groups on the Duncan scale, alongside the number per 1,000 who reported some form of job-related health limitation in 1989:

Duncan Scale Score (Limited to Blue Collar Occupations)	Mean IQ Percentile	No. per 1,000 with Job-Related Health Disability
0–9	35th	52
10–19	40th	55
20–29	48th	32
30–39	56th	26
40–49	59th	16

In short, the results of the regression analysis indicating that IQ has an important relationship to job disability even among blue-collar jobs, and even after taking age and years of education into account, are not explained away by the differences in the physical risks of these occupations. The same conclusion holds true when the analysis is conducted only for blue-collar workers and the variable "years of education" is added to the equation. The coefficient relating IQ to likelihood of disability is about four times the coefficient for years of education (with age as the other independent variable constant). Intriguingly, the opposite is true when the analysis is conducted just for white-collar workers: Years of education is important, wiping out any independent role for IQ. Interpreting this is difficult, both because health disability is such a rare phenomenon among white-collar workers and because IQ becomes so tightly linked to advanced education, which in turn is associated with jobs in which physical disability is virtually irrelevant (short of a stroke or other accident causing a mental impairment).

5. Terman and Oden 1947.

6. Hill 1980; Mayer and Treat 1977; O'Toole 1990; Smith and Kirkham 1982.

7. Grossman 1976; Kitagawa and Hauser 1960.

8. Restriction of range (see Chapter 3) might also reduce the independent role of IQ among college graduates.

Chapter 8

1. For a review of the literature about family decline, see Popenoe 1993.
2. U.S. Bureau of the Census 1992, Table 51.
3. Retherford 1986.
4. Garrison 1968; James 1989.
5. The cognitive elite did get married at somewhat older ages than others, and this difference will grow as the NLSY cohort gets older. Judging from other data, almost all of those in the bottom half of the IQ distribution who will ever marry have already married by 30, whereas many of that 29 percent unmarried in Class I will eventually marry, raising their mean age of marriage by some unknown amount. If all of them married at, say, age 40, the average age at marriage would approach 30, which may be taken as the highest mean that the NLSY could plausibly produce as it follows its sample into middle age.
6. In his famous lifetime study of intellectually gifted children born around 1910, Lewis Terman found that, as of the 1930s and 1940, highly gifted men eventually got married at higher rates than the national norms— about 84 percent, compared to a national rate of 67 percent for men of similar age. Gifted women married later than the average woman, but by their mid-30s they too had higher marriage rates than the general population, though the difference was not as great as for men: 84 percent compared to 78 percent (Terman and Oden 1947, p. 227).
7. Cherlin 1981, Figure 1-5. His estimation procedure suggests that the odds of eventual divorce in 1980 were 54 percent. Also see Raschke 1987.
8. We are here calculating odds ratios—the likelihood of marital survival divided by the likelihood of divorce within the first five years—from the table on page 174. The ratio of odds ratios for marital survival versus divorce during the first five years of marriage was 2.7, comparing Class I to Class V.
9. In addition to the standard variables (age, parental socioeconomic status, and IQ), we added "date of first marriage." We wished to add age at first marriage as well, but it was so highly correlated with the date of first marriage in the entire white sample ($r = +.81$) that the two variables could not be used together. It was possible to use them together in some of the subsamples we analyzed. The pattern of results was unchanged.
10. Different subsets of white youths, both the entire sample of those who had married and the subset of those who had reached the age of 30, and the subset below the age of 30 all yielded similar results.
11. E.g. Raschke 1987; Sweet and Bumpass 1987.
12. Higher socioeconomic status is also associated with a lower probability of divorce in the college sample, though the independent effect of parental SES is much smaller than the independent effect of IQ. Socioeconomic

status had an insignificantly direct relationship with divorce for the high school sample. Thinking back to the analysis of marriage, note a curious contrast: IQ makes a lot of difference in whether high school graduates get married but not in whether they get divorced. IQ makes little difference in whether college graduates get married by the age of 30 but a lot of difference in whether they get divorced. Why? We have no idea. In any case, embedded in this complicated set of findings are intriguing possibilities, which warrant a full-scale analysis.

13. Raschke 1987; Sweet and Bumpass 1987; Teachman et al. 1987.

14. Even a genetic component has been invoked to explain the fact that divorce runs in families. Not only do children tend to follow their parents' path toward divorce, but identical twins are more correlated in their likelihood of divorce than fraternal twins, a difference that often betrays some genetic influence. McGue and Lykken 1992.

15. Those living with only the father did as well as those living with both biological parents.

16. See references in Raschke 1987; South 1985.

17. Bronislaw Malinowski, *Sex, Culture, and Myth* (1930), quoted in Moynihan 1986, p. 170.

18. The production of illegitimate babies per unit population has also increased during this period, with the fastest growth occurring during the 1970s. In the jargon, the *rate* of illegitimate births has increased as well as the *ratio*. The distinction between rate and ratio raises a technical issue that has plagued the discussion of illegitimacy in recent years. Traditionally, illegitimacy rates have been computed by dividing the number of illegitimate births by the number of unmarried women. In a period when marital patterns are also shifting, this has the effect of confounding two different phenomena: the number of illegitimate births in the numerator of the ratio and the number of unmarried women in the denominator. To estimate the rate of change in the production of illegitimate children per unit population, it is essential to divide the number of illegitimate births by the entire population (or, if one prefers, by the number of women of childbearing age). This is almost never done, however, in nontechnical discussions (or in many of the technical ones, for that matter). For a discussion of the difference this makes in interpreting trends in illegitimacy, see Murray 1993.

19. Sweet and Bumpass 1987, p. 95. In 1960, there were 73,000 never-married mothers between the ages of 18 and 34; in 1980, there were 1,022,000.

20. Bachu 1991, Table 1. The figures for ages 18 to 34 are interpolated from the published figures for ages 15 to 34.

21. Not to mention that IQ has changed in the wrong direction to explain increasing illegitimacy (see the Flynn Effect, discussed in Chapters 13 and 15).

22. As in the case of school dropout, one may ask whether having a baby out of wedlock as a teenager caused school dropout, therefore resulting in an artificially low IQ score. As before, the cleanest way to test the hypothesis is to select all the women who had their first baby *after* they took the test in 1980 and repeat the analyses reported here, introducing a control for age at first birth. When this is done, the relationships reported continue to apply as strongly as, and in some cases more strongly than, they do for the entire sample.

    A similar causal tangle is associated with the age at first birth. Age at first birth is a powerful explanatory variable in a statistical sense. It can drastically change the parameters, especially the importance of socioeconomic status and IQ, in a regression equation. But, in the 1990s, what causes a girl in her teens to have a baby? Probably the same things that might cause her to have an illegitimate baby: She grew up in a low–status household where having a baby young was an accepted thing to do; she is not very bright and gets pregnant inadvertently or because she has not thought through the consequences; or she is poor and has a baby because it offers better rewards than not having a baby, whether those rewards are tangible in the form of an income and apartment of her own through welfare, or in the form of having someone to love. And in fact all three variables—parental SES, IQ, and whether she was living in poverty prior to the birth—are powerful predictors of age at first birth, explaining 36 percent of the variance. Furthermore, age at first birth cannot be a cause of parental SES and poverty in the year prior to birth. Empirically, it can be demonstrated not to be a "cause" of the AFQT score, using the same logic applied to the case of illegitimacy.

23. Rindfuss et al. 1980.

24. Abrahamse et al. 1988. The analysis is based on a sample of 13,061 girls who were sophomores in 1980 at the time of the High School and Beyond (HS&B) baseline survey and also responded to the first follow-up questionnaire in 1982.

25. The exact figures, going from the bottom to the top quartile in socioeconomic status, are 38.7 percent, 29.7 percent, 19.9 percent, and 11.7 percent, based on weighted data, computed by the authors from the HS&B database. Figures reported here and on other occasions when we refer to the RAND study will sometimes show minor discrepancies with the published account, because Abrahamse et al. used imputed figures for certain variables, based on schoolwide measures, when individual data were missing. Our calculations do not use any imputed figures. As in the RAND study, all results are based on weighted analyses using the HS&B population weights.

26. For mothers of an illegitimate baby, the mean on the test of cognitive abil-

ity was .73 SD below the mean for all girls who had babies, and .67 SD below the mean for all white girls (mothers and nonmothers).

27. Limiting the analysis to first births avoids a number of technical problems associated with differential number of children per woman by cognitive and socioeconomic class. Analyses based on all children born by the 1990 interview show essentially the same results, however. We also conducted a parallel set of analyses using as the dependent variable whether the woman had ever given birth to a child out of wedlock (thereby adding women without any children at all to the analysis). The interpretations of the results were not markedly different for any of the analyses presented in the text.

28. We are, as usual, comparing the effects of a shift equal to ±2 SDs around the mean for both independent variables, cognitive ability and socioeconomic status.

29. Bachu 1993, Table J.

30. Bachu 1993, Table J.

31. The comparable probabilities given parental SES standard scores of −2 and +2 were 31 percent and 19 percent.

32. The literature is extensive. Two recent reviews of the literature are Moffitt 1992 and Murray 1993. See also Murray 1994.

33. The writing on this topic is much more extensive for the black community than the white. See, for example, Anderson 1989; Duncan and Hoffman 1990; Furstenberg et al. 1987; Hogan and Kitagawa 1985; Lundberg and Plotnick 1990; Rowe and Rodgers 1992; Teachman 1985; Moffitt 1983.

34. For a detailed presentation of this argument, see Murray 1986b.

35. An analysis based not on the dichotomous variable, poverty, but on income had essentially the same outcome.

36. When we repeat the analysis yet again, adding in the presence of the biological father, these results are sustained. Poverty and cognitive ability remain as important as before; the parents' poor socioeconomic status does not increase the chances of illegitimate babies.

Chapter 9

1. Louchheim 1983, p. 175. See also Liebmann 1993.

2. Bane and Ellwood 1983; Ellwood 1986b; Hoffman 1987.

3. The studies are reviewed in Bendick and Cantu 1978.

4. Hopkins et al. 1987.

5. This figure includes women not reflected in the table who did not go on AFDC within the first year after birth, received welfare at some later date, but did not become chronic recipients.

6. In all cases, we limit the analysis to women for whom we have complete

data and whose child was born prior to January 1, 1989. We also conducted this analysis with another definition of short-term recipiency, limiting the sample to women whose children had been born prior to 1986, divided into women who had never received welfare subsequently and women who had received welfare up to half of the years that they were observed but did not qualify as chronic welfare recipients. The results were similar to the ones reported in the text, with a large negative effect of IQ and an insignificant role for SES.

7. Bane and Ellwood 1983; Ellwood 1986a; Murray 1986a.

8. Ellwood 1986a; Murray 1986a.

9. We conducted a parallel analysis comparing chronic welfare recipients with all other mothers, including those who had been on welfare but did not qualify as chronic. There are no important differences in interpretation for the results of the two sets of analyses.

10. Among all white women, only 16 percent had not gotten a high school diploma, and 27 percent had achieved at least a bachelor's degree.

11. Once again, this analysis has to be based on women with a high school diploma because there was no way to analyze welfare recipiency among white women with B.A.s. Only two white women with B.A.s in the NLSY had become chronic recipients. But for the high school graduates, the effect of parental SES is modest—slightly smaller than the independent effect of cognitive ability. This pattern was generally shared among women who had gone on to get their GED (recall that people with a GED are not included in the high school sample).

12. Some of the obvious explanations are not as important as one might expect. For example, most of the high school dropouts who became chronic welfare recipients were not poor; only 36 percent of them had been below the poverty line in the year before birth. Nor is it correct to assume that all of them had babies out of wedlock; nearly half (46 percent) of their first babies had been born within marriage. But 70 percent of the chronic welfare recipients among the high school dropouts had had their first child before they turned 19, which means that some very large proportion of them had the baby before they would normally have graduated. Among high school dropouts who had not had a child before their nineteenth birthday, the independent relationships of IQ and socioeconomic ststus shift back toward the familiar pattern, with the effects of IQ being much larger than those of socioeconomic status.

13. Indeed, the teenage mothers who did *not* become chronic welfare recipients had a slightly lower mean IQ than those who did (23d centile versus 26th centile). Meanwhile, the ones who did not become welfare recipients at all had a fractionally higher mean socioeconomic status than the ones who did (27th centile versus 26th).

14. Having a high school diploma was an important variable in all of the analyses of welfare, over and above the effects of either cognitive ability or socioeconomic background, and regarding either short-term or chronic welfare recipiency. The question is whether the high school diploma—and we are referring specifically to the high school diploma, not an equivalency degree—reflects a cause or a symptom. Does a high school education prepare the young woman for adulthood and the world of work, thereby tending to keep her off welfare? Or does the act of getting a high school diploma reflect the young woman's persistence and ability to cope that tend to keep her off welfare? It is an important question; unfortunately, we were unable to think of a way to answer it with the data we have.

15. All are mutually exclusive groups. Criteria follow those for temporary and chronic welfare recipiency defined earlier.

Chapter 10

1. Anderson 1936.
2. See Bronfenbrenner 1958, p. 424, for a review of the literature through the mid-1950s. For a recent empirical test, see Luster et al. 1989.
3. Kohn 1959.
4. Kohn 1959.
5. Kohn 1959, p. 366.
6. Heath 1983.
7. The study also includes "Trackton," a black lower-class community.
8. Heath 1982, p. 54.
9. Heath 1981, p. 61.
10. Heath 1982, p. 62.
11. Heath 1982, p. 63.
12. Gottfried 1984, p. 330.
13. Kadushin 1988, p. 150.
14. Drawn from Kadushin, 1988, pp. 150–151. Formally, neglect is defined by one of the leading authorities, Norman Polansky, as a situation in which the caretaker "permits the child to experience avoidable present suffering and/or fails to provide one or more ingredients generally deemed essential for developing a person's physical, intellectual or emotional capacities." Quoted in Kadushin, p. 150.
15. Kaplun, 1976; Smith and Adler, 1991; Steele 1987; Trickett et al. 1991.
16. E.g., Azar et al. 1984. For a discussion of weaknesses in the state of knowledge about causes and an argument for continuing to treat abuse and neglect separately, see Cicchetti and Rizley 1981. See also Bousha and Twentyman 1984; Herrenkohl et al. 1983.
17. Some recent reviews of the evidence on causation are Hegar and Yung-

man 1989; Polansky 1981; Zuravin 1989. The intergenerational explanation is one of the most widely known. For a review of the literature and some important qualifications to assumptions about intergenerational transmission, see Kaufman and Zigler 1987.

18. Besharov 1991.
19. D. Besharov and S. Besharov, quoted in Pelton 1978, p. 608.
20. Parke and Collmer 1975.
21. Coser 1965; Horowitz and Liebowitz 1969.
22. Jensen and Nicholas 1984; Osborne et al. 1988.
23. Leroy H. Pelton's literature review is still excellent on the studies through the mid-1970s, as is Garbarino's. See Garbarino and Crouter 1978; Pelton 1978. Also see Straus and Gelles 1986; Straus et al. 1980; Trickett et al. 1991. Unless otherwise noted, the literature review in this section is not restricted to whites.
24. U.S. Department of Health and Human Services 1988; Wolfe 1985.
25. Gil 1970.
26. Reported in Pelton 1978.
27. Young and Gately 1988, pp. 247, 248.
28. Reported in Pelton 1990–1991.
29. Klein and Stern 1971; Smith 1975.
30. Baldwin and Oliver 1975.
31. Cohen et al. 1966; Johnson and Morse 1968.
32. Smith et al. 1974.
33. Pelton 1978, pp. 612–613.
34. Gil 1970. Recall that Chapter 6 demonstrated that cognitive ability was a stronger predictor of school dropout than socioeconomic status.
35. Brayden et al. 1992.
36. Crittenden 1988, p. 179.
37. Drotar and Sturm 1989.
38. Azar et al. 1984. See Steele 1987 for supporting evidence and Kravitz and Driscoll 1983 for a contrary view.
39. Bennie 1969.
40. Dekovic and Gerris 1992. For findings in a similar vein, see Goodnow et al. 1984; Keller et al. 1984; and Knight and Goodnow 1988. For studies concluding that parental reasoning is not related to social class, see Newberger and Cook 1983.
41. Polansky 1981, p. 43.
42. Most tantalizing of all was a prospective study in Minnesota that gave an extensive battery of tests to young, socioeconomically disadvantaged women before they gave birth. In following up these mothers, two groups were identified: one consisting of thirty-eight young women with high-stress life events and adequate care of their children (HS-AC), and the

other of twelve young women with high-stress life events and inadequate care (HS-NC). In the article, data on all the tests are presented in commendable detail, except for IQ. In the "method" section that lists all the tests, an IQ test is not mentioned. Subsequently, there is this passage, which contains everything we are told about the mentioned test: "The only prenatal measure that was not given at 3 months [after birth] was the Shipley-Hartford IQ measure. The mean scores on this measure were 26.9 for the HS-AC group and 23.5 for the HS-NC group (p = .064)." Egeland 1980, p. 201. A marginally statistically significant difference with samples of 12 and 38 suggests a sizable IQ difference.

43. Friedman and Morse 1974; Reid and Tablin 1976; Smith and Hanson 1975.
44. Wolfe 1985.
45. Berger 1980.
46. Young 1964, cited by Berger 1980.
47. Wolfe 1985, pp. 473–474.
48. It is understandable that many survey studies cannot obtain a measure of IQ. But virtually all of the studies discussed called for extensive cooperation by the abusive parents. The addition of a short intelligence test would seem to have been readily feasible.
49. The actual quotation is dense but intriguing: "Moreover, they [the British researchers] have shown that parental competence (defined as sensitivity and responsiveness to infant cues, quality of verbalization, and physical contact, and related skills) and adjustment (e.g., low anxiety and adequate flexibility) were distinguishing abilities that moderated the impact of aversive life events" (Wolfe 1985, p. 478).
50. Honesty of the respondents apart, the NLSY data do not address this issue. The question about drinking asked how often a woman drank but not how much at any one time. Since a single glass of wine or beer a few times a week is not known to be harmful, the drinking data are not interpretable.
51. Roughly equal proportions of smokers in the low and high cognitive classes told the interviewers that they had cut down during pregnancy—about 60 percent of smokers in each case.
52. Leonard et al. 1990; Hack and others 1991.
53. "Low birth weight" is operationally defined as infants weighing less than 5.5 pounds at birth. This definition, however, mixes children who are carried to term and are nonetheless underweight with children who are born prematurely (which usually occurs for reasons over which the woman has no control) but who are otherwise of normal weight and development. In the jargon, these babies have a weight "appropriate for gestational age" (AGA). Babies who weighed less than 5.5 pounds but whose weight was equal to or higher than the medical definition of AGA (using the Colorado Intrauterine Growth Charts) were excluded from the analysis.

54. The dip in the proportion for Class V could also be an artifact of small sample sizes. The proportion (computed using sample weights) is produced by 9 out of 116 babies. Sample sizes for the other cognitive classes—II, III, and IV—were much larger: 573, 2,059, and 737, respectively.

55. Hardy and Mellis 1977.

56. Cramer 1987. In a revealing sign of the unpopularity of intelligence as an explanatory variable, Cramer treats years of education as a proxy measure of socioeconomic status. For other studies showing the relationship of education to infant mortality, see Bross and Shapiro 1982; Keller and Fetterly 1978.

57. This is a persistent issue in infant mortality research. There are varying opinions about how important the distinction between neonatal and infant deaths may be. See Eberstein and Parker 1984.

58. Duncan 1993.

59. The calculation assumes that the mother has average socioeconomic background.

60. It measures, among other things, the emotional and verbal responsiveness and involvement of the mother, provision of appropriate play materials, variety in the daily routine, use of punishment, and organization of the child's environment. The HOME index was created and tested by Bettye Caldwell and Robert Bradley (Caldwell and Bradley 1984).

61. From Class IV to Class II, they were the 48th, 60th, and 68th percentile, respectively. For most of the assessments, including the HOME index, the NLSY database contains raw scores, standardized scores, and centile scores. For technical reasons, it is more accurate to work with standardized scores than percentiles when computing group means, conducting regression analyses, and so forth. On the other hand, centiles are much more readily understood by the ordinary reader. We have conducted all analyses using standardized scores, then converted the final results as reported in the tables back into centiles. Thus, the centiles in the table are *not* those that will be produced by simply averaging the HOME centile scores in the NLSY.

62. We replicated all of these analyses using the HOME index as a continuous variable, and the substantive conclusions from those replications are consistent with the ones reported here.

63. The HOME index has different scoring for children younger than 3 years old, children ages 3 through 5, and children ages 6 and older. We examined the HOME results for the different age groups and found that they could be combined without significant loss of precision for the interpretations we describe in the text. There is some evidence that the mother's IQ was most important for the home environment of children ages 3 through 5 and least important for children ages 6 and older, but the differences are not dramatic.

64. E.g., Duncan 1993 and almost anything published by the Children's Defense Fund.
65. We also conducted analyses treating family income as a continuous variable, which showed consistent results.
66. The poverty measure is based on whether the mother was below the poverty line in the year prior to the HOME assessment. Independent variables were IQ, mother's socioeconomic background, mother's age, the test year, and the child's age group (for scoring the HOME index).
67. The table on page 222 shows the predicted odds of being in the bottom decile on the HOME index from a regression equation, using the child's sample weights, in which the dependent variable is a binary representation of whether an NLSY child had a HOME score in the bottom decile, and the independent variables were mother's IQ, mother's socioeconomic background, mother's age, and nominal variables representing the test year, the age category for scoring the HOME index, poverty in the calendar year prior to the administration of the HOME index, and receipt of AFDC in the calendar year prior to the administration of the HOME index.

Mother's IQ	Mother's Socioeconomic Background	In Poverty?	On Welfare?	Odds of Being in the Bottom Decile on the HOME Index
Average	Average	No	No	4%
Average	Average	Yes	No	8%
Average	Average	No	Yes	9%
Average	Average	Yes	Yes	16%
Average	Very low	No	No	7%
Average	Very low	Yes	No	12%
Average	Very low	No	Yes	14%
Average	Very low	Yes	Yes	24%
Very low	Average	No	No	10%
Very low	Average	Yes	No	18%
Very low	Average	No	Yes	21%
Very low	Average	Yes	Yes	34%

"Very low" is defined as two SDs below the mean. Poverty and welfare refer to the calendar year prior to the scoring of the HOME index.

68. The NLSY reported scores on these indexes for infants under 1 year of age, not analyzed here.

69. This statement applies to the full white sample. In the cross-sectional sample, used for the regression results in Appendix 4, the role of birth status (legitimate or illegitimate) was not significant when entered along with poverty and welfare receipt.

70. A technical note that applies to the means reported in the table on page 230 and in Chapter 15. In applying the national norms, the NLSY declined to estimate scores for very low-scoring children not covered in the PPVT's scoring tables, instead assigning them a score of zero. For purposes of computing the means above and in Chapter 15, we assigned a score of 40 (four SDs below the mean, and the lowest score assigned in the standard tables for scoring the PPVT) to all children with scores under 40.

71. Careful readers may be wondering why white children, who have had less than their fair share of the bottom decile for most of the other indicators, account for fully 10 percent of all NLSY children in the bottom decile. The reason is that the women of the NLSY sample (all races) have had a high proportion of low-IQ children, based on the national norms for the PPVT—fully 23 percent of all NLSY children ages 6 and older when they took the test had IQs of 80 or lower. For whites, 10 percent of the children who have been tested fall into the bottom decile. This news is not quite as bad as it looks. Just because the NLSY mothers were a nationally representative sample of women in a certain age group does not mean that their children are a nationally representative sample of children. But the news is nonetheless worrisome, with implications that are discussed in Chapter 15.

72. See Chapter 4 for the discussion of heritability of IQ.

Chapter 11

1. The proportional increases in property crime tracked more or less with the increases in violent crime until the late 1970s. Since then, property crime has moved within a narrow range and in 1992 was actually lower than it had been ten years earlier. This divergence between violent and property crimes is in itself a potentially significant phenomenon that has yet to be adequately explored.

2. For citations of the extensive literature on this subject, see Chaiken and Chaiken 1983; Wilson and Herrnstein 1985. The official statistics may have understated the increase in these "crimes that people consider serious enough to warrant reporting to the police," insofar as many burglaries, assaults, and street robberies that would have been reported in the 1950s (when there was a reasonable chance that the police would conduct a genuine investigation) are no longer reported in urban areas, where it is taken for granted that they are too minor to compete for limited police resources.

3. A more traditional way to sort the theories is to contrast classical theories,

which depict crime as the rational behavior of free agents, based on costs and benefits, with positive theories, which look for the causes of crime in society or in psychological makeup (for discussion of criminological theory, see, for example, Gottfredson and Hirschi 1990; Wilson and Herrnstein 1985). We are distinguishing only among positive theories, because the notion of criminals as rational agents seems to fit few actual criminals and the role of costs and benefits can readily be absorbed by a positive theory of criminal behavior (see Wilson and Herrnstein 1985, Chap. 2). A distinction similar to ours between psychological and sociological theories is one between "psychiatric" and "criminological" theories in Wessely and Taylor 1991.

4. Freeman 1983; Mayer and Jencks 1989; Wilson and Herrnstein 1985, Chaps. 11, 12.

5. Cleckley 1964; Colaizzi 1989.

6. Wilson and Herrnstein 1985.

7. Wilson and Herrnstein 1985.

8. In fact, within criminological theory, the distinction between being disposed to break the law and being disposed to obey it has some resonance, as illustrated in, for example, Gottfredson and Hirschi 1990. This is a fine point of theory, which we cannot elaborate on here.

9. For more extended discussion of the logic of the link between IQ and committing crime, see Gottfredson and Hirschi 1990; Hirschi 1969; Wilson and Herrnstein 1985.

10. Goring 1913.

11. Goddard 1914.

12. Murchison 1926. We know now that this was a peculiarity of a federal prison like Leavenworth, which had relatively few of the run-of-the-mill offenders typical in state prisons.

13. Sutherland 1931.

14. Haskell and Yablonsky 1978, p. 268.

15. Reid 1979, p. 156.

16. Hirschi and Hindelang 1977.

17. Reid 1982.

18. A balanced, recent summary says, "At this juncture it seems reasonable to conclude that the difference [between offenders and nonoffenders in intelligence] is real and not due to any of the possible methodological or confounding factors that have been noted in the literature" (Quay 1987 p. 107ff.).

19. The gap between offenders and nonoffenders is typically larger on verbal than on performance (i.e., nonverbal) intelligence tests (Wilson and Herrnstein 1985). It has been suggested that this is because the essential

difference between offenders and nonoffenders is the difference in *g;* it is well known that verbal scores are more dependent on *g* than performance scores (Gordon 1987; Jensen and Faulstich 1988). Another, not necessarily inconsistent, interpretation is that verbal intelligence scores do better at measuring the capacity for internalizing the prohibitions that help deter crime in nonoffenders (Wilson and Herrnstein 1985). Multiple offenders, as distinguished from offenders in general, also have significant deficits in logical reasoning ability per se (Reichel and Magnusson 1988). Whatever the reason for these patterns of differences, the methodological implications are clear: The rare study that fails to find much of an association between IQ and offending may have used nonverbal scores or scores that, for one reason or another, minimize individual differences in *g.*

20. E.g., Blumstein et al. 1985; Denno 1990. National studies of convicts who get rearrested after release also show that those with low levels of education (which are presumably correlated with low test scores) are at higher risk for recidivism (Beck and Shipley 1989).

21. Lipsitt et al. 1990.

22. Reichel and Magnusson 1988.

23. Hirschi 1969; Wilson and Herrnstein 1985.

24. Nicholson and Kugler 1991.

25. The evidence in fact suggests that smart offenders pick crimes with lesser likelihood of arrest and larger payoffs (Wilson and Herrnstein 1985).

26. Moffitt and Silva 1988; Hindelang et al. 1981; Hirschi and Hindelang 1977; Wilson and Herrnstein 1985.

27. Reichel and Magnusson 1988.

28. Kandel et al. 1988.

29. In this sample, there was no significant correlation between IQ and socioeconomic status, and IQ remained a significant predictor of offending even after the effects of parental SES and the sons' own level of education were entered as covariates in an analysis of covariance.

30. White et al. 1989.

31. Werner and Smith 1982.

32. Werner 1989; Werner and Smith 1982.

33. For an entry into this literature, see Farrington and West 1990; Gottfredson and Hirschi 1990; Mednick and others 1987; Wilson and Herrnstein 1985.

34. In this regard, it is perhaps worth mentioning that we originally intended for this book to be about individual differences generally and social policy, with intelligence as the centerpiece. We narrowed the focus to intelligence partly because it looms so much larger than any other individual trait in explaining what is going on, but also out of necessity: Only for criminal

behavior is the scientific literature extensive enough to have permitted a thoroughgoing presentation of individual differences other than intellectual.

35. The most serious problem is the established and pronounced tendency of black juveniles to underreport offenses (Hindelang 1978, 1981).

36. Not surprisingly, the most serious offenders are the ones who most often underreport their crimes. Serious offenders are also the ones most likely to go uninterviewed in survey research. At the other extreme, minor offenders brag about their criminal exploits. They inflate the real level of "crime" by putting minor incidents (for example, a school-yard fistfight, which can easily fit the technical definition of "aggravated assault") in the same category with authentically felonious attacks.

    Since we are focusing on the role of intelligence, self-report data pose a special problem, for it has been observed that people of low intelligence are less candid than brighter respondents. This bias would tend to weaken the correlation between IQ and crime in self-report data.

37. The authoritative source on self-report data for juveniles is still Hindelang et al. 1981. See also Hindelang 1978, 1981; Smith and Davidson 1986.

38. Wolfang, Figlio, and Sellin 1972; Wilson and Herrnstein 1985.

39. These results for the entire age range are substantially the same when age subgroups are examined, but some differences may be found. Those who become involved with the criminal justice system at an early age tended to have lower intelligence than those who first become involved later in their teens.

40. This represents the top decile of white males. To use the same index across racial groups is inadvisable because of the different reporting characteristics of whites and blacks.

41. For a review of the literature, see Wilson and Herrnstein 1985.

42. Elliott and Voss 1974.

43. Thornberry et al. 1985 uses the Philadelphia Cohort Study to demonstrate rising crime after dropout for that well-known sample.

44. The sample includes those who got a GED—most of whom had gotten it at the correctional institution in which they were incarcerated at the time of their interview. The results are shown in Appendix 4.

Chapter 12

1. Gove 1964. The definition is listed, sadly, as "obsolete." We can think of no modern word doing that semantic job now.

2. More recently, Walter Lippmann used *civility* in his worrying book (Lippmann 1955) about what he feared was disappearing with the rising "Jacobinism" of American political life, the shift he saw early in the century

away from representative government toward populist democracy. Early in his career as a journalist and social commentator (Lippmann 1922b), Lippmann noted that the ordinary, private person sets the concerns of governance very low on his or her list of priorities. To govern us, he said, we needed a special breed of person, leaders with the capacity to fathom, and the desire to promote, the public good. That capacity is what he called civility. For a reflection on Lippmann's conception of civility by a social scientist, see Burdick 1959.

3. There are other rationales for not voting, as, for example, the one promoted on a T-shirt favored by libertarians: "Don't vote. It only encourages them."

4. For an attempt to construe voting as a rational act from the economic standpoint, see Downs 1957.

5. Aristotle 1905 ed., p. 1129.

6. Although the sample was not strictly representative of the American population, it was a broad cross-section, unlikely to be atypical except as a result of its underrepresentation of rural and minority children. Hess and Torney 1967.

7. The second graders were excluded from some of the analyses because some questionnaire items evoked too high a rate of meaningless or nonresponses.

8. A measure of political efficacy was based on the children's "agree" or "disagree" responses to five statements, including: "I don't think public officials care much what people like me think." Or, "People like me don't have any say about what the government does."

9. Harvey and Harvey 1970.

10. The exceptions included the measures for political efficacy and political participation, both of which were barely correlated with intelligence, although slightly correlated with socioeconomic status (primarily via parental education, rather than family wealth). The authors speculated that the rising cynicism of the young during the later 1960s may in part account for these deviant results.

11. Like other studies (e.g., Neuman 1986, see below), this one also found that the more intelligent someone is, the more likely he or she is to be liberal on social issues and conservative on economic ones. Chauvinistic, militaristic, and anticommunistic attitude were inversely related to intelligence.

12. For a brief summary of this literature as of the late 1960s, see White 1969, who similarly concludes that political socialization, as he calls it, is highly dependent on intelligence itself rather than on socioeconomic status.

13. Sidney Verba and Norman Nie (1972), leading scholars of American voting, distinguish cogently between the study of politics as a political scien-

tist approaches it and political psychology. A political scientist mostly wants to understand how political participation shapes the choices a community makes; a political psychologist tries to understand the participation itself. This chapter comes closer to political psychology than to political science.

14. Campbell et al. 1960; Milbrath and Goel 1977; Verba and Nie 1972; Wolfinger and Rosenstone 1980.

15. Wolfinger and Rosenstone 1980, p. 13.

16. Verba and Nie 1972.

17. The one exception, the frequency with which an individual contacted political officials for matters of personal concern, showed no such correlation, but it is also the most ambiguously political. See Verba and Nie 1972.

18. There are hints, however, that, if socioeconomic status had been broken into components of educational level and income, educational level would have predicted political participation better than income. See Figures 6-1 to 6-3 in Verba and Nie 1972.

19. Wolfinger and Rosenstone 1980. In even-numbered years, the CPS, a survey conducted monthly of a nationally representative sample of tens of thousands of Americans, asks about voting in the November election. These surveys also include data on income, occupation, education, and other personal and regional variables. The Wolfinger and Rosenstone analysis was based on the entire sample of almost 100,000 respondents in the November surveys in 1972 and 1974 and a random subsample used for more detailed modeling. The main technique they used is the *probit analysis,* a form of multivariate analysis for estimating the changes in probability of some dependent variable—voting, in this case—associated with a change in an independent variable—educational attainment, for example—after the effects of the other variables—say, income or occupational level—are taken account of.

20. E.g., Peterson 1990.

21. Neuman 1986. This book aggregates data from nine studies of voting between 1948 and 1980 and comes up with a measure of "political sophistication," which seems to have considerable power in explaining much about voting, including simple turnout. The "key causal factor" for political sophistication, Neuman found, is education, which explained four times as much of the variance in sophistication as the next most influential factor in a list that included age, race, sex, the other components of socioeconomic status, parental behavior, and region of the country.

22. Wolfinger and Rosenstone 1980, p. 19.

23. Besides the works already cited, for other overviews coming to the same basic conclusion, see Campbell et al. 1960; Milbrath and Goel 1977; Neuman 1986.

24. "It is difficult to find support in our data for notions that a generic status variable plays any part in the motivational foundations of the decision to vote" (Wolfinger and Rosenstone 1980, p. 35). Perhaps there is some effect of income on voting at the lowest levels but throughout the range of income, it seems to have no independent predictive value of its own.

25. Verba and Nie 1972, p. 335.

26. How someone votes, rather than whether, can be more plausibly connected to the outward benefits gained from the outcome of an election. And many political scientists focus more on political preference than on level of engagement. Political preferences, too, have their individual correlates, but we will not try to summarize these results as well (but see, for example, Fletcher and Forbes, 1990; Granberg and Holmberg 1990; Milbrath 1977; Neuman 1986; Nie et al. 1976).

27. There is an indirect argument to be made by combining four observations: (1) We know for sure that one of the traits roughly measured by educational attainment is intelligence. (2) As we showed in Chapter 1, American educational opportunities are more efficiently distributed by cognitive ability than they have ever been, here or elsewhere. (3) It is here and now that we see the strongest correlations between voting and educational attainment. (4) In countries where education and cognitive ability are not so thoroughly enmeshed, education has less impact on voting. To fill in the story: During the 1950s and 1960s, the level of political participation rose more rapidly than the educational level of the population (Verba and Nie 1972, p. 252). Looking backward, we see the other side of the same coin. In 1870, only 2 percent of the American population had finished high school; even fewer were going to college. Yet voting rates may have been higher than they are now. Kleppner (1982) concludes that voting rates were more than 11 percentage points above where they should have been, had education had the same effects in the 1880s that they had in 1968. Shortridge (1981) has a lower estimate of voter turnout in the late nineteenth century, but still one that exceeds expectations, given the educational levels of the period. Proper historical comparisons must, of course, take into account changes in voting laws, in poll taxes, in registration requirements, as well as the effects of the extension of suffrage to women and to 18- to 20-year olds. However, after all those corrections are made, scholars agree that past voting rates (post–Civil War, nineteenth century, for example) are incommensurately high or present rates are incommensurately low, given the changes in levels of formal education of the general public. Except in the South of the Reconstruction, the correlation between education and voting rate was negative from 1876 to 1892, just the reverse of what it is now (see Kleppner 1982). The international data indicating that education is less important in voting where education is

not so enmeshed with cognitive ability come from Milbrath and Goel (1977).

28. Exposure to political print media was another influential factor, but this, too, turned out to be most strongly associated with rated intelligence (see Luskin 1990).
29. The so-called Bay Area Survey, described in Neuman 1981, 1986.
30. See note 21.
31. Neuman 1986, p. 117.
32. Useful summaries can be found in Abramson and Claggett 1991; Hill and Luttbeg 1983; Kleppner 1982; Peterson 1990; Rothenberg and Licht 1982.
33. E.g., Milbrath and Goel 1977. Biological and social scientists have lately tried to enrich our understanding of "political man" by showing the links to social behavior in other species. For background to the huge literature on the variety of influences on political behavior and attitudes, see Converse 1964; Kinder and Sears 1985; Rokeach 1973.
34. Harvey and Harvey 1970.
35. Neuman 1986.
36. Luskin 1990.

Chapter 13

1. For a useful recent critique of the treatment of race by psychologists, also demonstrating how difficult (impossible?) it is to be detached about this issue, see Yee et al. 1993.
2. Lynn 1991c.
3. Lynn 1987a. For a critique of Lynn's early work, see Stevenson and Azuma 1983.
4. For those who want to reconstruct the debate, Lynn's 1987 and 1991 review articles followed on earlier studies: Lynn 1977, 1978, 1982; Lynn and Hampson 1986b. For his response to Flynn's 1987 critique, see Lynn 1987b.
5. Chan and Vernon 1988.
6. Lynn and Song 1994.
7. Iwawaki and Vernon 1988; Vernon 1982.
8. Flynn 1991; Sue and Okazaki 1990.
9. Flynn 1991.
10. Lynn 1993b.
11. Lynn 1987a, 1987b, 1989, 1990a, 1990b, 1991b, 1991c, 1992, 1993a, 1993b; Lynn and Hattori 1990; Lynn, Pagliari, and Chan 1988.
12. Lynn, Hampson, and Iwawaki 1987.
13. Lynn 1991c.
14. Stevenson et al. 1985.

15. Lynn 1991a, p. 733. Lynn has noted that the mean white IQ in Minnesota is approximately 105, well above the average for the American white population. On the other hand, it is possible that the cities chosen in Japan and Taiwan were similarly elevated.

16. An excellent account of the literature may be found in Storfer 1990, pp. 314–321, from which our generalizations are taken. For Jews in Britain, see also Lynn 1992.

17. Storfer 1990, pp. 321–323.

18. As reported in Jensen 1984b, p. 479.

19. Sattler 1988.

20. A detailed and comprehensive review of the literature through 1980 may be found in Osborne and McGurk 1982; Shuey 1966. For an excellent one-volume synthesis and analysis, see Loehlin, Lindzey, and Spuhler 1975.

21. Standard deviations are explained in Appendix 1.

22. To qualify, all studies had to report data for both a white and black sample, with a sample size of at least fifty in each group, drawn from comparable populations that purported to be representative of the general population of that age and geographic area (studies of special populations such as delinquents were excluded). Socioeconomic status posed a special problem. If a study explicitly matched subjects by SES, it was excluded. If it simply drew its samples from a low-SES area, it was included, even though some degree of matching had occurred. The study had to use a standardized test of cognitive ability, although not all of them were IQ tests and not all included a complete battery. If the scores were reported as IQs, a standard deviation of 15 was imputed if no standard deviations for that sample were given.

23. To get the IQ equivalent of SD differences, multiply the SD difference by 15; hence, $1.08 \times 15 = 16.2$ IQ points.

24. This figure is based on non-Latino whites. The difference between blacks and the combined white-Latino sample in the NLSY is 1.12 SDs. Because the U.S. Latino population was proportionally very small until the 1970s, the NLSY figure for non-Latino whites is more comparable to the earlier tests, in terms of definition of the sample, than the figure for the combined white-Latino sample, and we shall use it exclusively in discussions of the NLSY data throughout the chapter.

25. The formula is $\sigma\,Diff. = \left(\overline{X}_w - \overline{X}_b\right)\Big/ \sqrt{\left(N_w\sigma_w^2 + N_b\sigma_b^2\right)\big/\left(N_w + N_b\right)}$, where N is the sample size, X is the sample mean, σ is the standard deviation, and w and b stand for white and black, respectively (taken from Jensen and Reynolds 1982, p. 425). Note that our white sample differs from the one used in Office of the Assistant Secretary of Defense (Manpower) (1982). The "white" sample in that report included all persons not identified as

Hispanic or black, whereas our "white" sample also excluded persons identifying themselves as American Indians or a member of an Asian or Pacific ethnic group. The NLSY and the AFQT are described in the Introduction to Part II and Appendix 2.

26. This is a very rough estimate. As of 1994 there were approximately 32.8 million blacks in America. If the estimate is computed based on the mean IQ (86.7) and standard deviation (12.4) of blacks in the NLSY, a table of the normal distribution indicates that only about 0.1 percent, or about 33,000, would have IQs of 125 or higher. If one applies the observed distribution in the NLSY and asks what proportion of blacks are in the top five percent of the AFQT distribution (roughly corresponding to an IQ of 125), the result, 0.4 percent, implies that the answer is about 131,000. There are reasons to think that both estimates err in different directions. We compromised with 100,000.

27. For example, no external evidence for bias has turned up with the WISC, WAIS, Stanford-Binet, Iowa Test of Educational Development, California Achievement Test, SAT, ACT, GRE, LSAT, MCAT, Wonderlic Personnel Test, GATB, and ASVAB (including the AFQT in particular).

28. If any bias has been found, it is primarily regarding performance in school, and it shows that test scores for blacks often "overpredict" performance; that is, the tests are biased "in favor" of blacks, tending for unknown reasons to predict higher performance than is actually observed. See Appendix 5 for details.

29. Weiss 1987, p. 121. A separate argument, made in Zoref and Williams (1980), adduced evidence that verbal items in IQ tests are disproportionately based on white males "in role-stereotyped representations." The authors do not present evidence that performance on these items varies by race or gender in ways that would indicate bias but rather indict the tests as a whole on the basis of their sexism and racism.

30. The reason why the "oarsman:regatta" example has been used so often in descriptions of cultural bias is that it is one of the few items in the SAT that looks so obviously guilty. Perhaps if a test consisted exclusively of items that were equivalent to the example, it would be possible to demonstrate cultural bias statistically, but no modern test has more than a few that come close to "oarsman:regatta."

31. The definitive assessment of internal evidence of bias is in Jensen 1980.

32. E.g., Valencia and Rankin 1988; Munford and Munoz 1980.

33. For a review, see Jensen 1980.

34. The NLSY has higher scores for whites than blacks on backward digit span and virtually no difference at all for forward digit span. In a similar way, SES differences within races are also greater for backward digit tests than forward digit tests (Jensen and Figueroa 1975).

35. Gordon 1984. See Farrell 1983, and the attached responses, for an attempt to explain the difference in digit span results through cultural bias hypotheses.

36. Another commonly used apparatus involves a home button and a pair of other buttons, for yes and no, in response to tasks presented by a computer console. The results from both types of apparatus are congruent.

37. The literature is extensive, and we are bypassing which aspect of reaction time in fact covaries with *g*. For our purposes, it is only necessary that some aspects do so. For some of the issues, see, for example, Barrett, Eysenck, and Lucking 1986; Matthews and Dorn 1989; Vernon 1983; Vernon et al. 1985.

38. Jensen and Munro 1979.

39. Jensen 1993b.

40. The dependent variable is age-equated IQ score, and the independent variables are a binary variable for race (white or black) and the parental SES index. The difference between the resulting predicted IQs is divided by the pooled weighted standard deviation.

41. Among the young women in the RAND study of adolescent pregnancy described in Chapter 8 (Abrahamse et al, 1988), drawn from the nationally representative High School and Beyond sample, the same procedure reduced the B/W difference by 32 percent. See also Jensen and Reynolds 1982 and Jensen and Figueroa 1975.

42. For some people, controlling for status is a tacit way of isolating the genetic difference between the races. This logic is as fallacious as the logic behind controlling for SES that ignores the ways in which IQ helps determine socioeconomic status. See later in the chapter for our views on genetics and the B/W difference.

43. In other major studies the B/W difference continues to widen even at the highest SES levels. In 1975, for example, Jensen and Figueroa (1975) obtained full-scale WISC IQ scores for 622 whites and 622 blacks, ages 5 to 12, from a random sample of ninety-eight California school districts. They broke down the scores into ten categories of SES, using Duncan's index of socioeconomic prestige based on occupation. They found a B/W discrepancy that went from a mere .13 SD in the lowest SES decile up to 1.20 SD in the highest SES decile. Going to the opposite type of test data, the Scholastic Aptitude Test taken by millions, self-selected with a bias toward the upper end of the cognitive distribution, the same pattern emerged. In 1991, to take a typical year, the B/W difference among students whose parents had less than a high school diploma was .58 SD (averaging verbal and mathematical scores), while the B/W difference among students whose parents had a graduate degree was .78 SD. (National Ethnic/Sex Data for 1991, unpublished data available by request from the College Board). In

their separate reviews of the literature, Audrey Shuey (whose review was published in 1966) and John Loehlin and his colleagues (review published in 1975) identified thirteen studies conducted from 1948 through the early 1970s that presented IQ means for low- and high-SES groups by race. In twelve of the thirteen studies, the black-white difference in IQ was higher for the higher-SES group than for the lower-SES group. For similar results for the 1981 standardization of the WAIS-R, see Reynolds et al. 1987. A final comment is that the NLSY also shows an increasing B/W difference at the upper end of the socioeconomic scale when the 1980 AFQT scoring system is used and the scores are not corrected for skew. See Appendix 2 for a discussion of the scoring issues.

44. Kendall, Verster, and Mollendorf 1988.

45. Kendall, Verster, and Mollendorf 1988. For another example, this time of an entire book devoted to testing in the African setting that fails to mention a single mean, see Schwarz and Krug 1972.

46. Lynn 1991c.

47. Boissiere et al. 1985.

48. Owen 1992.

49. Reynolds et al. 1987.

50. Vincent 1991.

51. Vincent also cites two nonnormative studies of children in which the B/W differences ranged from only one to nine points. These are the differences after controlling for SES, which, as we explain in the text, shrinks the B/W gap by about one-third.

52. Jensen 1984a; Jensen and Naglieri 1987; Naglieri 1986. They point out that the K-ABC test is less saturated with *g* than a conventional IQ measure and more dependent on memory, both of which would tend to reduce the B/W difference (Naglieri and Bardos 1987).

53. Jensen 1993b.

54. Based on the white and black SDs for 1980, the first year that standard deviations by race were published.

55. Wainer 1988.

56. Our reasons for concluding that the narrowing of the B/W differences on the SAT was real, despite the potential artifacts involved in SAT score, are as follows. Regarding the self-selection problem, the key consideration is that the proportion of blacks taking the test rose throughout the 1976–1993 period (including the subperiod 1980–1993). In 1976, blacks who took the SAT represented 10 percent of black 17-year-olds; in 1980, the proportion had risen to 13 percent; by 1993, it had risen to about 20 percent. While this does not necessarily mean that blacks taking the SAT were coming from lower socioeconomic groups (the data on parental edu-

cation and income from 1980 to 1993 indicate they were not), the pool probably became less selective insofar as it drew from lower portions of the ability distribution. The improvement in black scores is therefore more likely to be understated by the SAT data than exaggerated.

Howard Wainer (1988) has argued that changes in black test scores are uninterpretable because of anomalies that could be inferred from the test scores of students who did not disclose their ethnicity on the SAT background questionnaire (nonresponders). Apart from several technical questions about Wainer's conclusions that arise from his presentation, the key point is that the nonresponder population has diminished substantially. As it has diminished, there are no signs that the story told by the SAT is changing. The basic shape of the falling trendline for the black-white difference cannot plausibly be affected by nonresponders (though the true means in any given year might well be somewhat different from the means based on those who identify their ethnicity).

57. The range of .15 to .25 SD takes the data in both the text and Appendix 5 into account. To calculate the narrowing in IQ terms, we need to estimate the correlation between IQ and the various measures of educational preparation. A lower correlation would shrink the estimate of the amount of IQ narrowing between blacks and whites, and vice versa for a higher estimate. The two- to three-point estimate in the text assumes that this correlation is somewhere between .6 and .8. If we instead rely entirely on the SAT data and consider it to be a measure of intelligence per se, then the narrowing has been four points in IQ, but only for the population that actually takes the test.

58. A change of one IQ point in a generation for genetic reasons is not out of the realm of possibility, given sufficient differential fertility. However, the evidence on differential fertility (see Chapter 15) implies not a shrinking black-white gap but a growing one.

59. Jaynes and Williams 1989; Jencks and Peterson 1991.

60. Linear extrapolations are not to be taken seriously in these situations. A linear continuation of the black and white SAT trends from 1980 to 1990 would bring a convergence with the white mean in the year in 2035 on the Verbal and 2053 on the Math. And when it occurs, racial differences would not be ended, for if we apply the same logic to the Asian scores, in that year of 2053 when blacks and whites both have a mean of 555 on the Math test, the Asian mean would be 632. The Asian Verbal mean (again, based on 1980–1990) would be 510 in the year 2053, forty-seven points ahead of the white mean. But—such is the logic of linear extrapolations from a short time period—the black Verbal score would by that time have surpassed the white mean by thirty-seven points and would be 500, only

ten points behind the Asians. In 2069, the black Verbal mean would surpass the Asian Verbal mean. Linear trends over short periods of time cannot be sensibly extrapolated much into the future, notwithstanding how often one sees such extrapolations in the media.

61. See Appendix 5 for ACT results. In short, the mean rose from 16.2 to in 1986 to 17.1 in 1993. The number of black ACT students also continued to rise during this period, suggesting that the increase after 1986 was not the result of a more selective pool.

62. Chapter 18 explores this line of thought further.

63. SAT trends are subject to a variety of questions relating to the changing nature of the SAT pool. The discussion that follows is based on unreported analyses checking out the possibility that the results reflect these potential artifacts (e.g., changes in the proportion of Asians using English as their first language; changes in the proportion of students coming from homes where the parents did not go to college). The discussion of these matters may be found in Chapter 18.

64. The first year for which a frequency distribution of scores by ethnicity has been published is 1980.

65. Trying to predict trends on the basis of equivalent percentage changes from different baselines is a treacherous proposition. A comparison with black and Asian gains makes the point. For example, the percentage of blacks scoring in the 700s on the SAT-Verbal grew by 23 percent from 1980 to 1990, within a percentage point of the Asian proportional increase. For students scoring in the 600s, the black increase was 37 percent, not far below the Asian increase of 48 percent. The difficulty with using proportions in this instance is that the baselines are so different. Take the case of students scoring in the 600s on the SAT-V, for example. The proportions that produced that 37 percent increase for blacks were eleven students out of a thousand in 1980 versus fifteen students out of a thousand in 1990. The Asian change, put in the same metric, was from fifty-five students in 1980 to eighty-one students in 1990. For every four students per thousand that blacks gained in the 600 group, Asians gained twenty-six per thousand.

66. This statement is based on a calculation that assumes that the 1980 distribution of scores remained the same except for the categories of interest. To illustrate, in 1980, 19.8 percent of black students scored from 200 to 249. In 1993, only 13.1 percent scored in that range. Suppose that we treat the percentage distribution for 1980 as if it consisted of 1,000 students. In that year, 198 of those students scored in the 200 to 249 range. We then recompute the mean for the 1980 distribution, substituting 128 for 198 in the 200 to 249 point category (assigning midpoint values to all the intervals to reach a grouped mean), so in effect we are calculating a mean for a fictitious population of $1000 - 198 + 128 = 930$. (The actual calculations

used unrounded proportions based on the actual frequencies in each interval.)

A technical note for those who might wish to reproduce this analysis: When means are computed from grouped data, the midpoint of an interval is not necessarily the actual mean of people in that interval, usually because more than 50 percent of the scores will tend to be found in the fatter part of the distribution covered by the interval but also because scores may be bunched at the extreme categories. In the SAT-Math, for example, a disproportionate number of the people in the interval from 750 to 800 have scores of 800 and of those in the interval from 200 to 249 have scores of 200 (because they guessed wrong so often that their score is driven down to the minimum). Such effects can produce a noticeable bias in the estimated mean. For example, the actual verbal mean of black students in 1980 was 330. If one computes the mean based on the distribution published annually by the College Board, which run in fifty-point intervals from 200 to 800, the result is 336.4. The actual mean in 1990 was 352; the grouped mean is 357.9. The computed figure in the text is based on the surrogate mean as described above compared to the grouped 1980 and 1990 means, to provide a consistent framework.

67. The contrast with the Asian experience on the SATs is striking. The Asian Math mean rose from 509 to 535. Of this increase, *none* of it was due to decreases in students scoring less than 200 (compared to 22 percent for blacks), while a remarkable 54 percent was due to gains in the 700 and up group (compared to 3 percent for blacks). Meanwhile, on the Verbal test, the Asian mean rose from 396 to 415 from 1980 to 1993. Of this, only 17 percent occurred because of reductions in Asians scoring in the 200s (compared to 51 percent for blacks), while 9 percent occurred because of increases in Asians scoring in the 700s (compared to 0.4 percent for blacks). The Asian increase in test scores has been driven by improvements among the best students, while the black increase has been driven by improvements among the worst students. We are unable to find any artifacts in the changing nature of the black and Asian SAT pools that would explain these results. The continued Asian improvement makes it difficult to blame the slowdown in black improvement in the last decade on events that somehow made it impossible for any American students to make progress. Explanations could be advanced based on events specific to blacks.

68. Snyderman and Rothman 1988. The sample was based on random selections from the Members and Fellows of the American Educational Research Association, National Council on Measurement in Education, six divisions of the American Psychological Association (Developmental Psychology, Educational Psychology, Evaluation and Measurement, School

Psychology, Counseling Psychology, and Industrial and Organizational Psychology), the Behavior Genetics Association, the Cognitive Science Society, and the education division of the American Sociological Association.

69. Brody 1992, p. 309.
70. Gould 1984, pp. 26–27.
71. Gould 1984, p. 32. See Lewontin, Rose, and Kamin 1984, p. 127, for a similar argument.
72. Gould 1984, p. 33.
73. The ramifications for public policy are dealt with in detail in Chapters 19 and 20, concerning affirmative action.
74. We do not include in the text any discussion of Phillipe Rushton's intensely controversial writings on the differences among Asian, white, and black populations. For a brief account, see Appendix 5.
75. A similar example can be found in Lewontin 1970, one of the most outspoken critics of the IQ enterprise in all its manifestations.
76. The calculation proceeds as follows: The standard deviation of IQ being 15, the variance is therefore 225. We are stipulating that environment accounts for .4 of the variance, which equals 90. The standard deviation of the distribution of the environmental component of IQ is the square root of 90, or 9.49. The difference between group environments necessary to produce a fifteen-point difference in group means is 15/9.49, or 1.58, and the difference necessary to produce a three-point difference is 3/9.49, or .32. The comparable figures if heritability is assigned the lower bound value of .4 are 1.28 and .26. If heritability is assigned the upper-bound value of .8, then the comparable figures are 2.24 and .45.
77. Stevenson et al. 1985.
78. Lynn 1987a.
79. Frydman and Lynn 1989.
80. Iwawaki and Vernon 1988; McShane and Berry 1988.
81. Vernon, 1982 p. 28. It has been argued that the 110 figure is too high, but a verbal-visuospatial difference among Asian Americans is not disputed (Flynn 1989).
82. Supplemental evidence has been found among Chinese students living in China who were given the SAT. Several hundred Chinese students in Shanghai between the ages of 11 and 14 scored extremely high on the Math SAT, despite an almost total lack of familiarity with American cognitive ability testing. As a proportion of the total population, this represented a far greater density of high math scorers in Shanghai than in the United States. Further attempts to find high scorers in Chinese schools confirmed the original results in Shanghai (Stanley, Feng, and Zhu 1989).
83. The SAT data actually provide even more of a hint about genetic origins

for the test-score pattern, though a speculative one. The College Board reports scores for persons whose first language learned is English and for those whose first language is "English and another." It is plausible to assume that Asian students whose only "first language" was English contain a disproportionate number of children of mixed parentage, usually Asian and white, compared to those in whose homes both English and an Asian language were spoken from birth. With that hypothesis in mind, consider that the discrepancy between the Verbal and Math SATs was (in IQ points) only 1.7 points for the "English only" Asians and 5.3 points for the "English and another" first-language Asians. Nongenetic explanations are available. For example, one may hypothesize that although English and another language were both "first languages," English wasn't learned as well in those homes; hence the Verbal scores for the "English and another" homes were lower. But then one must also explain why the Math scores of the "English and another" Asians were twenty-one SAT points higher than the "English-only" homes. Here one could hypothesize that the "English-only" Asians were second- and third-generation Americans, more assimilated, and therefore didn't study math as hard as their less assimilated friends (although somehow they did quite well in the Verbal test). But while alternative hypotheses are available, the consistency with a genetic explanation suggests that it would be instructive to examine the scores of children of full and mixed Asian parentage.

84. A related topic that we do not review here is the comparison of blacks and whites on Level I and Level II abilities, using Jensen's two-level theory of mental abilities (Jensen and Figueroa 1975; Jensen and Inouye 1980). The findings are consistent with those presented under the discussion of WISC-R profiles and Spearman's hypothesis.

85. "Spearman's hypothesis" is named after an observation made by Charles Spearman in 1927. Noting that the black-white difference varied systematically for different kinds of tests, Spearman wrote that the mean difference "was most marked in just those [tests] which are known to be most saturated with g" (Spearman 1927, p. 379). Spearman himself never tried to develop his comment into a formal hypothesis or to test it.

86. Jensen and Reynolds 1982.

87. Jensen and Reynolds actually compared large sets of IQ scores with the full-scale IQ score held constant statistically.

88. Jensen and Reynolds 1982, p. 427; Reynolds and Jensen 1983.

89. Jensen and Reynolds 1982, pp. 428–429.

90. Jensen 1985, 1987a.

91. Jensen 1993b.

92. Braden 1989.

93. Jensen 1993b.

94. The correlations between g loading and black-white difference are typically in the .5 to .8 range.

95. A concrete example is provided by the Kaufman Assessment Battery for
Children (K-ABC), a test that attained some visibility in part because
the separation between black and white children on it is smaller than on
more standard intelligence tests. It was later found that K-ABC is a less
valid measure of g than the standard tests (Jensen 1984a; Kaufman and
Kaufman 1983; Naglieri and Bardos 1987).

96. E.g., Pedersen et al. 1992. Jensen limits himself to discussing Spearman's
hypothesis on the phenotypic level.

97. Jensen 1977.

98. Some other studies suggest a systematic sibling difference for national
populations, but it goes the other way: Elder siblings outscore younger
siblings in some data sets. However, this "birth-order" effect, when it occurs at all, is much smaller than the effect Jensen observed.

99. Jensen 1985, 1987a.

100. Various technical arguments were advanced against Jensen's claim that
blacks and whites differ the most on tests that are the most highly loaded
on g. Many of these were effectively resolved within the forum. One critic
hypothesized that Jensen's findings resulted from an artifact of varying
reliabilities (Baron 1985). Jensen was able to demonstrate that corrections for unreliability did not wash out the evidence for Spearman's hypothesis and that some of the tests with low g loadings had high
reliabilities to begin with, contrary to the critic's assumption. Another
commentator suggested that Jensen had inadvertently built into his own
analysis the very correlation between g loading and black-white difference that he purported to discover (Schonemann 1985; see also Wilson
1985). In the next round (the forum occupied two issues of the journal),
after being apprised of a response by physicist William Shockley (Shockley 1987), he withdrew his argument. A less serious criticism suggested
that black-white differences did indeed correlate with some general factor that turns up to varying degrees in different intelligence tests but that
the factor may not be g (Borkowski and Maxwell 1985). To this criticism,
Jensen was able to demonstrate that the g factor accounted for so large a
fraction of the total variance in test scores that no other general factor
could possibly be comparably correlated with black-white differences. A
still less serious criticism (indeed, barely a criticism at all), made by several commentators, was that the g that turns up in one battery of tests is
likely to differ from the g that turns up in another (e.g., Kline 1985).
Jensen accepted this point, noting, however, that the various g's are themselves intercorrelated.

A number of critics took a nontechnical tack. One set argued that Jensen's analysis was conceptually circular. For example, if *g* is defined as intelligence, then tests that are loaded on *g* will be considered tests of intelligence. If these happen, coincidentally, to be the tests that black and whites differ on, then Spearman's hypothesis will seem to be confirmed, though the link between the tests and intelligence was simply postulated, not proved (Brody 1987). For a related argument see Macphail 1985. Jensen acknowledged that he had not tried to discuss the relationship of *g* to intelligence in this particular article. Another set of critics made what could be called meta-critical comments, wondering why Jensen should want to uncover relationships that are not very interesting (Das 1985), hurtful to blacks (Das 1985), inimical to world peace (Bardis 1985), and likely to distract attention from the possibility of raising people's *g* by educational means (Whimbey 1985). None of these commentaries disputed that the data show what Jensen said they show.

A few years later, the last paper written by the noted psychometrician, Louis Guttman, before his death, attempted to demonstrate a mathematical circularity in Jensen's argument, concluding that Spearman's hypothesis is true by mathematical necessity (Guttman 1992). He argued that the factor analytic procedures that are used to extract an estimate of *g* cannot fail to produce a correlation between *g* and the B/W difference. If the correlation is present by necessity, concluded Guttman, it can't be telling us anything about nature. The gist of Guttman's case is that if *g* is the only source of correlation across tests, then the varying B/W differences across tests *must* be correlated with *g*. Jensen and others were quick to point out that no one now believes that *g* is the only source of correlation between tests, just the largest one. We will not try to reproduce Guttman's mathematical argument, not just because it would get us deep into algebra but because it was decisively refuted by other psychometricians who commented on it and seems to have found no other support since its publication. See Jensen 1992; Loehlin 1992; Roskam and Ellis 1992.

101. Gustafsson 1992.
102. Mercer 1984, pp. 297–310.
103. Mercer 1988.
104. Mercer 1988, p. 209.
105. It would be useful for the reader if we could present Mercer's results so that they parallel the method we have been using, in which the sociocultural variables and ethnicity are treated as independent variables predicting IQ, but her presentation does not include that analysis.
106. Mercer 1988, p. 208.

107. The critique of Mercer's position has been highly technical. Readers who have the patience will find an extended exchange between Mercer, Jensen, and Robert Gordon in Reynolds and Brown 1984.
108. Mercer 1984, Tables 6, 9; Jensen 1984b, pp. 580–582.
109. Boykin 1986, p. 61.
110. For review, see Boykin 1986.
111. Ogbu 1986.
112. Flynn 1984, 1987a, 1987b.
113. Merrill 1938.
114. Flynn 1984, 1987b; Lynn and Hampson 1986c.
115. Flynn 1987a, 1987b.
116. Lynn and Hampson 1986a.
117. Teasdale and Owen 1989.
118. For evidence that this is what has happened in the United States, see Murray and Herrnstein 1992.
119. If the mean IQ in 1776 had been 30 and the standard deviation was what it is today, then America in the Revolutionary period had only five men and women with IQs above 100.
120. Lynn and Hampson 1986a.
121. Consider the analogy of height. The average stature of Americans has risen several inches since the Pilgrims landed at Plymouth, but height has run in families nevertheless.
122. A shifting link between IQ and intelligence is not only possible but probable under certain conditions. For example, when the literacy level of a country rises rapidly, scores on conventional intelligence tests will also rise because more people will be better able to read the test. This rise is unlikely to be fully reflected in a rising intelligence level, at least with equal rapidity. Flynn 1987b discusses this general measurement issue.
123. Scarr and Weinberg 1976, 1978, 1983; Weinberg, Scarr and Waldman 1992.
124. Weinberg, Scarr, and Waldman 1992, Table 2. The progression of the IQ means from two black parents to one black/one white to two white parents is not as neatly supportive of a genetic hypothesis as might first appear, because there is reason to suspect that the mixed-race biological parents of the adopted children were disproportionately drawn from college students, which in turn would imply that the IQ of the black parent was well above the black mean.
125. Weinberg, Scarr, and Waldman 1992. For the technical debate, see Levin in press; Lynn in press, with a response by Scarr and Weinberg in Waldman, Weinberg, and Scarr in press.
126. Weinberg, Scarr, and Waldman 1992, Table 2. The overall decline in

scores for all groups was because a new test norm had been imposed in the interim, vitiating the Flynn effect for this group.

127. Waldman, Weinberg, and Scarr in press.

128. Eyferth 1961 For accounts in English, see Loehlin, Lindzey, and Spuhler 1975; Flynn 1980.

129. Loehlin, Lindzey, and Spuhler 1975, Chap. 5.

130. An earlier study showed no significant association between the amount of white ancestry in a sample of American blacks and their intelligence test scores (Scarr et al. 1977). If the whites who contributed this ancestry were a random sample of all whites, then this would be strong evidence of no genetic influence on black-white differences. There is no evidence one way or another about the nature of the white ancestors.

131. Lewontin, Rose, and Kamin 1984.

132. Scarr and Weinberg 1976, Table 12.

Chapter 14

1. U.S. Department of Labor 1993, Table 3.

2. U.S. Bureau of the Census 1993, Table 1.

3. The NLSY sample does not include GEDs. Nationally, the 1991 high school completion rate (signifying twelve years of school) was 87.0 percent for whites, 72.5 percent for blacks, and 55.4 percent for Latinos (National Center for Education Statistics 1993, p. 58).

4. These results refer to a logistic analysis in which the dependent variable was a binary variable representing obtaining a normal high school diploma. The independent variables were age and IQ.

5. For persons ages 25 to 29 in 1992, the proportions with bachelor's degrees were 26.7 percent for whites, 10.6 percent for blacks, and 11.4 percent for Latinos (National Center for Education Statistics 1993, p. 62).

6. Welch 1973.

7. For example, given the mean years of education for people entering the high-IQ occupations defined in Chapter 3 (16.6) and holding age constant at the mean, the probability that whites would be in a high-IQ occupation was 14.4 percent compared to 12.8 percent for blacks and 18.1 percent for Latinos.

8. Gottfredson 1986.

9. Gottfredson 1986 leaves room for the possibility that blacks at the upper end of the IQ distribution were disproportionately choosing medicine, engineering, or the other professions she happened to examine. Perhaps if she had examined other high-IQ occupations (one may hypothesize), she would have found blacks represented at or below expectations. Our analy-

sis, incorporating a broad range of high-IQ occupations, makes this hypothesis highly unlikely. The extension of the analysis in Chapter 20 rules it out altogether.

10. The proportions in high-IQ occupations were 5.8 percent for whites, 3.1 percent for blacks, and 3.7 percent for Latinos.

11. After controlling for IQ, the unrounded proportions in high-IQ occupations were 10.4 percent for whites, 24.5 percent for blacks, and 16.2 percent for Latinos.

12. "Year round" is defined as people who reported being employed for fifty-two weeks in calendar 1989 and reported wage income greater than 0 (excluding a small number who apparently were self-employed and did not pay themselves a wage).

13. This result is based on a regression analysis when the wage is the dependent variable, age is the independent variable, and the analysis is run separately for each race. The figures reported reflect the mean for a black and white of average age in the NLSY sample.

14. For a more detailed technical analysis of the NLSY experience, reaching the same conclusions, see O'Neill 1990. O'Neill's collateral findings about the joint role of education and IQ are taken up in Chapter 19.

15. U.S. Bureau of the Census 1993, Table 29.

16. Precisely, 64.4 percent higher, computed using unrounded poverty rates.

17. For various approaches, see Bianchi and Farley 1980; Jargowsky 1993; Massey and Eggers 1990; Smith and Welch 1987, Eggebeen and Lichter 1991. For a summary of the literature, see Jaynes and Williams 1989.

18. U.S. Department of Labor 1993, Table 3.

19. For civilian males not in school and not prevented from working by health problems.

20. Wilson 1987, Lemann 1991, Holzer 1986; Kasarda 1989; Topel 1993, Jaynes and Williams 1989.

21. The proportions in 1960 were 66 percent (blacks) and 72 percent (whites). Computed from Tables 1 and 16, National Center for Health Statistics 1993, and comparable tables in earlier editions.

22. William Julius Wilson is best known for the lack-of-marriageable-males thesis (Wilson 1987), which is currently thought to have some explanatory power (like IQ) but leaves the bulk of the discrepancy unexplained (as does IQ). See South 1993; Fossett and Kiecolt 1993; Bulcroft and Bulcroft 1993; Schoen and Kleugel 1988; Lichter, LeClere, and McLaughlin 1991. For other empirical work bearing on the thesis, see Bennett, Bloom, and Craig 1989; Tucker and Taylor 1989; South and Lloyd 1992; Spanier and Glick 1980; Staples 1985.

23. National Center for Health Statistics, 1993, Table 26. Figures in the text are for live births.

24. E.g., Anderson 1989; Bumpass and McLanahan 1989; Duncan and Laren 1990; Ellwood and Crane 1990; Furstenberg et al. 1987; Hogan and Kitagawa 1985; Lundberg and Plotnick 1990; Murray 1993; Rowe and Rodgers 1992; Teachman 1985.

25. Computed from Committee on Ways and Means and U.S. House of Representatives 1993, pp. 688, 697; SAUS 1993, Table 23.

26. These figures, already high, are even higher when the analysis is limited to mothers. The percentages of mothers who had ever been on welfare for blacks, Latinos, and whites, were 65.0, 40.5 and 21.8, respectively. We conducted parallel analyses limited to women who had borne a child prior to 1986, giving at least five years' "chance" for a woman to show up on the AFDC roles. This had the predictable effect of slightly increasing the percentages of women who had ever received AFDC, but yielded the same substantive conclusions.

27. Intergenerational transmission has some role. See McLanahan and Bumpass 1988; McLanahan 1988. For other discussions touching on racial differences in welfare recipiency, see An, Haveman, and Wolfe 1990; Bernstam and Swan 1986; Bianchi and Farley 1980; Donnelly and Voydanoff 1991; Duncan and Hoffman 1990; Hirschl and Rank 1991; Hofferth 1984; Hogan, Hao, and Paush 1990; Honig 1974; Hutchens, Jackson, and Schwartz 1987; Smith and Welch 1989; Wiseman 1984, Hoffman 1987; Rank 1988; Zabin et al. 1992.

28. National Center for Health Statistics 1993, Table 26.

29. Based on the Colorado Interuterine Growth Charts.

30. For discussions of reasons for the black-white gap in low-birth-weight babies see David 1990; Kempe et al. 1992; Mangold and Powell-Griner 1991.

31. U.S. Bureau of the Census 1993, Table 3. The Bureau of the Census does not break out "non-Latino whites" in the official statistics. If one assumes that all persons labeled as "Hispanic origin" were white, then 12.9 percent of non-Latino white children were under the poverty line. This is an underestimate for the actual figure, since many persons of Hispanic origin are classified as black. The figure of 14 percent in the text is an estimate that attempts to compensate roughly for the underestimate.

32. The reasons for the gap in black and white child poverty are discussed in the same literature that deals with differences in marriage rates and illegitimacy, which together account for much of the differing financial situations facing black and white mothers of young children.

33. Various approaches to ethnic differences in home environment are Heath 1982; Bardouille-Crema, Black, and Martin1986; Field et al. 1993; Kelley, Power, and Wimbush 1992; McLoyd 1990; Moore 1985; Pearson et al. 1990; Radin 1971; Tolson and Wilson 1990; Wasserman et al. 1990. A useful older account is Davis and Havighurst 1946.

34. See Jones 1992 on abortion, Abramson and Claggett 1991 on voting, and Elliott and Ageton 1980 on delinquency.
35. See the references (note 33) regarding ethnic differences in home environment.
36. Refers to arrests for index crimes in 1992 relative to the size of the black and white populations. Computed from Federal Bureau of Investigation 1993, Table 43, and *SAUS* 1993, Table 22. See also Wilson and Herrnstein 1985, Chap. 18.
37. U.S. Bureau of the Census 1993b, Table 305.
38. R. Gordon 1976, 1987.
39. We cannot use the NLSY self-report data for inter-racial comparisons. Self-report crime measures have consistently revealed marked differences in the willingness of black and white youths to disclose crimes. See Elliott and Ageton 1980; Hindelang 1981; Hindelang, Hirschi, and Weis 1981.
40. See the sixteen studies reviewed in Osborne and McGurk, 1982. See also the results from the Philadelphia delinquency cohort (Wolfgang, Figlio, and Sellin 1972).

Chapter 15

1. We would, of course, need to know something about the fathers' scores too. The more complete account comes later in the chapter.
2. Also see Ghiselin and Scudo 1986; Ingle 1973.
3. Soloway 1982.
4. Francis Galton's coined the term *eugenic*. See Galton 1883.
5. The eugenicists were active, but, as we noted in the Introduction, the intelligence testers were not. For an account of what happened prior to the passage of the xenophobic and nativist Immigration Restriction Act of 1924 and how it has gotten distorted in the retelling, see Snyderman and Herrnstein 1983.
6. "Intrinsic birth rates" are birth rates corrected for age distributions. Death rates also decline during the demographic transition, but they will not be discussed in any detail here. Demographers generally believe that differential death rates cease to be a major factor in population growth in modernized societies like ours. This is a supposition that needs to be reassessed, given the probable differential impact of infant mortalities, homicide rates, and AIDS in relation to tested intelligence. Of all the studies we summarize below, only Retherford and Sewell 1988 takes mortality rates into account, but it did not have a nationally representative sample to analyze. We may surmise that the intergenerational decline in intelligence is being mitigated somewhat by differential intrinsic death rates.
7. Retherford 1986; Retherford and Sewell 1988; Vining 1986; Wrong 1980.

8. Retherford 1986; Retherford and Sewell 1988.
9. Becker 1981.
10. E.g., Retherford and Sewell 1988; Rindfuss, Bumpass, and John 1980.
11. Vining 1982a, Vining 1986.
12. Vining 1986.
13. For a sampling of studies that indicate the importance of attitudinal variables for motherhood in many nations, see Booth and Duvall 1981; Hass 1972; Krishnan 1990; Mason and Palan 1981; Youssef 1978.
14. Estimating the phenotypic, as distinguished from the genotypic, change in intelligence across generations is conceptually little more than a matter of toting up the population yielded across the distribution of intelligence, then aggregating the subtotals to get the overall distribution of scores in the next generation, after first taking account of regression to the mean (Andrews 1990; Falconer 1966; Retherford and Sewell 1988). It is not necessary to include any estimate for the heritability of intelligence. This simplicity in conception should not be confused with simplicity in actually making these calculations. Parents in, say, successive deciles of intelligence may have differing intrinsic rates of population growth (or decline) because of varying lifetime fertilities, varying ages at reproduction, and varying mortality rates. Assortative mating by the parents (see Chapter 4) matters in calculation only insofar as it influences the correlation between parents and children. Hence, if fertility is lower at higher levels of intelligence, then assortative mating for intelligence will speed the decline of the population intelligence because it increases the correlation between parents and children. Some of the studies that we cite focus on the genotypic decline rather than the phenotypic (e.g., Retherford and Sewell 1988). Since children resemble the parents who rear them for environmental reasons as well as genetic, the population phenotype will change more rapidly than the population genotype.
15. The best review of the early studies is Anastasi 1956. See also Duncan 1952; Olneck, Wolfe, and Dean 1980; Retherford and Sewell 1988; Van Court and Bean 1985; Vining 1986.
16. Cattell 1936, Cattell 1937.
17. Retherford and Sewell 1988.
18. Cook, 1951 p. 6.
19. As Osborn and Bajema (1972) stated, "The distribution of births in an industrial welfare-state democracy would become more eugenic as the environment improved with respect to health, educational, and occupational opportunities, and particularly with respect to the spread of birth control to the point where freedom of parenthood became a reality for all citizens" (p. 344). The Eugenic Hypothesis was first stated in Osborn 1940.

20. Maxwell 1954; Scottish Council for Research in Education 1949.
21. Cattell 1951. See also Tuddenham 1948.
22. Higgins, Reed, and Reed 1962.
23. Bajema 1963, 1971; Olneck, Wolfe, and Dean 1980; Waller 1971. In addition, as we explained in Chapter 13, the Flynn Effect would have masked any decline in IQ by demographic processes.
24. Cattell 1974; Osborne 1975.
25. Retherford and Sewell 1988.
26. Vining 1982b.
27. VanCourt and Bean 1985.
28. Retherford and Sewell 1988.
29. Ree and Earles 1991a.
30. The simplest way to get around the estimates that scholars have derived would be to measure the IQs of successive generations, following parents and their children, but surprisingly few studies of any size measure cognitive ability in both parents and children, and those few have always been small studies conducted for specific purposes; none has met the crucial criterion of national representativeness. In the United States, the NLSY has the potential to yield such estimates, if the study continues long enough, because it has already initiated a program of testing the children of the NLSY mothers. As of now, however, it provides no interpretable data about the national population as a whole. The women of the NLSY are only partway through their childbearing years (ages 25 to 33 as of our last observation), and the children of the sample are atypical in that they were disproportionately born to young mothers, who may differ in their child-rearing practices from older mothers. The sample is still missing altogether many of the children of women who delay childbearing, who in turn are disproportionately women with advanced education—and high IQs. We can use the mother-child testing data to extract a few clues about ethnic differences, described later in this chapter.
31. See Chapter 17.
32. Not everyone agrees that it is worrisome. In a recent contribution to the fertility debate, Samuel Preston and Cameron Campbell (1993) challenge the premise that negative differential fertility on the microlevel must mean falling national intelligence on the macrolevel. Such negative differentials are compatible, they argue, with a constant, improving, or deteriorating intelligence distribution in the population as a whole. It all depends on how the current differentials relate to past and future fertility patterns. The argument is densely mathematical, and neither the article nor the two accompanying commentaries lend themselves to easy summary. Interpreting the argument is complicated by the fact that the authors operationalized their model with one of the only data sets in which the fertility differen-

tial is *not* negative. However, the narrowest mathematical implication of their model remains accurate: It is possible to postulate conditions that produce a constant or even rising IQ in the face of negative fertility differentials. There is no reason to suppose that those special conditions prevail now or have in the recent past. James Coleman (1993) similarly points out in his commentary that these hypothetical conditions do not have much to do with what is known about the history of fertility, concluding that "their rejection of the common belief about the effect of fertility differences is not warranted. What they have done is not to answer the questions involved, but to frame the problem in a most useful way" (p. 1032).

33. A population has a limited number of ova and an unlimited number of sperm. Therefore, what matters for replacement (net of migration) is how many females are born and what their fertilities are. Hence, since slightly more than 50 percent of births are males and since a few of the females do not reach the age of reproduction, the average woman needs to have approximately 2.1 births to attain replacement fertility.

34. Sweet and Rindfuss 1983, Fig. 2. Other countries similarly show the impact of education on fertility. A study of Mexican women in which urbanization, occupation, migration, and education were examined for their effects on fertility found that education was the main depressant. See Pick, Butler, and Pavgi 1988.

35. Based on completed fertility for women ages 35 to 44 in the Bureau of the Census's Current Population Survey, a nationally representative sample, in June 1992 (Bachu 1993, Table 2). The mean IQ represents the aggregated means by educational level. This calculation assumes that the mean IQ of women at various educational levels is the same for women born from 1948 to 1957 (the national sample represented in the figure on page 349) as it was for the NLSY women born from 1957 to 1964. Is this plausible? Women born from 1948 to 1957 graduated from high school from 1966 to 1975, after the percentage of students finishing high school had hit its peak, after the major shifts in educational recruitment to college had already changed for whites, and after aggressive affirmative action had begun for blacks and to some extent for Latinos. We can think of no reason to assume that the mean IQ of NLSY women (born from 1957 to 1964) at different levels of educational attainment was systematically different than for the cohort of women born from 1948 to 1957, though it could have been.

36. The data report the education of the mother at the time she has a child, but a very young mother may later go back to finish high school, and a woman with a bachelor's degree may return for a master's or a Ph.D. In ascribing IQs based on educational attainment, it is important to base them on the final attainment, not just on the years of education at the time of

birth. Our procedure for doing so was as follows: Using the NLSY, we first established the difference between education at the time of birth and education as of 1990, when the youngest woman in the NLSY was reaching 26. In the first version of our procedure, it was assumed that the proportion of women who gave birth at ages 26 to 33 (the age range of 98 percent of NLSY women by the 1990 interview) who would subsequently move into a new educational category (the categories were 0–11, 12, 13–15, 16, and 17 or more years of education) was extremely small. We then computed an adjusted version of the table showing births by age by race in National Center for Health Statistics 1993, Table 20, assuming eventual educational attainment equal to that observed in the NLSY (for example, 36.1 percent of NLSY women who had ten years of education when they first gave birth reported twelve years of education by 1990; we recomputed the NCHS cell assuming that 36.1 percent of the women in the NCHS figures who were shown as having ten years of education would eventually get twelve). We then used the adjusted matrix of births by age by race to estimate IQs, using the NLSY mean IQs for women with equivalent years of education. Note that this computation must be done using separate estimates by race, because of the large discrepancy between the IQs of blacks and whites of equivalent years of education. This first iteration yielded an estimated mean IQ of mothers for the 1991 U.S. birth cohort of 97.9. We then repeated the process, using a sample limited to births that occurred by the end of 1986, meaning that each mother had at least four years of postbirth observation to see if she went back to school. This version avoided the assumption that women ages 26 and over seldom go back to school, at the cost of reducing sample sizes and perhaps introducing some unrepresentativeness into the truncated sample. The estimated IQ for the mothers of 1991 U.S. birth cohort using this procedure was 98.0.

37. The actual figure, based on all births through 1990, was 95.7. It is produced by taking the mean (using sample weights as always) of the IQ associated with the mother of each child born to an NLSY mother.

38. Out of every 100 women ages 30 to 34 in 1990, only 2 had their first birth that year; after age 34, the proportion fell rapidly to near zero. See Bachu 1991, Table 4. We realize that many readers know personally of numerous women who had their first babies in their late thirties. It is one more useful example of the difference between the world in which most of our readers live and the rest of the country.

39. Women of the NLSY who had reached ages 32 to 33 may be expected to have borne about 83 percent of all the babies they will ever bear (interpolated from National Center for Health Statistics 1991, Table 2).

40. The biases will understate the age differential by cognitive class because (based on known patterns of childbearing by women of different educa-

tional groups) the largest change in the final mean age of births will occur among the brightest women.

41. Bachu 1993, Table 2.

42. This finding echoes points made in other places. We showed earlier (see Chapter 8) that it is not IQ per se that depresses fertility but the things that a higher IQ results in, such as more education (see Retherford and Sewell 1989; Rindfuss, Morgan, and Spicegood 1980). At given IQ scores, blacks get more schooling than either whites or Latinos (Chapters 13, 18). Hence we should not be surprised that, at given IQ scores, blacks have lower fertility than either of the other groups; they are more likely to be still in school.

43. Rindfuss, Morgan, and Spicegood 1980; Osborne 1973; Chen and Morgan 1991b.

44. Chen and Morgan 1991a; Rindfuss, Morgan, and Spicegood 1988.

45. The quotation is taken from Baker and Mott 1989, p. 24.

46. To mention just one of the most important reasons to hedge, the participation of Latino mothers in the NLSY testing program was comparatively low, making the white-Latino comparison quite tentative. And as we cautioned in Chapter 14, the PPVT is probably less valid for Latinos than for other groups. This may bear on the comparison between Latino-white differences among mothers and among children. In any case, the figure for the apparent dysgenic effect for the Latino-white comparison is small enough to deter strong conclusions.

In contrast, the black-white apparent dysgenic effect is large, and we examined it using several methods to see if it might be spurious. The table on page 356 reports the results using the children's sample weights, and comparing tested children with the mothers of those children, counting a mother more than once if she had more than one child and counting the same child more than once if he or she had been tested in more than one year (after turning 6). If we repeat the same calculation but including all children who were tested (including those under the age of 6), the black-white difference among the mothers is 13.9 points, compared to a difference among the children of 20.0 points, an even larger dysgenic difference than the one produced by the children ages 6 and older. Another approach is to discard the sample weights (which are problematic in several respects, when comparing across test years) and instead restrict the sample to children born to mothers who were in the cross-sectional NLSY sample. Doing so for all children who took the PPVT after the age of 6 produces a B/W difference of 14.8 points for the mothers and 18.1 points for the children, or a dysgenic difference of 3.3 points. Doing so for all children who took the PPVT produces a B/W difference of 14.9 points for the mothers and 19.4 for the children, or a dysgenic difference of 4.5 points.

Our next step was to examine separately the results from the three test years (1986, 1988, and 1990). For the children who were 6 or older when they took the test (which again shows a smaller difference than when the test includes all children), the B/W differences for the three test years, using sample weights, were 5.9, 1.9, and 3.0 points, respectively. The differences across test year did not affect the conclusion that a significant dysgenic effect exists, but the reasons for the differences are worth investigating.

In our attempt to see whether the dysgenic effect could be attenuated, we repeated all of these analyses with one difference: Instead of using the national norms for the PPVT (normed to a mean of 100 and SD of 15), we let the NLSY children be their own reference group, comparing the black and white scores using the observed mean and standard deviation for all NLSY children who took the test. This procedure reduces the estimate of the dysgenic effect. For example, the results, using sample weights, for the children who were 6 and older, showed an increasing B/W gap of 1.9 points instead of the 3.9 points produced by using the national norms. The difficulty in interpreting this finding is that the procedure itself has no good rationale. The PPVT national norms seem to have been properly determined. If anything, the Flynn effect should mean that the NLSY children, taking the test anywhere from seven to eleven years after the norms were established, should have a 2- to 3-point IQ edge when compared to the national norms. So we have no reason to think that the lower estimate is the correct one, but it does represent the best way we could concoct to minimize the B/W dysgenic effect.

Finally, we explored how the births to NLSY women might affect these findings by comparing black and white women who had not borne a child as of 1990. The mean IQ for the childless white women was 106.6, compared to 100.3 for childless black women. That black women without children have a mean of 100 is in itself striking evidence of the low fertility among the top part of the black IQ distribution, but even if subsequent fertility for the two groups is the same, the B/W gap in the next generation will presumably continue to diverge as the NLSY women complete their fertility.

47. *New York Times.* "Slighting words, fighting words." Feb. 13, 1990, p. A24.
48. The computation in the text counts each mother as many times as she had children who were tested. If instead each mother is counted only once, the white-black difference among mothers is 1.12 SDs. The white-Latino difference is 1.05 SDs.
49. Auster 1990; Bouvier 1991; Gould 1981; Simon 1989; Wattenberg 1987; Wattenberg and Zinsmeister 1990.
50. Holden 1988.

51. E.g., Higham 1973; Lukacs 1986.
52. Simon 1989. For a symposium, see Simon et al. 1993.
53. Auster 1990, and various contributors in Simon et al. 1993.
54. Bouvier and Davis 1982. This particular estimate is based on annual immigration of 1 million.
55. The figures for the 1950s, 1960s, and 1970s were 11 percent, 16 percent and 18 percent respectively. *SAUS* 1992, Table 14 (*SAUS* 1971, Table 4).
56. Lynn 1991.
57. *SAUS* 1992, Table 8. The figures also includes once-illegal immigrants who were granted permanent residence under the Immigration Reform and Control Act of 1986.
58. Sowell 1981.
59. A first, elementary consideration is that the NLSY data refer almost exclusively to the children of the adults who decided to immigrate. Whatever self-selection for IQ might have existed in the elders will be less visible in their offspring.
60. Carliner 1980; Chiswick 1978; Gabriel 1991.
61. Borjas 1987. Borjas's formulation also draws on Roy 1951 and Sjaastad 1962. In forthcoming papers, Borjas has since extended his analysis through the 1990 census, showing a continuation of the trends from 1970 to 1980. Borjas 1993, 1994.
62. Borjas 1987, Table 3.
63. Sowell 1981, p. 220.
64. Borjas 1987, Table 3.
65. Borjas 1987, p. 552.
66. The procedure is limited to the NLSY's cross-sectional sample (i.e., omitting the supplemental samples), so that sample weights are no longer an issue. Using random numbers, subjects with IQ scores above 97 had an equal chance of being discarded. Because different subsamples could yield different results, we created two separate samples with a mean of 97 and replicated all of the analyses. The data reported in the table on page 368 represent the average produced by the two replications, compared to the national mean as represented by unweighted calculations using the entire cross-sectional sample.
67. Cattell 1938, as reprinted in Cattell 1983.
68. Cattell 1983, pp. 167, 168.
69. Cattell 1983, pp. 167, 175.
70. Cattell 1983, pp. 167, 169.
71. The procedures parallel those used for the preceding analysis of a mean of 97.
72. In effect, our sample with a mean of 97 shows what happens when people with above-average IQs decrease their fertility, and our sample of 103 shows

what happens when people with below-average IQs decrease theirs. When we changed the NLSY sample so that the mean fell to 97, we used a random variable to delete people with IQs above 97 until the average reached 97. This did not do much to get rid of people who had the problems; most of its effect was to diminish the supply of people without problems. When we changed the NLSY sample so that the mean rose to 103, we were randomly deleting people with IQs below 103. In the course of that random deletion, a significant number of people toward the bottom of the distribution—our Classes IV and V—were deleted. Suppose instead we had lowered the IQ to 97 by randomly *duplicating* subjects with IQs below 97. In that case, we would have been simulating what happens when people with below-average IQs increase their fertility, and the results would have been more closely symmetrical with the effects shown for the 103 sample.

73. These figures continue to be based on the cross-sectional NLSY sample, used throughout this exercise. The 1989 poverty rate for the entire NLSY sample, calculated using sample weights, was 10.9 percent.

Chapter 16

1. A woman was classified as a chronic welfare recipient if she had received welfare for at least five years by the 1990 interview. Women with incomplete data on AFDC in the years following the birth of the first child or whose first child was born after 1985 were not scored on this variable.

2. We do not weight the computations for the overrepresentation of below-average IQ mothers, but we continue to use sample weights.

3. This represents the mean of the mothers of the NLSY children, with each mother counted once for each illegitimate child. Because of the inverse relationship between IQ and the number of illegitimate children, the mean counting each mother of an illegitimate child only once was higher: 89.

4. As in the case of illegitimacy, IQ and the number of children of divorced and separated mothers were inversely related. When the mother is counted only once regardless of the number of children, the mean is 94.

5. See Chapter 10 for a description of this intelligence test (the PPVT).

Chapter 17

1. A brief refresher (see Chapter 4): A heritability of 60 percent (a mid-range estimate) says that 40 percent of the observed variation in intelligence would disappear if a magic wand wiped out the differences in those aspects of the environment that bear on intelligence. Given that variance is the standard deviation squared and that the standard deviation of IQ is 15, this means that 40 percent of 15^2 is due to environmental variation, which is to say that the variance would drop from 225 to 135 and the standard de-

viation would contract to 11.6 instead of 15 if all the environmental sources of variation disappeared.

2. "A healthy mind in a healthy body." Some of the history is recounted in Lynn 1990b. Abstracts of a series of studies by Stephen Schoenthaler and his associates on the effects of diet on intelligence and on antisocial, criminal behavior are in Schoenthaler 1991.

3. Stein et al. 1972.

4. Lynn 1990b.

5. Benton and Roberts 1988.

6. At the age of 12 and 13, youngsters' scores rise during an eight-month period in the natural course of events. The dietary supplement, then, is affecting the rate of increase of the nonverbal, but not the verbal, scores.

7. Schoenthaler et al. 1991.

8. WISC-R. Block Design, a highly g-loaded subtest of WISC-R, showed little or no benefit of the food supplement.

9. Earlier work suggesting that reductions in refined sugar increase intelligence are now being reinterpreted as the effect not of sugar per se but of shifting the diet away from foods with little in the way of vitamins and minerals to more nutritious foods; see Schoenthaler et al. 1991; Schoenthaler Doraz, and Wakefield 1986. The basic point is that we have almost no idea of the pathway between diet or food supplements and intellectual development; assuming there is a path, it could be long and winding.

10. A child taking a pill that gives, say, one RDA is getting more than the recommended daily allowances, since the rest of his diet cannot be utterly devoid of vitamins and minerals.

11. For a failure to confirm an effect of vitamin-mineral supplements, see Crombie et al. 1990, and for a failure to find an effect on intelligence of diet short of chronic malnutrition, see Church and Katigbak 1991. For more general discussion of the issue, see Eysenck 1991; Lynn 1990; Yudkin 1991.

12. Later children are on the average born into larger families, which tend to be of lower average IQ. Hence, there is a decline with successive births that is a by-product of family size in and of itself. However, even after the family size effect is extracted, there may be a decline with birth order. The classic demonstration of declining scores with successive births independent of family size is a study based on a large sample of Dutch men (Belmont and Marolla 1973; Belmont, Stein, and Zybert 1978). Since then, subsequent studies have both confirmed and failed to confirm the basic relationship (e.g., Blake 1989; Retherford and Sewell 1991; Zajonc 1976). At present, there is no resolution of the varying findings.

13. Representative findings, on Japanese twins, are in Takuma 1966, described in Iwawaki and Vernon 1988.

14. For a review of the literature on twin differences in birth weight in relation to IQ as well as of other evidence that the uterine environment affects intelligence, see Storfer 1990.

15. Achenbach et al. 1990. This study compared two dozen low-birth-weight babies whose mothers received training in mothering with comparably small groups of normal-weight babies and low-birth-weight babies whose mothers did not receive the training. The encouraging outcome is that when the children were 7 years old, the usual deficit seems to have been forestalled by having trained the mothers in infant nurturing. However, the small scale of the study, the lack of random assignment to the three groups, and the puzzling near identity in scores for the underweight children whose mothers had been trained and the normal children suggest that the next step should to attempt to replicate the finding, as the authors themselves say.

16. For a helpful and balanced introduction to aptitude-treatment interactions, see Snow 1982.

17. Hativa 1988.

18. Atkinson 1974.

19. Cook et al. 1975.

20. Coleman et al. 1966. The report talked about educational "aptitude," but the measures used—vocabulary scores, reading comprehension, mathematical reasoning tasks, etc.—were taken from standard group tests of IQ.

21. See Mosteller and Moynihan 1972 for a collection of more or less critical articles; included also is Coleman's response to the most intense methodological criticisms (Coleman 1972). The combatants were often trying to answer different questions, with Coleman mostly interested in whether the objective differences among schools were responsible for the observed differences in abilities and his critics more interested in characterizing the objective differences in the schools. We cannot do justice to the range of issues that surfaced in the report and the subsequent commentary, but one of them deserves mention: The report uncovered evidence that the ethnic and socioeconomic mix of students in a school had a larger impact than the more standard investments in per pupil expenditures, teacher salaries, quality of physical plant, and the like. This, in turn, became a major argument for school busing. Soon after, school busing itself became a battleground for social researchers, a tale we will not tell here except to say that having a beneficial effect on intelligence is no longer used as an argument in favor of busing.

22. Coleman and Hoffer 1987.

23. It isn't hard to find what seems to be the opposite conclusion in educational writings (e.g., the Coleman report is "no longer taken seriously," Zigler and Muenchow 1992, p. 62) but no one has been able to show that the variables

examined in the report account for much of the variation in cognitive ability among American public school students. If they are in any sense not taken seriously, it is presumably because educational variables other than the ones that Coleman studied have been found to be significant. This chapter reviews the evidence about those other variables as well.

24. See Kozol 1992 for a passionate argument that disparities in school funding are a major cause of disparities in educational outcomes.

25. Husén and Tuijnman 1991.

26. The quantitative details of the study are not germane to contemporary times, but even then, when schooling varied so broadly, the direct link between IQ at the age of 10 and at 20 was a minimum of five times stronger than that between amount of schooling and IQ at 20, in terms of variance accounted for in a path analysis.

27. Flynn himself does not believe that educational equalization per se accounts for much of the rise in IQ in some countries such as Holland (Flynn 1987a), but then Flynn also does not believe that the rising national averages in IQ really reflect rising intelligence.

28. Stephen Ceci (1991) has summarized evidence, much of it from earlier in the century, for an impact of schooling on intelligence.

29. National Center for Education Statistics 1981, Table 161, 1992, Table 347.

30. McLaughlin 1977, p. 55.

31. McLaughlin 1977, p. 53 The failure of such compensatory efforts antedated the Great Society by many years, however. An early educational researcher writing of similar compensatory efforts in 1938 concluded that "whatever the number of years over which growth was studied; whatever the number of cases in the several groups used for comparisons; whatever the grade groups in which the IQs were obtained; whatever the length of the interval between initial and final testing; in short, whatever the comparison, no significant change in IQs has been found" (Lamson 1938, p. 70).

32. Office of Policy and Planning 1993.

33. For more on this distinction, see Adams 1989; Brown and Campione 1982; Jensen 1993a; Nickerson, Perkins, and Smith 1985.

34. "Chicago educator pushes common sense," *St. Louis Post Dispatch*, Dec. 2, 1990, p. 5D; "Marva Collins still expects, gets much," *St. Petersburg Times*, July 23, 1989, p. 6A; "Pioneering educator does not want post in a Clinton cabinet," *Minneapolis Star Tribune*, Oct. 25, 1992, p. 22A.

35. Spitz 1986. See also "Chicago schools get an education in muckraking," *Chicago Tribune*, May 8, 1989, p. 1C.

36. "Fairfax principal, 4 other educators disciplined in test-coaching," *Washington Post*, Aug. 7, 1987, p. C1.

37. "Pressure for high scores blamed in test cheating," *Los Angeles Times*, Sept. 18, 1988, p. 1.

38. "S.I. principal said to fudge school scores," *New York Times*, July 19, 1991, p. B1.

39. For a sense of the magnitude of the cheating problem, see "Schools for Scandal," *U.S. News & World Report*, April 27, 1992, p. 66.

40. The minister was Luis Alberto Machado, a high official in the ruling party at the time.

41. Based on estimates in the preceding years, the children in the two groups were chosen to be of comparable cognitive ability. For descriptions of the experiment, see Herrnstein et al. 1986; Nickerson 1986.

42. The teachers' manual for most of the lessons, translated into English, is available as Adams 1986.

43. See Brigham 1932 for the relevant background. Briefly, the SAT was originally designed to be an intelligence test targeted for the college-going population and was originally validated against existing intelligence tests. For a modern source showing how carefully the College Board avoids saying the SAT measures intelligence while presenting the evidence that it does, see Donlon 1984.

44. Fallows 1980; Slack and Porter 1980; Messick 1980; DerSimonian and Laird 1983; Dyer 1987; Becker 1990.

45. Messick and Jungeblut 1981.

46. From 1980 to 1992, the SAT-V standard deviation varied from 109 to 112 and the SAT-M standard deviation varied from 117 to 123. For the calculations, we assumed SDs of 110 and 120, respectively.

47. McCall 1979.

48. McCall 1987.

49. Alexander Pope (in his *Moral Essays*) is the poet, and the entire couplet is "'Tis education forms the common mind; / Just as the twig is bent the tree's inclined."

50. See Mastropieri 1987 for a review of the expert consensus on this point.

51. For a sympathetic rendition of the program and its history, see Zigler and Muenchow 1992. For a more critical account, see Spitz 1986. We try to keep our account as close to what these two have in common as we can.

52. "Project Rush-Rush" was what Head Start was called by those in Washington who thought that it was plunging ahead with more speed than deliberation (quoted in Caruso, Taylor, and Detterman 1982, p. 52).

53. Zigler and Muenchow 1992, reporting the conclusions of Leon Eisenberg and C. Keith Connors after the first summer program. Only slightly less grandiose were the claims of raising IQ scores "a point a month" that were often cited by enthusiasts.

54. Sargent Shriver, brother-in-law of the late president, John Kennedy, and former head of the Peace Corps.

55. The first comprehensive evaluation was the so-called Westinghouse study,

which the Office of Economic Opportunity sponsored. Its conclusion was that there were few or no cognitive benefits of Head Start within three years after the child completed it (Cicarelli, Evans, and Schiller 1969). Soon there was a mini-industry picking over the Westinghouse study, in addition to the one picking over Head Start. The consensus is now clear: Cognitive gains vanish before the end of primary school, e.g., Haskins 1989; McKey 1985; Spitz 1986; Zigler and Muenchow 1992. The new consensus has recently surfaced in the popular media (e.g., J. DeParle, "Sharp criticism for Head Start, even by friends," *New York Times*, Mar. 19, 1993, p. A1).

56. For a range of views, see Gamble and Zigler 1989; McKey 1985; Zigler and Muenchow 1992.

57. E.g. Haskins 1989.

58. Zigler and Muenchow 1992. Edward Zigler, one of the early research directors of Head Start and a professor at Yale, argues in his book that it was a mistake from the beginning to promise gains in intelligence to the public. The more general shift away from making increases in IQ the target of preschool programs is discussed in Garber and Hodge 1991; Locurto 1991; Schweinhart and Weikart 1991, pro and con.

59. Among the people promising gains in the 300 percent range is the president of the United States, as reported by Jason DeParle ("Sharp criticism for Head Start, even by friends," *New York Times*, Mar. 19, 1993). Even more of an optimist is economist Alan Blinder, who once promised a return of $4.75 for every dollar spent on preschool education (Blinder 1987).

60. For a review of such benefits from Head Start programs, see Haskins 1989, who concludes that the results "call for humility" (p. 280). The Head Start literature, he says, "will not support the claim that a program of national scope would yield lasting impacts on children's school performance nor substantial returns on the investment of public dollars" (p. 280). In short, there are no sleeper effects from Head Start. Even the evidence of cost-effective returns in the more intensive educational programs is highly restricted. For a literature review, see Barnett and Escobar 1987.

61. Most of the children were 3 years old and spent two years in the program; the 22 percent who were 4 spent only one year in it (Barnett 1985; Berrueta-Clement et al. 1984.

62. Half a school day, or about two and a half hours.

63. The lack of effect was indirectly confirmed in a subsequent study by the same group of workers. They failed to find any differential effect on IQ of three different forms of preschool: their own cognitive enrichment program, a language-enhancing program, and a conventional nursery school program (Weikart et al. 1978). There was no control group in this follow-up, so we cannot say how much, if at all, preschool per se influenced IQ.

64. For a critical reading of just how minimal these other effects of preschool may have been, see Spitz 1986.
65. Lazar and Darlington 1982.
66. Similar estimates can be found in a study of the early effects of Head Start and the consortium sample (Lee et al. 1990).
67. Lazar and Darlington 1982, p. 47 The people who do these studies often argue that other positive effects are not being picked up in the formal measurements (e.g., Ramey, MacPhee, and Yeates 1982).
68. Many publications have flowed from the project; useful summaries are in Ramey 1992; Ramey, MacPhee, and Yeates 1982.
69. Personal communication from Ron Haskins.
70. Ramey 1992.
71. These differences are clearer in the critical accounts of the project in Spitz 1986 and 1992 than in the report by Ramey, MacPhee, and Yeates 1982.
72. Herrnstein 1982; Sommer and Sommer 1983.
73. Page 1972; Page and Grandon 1981.
74. Garber 1988; Garber and Hodge 1991.
75. Jensen 1989; Locurto 1991. The problem of "teaching to the test" recurs in educational interventions. It is based on the test's being less than a perfect measure of intelligence (or g), so that it is possible to change the score without changing the underlying trait (see further discussion in Jensen 1993a).
76. Our topic here is the effect of adoption on raising IQ, not the implications of adoption data for estimating the heritability of IQ. For reviews of the adoption literature, see Herrnstein 1973; Locurto 1990; Munsinger 1975; Plomin and DeFries 1985. A comprehensive theoretical analysis of adoption studies of intelligence is in Turkheimer 1991.
77. Brown 1958, Chap. 5; Lane 1976; Lane and Pillard 1978.
78. Among others inspired by this evidence from "wild children" of the power over the mind of the human environment was an Italian physician trained at the end of the nineteenth century whose approach to education has survived the twentieth, Maria Montessori.
79. Locurto 1990; Plomin and DeFries 1985. In a refinement of this observation, it has been found that adopted children also score lower than the children in other homes that are socioeconomically the same as those of their adoptive parents but have no adopted children (thereby controlling for possible ways in which adoptive parents might be distinctive from nonadoptive parents).
80. Locurto 1990.
81. Dumaret and Stewart 1985; Schiff et al. 1982; Schiff and Lewontin 1986.
82. We will disregard in our analysis a number of considerations that would re-

duce estimates of the impact of home environment, such as that the IQ of the schoolmates of the nonadopted half-siblings (who presumably share comparable lower-class surroundings) averaged only seven points less than the adopted children, not twelve. This difference raises the possibility that the adopted-away child seemed brighter in infancy or had better intellectual prospects than the half-sibling who stayed at home because of the parent they did not share, or that the shift in home environments was even more extreme than the estimates below assume it was, as if the adopted child's biological family home was atypically poor, even for the poor neighborhoods they were in. This, as we explain below, would reduce the overall estimate of the impact of home environment.

83. The cell sizes in the 2 × 2 table of high- and low-SES adopting and biological parent families were only ten children or fewer.

84. Capron and Duyme 1989. This study showed an even larger benefit—equivalent to sixteen IQ points—of having high-SES biological parents, even when the child was not reared by them, which again points to a heritability greater than .5.

85. This, it should be remembered, is for childhood IQ, which is more subject to the influence of home environment than adult IQ. Recent work has also indicated that how a parent treats a child (presumably also an adopted child) is in part determined by the child's inherited characteristics. To that extent, speaking of home environment as if it were purely an environmental source of variation is incorrect (see Plomin and Bergeman 1991).

86. A twenty-point swing is easily reconciled with a heritability of .6 for IQ. Suppose the high- and low-SES homes in the French studies represent the 90th and 10th centile of environmental quality, as the text says. A twenty-point swing in IQ from the 2d to the 98th centile of environmental quality would then imply that the standard deviation of home environment effects on IQ is 4.69. Squared, this means a variance of 22 attributable to home environment. But as we noted in note 1, a heritability of .6 implies that there is a variance of $225 - 135$, or 90, attributable to environmental sources. The French adoption studies, in short, are consistent with the conclusion that about a quarter of environmental variance is the variance across homes (if our guesses about the adopting and biological home environments are not way off). Three-quarters of the environmental influence on intelligence must be uncorrelated with the family SES, according to the present analysis. Note again that the balance tips toward environmental factors outside families as being the more relevant than those provided by families in affecting IQ, as mentioned in Chapter 4.

87. For a discussion of cost-benefit considerations, see Haskins, 1989.

Chapter 18

1. "Sharpen your pencil, and begin now," *Wall Street Journal*, June 9, 1992, p. A16.
2. National Commission on Excellence in Education 1983, p. 5.
3. National Commission on Excellence in Education 1984, p. 58.
4. For an example of an alarmist view and a discussion of the various estimates, see Kozol 1985.
5. National Center for Education Statistics 1992, Table 12-4.
6. *DES* 1992, Table 95.
7. Ravitch and Finn 1987, p. 49.
8. Congressional Budget Office 1987, p. 16.
9. Congressional Budget Office 1987, p. 16.
10. Quoted in Kozol 1985, p. 9.
11. Four of the studies were conducted by the International Association for the Evaluation of Educational Achievement, known as the IEA. They were the First International Mathematics Study (FIMS), mid-1960s; the First International Science Study (FISS), 1966–1973; the Second International Mathematics Study (SIMS), 1981–1982; and the Second International Science Study (SISS), 1981–1982. The fifth study was initiated by the United States as a spin-off from NAEP. It was conducted in 1988 and is known as the First International Assessment of Educational Progress (IAEP-I) (Medrich and Griffith 1992).
12. Medrich and Griffith 1992, Appendix B.
13. National Center for Education Statistics 1992, pp. 208–215.
14. The best single source for understanding complexities of international comparisons is the summary and synthesis produced by National Center for Educational Statistics (Medrich and Griffith 1992). Other basic sources in this literature are Walker 1976; McKnight et al. 1989; Keeves 1991. There are cultural factors too. In his vigorous defense of American education, Gerald Bracey tells of the scene in a Korean classroom during one such international test: "As each Korean student's name was called to come to the testing area, that child stood and exited the classroom to loud applause. What a personal honor to be chosen to perform for the honor of the nation!" American children seldom react that way, Bracey observes (Bracey 1991, p. 113).
15. Bishop 1993b, National Center for Education Statistics 1992a, pp. 60–61.
16. In addition to Bishop 1989, reviewed below, see especially Carlson, Huelskamp, and Woodall 1993; Bracey 1991.
17. Bishop 1989.
18. The Flynn effect refers to gradually rising scores over time on cognitive ability tests, discussed in Chapter 13.

19. NAEP periodically tests representative samples of students at different age levels in mathematics, reading, science, and, more recently, in writing and in history and literature.

20. National Center for Education Statistics, 1991, Fig. 1. The tests were designed to have a mean of 250 and a standard deviation of 50 when taken across all three age groups. The exception to flat trend lines was science performance among 17-year-olds, which shows a fifteen-point decline from 1969 to 1990, somewhat more than .3 SD (we do not know the specific standard deviations for 17-year-olds on the science test; probably it is less than 50). Note also that science among 17-year-olds reflects disproportionately the performance of the above-average students who tend to take high school science—consistent with our broader theme that educational performance deteriorated primarily among the gifted.

21. Two large questions about the table on page 422 immediately present themselves. First, are the five studies accurate representations of the national samples that they purported to select, and are the five tests comparable with each other? The answer to the first half of the question is a qualified yes. The studies were not perfect, but all appear to have been well designed and executed. The qualification is that the data exclude youngsters who did not reach the junior year in high school. The answer to the second half of the question is cloudier, if only because sets of tests administered at different times to different samples always introduce incomparabilities with effects that cannot be assessed precisely. The prudent conclusion regarding the math scores is to discount the modest fall and rise from 1955 to 1983 and assume instead that math aptitude over that period was steady. Regarding the Verbal scores, it seems likely that they rose from 1955 to 1966 and dropped from sometime after 1966 to sometime between 1974 and 1983, with the magnitude and precise timing of those shifts still open to question. Before leaving the norm studies, we must add a proviso: the SAT scales got easier during 1963 to 1973 by about eight to thirteen points on the Verbal and perhaps ten to seventeen points on the Math. They seem to have been stable before and following this period (Modu and Stern 1975, 1977). The same person would, in other words, have earned a higher score on the later SATs than the earlier ones, owing purely to changes in the test scales themselves. Whether the PSAT, a much shorter test, experienced the same degree of drift is unknown, but it is a good idea to adjust mentally the 1974 and 1983 scores downward a bit, though this does not change the overall interpretation of the results.

22. Grades 10 and 11 show a similar pattern. Grade 12 remained slightly under its high (1965–1967) as of 1992, but it is likely that the deficit is explained by increases in the proportion of 17-year-olds retained in school.

The possibility remains open, however, that education in the post-slump period improved more in the lower grades than in the higher ones.

23. Congressional Budget Office 1986.

24. Medrich and Griffith 1992.

25. The College Board added new method of reporting test scores in 1967 based on seniors instead of all tests administered, and continued to report the means for both types of samples through 1977. During the years when both scores were available, the trends were visually almost indistinguishable. In the year when we employed the new measure in the graph on page 425, 1970, the scores for the two methods were identical.

26. Based on the 1963 standard deviations, .49 and .32 SD reductions respectively.

27. For a technical statement of this argument, see Carlson, Huelskamp, and Woodall 1993.

28. Readers can follow the journey through the numbers in Murray and Herrnstein 1992.

29. It is possible that the SAT pool was not getting democratized in the usual socioeconomic sense but was nevertheless beginning to dig deeper into the cognitive distribution. Responses in the SAT student questionnaire indicate that somewhat more students from the bottom of the class were taking the test in 1992 than in 1976, but this effect was extremely small for whites. In 1980, 72.2 percent of whites reported that they were in the top two-fifths of their high school class, compared to 71.5 percent in 1992. We nonetheless explored the possibility that the pool had become cognitively democratized, by looking at the scores of students who reported that they were in the top tenth, the second tenth, and the second fifth of their classes. If their scores went up while those for the entire SAT sample went down, that would be suggestive evidence (if we make certain assumptions about the consistency with which students reported their true class rank) that the pool was drawing from a cognitively broader segment of the population. Using 1980 (the end of the decline) to 1992 as the period of comparison, the Verbal scores of whites who reported they were in the top tenth, 2d tenth, and 2d fifth went up by five, seven, and eight points respectively, while that of the entire white SAT pool remained flat. In Math, the scores of the top tenth, 2d tenth, and 2d fifth went up by nine, thirteen, and fourteen points, respectively, while that of the pool rose by nine points. At first glance, this would seem to be evidence for a strong effect of cognitive democratization. But then we looked at what happened to the scores of white students reporting that they were in the 3d, 4th, and lowest fifths of their classes. Their scores went up by much more: nine, eleven, and ten points, respectively, in the Verbal; seventeen, seventeen, and nine in the Math. We are aware of Simpson's paradox, which shows how scores

in each interval can go up when scores in the aggregated group go down, but in this case the explanation appears to lie in changes either in the way that students report their class rank, the meaning of class rank, or both. We give "cognitive democratization" credit for two points each in the Verbal and Math, but it is not certain that even that much is warranted.

30. For an argument that the test score decline does in fact represent falling intelligence, see Itzkoff 1993.

31. For a broader discussion of falling SAT scores in the high-scoring segment of the pool, see Singal 1991.

32. From 1967, scores were reported for all test takers; from 1972 through 1976, ETS reported scores for all test takers and for college-bound seniors. To estimate college-bound seniors for 1967–1972, we computed the ratio of college-bound seniors to total test takers for the overlapping years of 1972–1976. For Verbal, the mean ratio was .82, with a high of .88 and a low of .77. For Math, the mean ratio was .78, with a high of .85 and a low of .71. The mean ratios were applied to the data from 1967 to 1972 to obtain an estimate of the number of college-bound seniors.

33. ETS keeps careful watch on changes in item difficulty, which are called "scale drift." It finds that scores of 650 and above were little affected by scale drift (Modu and Stern 1975; 1977).

34. The remaining possibility is that the increase in the SAT pool during the 1980s brought students into the pool who could score 700 but had not been taking the test before. This possibility is not subject to examination. It must be set against the evidence that extremely high proportions of the top students have been going to college since the early 1960s and that the best-of-the-best, represented by those who score more than 700 on the SAT, have been avidly seeking, and being sought by, elite colleges since the 1950s, which means that they have been taking the SAT. Note also that the proportion of SAT students who identify themselves as being in the top tenth of their high school class—where 700 scorers are almost certain to be—was virtually unchanged from 1981 to 1992. Finally, if highly talented new students were being drawn from some mysterious source, why did we see no improvement on the SAT-Verbal? It seems unlikely that the increase in the overall proportion of high school students taking the SAT can account for more than a small proportion, if any, of the remarkable improvement in Math scores among the most gifted during the 1980s.

35. Once again, the changes are not caused by changes in the ethnic composition of the pool (for example, by an influx of test takers who do not speak English as their native language). The trendline for whites since 1980 parallels that for the entire test population.

36. National Center for Education Statistics 1992, p. 57. We also examined the SAT achievement test results. They are harder to interpret than the

SATs because the test is regularly rescaled as the population of students taking the test changes. For a description of the equating and rescaling procedures used for the achievement tests, see Donlon 1984, pp. 21–27. The effects of these rescalings, which are too complex to describe here, are substantial. For example the average student who took the Biology achievement test in 1976 had an SAT-Math score that was 71 points above the national mean; by 1992, that gap had increased to 126 points. The same phenomenon has occurred with most of the other achievement tests (Math II, the more advanced of the two math achievement tests, is an exception). Put roughly, the students who take them are increasingly unrepresentative of the college-bound seniors who take the SAT, let alone of the national population. We focused on the students scoring 700 or higher by again assuming that since the 1960s, a very high proportion of the nation's students who could score higher than 700 on any given achievement test took the test. We examined trends on the English Composition, American History, Biology, and Math II tests from three perspectives: the students scoring above 700 as a proportion of (1) all students who took that achievement test; (2) all students who took the SAT; and (3) all 17-year-olds. Method 1 (as a proportion of students taking the achievement test) revealed flat trendlines—not surprisingly, given the nature of the rescaling. Methods 2 and 3 revealed similar patterns. With all the reservations appropriate to this way of examining what has happened, we find that the proportion scoring above 700 on English Composition and Math II mirrored the contrast we showed for Verbal and Math scores on the SAT: a sharp drop in the English Composition in the 1970s, with no recovery in the 1980s; an equally sharp and steep rise in the Math II scores beginning in the 1980s and continuing through the 1992 test. The results for American History and Biology were much flatter. Method 2 showed no consistent trend up or down, and only minor movement in either direction at any time. Method 3 showed similar shallow bowl-shaped curves: reductions during the 1970s, recovery during the 1980s that brought the American History results close to the first year of 1972, and brought Biology to a new high, although one that was only fractionally higher than the 1972 results. This is consistent with a broad theme that the sciences and math improved more in the 1980s than the humanities and social sciences did.

37. Diane Ravitch's account, one of the first, is still the best (Ravitch 1983), with Finn 1991; Sowell 1992; Ravitch 1985; Boyer 1983; and Porter 1990 providing perspectives on different pieces of the puzzle and guidance to the voluminous literature in magazines and journals regarding the educational changes in elementary and secondary schools. For basic texts by advocates of the reforms, see Goodman 1962; Kohl 1967; Silberman 1970; Kozol

1967; Featherstone 1971; Illich 1970; and the one that in some respects started it all, Neill 1960.

38. Fiske 1984; Gionfriddo 1985.

39. Sowell 1992, p. 7.

40. Bishop 1993b.

41. Bejar and Blew 1981; Breland 1976; Etzioni 1975; Walsh 1979.

42. By the early 1980s, when the worst of the educational crisis had already passed, the High School and Beyond survey found that students averaged only three and a half hours per week on homework (Bishop 1993b).

43. *DES* 1992b, Table 132.

44. *DES* 1992b, Table 129. The picture is not unambiguous, however. Measured in "Carnegie units," representing one credit for the completion of a one-hour, one-year course, high school graduates were still getting a smaller proportion of their education from academic units than from vocational or "personal" units (National Center for Education Statistics 1992, p. 69).

45. We do not exempt colleges altogether, but there are far more exceptions to the corruption as we mean it at the university level than at the high school level, in large part because high schools are so much more shaped by a few standardized textbooks.

46. Gionfriddo 1985.

47. Irwin 1992, Table 1. The programs we designated as for the disadvantaged were the Title I basic and concentration grants, Even Start, the programs for migratory children, handicapped children, neglected and delinquent children, the rural technical assistance centers, the state block grants, inexpensive book distribution, the Ellender fellowships, emergency immigrant education, the Title V (drug and alcohol abuse) state grants, national programs, and emergency grants, Title VI (dropout), and bilingual program grants.

48. *DES* 1992b, Table 347.

49. Calvin Lockridge, quoted in "Old debate haunts Banneker's future," *Washington Post*, March 29, 1993, p. A10.

50. Ibid.

51. Bishop 1993b.

52. For a coherent and attractive list of such reforms, see Bishop 1990b.

53. Stevenson et al. 1990.

54. E.g., 63 percent of respondents in a recent poll conducted by Mellman-Lazarus-Lake for the American Association of School Administrators thought that the nation's schools needed "major reform," compared to only 33 percent who thought their neighborhood schools needed major reform. Roper Organization 1993.

55. E.g., Powell, Farrar, and Cohen 1985.

56. Bishop has developed these arguments in several studies: Bishop 1988b, 1990a, 1990b, 1993a, 1993b.

57. Bishop 1993b (p. 20) cites the example of Nationwide Insurance, which in the single year of 1982 sent out over 1,200 requests for high school transcripts and got 93 responses.

58. Bishop 1988a, 1988b, 1990a, 1993a, 1993b.

59. Bishop 1990b.

60. Ibid.

61. The Wonderlic Personnel Test fits this description. For a description, see E. F. Wonderlic & Associates 1983. The value of a high school transcript applies mainly to recent high school graduates who have never held a job, so that employers can get a sense of whether this person is likely to come to work every day, on time. But after the first job, it is the job reference that will count, not what the student did in high school.

62. The purposes of such a program are primarily to put the federal government four-square on the side of academic excellence. It would not appreciably increase the number of high-scoring students going to college. Almost all of them already go. But one positive side effect would be to ease the financial burden on many middle-class and lower-middle-class parents who are too rich to qualify for most scholarships and too poor to send their children to private colleges.

Chapter 19

1. Quotas as such were ruled illegal by the Supreme Court in the famous *Bakke* case.

2. Except as otherwise noted, our account is taken from Maguire, 1992.

3. A. Pierce et al., "Degrees of success," *Washington Post,* May 8, 1991, p. A31.

4. Seven COFHE schools provided data on applicants and admitted students, but not on matriculated students. Those schools were Barnard, Bryn Mawr, Carleton, Mount Holyoke, Pomona, and Smith. The ethnic differences in scores of admitted students for these schools were in the same range as the differences for the schools shown in the figure on page 452. Yale did not supply any data by ethnicity. Data are taken from Consortium on Financing Higher Education 1992, Appendix D.

5. "Best Colleges," *U.S. News & World Report,* Oct. 4, 1993, pp. 107–27.

6. Data for the University of Virginia and University of California at Berkeley are for 1988 and were obtained from Sarich 1990 and L. Feinberg, "Black freshman enrollment rises 46% at U-Va," *Washington Post,* December 26, 1988, p. C1.

7. The figures for standard deviations and percentiles are based on the

COFHE schools, omitting Virginia and Berkeley. The COFHE Redbook provides the SAT scores for the mean, 25th percentile, and 75th percentile by school. We computed the estimated standard deviation for the combined SATs as follows:

Estimated standard deviation for each test (Verbal and Math): given the scores for the mean and any percentile, the corresponding SD is given by $(x-m)/z$, where x is the score for the percentile, m is the mean, and z is the standardized score for that percentile in a normal distribution. Two separate estimates were computed for each school, based on the 25th and 75th percentiles. These two estimates were averaged to reach the estimated standard deviation for each test.

The formula for estimating the standard deviation of combined tests is $\sqrt{\sigma_1^2 + \sigma_2^2 + 2\,r\,\sigma_1\,\sigma_2}$, where r is the correlation between the two tests and σ represents the standard deviation of the two tests. The correlation of the verbal and math SATs as administered to the entire SAT population is .67 (Donlon 1984, p. 55). The correlation for elite schools is much smaller. For purposes of this exercise, we err on the conservative side by continuing to use the correlation of .67. We further err on the safe side by using the standard deviation for the entire student population, which is inflated by the very affirmative action admissions that we are analyzing. If instead we were to use the more appropriate baseline measure, the standard deviation for the white students, the Harvard standard deviation (known from unpublished data provided by the Admissions Office) would be 105 instead of 122. For both reasons, the analysis of the gap between minority and white students in the COFHE data is understated. To give an idea of the magnitude, our procedure underestimated the known black-white gap at Harvard by 14 percent.

8. The Berkeley figure for Latinos is an unweighted average of Chicanos and other Latino means.

9. Scholars who have tried to do work in this area have had a tough time obtaining data, up to and including researchers from the Office for Civil Rights in the Department of Education (Chun and Zalokar 1992, note, p. 108).

10. The Berkeley figure for Latinos is an unweighted average of Chicanos and other Latino means. For Davis, only a Chicano category is broken out. Virginia had no figure for Latino students.

11. Chun and Zalokar 1992.

12. Committee on Minority Affairs 1984, p. 2.

13. Chan and Wang 1991; Hsia 1988; Li 1988; Takagi 1990; Bunzel and Au 1987.

14. K. Gewertz, "Acceptance rate increases to 76% for class of 1996," *Harvard University Gazette*, May 15, 1992, p. 1.

15. F. Butterfield, "Colleges luring black students with incentives," *New York Times*, Feb. 28, 1993, p. 1

16. For Chicano and other Latino students at Berkeley, the comparative position with whites also got worse. SAT scores did not rise significantly for Latino students during the 1978-1988 period, and the net gap increased from 165 to 254 points for the Chicanos and from 117 points to 214 points for other Latinos.

17. Powers 1977, as reported with supplementary analysis in Klitgaard 1985, Table A1.6, p. 205.

18. The 12–15 range cuts off the upper 11.5 percent, 14.9 percent, and 7.5 percent of matriculants with known MCAT scores for the biological sciences, physical sciences, and verbal reasoning tests respectively. By way of comparison, the top 10 percent in the SAT-Math in 1993 was a little above 650; in the SAT-Verbal, in the high 500s.

19. Shea and Fullilove 1985, Table 4, reporting 1979 and 1983 data, indicate that blacks with MCAT scores in the 5–7 range had approximately twice the chance of admission of white students. In another glimpse, a multivariate analysis of applicants to medical school from among the undergraduates at two University of California campuses (Berkeley and Davis) during the last half of the 1970s began with the average white male applicant, who had a 17.8 percent chance of being admitted. Holding other characteristics constant, being black raised the probability of admission to 94.6 percent. Being an American Indian or Chicano raised the probability to 95.0 percent (Olmstead and Sheffrin, 1980a). An Asian with identical age and academic credentials had a 25 percent chance of admission, higher than the white probability but not statistically significantly so. Williams, Cooper, and Lee 1979 present the odds from the opposite perspective: A study of ten medical schools by the Rand Corporation found that a minority student with a 50 percent chance of admission would have had about a 5 percent chance of admission if he were white with the same qualifications.

20. Klitgaard 1985.

21. Proponents of affirmative action commonly cite preference for children of the alumni and students from distant states as a justification for affirmative action. Given the size of the racial discrepancies we have reported, it would be useful to have an open comparison of the discrepancies associated with these other forms of preference. We have found data from only one school, Harvard, where the legacy of having a Harvard parent continues to be a plus in the admissions process but small in terms of test scores. For the decade starting in 1983, the average Verbal score of alumni chil-

dren admitted to Harvard was 674 compared to 687 earned by the admitted children of nonalumni; for Math scores, the comparable scores were 695 versus 718, respectively. Office of Civil Rights 1990.

22. Higham 1984. The arguments against admitting Jews were likely to mention that gentile families might not send their children to a college with "too many" Jews (institutional self-interest) or that anti-Semitism would make it hard for Jewish alumni to use their college education for society's welfare (social utility).

23. Berger 1987.

24. Lloyd 1990; Peller 1991.

25. The formal explication of this standard is Thorndike 1971. For a discussion of how slippery the notion of "acceptable" performance can be, see Brown 1980.

26. The comparisons are based on NLSY subjects who went to the same four-year colleges and universities (again, excluding historically black schools). Excluding junior colleges eliminates problems of interpretation if different proportions of different ethnic groups attended junior colleges rather than four-year institutions. Since the framework for the analysis assumes a multiracial campus, it seemed appropriate to exclude the 103 NLSY subjects (all but 6 of whom were black) who attended historically black institutions. For the record, the mean AFQT score of black students who first attended historically black institutions and blacks who first attended other four-year institutions were within two IQ points of each other.

27. We used the top and bottom half of socioeconomic status rather than a more restrictive definition (such as the top and bottom quartile) to give large enough sample sizes for us to have confidence in the results. When we used the more restrictive definitions, the results showed admissions decisions that were even farther out of line with the rationale, but with small samples numbering just 15 pairs for two of the cells. The procedure for the analysis was as follows: The NLSY includes the FICE (Federal Interagency Committee on Education) code for each institution the NLSY subjects attended. This analysis is based on the first such institution attended after high school. The matching procedure sometimes creates multiple lines for one member of the pair. For example, suppose that three whites and one black have attended the same school. One may either enter the black score three times or eliminate duplicates, entering the black score only once. We consider that the elimination of duplicates is likely to introduce more error, on the assumption that the differences among colleges can be large. Imagine a sample consisting of two schools: an unassuming state teachers' college, with three whites and three blacks in the NLSY sample, and Yale, with three whites and one black. The Yale scores are much higher than the teachers college scores. Eliminating duplicates—entering just one (high)

black score for Yale instead of the same score three times—would defeat the purpose of matching schools. The figures reported in the text are thus based on means that have counted some people more than once but control for institutional effects. The mean used to compute a cell entry is the intercept of a regression in which the dependent variable is IQ score and the independent variables are the institutions, coded as a vector of nominal variables. Note that we also reproduced this analysis eliminating duplicates. The results are so similar that the alternative numbers could be inserted in the text without requiring the change of any of the surrounding discussion.

In addition to this form of the analysis, we examined other ways of cutting off low and high socioeconomic status, ranging from the most general, which divided the deciles into the top and bottom five, to the most extreme, which considered only the top and bottom deciles. For the latter analyses, we used the entire sample of NLSY students who attended four-year institutions, to preserve large enough sample sizes to analyze. Those results were consistent with the ones presented in the text. A positive weight attached to being black until reaching the most extreme comparison, of a white student in the bottom socioeconomic status decile compared to a black student in the top decile, at which point the edge for the black student fell to close to zero (but never actually reached zero). We further examined the results when the sample consisted of NLSY subjects who had received a bachelor's degree (not just attended a four-year college). The pattern was identical for both blacks and Latinos, and even the magnitudes of the differences were similar except that, as in other replications, the gap between the disadvantaged white and disadvantaged black grew substantially over the one reported in the text.

28. The computation, using IQ scores, was (black mean − white mean)/(SD of all whites who attended a four-year institution as their first college). In understanding the way that affirmative action operates, we take it that the reference point is the white student population, which indeed squares with most qualitative discussions of the issue, pro and con.

29. Perhaps "low SES" for blacks meant a much worse background than "low SES" for whites? Not by much; the means for both groups were close (31st percentile for whites, 25th for blacks), and controlling for the difference did not appreciably change the story. Nor did it do any good to try to define "high" and "low" SES more strictly, such as people in the top and bottom quartiles. In that case, the disadvantaged blacks were admitted with even lower lower scores than disadvantaged whites, in the region of 1.5 standard deviations (depending on the specific form of the analysis)—and so on through the cells in the table.

30. We use this indirect measure because other more direct measures (e.g., the number of blacks enrolling in college out of high school, or the number of persons ages 20 to 21 enrolled in school) do not go back to the 1960s and 1950s.

    From 1950–1969, data are available only for "blacks and others." Overlapping data indicate that the figure for "blacks only" in the early 1970s was stable at approximately 95 percent of the "blacks and other" figure. The data for 1950–69 represent the "blacks and other" numbers multiplied by .95. If one assumes that the proportion was somewhat higher in the 1950s and early 1960s, this produces a fractional overestimate of the upward black trendline, but so small as to be visually imperceptible in the graph on page 469.

31. Carter 1991; D'Souza 1991; Sowell 1989; Sowell 1992; Steele 1991.

32. See, for example, Sarich 1990; Lynch 1991.

33. For a review of this literature through the 1970s, see Breland 1979. Research since then has not changed the picture. See also Linn 1983; Donlon 1984, pp. 155–159.

34. As in so many matters involving affirmative action, this indirect reasoning would be unnecessary if colleges and universities were to open their data on grades to researchers.

35. Altbach and Lomotey 1991; Bunzel 1992; D'Souza 1991.

36. E.g., Carter 1991; Steele 1991.

37. National Center for Education Statistics 1992, Tables 170, 249. In the NLSY sample, among all students who first entered a four-year nonblack university, 27 percent of the whites failed to get a bachelor's degree compared to 57 percent of the blacks and 55 percent of Latinos. "Dropout" in the NLSY is defined as having failed to have completed a bachelor's degree by the 1990 interview, despite having once entered a four-year college. By that time, the youngest members of the NLSY were 25 years old.

38. The real discrepancy in dropout rates involved Latinos. Using the same analysis, the probability that a Latino student with an IQ of 110 would get a bachelor's degree was only 49 percent. These results are produced when the analysis is run separately for each race.

39. A. Hu, "Hu's on first," *Asian Week*, May 12, 1989, p. 7; Consortium on Financing Higher Education 1992.

40. A. Hu, "Minorities need more support," *The Tech*, Mar. 17, 1987, p. 1.

41. Carter 1991; Sowell 1992; Steele 1991; D'Souza 1991; Murray 1984.

42. There should probably also be some contraints on the spread of the ability distributions in various groups, but such specificity would be out of place here.

Chapter 20

1. This statement assumes that the violation of the 80 percent rule is statistically significant. With sufficiently small numbers of hirees or promotions, these percentages will fluctuate widely by chance.

2. The Uniform Guidelines are just guidelines, not laws. In one notable 1982 case (*Connecticut* v. *Teal*), the Supreme Court ruled that even the practice of meeting the 80 percent rule by hiring larger numbers of test passers from the protected than from the unprotected groups still falls short if the test produces disparate impact. Disparate impact, in and of itself, said the Court in *Teal*, deprives protected applicants of equal opportunity, even if the disproportionate numbers are corrected at the bottom line. Under this ruling, an employer who hires a given number of blacks will be violating the law if the blacks have high ability test scores, but not violating the law if the same number of blacks are hired without recourse to the scores at all, and thus are bound to have lower scores on average. This eventuality was lauded by Kelman 1991, who argues (p. 1169) that hiring a larger proportion of test-passing blacks than test-failing blacks "stigmatizes" blacks because it implicitly validates a test on which blacks on average score below whites. Better, he suggests, not to test at all, tacitly assuming that the test has no predictive power worth considering. For another view of *Teal*, see Epstein 1992.

3. The Hartigan Report is discussed in Chapter 3.

4. E.g., Kelman 1991.

5. Heckman and Payner 1989, p. 138.

6. The categories are based on those defined by the federal government. The professional-technical category was chosen to represent high-status jobs. The clerical category was chosen both to represent lower-status skilled jobs and also because, among those categories (others are sales workers and the craft workers), clerical is the only category that shows a visibly steeper increase after 1959 than before it. Two technical points about the graph on page 485 are important. First, the job classification system used by the Census Bureau was altered in 1983. Figures for 1983–1990 conform to the classification system in use from 1959–1982. The professional-technical category for 1983–1990 consists of the sum of the headings of "professional specialty," "technical, sales, and administrative support," "accountants and auditors," and "personnel, training, and labor relations specialists." The clerical category consists of the sum of "administrative support, including clerical," and "cashiers." Second, the data in the graph are for blacks only, corrected for the "blacks and others" enumeration that was used until 1973. The correction is based on the known ratio of jobs held by the "others" in "blacks and others" for overlapping data as of 1973. This assumes that the

"others" (mostly Asian) held a constant proportion of clerical and professional jobs held by "blacks and others" from 1959–1973. If in fact the proportion went down (blacks acquired these jobs disproportionately), then the pre-1973 line in the graph slightly underestimates the slope of the black increase. If in fact the proportion went up (the "others" acquired these jobs disproportionately), then the pre-1973 line in the graph slightly overestimates the slope of the black increase. Note, however, that even as of 1973, blacks constituted 87.9 percent of the "black and other" population ages 18 and over, compared to 91.9 percent in 1960, so the degree of error is unlikely to be visually perceptible in the graph. The alternative was to show "blacks and others" consistently from 1959 into the 1990s, but from a technical perspective this becomes increasingly inaccurate as the percentage of "others" increases rapidly in the 1970s and 1980. Visually, graphs prepared under either method show the same story.

7. The main complications are, first, that the affirmative action policies evolved over a period of time, so that the landmark events are not as decisive as they may appear to be (see Appendix 7). Second, laws and regulations often institutionalize changes that were already under way for other reasons. This seems to be clearly the case with the hiring of minorities, and it, too, tends to blunt the impact of the laws and regulations when they come along. Third, different regions of the country probably reacted to the laws and regulations differently, thereby diluting their impact in national statistics.

8. Donohue and Heckman 1991; Epstein 1990; Freeman 1984; Heckman and Payner 1989; Heckman and Verkerke 1990; Leonard 1986; Welch 1981.

9. Brown and Erie, 1981 concluded that about 55 percent of the increase in black managerial, professional, and technical employment from 1960 to 1976 occurred in the public sector.

10. The classic exchange on this topic is Epstein 1992, Chap. 12; Heckman and Payner 1989.

11. The normative 1 standard deviation difference is assumed for this exercise. The observed difference in the NLSY is larger, hence would only exacerbate the conclusion suggested by the graphic on page 485.

12. Obviously, there will be employees who fall outside the range. But insofar as the tails at both ends are small and roughly equivalent, the calculation is not much affected. These particular numbers are based on the observed distribution of NLSY whites in these job categories. For clerical jobs, 90 percent of all white employees had IQs between 85.7 and 122.7, with a standard deviation of 11.3. For professional and technical jobs, 90 percent of all white employees had IQs of 98.0 and above, with a standard deviation of 11.8.

13. The assumptions used for the figure are extremely conservative. Most obviously, the standard deviation of 15 is too high. People within an occupational category will always tend to have a smaller dispersion than the general population. If we change nothing except reduce the standard deviations to 12 for both blacks and whites, in line with the observed standard deviations in the NLSY, the black-white ratios rise from 1.7 (professional-technical) and 1.6 (clerical) to 2.5 and 1.9 respectively. In addition, however, the graph on page 490 is conservative in using an IQ range that encompasses 90 percent of the white workers in an occupational category. The lower the bottom end of the range is, the more it disproportionately inflates the eligible portion of the black population (changes in the top end of the range are at the tail of the distribution and add very little to the eligible pool). Visualize the bell curve: By lowering the bottom cutoff for professional-technical professions from 100 to 98 (for example), everyone in that very fat part of the curve is treated as being just as eligible for a professional-technical occupation as anyone else—even though, in reality, they are much less likely than persons with higher IQs to get such jobs. If, for example, we base the range on the IQs that embrace 80 percent of the white workers in an occupation—more realistic in many respects—the black-white ratio in 1990 grows to 2.3 for professional-technical occupations and 1.8 for clerical. But the conclusions still hold even if we broaden the range still further than in the graph, to embrace 95 percent of all people in those occupations. In that case—which assumes, implausibly, that all people with IQs higher than 89.8 are equally likely to be hired for technical-professional jobs and that all people with IQs between 82.0 and 130.3 are equally likely to be hired for clerical jobs—the black-white ratio as of 1990 is still greater than 1 in both instances: 1.2 for professional-technical, 1.5 for clerical. In short, the differences produced by altering the assumptions can make substantial differences in the size of the estimates of disproportionate hiring, but even assumptions that go well beyond common sense and the available data do not change the overall conclusions drawn in the text.

14. The observations using the CPS and the NLSY are not completely independent, insofar as we took our estimate of the IQ range for clerical and professional-technical occupations from the data on NLSY whites. But those parameters did not constrain the results for blacks.

15. The sample in these analyses excluded persons who were still in school in 1990.

16. Jaynes and Williams 1989, Tables 4-1, 6-1.

17. Hartigan and Wigdor 1989. See also Chapters 3 and 13.

18. As of 1987, states had such a certification process. See Rudner 1988.

19. Straus and Sawyer 1986.

20. Lerner 1991.

21. In Pennsylvania, with the highest pass rates, the state commissioner of higher education openly acknowledged that Pennsylvania sought to avoid lawsuits alleging racial bias in the test by establishing a low cutoff score that they would subsequently try to raise. See H. Collins, "Minority groups are still lagging on teacher's exam," *Philadelphia Inquirer*, Aug. 5, 1989, p. B1.

22. The answer to the question of how such large differences can show up in otherwise credentialed teachers is, in effect, the topic of the preceding chapter, on affirmative action in higher education.

23. If we make the empirically more likely assumption that IQ does have a positive correlation with the nonintellectual skills, then the people with low intellectual skills will, on average, also have depressed nonintellectual job skills.

24. For examples of affirmative action programs in public bureaucracies, see Lynch 1991, pp. 24–32; Taylor 1992, Chaps. 4, 5.

25. Carlson 1993.

26. Carlson 1993, p. 28.

27. Carlson 1993, p. 30.

28. *Washington Post*, October 24–28, 1993.

29. Delattre 1989; Sechrest and Burns 1992.

30. Among the other stories we have located linking poor worker performance to hiring under affirmative action requirements are one reporting an increase in collisions and other accidents on the New York public transportation system (K. Foran, "TA lax on Safety," *Newsday*, Sept. 19, 1990, p. 5), another describing the rise in criminal behavior among Detroit's police officers (E. Salholz, "Going After Detroit's rogue cops," *Newsweek*, Sept. 5, 1988, p. 37), and one discussing the much higher rate of firings among Boston's black postal workers, compared to white workers (B. McAllister, "Researchers say Postal Service tried to block article on firings," *Washington Post*, Oct. 17, 1992, p. A3).

31. Silberberg 1985. See also Ford et al. 1986; Kraiger and Ford 1985.

32. Silberberg has his own interesting hypotheses about these differences, which we do not elaborate here. Nothing in his account is at variance with our conclusion that affirmative action procedures are exacting a cost in worker performance.

33. Hacker 1992, p. 25.

34. In fact, that was precisely the excuse often given by the major leagues for not hiring blacks.

35. For a detailed statement of this perspective, see Kelman 1991.

36. Quoted in Bolick 1988, p. 49. See also Taylor 1992, p. 126.

37. There is a presumption that if we cannot explain a group difference, it is

appropriate to assume that there is no good reason for it. This is bad logic. Not knowing a good reason for a difference is not the same as knowing that there is no good reason.

38. We understand the argument that, in the long term, and taking the broadest possible view, if all businesses were to behave in "socially responsible" ways, there would result a better society that would provide a healthy climate for the businesses themselves. Our argument is somewhat more direct: Can a university president, thinking realistically about the foreseeable future, see that his university will be better qua university by admitting some students who are academically less qualified than their competitors? Generally, yes. Can the owner of a business, thinking realistically about the foreseeable future, see that his business will be better qua business by hiring people who are less productive than their competitors? Generally, no.

39. D. Pitt, "Despite revisions, few blacks passed police sergeant test," *New York Times,* January 13, 1989, p. 1.

40. See Taylor 1992, pp. 129–137, for an account of some of the more egregious examples.

41. The largest difference, 1.6 SDs, was for persons with advanced degrees. For Latinos, the gap with whites ranged from .6 to 1.0 SDs.

42. Other approaches for contending with affirmative action constraints have surfaced. For example, New York's Sanitation Department used a test on which 23,078 applicants out of 24,000 got perfect scores, and its Fire Department used a test with multiple choice questions for which a point of credit was given if the first choice is correct, a half-point if the second choice is correct, or a quarter-point if the third choice is correct, thereby inflating the grades for people who get lots of items wrong (Taylor 1992).

43. Hartigan and Wigdor 1989; Hunter and Hunter 1984.

44. For an account, see Hartigan and Wigdor 1989.

45. E. F. Wonderlic & Associates, 1983, Table 18, p. 25. The scores of Asians are lower than the national mean (in contrast to results of IQ studies) probably because the Wonderlic, a pencil-and-paper test, is language sensitive and is widely used for lower-level jobs. It seems likely that substantial proportions of Asians who take the Wonderlic are recent immigrants for whom English is a second and often newly acquired language.

46. Summarized in Lynch 1991. See also Detlefsen 1991.

Chapter 21

1. Kaus 1992. Kaus's analysis runs parallel with our own in many respects— among other things, in his use of the Herrnstein syllogism (Herrnstein 1971, 1973) to think about the stratifying influence of intelligence.

2. The remark appeared in the manuscript of *The End of Equality*. It is used here with permission of the author.
3. Quoted in Novak 1992, p. 24.
4. Surveys by the Roper Organization (Roper Reports 92–5), as reported in *American Enterprise* (May–June 1993): 86.
5. U.S. Bureau of the Census 1992, Table B-6, 1975.
6. U.S. Bureau of the Census, 1991, Table B-3. All data are based on pretax income, so the tax reforms of the 1980s are not implicated.
7. Reich 1991.
8. Voting estimated from Jennings 1991, Tables 7, 10, 13.
9. Overall, 19.2 percent of children born to NLSY women from the mid-1970s through 1990 were born to unmarried mothers with below-average IQs. The national illegitimacy ratio grew steadily throughout that period.
10. "White" includes births to Caucasian Latinos. The National Center for Health Statistics has provided Latino/non-Latino breakdowns only since 1986. During that period, the non-Latino white illegitimacy ratio increased from 13.2 percent to 18.0 percent in 1991, the latest figures as we write.
11. Data refer to poverty in the year prior to birth, and to non-Latino and Latino whites combined, to be consistent with the use of "white" in this discussion. The proportions for non-Latino white women above and below the poverty line were quite similar, however: 6 percent and 44 percent respectively.
12. Unpublished detailed tables for Bachu 1993, available from the Bureau of the Census.
13. These continue to be figures for Latino and non-Latino whites combined. The figures for non-Latino whites may be found in Chapter 8. They are not so different (because non-Latino whites so dominate the total). Seventy-two percent of illegitimate children of non-Latino white mothers in the NLSY had IQs below 100, and 39 percent had IQs below 90.
14. Wilson 1987. For a complementary view, see Massey and Denton 1993.
15. In the NLSY, blacks from the lowest quartile of socioeconomic background had a mean IQ equivalent of 82.
16. For an early statement of this argument, see Murray 1988a.
17. Jencks and Peterson 1991.
18. Chapter 16 discussed some of these efforts with regard to intelligence. For broader-ranging assessments, see Murray 1984; Stromsdorfer 1987; Rossi 1987; Glazer 1988.

Chapter 22

1. The phrasing draws from Rawls 1971, pp. 14–15.
2. For discussion of this transformation, see, for example, Brown 1988.
3. Thomas Hobbes postulated an axiom—Hobbes saw it as literally an axiom, in the mathematical sense—for governing people with equal rights to liberty: "That a man be willing, when others are so too . . . to lay down this right to all things; and be contented with so much liberty against other men, as he would allow other men against himself." Hobbes 1651, Chap. 14.
4. Hobbes expressed the gloomy prospect of perfect anarchy in the one sentence for which he is best remembered: "And the life of man [would be] solitary, poore, nasty, brutish and short." Hobbes 1651, Chap. 13.
5. Locke 1689, Second Treatise, sec. 4.
6. Locke 1689 Bk. IV, Chap. XX.
7. See, for example, Wills 1978; Beer 1993.
8. Mayo 1942, pp. 77–78.
9. Costopoulos 1990, p. 50.
10. Costopoulos 1990, p. 47.
11. Mayo 1942, p. 78.
12. Costopoulos 1990, p. 47.
13. Quoted in Diamond 1976, p. 16.
14. Costopoulos 1990, p. 48.
15. That fact, combined with the "irresistible corruption" that Adams saw as infecting all political systems, caused him to be deeply pessimistic about the survival of the experiment in human government that he had been so instrumental in founding. He sometimes wondered gloomily whether a hereditary aristocracy on the British model might be necessary to offset the unrestrained avarice and factiousness of Jefferson's natural aristocracy.
16. Aristotle 1905 ed., p. 207.
17. Hamilton et al. 1787, No. 10.
18. White 1958, p. 122.
19. Huber 1988; Olson 1991.
20. Bureau of Labor Statistics 1982, Table C-23, 1989, Table 42.
21. In 1990 dollars in all cases: the annual income of male year-round, full-time nonfarm, non-mine laborers was $16,843 in 1958. (*SAUS* 1970, Table 347). The comparable earnings for "handlers, equipment cleaners, helpers, and laborers" in 1991 was $16,777. U.S. Bureau of the Census, 1992, Table 32. The full-time weekly earnings of "lower-skilled labor" in 1920 was $169 in 1990 dollars, or $8,459 for a fifty-week year (U.S. Bureau of the Census 1975, Series D 765-778).

22. For a full presentation of the following argument, see Murray 1988b, Chap. 12.

23. Wilson 1993.

24. It is doubtless harder even for bright people to lead law-abiding lives when the laws become more complex, but the marginal effects will be smaller on them than on the less bright.

25. Ellwood 1988.

26. For an accessible discussion of the pros and cons of the EITC, see Kosters 1993. A more ambitious approach that we think deserves consideration would replace the entire structure of federal transfers to individuals—income supplements, welfare, in-kind benefits, farm subsidies, and even social security—with a negative income tax of the kind proposed by Milton Friedman in Friedman 1962. Like Friedman, we are attracted to this strategy only if it replaces everything else, a possibility so unlikely that it is hard to talk about seriously. This does not diminish its potential merit.

Appendix 1

1. The figure depicts 250 18-year-old males drawn randomly from the NLSY sample.

2. Based on the NLSY subjects, born from 1957 through 1964, as of 1982, when the youngest was 18 years old, the mean height of contemporary Americans is a little over 5 feet 7 inches, with a standard deviation of about 4 inches.

3. Based on the 1983 ETS norm study (Braun and King 1987) and dropout rates in the 1980s, we estimate the mean for all 18-year-olds (including dropouts) at 325, with an standard deviation of 105. This would indicate that the 99th centile begins at a score of 569. The example in the text is phrased conservatively.

4. The Pearson's r is .501 in both cases. The number 3,068 refers to males with weight and height data in 1982.

5. For simplicity's sake, we are assuming that the variables can have only linear relationships with each other.

Appendix 2

1. The NLSY on CD-ROM disk is available for a nominal fee from the Center for Human Resource Research, Ohio State University.

2. Inquiries should be directed to Prof. Richard J. Herrnstein, Department of Psychology, William James Hall, Harvard University, Cambridge, MA 02138, or to Dr. Charles Murray, American Enterprise Institute, 1150 17th St. NW, Washington, DC 20036.

3. Data for 1991 had become available in time to be used for the analysis, but for budgetary reasons, the NLSY had to cut the supplementary sample of low-income whites as of 1991. We decided that the advantages of including low-income whites in the analysis outweighed the advantages of an additional year of data.

4. We followed the armed forces' convention of limiting subtest scores to a maximum of three standard deviations from the mean. We gratefully acknowledge the assistance of Dr. Malcolm J. Ree, who led the revision of the AFQT, in computing the revised scores for the NLSY.

5. This procedure is facilitated by the large sample sizes (at least 1,265 with valid AFQT scores in each birth year, which are as large as the samples commonly used for national norms in tests such as the WISC and WAIS), and the fact that the NLSY sample was balanced for ethnic group and gender within birth years.

6. We also experimented with groupings based not on the calendar year, but the school year. The differences in centile produced by the two procedures were never as much as two, so we remained with calendar year as the basis.

7. See *Users Guide* 1993, pp. 157–162.

Appendix 3

1. The subtests are General Science (GS), Arithmetic Reasoning (AR), Work Knowledge (WK), Paragraph Comprehension (PC), Numerical Operations (NO), Coding Speed (CS), Auto/Shop Information (AS), Mathematics Knowledge (MK), Mechanical Comprehension (MC), and Electronics Information (EL). Two subtests (Numerical Operations and Coding Speed) are highly speeded; the other eight are "power" rather than speed tests.

2. Ree and Earles 1990a, 1990b, 1991c.

3. We use the term *factor* in a generic sense. Within psychometrics, terms like *factor* and *component* are used selectively, depending on the particular method of analysis used to extract the measures.

4. E.g., Gould 1981.

5. Jensen 1987a, 1987b; Ree and Earles 1991c; Welsh, Watson, and Ree 1990.

6. To account for literally 100 percent of the variance takes ten factors (because there are ten subtests), with the final few of them making increasingly negligible contributions. In the case of ASVAB, the final five factors collectively account for only 10 percent of the total variance in scores.

7. Sperl, Ree and Steuck 1990.

8. Carroll 1988; Jensen 1987a.

9. Ree and Earles, 1990a, 1990b, 1991c.

10. Gordon 1984; Jensen and Figueroa 1975.

11. Note that the General Science subtest and the Electronics Information subtest are as highly g-loaded as the subtests used in the AFQT. Why not use them as well? Because they draw on knowledge that is specific to certain courses that many youths might not have taken, whereas the mathematics and reading subtests require only material that is ordinarily covered in the courses taken by every student who goes to elementary and secondary school. But this is a good illustration of a phenomenon associated with IQ tests: People who acquire knowledge about electronics and science also tend to have high mathematics and verbal ability.

12. Jensen 1980, Table 6.10.

13. Within a single test, the test score might mean any of several percentile scores, depending on the age of the student; hence the reason for using percentiles. For the analyses in the text, scores were used only if both a test score and a percentile were recorded. Anomalous scores were discarded as follows: For the California Test of Mental Maturity, one test score of 700. For the Otis-Lennon Mental Ability Test, eight cases in which the test score was under 30 and the percentile was over 70; one case in which the test score was 176 and the percentile was only 84. For the Henmon-Nelson Test of Mental Maturity, one test score of 374. For the Differential Aptitude Test, sixteen test scores over 100. For the Lorge-Thorndike Intelligence Test and the Kuhlmann-Anderson Intelligence Test, which showed uninterpretable scatter plots of test scores against percentiles, cases were retained if the test score normed according to a mean of 100 and a standard deviation of 15 was within 10 centiles of the reported percentile score. The number of eligible scores on the Stanford-Binet and the Wechsler Intelligence Scale for Children (18 and 16, respectively) was too small to analyze.

14. Jensen 1980, Table 8.5.

15. This list is taken from Jensen 1980, p. 72. Jensen devotes a chapter (Chap. 4) to the distribution of mental ability, which we recommend as an excellent single source for readers who want to pursue this issue.

16. For an exploration of the relationships as of the late 1960s, see Jencks et al. 1972, Appendix B. For separate studies, see Rutter 1985; Hale, Raymond, and Gajar 1982; Wolfe 1982; Schiff and Lewontin, 1986.

17. Husén and Tuijnman, 1991. See also Ceci 1991, for a case that schooling has a greater influence on IQ than has generally been accepted, drawing heavily on data from earlier decades when the natural variation in schooling was large.

Appendix 5

1. Validity is measured by the correlation between predictor and outcome, which, multiplied by the ratio of the standard deviations of the outcome to the predictor, gives the regression coefficient of the outcome on the predictor. To keep this discussion simple, we assume an increasing monotonic relationship between the validity and the regression coefficient here. For a discussion that does not make this simplifying assumption, see Jensen 1980.

2. In the following sources, one can find varying estimates of the magnitude of predictive validity of intelligence tests and varying opinions about whether the tests are a net benefit to society, but they unanimously accept the conclusion that no bias against blacks in educational or occupational prediction has been found: Breland, 1979; Crouse and Trusheim 1988; Hartigan and Wigdor 1989; Hunter and Schmidt 1990; Jensen 1980; Klitgaard 1985; Reynolds and Brown 1984; Schmidt 1988.

3. For a discussion of the sources of error and their relevance to meta-analyses of occupational outcomes in particular, see Hunter and Schmidt 1990. For a more general discussion, including educational outcomes, see Jensen 1980.

4. Jensen 1984b, p. 523.

5. Occasionally, one may find a study that finds differential predictive validity for one ethnic group or another for a particular test—e.g., the K-ABC test for Latinos and non-Latino whites (Valencia and Rankin 1988). But even for Latinos, validity generalization has generally been confirmed (e.g., Reynolds and Gutkin 1980; Valdez and Valdez 1983).

6. Jensen 1980, Table 10.4.

7. Breland 1979, Table 3b.

8. Ibid.

9. Hartigan and Wigdor 1989, Table 9.5.

10. Ibid.

11. The example given here is a special case of a more general phenomenon: As long as the product of the regression coefficient (which is assumed not to differ for the groups) and the mean difference between groups in the predictor is smaller than the mean difference in the outcome, there will be overprediction for the lower-scoring group.

12. For a review of the literature through the early 1980s, see Jensen 1985, also discussed in Chapter 13. For studies since then, see Braden 1989; Jensen 1992, 1993b. The single contrary study extant is Gustafsson 1992.

13. McGurk 1951. Also in 1951, Kenneth Eells's doctoral thesis at the University of Chicago showed that test item difficulty did not vary much across white ethnics of different types, thereby failing to support the intuition

that cultural factors are dominant (Eells et al. 1951). See Jensen 1980, Chap. 11, for more on McGurk's and Eells's work and on other early studies of test item bias.

14. For a review of the literature through the late 1970s, see Jensen 1980, Chap. 11. For studies since 1980, see Bart et al. 1986; Ross-Reynolds and Reschly 1983; Sandoval et al. 1983; Jensen and McGurk 1987; Cook 1987; Koh, Abbatiello, and Mcloughlin 1984; Reschly and Ross-Reynolds 1982; Mishra 1983. All found no item differences, or differences that explained only a fraction of the differences in group scores. Are there any exceptions? We identified one such study for blacks (Montie and Fagan 1988), based on 3-year-olds. There may very well be other studies of similar size (the sample in Montie and Fagan was 86) that are lurking in the literature, but we know of no studies using large-scale representative samples that establish item bias against blacks. Some studies of Latinos have found evidence of bias, mostly associated with Spanish and English language characteristics. See Valencia and Rankin 1988; Whitworth and Chrisman 1987, Munford and Munoz 1980. But the factor structure of the test results has generally been found to be the same for Latino and non-Latinos (e.g., see Mishra 1981).

15. See Jensen 1980, Table 11.12. Also see Miele 1979.

16. Scheuneman 1987.

17. For a literature review, see Jensen 1980, Chap. 12.

18. Dyer 1970.

19. For studies specifically dealing with differential racial effects of coaching and practice through the late 1970s, see Baughman and Dahlstrom 1968; Costello 1970; Dubin, Osburn, and Winick 1969; Jensen 1980. For studies bearing on the issue since 1980 (but not addressing it as directly as the earlier ones), see Powers 1987; Terrell and Terrell 1983; Johnson and Wallace 1989; Cole 1987.

20. For literature reviews, see Sattler and Gwynne 1982; Jensen 1980.

21. For a literature review, see Jensen 1980, Chap. 12.

22. For a literature review, see Jensen 1980, Chap. 12.

23. Jensen 1980, Chap. 12. See also note 14 regarding item bias for Latinos.

24. Jensen 1980, Chap. 12.

25. Quay 1971, 1972, 1974.

26. Farrell 1983 and the attached responses.

27. Johnson et al. 1984; Frederiksen 1986; Johnson 1988; Kerr et al. 1986; Madhere 1989; Scheuneman 1987; White et al. 1988

28. Rock et al. 1985 details the changes between the two administrations, concluding that "the cautious position would be that neither administration had an advantage. A less cautious conclusion is that the 1980 subjects probably had some small advantage" (p. 18).

29. Based on the white standard deviation for 1980, the first year that standard deviations by race were published.
30. Congressional Budget Office, 1986, Fig. E-3.
31. Contrary to popular belief, on the proposition whether brain size is correlated with IQ, the evidence strongly favors the pros over the cons, even after correcting for stature. A sampling of contemporary positions in this mini-controversy is Cain and Vanderwolf 1990; Gould 1978, 1981; Lynn 1989; Michael 1988; Passingham 1982; Rushton 1990d, in press; Valen 1974. Brain size is, however, not necessarily wholly determined by the genes; it could also be associated with nutrition or general health.
32. The Rushton controversy has unfolded in a rapidly expanding scholarly literature. Some of the papers, pro and con, are Cain and Vanderwolf 1990; Lynn 1989b; Roberts and Gabor 1990; Rushton 1985, 1987, 1988, 1990a, 1990b, 1990c, 1990d, 1991a, 1991b; Rushton and Bogaert, 1978, 1988; Silverman 1990; Weitzmann et al. 1990; Zuckerman and Brody 1988. For further substantiation of some of the race differences that Rushton invokes, see Ellis and Nyborg 1992; Lynn 1990c; Mangold and Powell-Griner 1991; Rowe, Rodgers, and Meseck-Bushey 1988; Valen 1974.
33. Almost as all encompassing a thesis as Rushton's is Richard Lynn's account of the evolution of racial differences in intelligence in terms of the ancestral migrations of groups of early hominids from the relatively benign environments of Africa to the harsher and more demanding Eurasian latitudes (Lynn 1991c), where they branched into the Caucasoids and Mongoloids. Such theories were not uncommon among anthropologists and biologists of a generation or two ago (e.g., Darlington 1969). As the biological outlook on human behavior became controversial, this kind of theorizing has almost vanished. The modern version relies much more on psychological measurements of contemporary populations than the earlier version.

Appendix 7

1. For a comprehensive discussion, see Epstein 1992.
2. Any one of these court cases may involve heroic efforts: "Some courts have expressed concern at the spectacle of trials lasting for weeks, following years of discovery, and involving a multitude of statistical and other experts and seemingly endless testimony about the credentials of a single [job] candidate." Bartholet 1982, p. 1002.
3. Quoted in Patterson 1989, p. 87.
4. Patterson 1989.
5. Patterson 1989.
6. 401 U. S. 424 (1971).

7. Lynch 1991; Murray 1984; Patterson 1989.

8. For a clear account, see Patterson 1989.

9. 401 U.S. 432.

10. Ibid.

11. There is good evidence that the Duke Power Co. had no discriminatory intent in using the test or the educational credential; it was using the same criteria at a time when it was frankly pursuing a race-segregationist hiring policy. This earlier conduct gives credence to its claim that it wanted to improve its employees' intellectual level.

12. Some legal scholars criticize the Court for not having interpreted the Constitution itself, in the Fourteenth Amendment, as providing protection against disparate impact (e.g., Tribe 1988).

13. Ironically, the particular wording in the relevant part of Title VII was an accommodation to one of the act's most uneasy opponents, Senator John Tower of Texas, who was concerned that the law not be used in precisely the manner that, in Griggs, the court ruled that it should be used (Wilson 1972).

14. For an excellent discussion, see Epstein 1992, whose reading of the record strongly confirms ours. Epstein makes the point that had the Congress known in 1964 what interpretation the Court was to place on Title VII in Griggs, it "would have gone down to thundering defeat" (p. 197). From the legislative record, that appears to us to be a fair assessment.

15. Quoted in Wilson 1972, pp. 854ff.

16. Quotes attributed to S. Rep. 92-415, 92d Cong., 1st sess. 5 (1971), the report of the Senate Committee on Labor and Public Welfare, in Patterson 1989.

17. Wilson 1972.

18. Bartholet 1982, p. 958.

19. 422 U.S. 405 (1975).

20. Our discussion here has drawn on Braun 1992.

21. Courts other than the Supreme Court have imposed on the employer itself the burden of seeking less discriminatory alternatives (Patterson, 1989).

22. For references to the relevant government documents, see Patterson 1989.

23. For a similar conclusion, and some detail to back it up, see Potter 1986.

24. 490 U.S. 642 (1989).

25. 490 U.S. 659.

26. Cathcart and Snyderman 1992.

Bibliography

Abrahamse, A. F., Morrison, P. A., and Waite, L. J. 1988. *Beyond Stereotypes: Who Becomes a Single Teenage Mother?* R-3489–HHS/NICHD. Santa Monica, Cal.: Rand Corporation.

Abramson, P. R., and Claggett, W. 1991. Racial differences in self-reported and validated turnout in the 1988 presidential election. *J. of Politics* 53:186–197.

Achenbach, T. M., Phares, V., Howell, C. T., and Rauh, V. A. 1990. Seven-year outcome of the Vermont Intervention Program for low-birthweight infants. *Child Development* 61:1672–1681.

Ackerman, P. L. 1987. Individual differences in skill learning: An integration of psychometric and information processing perspectives. *Psychological Bull.* 102:3–27.

Adams, M. J. 1986. *Odyssey: A Curriculum for Thinking.* Watertown, Mass.: Mastery Education Corporation.

Adams, M. J. 1989. Thinking skills curricula: Their promise and progress. *Educational Psychologist* 24:25–77.

Ahern, F. M., Johnson, R. C., and Cole, R. E. 1983. Generational differences in spouse similarity in educational attainment. *Behavior Genetics* 13:95–98.

Alderman, D. L., and Powers, D. E. 1979. *The Effects of Special Preparation on SAT-Verbal Scores.* Princeton, N.J.: Educational Testing Service.

Alexander, K. L., Natriello, G., and Pallas, A. M. 1985. For whom the school bell tolls: The impact of dropping out on cognitive performance. *Am. Sociological Rev.* 50:409–420.

Altbach, P. G., and Lomotey, K. (eds.). 1991. *The Racial Crisis in American Higher Education.* Albany: State University of New York Press.

An, C.-B., Haveman, R., and Wolfe, B. 1990. Teen out-of-wedlock births and welfare receipt: The role of childhood events and economic circumstances. *Rev. of Economics and Statistics* 75:195–208.

Anastasi, A. 1956. Intelligence and family size. *Psychological Bull.* 53:187–209.

Anderson, E. 1989. Sex codes and family life among poor inner-city youths. *Annals of the Am. Academy of Political and Social Science* 501:59–78.

Anderson, J. E. 1936. *The Young Child in the Home.* White House Conference on Child Health and Protection. Washington, D.C.: Government Printing Office.

Andrews, W. J. 1990. Eugenics revisited. *Mankind Quarterly* 30:235–302.

Angoff, W. H., and Ford, S. F. 1973. Item-race interaction on a test of scholastic aptitude. *J. of Educational Measurement* 10:95–106.

Angrist, J. D., and Krueger, A. B. 1991a. Does compulsory school attendance affect schooling and earnings? *Quarterly J. of Economics* 106:979–1014.

Angrist, J. D., and Krueger, A. B. 1991b. *Estimating the Payoff to Schooling Using the Vietnam-Era Draft Lottery.* Industrial Relations Section, Working Paper 290. Princeton, N.J.: Princeton University.

Aristotle. *Politics.* Translated by Benjamin Jowett. 1905 ed. Oxford: Clarendon Press.

Arrow, K. 1973. Higher education as a filter. *J. of Public Economics* 2:193–216.

Atkinson, A. B., Maynard, A. K., and Trinder, C. G. 1983. *Parents and Children: Incomes in Two Generations.* London: Heinemann.

Atkinson, R. C. 1974. Teaching children to read using a computer. *Am. Psychologist* 29:169–178.

Auster, L. 1990. *The Path to National Suicide: An Essay on Immigration and Multiculturalism.* Monterey, Va.: American Immigration Control Foundation.

Azar, S. T., Robinson, D. R., Hekiman, E., and Twentyman, C. T. 1984. Unrealistic expectations and problem-solving ability in maltreating and comparison mothers. *J. of Consulting and Clinical Psych.* 52:687–691.

Bachman, J. G. III, Green, S., and Wirtanen, I. D. 1971. *Dropping Out—Problem or Symptom?* Youth in Transition, vol. 3. Ann Arbor, Mich.: Institute for Social Research.

Bachu, A. 1991. *Fertility of American Women: June 1990.* U.S. Bureau of the Census. Current Population Report Series P-20, No. 454. Washington, D.C.: Government Printing Office.

Bachu, A. 1993. *Fertility of American Women: June 1992.* U.S. Bureau of the Census. Current Population Report Series P-20, No. 470. Washington, D.C.: Government Printing Office.

Bajema, C. J. 1963. Estimation of the direction and intensity of natural selection in relation to human intelligence by means of the intrinsic rate of natural increase. *Eugenics Quarterly* 10:175–187.

Bajema, C. J. 1971. Natural selection and intelligence: The relationship between intelligence and completed fertility among Third Harvard Growth Study participants. *Am. J. of Physical Anthropology* 31:273.

Baker, P. C., and Mott, F. L. 1989. *NLSY Child Handbook 1989.* Columbus, Ohio: Center for Human Resource Research.

Baldwin, J. A., and Oliver, J. E. 1975. Epidemiology and family characteristics of severely abused children. *British J. of Preventive Social Medicine* 29:205–221.

Bangert-Drowns, R. L. 1986. Review of developments in meta-analytic method. *Psychological Bull.* 99:388–399.

Bank, L., Forgatch, M. S., Patterson, G. R., and Fetrow, R. A. 1993. Parenting practices of single mothers: Mediators of negative contextual factors. *J. of Marriage and the Family* 55:371–384.

Bardis, P. D. 1985. Jensen, Spearman's g, and Ghazali's dates: A comment on interracial peace. *Behavioral and Brain Sciences* 8:219–220.

Bardouille-Crema, A., Black, K. B., and Martin, H. P. 1986. Performance on Piagetian tasks of black children of differing socioeconomic levels. *Developmental Psych.* 22:841–44.

Barnes, B. J., and Carr, R. A. 1993. *1991–92 National Decision Profiles.* Newtown, Pa.: Law School Admission Services.

Barnes, V., Potter, E. H., and Fiedler, F. E. 1983. Effect of interpersonal stress on the prediction of academic performance. *J. of Applied Psych.* 68:686–697.

Barnett, W. S. 1985. *The Perry Preschool Program and Its Long-Term Effects: A Benefit-Cost Analysis.* Ypsilanti, Mich.: High/Scope Educational Research Foundation.

Barnett, W. S., and Escobar, C. M. 1987. The economics of early educational intervention: A review. *Rev. of Educational Research* 57:387–414.

Baron, J. 1985. Reliability and g. *Behavioral and Brain Sciences* 8:220–221.

Barrett, P., Eysenck, H. J., and Lucking, S. 1986. Reaction time and intelligence: A replicated study. *Intelligence* 10:9–40.

Barro, S. M., and Kolstad, A. 1987. *Who Drops Out of High School?* Washington, D.C.: Center for Education Statistics, U.S. Department of Education.

Bart, W., et al. 1986. An ordering-analytic approach to the study of group differences in intelligence. *Educational and Psychological Measurement* 46:799–810.

Bartholet, E. 1982. Application of Title VII to jobs in high places. *Harvard Law Rev.* 95:945–1027.

Baughman, E. E., and Dahlstrom, W. G. 1968. *Negro and White Children: A Psychological Study in the Rural South.* New York: Academic Press.

Beck, A. J., and Shipley, B. E. 1989. *Recidivism of Prisoners Released in 1983.* Bureau of Justice Statistics Special Report NCJ-116261. Washington, D.C.: U.S. Department of Justice.

Becker, B. E., and Huselid, M. A. 1992. Direct estimates of SD_y and the implications for utility analysis. *J. of Applied Psych.* 77:227–233.

Becker, B. J. 1990. Coaching for the Scholastic Aptitude Test: Further synthesis and appraisal. *Rev. of Educational Research* 60:373–417.

Becker, G. S. 1981. *A Treatise on the Family.* Cambridge, Mass.: Harvard University Press.

Beer, S. H. 1993. *To Make a Nation: The Rediscovery of American Federalism.* Cambridge, Mass.: Harvard University Press.

Bejar, I. I., and Blew, E. O. 1981. Grade inflation and the validity of the Scholastic Aptitude Test. *Am. Educational Research Journal* 18:143.

Belmont, L., and Marolla, F. A. 1973. Birth order, family size, and intelligence. *Science* 182:1096–1101.

Belmont, L., Stein, Z., and Zybert, P. 1978. Child spacing and birth order: Effect on intellectual ability in two-child families. *Science* 202:995–996.

Bender, W. J. 1960. *Final Report of W. J. Bender, Chairman of the Admission and Scholarship Committee and Dean of Admissions and Financial Aids, 1952–1960.* Cambridge, Mass.: Harvard University.

Bendick, M. J., and Cantu, M. G. 1978. The literacy of welfare clients. *Social Science Rev.* 52:56–68.

Bendix, R. 1949. *Higher Civil Servants in American Society: A Study of the Social Origins, the Careers, and the Power-Position of Higher Federal Administrators.* Westport, Conn.: Greenwood Press.

Bennett, N. G., Bloom, D. E., and Craig, P. H. 1989. The divergence of black and white marriage patterns. *Am. J. of Sociology* 95:692–722.

Bennie, E. H. 1969. The battered child syndrome. *Am. J. of Psychiatry* 125:975–979.

Benton, D., and Roberts, G. 1988. Effect of vitamin and mineral supplementation on intelligence of a sample of schoolchildren. *Lancet* 1:140–144.

Berger, A. M. 1980. The child abusing family: II. Child and child-rearing variables, environmental factors and typologies of abusing families. *Am. J. of Family Therapy* 8:52–68.

Bernal, E. M. 1984a. Bias in mental testing: Evidence for an alternative to the heredity-environment controversy. In *Perspectives on "Bias in Mental Testing."* C. R. Reynolds and R. T. Brown (eds.). New York: Plenum Press, pp. 171–187.

Bernal, E. M. 1984b. Postscript: Bernal replies. In *Perspectives on "Bias in Mental Testing."* C. R. Reynolds and R. T. Brown (eds.). New York: Plenum Press, pp. 587–593.

Bernstam, M. S., and Swan, P. L. 1986. *The State as Marriage Partner of Last Resort: A Labor Market Approach to Illegitimacy in the United States, 1960–1980.* University of New South Wales, Australia. Photocopy.

Berrueta-Clement, J. R., Schweinhart, L. J., Barnett, W. S., Epstein, A. S., and Weikart, D. P. 1984. *Changed Lives: The Effects of the Perry Preschool Program through Age 19.* Ypsilanti, Mich.: High/Scope Educational Research Foundation.

Bianchi, S. M., and Farley, R. 1979. Racial differences in family living arrangements and economic well-being: An analysis of recent trends. *J. of Marriage and the Family* 41:537–551.

Bingham, W. V. D. 1937. *Aptitudes and Aptitude Testing.* New York: Harper & Bros.

Bishop, J. H. 1988a. Employment testing and incentives to learn. *J. of Vocational Behavior* 33:404–423.

Bishop, J. H. 1988b. The skills shortage and the payoff to vocational education. Working Paper 90–08. Ithaca, N.Y.: Center for Advanced Human Resource Studies, Cornell University.

Bishop, J. H. 1989. Is the test score decline responsible for the productivity growth decline? *Am. Econ. Rev.* 79:178–194.

Bishop, J. H. 1990a. The productivity consequences of what is learned in high school. *J. of Curriculum Studies* 22:101–126.

Bishop, J. H. 1990b. What's wrong with American secondary schools: Can state governments fix it? Working Paper 90–17. Ithaca, N.Y.: Center for Advanced Human Resource Studies, Cornell University.

Bishop, J. H. 1993a. Educational reform and technical education. Working Paper 93–04. Ithaca, N.Y.: Center for Advanced Human Resource Studies, Cornell University.

Bishop, J. H. 1993b. Incentives to study and the organization of secondary instruction. Working Paper 93–08. Ithaca, N.Y.: Center for Advanced Human Resource Studies, Cornell University.

Blackburn, M. L., Bloom, D. E., and Freeman, R. B. 1990. The declining economic position of less skilled men. In *A Future of Lousy Jobs? The Changing Structure of U.S. Wages.* G. Burtless (ed.). Washington, D.C.: Brookings Institution, pp. 31–76.

Blackburn, M., and Neumark, D. 1991a. *Unobserved Ability, Efficiency Wages, and Interindustry Wage Differentials.* Cambridge, Mass.: National Bureau of Economic Research.

Blackburn, M. L., and Neumark, D. 1991b. Omitted-ability bias and the increase in the return to schooling. *J. of Labor Economics* 11:521–544.

Blake, J. 1989. *Family Size and Achievement.* Berkeley, Cal.: University of California Press.

Blankenship, A. B., and Taylor, H. R. 1938. Prediction of vocational proficiency in three machine operations. *J. of Applied Psych.* 22:518–526.

Blinder, A. S. 1987. Improving the chances of our weakest underdogs—poor children. *Business Week*, December 14, p. 20.

Block, N. J., and Dworkin, G. 1974. IQ: Heritability and Inequality, Part I. *Philosophy and Public Affairs* 3:331–409.

Bloom, B. S. 1964. *Stability and Change in Human Characteristics.* New York: Wiley.

Bluestone, B., and Harrison, B. 1988. The growth of low-wage employment: 1963–86. *AEA Papers and Proceedings* 78:124–128.

Blumstein, A., Farrington, D. P., and Moitra, S. 1985. Delinquency careers: Innocents, desisters, and persisters. In *Crime and Justice: An Annual Review of Research.* Vol. 6. M. Tonry and N. Morris (eds.). Chicago: University of Chicago Press, pp. 187–219.

Bock, R. D., and Moore, E. G. J. 1986. *Advantage and Disadvantage: A Profile of American Youth.* Hillsdale, N.J.: Lawrence Erlbaum Associates.

Boissiere, M., Knight, J. B., and Sabot, R. H. 1985. Earnings, schooling, ability, and cognitive skills. *Am. Econ. Rev.* 75:1016–1029.

Bok, D. 1985a. Admitting success. *New Republic*, February 4, pp. 14–16.

Bok, D. 1985b. A view from the top: An interview with Derek Bok. *Harvard Political Rev.* (Spring): 9.

Bolick, C. 1988. *Changing Course: Civil Rights at the Crossroads.* New Brunswick, N.J.: Transaction Books.

Booth, A., and Duvall, D. 1981. Sex roles and the link between fertility and employment. *Sex Roles* 7:847–856.

Borjas, G. J. 1987. Self-selection and the earnings of immigrants. *Am. Econ. Rev.* 77:531–553.

Borjas, G. J. 1993. Immigration and welfare, 1970–1990. University of San Diego. Photocopy.

Borjas, G. J. 1994. Assimilation and changes in cohort quality revisited: What happened to immigrant earnings in the 1980s? University of San Diego. Photocopy

Borkowski, J. G., and Maxwell, S. E. 1985. Looking for Mr. Good-*g*: General intelligence and processing speed. *Behavioral and Brain Sciences* 8:221–222.

Bouchard, T. J., Jr. 1981. Familial studies of intelligence: A review. *Science.* 212:1055–1059.

Bouchard, T. J., Jr., Lykken, D. T., McGue, M., Segal, N. L., and Tellegen, A. 1990. Sources of human psychological differences: The Minnesota study of twins reared apart. *Science* 250:223–228.

Bousha, D. M., and Twentyman, C. T. 1984. Mother-child interactional style in abuse, neglect, and control groups: Naturalistic observations in the home. *J. of Abnormal Psych.* 93:106–114.

Bouvier, L. F., and Davis, C. B. 1982. *Immigration and the Future Racial Composition of the United States.* Alexandria, Va.: Center for Immigration Research and Education.

Bouvier, L. J. 1991. *Fifty Million Californians.* Washington, D.C.: Center for Immigration Studies.

Bowles, S., and Gintis, H. 1976. *Schooling in Capitalist America: Educational Reform and the Contradictions of Economic Life.* New York: Basic Books.

Boyer, E. L. 1983. *High School: A Report on Secondary Education in America.* New York: Harper & Row.

Boykin, A. W. 1986. The triple quandary and the schooling of Afro-American children. In *The School Achievement of Minority Children.* U. Neisser (ed.). Hillsdale, N.J.: Lawrence Erlbaum Associates, pp. 57–92.

Bracey, G. W. 1991. The big lie about U.S. education. *Phi Delta Kappan* (October): 105–117.

Braden, J. P. 1989. Fact or artifact? An empirical test of Spearman's hypothesis. *Intelligence* 13:149–155.

Bradley, R. H., et al. 1977. Home environment, social status, and mental test performance. *J. of Educational Psych.* 69:697–701.

Brandt, E. A. 1984. The cognitive functioning of American Indian children: A critique of McShane and Plas. *School Psych. Rev.* 13:74–82.

Braun, H. I., Centra, J., and King, B. F. 1987. *Verbal and Mathematical Ability of High School Juniors and Seniors in 1983: A Norm Study of the PSAT/NMSQT and the SAT*. Princeton, N.J.: Educational Testing Service.

Braun, L. W. 1992. *Psychologists v. the law: The debate over employment testing*. Third-year paper. Harvard Law School.

Brayden, R. M., Altemeier, W. A., Tucker, D. D., Dietrich, M. S., and Vietze, P. 1992. Antecedents of child neglect in the first two years of life. *J. of Pediatrics* 120:426–429.

Breland, H. M. 1976. *Grade Inflation and Declining SAT Scores: A Research Viewpoint*. Princeton, N.J.: Educational Testing Service.

Breland, H. M. 1979. *Population Validity and College Entrance Measures*. New York: College Board.

Brigham, C. C. 1923. *A Study of American Intelligence*. Princeton, N.J.: Princeton University Press.

Brigham, C. C. 1932. *A Study of Error: A Summary and Evaluation of Methods Used in Six Years of Study of the Scholastic Aptitude Test of the College Entrance Examination Board*. New York: College Entrance Examination Board.

Brodnick, R. J., and Ree, M. J. 1993. A structural model of academic performance, socioeconomic status, and Spearman's g. San Antonio: St. Mary's University of Texas. Photocopy.

Brody, N. 1987. Jensen, Gottfredson, and the black-white difference in intelligence test scores. *Behavioral and Brain Sciences* 10:507–508.

Brody, N. 1992. *Intelligence*. 2d ed., San Diego: Academic Press.

Brogden, H. E. 1949. When testing pays off. *Personnel Psych.* 2:171–183.

Bronfenbrenner, U. 1958. Socialization and social class through time and space. In *Readings in Social Psychology*. Eleanor E. Maccoby, T. M. Newcomb, and E. L. Hartley (eds.). New York: Holt, pp. 400–425.

Brooks-Gunn, J., Liaw, F., and Klebanov, P. K. 1992. Effects of early intervention on cognitive function of low birth weight preterm infants. *J. of Pediatrics* 120:350–359.

Bross, D. S., and Shapiro, S. 1982. Direct and indirect association of five factors with infant mortality. *Am. J. of Epidemiology* 115:78–91.

Brown, A. L., and Campione, J. C. 1982. Modifying intelligence or modifying cognitive skills: More than a semantic quibble? In *How and How Much Can Intelligence Be Increased*. D. K. Detterman and R. J. Sternberg (eds.). Norwood, N.J.: Ablex Publishing Corp., pp. 215–230.

Brown, C. 1980. A note on the determination of "acceptable" performance in Thorndike's standard of fair selection. *J. of Educational Measurement* 17:203–209.

Brown, H. P. 1988. *Egalitarianism and the Generation of Inequality.* Oxford: Clarendon Press.

Brown, M. K., and Erie, S. P. 1981. Blacks and the legacy of the Great Society. *Public Policy* 12:299–330.

Brown, R. 1958. *Words and Things: An Introduction to Language.* New York: Free Press.

Buenning, M., and Tollefson, N. 1987. The cultural gap hypothesis as an explanation for the achievement patterns of Mexican-American students. *Psych. in the Schools* 24:264–272.

Bulcroft, R. A., and Bulcroft, K. A. 1993. Race differences in attitudinal and motivational factors in the decision to marry. *J. of Marriage and the Family* 55:338–355.

Bumpass, L., and McLanahan, S. 1989. Unmarried motherhood: Recent trends, composition, and black-white differences. *Demography* 26:279–286.

Bundy, M. 1955. Four subjects and four hopes. *College Board Rev.* 27:17–20.

Bunzel, J. H. 1992. *Race Relations on Campus: Stanford Students Speak.* The Portable Stanford. Stanford: Stanford Alumni Association.

Bunzel, J. H., and Au, J. K. D. 1987. Diversity or discrimination—Asian Americans in college. *Public Interest* 87:49–62.

Burck, C. G. 1976. A group profile of the Fortune 500 chief executive. *Fortune* (May): 173–177.

Burdick, E. 1959. Political theory and the voting studies. In *American Voting Behavior.* E. Burdick and A. J. Brodbeck (eds.). Glencoe, Ill.: Free Press, pp. 136–149.

Bureau of Labor Statistics. 1982. *Labor Force Statistics Derived from the Current Population Survey: A Databook.* Vol. 1. U.S. Department of Labor Bulletin 2096. Washington, D.C.: Government Printing Office.

Bureau of Labor Statistics. 1983. *Handbook of Labor Statistics.* U.S. Department of Labor, Bulletin 2175. Washington, D.C.: Government Printing Office.

Bureau of Labor Statistics. 1989. *Handbook of Labor Statistics.* U.S. Department of Labor, Bulletin 2340. Washington, D.C.: Government Printing Office.

Burgess, E. W., and Wallin, P. 1943. Homogamy in social characteristics. *Am. J. of Sociology* 49:109–124.

Burke, M. J., and Frederick, J. T. 1984. Two modified procedures for estimating standard deviations in utility analyses. *J. of Applied Psych.* 69:482–489.

Burt, C. 1963. Is intelligence distributed normally? *British J. of Statistical Psych.* 16:175–190.

Buss, D. M. 1987. Sex differences in human mate selection criteria: An evolutionary perspective. In *Sociobiology and Psychology: Ideas, Issues and Applications*. C. C., M. Smith, and D. Krebs (eds.). Hillsdale, N.J.: Lawrence Erlbaum Associates, pp. 335–351.

Buss, D. M. 1989. Sex differences in human mate preferences: Evolutionary hypotheses tested in 37 cultures. *Behavioral and Brain Sciences* 12:1–49.

Butler, R. P., and McCauley, C. 1987. Extraordinary stability and ordinary predictability of academic success at the United States Military Academy. *J. of Educational Psych*. 79:83–86.

Cain, D. P., and Vanderwolf, C. H. 1990. A critique of Rushton on race, brain size, and intelligence. *Personality and Individual Differences* 11:777–784.

Caldwell, B. M., and Bradley, R. H. 1984. *Home Observation for Measurement of the Environment*. Little Rock, Ark.: University of Arkansas Press.

Camayd-Freixas, Y., and Horst, L. 1987. *Dropouts in 1987*. Boston: School Committee of the City of Boston, Office of Research and Development.

Cameron, S. V., and Heckman, J. J. 1992. *The nonequivalence of high school equivalents*. University of Chicago, Chicago, Ill. Photocopy.

Cameron, S. V., and Heckman, J. J. 1993. Determinants of young male schooling and training choices. Working Paper 4327. Cambridge, Mass.: National Bureau of Economic Research.

Campbell, A., Converse, P. E., Miller, W. E., and Stokes, D. E. 1960. *The American Voter*. New York: Wiley.

Capron, C., and Duyme, M. 1989. Assessment of effects of socioeconomic status on IQ in a full cross-fostering study. *Nature* 340:552–553.

Card, D., and Kreuger, A. B. 1993. Trends in relative black-white earnings revisited. *Am. Econ. Rev*. 83:85–91.

Carliner, G. 1980. Wages, earnings, and hours of first, second and third generation American males. *Econ. Inquiry* 18:87–102.

Carlson, C. C., Huelskamp, R. M., and Woodall, T. D. 1993. Perspectives on education in America: An annotated briefing. *J. of Educational Research* 86:259–310.

Carlson, T. 1993. D.C. blues: The rap sheet on the Washington police. *Policy Rev*. (Winter): 26–33.

Carroll, J. B. 1988. Individual differences in cognitive functioning. In *Stevens' Handbook of Experimental Psych*.. R. C. Atkinson, R. J. Herrnstein, G. Lindzey, and R. D. Luce (eds.). New York: Wiley-Interscience, 2:813–862.

Carter, S. 1991. *Reflections of an Affirmative Action Baby*. New York: Basic Books.

Caruso, D. R., Taylor, J. J., and Detterman, D. K. 1982. Intelligence research and intelligent policy. In *How and How Much Can Intelligence Be Increased*. D. K. Detterman and R. J. Sternberg (eds.). Norwood, N.J.: Ablex Publishing Corp., pp. 45–65.

Cathcart, D. A., and Snyderman, M. 1992. The Civil Rights Act of 1991. The Labor Lawyer 8:849–922.

Cattell, R. B. 1936. Is our national intelligence declining? *Eugenics Rev.* 28:181–203.

Cattell, R. B. 1937. *The Fight for Our National Intelligence.* London: King & Sons.

Cattell, R. B. 1938. Some changes in social life in a community with a falling intelligence quotient. *British J. of Psych.* 28:430–450.

Cattell, R. B. 1951. The fate of national intelligence: Test of a thirteen-year prediction. *Eugenics Rev.* 42:136–148.

Cattell, R. B. 1971. *Abilities: Their Structure, Growth, and Action.* Boston: Houghton Mifflin.

Cattell, R. B. 1974. Differential fertility and normal selection for IQ: Some required conditions in their investigation. *Social Biology* 21:168–177.

Cattell, R. B. 1979. Are culture fair intelligence tests possible and necessary? *J. of Research and Development in Education* 12:3–13.

Cattell, R. B. 1983. *Intelligence and National Achievement.* Washington, D.C.: Institute for the Study of Man.

Ceci, S. J. 1991. How much does schooling influence general intelligence and its cognitive components? A reassessment of the evidence. *Developmental Psych.* 27:703–722.

Ceci, S. J., and Liker, J. K. 1986. A day at the races: A study of IQ, expertise, and cognitive complexity. *J. of Experimental Psych.* 115:255–266.

Chaiken, J. M., and Chaiken, M. R. 1983. Crime rates and the active criminal. In *Crime and Public Policy.* J. Q. Wilson (ed.). San Francisco: ICS Press, pp. 11–30.

Chan, J. W. C., and Vernon, P. E. 1988. Individual differences among the peoples of China. In *Human Abilities in Cultural Context.* S. H. Irvine and J. W. Berry (eds.). New York: Cambridge University Press, pp. 340–357.

Chan, S., and Wang, L.-C. 1991. Racism and the model minority: Asian-Americans in higher education. In *The Racial Crisis in American Higher Education.* P. G. Altbach and K. Lomotey (eds.). Albany, N.Y.: State University of New York Press, pp. 43–68.

Chen, R., and Morgan, S. P. 1991. Recent trends in the timing of first births in the United States. *Demography* 28:513–533.

Cherlin, A. J. 1981. *Marriage, Divorce, Remarriage.* Cambridge, Mass.: Harvard University Press.

Chipuer, H. M., Rovine, M. J., and Plomin, R. 1990. LISREL modeling: Genetic and environmental influences on IQ revisited. *Intelligence* 14:11–21.

Chiswick, B. R. 1978. The effect of Americanization on the earnings of foreign-born men. *J. of Political Econ.* 86:897–921.

Chun, K.-T., and Zalokar, N. 1992. *Civil Rights Issues Facing Asian Americans in the 1990s.* Washington, D.C.: U.S. Commission on Civil Rights.

Church, A. T., and Katigbak, M. S. 1991. Home environment, nutritional status, and maternal intelligence as determinants of intellectual development in rural Philippine preschool children. *Intelligence* 15:49–78.

Cicarelli, V. G., Evans, J. W., and Schiller, J. S. 1969. *The Impact of Head Start: An Evaluation of the Effects of Head Start on Children's Cognitive and Affective Development.* Athens, Ohio: Westinghouse Learning Corporation and Ohio University.

Cicchetti, D., and Rizley, R. 1981. Developmental perspectives on the etiology, intergenerational transmission, and sequelae of child maltreatment. *New Directions for Child Development* 11:31–55.

Clark, C. D., and Gist, N. P. 1938. Intelligence as a factor in occupational choice. *Am. Sociological Rev.* 3:683–694.

Cleckley, H. 1964. *The Mask of Sanity.* St. Louis: Mosby.

Clews, H. 1908. *Fifty Years in Wall Street.* New York: Irving Publishing Co.

Clignet, R. 1974. *Liberty and Equality in the Educational Process: A Comparative Sociology of Education.* New York: Wiley.

Clotfelter, C. T. 1990. Undergraduate Enrollments in the 1980s. Working Paper. Cambridge, Mass.: National Bureau for Economic Research.

Cogan, J. 1982. The decline in black teenage employment: 1950–70. *Am. Econ. Rev.* 72:621–638.

Cohen, M. I., Raphling, D. L., and Green, P. E. 1966. Psychological aspects of the maltreatment syndrome in childhood. *J. of Pediatrics* 69:279–284.

Colaizzi, J. 1989. *Homicidal Insanity. 1800–1985.* Tuscaloosa, Ala.: University of Alabama Press.

Cole, B. P. 1987. College admissions and coaching. *Negro Educational Rev.* 38:125–135.

Cole, C. C., Jr. 1955. Who's going to college? *College Board Rev.* 27:13–16.

Coleman, J. S. 1972. The evaluation of Equality of Educational Opportunity. In *On Equality of Educational Opportunity.* F. Mosteller and D. P. Moynihan (eds.). New York: Random House, pp. 146–167.

Coleman, J. S. 1993. Comment on Preston and Campbell's "Differential fertility and the distribution of traits." *Am. J. of Sociology* 98:1020–1032.

Coleman, J. S., and Hoffer, T. 1987. *Public and Private Schools: The Impact of Communities.* New York: Basic Books.

Coleman, J. S., et al. 1966. *Equality of Educational Opportunity, Supplemental Appendix 9.10.* Washington, D.C.: U.S. Office of Education.

Coles, R. 1967. *Migrants, Sharecroppers, and Mountaineers.* Children of Crisis, vol. 2. Boston: Little, Brown.

College Entrance Examination Board. 1961. *College Profiles.* New York: College Entrance Examination Board.

Collins, J. W. 1992. Disparate black and white neonatal mortality rates among infants of normal birth weight in Chicago: A population study. *J. of Pediatrics* 120:954–960.

Committee on Minority Affairs. 1984. *Report to the Corporation Committee on Minority Affairs from Its Subcommittee on Asian American Admissions.* Providence, R.I.: Brown University Corporation.

Committee on Ways and Means and U.S. House of Representatives. 1993. *1993 Green Book: Background Material and Data on Programs within the Jurisdiction of the Committee on Ways and Means.* WMCP 103–18. Washington, D.C.: Government Printing Office.

Congressional Budget Office. 1986. *Trends in Educational Achievement.* Congress of the United States. Washington, D.C.: Government Printing Office.

Congressional Budget Office. 1987. *Educational Achievement: Explanations and Implications of Recent Trends.* Congress of the United States. Washington, D.C.: Government Printing Office.

Consortium on Financing Higher Education. 1992. *COFHE Admissions Statistics: Classes Entering 1991 and 1992 (Redbook XVII).*Cambridge, Mass.: Consortium on Financing Higher Education.

Converse, P. E. 1964. The nature of belief systems in mass publics. In *Ideology and Discontent* D. E. Apter (ed.). New York: Free Press, pp. 206–261.

Cook, P. C. 1987. Cultural bias in the California Achievement Tests: A focus on internal indices. *Dissertations Abstracts International* 48(2–A):339.

Cook, P. J., and Frank, R. H. 1991. The growing concentration of top students at elite schools. In *The Economics of Higher Education.* C. Clotfelter and M. Rothschild (eds.) Chicago: NBER-University of Chicago Press.

Cook, R. C. 1951. *Human Fertility: The Modern Dilemma.* New York: Sloane.

Cook, T. K., Appleton, H., Conner, R. F., Shaffer, A., Tamkin, G., and Weber, S. J. 1975. *"Sesame Street" Revisited.* New York: Russell Sage Foundation.

Cooksey, E. C. 1990. Factors in the resolution of adolescent premarital pregnancies. *Demography* 27:207–218.

Coser, L. 1965. The sociology of poverty. *Social Problems* 13:140–148.

Costello, J. 1970. Effects of pretesting and examiner characteristics on test performance of young disadvantaged children. *Proceedings of the 78th Annual Convention, Am. Psychological Assoc.* 5:309–310.

Costopoulos, P. J. 1990. Jefferson, Adams, and the natural aristocracy. *First Things* 1:46–52.

Cramer, J. C. 1987. Social factors and infant mortality: Identifying high-risk groups and proximate causes. *Demography* 24:299–322.

Crawford-Nutt, D. H. 1976. Are black scores on Raven's Standard Progressive Matrices an artifact of method of test presentation? *Psychologia Africana* 16:201–206.

Crittenden, P. 1988. Family and dyadic patterns of functioning in maltreating families. In *Early Prediction and Prevention of Child Abuse*. K. Browne, C. Davies, and P. Stratton (eds.). New York: Wiley, pp. 161–189.

Crombie, I. K., Todman, J., McNeill, G., Florey, C. D. V., Menzies, I., and Kennedy, R. A. 1990. Effect of vitamin and mineral supplementation on verbal and non-verbal reasoning of school children. *Lancet* 335:744–747.

Cronbach, L. J., and Gleser, G. C. 1965. *Psychological Tests and Personnel Decisions*. 2d ed., Urbana, Ill.: University of Illinois Press.

Crouse, J., and Trusheim, D. 1988. *The Case against the SAT*. Chicago: University of Chicago Press.

Cutler, D. M., and Katz, L. F. 1991. *Macroeconomic Performance and the Disadvantaged*. Cambridge, Mass.: Harvard University and NEBR.

Cyphers, L. H., Fulker, D. W., Plomin, R., and DeFries, J. C. 1989. Cognitive abilities in the early school years: No effects of shared environment between parents and offspring. *Intelligence* 13:369–386.

D'Souza, D. 1991. *Illiberal Education*. New York: Free Press.

Darlington, C. D. 1969. *The Evolution of Man and Society*. New York: Simon and Schuster.

Das, J. P. 1985. Interpretations for a class on minority assessment. *Behavioral and Brain Sciences* 8:228.

David, R. 1990. Race, birth weight, and mortality rates. *J. of Pediatrics* 116:101–102.

Davis, A., and Havighurst, R. J. 1946. Social class and color differences in child-rearing. *Am. Sociological Rev.* 11:698–710.

DeFries, J. C., Johnson, R. C., Kuse, A. R., McClearn, G. E., Polovina, J., Vandenberg, S. G., and Wilson, J. R. 1979. Familial resemblance for specific cognitive abilities. *Behavior Genetics* 9:23–43.

Dekovic, M., and Gerris, J. R. M. 1992. Parental reasoning complexity, social class, and child-rearing behaviors. *J. of Marriage and the Family* 54:675–685.

Delattre, E. J. 1989. *Character and Cops: Ethics in Policing*. Washington, D. C.: American Enterprise Institute.

Denno, D. W. 1990. *Biology and Violence: From Birth to Adulthood*. New York: Cambridge University Press.

DerSimonian, R., and Laird, N. M. Evaluating the effect of coaching on SAT scores: A meta-analysis. *Harvard Educational Rev.* 53:1–15.

Detlefsen, R. R. 1991. *Civil Rights under Reagan*. San Francisco: ICS Press.

Diamond, M. 1976. The American idea of man: The view from the founding. In *The Americans: 1976. An Inquiry into Fundamental Concepts of Man Underlying Various U.S. Institutions*. Vol. 2. I. Kristol and P. Weaver (eds.). Lexington, Mass.: Lexington Books, pp. 1–23.

Dillon, H. J. 1949. *Early School Leavers: A Major Educational Problem*. New York: National Child Labor Committee.

Dilts, S. W. (ed.). 1991. *Peterson's Guide to Four-Year Colleges.* 21st ed. Princeton, N.J.: Peterson's Guides.

Donlon, T. F. (ed.). 1984. *The College Board Technical Handbook for the Scholastic Aptitude Test and Achievement Tests.* New York: College Entrance Examination Board.

Donnelly, B. W., and Voydanoff, P. 1991. Factors associated with releasing for adoption among adolescent mothers. *Family Relations* 40:404–410.

Donohue, J. J., III, and Heckman, J. 1991. Continuous versus episodic change: The impact of civil rights policy on the economic status of blacks. *J. of Econ. Literature* 29:1603–1643.

Downs, A. 1957. *An Economic Theory of Democracy.* New York: Harper.

Drotar, D., and Sturm, L. 1989. Influences on the home environment of preschool children with early histories of nonorganic failure-to-thrive. *Developmental and Behavioral Pediatrics* 10:229–235.

Dubin, J. A., Osburn, H., and Winick, D. M. 1969. Speed and practice: Effects on Negro and white test performance. *J. of Applied Psych.* 53:19–23.

Dumaret, A., and Stewart, J. T. 1985. IQ, scholastic performance and behaviour of sibs raised in contrasting environments. *J. of Child Psych., and Psychiatry and Allied Disciplines* 26:553–580.

Duncan, G. J. 1993. *Economic deprivation and early-childhood development.* Ann Arbor, Mich.: Social Science Research Center. Photocopy.

Duncan, G. J., and Hoffman, S. D. 1990. Welfare benefits, economic opportunities, and out-of-wedlock births among black teenage girls. *Demography* 27:519–535.

Duncan, G. J., and Laren, D. 1990. *Neighborhood Correlates of Teen Births and Dropping Out: Preliminary Results from the PSID-Geocode File.* Ann Arbor, Mich.: SSRC Working Group on Communities and Neighborhoods, Family Processes and Individual Development. Social Science Research Center.

Duncan, O. D. 1952. Is the intelligence of the general population declining? *Am. Sociological Rev.* 17:401–407.

Duncan, O. D. 1968. Ability and achievement. *Eugenics Quarterly* 15:1–11.

Dunnette, M. D. 1976. Aptitudes, abilities, and skills. In *Handbook of Industrial and Organizational Psychology.* M. D. Dunnette (ed.). Chicago: Rand McNally College Publishing Company, pp. 473–520.

Dyer, H. S. 1987. The effects of coaching for Scholastic Aptitude. *NASSP Bull.* 71:46–53.

Dyer, P. J. 1970. *Effects of test conditions on Negro-white differences in test scores.* Ph.D. dissertation, Columbia University.

E. F. Wonderlic & Associates, I. 1983. *Wonderlic Personnel Test Manual.* Northfield, Ill.: E. F. Wonderlic & Associates.

Eagle, E. 1988a. *High School and Beyond: Educational Experiences of the 1980 Senior Class.* Berkeley, Cal.: MPR Associates.

Eagle, E. 1988b. *National Longitudinal Study 1972: Educational Experiences of the 1972 Senior Class*. Berkeley, Cal.: MPR Associates.

Eberstein, I. W., and Parker, J. R. 1984. Racial differences in infant mortality by cause of death: The impact of birth weight and maternal age. *Demography* 21:309–321.

Eells, K., et al. 1951. *Intelligence and Cultural Differences*. Chicago: University of Chicago Press.

Egeland, B., Breitenbucher, M., and Rosenberg, D. 1980. Prospective study of the significance of life stress in the etiology of child abuse. *J. of Consulting and Clinical Psych.* 48:195–205.

Eggebeen, D. J., and Lichter, D. T. 1991. Race, family structure, and changing poverty among American children. *Am. Sociological Rev.* 56:801–817.

Elliot, R. 1988. Tests, abilities, race, and conflict. *Intelligence* 12:333–350.

Elliott, D. S., and Ageton, S. S. 1980. Reconciling race and class differences in self-reported and official estimates of delinquency. *Am. Sociological Rev.* 45:95–110.

Elliott, D. S., and Voss, H. 1974. *Delinquency and Dropout*. Lexington Mass.: Lexington Books.

Elliott, R. 1987. *Litigating Intelligence: IQ Tests, Special Education, and Social Science in the Courtroom*. Dover, Mass.: Auburn House.

Ellis, L., and Nyborg, H. 1992. Racial/ethnic variations in male testosterone levels: A probable contributor to group differences in health. *Steroids* 57:1–4.

Ellwood, D. 1986a. *Targeting the "Would-Be" Long-Term Recipient: Who Should Be Served?* Princeton, N.J.: Mathematica Policy Research.

Ellwood, D. T. 1986b. The spatial mismatch hypothesis. In *The Black Youth Employment Crisis*. R. B. Freeman and H. J. Holzer (eds.). Chicago: University of Chicago Press.

Ellwood, D. T. 1988. *Poor Support: Poverty in the American Family*. New York: Basic Books.

Ellwood, D., and Bane, M. J. 1985. The impact of AFDC on family structure and living arrangements. In *Research in Labor Economics*, Vol. 7. R. G. Ehrenberg (ed.). Greenwich, Conn.: JAI Press, pp. 137–207.

Ellwood, D. T., and Crane, J. 1990. Family change among black Americans: What do we know? *J. of Econ. Perspectives* 4:65–84.

Epstein, R. A. 1990. The paradox of civil rights. *Yale Law and Policy Rev.* 8:299–319.

Epstein, R. A. 1992. *Forbidden Grounds: The Case against Employment Discrimination Laws*. Cambridge, Mass.: Harvard University Press.

Ervin, L., Hogrebe, M. C., Dwinell, P. L., and Newman, I. 1984. Comparison of the prediction of academic performance for college developmental students and regularly admitted students. *Psychological Reports* 54:319–327.

Etzioni, A. 1975. Grade inflation. *Science* 190:101.

Eyferth, K. 1961. Leistungen verschiedener Gruppen von Besatzungskindern in Hamburg-Wechsler Intelligenztest für Kinder (HAWIK). *Archiv für die gesamte Psychologie* 113:222–241.

Eysenck, H. J. 1991. Raising I.Q. through vitamin and mineral supplementation: An introduction. *Personality and Individual Differences* 12:329–333.

Faculty of Arts and Sciences. 1960. *Admission to Harvard College*. Report by the Special Committee on College Admission Policy. Cambridge, Mass.: Harvard University.

Falconer, D. S. 1966. Genetic consequences of selection pressure. In *Genetic and Environmental Factors in Human Ability*. J. E. Meade and A. S. Parkes (eds.). Edinburgh: Oliver & Boyd, pp. 219–232.

Falconer, D. S. 1989. *An Introduction to Quantitative Genetics*. 3d ed. New York: Wiley.

Fallows, J. 1980. The tests and the brightest: How fair are the College Boards? *Atlantic Monthly* (February): 37–48.

Fallows, J. 1985. The case against credentialism. *Atlantic Monthly* (December): 49–67.

Farrell, T. J. 1983. IQ and standard English. *College Composition and Communication* 34:470–484.

Farrington, D. P., and West, D. J. 1990. The Cambridge Study in Delinquent Development: A long-term follow-up of 411 London males. In *Criminality: Personality, Behavior, Life History*. H. J. Kerner and G. Kaiser (eds.). New York: Springer-Verlag, pp. 115–138.

Farver, A. S., Sedlacek, W. E., and Brooks, G. C. 1975. Longitudinal predictions of university grades for blacks and whites. *Measurement and Evaluation in Guidance* 7:243–250.

Featherstone, J. 1971. *Schools Where Children Learn*. New York: Liveright.

Federal Bureau of Investigation. 1993. *Crime in the United States 1992: Uniform Crime Reports*. Washington, D.C.: Government Printing Office.

Feinberg, L. 1988. Black freshman enrollment rises 46% at U-Va. *The Washington Post*, Dec. 26, p. C1.

Field, T. M., Widmayer, S. M., Stringer, S., and Ignatoff, E. 1993. Teenage, lower-class, black mothers and their preterm infants: An intervention and developmental follow-up. *Child Development* 51:426–436.

Fierman, J. 1987. What it takes to be rich in America. *Fortune*, April 13, pp. 22–29.

Figueroa, R. A. 1983. Test bias and Hispanic children. *J. of Special Education* 17:431–440.

Figueroa, R. A., and Sassenrath, J. M. 1989. A Longitudinal Study of the Predictive Validity of the System of Multicultural Pluralistic Assessment (SOMPA). *Psych. in the Schools* 26:5–15.

Filer, R. K. 1981. The influence of affective human capital on the wage equation. In *Research in Labor Economics*, vol. IV. R. Ehrenberg (ed.). Greenwich, Conn.: JAI Press, pp. 367–409.

Finch, F. E. 1946. *Enrollment Increases and Changes in the Mental Level of the High School Population*. Stanford, Cal.: Stanford University Press.

Finn, C. E., Jr. 1991. *We Must Take Charge: Our Schools and Our Future*. New York: Free Press.

Fisher, A. B. 1992. The new debate over the very rich. *Fortune*, June 29, pp. 42–54.

Fiske, E. B. 1984. Are they "dumbing down" the textbooks? *Principal* 64:44.

Fletcher, J. F., and Forbes, H. D. 1990. Education, occupation and vote in Canada, 1965–1984. *Canadian Rev. of Sociology and Anthropology* 27:441–461.

Fletcher, R. 1991. Intelligence, equality, character, and education. *Intelligence* 15:139–149.

Flinn, C. J., and Heckman, J. J. 1983. Are unemployment and out of the labor force behaviorally distinct labor force states? *J. of Labor Economics* 1:28–42.

Flynn, J. R. 1980. *Race, IQ, and Jensen*. London: Routledge and Kegan Paul.

Flynn, J. R. 1984. The mean IQ of Americans: Massive gains 1932 to 1978. *Psychological Bull.* 95:29–51.

Flynn, J. R. 1987a. Massive IQ gains in 14 nations: What IQ tests really measure. *Psychological Bull.* 101:171–191.

Flynn, J. R. 1987b. The ontology of intelligence. In *Measurement, Realism, and Objectivity*. J. Forge (ed.). New York: D. Reidel, pp. 1–40.

Flynn, J. R. 1989. Rushton, evolution and race: An essay on intelligence and virtue. *Psychologist* 2:363–366.

Flynn, J. R. 1991. *Asian Americans: Achievement beyond IQ*. Hillsdale, N.J.: Lawrence Erlbaum Associates.

Flynn, T. M. 1984. Counterstatement: Responses to Thomas J. Farrell, "IQ and standard English" (with a reply by Thomas J. Farrell). *College Composition and Communication* 35:455–479.

Fogel, R. W. 1992. Egalitarianism: The economic revolution of the twentieth century. New Haven, Conn.: Yale University. Photocopy.

Ford, J. K., Kraiger, K., and Schechtman, S. L. 1986. Study of race effects in objective indices and subjective evaluations of performance: A meta-analysis of performance criteria. *Psychological Bull.* 99:330–337.

Forrest, D. W. 1974. *Francis Galton: The Life and Work of a Victorian Genius*. New York: Taplinger.

Fossett, M. A., and Kiecolt, K. J. 1993. Mate availability and family structure among African Americans in U.S. metropolitan areas. *J. of Marriage and the Family* 55:288–302.

Frederiksen, N. 1986. Toward a broader conception of human intelligence. *Am. Psychologist* 41:445–452.

Freeman, R. B. 1976. *The Overeducated American.* New York: Academic Press.

Freeman, R. B. 1983. Crime and unemployment. In *Crime and Public Policy.* J. Q. Wilson (ed.). San Francisco: Institute for Contemporary Studies, pp. 89–106.

Freeman, R. B. 1984. Affirmative action: Good, bad, or irrelevant? *New Perspectives* 16:23–27.

Friedman, M. 1962. *Capitalism and Freedom.* Chicago: University of Chicago Press.

Friedman, S. B., and Morse, C. W. 1974. Child abuse: A 5-year follow-up of early case finding in the emergency department. *Pediatrics* 54:404–410.

Friedman, T., and Williams, E. B. 1982. Current use of tests for employment. In *Ability Testing: Uses, Consequences, and Controversies,* Vol. 2. A. K. Wigdor and W. R. Garner (eds.). Washington, D.C.: National Academy Press, pp. 99–169.

Frydman, M., and Lynn, R. 1989. The intelligence of Korean children adopted in Belgium. *Personality and Individual Differences* 10:1323–1325.

Fryer, D. 1922. Occupational-intelligence standards. *School and Society* 16:273–276.

Fuchs, D., and Fuchs, L. S. 1986. Test procedure bias: A meta-analysis of examiner familiarity effects. *Rev. of Educational Research* 56:243–262.

Furstenberg, F. F., Jr., Morgan, S. P., Moore, K. A., and Peterson, J. L. 1987. Race differences in the timing of adolescent intercourse. *Am. Sociological Rev.* 52:511–518.

Gabriel, P. E. 1991. A comparison of the occupational distributions of native- and foreign-born males: An immigration consideration. *Am. J. of Econ. and Sociology* 50:351–364.

Galton, F. 1869. *Hereditary Genius: An Inquiry into Its Laws and Consequences.* 1892 ed. London: Macmillan.

Galton, F. 1883. *Inquiries into Human Faculty and Its Development.* London: Macmillan.

Galton, F. 1888. Co-relations and their measurement, chiefly from anthropological data. *Proceedings of the Royal Society of London* 45:135–145.

Gamble, T. J., and Zigler, E. 1989. The Head Start synthesis project: A critique. *J. of Applied Developmental Psych.* 10:267–274.

Garbarino, J., and Crouter, A. 1978. Defining the community context for parent-child relations: The correlates of child maltreatment. *Child Development* 49:604–616.

Garber, H. L. 1988. *The Milwaukee Project: Preventing Mental Retardation in Children at Risk.* Washington, D.C.: American Association on Mental Retardation.

Garber, H. L., and Hodge, J. D. 1991. Understanding intervention, inoculation, and risk for intellectual deceleration: A reply to Locurto. *Intelligence* 15:317–325.

Gardner, H. 1983. *Frames of Mind: The Theory of Multiple Intelligences*. New York: Basic Books.

Gergen, K. J., and Ullman, M. 1977. Socialization and the characterological basis of political activism. In *Handbook of Political Socialization*. S. A. Renshon (ed.). New York: Free Press, pp. 411–442.

Ghiselin, M. T., and Scudo, F. M. 1986. The bioeconomics of phenotypic selection. *Behavioral and Brain Sciences* 9:194–195.

Ghiselli, E. E. 1966. *The Validity of Occupational Aptitude Tests*. New York: Wiley.

Ghiselli, E. E. 1973. The validity of aptitude tests in personnel selection. *Personnel Psych.* 26:461–477.

Ghiselli, E. E., and Brown, C. W. 1947. Learning in accident reduction. *J. of Applied Psych.* 31:580–582.

Gifford, B. R. (ed.). 1989. *Test Policy and the Politics of Opportunity Allocation: The Workplace and the Law*. Boston: Kluwer Academic.

Gil, D. 1970. *Violence Against Children*. Cambridge, Mass.: Harvard University Press.

Gilder, G. 1986. *Men and Marriage*. Gretna, La.: Pelican Publishing.

Gionfriddo, J. J. 1985. The Dumbing Down of Textbooks: An Analysis of Six Textbook Editions during a Twelve Year Span. Ph.D. dissertation, Kean College.

Glass, G. V. 1976. Primary, secondary, and meta-analytic research. *Educational Researcher* 5:3–8.

Glass, G. V., McGaw, B., and Smith, M. L. 1981. *Meta-Analysis in Social Research*. Beverly Hills, Cal.: Sage Publications.

Glazer, N. 1988. *The Limits of Social Policy*. Cambridge, Mass.: Harvard University Press.

Goddard, H. H. 1914. *Feeble-Mindedness. Its Causes and Consequences*. New York: Macmillan.

Goldman, R. D., and Hewitt, B. N. 1976. Predicting the success of black, Chicano, Oriental and white college students. *J. of Educational Measurement* 13:107–117.

Goldman, R. D., and Richards, R. 1974. The SAT prediction of grades for Mexican-American versus Anglo-American students at the University of California, Riverside. *J. of Educational Measurement* 11:129–135.

Goldman, R. D., and Widawski, M. H. 1976. An analysis of types of errors in the selection of minority college students. *J. of Educational Measurement* 13:185–200.

Goodman, P. 1962. *Growing Up Absurd: Problems of Youth in the Organized Society*. New York: Vintage Books.

Goodnow, J. J., Cashmore, J., Cotton, S., and Knight, R. 1984. Mothers' developmental timetables in two cultural groups. *International J. of Psych.* 19:193–205.

Gordon, R. A. 1984. Digits backward and the Mercer-Kamin Law: An empirical response to Mercer's treatment of internal validity of IQ tests. In *Perspectives on "Bias in Mental Testing."* C. R. Reynolds and R. T. Brown (eds.). New York: Plenum Press, pp. 357–506.

Gordon, R. A. 1987. SES versus IQ in the race-IQ-delinquency model. *International J. of Sociology and Social Policy* 7:30–96.

Gordon, R. A. 1976. Prevalence: The rare datum in delinquency measurement and its implications for the theory of delinquency. In *The Juvenile Justice System.* M. W. Klein (ed.). Beverly Hills, Cal.: Sage Publications, pp. 201–284.

Goring, C. 1913. *The English Convict: A Statistical Study.* London: Darling and Son.

Gottfredson, L. S. 1986. Societal consequences of the g factor in employment. *J. of Vocational Behavior* 29:379–410.

Gottfredson, M. R., and Hirschi, T. 1990. *A General Theory of Crime.* Stanford, Cal.: Stanford University Press.

Gottfried, A. W. 1984. Home environment and early cognitive development: Integration, meta-analyses, and conclusions. In *Home Environment and Early Cognitive Development.* A. W. Gottfried (ed.). Orlando, Fla.: Academic Press, pp. 329–342.

Gould, S. J. 1978. Morton's ranking of races by cranial capacity. *Science* 200:503–509.

Gould, S. J. 1981. *The Mismeasure of Man.* New York: W. W. Norton.

Gould, S. J. 1984. Human equality is a contingent fact of history. *Natural History,* November, pp. 26–33.

Gove, P. B. (ed.). 1964. *Webster's Third New International Dictionary of the English Language Unabridged.* Springfield, Mass.: G. & C. Merriam.

Granberg, D., and Holmberg, S. 1990. The intention-behavior relationship among U.S., and Swedish voters. *Social Psych. Quarterly* 53:44–54.

Griliches, Z. 1970. Notes on the role of education in production functions and growth accounting. *Education, Income and Human Capital* 35:71–127.

Grossman, M. 1975. The correlation between health and schooling. In *Household Production and Consumption.* N. E. Terleckyj (ed.). New York: Columbia University Press, pp. 147–211.

Guilford, J. P. 1967. *The Nature of Human Intelligence.* New York: McGraw-Hill.

Guion, R. M. 1983. Comments on Hunter. In *Performance Measurement and Theory.* Frank Landy, S. Zedeck, and J. Cleveland (eds.). Hillsdale, N.J.: Lawrence Erlbaum Associates, pp. 267–275.

Gustafsson, J.-E. 1992. The "Spearman hypothesis" is false. *Multivariate Behavioral Research* 27:265–267.

Guterman, S. S. 1979. IQ tests in research on social stratification: The cross-class validity of the tests. *Sociology of Education* 52:163–173.

Guttman, L. 1992. The irrelevance of factor analysis for the study of group differences. *Multivariate Behavioral Research* 27:175–204.

Hack, M., Breslau, N., Weissman, B., Aram, D., Klein, N., and Borawski, E. 1991. Effect of very low birth weight and subnormal head size on cognitive abilities at school age. *New England J. of Medicine* 325:231–237.

Hacker, A. 1992. An affirmative vote for affirmative action. *Academic Questions* 5:24–28.

Hahn, A., and Lefkowitz, J. 1987. *Dropouts in America: Enough Is Known for Action*. Washington, D.C.: Institute for Educational Leadership.

Hale, R. L. 1983. An examination for construct bias in the WISC-R across socioeconomic status. *J. of School Psych.* 21:153–156.

Hale, R. L., Raymond, M. R., and Gajar, A. H. 1982. Evaluating socioeconomic status bias in the WISC-R. *J. of School Psych.* 20:145–149.

Hall, V. C., and Turner, R. R. 1974. The validity of the "different language explanation" for poor scholastic performance by black students. *Rev. of Educational Research* 44:69–81.

Hamilton, A., Madison, J., and Jay, J. 1787. *The Federalist Papers*. New York: New American Library, 1982.

Hanson, S. L., Morrison, D. R., and Ginsburg, A. L. 1989. The antecedents of teenage fatherhood. *Demography* 26:579–596.

Hartigan, J. A., and Wigdor, A. K. (eds.). 1989. *Fairness in Employment Testing: Validity Generalization, Minority Issues, and the General Aptitude Test Battery*. Washington, D.C.: National Academy Press.

Harvey, S. K., and Harvey, T. G. 1970. Adolescent political outlook: The effects of intelligence as an independent variable. *Midwest J. of Political Science* 14:565–595.

Haskell, M. R., and Yablonsky, L. 1978. *Criminology: Crime and Criminality*. 2d ed. Chicago: Rand McNally.

Haskins, R. 1989. Beyond metaphor: The efficacy of early childhood education. *Am. Psychologist* 44:274–282.

Hass, P. H. 1972. Maternal role incompatibility and fertility in urban Latin America. *J. of Social Issues* 28:111–127.

Hativa, N. 1988. Computer-based drill and practice in arithmetic: Widening the gap between high- and low-achieving students. *Am. Educational Research Journal* 25:366–397.

Hawk, J. 1970. Linearity of criterion-GATB aptitude relationships. *Measurement and Evaluation in Guidance* 2:249–251.

Hawk, J. 1986. Real world implications of g. *J. of Vocational Behavior* 29:411–414.

Heath, A. C., et al. 1985. No decline in assortative mating for educational level. *Behavior Genetics* 15:349–369.

Heath, A. C., Eaves, L. J., Nance, W. E., and Corey, L. A. 1987. Social inequality and assortative mating: Cause or consequence? *Behavior Genetics* 17:9–17.

Heath, S. 1983. *Ways with Words*. New York: Cambridge University Press.

Heath, S. B. 1982. What no bedtime story means: Narrative skills at home and school. *Language and Society* 11:49–76.

Heckman, J. J. 1993. What have we learned about labor supply in the past twenty years? *Am. Econ. Rev.* 83:116–126.

Heckman, J. J., and Payner, B. 1989. Determining the impact of federal antidiscrimination policy on the economic status of blacks: A study of South Carolina. *Am. Econ. Rev.* 79:138–177.

Heckman, J. J., and Verkerke, J. H. 1990. Racial disparity and employment discrimination law: An economic perspective. *Yale Law and Policy Rev.* 8: 276–298.

Hegar, R. L., and Yungman, J. J. 1989. Toward a causal typology of child neglect. *Children and Youth Services Rev.* 11:203–220.

Heilman, M. E., Block, C. J., and Lucas, J. A. 1992. Presumed incompetent? Stigmatization and affirmative action efforts. *J. of Applied Psych.* 77:536–544.

Helms, J. E. 1992. Why is there no study of cultural equivalence in standardized cognitive ability testing? *Am. Psychologist* 47:1083–1101.

Herrenkohl, R. C., Herrenkohl, E. C., and Egolf, B. P. 1983. Circumstances surrounding the occurrence of child maltreatment. *J. of Consulting and Clinical Psych.* 51:424–431.

Herrnstein, R. J. 1971. I.Q. *Atlantic Monthly* (September): 43–64.

Herrnstein, R. J. 1973. *IQ in the Meritocracy*. Boston: Atlantic–Little Brown.

Herrnstein, R. J. 1982. IQ testing and the media. *Atlantic Monthly* (August): 68–74.

Herrnstein, R. J., Belke, T., and Taylor, J. 1990. New York City Police Dept. Class of June 1940: A Preliminary Report. Harvard University. Photocopy.

Herrnstein, R. J., and Boring, E. G. 1965. *A Source Book in the History of Psychology*. Cambridge, Mass.: Harvard University Press.

Herrnstein, R. J., Nickerson, R. S., De Sanchez, M., and Swets, J. A. 1986. Teaching thinking skills. *Am. Psychologist* 41:1279–1289.

Hess, R. D., and Torney, J. V. 1967. *The Development of Political Attitudes in Children*. Chicago: Aldine.

Hickman, J. A., and Reynolds, C. R. 1987. Are race differences in mental test scores an artifact of psychometric methods? A test of Harrington's experimental model. *J. of Special Education* 20:409–430.

Higgins, J. V., Reed, E. W., and Reed, S. C. 1962. Intelligence and family size: A paradox resolved. *Social Biology* 9:84–90.

Higham, J. 1973. *Strangers in the Land*. New York: Atheneum.

Higham, J. 1984. *Send These to Me: Immigrants in Urban America*. Rev. ed. Baltimore: Johns Hopkins University Press.

Hill, C. R. 1979. Capacities, opportunities and educational investments: The case of the high school dropout. *Rev. of Economics and Statistics* 61:9–20.

Hill, D. B., and Luttbeg, N. R. 1983. *Trends in American Electoral Behavior*. 2d ed. Itasca, Ill.: F. E. Peacock Publishers.

Hilliard, A. G., III. 1979. Standardization and cultural bias impediments to the scientific study and validation of "intelligence." *J. of Research and Development in Education* 12:47–58.

Hilliard, A. G. III. 1984. IQ Testing as the emperor's new clothes: A critique of Jensen's "Bias in Mental Testing." In *Perspectives on "Bias in Mental Testing."* C. R. Reynolds and R. T. Brown (eds.). New York: Plenum Press, pp. 139–169.

Hills, B. J. 1980. Vision, visibility, and perception in driving. *Perception* 9:183–216.

Himmelfarb, G. 1984. *The Idea of Poverty: England in the Early Industrial Age.* New York: Alfred A. Knopf.

Hindelang, M. J. 1978. Race and involvement in common law personal crimes. *Am. Sociological Rev.* 43:93–109.

Hindelang, M. J. 1981. Variations in sex-race-age-specific incidence rates of offending. *Am. Sociological Rev.* 46:461–474.

Hindelang, M. J., Hirschi, T., and Weis, J. G. 1981. *Measuring Delinquency.* Beverly Hills, Cal.: Sage Publications.

Hirsch, J. 1975. The bankruptcy of "science" without scholarship. *Educational Theory* 25:3–28.

Hirschi, T. 1969. *Causes of Delinquency.* Berkeley, Cal.: University of California Press.

Hirschi, T., and Hindelang, M. J. 1977. Intelligence and delinquency: A revisionist review. *Am. Sociological Rev.* 42:571–587.

Hirschl, T. A., and Rank, M. R. 1991. The effect of population density on welfare participation. *Social Forces* 70:225–235.

Hobbes, T. 1651. *Leviathan.* 1950 ed., New York: Dutton.

Hofferth, S. L. 1984. Kin networks, race, and family structure. *J. of Marriage and the Family* 46:791–801.

Hoffman, S. D. 1987. Correlates of welfare receipt and dependency. In *Welfare Dependency: Behavior, Culture and Public Policy.* K. R. Hopkins (ed.). Alexandria, Va.: Hudson Institute, pp. 3.1–3.30.

Hogan, D. P., Hao, L.-X., and Parish, W. L. 1990. Race, kin networks, and assistance to mother-headed families. *Social Forces* 68:797–812.

Hogan, D. P., and Kitagawa, E. M. 1985. The impact of social status, family structure, and neighborhood on the fertility of black adolescents. *Am. J. of Sociology* 90:825–855.

Holden, C. 1988. Debate warming up on legal immigration policy. *Science* 241:288–290.

Holzer, H. J. 1986. Reservation wages and their labor market effects for black and white male youth. *J. of Human Resources* 21:157–178.

Honig, M. 1974. AFDC income, recipient rates, and family dissolution. *J. of Human Resources* 9:303–322.

Hopkins, K. R., Newitt, J., and Doyle, D. 1987. Educational performance and attainment. In *Welfare Dependency: Behavior, Culture and Public Policy*. K. R. Hopkins (ed.). Alexandria, Va.: Hudson Institute, pp. 8.1–8.68.

Horowitz, I. L., and Liebowitz, L. 1969. Social deviance and political marginality: Toward a redefinition of the relation between sociology and politics. *Social Problems* 25:280–296.

Hsia, J. 1988. Limits of affirmative action: Asian American access to higher education. *Educational Policy* 2:117–136.

Huber, P. W. 1988. *Liability: The Legal Revolution and Its Consequences*. New York: Basic Books.

Humphreys, L. G. 1968. The fleeting nature of the prediction of college academic success. *J. of Educational Psych.* 59:375–380.

Humphreys, L. G. 1973. Postdiction study of the graduate record examination and eight semesters of college grades. *J. of Educational Measurement* 10:179–184.

Humphreys, L. G. 1986. Commentary on "The *g* factor in employment." *J. of Vocational Behavior* 29:421–437.

Humphreys, L. G., and Taber, T. 1973. Ability factors as a function of advantaged and disadvantaged groups. *J. of Educational Measurement* 10:107–115.

Hunter, J. E. 1979. *An Analysis of Validity, Differential Validity, Test Fairness, and Utility for the Philadelphia Police Officers Selection Examination Prepared by the Educational Testing Service*. Report to the Philadelphia Federal District Court, Alvarez v. City of Philadelphia.

Hunter, J. E. 1980. *Test Validation for 12,000 Jobs: An Application of Synthetic Validity and Validity Generalization to the General Aptitude Battery (GATB)*. U.S. Employment Service, U.S. Department of Labor. Washington, D.C.: Government Printing Office.

Hunter, J. E. 1983. A causal analysis of cognitive ability, job knowledge, job performance, and supervisor ratings. In *Performance Measurement and Theory*. F. Landy, S. Zedeck, and J. Cleveland (eds.). Hillsdale, N.J.: Lawrence Erlbaum Associates, pp. 257–266.

Hunter, J. E. 1985. *Differential validity across jobs in the military*. Rockville, Md.: Research Applications.

Hunter, J. E. 1986. Cognitive ability, cognitive aptitudes, job knowledge, and job performance. *J. of Vocational Behavior* 29:340–362.

Hunter, J. E. 1989. *The Wonderlic Personnel Test as a Predictor of Training Success and Job Performance.* Northfield, Ill.: E. F. Wonderlic Personnel Test.

Hunter, J. E., and Hunter, R. F. 1984. Validity and utility of alternative predictors of job performance. *Psychological Bull.* 96:72–98.

Hunter, J. E., and Schmidt, F. L. 1982. Fitting people to jobs: The impact of personnel selection on national productivity. In *Human Performance and Productivity: Human Capability Assessment,* vol. 1. M. D. Dunnette and E. A. Fleishman (eds.). Hillsdale, N.J.: Lawrence Erlbaum Associates, pp. 233–284.

Hunter, J. E., and Schmidt, F. L. 1990. *Methods of Meta-Analysis: Correcting Error and Bias in Research Findings.* Newbury Park, Cal.: Sage Publications.

Hunter, J. E., Schmidt, F. L., and Judiesch, M. K. 1990. Individual differences in output variability as a function of job complexity. *J. of Applied Psych.* 75:28–42.

Husby, R. D. 1993. The minimum wage, wage subsidies, and poverty. *Contemporary Policy Issues* 11:30–38.

Husén, T., and Tuijnman, A. 1991. The contribution of formal schooling to the increase in intellectual capital. *Educational Researcher* 20:17–25.

Hutchens, R., Jakubson, G., and Schwartz, S. 1987. AFDC and the formation of subfamilies. Discussion Paper 832–87. Madison, Wis.: Institute for Research on Poverty.

Ilai, D., and Willerman, L. 1989. Sex differences in WAIS-R item performance. *Intelligence* 13:225–234.

Illich, I. 1970. *Deschooling Society.* New York: Harper & Row.

Ingle, D. J. 1973. *Who Should Have Children? An Environmental and Genetic Approach.* New York: Bobbs-Merrill.

Iowa State Department of Public Instruction. 1965. *Dropouts: Iowa Public Schools.* Des Moines, Iowa: State of Iowa.

Irwin, P. M. 1992. *Elementary and Secondary Education Act of 1965: FY 1993 Guide To Programs.* Congressional Research Service. Washington, D.C.: Government Printing Office.

Itzkoff, S. W. 1993. America's unspoken economic dilemma: Falling intelligence levels. *J. of Social, Econ., and Political Studies* 18:311–326.

Iwawaki, S., and Vernon, P. E. 1988. Japanese abilities and achievements. In *Human Abilities in Cultural Context.* S. H. Irvine and J. W. Berry (eds.). New York: Cambridge University Press, pp. 358–384.

Jargowsky, P. 1993. Ghetto poverty among blacks in the 1980's. University of Texas at Dallas. Photocopy.

Jaynes, G. D., and R. M. Williams (eds.). 1989. *A Common Destiny: Blacks and American Society.* Washington, D.C.: National Academy Press.

Jencks, C. 1979. *Who Gets Ahead? The Determinants of Economic Success in America.* New York: Basic Books.

Jencks, C., and Peterson, P. E. (eds.). 1991. *The Urban Underclass.* Washington, D.C.: Brookings Institution.

Jencks, C., Smith, M., Acland, H., Bane, M. J., Cohen, D., Gintis, H., Heyns, B., and Michelson, S. 1972. *Inequality: A Reassessment of the Effect of Family and Schooling in America.* New York: Basic Books.

Jennings, J. T. 1991. *Voting and Registration in the Election of Nov. 1990.* Current Population Report Series P-20, No. 453. U.S. Bureau of the Census. Washington, D.C.: Government Printing Office.

Jensen, A. R. 1969. How much can we boost IQ and scholastic achievement? *Harvard Educational Rev.* 39:1–123.

Jensen, A. R. 1974. How biased are culture-loaded tests? *Genetic Psych. Monographs* 90:185–244.

Jensen, A. R. 1977. Cumulative deficit in IQ of blacks in the rural South. *Developmental Psych.* 13:184–191.

Jensen, A. R. 1978. Genetic and behavioral effects of nonrandom mating. In *Human Variation: Biopsychology of Age, Race, and Sex.* R. T. Osborne, C. E. Noble, and N. Weyl (eds.). New York: Academic Press, pp. 5–105.

Jensen, A. R. 1980. *Bias in Mental Testing.* New York: Free Press.

Jensen, A. R. 1984a. The black-white difference on the K-ABC: Implications for future tests. *J. of Special Education* 18:377–408.

Jensen, A. R. 1984b. Test bias: Concepts and criticisms. In *Perspectives on "Bias in Mental Testing."* C. R. Reynolds and R. T. Brown (eds.). New York: Plenum Press, pp. 507–586.

Jensen, A. R. 1985. The nature of the black-white difference on various psychometric tests: Spearman's hypothesis. *The Behavioral and Brain Sciences.* 8:193–258.

Jensen, A. R. 1986. *g:* Artifact or reality? *J. of Vocational Behavior* 29:301–331.

Jensen, A. R. 1987a. Continuing commentary on "The nature of the black-white difference on various psychometric tests: Spearman's hypothesis." *The Behavioral and Brain Sciences.* 10:507–537.

Jensen, A. R. 1987b. The *g* beyond factor analysis. In *The Influence of Cognitive Psych. on Testing.* Royce R. Ronning, J. A. Glover, J. C. Conoley, and J. C. Witt (eds.). Hillsdale, N.J.: Lawrence Erlbaum Associates, pp. 87–142.

Jensen, A. R. 1989. Raising IQ without increasing *g?* A review of "The Milwaukee Project: Preventing Mental Retardation in Children at Risk." *Developmental Review* 9:234–258.

Jensen, A. R. 1990. Speed of information processing in a calculating prodigy. *Intelligence* 14:259–274.

Jensen, A. R. 1992. Spearman's hypothesis: Methodology and evidence. *Multivariate Behavioral Research* 27:225–233.

Jensen, A. R. 1993a. Psychometric *g* and achievement. In *Policy Perspectives on Educational Testing*. B. R. Gifford (ed.). Boston: Kluwer Academic Publishers, pp. 117–227.

Jensen, A. R. 1993b. Spearman's hypothesis tested with chronometric information-processing tasks. *Intelligence* 17:44–77.

Jensen, A. R., and Faulstich, M. E. 1988. Difference between prisoners and the general population in psychometric g. *Personality and Individual Differences* 9:925–928.

Jensen, A. R., and Figueroa, R. A. 1975. Forward and backward digit span interaction with race and IQ: Predictions from Jensen's theory. *J. of Educational Psych.* 67:882–893.

Jensen, A. R., and Inouye, A. R. 1980. Level I and Level II abilities in Asian, white, and black children. *Intelligence* 4:41–49.

Jensen, A. R., and McGurk, F. C. J. 1987. Black-white bias in "cultural" and "noncultural" test items. *Personality and Individual Differences*. 8:295–301.

Jensen, A. R., and Munro, E. 1979. Reaction time, movement time, and intelligence. *Intelligence* 3:121–126.

Jensen, A. R., and Naglieri, J. A. 1987. Comparison of black-white differences on the WISC-R and the K-ABC: Spearman's hypothesis. *Intelligence* 11:21.

Jensen, A. R., and Reynolds, C. R. 1982. Race, social class and ability patterns on the WISC-R. *Personality and Individual Differences* 3:423–438.

Jensen, R. F., and Nicholas, K. B. 1984. Influence of the social characteristics of both father and child on the tendency to report child abuse. *Professional Psych.: Research and Practice* 15:121–128.

Johnson, B., and Morse, H. A. 1968. Injured children and their parents. *Children* 15:147–152.

Johnson, K.M., et al. 1984. The nature of human ability: An historical perspective on intelligence. Paper presented at the annual meeting of the American Educational Research Association, New Orleans.

Johnson, R. C., Ahern, F. M., and Cole, R. E. 1980. Secular change in degree of assortative mating for ability? *Behavioral Genetics* 10:1–8.

Johnson, R. C., Nagoshi, C. T., and Ahern, F. M. 1987. A reply to Heath et al. on assortative mating for educational level. *Behavioral Genetics* 17:1–7.

Johnson, S. T. 1988. Test fairness and bias: Measuring academic achievement among black youth. *Urban League Rev.* 11:76–92.

Johnson, S. T., and Wallace, M. B. 1989. Characteristics of SAT quantitative items showing improvement after coaching among black students from low-income families: An exploratory study. Special Issue: The test item. *J. of Educational Measurement* 26:133–145.

Jones, E. F. and Forrest, J. D. 1992. Underreporting of abortion in surveys of U.S. women: 1976 to 1988. *Demography* 29:113–126.

Jones, G. E. 1988. Investigation of the efficacy of general ability versus specific ability as predictors of occupational success. Master's thesis, St. Mary's University.

Joynson, R. B. 1989. *The Burt Affair*. London: Routledge.

Juhn, C., Murphy, K. M., and Pierce, B. 1990. Wage inequality and the rise in returns to skill. University of Chicago. Photocopy.

Kadushin, A. 1988. Neglect in families. In *Mental Illness, Delinquency, Addictions, and Neglect*. E. W. Nunnally, C. S. Chilman, and F.M. Cox (eds.). Newbury Park, Calif.: Sage, pp. 147–166.

Kamin, L. 1974. *The Science and Politics of IQ*. Hillsdale, N.J.: Lawrence Erlbaum Associates.

Kandel, E., Mednick, S. A., Kirkegaard-Sorensen, L., Hutchings, B., Knop, J., Rosenberg, R., and Schulsinger, F. 1988. IQ as a protective factor for subjects at high risk for antisocial behavior. *J. of Consulting and Clinical Psych.* 56:224–226.

Karen, D. 1991. "Achievement" and "ascription" in admission to an elite college: A political-organizational analysis. *Sociological Forum* 6:349–380.

Karmel, L. J., and Karmel, M. O. 1978. *Measurement and Evaluation in the Schools*. 2d ed. New York: Macmillan.

Kasarda, J. D. 1989. Urban industrial transition and the underclass. *Annals of the Am. Academy of Political and Social Science* 501:26–47.

Katz, L. F., and Murphy, K. M. 1990. *Changes in Relative Wages, 1963–1987: Supply and Demand Factors*. Cambridge, Mass.: National Bureau of Economic Research.

Kaufman, A. S., and Kaufman, N. L. 1983. *Kaufman Assessment Battery for Children: Interpretive Manual*. Circle Pines, Minn.: American Guidance Service.

Kaufman, J., and Zigler, E. 1987. Do abused children become abusive parents? *Am. J. of Orthopsychiatry* 57:186–192.

Kaus, M. 1992. *The End of Equality*. New York: Basic Books.

Keene, K., and Ladd, E. C. 1991. Politics of the professoriate. *Am. Enterprise* (July/August): 86–87.

Keeves, J. (ed.). 1991. *The IEA Study of Science III: Changes in Science Education and Achievement 1970–84*. Oxford: Pergamon Press.

Keller, C., and Fetterly, K. 1978. Legitimacy and mother's education as risk factors in post neonatal mortality. Paper presented at the American Public Health Association Annual Meeting, Los Angeles.

Keller, H., Miranda, D., and Gauda, G. 1984. The naive theory of the infant and some maternal attitudes. *J. of Cross-Cultural Psych.* 15:165–179.

Kelley, M. L., Power, T. G., and Wimbush, D. D. 1992. Determinants of disciplinary practices in low-income black mothers. *Child Development* 63:573–582.

Kelman, M. 1991. Concepts of discrimination in "general ability" job testing. *Harvard Law Rev.* 104:1158–1247.

Kempe, A., et al. 1992. Clinical determinants of the racial disparity in very low birth weight. *New England J. of Medicine* 327:969–973.

Kendall, I. M., Verster, M. A., and Mollendorf, J. W. V. 1988. Test performance of blacks in Southern Africa. In *Human Abilities in Cultural Context*. S. H. Irvine and J. W. Berry (eds.). Cambridge: Cambridge University Press, pp. 299–339.

Keogh, B. K., and MacMillan, D. L. 1970. Effects of motivational and presentation conditions on digit recall of children of differing socioeconomic, racial, and intelligence groups. *Am. Educational Research J.* 8:27–38.

Kevles, D. J. 1985. *In the Name of Eugenics: Genetics and the Uses of Human Heredity*. New York: Alfred A. Knopf.

Kinder, D. R., and Sears, D. O. 1985. Public opinion and political action. In *Handbook of Social Psychology*. vol. 2. G. Lindzey and E. Aronson (eds.). New York: Random House, pp. 659–741.

Kitagawa, E., and Hauser, P. M. 1960. Education differences in mortality by cause of death. *Demography* 5:318–353.

Klein, M., and Stern, L. 1971. Low birth weight and the battered child syndrome. *Am. J. of Diseases of Children* 122:15–18.

Kleppner, P. 1982. *Who Voted? The Dynamics of Electoral Turnout, 1870–1980*. New York: Praeger.

Kline, P. 1985. The nature of psychometric g. *Behavioral and Brain Sciences* 8:234.

Klitgaard, R. 1985. *Choosing Elites: Selecting "The Best and the Brightest" at Top Universities and Elsewhere*. New York: Basic Books.

Knight, R. A., and Goodnow, J. J. 1988. Parents' beliefs about influences over cognitive and social development. *International J. of Behavioral Development* 11:517–527.

Koh, T., Abbatiello, A., and McLoughlin, C. S. 1984. Cultural bias in WISC subtest items: A response to Judge Grady's suggestion in relation to the PASE case. *School Psych. Rev.* 13:89–94.

Kohl, H. 1967. *36 Children*. New York: New American Library.

Kohn, M. L. 1959. Social class and parental values. *Am. J. of Sociology* 64:337–351.

Kominski, R. 1990. Estimating the national high school dropout rate. *Demography* 27:303–311.

Kosters, M. H. 1993. The earned income tax credit and the working poor. *Am. Enterprise* (May–June): 64–72.

Kozol, J. 1967. *Death at an Early Age: The Destruction of the Hearts and Minds of Negro Children*. Boston: Houghton Mifflin.

Kozol, J. 1985. *Illiterate America*. Garden City, N.Y.: Anchor Press/Doubleday.

Kozol, J. 1992. *Savage Inequalities: Children in America's Schools*. New York: HarperCollins.

Kraiger, K., and Ford, J. K. 1985. A meta-analysis of race effects in performance ratings. *J. of Applied Psych.* 70:56–65.

Kravitz, R. I., and Driscoll, J. M. 1983. Expectations for childhood development among child-abusing and nonabusing parents. *Am. J. of Orthopsychiatry* 53:345–352.

Krishnan, V. 1990. A causal approach to the study of fertility and familism. *Social Biology* 37:59–68.

Krohn, E. J., Lamp, R. E., and Phelps, C. G. 1988. Validity of the K-ABC for a black preschool population. *Psych. in the Schools* 25:15–21.

Kronick, R. F., and Hargis, C. H. 1990. *Dropouts: Who Drops Out and Why—and the Recommended Action.* Springfield, Ill.: Charles C. Thomas.

Lam, D. A., and Miron, J. A. 1991. Seasonality of births in human populations. *Social Biology* 38:51–78.

Lambert, C. 1993. Desperately seeking summa. *Harvard Magazine* (May–June): 36–30.

Lamson, E. E. 1938. To what extent are intelligence quotients increased by children who participate in a rich vital school curriculum? *J. of Educational Psych.* 29:67–70.

Lane, H. 1976. *The Wild Boy of Aveyron.* Cambridge, Mass.: Harvard University Press.

Lane, H., and Pillard, R. 1978. *The Wild Boy of Burundi: A Study of an Outcast Child.* New York: Random House.

Lazar, I., and Darlington, R. 1982. Lasting effects of early education: A report from the consortium for longitudinal studies. *Monographs of the Society for Research in Child Development* 47, issues 2–3.

Learned, W. S., and Wood, B. D. 1938. *The Student and His Knowledge, A Report to the Carnegie Foundation on the Results of the High School and College Examinations of 1928, 1930, and 1932.* New York: Carnegie Foundation for the Advancement of Teaching.

Lee, V. E., Brooks-Gunn, J., Schnur, E., and Liaw, F.-R. 1990. Are Head Start effects sustained? A longitudinal follow-up comparison of disadvantaged children attending Head Start, no preschool, and other preschool programs. *Child Development* 61:495–507.

Lemann, N. 1991. *The Promised Land: The Great Black Migration and How It Changed America.* New York: Alfred A. Knopf.

Leonard, C. H., et al. 1990. Effect of medical and social risk factors on outcome of prematurity and very low birth weight. *J. of Pediatrics* 116:620–626.

Leonard, J. S. 1984. Employment and occupational advance under affirmative action. *Rev. of Economics and Statistics* 66:377–385.

Leonard, J. S. 1986. The effectiveness of equal employment law and affirmative action regulations. In *Research in Labor Economics,* vol. 8, Part B. R. G. Ehrenberg (ed.). Greenwich, Conn.: JAI Press, pp. 85–140.

Lerner, B. 1991. Good news about American education. *Commentary* (March): 19–25.

Levin, H. M. 1989. Economics of investment in educationally disadvantaged students. *Am. Econ. Rev.* 79:52–56.

Levin, M. In press. Comment on Minnesota transracial adoption study. *Intelligence*.

Levy, F., and Murnane, R. J. 1992. U.S. earnings levels and earnings inequality: A review of recent trends and proposed explanations. *J. of Econ. Literature* 30:133–1381.

Lewontin, R. C. 1970. Race and intelligence. *Bull. of the Atomic Scientists* 26:2–8.

Lewontin, R., Rose, S., and Kamin, L. 1984. *Not in Our Genes*. New York: Pantheon Books.

Li, V. H. 1988. Asian discrimination: Fact or fiction? *College Board Rev.* 149: 20–32.

Lichter, D. T., LeClere, F. B., and McLaughlin, D. K. 1991. Local marriage markets and the marital behavior of black and white women. *Am. J. of Sociology* 96:843–867.

Liebmann, G. W. 1993. The AFDC conundrum: A new look at an old institution. *Social Work* 38:36–43.

Linn, R. L. 1983. Predictive bias as an artifact of selection procedures. In *Principles of Modern Psychological Measurement: A Festschrift for Frederic M. Lord*. H. Wainer and S. Messick (eds.). Hillsdale, N.J.: Lawrence Erlbaum Associates, pp. 27–40.

Linn, R. L. 1986. Comments on the *g* factor in employment testing. *J. of Vocational Behavior* 29:438–44.

Lippmann, W. 1922a. A future for the tests. *New Republic* (November 29): 9–10.

Lippmann, W. 1922b. *Public Opinion*. New York: Macmillan.

Lippmann, W. 1923. The great confusion. *New Republic* (January 3):145–146.

Lippmann, W. 1955. *Essays in the Public Philosophy*. Boston: Little, Brown.

Lipsitt, P. D., Buka, S. L., and Lipsitt, L. P. 1990. Early intelligence scores and subsequent delinquency: A prospective study. *Am. J. of Family Therapy* 18:197–208.

Lloyd, D. 1990. Throwing stones in glass houses. *California Monthly* (September): 17, 19.

Locke, J. 1689. *Two Treatises of Government.*. 1960 ed. Cambridge: Cambridge University Press, 1960.

Locke, J. *Essays*. 1975 ed. Oxford: Oxford University Press.

Locurto, C. 1990. The malleability of IQ as judged from adoption studies. *Intelligence* 14:275–292.

Locurto, C. 1991. Beyond IQ in preschool programs? *Intelligence* 15:295–312.

Loehlin, J. C. 1992. Guttman on factor analysis and group differences: A comment. *Multivariate Behavioral Research* 27:235–237.

Loehlin, J. C., Lindzey, G., and Spuhler, J. N. 1975. *Race Differences in Intelligence*. San Francisco: W. H. Freeman and Company.

Lorge, I. 1942. The "last school grade completed" as an index of intellectual level. *School and Society* 56:529–531.

Louchheim, K. (ed.). 1983. *The Making of the New Deal: The Insiders Speak*. Cambridge, Mass.: Harvard University Press.

Loury, L. D., and Garman, D. 1993a. Affirmative action in higher education. *Am. Econ. Rev.* 83:99–103.

Loury, L. D., and Garman, D. 1993b. College selectivity and earnings. Medford, Mass.: Tufts University. Photocopy.

Lukacs, J. 1986. *Immigration and Migration—A Historical Perspective*. Monograph Series, Paper 5. Monterey, Va.: American Immigration Control Foundation.

Lundberg, S., and Plotnick, R. D. 1990. Adolescent premarital childbearing: Do opportunity costs matter? Discussion Paper 90–23. Seattle, Wash.: Institute for Economic Research, University of Washington.

Luskin, R. C. 1990. Explaining political sophistication. *Political Behavior* 4:331–361.

Luster, T., Rhoades, K., and Haas, B. 1989. The relation between parental values and parenting behavior: A test of the Kohn hypothesis. *J. of Marriage and the Family* 51:138–147.

Lynch, F. R. 1991. *Invisible Victims: White Males and the Crisis of Affirmative Action*. New York: Praeger.

Lynn, M. 1989. Race differences in sexual behavior: A critique of Rushton and Bogaert's evolutionary hypothesis. *J. of Research in Personality* 23:1–6.

Lynn, R. 1977. The intelligence of the Japanese. *Bull. of the British Psychological Society* 30:69–72.

Lynn, R. 1978. Ethnic and racial differences in intelligence: International comparisons. In *Human Variation: The Biopsychology of Age, Race, and Sex*. R. T. Osborne, C. E. Noble, and N. Weyl (eds.). New York: Academic Press, pp. 261–286.

Lynn, R. 1982. IQ in Japan and the United States shows a growing disparity. *Nature* 297:222–223.

Lynn, R. 1987a. The intelligence of the mongoloids: A psychometric, evolutionary and neurological theory. *Personality and Individual Differences* 8:813–844.

Lynn, R. 1987b. Japan: Land of the rising IQ: A reply to Flynn. *Bull. of the British Psychological Society* 40:464–468.

Lynn, R. 1989. Positive correlations between head size and IQ. *British J. of Educational Psych.* 59:372–377.

Lynn, R. 1990a. Differential rates of secular increase of five major primary abilities. *Social Biology* 37:137–141.

Lynn, R. 1990b. The role of nutrition in secular increases in intelligence. *Personality and Individual Differences* 3:273–285.

Lynn, R. 1990c. Testosterone and gonadotropin levels and r/K reproductive strategies. *Psychological Report* 67:1203–1206.

Lynn, R. 1991a. Comment on "Educational achievements of Asian Americans." *Am. Psychologist* 46:875–876.

Lynn, R. 1991b. The evolution of racial differences in intelligence. *Mankind Quarterly* 32:99–121.

Lynn, R. 1991c. Race differences in intelligence: A global perspective. *Mankind Quarterly* 31:254–296.

Lynn, R. 1992. Intelligence: Ethnicity and culture. In *Cultural Diversity and the Schools*. J. Lynch and C. Modgil (eds.). London: Falmer Press, pp. 361–387.

Lynn, R. 1993a. Further evidence for the existence of race and sex differences in cranial capacity. *Social Behavior and Personality* 21:89–92.

Lynn, R. 1993b. Oriental Americans: Their IQ, educational attainment and socio-economic status. *Personality and Individual Differences* 15:237–242.

Lynn, R. In press. Some reinterpretations of the Minnesota Transracial Adoption study. *Intelligence*.

Lynn, R., and Hampson, S. 1986a. Further evidence for secular increases in intelligence in Britain, Japan, and the United States. *Behavioral and Brain Sciences* 9:203–204.

Lynn, R., and Hampson, S. 1986b. Intellectual abilities of Japanese children: An assessment of 2 1/2–8 1/2-year-olds derived from the McCarthy Scales of Children's Abilities. *Intelligence* 10:41.

Lynn, R., and Hampson, S. 1986c. The rise of national intelligence: Evidence from Britain, Japan, and the U.S.A. *Personality and Individual Differences* 7:23–32.

Lynn, R., Hampson, S. L., and Iwawaki, S. 1987. Abstract reasoning and spatial abilities in American, British and Japanese adolescents. *Mankind Quarterly* 27:379–405.

Lynn, R., and Hattori, K. 1990. The heritability of intelligence in Japan. *Behavior Genetics* 20:545–546.

Lynn, R., Pagliari, C., and Chan, J. 1988. Intelligence in Hong Kong measured for Spearman's *g* and the visuospatial and verbal primaries. *Intelligence* 12:423–433.

Lynn, R., and Song, M. J. 1994. General intelligence, visuospatial and verbal abilities in Korean children. *Personality and Individual Differences* 16:363–364.

McCall, R. B. 1977. Childhood IQ's as predictors of adult educational and occupational status. *Science* 197:482–483.

McCall, R. B. 1979. The development of intellectual functioning in infancy and the prediction of later IQ. In *Handbook of Infant Development*. J. D. Osofsky (ed.). New York: Wiley, pp. 707–741.

McCall, R. B. 1987. Developmental function, individual differences, and the plasticity of intelligence. In *The Malleability of Children*. J. J. Gallagher and C. T. Ramey (eds.). Baltimore: Paul H. Brookes, pp. 25–35.

McClelland, D. C. 1973. Testing for competence rather than for "intelligence." *Am. Psychologist* 28:1–14.

McCornack, R. L. 1983. Bias in the validity of predicted college grades in four ethnic minority groups. *Educational and Psychological Measurement* 18:54–58.

McDaniel, M. A., Schmidt, F. L., and Hunter, J. E. 1986. *The Evaluation of a Causal Model of Job Performance: The Relationship of Job Experience and General Mental Ability to Job Performance*. U.S. Office of Personnel Management, Washington, D.C.: Government Printing Office.

McGue, M., and Lykken, D. T. 1992. Genetic influence on risk of divorce. *Psychological Science* 3:368–373.

McGurk, F. C. J. 1951. *Comparison of the Performance of Negro and White High School Seniors on Cultural and Noncultural Psychological Test Questions*. Washington, D.C.: Catholic University Press.

McGurk, F. C. J. 1953a. On white and Negro test performance and socioeconomic factors. *J. of Abnormal Social Psych.* 48:448–450.

McGurk, F. C. J. 1953b. Socioeconomic status and culturally weighted test scores of Negro subjects. *J. of Applied Psych.* 37:276–277.

McGurk, F. C. J. 1967. The culture hypothesis and psychological tests. In *Race and Modern Science*, vol. 37. R. E. Kuttner (ed.). New York: Social Science Press, pp. 367–381.

McKey, R. H. 1985. *The Impact of Head Start on Children, Families, and Communities*. A. N. Smith and S. S. Aitken (eds.). Washington, D.C.: U.S. Department of Health and Human Services.

McKnight, C., et al. 1989. *The Underachieving Curriculum: Assessing U.S. Mathematics from an International Perspective*. Champaign, Ill.: Stipes.

McLanahan, S. S. 1988. Family structure and dependency: Early transitions to female household headship. *Demography* 25:1–16.

McLanahan, S., and Bumpass, L. 1988. Intergenerational consequences of family disruption. *Am. J. of Sociology* 94:130–152.

McLaughlin, D. H. 1977. *Title I, 1965–1975: A Synthesis of the Findings of Federal Studies*. Palo Alto, Cal.: American Institutes for Research.

McLoyd, V. 1990. The impact of economic hardship on black families and children: Psychological distress, parenting, and socioemotional development. *Child Development* 61:311–346.

MacMahon, A. W., and Millett, J. D. 1939. *Federal Administrators: A Bio-*

graphical Approach to the Problem of Departmental Management. New York: Columbia University Press.

Macphail, E. M. 1985. Comparative studies of animal intelligence: Is Spearman's *g* really Hull's D? *Behavioral and Brain Sciences* 8:234–235.

McShane, D., and Berry, J. W. 1988. Native North Americans: Indians and Inuit abilities. In *Human Abilities in Cultural Context.* S. H. Irvine and J. W. Berry (eds.). Cambridge: Cambridge University Press, pp. 385–426.

Madhere, S. 1989. Models of intelligence and the black intellect. *J. of Negro Education* 58:189–202.

Maguire, T. 1992. My bout with affirmative action. *Commentary* (April): 50–52.

Maier, M. H., and Hiatt, C. M. 1985. *On the Content and Measurement Validity of Hands-On Job Performance Tests.* CRM 85–79.Washington, D.C.: Center for Naval Analyses.

Maier, N. R. F., and Schneirla, T. C. 1935. *Principles of Animal Psychology.* New York: McGraw-Hill.

Manchester, W. 1983. *The Last Lion: Winston Spencer Churchill.* Boston: Little, Brown.

Mangold, W. D., and Powell-Griner, E. 1991. Race of parents and infant birthweight in the United States. *Social Biology* 38:13–27.

Mare, R. D. 1991. Five decades of educational assortative mating. *Am. Sociological Rev.* 56:15–32.

Mascie-Taylor, C. G. N. 1989. Spouse similarity for IQ and personality and convergence. *Behavior Genetics* 19:223–227.

Mascie-Taylor, C. G. N. 1990. The biology of social class. In *Biosocial Aspects of Social Class.* C. G. N. Mascie-Taylor (ed.). New York: Oxford University Press, pp. 117–142.

Mascie-Taylor, C. G. N., and Vandenberg, S. G. 1988. Assortative mating for IQ and personality due to propinquity and personal preference. *Behavior Genetics* 18:339–345.

Mason, K. O., and Palan, V. T. 1981. Female employment and fertility in peninsular Malaysia: The maternal role incompatibility hypothesis reconsidered. *Demography* 18:549–575.

Massey, D. S., and Denton, N. A. 1993. *American Apartheid: Segregation and the Making of the Underclass.* Cambridge, Mass.: Harvard University Press.

Massey, D. S., and Eggers, M. L. 1990. The ecology of inequality: Minorities and the concentration of poverty, 1970–1980. *Am. J. of Sociology* 95:1153–1188.

Mastropieri, M. A. 1987. Age at start as a correlate of intervention effectiveness. *Psych. in the Schools* 24:59–62.

Matarazzo, J. D. 1972. *Wechsler's Measurement and Appraisal of Adult Intelligence.* New York: Oxford University Press.

Matthews, G., and Dorn, L. 1989. IQ and choice reaction time: An information processing analysis. *Intelligence* 13:299–317.

Maxwell, J. 1954. Intelligence, fertility, and the future: A report on the 1947 Scottish Mental Survey. *Eugenics Quarterly* 1:244–247.

Mayer, R. E., and Treat, J. R. 1977. Psychological, social and cognitive characteristics of high-risk drivers: A pilot study. *Accident Analysis and Prevention* 9:1–8.

Mayo, B. 1942. *Jefferson Himself*. New York: Houghton Mifflin.

Mednick, S. A., Moffitt, T. E., and Stack, S. A. (eds.). 1987. *The Causes of Crime: New Biological Approaches*. New York: Cambridge University Press.

Medrich, E. A., and Griffith, J. E. 1992. *International Mathematics and Science Assessments: What Have We Learned?* NCES 92–011. Office of Educational Research and Improvement, National Center for Education Statistics. Washington, D.C.: Government Printing Office.

Mercer, J. R. 1984. What is a racially and culturally nondiscriminatory test? A sociological and pluralistic perspective. In *Perspectives on "Bias in Mental Testing."* C. R. Reynolds and R. T. Brown (eds.). New York: Plenum Press, pp. 293–356.

Mercer, J. R. 1988. Ethnic differences in IQ scores: What do they mean? (A response to Lloyd Dunn). *Hispanic J. of Behavioral Sciences* 10:199–218.

Merrill, M. A. 1938. The significance of IQ's on the revised Stanford-Binet scales. *J. of Educational Psych.* 29:641–651.

Messé, L. A., Crano, W. D., Messé, S. R., and Rice, W. 1979. Evaluation of the predictive validity of tests of mental ability for classroom performance in elementary grades. *J. of Educational Psych.* 71:233–241.

Messick, S. 1980. *The Effectiveness of Coaching for the SAT: Review, and Reanalysis of Research from the Fifties to the FTC*. Princeton, N.J.: Educational Testing Service.

Messick, S., and Jungeblut, A. 1981. Time and method in coaching for the SAT. *Psychological Bull.* 89:191–216.

Michael, J. S. 1988. A new look at Morton's craniological research. *Current Anthropology* 29:349–354.

Miele, F. 1979. Cultural bias in the WISC. *Intelligence* 3:149–164.

Milbrath, L. W., and Goel, M. L. 1977. *Political Participation: How and Why Do People Get Involved in Politics?* 2d ed. Chicago: Rand McNally.

Miller, B. C. 1993. Families, science, and values: Alternative views of parenting effects and adolescent pregnancy. *J. of Marriage and the Family* 55:7–21.

Miller, J. J. 1993. The U Mass morass. *Am. Experiment* 1:6–7.

Miller-Jones, D. 1989. Culture and testing. *Am. Psychologist* 44:360–366.

Mishra, S. P. 1981. Factor analysis of the McCarthy scales for groups of white and Mexican-American children. *J. of School Psych.* 19:178–182.

Mishra, S. P. 1982. The WISC-R and evidence of item bias for native-American Navajos. *Psych. in the Schools* 19:458–460.

Mishra, S. P. 1983. Ethnic group bias in WISC-R verbal items. Paper presented at the annual meeting of the American Psychological Association, Anaheim, Cal.

Modu, C. C., and Stern, J. 1975. *The Stability of the SAT Score Scale*. College Entrance Examination Board Research and Development Report 74–75, No. 3. Princeton, N.J.: Educational Testing Service.

Modu, C. C., and Stern, J. 1977. The stability of the SAT-Verbal score scale. In the appendixes to *On Further Examination: Report of the Advisory Panel on the Scholastic Aptitude Test Score Decline*. Princeton, N.J.: College Board, pp. 1–17.

Moffitt, R. 1983. An economic model of welfare stigma. *Am. Econ. Rev.* 73:1023–1035.

Moffitt, R. 1992. Incentive effects of the U.S. welfare system: A review. *J. of Econ. Literature* 30:1–61.

Moffitt, T. E., and Silva, P. A. 1988. IQ and delinquency: A direct test of the differential detection hypothesis. *J. of Abnormal Psych.* 97:330–333.

Moffitt, T. E., et al. 1981. Socioeconomic status, IQ, and delinquency. *J. of Abnormal Psych.* 90:152–56.

Montie, J. E., and Fagan, J. F. I. 1988. Racial differences in IQ: Item analysis of the Stanford-Binet at three years. *Intelligence* 12:315–332.

Moore, E. G. J. 1985. Ethnicity as a variable in child development. In *Beginnings: The Social and Affective Development of Black Children*. M. B. Spencer, G. K. Brookins, and W. R. Allen (eds.). Hillsdale, N.J.: Lawrence Erlbaum Associates, pp. 101–115.

Moore, E. G. J. 1986. Family socialization and the IQ test performance of traditionally and transracially adopted black children. *Developmental Psych.* 22:317–326.

Mordechai, M. 1975. A study of cross-cultural factorial structure of intelligence. *Psychologia: An International J. of Psych. in the Orient* 18:92–94.

Mosteller, F., and Moynihan, D. P. (eds.). 1972. *On Equality of Educational Opportunity*. New York: Random House.

Moynihan, D. P. 1986. *Family and Nation*. New York: Harcourt Brace Jovanovich.

Munford, P. R., and Munoz, A. 1980. A comparison of the WISC and WISC-R on Hispanic children. *J. of Clinical Psych.* 36:452–458.

Munsinger, H. 1975. The adopted child's IQ: A critical review. *Psychological Bull.* 82:623–659.

Murchison, C. 1926. *Criminal Intelligence*. Worcester, Mass.: Clark University.

Murphy, K. M., and Welch, F. 1989. Wage differentials in the 1980s: The role of international trade. Applied Econometrics Discussion Paper 23. Chicago: University of Chicago.

Murphy, K. M., and Welch, F. 1993a. Inequality and relative wages. *Am. Econ. Rev.* 83:104–109.

Murphy, K. M., and Welch, F. 1993b. Occupational change and the demand for skill, 1940–1990. *Am. Econ. Rev.* 83:122–126.

Murphy, K. R. 1986. When your top choice turns you down: Effect of rejected offers on the utility of selection tests. *Psychological Bull.* 99:133–138.

Murray, C. 1984. *Losing Ground: American Social Policy, 1950–1980.* New York: Basic Books.

Murray, C. 1986a. *According to age: Longitudinal profiles of AFDC recipients and the poor by age group.* Working seminar on the Family and American Welfare Policy. Washington, D.C.: American Enterprise Institute.

Murray, C. 1986b. No, welfare isn't really the problem. *Public Interest* no. 84:3–11.

Murray, C. 1988a. The coming of custodial democracy. *Commentary* 86:19–24.

Murray, C. 1988b. *In Pursuit: Of Happiness and Good Government.* New York: Simon & Schuster.

Murray, C. 1993. Welfare and the family: The American experience. *J. of Labor Economics* 11:224–262.

Murray, C. 1994. Does welfare bring more babies? *Public Interest,* no. 115:17–30.

Murray, C., and Herrnstein, R. J. 1992. What's really behind the SAT-score decline? *Public Interest,* no. 106:32–56.

Naglieri, J. A. 1986. WISC-R and K-ABC comparison for matched samples of black and white children. *J. of School Psych.* 24:81–88.

National Center for Education Statistics. 1991. *Trends in Academic Progress: Achievement of American Students in Science, 1970–90, Mathematics, 1973–90, Reading, 1971–90, and Writing, 1984–90.* Washington, D.C.: National Center for Education Statistics.

National Center for Education Statistics. 1992. *The Condition of Education 1992.* Washington, D.C.: Government Printing Office.

National Center for Education Statistics. *Digest of Education Statistics.* Annual. Washington, D.C.: Government Printing Office.

National Center for Health Statistics. 1991. Advance report of final natality statistics, 1989. *Monthly Vital Statistics Report* 40, no. 8.

National Center for Health Statistics. 1993. Advance report of final natality statistics, 1991. *Monthly Vital Statistics Report* 42, no. 3.

National Commission on Excellence in Education. 1983. *A Nation at Risk: The Imperative for Educational Reform.* Washington, D.C.: Government Printing Office.

National Commission on Excellence in Education. 1984. *A Nation at Risk: The Full Account.* Cambridge, Mass.: U.S.A. Research.

Neale, M. C., and McArdle, J. J. 1990. The analysis of assortative mating: A LISREL model. *Behavior Genetics* 20:287–296.

Neill, A. S. 1960. *Summerhill: A Radical Approach to Child Rearing*. New York: Hart.

Neuman, W. R. 1981. Differentiation and integration: Two dimensions of political thinking. *Am. J. of Sociology* 86:1236–1268.

Neuman, W. R. 1986. *The Paradox of Mass Politics: Knowledge and Opinion in the American Electorate*. Cambridge, Mass.: Harvard University Press.

Newberger, C. M., and Cook, S. L. 1983. Parental awareness and child abuse: A cognitive developmental analysis of urban and rural samples. *Am. J. of Orthopsychiatry* 53:512–524.

Newcomer, M. 1955. *The Big Business Executive: The Factors That Made Him, 1900–1950*. New York: Columbia University Press.

Nicholson, R. A., and Kugler, K. E. 1991. Competent and incompetent criminal defendants: A quantitative review of comparative research. *Psychological Bull.* 109:355–370.

Nickerson, R. S. 1986. Project intelligence: An account and some reflections. In *Facilitating Development: International Perspectives, Programs, and Practices*. M. Schwebel and C. A. Maher (eds.). New York: Haworth Press, pp. 83–102.

Nickerson, R. S., Perkins, D. N., and Smith, E. E. 1985. *The Teaching of Thinking*. Hillsdale, N.J.: Lawrence Erlbaum Associates.

Nie, N. H., Verba, S., and Petrocik, J. R. 1976. *The Changing American Voter*. Cambridge, Mass.: Harvard University Press.

Novak, M. 1992. The longtime-Democrat blues. *National Rev.*, July 20, pp. 24–26.

Oakland, T., and Feigenbaum, D. 1979. Multiple sources of test bias on the WISC-R and Bender-Gestalt Test. *J. of Consulting and Clinical Psych.* 47:968–974.

O'Brien, F. P. 1928. Mental ability with reference to selection and retention of college students. *J. of Educational Research* 18:136–143.

O'Connor, N., and Hermelin, B. 1987. Visual memory and motor programmes: Their use by idiot-savant artists and controls. *British J. of Psych.* 78:307–323.

Office of Civil Rights. 1990. *Statement of Findings (for Compliance Rev. No. 01–88–6009 on Harvard University)*. Washington, D.C.: U.S. Department of Education.

Office of Policy and Planning. 1993. *Reinventing Chapter 1: The Current Chapter 1 Program and New Directions*. Washington, D.C.: U.S. Department of Education.

Office of the Assistant Secretary of Defense (Manpower, R. A., and Logistics). 1980. *Implementation of New Armed Services Vocational Aptitude Battery and Actions to Improve the Enlistment Standards Process*. Report to the House and Senate Committees on Armed Services. Washington, D.C.: Department of Defense.

Office of the Assistant Secretary of Defense (Manpower, R. A., and Logistics).

1982. *Profile of American Youth: 1980 Nationwide Administration of the Armed Services Vocational Aptitude Battery.* Washington, D.C.: Department of Defense.

Office of the Assistant Secretary of Defense for Force Management and Personnel. 1989. *Joint-Service Efforts to Link Enlistment Standards to Job Performance: Recruit Quality and Military Readiness.* Report to the House Committee on Appropriations. Washington, D.C.: Department of Defense.

Ogbu, J. U. 1986. The consequences of the American caste system. In *The School Achievement of Minority Children.* U. Neisser (ed.). Hillsdale, N.J.: Lawrence Erlbaum Associates, pp. 19–56.

Olasky, M. 1992. *The Tragedy of American Compassion.* Washington, D.C.: Regnery Gateway.

Olasky, M. 1993. The war on adoption. *National Rev.,* June 7, pp. 38–44.

Olmstead, A. L., and Sheffrin, S. M. 1980a. Affirmative action in medical schools: Econometric evidence and legal doctrine. In *Research in Law and Economics,* vol. 3. Greenwich, Conn.: JAI Press, pp. 207–223.

Olmstead, A. L., and Sheffrin, S. M. 1980b. Medical school admission and affirmative action. Working Paper 146. Davis, Cal.: Department of Economics, University of California at Davis.

Olneck, M. R., Wolfe, B. L., and Dean, C. 1980. Intelligence and family size: Another look. *Rev. of Economics and Statistics* 62:241–247.

Olson, W. K. 1991. *The Litigation Explosion: What Happened When America Unleashed the Lawsuit.* New York: Dutton.

O'Neill, J. 1990. The role of human capital in earnings differences between black and white men. *J. of Econ. Perspectives* 4:25–45.

Oppenheimer, V. K. 1988. A theory of marriage timing: Assortative mating under varying degrees of uncertainty. *Am. J. of Sociology* 94:563–591.

Orr, D. P., et al. 1992. Factors associated with condom use among sexually active female adolescents. *J. of Pediatrics* 120:311–317.

Osborn, F. 1940. *Preface to Eugenics.* New York: Harper & Row.

Osborn, F., and Bajema, C. J. 1972. The eugenic hypothesis. *Social Biology* 19:337–345.

Osborne, R. T. 1973. Fertility ratio: Its relationship to mental ability, school achievement, and race. *J. of Psych.* 84:159–164.

Osborne, R. T. 1975. Fertility, IQ, and school achievement. *Psychological Reports* 37:1067–1073.

Osborne, R. T., and McGurk, F. C. J. (eds.). 1982. *The Testing of Negro Intelligence,* vol. 2. Athens, Ga.: Foundation for Human Understanding.

Osborne, Y. H., Hinz, L. D., Rappaport, N. B., Williams, H. S., and Tuma, J. M. 1988. Parent social attractiveness, parent sex, child temperament, and socioeconomic status as predictors of tendency to report child abuse. *J. of Social and Clinical Psych.* 6:69–76.

O'Toole, B. I. 1990. Intelligence and behaviour and motor vehicle accident mortality. *Accident Analysis and Prevention* 22:211–221.

Owen, D. 1985. *None of the Above: Behind the Myth of Scholastic Aptitude.* Boston: Houghton Mifflin.

Page, E. B. 1972. Miracle in Milwaukee: Raising the IQ. *Educational Researcher* 1:8–15.

Page, E. B., and Grandon, G. M. 1981. Massive intervention and child intelligence: The Milwaukee Project in critical perspective. *J. of Special Education* 15:239–256.

Parke, R., and Collmer, C. W. 1975. Child abuse: An interdisciplinary analysis. In *Review of Child Development Research*, vol. 5. E. M. Hetherington (ed.). Chicago: University of Chicago Press, pp. 150–184.

Parker, S. J., Zahr, L. K., Cole, J. G., and Brecht, M.-L. 1992. Outcome after developmental intervention in the neonatal intensive care unit for mothers of preterm infants with low socioeconomic status. *J. of Pediatrics* 120:780–785.

Passingham, R. E. 1982. *The Human Primate.* San Francisco: Freeman.

Patterson, P. O. 1989. Employment testing and Title VII of the Civil Rights Act of 1964. In *Test Policy and the Politics of Opportunity Allocation: The Workplace and the Law.* B. R. Gifford (ed.). Boston: Kluwer Academic Publishers.

Pearson, J., Hunder, A., Ensminger, M., and Kellam, S. 1990. Black grandmothers in multigenerational households: Diversity in family structure and parenting involvement in Woodlawn community. *Child Development* 61:434–442.

Pearson, R. (ed.). 1992. *Shockley on Eugenics and Race.* Washington, D.C.: Scott-Townsend.

Pedersen, N. L., Plomin, R., Nesselroade, J. R., and McClearn, G. E. 1992. A quantitative genetic analysis of cognitive abilities during the second half of the life span. *Psychological Science* 3:346–353.

Peller, G. 1991. Espousing a positive vision of affirmative-action policies. *Chronicle of Higher Education*, December 18, sec. 2.

Pelton, L. H. 1978. Child abuse and neglect: The myth of classlessness. *Am. J. of Orthopsychiatry* 48:608–617.

Pelton, L. H. 1990–1991. Poverty and child protection. *Protecting Children* (Winter): 3–5.

Peterson, S. A. 1990. *Political Behavior: Patterns in Everyday Life.* Newbury Park, Cal.: Sage Publications.

Phillips, K., Fulker, D. W., Carey, G., and Nagoshi, C. T. 1988. Direct marital assortment for cognitive and personality variables. *Behavior Genetics* 18:347–356.

Piaget, J. 1952. Autobiographical essay. In *A History of Psychology in Autobiog-*

raphy, vol. 4. E. G. Boring, H. S. Langfeld, H. Werner, and R. M. Yerkes (eds.). Worcester, Mass.: Clark University Press, pp. 237–256.

Pick, J. B., Butler, E. W., and Pavgi, S. 1988. Socioeconomic determinants of fertility: Selected Mexican regions, 1976–1977. *Social Biology* 35:137–157.

Pierson, G. W. 1969. *The Education of American Leaders: Comparative Contributions of U.S. Colleges and Universities*. New York: Praeger.

Plomin, R., and Bergeman, C. S. 1987. Why are children in the same family so different from one another? *Behavioral and Brain Sciences* 10:1–60.

Plomin, R., and Bergeman, C. S. 1991. The nature of nurture: Genetic influence on "environmental" measures. *Behavioral and Brain Sciences* 14:373–427.

Plomin, R., and DeFries, J. C. 1980. Genetics and intelligence: Recent data. *Intelligence* 4:15–24.

Plomin, R., and DeFries, J. C. 1985. *Origins of Individual Differences in Infancy: The Colorado Adoption Project*. Orlando, Fla.: Academic Press.

Plomin, R., and Loehlin, J. C. 1989. Direct and indirect IQ heritability estimates: A puzzle. *Behavior Genetics* 19:331–342.

Polansky, N. 1981. *Damaged Parents: An Anatomy of Child Neglect*. Chicago: University of Chicago Press.

Pond, M. 1933. Occupations, intelligence, age, and schooling: Their relationship and distribution in a factory population. *Personnel Journal* 11:373–382.

Popenoe, D. 1993. American family decline, 1960–1990: A review and appraisal. *J. of Marriage and the Family* 55:527–555.

Porter, R. P. 1990. *Forked Tongue: The Politics of Bilingual Education*. New York: Basic Books.

Potter, E. E. 1986. *Employee Selection: Legal and Practical Alternatives to Compliance and Litigation*. Washington, D.C.: National Foundation for the Study of Equal Employment Policy.

Powell, A., Farrar, E., and Cohen, D. 1985. *The Shopping Mall High School*. Boston: Houghton Mifflin.

Powers, D. E. 1977. Comparing predictions of law school performance for black, Chicano, and white law students. In *Reports of LSAC Sponsored Research*. Princeton, N.J.: Law School Admissions Council.

Powers, D. E. 1987. Who benefits most from preparing for a "coachable" admissions test? *Journal of Educational Measurement* 24:247–262.

Preston, S. H., and Campbell, C. 1993. Differential fertility and the distribution of traits: The case of IQ. *Am. J. of Sociology* 98:997–1019.

Price, R. A., and Vandenberg, S. G. 1980. Spouse similarity in American and Swedish couples. *Behavioral Genetics* 10:59–71.

Priest, T. B. 1982. Education and career among corporate chief executive officers: A historical note. *Social Science Quarterly* 63:342–349.

Qian, Z., and Preston, S. H. 1993. Changes in American marriage, 1972–1987:

Availability and forces of attraction by age and education. *Am. Sociological Rev.* 58:482–495.

Quay, H. C. 1987. Intelligence. In *Handbook of Juvenile Delinquency*. H. C. Quay (ed.). New York: Wiley, pp. 106–117.

Quay, L. C. 1971. Language, dialect, reinforcement, and the intelligence test performance of Negro children. *Child Development* 42:5–15.

Quay, L. C. 1972. Negro dialect and Binet performance in severely disadvantaged black four-year-olds. *Child Development* 43:245–250.

Quay, L. C. 1974. Language dialect, age, and intelligence-test performance in disadvantaged black children. *Child Development* 45:463–468.

Radin, N. 1971. Maternal warmth, achievement motivation, and cognitive functioning in lower-class preschool children. *Child Development* 42:1560–1565.

Ramey, C. T. 1992. High-risk children and IQ: Altering intergenerational patterns. *Intelligence* 16:239–256.

Ramey, C. T., MacPhee, D., and Yeates, K. O. 1982. Preventing developmental retardation: A general systems model. In *How and How Much Can Intelligence Be Increased*. D. K. Detterman and R. J. Sternberg (eds.). Norwood, N.J.: Ablex Publishing Corp., pp. 67–119.

Rank, M., and Hirschl, T. A. 1988. A rural-urban comparison of welfare exits: The importance of population density. *Rural Sociology* 53:190–206.

Raschke, H. J. 1987. Divorce. In *Handbook of Marriage and the Family*. M. B. Sussman and S. K. Steinmetz (eds.). New York: Plenum Press, pp. 597–624.

Ravitch, D. 1983. *The Troubled Crusade: American Education, 1945–1980*. New York: Basic Books.

Ravitch, D. 1985. *The Schools We Deserve: Reflections on the Educational Crises of Our Time*. New York: Basic Books.

Ravitch, D., and Finn, C. E., Jr. 1987. *What Do Our 17-Year-Olds Know?* New York: Harper & Row.

Rawls, J. 1971. *A Theory of Justice*. Cambridge, Mass.: Harvard University Press.

Ree, M. J., and Earles, J. A. 1990a. *Differential Validity of a Differential Aptitude Test*. AFHRL-TR-89–59. Brooks Air Force Base, Tex.: Manpower and Personnel Division,

Ree, M. J., and Earles, J. A. 1990b. *Estimating the General Cognitive Component of the Armed Services Vocational Aptitude Battery (ASVAB): Three Faces of g*. AFHRL-TR-90–38. Brooks Air Force Base, Tex.: Air Force Systems Command.

Ree, M. J., and Earles, J. A. 1991a. *Aptitude of future manpower: Consequences of demographic change*. Brooks Air Force Base, Tex.: Manpower and Personnel Division, Air Force Systems Command.

Ree, M. J., and Earles, J. A. 1991b. General cognitive ability predicts job performance. Interim technical paper AL-TP-1991–0057. Brooks Air Force

Base, Tex.: Manpower and Personnel Research Division, Air Force Systems Command.

Ree, M. J., and Earles, J. A. 1991c. The stability of *g* across different methods of estimation. *Intelligence* 15:271–278.

Reich, R. B. 1991. *The Work of Nations: Preparing Ourselves for 21st-Century Capitalism.* New York: Alfred A. Knopf.

Reichel, H., and Magnusson, D. 1988. The relationship of intelligence to registered criminality. Reports from the Department of Psychology 676. Stockholm, Sweden: University of Stockholm.

Reid, J. B., and Tablin, P. S. 1976. A social interactional approach to the treatment of abusive families. Paper presented to the American Psychological Association, Washington, D.C.

Reid, S. T. 1979. *Crime and Criminology.* 2d ed. New York: Holt, Rinehart and Winston.

Reid, S. T. 1982. *Crime and Criminology.* 3d ed., New York: Holt, Rinehart and Winston.

Reschly, D.J., and Ross-Reynolds, J. 1982. An investigation of WISC-R item bias with black, Chicano, Native American, Papago, and white children: Implications for nondiscriminatory assessment. Iowa City, Ia.: University of Iowa. Photocopy.

Retherford, R. D. 1986. Demographic transition and the evolution of intelligence: Theory and evidence. Working Paper 40. Honolulu: East-West Population Institute.

Retherford, R. D., and Sewell, W. H. 1988. Intelligence and family size reconsidered. *Social Biology* 35:1–40.

Retherford, R. D., and Sewell, W. H. 1989. How intelligence affects fertility. *Intelligence* 13:169–185.

Retherford, R. D., and Sewell, W. H. 1991. Birth order and intelligence: Further tests of the confluence model. *Am. Sociological Rev.* 56:141–158.

Reuning, H. 1988. Testing Bushmen in the central Kalahari. In *Human Abilities in Cultural Context.* S. H. Irvine and J. W. Berry (eds.). Cambridge: Cambridge University Press, pp. 453–486.

Reynolds, A. J., et al. 1988. An analysis of a PSAT coaching program for urban gifted students. *J. of Educational Research* 81:155–164.

Reynolds, C. R., and Brown, R. T. (eds.). 1984. *Perspectives on "Bias in Mental Testing."* New York: Plenum Press.

Reynolds, C. R., Chastain, R. L., Kaufman, A. S., and McLean, J. E. 1987. Demographic characteristics and IQ among adults: Analysis of the WAIS-R standardization sample as a function of the stratification variables. *J. of School Psych.* 25:323–342.

Reynolds, C. R., and Gutkin, T. B. 1980. Predictive validity of the WISC-R for white and Mexican-American children. Paper presented at the annual meeting of the American Educational Research Association, Boston.

Reynolds, C. R., and Jensen, A. R. 1983. WISC-R subscale patterns of abilities of blacks and whites matched on full scale IQ. *J. of Educational Psych.* 75:207–214.

Rindfuss, R. R., Bumpass, L., and John, C. S. 1980. Education and fertility: Implications for the roles women occupy. *Am. Sociological Rev.* 45:431–447.

Rindfuss, R. R., Morgan, S. P., and Spicegood, C. G. 1988. *First Births in America: Changes in the Timing of Parenthood.* Berkeley: University of California Press.

Roberts, J. 1971. *Intellectual Development of Children by Demographic and Socioeconomic Factors.* DHEW No. 72–1012. Washington, D.C.: Government Printing Office.

Roberts, J. V., and Gabor, T. 1990. Lombrosian wine in a new bottle: Research on crime and race. *Canadian J. of Criminology* 32:291–313.

Rock, D. A., Hilton, T. L., Pollack, J., Ekstrom, R. B., and Goertz, M. E. 1985. *Psychometric Analysis of the NLS and the High School and Beyond Test Batteries.* Princeton, N.J.: Educational Testing Service.

Rokeach, M. 1973. *The Nature of Human Values.* New York: Free Press.

Roper Organization. 1993. *Roper Reports* 93–8.

Roskam, E. E., and Ellis, J. 1992. Commentary on Guttman: The irrelevance of factor analysis for the study of group differences. *Multivariate Behavioral Research* 27:205–218.

Ross, C., Danziger, S., and Smolensky, E. 1987. The level and trend of poverty in the United States, 1939–1979. *Demography* 24:587–600.

Ross-Reynolds, J., and Reschly, D. J. 1983. An investigation of item bias on the WISC-R with four sociocultural groups. *J. of Consulting and Clinical Psych.* 51:144–146.

Rossi, P. 1987. The iron law of evaluation and other metallic rules. In *Research in Social Problems and Public Policy,* vol. 4. J. Miller and M. Lewis (eds.). Greenwich, Conn.: JAI Press, pp. 3–20.

Rothenberg, S., and Licht, E. 1982. *Ethnic Voters and National Issues.* Washington, D.C.: Free Congress Research and Education Foundation.

Rounds, J., and Andersen, D. 1985. Assessment for entrance to community college: Research studies of three major standardized tests. *J. of Research and Development in Education* 18:54–58.

Rowe, D. C., and Plomin, R. 1981. The importance of nonshared (E_1) environmental influences on behavioral development. *Developmental Psych.* 17:517–531.

Rowe, D. C., and Rodgers, J. L. 1992. A social contagion model of adolescent sexual behavior. Tucson: University of Arizona. Photocopy.

Rowe, D. C., Rodgers, J. L., and Meseck-Bushey, S. 1988. An "epidemic" model of sexual intercourse prevalences for black and white adolescents. *Social Biology* 36:127–145.

Roy, A. D. 1951. Some thoughts on the distribution of earnings. *Oxford Econ. Papers* 3:135–146.

Rudner, L. M. 1988. Teacher testing—an update. *Educational Measurement: Issues and Practice* 7:16–19.

Rushton, J. P. 1985. Differential K theory: The sociobiology of individual and group differences. *Personality and Individual Differences* 6:441–452.

Rushton, J. P. 1988. Race differences in behaviour: A review and evolutionary analysis. *Personality and Individual Differences* 9:1009–1024.

Rushton, J. P. 1990a. Race and crime: A reply to Roberts and Gabor. *Canadian J. of Criminology* 32:315–334.

Rushton, J. P. 1990b. Race differences and r/K theory: A reply to Silverman. *Ethnology and Sociobiology* 11:131–140.

Rushton, J. P. 1990c. Race, brain size and intelligence: A rejoinder to Cain and Vanderwolf. *Personality and Individual Differences* 11:785–794.

Rushton, J. P. 1990d. Race, brain size and intelligence: A rejoinder to Cain and Vanderwolf. *Personality and Individual Differences* 11:785–794.

Rushton, J. P. 1991a. Do r-K strategies underlie human race differences? A reply to Weitzman et al. *Canadian Psych.* 32:29–42.

Rushton, J. P. 1991b. Mongoloid-Caucasoid differences in brain size from military samples. *Intelligence* 15:351–359.

Rushton, J. P. In press. Cranial capacity related to sex, rank, and race in a stratified random sample of 6325 U.S. military personnel. *Intelligence*

Rushton, J. P., and Bogaert, A. F. 1987. Race differences in sexual behavior: Testing an evolutionary hypothesis. *J. of Research in Personality*, 21:529–551.

Rushton, J. P., and Bogaert, A. F. 1988. Race versus social class differences in sexual behavior: A follow-up test of the r/K dimension. *J. Res. Per.* 22:259–272.

Rutter, M. 1985. Family and school influences on cognitive development. *J. of Child Psych., and Psychiatry and Allied Disciplines* 26:683–704.

Ryan, W. 1971. *Blaming the Victim.* 1976 ed. New York: Vintage.

Saigal, S., Szatmari, P., Rosenbaum, P., Campbell, D., and King, S. 1991. Cognitive abilities and school performance of extremely low birth weight children and matched term control children at age 8 years: A regional study. *J. of Pediatrics* 118:751–760.

Sandoval, J., et al. 1983. Cultural differences on WISC-R verbal items. *J. of School Psych.* 21:49–55.

Sarich, V. 1990. The institutionalization of racism at the University of California at Berkeley. *Academic Questions* 4:72–81.

Sattler, J. 1988. *Assessment of Children's Intelligence and Other Special Abilities.* 2d ed. Boston: Allyn and Bacon.

Sattler, J. M and Gwynne, J. 1982. White examiners generally do not impede the intelligence test performance of black children: To debunk a myth. *Journal of Consulting and Clinical Psych.* 50:196–200.

Scarr, S., and Weinberg, R. A. 1976. IQ test performance of black children adopted by white families. *Am. Psychologist* 31:726–739.

Scarr, S., and Weinberg, R. A. 1978. The influence of "family background" on intellectual attainment. *Am. Sociological Rev.* 43:674–692.

Scarr, S., and Weinberg, R. A. 1983. The Minnesota adoption studies: Genetic differences and malleability. *Child Development* 54:260–267.

Scarr, S., Pakstis, A., Katz, S. H., and Barker, W. 1977. The absence of a relationship between degree of white ancestry and intellectual skills within the black population. *Human Genetics* 39:69–86.

Scheuneman, J. D. 1987. An experimental, exploratory study of causes of bias in test items. *J. of Educational Measurement* 24:97–118.

Schiff, M., Duyme, M., Dumaret, A., and Tomkiewicz, S. 1982. How much could we boost scholastic achievement and IQ scores? A direct answer from a French adoption study. *Cognition* 12:165–196.

Schiff, M., and Lewontin, R. 1986. *Education and Class: The Irrelevance of IQ Genetic Studies.* Oxford: Clarendon.

Schmidt, F. L. 1988. The problem of group differences in ability test scores in employment selection. *J. of Vocational Behavior* 33:272–292.

Schmidt, F. L., and Hunter, J. E. 1981. Employment testing: Old theories and new research findings. *Am. Psychologist* 36:1128–1137.

Schmidt, F. L., and Hunter, J. E. 1983. Individual differences in productivity: An empirical test of estimates derived from studies of selection procedure utilities. *J. of Applied Psych.* 68:407–414.

Schmidt, F. L., and Hunter, J. E. 1991. *Causal Modeling of Processes Determining Job Performance.* Iowa City: University of Iowa. Photocopy.

Schmidt, F. L., Hunter, J. E., McKenzie, R. C., and Muldrow, T. W. 1979. The impact of a valid selection procedure on work-force productivity. *J. of Applied Psych.* 64:609–626.

Schmidt, F. L., Hunter, J. E., Outerbridge, A. C., and Goff, S. 1988. Joint relation of experience and ability with job performance: A test of three hypotheses. *J. of Applied Psych.* 73:46–57.

Schmidt, F. L., Mack, M. J., and Hunter, J. E. 1984. Selection utility in the occupation of U.S. park ranger for three modes of test use. *J. of Applied Psych.* 69:490–497.

Schmidt, F. L., and Ones, D. S. 1992. Personnel selection. *Annual Rev. of Psych.* 43:627–670.

Schoen, R., and Kleugel, J. R. 1988. The widening gap in black and white marriage rates: The impact of population composition and differential marriage propensities. *Am. Sociological Rev.* 53:895–907.

Schoendorf, K. C., Hogue, C. J. R., Kleinman, J. C., and Rowley, D. 1992. Mortality among infants of black as compared with white college-educated parents. *New England J. of Medicine* 326:1522–1526.

Schoenthaler, S. J. 1991. Abstracts of early papers on the effects of vitamin and mineral supplementation on IQ and behaviour. *Personality and Individual Differences* 12:335–341.

Schoenthaler, S. J., Amos, S. P., Eysenck, H. J., Peritz, E., and Yudkin, J. 1991. Controlled trial of vitamin-mineral supplementation: Effects on intelligence and performance. *Personality and Individual Differences* 12:351–362.

Schoenthaler, S. J., Doraz, W. E., and Wakefield, J. A., Jr. 1986. The impact of a low full additive and sucrose diet on academic performance in 803 New York City public schools. *International J. of Biosocial Research* 8:185–195.

Schonemann, P. H. 1985. On artificial intelligence. *Behavioral and Brain Sciences* 8:241–242.

Schwarz, P. A., and Krug, R. E. 1972. *Ability Testing in Developing Countries: A Handbook of Principles and Techniques.* New York: Praeger.

Schweinhart, L. J., and Weikart, D. P. 1991. Response to "Beyond IQ in preschool programs?" *Intelligence* 15:313–315.

Scottish Council for Research in Education. 1949. *The Trend of Scottish Intelligence.* London: University of London Press.

Sechrest, D. K., and Burns, P. 1992. Police corruption: The Miami case. *Criminal Justice Behavior* 19:294–313.

Seibel, D. W. 1962. *Follow-Up Study of a National Sample of High School Seniors.* SR-62-56. Princeton, N.J.: Educational Testing Service.

Seligman, D. 1992. *A Question of Intelligence: The IQ Debate in America.* New York: Birch Lane Press.

Sewell, W. H., and Hauser, R. M. 1975. *Education, Occupation, and Earnings: Achievement in the Early Career.* New York: Academic Press.

Seymour, R. T. 1988. Why plaintiffs' counsel challenge tests, and how they can successfully challenge the theory of "validity generalization." *J. of Vocational Behavior* 33:331–364.

Shea, S., and Fullilove, M. T. 1985. Entry of black and other minority students into U.S. medical schools. *New England J. of Medicine* 313:933–939.

Shockley, W. 1987. Jensen's data on Spearman's hypothesis: No artifact. *Behavioral and Brain Sciences* 10:512.

Shortridge, R. M. 1981. Estimating voter participation. In *Analyzing Electoral History: A Guide to the Study of American Voter Behavior.* J. M. Clubb, W. H. Flanigan, and N. H. Zingale (eds.). Beverly Hills, Cal.: Sage, pp. 137–152.

Shuey, A. M. 1966. *The Testing of Negro Intelligence.* 2d ed. New York: Social Science Press.

Silberberg, E. 1985. Race, recent entry, and labor market participation. *Am. Econ. Rev.* 75:1168–77.

Silberman, C. 1970. *Crisis in the Classroom.* New York: Random House.

Silverman, I. 1990. The r/K theory of human individual differences: Scientific and social issues. *Ethnology and Sociobiology* 11:1–9.

Simon, J. L. 1989. *The Economic Consequences of Immigration.* Oxford: Basil Blackwell.

Simon, J. L., Borjas, G. J., Wattenberg, B. J., Stein, D., Bartley, R. L., and Brimelow, P. 1993. An immigration debate: Why control the borders? *National Rev.,* February 1, pp. 27–34.

Simon, R. J., and Danner, M. J. E. 1990. Gender, race, and the predictive value of the LSAT. *J. of Legal Education* 40:525–529.

Simons, R. L., Beaman, J., Conger, R. D., and Chao, W. 1993. Stress, support, and antisocial behavior trait as determinants of emotional well-being and parenting practices among single mothers. *J. of Marriage and the Family* 55:385–398.

Singal, D. J. 1991. The other crisis in American education. *Atlantic Monthly* (Nov.): 59ff.

Sjaastad, L. A. 1962. The costs and returns of human migration. *J. of Political Econ.* 70:80–93.

Skinner, B. F. 1938. *The Behavior of Organisms: An Experimental Analysis.* New York: Appleton-Century-Crofts.

Skinner, B. F. 1953. *Science and Human Behavior.* New York: Macmillan.

Skinner, B. F. 1971. *Beyond Freedom and Dignity.* New York: Alfred A. Knopf.

Slack, W. V., and Porter, D. 1980. The Scholastic Aptitude Test: A critical appraisal. *Harvard Educational Rev.* 50:154–175.

Smith, D. A., and Davidson, L. A. 1986. Interfacing indicators and constructs in criminological research: A note on the comparability of self-report violence data for race and sex groups. *Criminology* 24:473–487.

Smith, D. I., and Kirkham, R. W. 1982. Relationship between intelligence and driving record. *Accident Analysis and Prevention* 14:439–442.

Smith, J. P. 1984. Race and human capital. *Am. Econ. Rev.* 74:685–698.

Smith, J. P. 1989. Children among the poor. *Demography* 26:235–248.

Smith, J. P., and Welch, F. 1987. Race and poverty: A forty-year record. *AEA Papers and Proceedings* 77:152–158.

Smith, J. P., and Welch, F. R. 1989. Black economic progress after Myrdal. *J. of Econ. Literature* 27:519–564.

Smith, S. M. 1975. *The Battered Child Syndrome.* London: Butterworth.

Smith, S. M., and Hanson, R. 1975. Interpersonal relationships and child-rearing practices in 214 parents of battered children. *British J. of Psychiatry* 125:513–525.

Smith, S. M., Hanson, R., and Noble, S. 1974. Social aspects of the battered baby syndrome. *British J. of Psychiatry* 125:568–582.

Snow, R. E. 1982. The training of intellectual aptitude. In *How and How Much Can Intelligence Be Increased*. D. K. Detterman and R. J. Sternberg (eds.). Norwood, N.J.: Ablex Publishing Corp., pp. 1–37.

Snyderman, M., and Herrnstein, R. J. 1983. Intelligence tests and the Immigration Act of 1924. *Am. Psychologist* 38:986–995.

Snyderman, M., and Rothman, S. 1988. *The IQ Controversy: The Media and Public Policy*. New Brunswick, N.J.: Transaction Books.

Solon, G. 1992. Intergenerational income mobility in the United States. *Am. Econ. Rev.* 82:393–408.

Soloway, R. A. 1982. *Birth Control and the Population Question in England, 1877–1930*. Chapel Hill, N.C.: University of North Carolina Press.

Sommer, R., and Sommer, B. A. 1983. Mystery in Milwaukee: Early intervention, IQ, and psychology textbooks. *Am. Psychologist* 38:982–985.

South, S. J. 1985. Economic conditions and the divorce rate: A time-series analysis of the postwar United States. *J. of Marriage and the Family* 47:31–41.

South, S. J. 1993. Racial and ethnic differences in the desire to marry. *J. of Marriage and the Family* 55:357–370.

South, S. J., and Lloyd, K. M. 1992. Marriage markets and nonmarital fertility in the United States. *Demography* 29:247–264.

Sowell, T. 1981. *Ethnic America: A History*. New York: Basic Books.

Sowell, T. 1989. The new racism on campus. *Fortune*, February 13, pp. 115–116.

Sowell, T. 1992. *Inside American Education: The Decline, the Deception, the Dogmas*. New York: Free Press.

Spanier, G. B., and Glick, P. C. 1980. Mate selection differentials between whites and blacks in the United States. *Social Forces* 58:707–725.

Spearman, C. S. 1904. "General intelligence," objectively determined and measured. *Am. J. of Psych.* 15:201–209.

Spearman, C. 1927. *The Abilities of Man*. New York: Macmillan.

Sperl, T. C., Ree, M. J., and Steuck, K. W. 1990. *Air Force Officer Qualifying Test (AFOQT) and Armed Services Vocational Aptitude Battery (ASVAB): Analysis of Common Measurement Attributes*. Brooks Air Force Base, Tex.: Air Force Systems Command.

Spitz, H. H. 1986. *The Raising of Intelligence: A Selected History of Attempts to Raise Retarded Intelligence*. Hillsdale, N.J.: Lawrence Erlbaum Associates.

Spitz, H. H. 1992. Does the Carolina Abecedarian early intervention project prevent sociocultural mental retardation? *Intelligence* 16:225–237.

Spuhler, J. N. 1968. Assortative mating with respect to physical characteristics. *Social Biology* 15:128–140.

Stanley, D. T., Mann, D. E., and Doig, J. W. 1967. *Men Who Govern: A Biographical Profile of Federal Political Executives*. Washington, D.C.: Brookings Institution.

Stanley, J. C., Feng, C. D., and Zhu, X. 1989. Chinese youths who reason extremely well mathematically: Threat or bonanza? In *Network News and Views*, vol. 8. Washington, D.C.: Educational Excellence Network, pp. 33–39.

Staples, R. 1985. Changes in black family structure: The conflict between family ideology and structural conditions. *J. of Marriage and the Family* 47:1005–1013.

Steele, B. 1987. Psychodynamic factors in child abuse. In *The Battered Child*. 4th ed. R. E. Helfer and R. S. Kempe (eds.). Chicago: University of Chicago Press, pp. 81–114.

Steele, S. 1991. *The Content of Our Character*. New York: Basic Books.

Stein, Z., Susser, M., Saenger, G., and Marolla, F. 1972. Nutrition and mental performance. *Science* 178:708–713.

Stephen, E. H., Rindfuss, R. R., and Bean, F. D. 1988. Racial differences in contraceptive choice: Complexity and implications. *Demography* 25:53–70.

Sternberg, R. J. 1985. General intellectual ability. In *Human Abilities: An Information-Processing Approach*. R. J. Sternberg (ed.). New York: W.H. Freeman and Company, pp. 5–30.

Sternberg, R. J. 1988. *The Triarchic Mind: A New Theory of Human Intelligence*. New York: Penguin.

Stevenson, H. W., and Azuma, H. 1983. IQ in Japan and the United States: Methodological problems in Lynn's analysis. *Nature* 306:291–292.

Stevenson, H., Lee, S.-Y., Chen, C., Lummis, M., Stigler, J., Fan, L., and Ge, F. 1990. Mathematics achievement of children in China and the United States. *Child Development* 61:1053–1066.

Stevenson, H., Stigler, J. W., Lee, S., Lucker, G. W., Kitamura, S., and Hsu, C. 1985. Cognitive performance of Japanese, Chinese, and American children. *Child Development* 56:718–734.

Stewart, N. 1947. A.G.C.T. scores of army personnel grouped by occupation. *Occupation* 26:5–41.

Stigler, S. S. 1986. *The History of Statistics: The Measurement of Uncertainty before 1900*. Cambridge, Mass.: Harvard University Press.

Storfer, M. D. 1990. *Intelligence and Giftedness: The Contributions of Heredity and Early Environment*. San Francisco: Jossey-Bass.

Straus, M. A., and Gelles, R. J. 1986. Societal change and change in family violence from 1975 to 1985 as revealed in two national surveys. *J. of Marriage and the Family* 48:465–479.

Straus, M. A., Gelles, R. J., and Steinmetz, S. K. 1980. *Behind Closed Doors: Violence in the American Family.* New York: Anchor Books.

Straus, R. P., and Sawyer, E. A. 1986. Some new evidence on teacher and student competencies. *Economics of Education Rev.* 5:41–48.

Stromsdorfer, E. W. 1987. Economic evaluation of the Comprehensive Employment and Training Act. *Evaluation Rev.* 11:387–393.

Sturdivant, F. D., and Adler, R. D. 1976. Executive origins: Still a gray flannel world? *Harvard Business Rev.* 54:125–132.

Sue, S., and Okazaki, S. 1990. Asian-American educational achievements: A phenomenon in search of an explanation. *Am. Psychologist* 45:913–920.

Sussman, M. B., and Steinmetz, S. K. (eds.). 1987. *Handbook of Marriage and the Family.* New York: Plenum Press.

Sutherland, E. H. 1931. Mental deficiency and crime. In *Social Attitudes.* K. Young (ed.). New York: Holt, pp. 357–375.

Sweet, J. A., and Bumpass, L. L. 1987. *American Families and Households.* New York: Russell Sage Foundation.

Sweet, J. A., and Rindfuss, R. R. 1983. Those ubiquitous fertility trends: United States, 1945–1979. *Social Biology* 30:127–139.

Takagi, D. Y. 1990. From discrimination to affirmative action: Facts in the Asian American admissions controversy. *Social Problems* 37:578–592.

Takuma, T. 1966. On the early physical conditions influencing the development of intelligence. *Japanese J. of Psych.* 37:257–268.

Tambs, K., Sundet, J. M., Magnus, P., and Berg, K. 1989. Genetic and environmental contributions to the covariance between occupational status, educational attainment, and IQ: A study of twins. *Behavior Genetics* 19:209–222.

Taubman, P., and Wales, T. 1972. *Mental Ability and Higher Educational Attainment in the 20th Century.* New York: McGraw-Hill.

Taylor, J. 1992. *Paved with Good Intentions: The Failure of Race Relations in Contemporary America.* New York: Carroll & Graf.

Taylor, J. G., and Smith, P. C. 1956. An investigation of the shape of learning curves for industrial motor tasks. *J. of Applied Psych.* 40: 142–149.

Taylor, L., and Skanes, G. 1977. A cross-cultural examination of some of Jensen's hypotheses. *Canadian J. of Behavioural Sciences* 9:315–322.

Teachman, J. D. 1985. Historical and subgroup variations in the association between marriage and first childbirth: A life-course perspective. *J. of Family History* 10:379–401.

Teachman, J. D., Polonko, K. A., and Scanzoni, J. 1987. Demography of the family. In *Handbook of Marriage and the Family.* M. B. Sussman and S. K. Steinmetz (eds.). New York: Plenum Press, pp. 3–36.

Teasdale, T. W., and Owen, D. R. 1989. Continuing secular increases in intelligence and a stable prevalence of high intelligence levels. *Intelligence* 13:255–262.

Teasdale, T. W., Sørenson, T. I. A., and Owen, D. R. 1984. Social class in adopted and nonadopted siblings. *Behavior Genetics* 14:587–593.

Terman, L. M. 1942. The vocational successes of intellectually gifted individuals. *Occupations* 20:493–498.

Terman, L. M., and Oden, M. H. 1947. *The Gifted Child Grows Up: Twenty-Five Years' Follow-up of a Superior Group.* Genetic Studies of Genius, vol. 4. Stanford, Cal.: Stanford University Press.

Terrell, F., and Terrell, S. L. 1983. The relationship between race of examiner, cultural mistrust, and the intelligence test performance of black children. *Psych. in the Schools* 20:367–369.

Thornberry, T. P., Moore, M., and Christianson, R. L. 1985. The effect of dropping out of high school on subsequent criminal behavior. *Criminology* 23:3–18.

Thorndike, R. L. 1971. Concepts of culture fairness. *J. of Educational Measurement* 8:63–70.

Thorndike, R. L. 1986. The role of general ability in prediction. *J. of Vocational Behavior* 29:332–339.

Thurstone, L. L. 1938. *Primary Mental Abilities.* Psychometric Monographs 1. Chicago: University of Chicago Press.

Tildsley, J. L. 1936. *The Mounting Waste of the American Secondary School.* Cambridge, Mass.: Harvard University Press.

Tolson, T., and Wilson, M. 1990. The impact of two- and three-generational black family structure on perceived family climate. *Child Development* 61:416–428.

Topel, R. 1993. What have we learned from empirical studies of unemployment and turnover? *Am. Econ. Rev.* 83:110–115.

Tribe, L. H. 1988. *American Constitutional Law.* New York: Foundation Press.

Trickett, P. K., Aber, J. L., Carlson, V., and Cicchetti, D. 1991. Relationship of socioeconomic status to the etiology and developmental sequelae of physical child abuse. *Developmental Psych.* 27:148–158.

Tucker, M. B., and Taylor, R. J. 1989. Demographic correlates of relationship status among black Americans. *J. of Marriage and the Family* 51:655–665.

Tuddenham, R. D. 1948. Soldier intelligence in World Wars I and II. *Am. Psychologist* 3:54–56.

Turkheimer, E. 1991. Individual and group differences in adoption studies of IQ. *Psychological Bull.* 110:392–405.

Turner, R., Hall, V., and Grimmett, S. 1973. Effects of familiarization feedback on the performance of lower-class and middle-class kindergarteners on the Raven Colored Progressive Matrices. *J. of Educational Psych.* 65:356–363.

U.S. Bureau of the Census. 1975. *Historical Statistics of the United States, Colonial Times to 1970,* vol. 1. Washington, D.C.: Government Printing Office.

U.S. Bureau of the Census. *Money Income of Households, Families, and Persons in the United States*. Series P-60. Annual. Washington, D.C.: Government Printing Office.

U.S. Bureau of the Census. *Poverty in the United States*. Series P-60. Annual. Washington, D.C.: Government Printing Office.

U.S. Bureau of the Census. *Statistical Abstract of the United States*, Annual. Washington, D.C.: Government Printing Office.

U.S. Department of Health and Human Services. 1988. *Study of National Incidence and Prevalence of Child Abuse and Neglect*. Washington, D.C.: Office of Human Development Services.

U.S. Department of Labor. 1970. *Manual for the USTES General Aptitude Test Battery*. 4th ed. Washington, D.C.: Government Printing Office.

U.S. Department of Labor. 1993. *Employment and Earnings*. 40:1.

Valdez, R. S., and Valdez, C. 1983. Detecting predictive bias: The WISC-R vs. achievement scores of Mexican-American and non-minority students. *Learning Disability Quarterly* 6:440–447.

Valen, L. V. 1974. Brain size and intelligence in man. *Am. J. of Physical Anthropology* 40:417–423.

Valencia, R. R., and Rankin, R. J. 1988. Evidence of bias in predictive validity on the Kaufman Assessment Battery for children in samples of Anglo and Mexican American children. *Psych. in the Schools* 25:257–266.

Valencia, R. R., and Rankin, R. J. 1985. Evidence of context bias on the McCarthy Scales with Mexican American children: Implications for test translation and nonbiased assessment. *J.of Educational Psych.* 77:197–207.

Vance, S. C. 1966. Higher education for the executive elite. *California Management Rev.* 8:21–30.

VanCourt, M., and Bean, F. D. 1985. Intelligence and fertility in the United States: 1912–1982. *Intelligence* 9:23–32.

Verba, S., and Nie, N. H. 1972. *Participation in America: Political Democracy and Social Equality*. Chicago: University of Chicago Press.

Vernon, P. A. 1982. *The Abilities and Achievements of Orientals in North America*. New York: Academic Press.

Vernon, P. A. 1983. Speed of information processing and general intelligence. *Intelligence* 7:53–70.

Vernon, P. A., et al. 1985. Reaction times and speed of processing: Their relationship to timed and untimed measures of intelligence. *Intelligence* 9:357.

Vernon, P. E. 1950. *The Structure of Human Abilities*. New York: Wiley.

Vincent, K. R. 1991. Black/white IQ differences: Does age make the difference? *J. of Clinical Psych.* 47:266–270.

Vining, D. R., Jr. 1982a. Fertility differentials and the status of nations: A speculative essay on Japan and the West. *Mankind Quarterly* 22:311–353.

Vining, D. R., Jr. 1982b. On the possibility of the reemergence of a dysgenic trend with respect to intelligence in American fertility differentials. *Intelligence* 6:241–264.

Vining, D. R., Jr. 1986. Social versus reproductive success: The central theoretical problem of human sociobiology. *Behavioral and Brain Sciences* 9:167–216.

Wah, D. M., and Robinson, D. S. 1990. *Examinee and score trends for the GRE general test: 1977–78, 1982–83, 1986–87, and 1987–88.* Princeton, N.J.: Educational Testing Service.

Wainer, H. 1988. How accurately can we assess changes in minority performance on the SAT? *Am. Psychologist* 43:774–778.

Waldman, I. D., Weinberg, R. A., and Scarr, S. In press. Racial group differences in IQ in the Minnesota transracial adoption study: A reply to Levin and Lynn. *Intelligence*.

Walker, D. A. 1976. *The IEA Six Subject Survey: An Empirical Study of Education in Twenty-one Countries.* New York: Wiley.

Waller, J. H. 1971. Differential reproduction: Its relation to IQ test score, education, and occupation. *Social Biology* 18:122–136.

Walsh, J. 1979. Does high school grade inflation mask a more alarming trend? *Science* 203:982.

Warner, W. L., and Abegglen, J. C. *Big Business Leaders in America.* New York: Harper & Bros.

Wasserman, G., Rauh, V., Brunelli, S., Garcia-Castro, M., and Necos, B. 1990. Psychosocial attributes and life experiences of disadvantaged minority mothers: Age and ethnic variations. *Child Development* 61:566–580.

Watkins, M. P., and Meredith, W. 1981. Spouse similarity in newly-weds with respect to specific cognitive abilities, socio-economic status and education. *Behavioral Genetics* 11:1–11.

Wattenberg, B. J. 1987. *The Birth Dearth.* New York: Pharos Books.

Wattenberg, B. J., and Zinsmeister, K. 1990. The case for more immigration. *Commentary* (April): 19–25.

Weekley, J. A., et al. 1985. A comparison of three methods of estimating the standard deviation of performance in dollars. *J. of Applied Psych.* 70:122–126.

Weikart, D. P., Epstein, A. S., Schweinhart, L., and Bond, J. T. 1978. *The Ypsilanti Preschool Curriculum Demonstration Project: Preschool Years and Longitudinal Results.* Ypsilanti, Mich.: High/Scope Educational Research Foundation.

Weinberg, R. A., Scarr, S., and Waldman, I. D. 1992. The Minnesota transracial adoption study: A follow-up of IQ test performance at adolescence. *Intelligence* 16:117–135.

Weiss, J. G. 1987. It's time to examine the examiners. *Negro Educational Rev.* 38:107–124.

Weitzman, R. A. 1982. The prediction of college achievement by the Scholastic Aptitude Test and the high school record. *J. of Educational Measurement* 19:179–191.

Weitzmann, F., Wiener, N. I., Wiesenthal, D. L., and Ziegler, M. 1990. Differential K theory and racial hierarchies. *Canadian Psych.* 31:1–13.

Welch, F. 1973. Black-white differences in returns to schooling. *Am. Econ. Rev.* 63:893–907.

Welch, F. 1981. Affirmative action and its enforcement. *Am. Econ. Rev.* 71:127–133.

Welsh, J. R., Jr., Watson, T. W., and Ree, M. J. 1990. *Armed Services Vocational Aptitude Battery (ASVAB): Predicting Military Criteria from General and Specific Abilities.* AFHRL-TR-90–63. Brooks Air Force Base, Tex.: Air Force Systems Command.

Werner, E. E. 1989. High risk children in young adulthood: A longitudinal study from birth to 32 years. *Am. J. of Orthopsychiatry* 59:72–81.

Werner, E. E., and Smith, R. S. 1982. *Vulnerable But Invincible: A Longitudinal Study of Resilient Children and Youth.* New York: McGraw-Hill.

Wessely, S., and Taylor, P. J. 1991. Madness and crime: Criminology versus psychiatry. *Criminal Behaviour and Mental Health* 1:193–228.

Whimbey, A. 1985. Focusing on trainable *g. Behavioral and Brain Sciences* 8:245–246.

White, E. 1969. Intelligence, individual differences, and learning: An approach to political sophistication. *British J. of Sociology* 20:50–68.

White, J. L., Moffitt, T. E., and Silva, P. A. 1989. A prospective replication of the protective effects of IQ in subjects at high risk for juvenile delinquency. *J. of Consulting and Clinical Psych.* 57:719–724.

White, S., et al. 1988. Beyond intelligence testing. *National Forum: Phi Kappa Phi J.* 68:2–29.

White, T. H. 1958. *The Once and Future King.* New York: Putnam.

White, W. F., Nylin, W. C., and Esser, P. R. 1985. Academic course grades as better predictors of graduation from a commuter-type college than SAT scores. *Psychological Reports* 56:375–378.

Whitworth, R. H., and Chrisman, S. M. 1987. Validation of the Kaufman assessment battery for children comparing Anglo and Mexican-American preschoolers. *Educational and Psychological Measurement.* 47:695–698.

Whitworth, R. H., and Gibbons, R. T. 1986. Cross-racial comparison of the WAIS and WAIS-R. *Educational and Psychological Measurement* 46:1041–49.

Williams, A. P., Cooper, W. D., and Lee, C. L. 1979. *Factors Affecting Medical School Admission Decisions for Minority and Majority Applicants: A Comparative Study of Ten Schools.* R-2030–HEW. Santa Monica, Cal.: Rand Corporation.

Williams, M. J. 1987. How the wealthy get that way. *Fortune*, April 13, pp. 32–38.

Wills, G. 1978. *Inventing America: Jefferson's Declaration of Independence*. New York: Vintage.

Wilson, J. Q. 1993. *The Moral Sense*. New York: Free Press.

Wilson, J. Q., and Herrnstein, R. J. 1985. *Crime and Human Nature*. New York: Simon and Schuster.

Wilson, J. R. 1985. Jensen's support for Spearman's hypothesis is support for a circular argument. *Behavioral and Brain Sciences* 8:246.

Wilson, K. M. 1983. *A Review of Research on the Prediction of Academic Performance after the Freshman Year*. RR-83–11. Princeton, N.J.: Educational Testing Service.

Wilson, W. J. 1987. *The Truly Disadvantaged: The Inner City, the Underclass, and Public Policy*. Chicago: University of Chicago Press.

Wise, L. L., McLaughlin, D. H., and Gilmartin, K. J. 1977. *The American Citizen: 11 Years After High School*. Vol. 2. Palo Alto: American Institutes for Research.

Wiseman, M. 1984. Turnover and family fragmentation in Aid to Families with Dependent Children. Working Paper 84–10 (Revised). Berkeley, Cal.: Institute of Business and Economic Research, University of California.

Wojtkiewicz, R. A., McLanahan, S. S., and Garfinkel, I. 1990. The growth of families headed by women: 1950–1980. *Demography* 27:19–30.

Wolfe, D. A. 1985. Child-abusive parents: An empirical review and analysis. *Psychological Bull.* 97:462–482.

Wolfe, J. R. 1982. The impact of family resources on childhood IQ. *J. of Human Resources* 17:213–235.

Wolfgang, M. E., Figlio, R. M., and Sellin, T. 1972. *Delinquency in a Birth Cohort*. Chicago: University of Chicago Press.

Wolfinger, R. E., and Rosenstone, S. J. 1980. *Who Votes?* New Haven, Conn.: Yale University Press.

Wolpin, K. I. 1992. The determinants of black-white differences in early employment careers: Search, layoffs, quits, and endogenous wage growth. *J. of Political Econ.* 100:535–560.

Wrong, D. 1980. *Class Fertility Trends in Western Nations*. New York: Arno.

Yee, A. H., Fairchild, H. H., Weizmann, F., and Wyatt, G. E. 1993. Addressing psychology's problems with race. *Am. Psychologist* 48:1132–1140.

Young, G., and Gately, T. 1988. Neighborhood impoverishment and child maltreatment. *J. of Family Issues* 9:240–254.

Young, L. 1964. *Wednesday's Children: A Study of Child Neglect and Abuse*. New York: McGraw-Hill.

Youssef, N. H. 1978. The status and fertility patterns of Muslim women. In

Women in the Muslim World. L. Beck and N. Keddie (eds.). Cambridge, Mass.: Harvard University Press, pp. 69–99.

Yudkin, J. 1991. Intelligence of children and vitamin-mineral supplements: The DRF study. Discussion, conclusion and consequences. *Personality and Individual Differences* 12:363–365.

Zabin, L. S., Wong, R., Weinick, R. M., and Emerson, M. R. 1992. Dependency in urban black families following the birth of an adolescent's child. *J. of Marriage and the Family* 54:496–507.

Zajonc, R. B. 1976. Family configuration and intelligence. *Science* 192:227–236.

Zigler, E., and Muenchow, S. 1992. *Head Start: The Inside Story of America's Most Successful Educational Experiment*. New York: Basic Books.

Zimmerman, D. J. 1992. Regression toward mediocrity in economic stature. *Am. Econ. Rev.* 82:409–429.

Zoref, L. S., and Williams, P. B. 1980. A look at content bias in IQ tests. *J. of Educational Measurement* 17:313–322.

Zuckerman, M., and Brody, N. 1988. Oysters, rabbits and people: A critique of "race differences in behaviour" by J. P. Rushton. *Personality and Individual Differences* 9:1025–1033.

Zuravin, S. J. 1989. The ecology of child abuse and neglect: Review of the literature and presentation of data. *Violence and Victims* 4:101–120.

Index